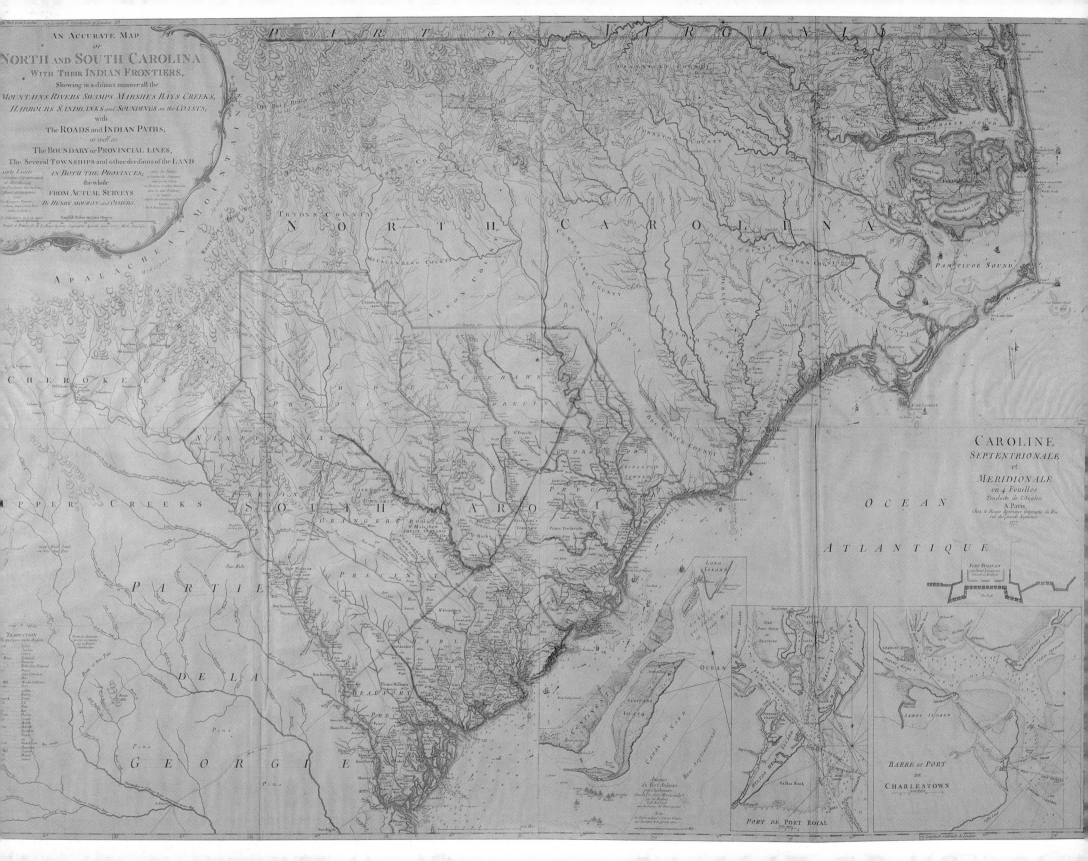

PART OF VIRGINIA

AN ACCURATE MAP
OF
NORTH AND SOUTH CAROLINA
WITH THEIR INDIAN FRONTIERS,
Shewing in a distinct manner all the
MOUNTAINS RIVERS SWAMPS MARSHES BAYS CREEKS,
HARBOURS SANDBANKS and SOUNDINGS on the COASTS;
with
The ROADS and INDIAN PATHS;
as well as
The BOUNDARY or PROVINCIAL LINES,
The Several TOWNSHIPS and other divisions of the LAND
IN BOTH THE PROVINCES;
the whole
FROM ACTUAL SURVEYS
By HENRY MOUZON and OTHERS.

NORTH CAROLINA

APALACHEAN MOUNTAINS

CHEROKEES

UPPER CREEKS

SOUTH CAROLINA

PARTIE

DE LA

GEORGIE

CAROLINE
SEPTENTRIONALE
et
MERIDIONALE
en 4 Feuilles
Traduite de l'Anglois
A Paris,

OCEAN

ATLANTIQUE

PAMTICOE SOUND

LONG ISLAND

OCEAN

CONTINENT

SULLIVANS
ISLAND

CANAL DE NORD

Bras Septentrional

FORT SULLIVAN

PORT DE PORT ROYAL

BARRE ET PORT
DE
CHARLESTOWN

CHARLESTON'S MARITIME
HERITAGE 1670–1865

CHARLESTON'S MARITIME HERITAGE 1670–1865

an illustrated history

by P. C. Coker III

CokerCraft Press
Charleston,
South Carolina

Works by P. C. Coker

Building Warship Models   1974

Charleston's Maritime Heritage 1670-1865   1987

Editors
Bertram C. Cooper
W. M. P. Dunne
Caroline G. Pocari, Ph.D.
Katherine S. Talmadge

CokerCraft Press
P. O. Box 176
Charleston, S. C. 29402

Copyright © 1987
by P. C. Coker III
Charleston, South Carolina

Library of Congress Cataloging-in-Publication Data

Coker, P. C. 1942–

    Charleston's maritime heritage 1670-1865.

    Bibliography: p.
    Includes index.
    1. Navigation—South Carolina—Charleston
Region—History. 2. Charleston Region (S.C.)—
History, Naval. 3. Shipbuilding —South
Carolina—Charleston Region— History. I. Title.

VK25.C3C65 1987   387.5'09757'915

87-70684

ISBN 0-914432-03-6

Printed in Korea
Through Overseas Printing Corporation
San Francisco, California

Half Title Page: **Showing Charleston's flag on far-flung seas, the Ravenel & Company's sailing ship *John Ravenel* in the Bay of Naples sometime in the 1850s.**

Title Page: **Charleston harbor circa 1838 as viewed from Hog Island, now Patriots' Point, by G. Cooke. The smoke rising in the background is supposedly from the fire of 1838, which destroyed much of the Ansonborough section of the city. The plethora of shipping shows a wide diversity of types in both sail and steam. The steamer at right was the ferry to Hobcaw.**

For Caroline, Cooper, and Rachel

as part of their Charleston Legacy

Contents

CHARLESTON'S MARITIME HERITAGE 1670–1865

W.H. Brooke, F.S.A.   T.A. Prior.

Introduction

As undergraduate students in history at the University of South Carolina in the early 1960s, we were encouraged to write our senior theses on a South Carolina subject. At the time the world was opening up to me, and South Carolina history seemed dull and uninteresting—a backwater to the larger national and international currents which dominated the scene.

I was wrong. The resurgence—primarily economic—of South Carolina in the 1960s, 70s, and 80s turned up vast amounts of information on this state's history. Much of this information has now been disseminated, and what a marvelous and exciting history it is. Instead of a backwater, South Carolina was the leading state in the South until the port of New Orleans allowed Louisiana to surpass her economically after the War of 1812. Politically, South Carolina continued to dominate the South until 1865. Virginia may take exception to this, but when one looks at the number of cabinet officers and other ministers in the national government prior to 1860, the large number of South Carolinians who played a part on the national stage must be recognized, especially her great statesman, John C. Calhoun. South Carolina's wealth and culture, while relatively unnoticed in the North, set the tone and pace in the South until the 1840s.

In conjunction with the casual treatment of the South in American history went the almost total disregard of Charleston's maritime history. There are very few accounts of this city's contribution to American maritime history and development, and most of these are rooted solely in the Confederate War. Whether this is due to the destruction of records over the years or to the Southern people's natural tendency toward interests other than maritime is open to question.

One particularly interesting phenomenon is the scarcity of illustrations, models, and plans of ships connected with this city before 1860. Of the illustrations herein, only a half dozen or so are in collections in Charleston. The rest are elsewhere, the majority outside the South.

One person sorely missed in the writing of this book is the late Milby Burton, for many years the director of the Charleston Museum, an able historian, and a nationally known figure in the antiques field. The many hours we spent discussing ships and naval history are treasured memories.

The late Harold Mouzon, a maritime attorney in Charleston, left a fascinating collection of writings on ships connected with Charleston. While most of it was drawn from newspaper accounts of the period and concentrated on privateers, his research has been invaluable to me. Without it I may have never connected some of the Bevan scenes of privateers with Charleston.

It is the passing of these gentlemen that prompted me to set down in writing what has been gathered on this subject. Because of my contacts around the world in the ship model field, I have been able to gather illustrations and information on Charleston ships and ship types that one person alone may never discover again. Hopefully what is set forth herein will give the reader a good understanding of this city's almost forgotten maritime heritage.

Most of us tend to regard our professions as of interest only to ourselves and our colleagues. For years this was my reaction to my work in the maritime field. However, as the large sweep of South Carolina's involvement in maritime matters over the past 300 years began to unfold, I slowly realized what a fascinating story it is, covering so many significant periods. While many seaports can claim leadership or historical connection in one period or another, Charleston is one of the few that can claim an almost unbroken dynamic history from 1670 to 1865.

What served to bring Charleston's maritime history into perspective for me was my ship model work on Confederate ironclads for the U. S. Navy. In doing research on this ship type, I found that Charleston's ironclads were better documented and illustrated than most of those built in the other Confederate seaports; as a result, I began to piece together the ships connected with Charleston from earlier periods, and one thing built upon another until this volume was well underway.

A ship model builder's craft must engage the skills of the artist, historian, and detective to uncover the past. These talents have all come together in the production of this work and have been aided by a final prerequisite, the old academic axiom of "publish or perish." A ship model builder does not succeed without writing, both for professional and financial reasons.

A book such as this can never be the work of one person. While my name may appear as author, I would not be so presumptuous as to consider that it is my work alone. Many of my friends and colleagues through the years have contributed appreciably to the expansion of my historical awareness. I am particularly indebted to great ship model builders: Lloyd McCaffrey of Boulder, Colorado, the Fabergé of the ship model world, for pictures of his exquisite miniatures of *Wasp* and *Fair American*; Harold Hahn for the illustrations of his magnificent Colonial Shipyard diorama in the Mariners' Museum in Newport News, Virginia, and his model of HMS *Roebuck*; and Robert Lightley of Cape Town, South Africa, for his beautiful illustrations of the Deptford Diorama, USS *Vixen*, and the American gunboats. These gentlemen are artists in the truest sense of the word, and I am honored that they allowed me to use their work in the illustration of this book.

Additional thanks go to the American naval historian W. M. P. Dunne for making available his research into the early U. S. Navy and its connection with Charleston, especially the frigate *John Adams*, which has all but been forgotten by her birthright city; Berkeley Grimball for the use of his master's thesis on Commodore Gillon of the South Carolina State Navy; and Stephen R. Wise, Ph.D. for the use of his dissertation, *Lifeline of the Confederacy: Blockade Running During the American Civil War*, which will soon be published by the University of South Carolina Press.

Special thanks go to Lois Oglesby and Tom Crew of the Mariners' Museum, Newport News, Virginia, for their diligent help in securing illustrations and doing research in that institution's archives. Dr. Ferdinand E. Chatard of the Maryland Historical Society was able to locate the sole known illustration of the frigate *John Adams* that can be considered accurate, along with those of two other Charleston-connected ships. Others to whom thanks go are Kathy Flynn for her help with illustrations in the Peabody Museum; Rusty Fleetwood of Savannah for his help with pre-Revolutionary South Carolina vessels; Emmett Robinson of Charleston for making his files on early Charleston available; Don Canney of Columbus, Ohio, for his help on antebellum steamships; Elias Bull of Charleston for reading the manuscript for factual errors and providing leads on locating the illustrations of early Charleston wharves; and Chuck Haberlein of the Naval Historical Center in Washington for his diligent help in tracking down obscure items. Additional thanks go to W. M. P. Dunne of Hampton Bays, New York and Stephen L. Thomas of Columbia, S. C. for reading the manuscript and offering their suggestions.

The success of *Charleston's Maritime Heritage* could not have been achieved without the exquisite paintings specifically commissioned for it. Tom Freeman's eight illustrations of maritime events of this city's past give an insight that has hitherto been missed. Mark Myers has portrayed with skillful accuracy the British ships that were such a large part of this city's colonial and Revolutionary history. The German artist Peter Dewitz has captured the essence of the vessels of the Confederate War. Special thanks go to Darby Erd of Columbia, South Carolina, for his perceptive interpretations of the early South Carolina vessels, and Daniel Dowdy, also of Columbia, for his renderings of Confederate ironclads.

I am deeply indebted to my wife, Cynthia, for the many hours of torture that she has endured throughout the writing of this book. Thanks also go to my sister, Caroline Gibbons Pocari, Ph.D. of Columbia, for her many hours of painstaking work on the first draft of the text and to Yvonne Walker for her comments and additions. If there is any lustre in the text, it comes from the thought processes of Bertram Cooper of Fairfax, Virginia, who went above and beyond the call of friendship to put this text into viable form. The final editing could not have been accomplished without the painstaking attention to detail of Kathy Talmadge of Boxborough, Massachusetts, for which I am most grateful.

In closing I make a plea for information on the location of any hitherto unknown or unpublished illustrations of ships connected with Charleston, no matter where they are now located. Of special interest would be a contemporary painting, drawing, or engraving of the frigate *John Adams* as she appeared during the period 1799–1807, in her original rig.

P. C. Coker III
Charleston, South Carolina
June 1987

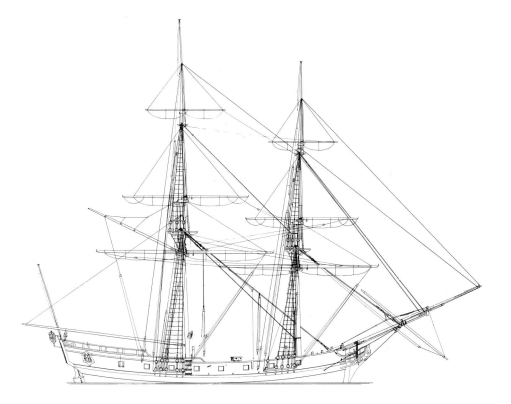

Foreword

Since its settlement in 1670, Charleston's *raison d'être* has been maritime commerce, a city where goods and materials were brought to ships for delivery elsewhere, and a place where ships brought goods and materials to be sold or shipped. Today little remains of Charleston's maritime past. When one considers the numbers and types of ships that have called in Charleston, been built here, and are otherwise connected with this city, the almost total lack of records and illustrations is unusual. Part of this missing link in the city's history is due to the Southern proclivity for agriculture and for the military arm of the defense establishment, the rest to the destruction of war, fires, and social neglect. The quick money from agriculture succeeded in focusing the concern of the city away from the significance of its maritime role. As a result records and illustrations are sparse.

By and large, the South has shown little concern for nautical lore. Within a century after Charleston's founding, local fortunes had been made in agriculture. As long as agriculture proved profitable, there was little incentive to expand into other pursuits. Shipbuilding declined and the city became dependent on ships built and owned by foreigners from the North or England. In the thirty years preceding the American Revolution, an average of less than one ocean-going vessel a year was built in Charleston. The local ship builders and owners fell on hard times. Before the start of the Confederate War in 1861, only fourteen ocean-going vessels calling regularly at Charleston were locally owned.

During the eighteenth and early nineteenth centuries, the plantocracy was the social elite, and those who engaged in other pursuits were looked down upon. As long as agriculture was profitable there was limited incentive by the controllers of capital to engage in shipping, shipbuilding, and related pursuits. Once the colony's coastal croplands reached peak development in the 1730s, only then did entrepreneurs look to new areas for profits. By the 1850s, mercantile pursuits had developed to the point that merchants attained equal wealth and social standing with planters. Many historians consider the American Civil War to be the last gasp of the Southern plantocracy; and it certainly ended its political and economic power.

Much has been written about the political, social, and military history of Charleston, but little has been told of her maritime past. Furthermore, what has been written omits large segments of that history. It was to fill those gaps that I embarked on this book.

There have been many criticisms leveled at the various histories of South Carolina, and Charleston's in particular. Those written by outsiders often treat Charleston as a backwater to the broad thrust of Western Civilization, a city where time has stopped. On the other hand, those histories written by Charlestonians tend to view Charleston as if it were the center of the universe. Historical accuracy lies between these two extremes. In concentrating on the maritime aspect of the city's economy and culture, I hope to show that Charleston's leaders, far from being the reactionary people that they have been depicted, were bold, innovative individuals, not lacking in initiative, but at the same time aware of and subject to the broad currents of Western Civilization.

The two centuries of maritime development covered in this volume span the heyday of European expansion under sail to the introduction of steam power in warships. The changes in ship construction were evolutionary until 1830, when the use of steam for power forced revolutionary changes. For example, with very little retraining, soldiers who repelled the first attack on Charles Towne[1] in 1706 could fit into the infantry ranks that stood at Secessionville in June 1862. Similarly, those sailors that arrived on the *Carolina* in 1670, or sailed with Jean Ribaut a century earlier, would have easily made the transition to crewmen on *John Adams* when she left Charleston on her maiden voyage in 1799. Without major retraining, however, they would have had a difficult time manning one of Duncan Ingraham's ironclads in 1863.

While we live in a revolutionary age of computer technology and space exploration, the seventeenth- and eighteenth-century equivalent was the sailing ship, and especially the sailing warship. These were the most complex instruments of man's industrial development until the railroad, or its nautical equivalent, the steamship. Nothing that man built in widespread use prior to this time was as complex and as expensive as the sailing ship. There is no better key to the creativity of man's industrial fabric.

In spite of the gradual changes in ship design, few forces of Western Civilization modernized faster than naval architecture during the age of sail. Ships and the men who sailed them were constantly moving from place to place. At each new destination, the ships' officers and crews would come in contact with similar men from other areas. If they did not exchange innovations and ideas directly, they would hear about them from fellow seamen, or by observing other vessels in port. Those that adapted to the successful improvements were one step ahead in the fierce competition to carry material about the world.

---

[1] Charleston was originally named for King Charles II of England. The first spelling was *Charles Towne*. By the early eighteenth century the last *e* had been dropped. Prior to the Revolution the name was spelled *Charlestown*. When the city received its charter of incorporation from the State of South Carolina in 1783, the name was altered for the final time to *Charleston*. The spelling of the name of the city throughout the text will correspond to that of the period under discussion.

Ship captains and crews are basically a conservative lot; thus advancement was not rapid. Innovation came about slowly until the steam age arrived. This pace allowed for lengthy intercourse and the exchange of ideas among people both on land and sea. However, if we look at many of the earlier innovations, they were spread about mostly by contact with seamen and those astute observers who went to sea.

During the era of the sailing ship, landsmen did not have much opportunity to travel. Travel was arduous, time-consuming, expensive, and dangerous. Those that did not have to travel on business or on government missions stayed close to home. Their contacts with outsiders were limited, and the exchange of ideas and innovations was through written means with limited accessibility. Therefore, intercourse among the various peoples of the world was largely conductd by seafarers.

While Charleston may seem to have basked in relative obscurity on the southeastern coast of North America, she was very much a part of the fabric of the British Empire as a result of her trade. Starting in the earliest days, there was pressure to become self-sufficient and turn a profit for the Proprietors of South Carolina. In order to achieve this aim, the city had to market commodities that were in demand elsewhere; as a consequence her citizens were subjected to the forces of world civilization and intercourse with other people. War three thousand miles across the ocean may have seemed remote, but Charleston felt its impact in changing political decisions and in prices for her exports and imports.

Those outside the South today perceive Charleston as a sleepy, static community; however, those who know the community well are often awestruck by its sophistication, its pride, and its vitality. These traits did not arise overnight, but are the consequence of centuries of evolution. This volume will show that many of these traits were formed through the city's trade and maritime development, which allowed it to become refined and to attain the wealth to develop in other areas.

The reason why this chronicle ends in 1865 is that the maritime history of Charleston during the last 120 years has centered largely around the development of the U. S. Naval Base and the S. C. State Ports Authority. The story of the former has been well told in Jim McNeil's *Charleston's Navy Yard* (CokerCraft Press, 1986) and the story of the State Ports Authority will probably be best told by someone connected with that agency's development and recent growth.

Throughout the city's development it has been associated with mid-sized and smaller ocean craft. This book, however, will be limited to the discussion of ocean-going vessels, except where smaller vessels may have had an effect. For those interested in the smaller coastal and inland vessels, the author recommends the splendid volume *Tidecraft*, by Rusty Fleetwood (Coastal Heritage Society, 1982).

South Carolina's first involvement with the sea arose when early Spanish, English, and French explorers arrived in small vessels, not unlike those that made up Columbus's fleet. They were generally square rigged, and some had a lateen-rigged sail on the aft or mizzenmast. They changed little over the next century except in size. By the mid-seventeenth century the Dutch, English, and French competition at sea had made great strides in naval architecture. Ships grew larger, with greater capacity; improved sails and rigging increased speed.

By the early eighteenth century the necessity for speed had made the small, fast Bermuda sloop the mainstay of the pirates, privateers, and many merchantmen, and would remain the favorite colonial vessel almost to the Revolution. It would be replaced by the easier-to-handle colonial sloops and schooners, which would in turn be replaced with larger merchant ships after the War for Independence.

The word *ship* can carry several connotations. In layman's language, it is a generic term for any ocean-going vessel. In precisely correct terminology, *ship* means a three-masted sailing vessel with square-rigged sails on each mast. Although it will be used interchangeably in this volume, the precise terminology is the major emphasis. The context in which it is used will be the key. Generally speaking, if the word *ship* is used in series with other types of vessels, it will mean the three-masted, square-rigged variety; if used alone it will also designate any ocean-going vessel.

General Background on Ships of the Period

Uninformed Europeans considered colonial America a backwoods, a crude outpost of English civilization. Those who have investigated it more closely have been surprised by the degree of sophisticated innovation in the crafts of pre-Revolutionary America. This backwoods concept was especially true in European shipbuilding circles, where the colonial shipbuilder was pictured as a primitive artisan, isolated from European developments and dependent upon only native intelligence, which naturally produced only the most primitive vessels. This was a false impression; Charles Town's shipbuilders maintained a level of skill equal to any in the field. There was nothing primitive in the art of marine construction in America. Contrary to existing prejudices, a skilled ship builder in America could produce a vessel patterned after any model that an owner might choose.

When the *Carolina* Expedition sailed to South Carolina in 1670, shipbuilding was a well-established art dictated by rules developed and laid down over the preceding 1,000 or more years. For the construction of wooden ships, this "establishment" or rules pertaining to ship construction would remain and carry over into the iron and steel shipbuilding that we know today with few fundamental alterations.

While English principles of ship construction were the major influence in Charles Town shipbuilding, Dutch and French innovations also had an impact. By the seventeenth century, the design and construction of warships in Europe had been standardized. Ships were built according to "establishments" as set down by each nation's naval hierarchy. This step, in effect, froze warship design for over 100 years. In England, the Admiralty set the minimum dimensions for each class, or rate, of warships. First-rates of 90 to 100 guns were the largest, and sixth-rates at 20 guns were the smallest. The rules governing the design and construction of merchant vessels were not as rigid as those laid down by the Admiralty. As a result, most advances in naval architecture were introduced first in the design and construction of merchant vessels.

Most colonial shipwrights had served long periods as apprentices to shipbuilders in Europe or in American yards, which helped to maintain conformity. In colonial America, far from the seat of power, more experimentation and variety were possible in designing the ships for speed and in the use of native building materials.

By the late seventeenth century, the colonial sailing ship had developed the basic form it would hold for the next two centuries. The bow had a stem, or prow extending from it. This supported the forward structure, much as an upward extension of the keel. The forward end of the ship was one deck higher (forecastle deck) than the mid-section or waist just forward of the main mast. Smaller vessels usually had no forecastle deck, and the curve of the main deck sloped more sharply upward from the midship section toward the bow and stern.

This resulted in higher sides at the forward end, which helped to keep water from coming directly over the bow in a seaway. The sterns were usually one deck higher than the mid-section and covered the aft part of the length of the hull. The high sterns gave the men controlling the rudder a view over the bow. On a disabled vessel, the high stern served as a weather vane to keep the craft pointed into the wind and waves for stability. Here toward the stern would be found the captain's cabin and, on larger ships, the officers' quarters. From these accommodations we derive the term *quarters*, meaning "a place to live," because it was under the quarterdeck, which was on the aft two-quarters of the ship.

number of masts was the first indication. The shape of the hull was seldom mentioned after 1850; in the early eighteenth century, the shape of the stern became almost uniform in ocean-going vessels. The pointed stern of the pinks gave way to the transom stern, which had been found to give better support to the after-superstructure and provided additional room for accommodations. References remained to the double-ended or pointed stern pinks, but these had almost disappeared by 1750 except in the fishing trade.

Square sails, the lowest of which were the Courses, proceeding upwards to the Topsails, Topgallant sails, and, in some cases, Royals at the very top, were the principal motive power. They were supplemented by a series of fore and aft sails, including the jibs at the bow; lateen, or gaff-rigged, sails on the mizzenmast; and staysails, similar to jibs, between the masts. Ocean-going sailing vessels had bowsprits or spars extending forward from the bow. Small vessels had only masts, and the smallest had only one.

The arrangement of the masts is used to describe vessels in today's terminology:

Typical arrangement of decks in an early seventeenth-century sailing ship.

The hull of a ship usually contained two decks, one on the top of the hull and a second one below, inside the hull. The latter often did not run continuously from bow to stern, but was arranged to suit the needs of the vessel for the service in which it would be employed. Between the lowest deck and the keel was an area running the length of the ship known as the hold. In this area was stowed the cargo; food; water; spare items needed for a voyage; ballast; and, on warships, the ammunition.

Most vessels, except the very smallest, had guns mounted on the main or uppermost continuous deck of the hull. These were for defense against pirates or other marauders. They were mostly for intimidation; few merchant ships had sufficient crewmen to man them. Even when manned, they could do little damage because of their small caliber. Sea battles up to 1750 were largely determined by armed men boarding an enemy ship to engage in hand-to-hand combat.

In looking at each vessel, the variations of its masts and spars are the most noticeable. Modern descriptions use the rig to describe a particular vessel, whereas in colonial times a vessel was most often described by her hull. As hulls became similar, a vessel came to be called a schooner, brig, and so on because the visible difference was then its type of rig; the

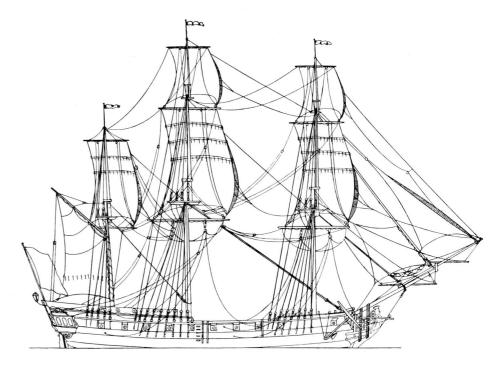

Ship: three masts with square sails on all masts

Brig: two masts (fore and main) with square sails on both masts. A brig is basically a shortened ship without a mizzenmast. A brigantine was a variation of a brig in that it had square sails only on the foremast.

Schooner: two-masted vessel with fore and aft sails. Some carried additional small square sails on the foremast and were called "topsail schooners." At first glance, a topsail schooner would appear similar to a brig or brigantine, but, on closer examination, the sharper rake or slant of the schooner's masts and the narrower flush-decked hull would be apparent.

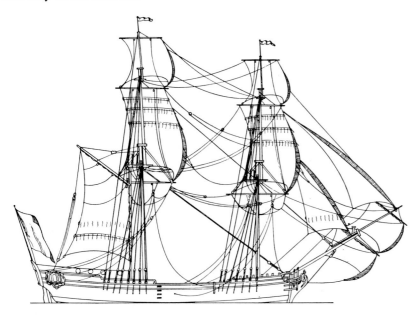

Snow: same as a brig but with a small pole mounted about a foot behind, or abaft, the mizzenmast for carrying the spanker, or gaff-rigged sail, on that mast.

Ketch: similar to a ship, but without a foremast. A ketch is similar to a brig, except it has a main and mizzenmast instead of a fore and mainmast, but the masts are placed further aft on the hull. Ketches were usually employed as warships with mortars in place of the foremast, and until about 1700 as ocean fishing boats.

Sloop: single-masted vessel with either square or fore and aft sails including a large-gaff rigged spanker and often a jibboom on the fixed bowsprit; this inclined upward at a sharper angle than the cutter's, which did not have a jibboom.

Cutter: similar to a sloop, but with a running bowsprit, and no quarterdeck.

The most popular vessel with the first Charles Town builders was the sloop—a small, fast, one-masted craft that was probably adapted from the earlier shallops. It had more sail area and the fore and aft rig made it a nimble craft for coastal trading in narrow, winding channels with small crews. The local shipowners quickly began to rely on the West Indies as the source for this ship type, and local builders turned to the schooners shortly after 1700. The sloop continued to be the most common vessel seen in Charles Town harbor in the first half of the eighteenth century. These vessels were the smallest of the ocean-going trading vessels, averaging 25 tons. Only about one-fourth of them were armed.

A shallop was originally a large boat that was carried on the decks in the waist (midship area) of the larger ships that brought the first colonists to America. These shallops were used for coastal exploration but, not being decked over, their seaworthiness was limited. Remaining popular as time passed, they soon had a deck added. As sizes increased, they were altered and became two-masted schooners. The name *shallop* gradually fell out of use in the early 1700s. They were to be rechristened *longboat* or *launch*.

Colonial shallop. The earlier vessels of this type were open; this one is partially decked over. As sizes increased the deck completely covered the hull.

The rounded sterns on the earlier shallops gave way to transom sterns, and the vessels increased in size. It was thus that the schooner developed. The schooner was fast for the period. Its easy-to-handle rig and shallow draft made it quite popular in the early eighteenth-century colonial coastal trade. With two masts, a small crew of two to six men could easily handle her. When heavy weather threatened, the crew could shorten or adjust sail, one mast at a time.

The first mention of a schooner in Charles Town was in 1717, when one is listed as having cleared the port. They varied in size and rig, but the hulls were quite similar, seldom over fifty tons. While American schooners of the period were largely alike, the Southern-built vessels were smaller and of shallower draft as opposed to the Northern-built ones. This allowed them to navigate Southern inlets and coastal waters.

Next to the rig, the vessel's carrying capacity was the important consideration. In the seventeenth century this was measured by the following formula, called Baker's rule:

keel length x greatest breadth inside the hull x the depth perpendicular from the breadth to the upper edge of the keel divided by 100

This formula gave the burden, or carrying capacity, of the vessel in tons, its most important characteristic as far as merchant vessels went. The *actual* tonnage of the vessel usually ran up to 40 percent over the figure derived by this formula, but that was less important. A vessel with a keel length of 100 feet, 20 feet wide, and 10 feet in depth at the midship point would have a burden of 200 tons, an above-average size for an ocean-going merchant ship of 1700. This same formula was used in assessing port charges and duties.

The formula was constantly being tinkered with. In 1664 Parliament changed the denominator from 100 to 94, the breadth measurement from outside to outside, and the depth measurement to one-half of the breadth. This tempted shipowners and builders to "pinch the beams," resulting in narrower vessels. Some were altered to the point of being rendered unseaworthy; but the overall result was speedier vessels, as narrow ships tend to be faster than wide ones.

In considering the form of the hull, the builder would opt for speed, carrying capacity, or a combination of these factors. Speed was not considered a priority at first. The ships were small; seaworthiness and carrying capacity were more important. Seaworthiness meant blunt ends, which hindered speed but increased carrying capacity. A blunt, or apple-cheeked, bow would keep the vessel from pitching into the waves and make the hull a more stable platform on which the crew could go about their work without having to hang on for dear life. For a warship, this was especially important. More than speed, a stable gun platform was the key to success in battle.

Accepted colonial shipbuilding practice defined that the underwater part of a ship should have "the head of a cod and the tail of a mackerel." This hull form would allow the blunt bow to give some stability from pitching in rough water, while the sharp stern would allow for good rudder control in steering. The widest point was one-third of the way back from the bow.

Speed was given more consideration in colonial waters than in European waters, where shorter distances and more-established authority kept reasonable controls on marauders. The lawlessness prevalent in the colonies demanded defensive measures. Any vessel that could not outfight an attacker had to be able to outsail it. Speed became the best insurance because it would preserve not only the vessel and cargo, but the lives and liberty of the crew. Further-

more, well-armed ships were expensive to build and man, and the weapons and ammunition took up space that could be devoted to cargo. In addition, small fast vessels were the favorite of both pirate and smuggler for they could slip in and out of shallow areas that would be denied to deeper-draft vessels.

Once the period of threats from pirates, privateers, and enemy warships was past, the shipowners reverted to the slower vessels that could carry more cargo on the same size hull. But when the threat manifested itself again, these slower ships were the first to fall prey. This topsy-turvy state of affairs existed throughout the eighteenth century, as the competition to build ships large, albeit slow, to transport goods was fierce. As a result colonial merchants suffered heavy wartime losses to enemy marauders.

Prior to 1700, greater speed was accomplished by moving the widest point of each frame upward in the forward end of the ship, resulting in a finer entry into the water. Elongating the hull vertically at the bow did not sufficiently improve a vessel's movement through the water and other refinements in hull form were gradually introduced. The early necessity for speed due to the lawlessness in the New World made American shipbuilders the leaders in the development of the fast-sailing ship. This culminated in the clipper ship era.

According to the physics of hydrodynamics, the speed of a sailing vessel is a function of the length of the waterline. (This does not apply to small vessels that can plane on the surface of the water, reducing their drag considerably.) Speed is calculated on paper at 1.3 times the square root of the waterline length. Accordingly, a 100-foot vessel would have a

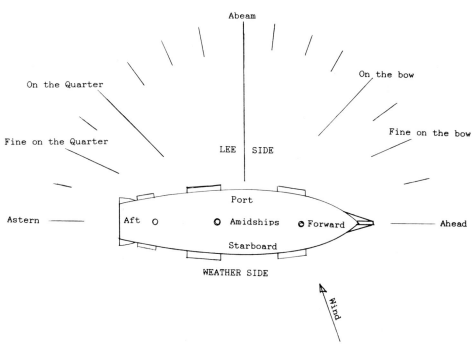

SHIPBOARD DIRECTIONS.

theoretical top speed of 13 knots (10 × 1.3). On occasion, some sailing vessels attained speeds as high as 1.5 times the square root of the waterline length, but any vessel with a factor above 1.25 was considered fast. The best possible speeds are attained under such favorable conditions as a wind on or abaft the beam, relatively calm sea, and a good hull-form designed to move through the water. The third consideration meant a sharp bow, which most colonial ships did not have.

In light winds, a small vessel with a large sail area would be favored for speed. In contrast, a large one with similarly proportioned sail area would be favored in a heavy wind and sea, as its heavier weight would provide more stability in addition to the advantage of the longer waterline. Rough water would slow the smaller vessel and make her bob around constantly, shaking the wind out of the sails.

The first colonial records of the necessity of speed came out of the French and Spanish sweeps of colonial shipping in Queen Anne's War. Only the fast or lucky ones escaped capture. Some colonial fleets were all but wiped out. This led to the need for small, fast ocean-going vessels that could be hidden in small coves or inlets.

Caribbean shipbuilders responded with the Jamaica-sloop, which had a keel deeper at the stern. This drag to the keel gave excellent rudder control. The raking mast, sharp deadrise or V-shaped hull, raking stem and stern, low freeboard (sides), and considerable rise of the deck fore to aft from the midship point, gave these Jamaica sloops a distinctive line. So many of them were built that Jamaica's timber was depleted. This forced the builders to move to Bermuda. Thus, we have the name derived for this ship type. The so-called Bermuda sloop was the favorite vessel of pirates because of its speed and ability to sail close to the wind (upwind). They were still popular and common as late as 1750. Few, however, were built in Charles Town, as local builders preferred the schooner.

Principles of Ship Construction

The shipbuilder and the future owner decided together on the size of the vessel to be built. A contract for the construction of a schooner at Charles Town in 1759 between George Powell, the builder, and the planters Nicholas Harleston, Elias Ball, and John Ball called for "a well-made vessel forty-four feet on the keel with a fifteen-foot beam and a six-foot hold."[2] It was to be supplied, rigged, and ready to sail for £605 in Carolina currency, considerably less than pound sterling. According to the contract, £200 was to be supplied upon completion of the framework; £200 upon planking; and the balance upon launch, completion, and delivery.

Once the builder and owner had decided upon the overall dimensions, the lines and a few of the hull sections would be laid out according to the standard shipbuilding formulas as set down in various reference works of the time. These early books on naval architecture were rare and valuable, carefully treasured by any shipbuilder who might be lucky enough to own one. In his will of 1850, the Charleston builder James Marsh bequeathed to his son his "Book of Naval Architecture[3] which formerly belonged to my Grand Father, dated 16 February 1756." From this we can gather that these books retained their utility for several generations.

Ships were built on a ramp-like structure called a shipbuilding way. This was laid out on an incline at right angles to the water, so that when the hull of the ship was completed, its weight would carry it downhill into the river at the proper time. The building way could vary from a few heavy planks laid into the earth, to heavy granite stones forming an elaborate roadway into the water. Whatever it was made from, it had to support the weight of the finished hull of the vessel, which could range from two to three hundred tons in eighteenth-century Charles Town.

The shipbuilders would take great pains to select the correct tree for the keel, as it was important to cut it from as few pieces as possible. Any joints would be weak and potential trouble points, as the keel was the backbone of the vessel on which the rest of the hull structure was built. After the keel timber was cut and shaped, it was laid on the building way on top of perpendicular support timbers. Precise positioning was important to keep the keel off the ground, allowing additional working room underneath the hull. To the keel was attached the stem and stern post. In between these, the frames were erected; the resulting structure looked much like the ribs and backbone of a huge animal. In South Carolina, native long-leaf heart pine was found to be the best material for keel construction because of its lateral strength, trueness, and durability in salt water.

Each frame consisted of several parts. The floor timbers were at the bottom, resting on top of the keel. Then curved sections, called *futtocks*, made up each side. The futtocks at the top of each frame were called the top timbers. The square-shaped floor timbers were placed on top of the keel with spaces between them that approximated their thickness. To the floor

Colonial Shipbuilding.

[2] Measures 52 62/94 tons.

[3] by Mango Murray, uncle of one of Marsh's predecessors, James Stewart.

timbers were attached the futtocks, overlapping by two to four feet, and attached to each other by wooden pegs or metal spikes in scarph joints. To make up each side of a frame, large vessels would have up to four futtocks; smaller vessels had one or two. The top timbers were scarphed to the top futtock of the frame.

The frames grew thinner as they went higher in the hull; most strength was required where the frames joined the keel. In the early days of the colony, framing was not as precise a science as it later became. Only every third or fourth frame was laid out and cut precisely before being erected on the keel. The others were shaped by eyesight. The builder relied on the planking to hold the entire structure together. Over the course of the eighteenth century, more and more of the frames were laid out and cut to precise shape before being pegged into the keel. By the mid-nineteenth century, all of the parts of the frame were laid out and precisely cut before assembly. Likewise, each frame was completely assembled before being erected on the keel, rather than being attached futtock by futtock.

To give extra strength to the joint between the floor timber and the first futtock, the inner planking, or ceiling, was made extra heavy and pegged into each frame. On the outside of the hull along the sides, extra-thick planks or wales were attached for added strength. These were the first part of the exterior planking attached to the hull's framework. When laymen see these wales in paintings, they mistake them for the outline of the decks on the inside, but no sailor could function on a ship's deck that followed the curves of the wales. Actually, they followed the outermost point of each frame, with the hull sloping inward above and below the wale. Above the wale, this inward slope was called "tumblehome".[4] It was a

[4] "Tumblehome" was used to move the mass of the upper decks inward toward the centerline of the ship to improve stability. On warships the added advantage of the slanting sides served to help deflect cannonballs in combat.

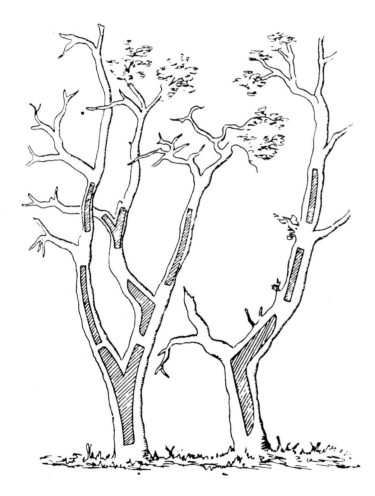

Typical tree showing the areas from which were cut the various timbers for wooden ships.

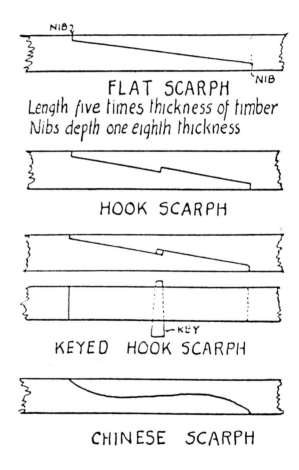

Typical Scarph Joints

Scarph joints were made by chamfering, halving, notching, or otherwise cutting away two pieces to correspond to each other, and then securing them together.

distinct characteristic of eighteenth-century ships. At the bow and stern, the wales were cut and sawed to shape rather than bent. On the inside of the hull, additional heavy longitudinal members were attached to the frames to support the deck beams (clamp or shelf), backed up by vertical (hanging) and horizontal (lodging) knees or trusses cut from the crotch of a tree.

Once the frames were in place, the outer and inner planking was applied. This was usually cut one and a half to two inches thick from long-leaf heart pine. However, in warships it was found that heart pine splintered badly when hit by cannonballs. These flying wooden splinters caused most of the casualties in naval battles. White oak was occasionally substituted, but it was less durable. The planks were attached to the frame with wooden pegs called *treenails* (trunnels). Planks had to be heated or scorched (later bent by steam) to curve

around the bow and stern of the vessel. When the planking was finished, the skin of the hull was similar to modern plywood, with the grain of the outer and inner planking running in one direction and the middle layer (frames) running perpendicular to it, making for a strong, rigid structure.

The decks were also cut from long-leaf pine and pegged into position. Then finishing touches were added and the bottom was covered, usually with a mixture of tallow and sulphur, to fend off the teredo navalis, a type of wood borer (related to the clam) that lives in salt water from the polar regions to the tropics. Other methods, such as lead sheathing or a coating of hair and tar sandwiched between two layers of planking, were also used; however, none was successful in protecting the bottoms of ships until copper sheeting was introduced

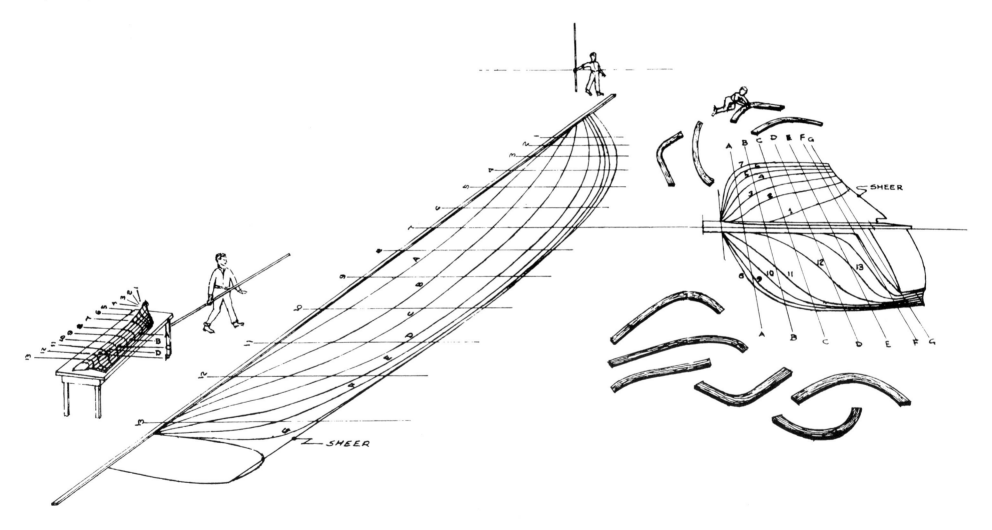

Laying down a small vessel in the mould loft. The vertical lines and station numbers aided the loftsman in marking his reference points on the grid he had drawn on the loft floor. From the **layout of the body plan at the right, the timbers would be cut to make up the frames in the hull.**

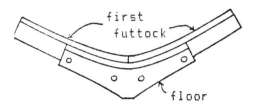

first
futtock

floor

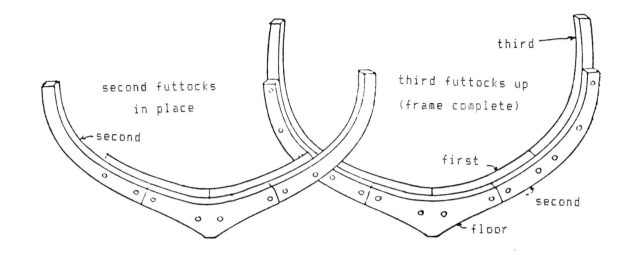

second futtocks
in place

second

third

third futtocks up
(frame complete)

first

second

floor

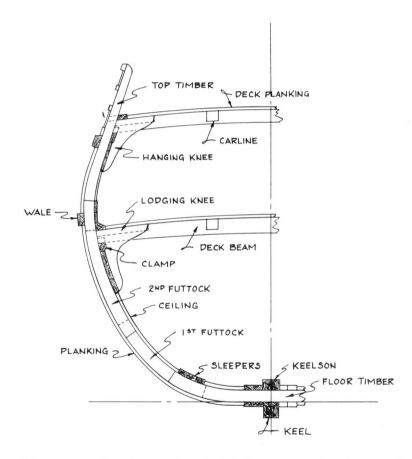

TOP TIMBER

DECK PLANKING

CARLINE

HANGING KNEE

LODGING KNEE

WALE

DECK BEAM

CLAMP

2ND FUTTOCK

CEILING

1ST FUTTOCK

PLANKING

SLEEPERS

KEELSON

FLOOR TIMBER

KEEL

Transverse section of a typical vessel of the late seventeenth and early eighteenth centuries. This method of hull framing would remain basically unchanged to the end of the era of the wooden sailing ship. Note the keel, floor timbers, and futtocks that make up each frame. To these were attached the side planking and ceiling or inside planking.

The first steps in constructing a wooden ship. The well-braced stem, stern, and first frames being erected on the keel on a building way. See page 51.

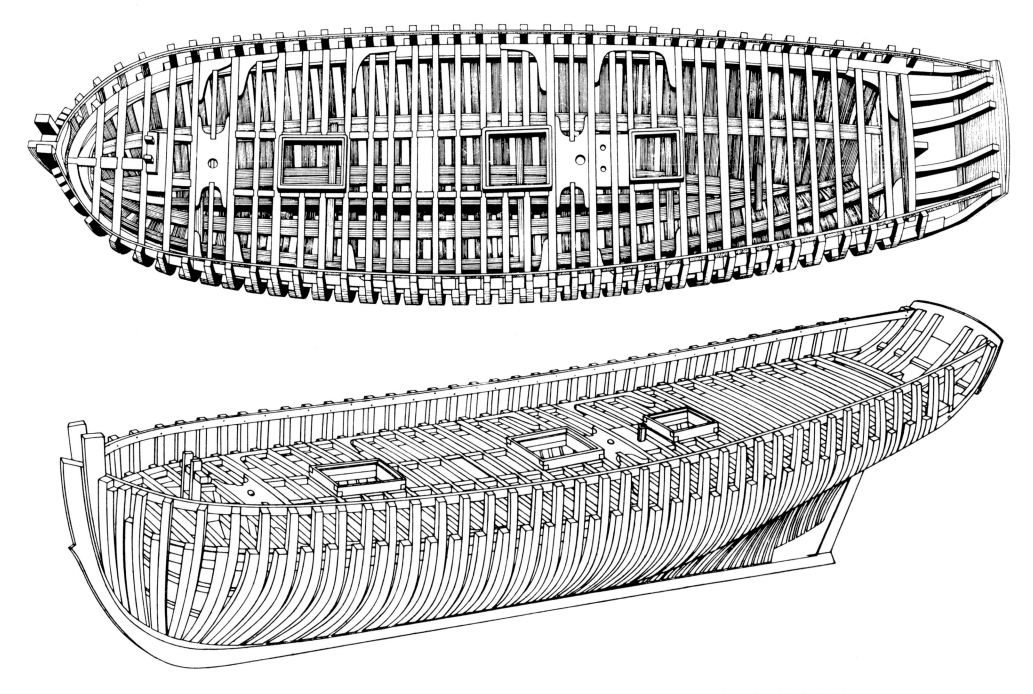

The hull of an eighteenth-century brig with frames, deck beams, and hull structure ready to receive the exterior hull and deck planking.

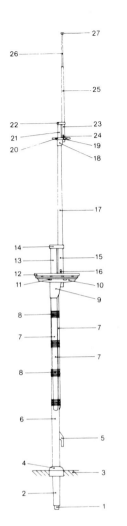

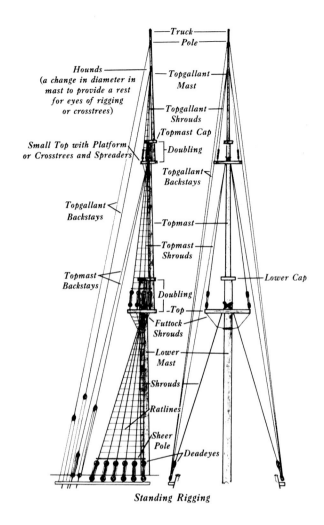

Standing Rigging

in Europe before the Revolution. Until the 1790s copper was too expensive and scarce in America to be used by local shipbuilders.

When the hull structure was complete, the vessel was launched with much fanfare and celebration. The uncompleted vessel was then taken to a fitting-out dock. There the masts and rigging were installed. The masts were constructed in pieces, with the lower masts being heavier. Overlapping the lower mast by a few feet was the topmast. At the doublings, or joints, between the masts were a pair of trestle trees on which the topmast could stand, with a band around both masts a few feet higher up. This system enabled the crew to remove the upper masts for repairs. Large vessels would carry topgallant masts above the topmasts, similarly attached, and larger vessels had royals.

As the masts went into position, the miles of cordage required for the rigging were piled on and around the spars. Shrouds and backstays ran from the mast tops to channels or chainplates on the sides, and stays ran from the mast tops to lower positions on the centerline—either to the deck, mast, or bowsprit ahead.

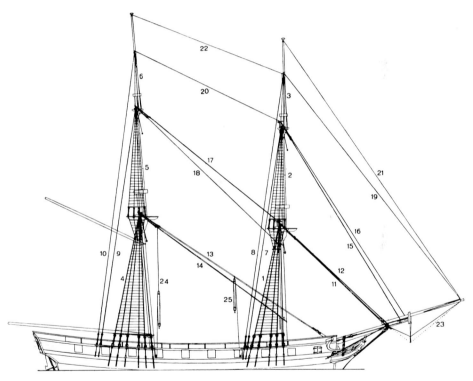

Standing Rigging of a British *Cruizer*-class Brig-of-war (early nineteenth century)

1 & 4 lower shrouds	15 & 16 fore topmast stay; fore topmast spring stay
2 & 5 topmast shrouds	17 & 18 main topmast stay; main topmast spring stay
3 & 6 topgallant shrouds	19 & 20 topgallant stays
7 & 9 topmast backstays	21 & 22 royal stays
8 & 10 topgallant backstays	23 martingale stays
11 & 12 forestay; fore spring stay	24 & 25 stay tackles for lifting loads
13 & 14 mainstay: main spring stay	

Mast Components

1 heel tenon	15 topmast heel
2 mast heel	16 fid
3 deck	17 topmast
4 mast wedges and collar	18 topmast cheeks
5 mast cleat	19 topmast trestle trees
6 lower mast	20 topmast cross trees
7 fish	21 topmast head
8 wooldings	22 topmast cap
9 mast cheeks	23 topgallant mast heel
10 lower mast trestle trees	24 fid
11 lower mast cross trees	25 topgallant mast
12 top	26 royal mast or pole
13 mast head	27 truck
14 cap	

Running rigging controlled the movement of the horizontal spars or yards on which the square sails hung; and of the sails, enabling them to be worked from positions on the deck rather than sending men aloft to set them. The crew would go aloft only to work on the masts and furl and unfurl the sails, not to position them to catch the wind. In light weather, additional square sails called steering or studding sails (stuns'ls) could be set by means of extensions lashed onto the ends of the yards.

Because of expense, paint was used only for decoration until the nineteenth century. As a result, the sides above the waterline were often covered with pine or linseed oil, which dried to a tough, dark brown preservative coating. In the years before the Revolution some owners began to disguise the age of their ships (the older the ship, the darker the color) by adding ochre to the finish, which varied from a mustard-yellow to a light brown hue. Regardless of whether stain or paint was used, the wales were most often covered with pitch or pine tar to prevent the hull from being scuffed or damaged when it rubbed against wharves or other ships.

European ships, particularly warships of the eighteenth century, were marked by elaborate color decorations, carvings, and gilt work. The colonies had to be more frugal in their approach to shipbuilding, in order to compete. The figurehead and the stern and quarter galleries were usually the only decorations on colonial ships. However, although starkness was the rule, successful shipowners would display their wealth with more elaborate decorations.

Sails on a Ship

1 flying jib
3 jib
4 fore topmast staysail
5 spritsail topsail
6 spritsail
7 fore royal
8 fore topgallant sail
9 fore topsail
10 fore course or fore sail
11 main topgallant staysail
12 middle staysail

13 main topmast staysail
14 main staysail
15 main royal
16 main topgallant sail
17 main topsail
18 main course or mainsail
19 mizzen topmast staysail
20 mizzen staysail
21 mizzen topgallant sail
22 mizzen topsail
23 mizzen sail (later spanker)

Starboard braces on a ship (arrows denote direction of movement).

CHARLES TOWNE SHIPS 1670–1750

Scale 1″ = 50′

Adventure **1690**

Bermuda Sloop 1700–1770

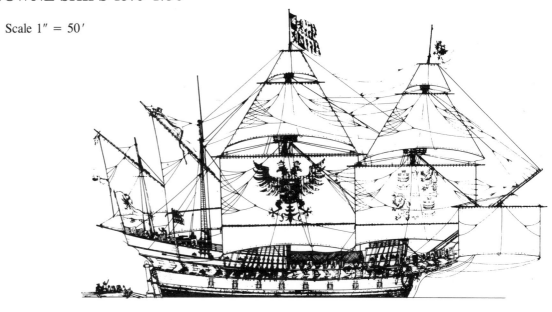

Spanish Galleon, late sixteenth century

shallop

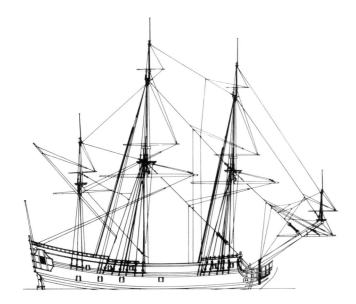

Carolina **1670**

English Sixth-rate Warship 1720–1774

Part I

CARVING A NEW SOCIETY FROM THE WILDERNESS

The colonization of South Carolina by Europeans was not a spontaneous, sudden event. Rather, it was the climax of decades of exploration and conflicts. Early records disagree in identifying the first Europeans to view what is now South Carolina, a land the natives called "Chicora." Some claim that John Cabot discovered it on a voyage in 1497, but no official concession was made to the territory. The gold of Mexico and Peru occupied the initial attention of the Spanish explorers, but eventually they sent explorers to Florida and points north. Spain had two interests in Chicora: one was to settle the area for development; the other, to deny it to others as a base for attacking their treasure fleets sailing up the coast on the way home to Spain. Because of the prevailing winds over the North Atlantic Ocean, sailing ships traveling between North America and Europe had to move along a clockwise route around the Atlantic's rim. Thus, any vessel leaving the Caribbean had to travel up the east coast of North America before setting off across the Atlantic. Anyone seeking to plunder these vessels merely had to lie in wait. Any coastal settlements were potential threats to these ships. By the same token, any ships coming from Europe to North America had to travel first to the Azores and then to the West Indies before proceeding up the coast. The southerly route made them vulnerable to unfriendly settlements in the Caribbean.

Early Explorers and Attempts at Colonization

In 1520, an expedition under Francisco Gordillo explored the Carolina coast, landing at Santa Elena (now Port Royal), Cape Fear, and Winyah Bay (St. John the Baptist Bay to the Spaniards). Another expedition in 1525 came to Winyah, but only to explore the area. The next year, a more ambitious expedition set out from Hispaniola in six ships with over 500 potential settlers under Lucas Vazquez de Ayllon. Hard times beset them on the North Carolina coast. They found Cape Fear not to their liking, their flagship wrecked, and they were deserted by their Indian guides. They moved south to Winyah Bay; some came overland and the remainder by ship. Here they established the town of San Miguel de Gualdape near the mouth of the Waccamaw River on lower Waccamaw Neck, across Winyah Bay from present-day Georgetown. San Miguel de Gualdape was the first Spanish settlement on the continent of North America north of Mexico. While there, the settlers constructed a small vessel to replace the flagship lost at Cape Fear. This was the first known instance of shipbuilding in South Carolina. Nothing is known about this vessel, but it must be assumed to have been small, since it was probably to be used for coastal exploring with oars or sails. Malaria decimated the population, including Ayllon, and jealousy and rivalry among his successors led to mutiny and harsh repression. By winter, discouragement among the survivors in the wilderness led them to abandon the settlement. Early in 1527, only about 150 sick and despondent colonists reached home.

During this time Spain withheld from other nations any knowledge of the vast wealth it had found in America, even going so far as to handle maps and charts as top-secret documents and to conceal the movements of its ships. Only Spanish seamen were allowed as crewmen on her vessels, which were under the control of the Council of the Indies. A sea captain sailing under license was given the use of charts and nautical information, but he was forbidden to pass it on. Upon his return from a voyage, he reported his activities to the Council of the Indies, which made due note of his sightings. Eventually, Spain found it was impossible to conceal the fabulous wealth she was reaping from America. Vessels from other nations were soon preying on Spain's treasure, forcing the Spanish fleets into a convoy system.

In the mid-sixteenth century, the religious politics of the Reformation were dominating Western Europe. In France the industrious Protestants, or Huguenots, had gained such influence that the crown gave tacit approval to their colonization efforts, mostly to get them out of the country. If the colony failed, the crown could consider them expendable. If it succeeded, France had a new colony at Spain's expense.

In 1562, the French admiral Gaspard de Coligny, a Huguenot, sent two ships to explore the southeast coast of North America under Jean Ribaut, a captain in the French Navy and fellow Protestant from the Norman port of Dieppe. The expedition of three small but well-armed ships was manned mostly by Huguenots who despised Catholic Spain. They sailed from Le Havre-de-Grâce in February 1562. Ribaut landed at several places along the Carolina coast, including Santa Elena. It was he who changed the name to Port Royal, the only French placename to remain in South Carolina. He took possession of the land in the name of the King of France, Charles IX, in whose honor he called the land "Carolina," derived from *Carolus*, the Latin name for Charles. The natives were friendly, so on what is today known as Parris Island, he built Charlesfort, also named in honor of the king. Here he left a small garrison of twenty-six men to hold the land while he returned to France for supplies in June 1562. As the ships departed they exchanged salutes with the fort.

Peace in the settlement soon dissolved into internal strife brought on by Captain Pierra, a dictatorial leader who was eventually killed by his men. Figuring that Ribaut would not return, the survivors then constructed a crude pinnace, or large boat, in which to return home. One account says that it was about forty feet and some twenty tons with two masts, probably lateen-rigged. Though none was a skilled shipwright, necessity taught them a method. They used moss and pitch as caulk, their clothes as sails, and cordage made by the Indians from tree bark. The survivors set sail. One young man, Guillaume Rouffi, stayed behind; he chose to remain with his Indian friends. While the craft may have been sea-worthy, its crew had little knowledge of navigation or seamanship. The food quickly ran out and the craft was becalmed for several days. A chance encounter with an English bark saved them from certain death only after they had resorted to cannibalism.

Ribaut had reached France in less than six weeks only to find civil war brewing and a relief expedition for his colony out of the question. In vain he sought help elsewhere. In the meantime, the Spanish ambassador in France reported Ribaut's activities to his sovereign. The governor of Cuba was directed to send an expedition to destroy the French settlement. After much searching, it found and destroyed Charlesfort, dug up Ribaut's marker claiming the area for France, and took Rouffi back to Cuba.

Two years later, Admiral Coligny dispatched another expedition under Ribaut's lieutenant, René de Laudonniere. They chose to make a settlement, Fort Caroline, on the St. Johns River in Florida in order to prey on Spanish ships off the coast. When the delivering ships returned to France, this second settlement also fell into discontent. By early 1565, the food was gone. By chance, the English sea captain John Hawkins anchored his squadron in the river, replenished their supplies, and sold them a ship. By summer the supplies had given out again, but as the survivors made ready to sail for France, Ribaut arrived in six ships with 300 new colonists.

A week after Ribaut's arrival, a Spanish squadron arrived but withdrew to St. Augustine after an inconclusive battle. From there the Spanish marched overland and, surprising Fort

Caroline at night, massacred the garrison. A few Frenchmen swam to the ships in the river. Some of the ships escaped to sea, but several were wrecked in a storm. Ribaut and most of his men had not escaped. The Spanish troops massacred them—not because they were French, but because they were Protestants. Laudonniere returned to France with the few

French ship of the type that Ribaut would have used in exploring the South Carolina Coast.

survivors. In 1568, the French returned to the St. Johns River under the command of Captain de Gourgues. They attacked and killed most of the Spanish, and demolished their fortifications. Political unrest in France, however, forced Laudonniere to return before a permanent settlement could be established.

In 1566, the Spanish returned to Port Royal and erected Fort San Felipe on Parris Island, not far from the remains of Charlesfort. For ten years this and a subsequent garrison struggled to survive in a seesaw relationship with the local Indians, who were aided from time to time by raids from French explorer/pirates. The Spanish hung on at Port Royal until 1586, when Sir Francis Drake looted and burned St. Augustine. This forced a drastic reduction of the strategic Spanish frontier posts. For the next century, Spanish priests continued to spread the gospel along the Carolina coast; but it was an uphill struggle—mostly because of deteriorating relations with the Indians. The Spaniards had failed to establish a commercially viable community. Neither were they able to provide their own food, and thus became a liability to the Indians whom they sought to convert.

England Enters the Contest

For the next century few Europeans set foot on South Carolina soil, but the French corsairs used the inlets and coves as bases to attack the Spanish treasure fleets. Constant fighting between the two and their Indian allies continued off and on until English, Portuguese, and Dutch vessels joined in the attacks on the Spanish. These were all sporadic skirmishes with no attempt to establish permanent settlements.

England had remained out of the contest largely due to her submission to Catholic authority. As a result she continued to recognize the Treaty of Tordesillas (1494), which had divided the New World between Spain and Portugal. The success of Drake, Frobisher, Hawkins, and other English corsairs against the Spanish led to a change of heart. At the same time England became convinced that her claim in North America was legitimate as a result of the discoveries of John Cabot. During the reign of Elizabeth I, the Reformation's ideas caught hold. England's attitude toward America changed and Rome's authority over her ended.

With England's unrestrained entry into the contest for America, an English settlement was established in North Carolina in 1584. As warfare between England and Spain broke out in the next year, the colonists were taken home by Sir Francis Drake in 1586. A new settlement was established the following year on nearby Roanoke Island, but supplies were delayed and did not reach the island until 1591. By then the colony had disappeared.

In 1629, Charles I granted a charter to Sir Robert Heath, Chief Justice of his Court of Common Pleas, to a province called "Carolana," after his Latin name. The following year, an expedition of former French Protestants set out to settle there; but they ended up in Virginia. Later, Heath's charter was exchanged for land in New York. Another settlement on the Cape Fear River was attempted in 1661 by a group from New England, but this expedition also failed.

By the mid-seventeenth century, England had established several colonies in North America, but none south of Virginia. The English civil war and the establishment of Cromwell's Protectorate from 1640 until the restoration of the monarchy in 1660 halted further overseas ventures. However, during these parlous years, many—mostly royalists—fled to the established areas in the New World to escape the fighting and then the retribution when the

war ended. Once Charles II was firmly on the throne, he set about repaying his supporters. To one group, he gave the large area south of Virginia called "Carolina" to be developed as they saw fit. The initial mover behind this charter was Sir John Colleton, who had extensive holdings in Barbados, which even by then was overcrowded and overdeveloped. He sought new lands on the continent to absorb the excess population of the island. Colleton and the others were called the Lords Proprietors. They were: the Earl of Clarendon; the Duke of Albemarle; Lord Craven; Lord Berkeley; Anthony Ashley Cooper, the Earl of Shaftsbury; Sir George Carteret; Sir William Berkeley; and Sir John Colleton, names that dot the landscape of the Carolinas today. Anthony Ashley Cooper would furnish most of the enthusiasm for the venture. Meanwhile, the crush of the crowd on Barbados was prompting its inhabitants to look toward the mainland for settlement. In 1663, Captain William Hilton of Barbados explored the Carolina coast in the ship *Adventure*. He found the land favorable for settlement and was warmly received by the Edisto Indians. They showed him the ruins of the French and Spanish forts at Parris Island, where he had a friendly encounter with a Spanish ship and exchanged gifts. Hilton induced the Indians to free some shipwrecked English sailors who had been enslaved. When the Lords Proprietors heard Hilton's accounts of his exploration on the Carolina coast, they ordered an expedition from Barbados to resettle Cape Fear. Although a storm damaged the ships, and one was lost on entering the river, the settlement took hold and was called Charles Town on the Charles River, the present-day Cape Fear River. It soon had some 800 inhabitants.

In June of 1666, an expedition under Robert Sandford set out from Charles Town on the Charles River and explored the areas of the North Edisto River, the Dawhoo River, the South Edisto River, and Port Royal. Because the Indians were friendly and helpful, a young Englishman, Henry Woodward, was left at Port Royal with them. He remained there for three years. He is known as the first English settler of Carolina. Later, he was captured by the Spanish and imprisoned at St. Augustine; there, the English buccaneer Robert Searle rescued him in time for him to participate in the settlement of Charles Towne on the Ashley River.

The cacique of Cayagua, or Kiawah, went back north with Sandford to pilot him into his harbor, still known by the Spanish name of San Jorge Bay, but conditions were not suitable for them to enter the harbor. Sandford named the river "Ashley" and disembarked the cacique before returning north. When he returned to Cape Fear, Sandford found the settlers despondent over their prospects. In 1667, the colony was abandoned and most of the settlers moved to previously established communities to the north, in Virginia.

The *Carolina* Expedition

When the Second Anglo-Dutch War of 1665–68 eliminated the Dutch from New York, the English were left in possession of the entire east coast of North America from French Canada to Spanish Florida. However, Franco-Dutch attacks on English islands in the West Indies during the 1665–1668 war revealed a renewed French interest in establishing colonies in America. Armed conflict seemed inevitable. To beat the French in colonization and to relieve the overcrowding on Barbados, the English began immediately to plan to send another group of settlers from England to Port Royal.

But it took two years of preparation for the expedition. In August of 1669, three small vessels sailed from Devon in the south of England. The largest was the frigate *Carolina*, a

Model of *Carolina* at Charles Towne Landing that was built by Erik A. R. Ronnberg, Jr., of Rockport, Massachusetts, from plans by the late William Avery Baker. *Carolina* displaced about 200 tons and was about 100 feet long. No records remain of the vessel, so this model was built on assumptions based on contemporary vessels. Note the bluff (apple-cheeked) bow common to the period. Ships of this time were small and built for seaworthiness, not speed.

ship of about 200 tons.[1] The others were *Port Royal*, a similar vessel but about half as large, and the two-masted sloop, or shallop, *Albemarle* of 30 tons.

Command of the expedition was given to Joseph West, who had been appointed Governor. He had evidently shown much promise as a subaltern of Sir George Carteret's son, James, on the fourth rates HMS[2] *Jersey* and *Foresight* in the West Indies battles against the French and Dutch in 1667–1668. Since naval service during the age of sail was one of the best possible preparations for high administrative duty, West undoubtedly had shown much talent to his superiors. He lived up to every expectation. To him, walking the thin line between the colonists and the Proprietors, goes much of the credit for getting the colony off to a good start.

Carolina carried 93 passengers of mixed backgrounds—servants, artisans, gentlemen, and representatives of the Proprietors. Her cost to the Proprietors was £430. Roughly translated into today's costs, the entire expedition amounted to about a quarter of a million dollars. This was a mere pittance compared to what the ultimate return was. But it was a great gamble in light of the failures that had preceded it. The squadron stopped at Kinsale, Ireland, where they hoped to pick up additional settlers, but they found none who were ready to join Englishmen and risk the adventure of settling in the strange new land. At this stop some of the original, more timorous passengers deserted. From Ireland, the squadron set out on a forty-day passage to Barbados. On their arrival there, on November 2, a storm drove *Albemarle* ashore. She was a total loss, but the other ships received minor, repairable injury.

The single masted-sloop *Three Brothers* was purchased to replace *Albemarle*. She was probably about 65 feet long and drew more water aft than forward. Her main deck at the waist was apparently low, but the deck was crowned with high bulwarks and a short quarterdeck, for a stern cabin. Sir John Yeamans of Barbados took command of the fleet, and the voyage to Carolina was resumed at the end of November. More settlers joined the expedition before it moved on.

Near the island of Nevis the fleet was driven into port by hurricanes, but the delay proved to be a fortuitous diversion; here the expedition picked up the redoubtable Henry Woodward.

After his liberation from St. Augustine, Woodward had joined a privateer in his effort to return home. The vessel, however, was wrecked at Nevis. When the Carolina colonists persuaded him to join them, they did not know that his knowledge and earlier friendship with the Indians would be an invaluable aid in the coming years.

When the weather cleared, the fleet got underway and headed north to Bermuda. As they neared the south of the island, *Port Royal* was ordered to proceed directly to Carolina. En route, she ran short of water and headed southwest before a favorable wind to the Bahamas. While heading upwind through these islands, she piled up on the rocks near Great

Abaco on January 12. The vessel was a complete loss, but the passengers and crew made it to shore. There a vessel was built from the wreckage of *Port Royal* to carry them to Eleuthera, about 100 miles away. From Eleuthera the crew made it to New Providence and from there to Bermuda in time to rejoin *Carolina* before she sailed.

Three Brothers and *Carolina*, whose stern was battered in by another hurricane, proceeded to Bermuda. En route, *Three Brothers* became separated from *Carolina*. When the latter arrived at Bermuda, Colonel William Sayle of that island was appointed by Sir John Yeamans, the only Proprietor to attend any part of the voyage, to be the first governor of Carolina. Sayle joined the expedition while Yeamans stepped aside. Sayle had long been connected with colonization efforts in Bermuda and the Bahamas and was an able colonial administrator of high character. By making him the leader, it was hoped that additional settlers from Bermuda would join the expedition. While an experienced and able person, Sayle caused dissent among the colonists because of his age (eighty) and religion ("a dissenting zealot"). West did eventually become governor later in 1671 upon Sayle's death.

The hurricane that damaged *Carolina's* stern caused *Three Brothers* to miss her landfall at Bermuda. She was consequently driven on to Virginia. A Bermuda shallop or sloop was substituted for her. Of the original vessels, only *Carolina* made it to the land of Chicora on March 17, 1670. The first landing was at Bull Harbor, a wide inlet at the east end of Bull's Island where a safe anchorage and access to fresh water could be had. The Indians living there gave the settlers a warm reception. After several days the ubiquitous Cacique of Kiawah (Cayagua) came to meet them. He persuaded the settlers, who had intended to land at Port Royal, to proceed to his domain along the Ashley River. As South Carolina's first real estate promoter, he sought the protection of the English against his enemies, the cannibalistic Westoes of Georgia, who were probably Spanish allies.

Carolina proceeded to Port Royal while the sloop explored the Cacique's land. The sloop rejoined *Carolina* at Port Royal with a favorable report that convinced the settlers to establish themselves on St. George's Bay. Added to this, the Indians at Port Royal were hard pressed by their enemies, the Westoes. Although no supplies had yet been landed, the free men of the expedition elected five men to the governing council, the first election in South Carolina, and the little squadron headed north.

Settlement at Charles Towne

Known to the Spanish as San Jorge and to the English as St. George's Bay, Charleston harbor presented a wide expanse of water to the new settlers as they entered it sometime in the first part of April 1670 on *Carolina* and her consort. The two vessels proceeded up the Ashley River to what is now Old Town Creek on the west bank and landed on a high bluff out of sight of the ocean. This peninsula of land, named Albemarle Point, was only 50 yards wide at the neck, guarded by a creek on one side and marsh on the other. A short distance away was the Cacique's main village.

A month later, *Three Brothers* arrived after a brush with the Spaniards and their Indian allies near St. Catherine's Island in Georgia. The ship had sent a landing party ashore led by the captain. They were captured and some killed. While the Indians at Town Creek seemed to pose no threat, the settlers were concerned about the large Spanish garrison at St. Augustine, 200 miles to the south. They busied themselves constructing defenses. It took them

---

[1] At that time, a frigate was any ship-rigged vessel, lightly built with a flat transom as opposed to a pointed stern.

[2] The usage of HMS for His or Her Majesty's Ship did not become official until after 1850 in the Royal Navy. HMS will be used throughout this book to distinguish British warships from those of other navies.

Carolina at anchor for the first time in Charles Towne harbor.

some two years to complete the moat and palisades fortifications with its seven cannon.[3]

The Proprietors had promised each settler and servant 150 acres of land on which to establish themselves. Ten years later new settlers were still being promised at least 50 acres of land. The local Indians made up the food deficit until the spring of 1673, when the colonists had become more or less self-sufficient.

Apprehensions of a Spanish attack were too soon confirmed. In September 1670, friendly Indians reported that three Spanish ships accompanied by a number of large Indian canoes, or periaguas, were at Stono Inlet preparing to attack. For ten days the colonists waited for the expected battle. A group of enemy Indians encamped on Morris Island almost trapped *Carolina*, which was returning from Virginia with supplies. A few shots were exchanged, but the ship got away without damage. A storm soon dispersed the threatening Spanish fleet. This gave the fledgling colony a welcome respite.

Early in 1671, the arrival of additional settlers swelled the population of the village. The next year, a census was taken; there were almost 400 people in the colony. In this year the first settlers began moving to Oyster Point, the present site of Charleston. By 1676 clearing of the land on Oyster Point began in earnest, with the simultaneous raising of defense works.

This area was picked because of its high clay bluff running along present day East Bay Street from Water to Market Streets. In addition there was little or no marsh between the land and the river, making it a good site for wharves. Creeks on the northern and southern flanks offered some protection against land attack.

It was not until the end of 1679 that the decree from the Proprietors arrived. The settlers were given official authorization to move the town to Oyster Point. A clerk on HMS *Richmond*, which arrived in 1680 with 45 French Protestants under the leadership of René Petit and Jacob Guerard, reported that 1,000 to 1,200 people already inhabited the town with some sixteen vessels in the harbor. The settlement in Charles Towne seemed firmly and safely established. Two years later over 100 wooden houses were reported built at Oyster Point. The population by then had more than doubled. A lot of the increase was due to dissenters fleeing England and others leaving in anticipation of renewed religious strife when the Catholic James II would ascend the throne.

The City's Early Defenses

The settlement at Oyster Point was fortified well. Its defenses were constantly expanded and improved until the town was surrounded by earthworks and palisades, making Charles Towne one of only four medieval-type walled cities in North America. The walled fortress enclosed an area about a mile along the Cooper River and about a half-mile deep. Two regiments of militia manned the ramparts in time of crisis, but a full-time captain of the fort was appointed by the governor to care for the guns and powder. During peacetime, guard duty was rotated two at a time among the sixteen companies comprising the local militia regiments.

Six brick bastions some twenty feet high dotted the works, diamond-shaped ones at each

---

[3] A replica of the original settlement at Charles Towne can be seen today at Charles Towne Landing. It is similar to the seventeenth-century replicas at Jamestown, Virginia, and Plymouth, Massachusetts.

Plan of the original walls of Charles Towne superimposed on the present city's street plan.

A Granville Bastion 1702
B Half Moon Battery (site of the Exchange in 1772)
C Craven Bastion
D Carteret Bastion
E Johnson's Half Moon
F Colleton Bastion
G St. Philip's Church
H St. Michael's Church
I Oyster Point (White Point)
J Powder Magazine 1704

corner with two half-moon batteries in the middle of the long legs. Between these were triangular shaped redans, all armed with cannon of various caliber. A moat backed by earthworks lined the land defenses on the west side of the city.

Near the center of the northern wall, a powder magazine was constructed[4] around 1703. It faced the creek, which ran along present-day Market Street; the location of the creek supposedly would keep enemy cannon at long range on this side of the city.

The Proprietors sent guns for these defenses. They included some eighty-three 18- to 24-pounder culverins, demi-culverins (9-pounders), cannon, and sakers. The largest were mounted on Granville Bastion, since it would bear the brunt of an enemy naval attack. Craven had the next largest number, followed by Carteret and Colleton on the west side.

These bastions were really separate forts constructed of earth, wood, and bricks, protruding beyond the walls. The essential components of the city's defenses remained until the War of Austrian Succession in 1745–1746, when a new wall with five bastions was built along Market and Beaufain Streets to the Ashley River. A hurricane in September 1752 destroyed most of the works facing the Cooper River. Extensive repairs were required, but after the British victory ousted France and Spain from the east coast of North America in 1763, it went to ruin. Some of the bastions were repaired again during the Revolution, but by the end of the eighteenth century, little of the original fortifications were left.

In addition to the walled fortifications, a system of lookouts and watch houses was established along the coast to guard against surprise attack by the Indians and Spaniards. The best known of these lookouts was the one at the harbor entrance, first manned in 1674 by the Irish soldier of fortune Florence O'Sullivan, who came with the first settlers. He was placed there with a signal gun to be fired when any ship was sighted. The number of times it fired indicated the number of ships. By the time of Queen Anne's War in 1703, the lookouts had been expanded to extend from Daufuskie Island in the south to Bull's Island in the north.

In August 1686, a Spanish expedition of three periaguas, or large Indian canoes, put into Port Royal sound and attacked the Scottish settlement at Stuart's Towne below the present-day town of Beaufort. While the inhabitants fled into the forests, the enemy sacked and burned the buildings. The militia set out to James Island to defend the city from attack in case the enemy moved northward. In the meantime the Spanish had landed on Edisto Island and burned Paul Grimball's house. When the Spanish realized that the militia was moving toward them, they began a retreat to Port Royal. The militia forces that were pursuing them made plans to proceed there when news came that a storm that brushed the coast had sunk one of the enemy's periaguas with the commander of the expedition, Senor Alexandro, on board. The same storm did considerable damage to the ships in Charles Towne's harbor, with many being driven upon the shore or lost.

With the removal of this first Spanish threat, the colony seemed to prosper; commerce was excellent and trade was brisk, but progress did not come easily. After the turn of the century, fire, disease, and hurricanes devastated the city. Coming after so many other disasters, the storm contributed toward widespread despair. Many colonists thought of giving up and moving north. Yet courage and determination prevailed, so that the city could be rebuilt on its ruins and look to the future.

[4] This powder magazine still stands on Cumberland Street—the oldest public structure remaining in the city.

Cooper River waterfront, circa 1740. Charles Towne was one of only four moated and walled cities in North America, although it remained such for less than half a century.

The Pirates, Part 1

The latter part of the seventeenth century was a period of aggressive expansion of seafaring trade. A multitude of ships of all sizes, shapes, and nationalities plied the complex network of shipping lanes around the world. Their valuable cargoes naturally attracted hordes of pirates to the sea lanes. It is little wonder that the years from 1690 to 1720 are known as the "Golden Age of Piracy." When the gold from Spanish America began to diminish, the commodity cargoes to and from England replaced it. Needing a market for their booty, the pirates found a great demand in North America, which was being carved from the wilderness. Since government authority was weak, the pirates got a sympathetic reception from the various governors who were beset by financial problems to which the mother country turned a deaf ear, but which the local citizens understood. Merchants, for example, liked the lack of haggling with customs officials, payment of duties, and the strict conformity to trade laws that pirate goods offered. Resentment of the rich and of those in authority among the average law-abiding citizens ashore was the basis for the popular support of the pirates. Many of them had come to America to escape the autocratic authority of European despots.

There were no class distinctions on pirate ships. Matters were run by a show of hands. Some ships changed captains frequently, while others kept one leader for years. It was democracy in its purest form. Those who disagreed were sometimes allowed to depart or form a crew for a captured ship; others were set adrift in a boat or marooned. As for the punishment of walking the plank, no pirate crew would have gone to the trouble of erecting a "plank" for an outcast or victim to "walk" and plunge to his demise. They would have tossed the man overboard and been done with it. These punishments were mild compared to what many pirates meted out to their captives, especially women.

The pirate crews were quick to judge the competency of their leaders and knew what dangers lurked at sea. The "captain" was often captain in name only. A few captains took up quarters in the great cabin, but even here, the crew came and went at will with no regard for the protocol of the sea. Once the shooting started, the captain's authority was absolute; he would often kill any man on the spot who did not obey his command. Second to him was the quartermaster, who more or less administered the running of the ship. Under him was the sailing master, who directed the trim of the sails and oversaw navigation of the vessel. The pirate ship operated very similarly to warships flying national flags.

Skilled in psychological warfare, pirates employed fear and intimidation to attain their goals. They retreated in the face of strength, and attacked weakness. Unless cornered, few pirates would engage a warship.

While piracy has been called one of civilization's oldest professions, most men were lured to it by unemployment, the spirit of adventure, and their aversion to the strict discipline and the brutal punishments in navies. These were the bonds of all pirates, but few showed loyalty to anyone. While discipline at sea was bad, it was worse ashore. But life in the seventeenth century was generally hard for everyone except the few at the very top. A seaman might make a pound sterling a month, but a laborer ashore made half that. Yet, in one haul, a pirate crewman might make the equivalent of several lifetimes at those wages. Living within the law, they would be hung for stealing a shilling; as pirates, they could steal a fortune at no greater risk!

The dividing line between pirate and privateersman has always been ambiguous, much as the line that differentiates terrorist and freedom fighter today. It was largely a matter of perspective. Even the most upstanding privateer captain had his brutal and bloodthirsty side. Once out of sight of land and the clutches of civilization, many would show a side that would make a modern villain recoil in horror.

One historian's claim that South Carolina was settled by the outcasts of European society who tolerated these buccaneers is less than correct. The Proprietors went out of their way to encourage men of means to settle the colony; however, during the hardships of the early days, the local authorities were hardly able to control the general population, much less the lawless. In addition, pirate attacks on the Spanish enemies of the colony helped to hold the Spanish at bay. As long as the pirates behaved themselves in Charles Towne, it was "live and let live." Only the Proprietors criticized the citizens' tolerance of piracy. It was very important that they remain in the good graces of the government and colonial interests in London.

An additional reason for Charles Towne's general tolerance of pirates was that most of the seized ships were English rather than locally owned. The local goods that they carried were not of great value, and a few losses were expected. However, the English shipowners complained to the government, which passed the complaints on to the Proprietors, who in turn told the local authorities to clamp down.

First Pirates

The Carolina coast had been a haunt for pirates and privateersmen since the mid-sixteenth century. The earliest record of pirate activity involves one of the three relief ships under Laudonniere that came to relieve Jean Ribaut's colony at Port Royal in 1564. A vessel was seized by a mutinous crew who had joined the expedition because of the exaggerated accounts of Carolina's wealth. Finding reality less than that promised, they decided to try their luck as pirates in the Caribbean. Once Laudonniere refused to allow them to leave, the group mutinied, stole a ship, and set sail for the Caribbean. There they were successful; they even terrorized Jamaica. After another battle with the Spanish, they returned to Port Royal; there Laudonniere had them arrested and publicly executed as an example. Soon after, word of the wealth of Spain's treasure fleets leaked out, and daring English and French sea captains began to prey on them. The coves and inlets of the Carolina coast were perfect hiding places and rest points; later, they also became bases of operations and, if legends are correct, places to bury treasure. Of the places near Charles Towne, Bull's Bay and the estuary of the North Edisto River were the most popular. The modern coastal towns of McClellanville and Rockville were most likely the occasional sites for early pirate bases. From there it was an easy transformation to fishing village and then summer resort.

Additionally, pirates could take their ill-gotten gains and then put into nearby Charles Towne to enjoy the benefits of civilization, exchange their booty for other items, and gain new recruits. The authorities of the fledgling colony were in no position to challenge them. In fact, they may have encouraged these outlaws of the sea, since their booty was scattered around generously. It was practically the only specie seen. Pirates who seized goods instead

of gold came into port and sold them cheaply. Few people asked questions, being grateful to get foreign merchandise at a good price. Carrying commissions from the king to sail as privateers, powerfully armed pirates were not awed by the local authorities. And the citizens looked upon pirate attacks, especially on Spanish ships, as patriotic duty rather than lawlessness.

King Charles himself did not set a good example when he knighted the buccaneer Henry Morgan, much as Queen Elizabeth had knighted Francis Drake a century earlier. The king added insult to Spain's injury by making Morgan lieutenant governor of Jamaica as a reward for sacking Panama, an act which was strictly piratical. By bestowing this honor on Morgan, the king strengthened the hand of the pirates, particularly in the Caribbean. From there it was a small step to attacking English ships.

Added to London's tolerance of Morgan was local tolerance of pirates and privateers. While England and Spain were at peace, Thomas Newe wrote from Charles Towne in 1682 of privateers and other vessels taking on stores, and of a French privateer of four guns and thirty men bringing in a Spanish prize of sixteen guns and one hundred men. During the war between France and Spain that started in 1684, numerous privateers sallied forth from Charles Towne to plunder the ships of the warring parties off the coast. Spanish prizes were brought into the port; even Henry Morgan paid a visit, with the encouragement of Governor Morton and Council. Since Morgan had been given the king's seal of approval, it would hardly have been fitting for the governor and council to exclude him. Furthermore, his powerful ships were the colony's best defense against the Spanish. The Royal Navy was hard pressed at home and had no warships to spare for Charles Towne. King Charles soon after ordered that the issuance of privateer commissions be halted and the Jamaica anti-piracy laws strictly enforced. Governor Quarry flagrantly ignored enforcement of the anti-piracy laws and encouraged pirates. It is considered that this encouragement of piracy prompted the Spanish attack on the Edisto and Port Royal settlements in 1686.

After the Spanish attack, the colonists organized an expedition to St. Augustine, but the new governor, James Colleton, halted it. His administration made the first real effort to stamp out piracy, but he was less than successful. His first act was to expel one John Boon from Council for cooperating with the pirates.

London also realized that commerce with the colonies was suffering due to the pirates. In 1687, Sir Robert Holmes was commissioned by King James II to proceed to the West Indies with a fleet to eradicate the menace. Orders also came to the authorities in Charles Towne to do likewise. This led to Council passing in February of that year an act for the suppression of the pirates. Holmes was not entirely successful, but at least it showed the colonists that the royal government was serious about ending piracy. With this shift in official policy, caution began to be used in dealing with the buccaneers.

The local effort against the pirates came to an end in 1689, when the colony became embroiled in a battle between the South Carolina Commons on one hand and the governor and Proprietors on the other. Governor Sothell, in order to silence his enemies, accused them among other things of consorting with the pirates. At the very time he made these accusations, it was widely rumored that he was receiving bribes from the culprits. His governorship caused the sea rovers to return to greater favor with the citizens. When Philip Ludwell succeeded him as governor, the pirates had arrived at the height of their power. At first, Governor Ludwell made some efforts to enforce the anti-piracy laws. But his resources were meager, and he, too, got caught up in bribery and corruption. The Proprietors' stingy policies allowed only token means for the governors to enforce the law. In his 1697 report to the

Board of Trade, Edward Randolph censured Ludwell for his disruption of the political life in the colony through arbitrary proceedings, and also for his "encouragement to pirates."

Soon after Ludwell had taken office, a suspicious vessel, *Royal Jamaica*, arrived with forty men and large quantities of silver and gold. With this loot the crew was in immediate favor around town, and they wished to remain within the confines of civilized authority. The local authorities, unsure of their character, allowed them to remain in exchange for a bond (or bribe), while their record was checked with London. Once London cleared their record they were free; those that were wanted for piracy were transported there for trial.

Another vessel was wrecked on the coast and the crew came to Charles Towne. Here they boasted openly of having been as far as the Red Sea, where they supposedly plundered vessels belonging to the Grand Mogul. This crew too was not molested by the local officials. It was the reports of these doings that prompted the first high-level criticisms launched against the Proprietors by Edward Randolph. He singled out for attack their laxness in enforcing the Navigation Acts and in suppressing the pirates.

Some crews were brought to trial, but they managed to bribe their way out. Things went from bad to worse, until it seemed as if the pirates were running the colony. The authority of the Proprietors and of the king was no match for the glitter of buccaneer gold. In 1692 during Ludwell's administration, the colony reached the nadir of its fortunes, both morally and commercially.

In November 1693, Thomas Smith became governor. He had served honorably on Ludwell's council, and in return for his public service, he had been rewarded with the title "Landgrave." Smith was familiar with the scandals of Ludwell's administration and was determined that his term would not go down in such ignominy. One of the first moves he made as governor was an attempt to enforce the anti-piracy laws honestly. It proved too much for him. After a year, he died in office in 1694.

As fallout from Smith's efforts at reform, rumors swept the uneasy city: the pirates were preparing to plunder and burn Charles Towne in retaliation. Such had been the fate of Panama and Porto Bello earlier in the century. The city was numb with panic, but nothing happened. Panic subsided and, skittishly, life continued.

In the last half of the 1690s, Charles Towne's attitude toward piracy began to change. The prosperity of the merchants on both sides of the Atlantic demanded an end to the rampant brigandage. Corrupt officials refused to acquiesce; the frontier spirit, now on the wane, dictated otherwise. The Proprietors did not help matters. Exercising ultimate authority from across the ocean, they were either too lenient or appointed weak or corrupt governors when the situation called for a firm hand. Regardless, the forces of change were blowing through the young city.

Charles Towne's Change of Attitude Toward the Pirates

By the late 1690s the colony began to reap the benefits of the new rice trade. England took very little of the crop, as rice was not a major part of the English diet. Most of it went to more lucrative foreign markets. Naturally the pirates descended upon the imports that the profits from rice brought. The subsequent losses aroused the ire of Charles Towne merchants against the pirates. For the first time in years pirate ships were denied entry to Charles Towne harbor.

The arrival of the Huguenot refugees who had been thrown out of France in 1685 by the revocation of the Edict of Nantes, and of middle-class English Dissenters contributed greatly to the change in the city's posture. These were people of high principle who were not going to yield their gains to a lawless horde, even though a few of them had been corrupted by the colony.

Another factor causing the public's change of attitude was the growing strength and numbers of the pirates and the physical threat that they posed to the city. People realized that if enough pirates banded together, they could attack the city and sack and burn it. Lamentably some local officials continued to tolerate and even benefit from pirate ships and crews, but it became increasingly apparent that the city's existence now depended upon the safe transport of her products across the sea.

In 1699, a motley crew of about forty-five pirates in a ship outfitted at Havana lay off Charles Towne for some time. They captured several vessels and put the crews ashore. Before long, they began to dispute the division of the spoils. Nine Englishmen in the crew lost out and were set adrift; they landed at Bull's (Sewee) Bay. From there, they came by land to the city, where they made up a story about being shipwrecked. However, they were identified as pirates by some of the crews whom they had earlier plundered. The pirates were brought to trial; seven were executed. With this act the pirates began a general exodus from the colony. A few confessed and declared their intent to change their lives; they were allowed to remain undisturbed, but only in lawful pursuits.

In March 1701, King William proclaimed a pardon for those pirates who wanted to end their careers in crime and embark upon an honest life. They only had to surrender and then take the oath of allegiance within twelve months. Some of the infamous Captain Kidd's crew who were in the province promptly surrendered and took the oath. A letter written by William Penn at the time mentions that several of Kidd's men had settled in Carolina and had become planters.

In the northern colonies, a renewed assault on the pirates drove many of them from New England, New York, and Virginia. In 1701, the start of the War of the Spanish Succession, or Queen Anne's War, in which England fought France and Spain, saw many of the buccaneers flocking to join the privateers of the British irregular navy. Some of them obtained commissions as privateers; their pirate vessels then became legal men-of-war.

Throughout this war, hundreds of privateers operated out of American ports. While the losses in battle were high, the enthusiasm for privateering also remained high. This was especially true after 1708 when Parliament renounced its 10-percent claim of all prizes. Before the war ended, more than 2,000 prizes had been taken, most of them French.

The seventeenth-century history of Charles Towne was lacking in redemption. One can speculate that if the colony had disappeared in 1700, little note would be made of it today. As the eighteenth century began, changes were in the wind: the economy and the politics of the city took on new meaning. Once the harbor for some of the greatest buccaneers of the Western world, Charles Towne now strung up pirates at the entrance of the port. As a result, the freebooters began to leave the South Carolina coast. They moved northward or to the Bahamas; the colony was given a respite, which was also helped by the war in Europe.

Rice crops were lucrative, bringing honest earnings to replace that of pirate booty. Another essential commodity was also becoming a significant contributor to the economy: naval stores. The colony now had two very important crops. Governor Moore's administration, which began the new century, brought a period of prosperity and relative calm. Charles Towne had effected a complete about-face; she was now the enemy of the pirates. Her record henceforth on this account is one of the best. As a city, her contribution to the eradication of lawlessness on the high seas is unrivaled.

The Attack of the French Squadron

From time to time the various colonies in America found themselves actively embroiled in the wars that affected their respective mother countries in Europe. Hitherto, Charles Towne had done little other than serve as a base for the privateers who were engaged in these wars. From the very beginning the colony had been threatened by the Spanish; and the Spanish raids to the south of the city in 1686 were vivid memories. However, during Queen Anne's War (1702–1713), a real threat manifested itself—direct assault from the sea.

In May of 1702, shortly before the actual declaration of hostilities, a Spanish and Apalachee Indian army headed for South Carolina. They were stopped in Georgia by Creek Indians who had allied themselves with the English. This aborted attack by the Spanish instigated the organization of a counterattack by the colony. The target was the main Spanish base at St. Augustine. With 500 to 600 militia troops, ten vessels sailed from Port Royal in September. The main force under Governor James Moore proceeded directly by sea. With 100 men Colonel Robert Daniel moved overland. The city of St. Augustine fell to the invaders and the Spanish retired to the impregnable Castillo de San Marcos overlooking St. Augustine harbor. When Governor Moore's fleet arrived, the combined forces besieged the fortress. Without heavy artillery, however, they had little chance of taking it.

Attempts were made to obtain siege guns from Jamaica, but while waiting for the artillery, they spied two enemy ships off shore. Believing them to be part of a powerful fleet, Moore quickly lifted the siege, abandoned his ships and provisions, and retreated toward Charles Towne by land. The operation had lasted three months and expended much of the colony's short supply of funds. Charles Towne was now vulnerable to a counterattack.

In January 1704, Moore redeemed his honor with a thrust into the very heart of Spain's possessions around Apalachee Bay, Florida. Causing even greater damage to the commerce of Spain and France were the swarms of privateers that operated out of Charles Towne during the war. Because of Moore's attack on St. Augustine, the privateer operations, and the French alarm for the safety of Mobile, the colonial administrators of Spain and France decided to execute Louisiana Governor Bienville's plan of 1702 for the crushing of Carolina.

As early as 1702, Spain and France had begun planning an invasion of South Carolina. Operating through its many trade contacts in the Caribbean, the colony's intelligence network sent word of the plans. In response Governor Johnson ordered the fortifications around Charles Towne to be strengthened and lookouts stationed at regular intervals along the coast.

The French Squadron Arrives

On Saturday, August 24, 1706, a Dutch privateer sloop from New York belonging to Captain Stool anchored in Charles Towne harbor. The crew reported that while off St. Augustine a few days earlier, they had fallen in with a French ship which was planning to attack the city. Captain Stool had gone to St. Augustine to intercept a Spanish ship expected from Havana with money for the Spanish garrison at St. Augustine. Captain Stool had hardly made his report when six columns of smoke appeared on Sullivan's Island, the signal that that many ships were off the bar. These ships were a French squadron from Martinique that had assembled at Havana. A storm had dispersed the ships as they sailed up the coast. The main body assembled in the North Edisto River and then proceeded toward Charles Towne. Two other vessels later made landfall at Sewee (Bull's) Bay to the north.

Led by Captain De Feboure [le Fevre?], the squadron consisted of the frigate *Soleil* of 22 guns, two 8-gun sloops under Captains Sorbay and la Pierriere, two smaller sloops, and a galley. Some accounts list the ships as privateers with commissions from Paris; but, there was speculation that they were warships of the French Navy. There was a privateer named *Soleil* operating out of the French port of Dunkerque during the period 1703–1707, and she may have been the ship that served as flagship of the squadron that attacked Charles Towne.

On board the ships were about 700 Spanish soldiers under General D'Arbousset and 200 Indian allies. The Spanish had encouraged the attack, but they misled the French as to the defenses and conditions at Charles Towne, saying it was ripe for the picking and plundering, due to an epidemic of yellow fever.

Some of the Spanish soldiers landed on James Island. They burned a plantation while the boats from the French ships sounded the bar. The shallow entrance to the harbor that was

Frigate a la Voile,

French warship similar to *Soleil*.

to plague the commerce of the city for some 150 years showed its beneficial side for the first time by delaying an enemy attack, thus giving the city time to marshal its defenses.

On August 27, the enemy ships crossed the bar and anchored off Sullivan's Island to await suitable winds to run into the harbor. The next day when a flag of truce appeared, Governor Johnson sent a galley to make inquiry. A French officer was blindfolded and then conducted ashore to Granville Bastion, where he was held until the governor was ready to receive him. The gun emplacement on this bastion had recently been completed as the southeastern anchor of the city's walled defenses.

Upon being brought before Johnson, the French officer demanded the surrender of the city within an hour. Governor Johnson, with the skill of an expert poker player, replied that he would not need a minute to reply in the negative. One local story has it that as the French officer was being led to the governor with eyes uncovered, the colonial militia was drawn up to their best advantage. As he was conducted up the street to meet with the governor, he saw soldiers stationed between buildings and down the side streets. He was impressed: the town seemed to be defended by four times the number of soldiers that he had expected. He did not realize that he was actually looking at the same militia units again and again; as soon as he passed one site, they ran behind the buildings to fall in at the next opening, just in time to be seen again!

A galley-built ship of the early eighteenth century of the type that would have been used in repelling the French attack on Charles Towne.

Skirmishes Ashore

On August 29, the morning after the meeting between Johnson and the French officer, about 160 Spanish troops landed on the mainland at Mount Pleasant. They ranged among the plantations, burning and plundering the houses. Two vessels at the Hobcaw Creek shipyard were burned. In one of the galleys, Governor Johnson sent 100 men to repel the enemy. Upon their approach, the Spanish troops were recalled to their ships. The South Carolinians also withdrew. It was apparent to the French and Spanish forces that the South Carolinians were more determined and better able to defend themselves than they had expected.

At the same time, about 40 men from the French ships landed on James Island, where they ravaged the countryside. Captain Drake's galley immediately set out with 60 men and 20 Indians to repulse the invaders. On their approach, the enemy retreated to their galley under fire from the Indians.

That night, about 300 French marines returned to the Shem Creek area of Mount Pleasant. Captain Cantey was sent with 100 men from the city to drive them off. His force landed at night at Hobcaw and marched overland the short distance to the creek. At daybreak, they attacked. Two or three volleys were exchanged. The enemy broke and ran; they were pursued by the Indians, who took 58 prisoners. Several of the French were drowned while trying to get across Shem Creek. The colonials lost only one man.

Naval Preparations

An improvised fleet had been organized to repel the enemy fleet. Some of them were probably former pirates of the previous decade, now turned privateersmen. Made up mostly of merchant ships in the harbor, the fleet consisted of:

flagship *Crown Galley* 12 guns (Lt. Colonel William Rhett)
galley[1] *Mermaid* 12 guns (Thomas Cary of North Carolina)
galley *Richard*[2] 16 guns, 6 patteraroes (small mortars) and 146 men (Thomas Spread)
galley *William* (Captain Kember)
sloop *Flying Horse* 8 guns and 80 men (Peter Stool)
Bermuda sloop *Seaflower* 100 men (Captain Watson)

---

[1] The term *galley* used here did not necessarily apply to a vessel whose primary means of propulsion was oars. The name was applied to any nimble vessel that could easily be rowed because of her relatively light construction and fine, shallow draft. These were usually smaller, lightly constructed vessels; they were great assets in the narrow channels and light winds of the Carolina coast. For such galleys, oars were strictly an auxiliary to sails for propulsion. With the Mediterranean galley, oars and oarsmen were as much the means of propulsion as the sails.

[2] *Richard* with 16 guns was fairly large for a merchant galley, although the Royal Navy commissioned some that mounted up to 24 guns. The development of these galleys as merchant ships was a direct result of the staggering losses of colonial shipping during King William's War (1689–1697). The Royal Navy was unable to furnish adequate protection to colonial ships, so speed and maneuverability became a merchantman's best defense.

The French squadron retreats over the bar as Colonel
William Rhett leads the colonial squadron to the attack.

The local squadron set sail on August 31 to engage the attackers. The French ships, however, were favored by the northeasterly wind and, having seen enough action, set sail and passed over the bar. The colonial ships returned to the city without fighting.

Mopping Up

The two vessels of the French squadron that had earlier become separated from the main force during the storm made landfall at Sewee Bay. These were the French brig *Brillante* of 6 guns under Captain Lewis Pasquereau, and another vessel. A landing party from the two ships set out overland for Charles Towne. They reached Remley's Point near Hobcaw, from where they could see the city, but they had no way to cross the Cooper River. Troops and Indians were dispatched from Charles Towne. They landed and pursued them to Victory Point (Porcher's Bluff). In the battle that ensued, seven of the enemy were killed, fifty-six taken prisoner, and the rest put to flight.

Two days later Governor Johnson received word of the arrival of *Brillante* and the other vessel at Sewee Bay. Two sloops manned with 160 men set out under Colonel Rhett to attack them. Colonel Rhett's force came upon *Brillante* aground. She surrendered without firing a shot. Most of her crewmen were already prisoners ashore! The other vessel escaped. The prisoners and their ship were brought to the city. Later, the 230 or so Spanish and French prisoners taken in the entire operation were sent to Virginia, where they were ransomed for 10,000 pieces of eight.

Aftermath

The French attack clearly demonstrated the resourcefulness of the colony under attack and the resolve of the citizens to defend it. The struggle to tame the wilderness and the Indian battles had made the colonists able fighters. Furthermore they were able to take advantage of the terrain of the South Carolina Lowcountry, which had become home territory to them.

These engagements made the colony realize how vulnerable it was from the sea. In 1708, Fort Johnson was constructed on a low hill at Windmill Point on the east end of James Island, where a watch house had been established as early as 1685. The new fort was triangular in shape with three bastions, one at each corner, each mounted with cannon. A battery of heavy cannon mounted at the fort's base guarded the harbor entrance. The battery wall, constructed of earth retained by driven piles, was protected from the sea by ballast stones. The walls of the fort were built of mud, oyster shells, and pine saplings. A moat surrounded the structure on the land side. Inside, the buildings varied with time, but most were wooden. They included a commander's house, barracks, magazine, and storehouse. Only during time of crisis was the fort kept in good repair. The sea and rain constantly ate away at the earthworks and rotted the wooden structure. Local troops garrisoned the fort throughout the colonial period.

In 1702, prior to the French attack, a system of scout boats to augment the lookout system had been proposed by a resolution of the Commons House of Assembly. The resolution ordered that there be with all possible expedition bought for the use of the public, six cypress periaguas, forty feet long and five wide, at least with up to a dozen pair of oars for each vessel to be kept, one in the North Edisto, two near the head of the Stono River, and three near Charles Towne, for the carrying of men in case of an invasion. This was the beginning of a navy for South Carolina. Few if any of the periaguas were in service before 1713.

In 1703 the sloop *Scout* was purchased as part of the scout system. When the 1713 act was passed the system actually went into effect, with two scout boats placed in service. Of these first boats, one covered the area between Port Royal and St. Augustine, the other the area between the Stono River and Port Royal. During the Yemassee Indian uprising of 1715 these boats rendered valuable service transporting militia units around the coastal waterways.

The scout boats were light and strong with shallow draft. They were designed to be used for the rapid movement of small numbers of troops or marines along the coast. Armed with swivel guns, they were forerunners of the galleys that would fight in the Revolution. Two vessels of this type were probably the so-called "galleys" that made up Colonel Rhett's squadron. They were made from a large hollow cypress[3] log, which was sawn vertically down the middle of the boat's length. The two parts were reattached with a plank inserted horizontally between the halves and joined together with pegs. The middle plank enabled the builder to make the boats wider than an average large tree trunk. Each boat carried at least one mast, either with Bermuda-type fore and aft, or lateen-rigged sails. The main propulsion, however, was four to twelve large oars.

The scout system was maintained and increased with larger craft until 1736, when it was discontinued. Two years later, with the prospect of a new Spanish war on the horizon, they were reinstated. These scouts remained in service until 1763, when the boats were sold.

Ideally, the scout boat system consisted of groups of two periaguas carrying marines who were able to fight on land or water, using a small strategically placed base. One boat would patrol while the crew of the other manned the base, which was little more than a lightly built clapboard building with a crude observation tower. Some had cannon to signal the approach of a hostile force; others used beacon fires. Their principal duty was to ply the coastal waterways on the lookout for waterborne Indian or Spanish raiding parties, or runaway slaves. The manpower shortage in the colony hampered its ideal implementation.

After the ignominious failure of the French attack, Spain continued her attempts to subdue the English colony. Another expedition was planned. Rumors of a new attack peaked in 1709. The captain of the English merchantman *Boaz Bell* reported that Spanish vessels had actually been designated for the assault. These reports came as part of the voluminous correspondence among high officials of the various English colonies in the region. Rumor evidently fed upon rumor, as another attack did not come until years later.

An expedition was prepared in 1719, as part of a proposed Spanish sweep of the southern English colonies. Fortunately, the Spanish fleet was so battered after its attack on Nassau and a subsequent storm that it did not venture further north.

---

[3] Cypress is a soft wood that is very durable in water. Cypress trees grow in swamps and the core is naturally hollow.

Renewal of Piracy

After several years of peace at sea, in 1712 the Provincial Assembly passed a bill to strengthen local anti-piracy statutes that enforced the English pirate laws. There was no particular reason for this action, but it did serve to warn the sea rovers that they were still unwelcome in Charles Towne.

In the fall of 1712, South Carolina sent aid to its neighbors in North Carolina who were fighting an Indian uprising. Shortly afterward Indian warfare spread south in what is known as the Yemassee Indian War of 1715. The two uprisings exhausted the local treasury and caused economic loss to the merchants. The colony's crops were its sole export, and these were laid to waste by the fighting; the Yemassee War was the most devastating Indian war that the colony endured. Aid came from Virginia, and with this help Governor Craven succeeded in forcing the Indians to a kind of armed peace, but not until the entire colony beyond twenty-five or thirty miles of Charles Towne had been devastated.

Following the Indian fighting, a new threat arose at sea. After the signing of the Peace of Utrecht ended Queen Anne's War in 1713, the European navies dismissed from their service thousands of unneeded sailors. The recruitment of the pirates into the navies when the war began was now reversed. Many found their way into the growing merchant trade, but many others were unemployed. They were a natural source for pirate crews.

Wartime privateersmen went from plundering the enemy to plundering anything that came along. From all sides, the world's trade routes were prey to pirates. It is possible that successful pirates like Sir Francis Drake, who a century earlier had captured the public's imagination in England, still were hero figures. The more isolated a route was, the more it appealed to pirates. One of the more vulnerable of these routes was that of the Spanish treasure fleets as they made their way up the eastern coast of North America on their way home. Another was the trade routes from Charles Towne to the West Indies, and to England.

The principal operating base for these new pirates was the island of New Providence in the Bahamas. The Bahama Islands had been fought over during the war; sacked by both the Spanish and French, they were in such bad shape that the British authority abandoned them. In came the buccaneers! By late 1712, the number of pirates living there mushroomed, and by 1716, 2,000 pirates were living and operating out of what we know as Nassau. That year, Governor Spotswood of Virginia gave the first warning to London of the threat that these pirates posed. He went so far as to name the pirate Thomas Barrow as the unofficial governor of the Bahamas. Barrow is better known today as Blackbeard.

The Royal Navy had been so shrunk after the Treaty of Utrecht that it had neither the manpower nor the equipment to cope with the problem of the pirates. The paltry fees that were paid for convoy work encouraged ship commanders to make under-the-table deals with the pirates. In some instances the warships acted as merchantmen, carrying cargoes at reduced rates for pocket money for the warship captains. The pirates did not attack these warships and in turn they reciprocated by not attacking the pirates. This truce played hob with Carolina's growing commerce.

Charles Towne Weakened

The British Navy no longer was able to patrol the seas adequately; the pirates were flourishing; and Carolina had become a thriving economy, but an economy dependent on a market across the ocean, which was in turn dependent on protection from brigands.

Weakened by the Indian wars, the colony now faced the threat of rampant piracy. Charles Towne was innocent; it now sheltered none of the pirates. But the Bahamas to the south, and the almost deserted Cape Fear River and the sounds of the North Carolina Coast to the north, provided them snug harbor. From there, they sortied to sack any merchant fleets they caught in the shipping lanes. By 1715, losses had become so great that severe action was demanded; communication with Europe was in jeopardy, and, more important, the commerce of the colony was in dire peril. Pleas to the Proprietors in London went unheeded. They had apparently lost interest in their remote American holdings that had become a financial drain on their pocketbooks. Finally, the colony's London agent approached Parliament and the Crown directly. His plea fell on receptive ears. There was only one condition: the Proprietors in turn would vest the colony in the Crown. Lord Carteret, one of the Proprietors, offered such a proposal to the trade commissioners. But no action was taken, no decision made; it was tabled.

Even in its weakened state, the colony began to confront the threat from the sea. Nine men charged with the seizure of the sloop *Providence* were brought to trial. Though probably guilty, this group was acquitted; but four other pirates were hanged after a due process trial. Then the British fifth-rate *Shoreham*[1] stopped in the harbor, giving a boost to the city's morale. Though *Shoreham's* visit was brief, it was a portent of things to come. In 1717 the pirate Christopher Moody with two ships made one of several hit-and-run visits to the bar, capturing several vessels.

When Robert Johnson began his administration as governor in 1717, the times and the man came together fortuitously for the final assault on the scourge of the sea. In London, those who had really benefited from the colonial trade were now in high social or political positions. By and large they were middle-class merchants who had grown to depend on the shipments from Charles Towne. They began to argue the colonists' case. But King George I was busily occupied with the movements of Sweden against his Hanovarian Electorate. With the ships of his navy thus employed, he chose to brush the colonial problem aside; it was easier to deal with matters closer at hand. He granted an amnesty to the pirates, apparently thinking that this would turn them from their evil ways. It did not work.

The Royal Navy Enters the Fray

Some pirates took the oath of fealty, but most ignored it. By the fall of 1717, it had become apparent that the king's pardon had had little effect. London dispatched Captain

---

[1] Launched in January 1694, the 32-gun *Shoreham*, while a fifth-rate, was smaller (103') than the sixth-rates that would call Charles Towne home in the subsequent decades.

Woodes Rogers to New Providence with several small warships; his instructions were to exterminate the outlaws living there, and to reestablish a government under the British Crown.

Rogers is one of the unsung heroes of British naval history. Having taken two privateers around the world in the last war with Spain, he captured Spain's rich Manila galleon in the Pacific. In July 1718, Rogers arrived at New Providence and found a large number of pirates. Some, including the notorious Edward Teach, had already fled when they learned of Rogers' imminent arrival. Of those remaining, all surrendered to the Crown except Charles Vane [or Vaughn], who had made his reputation plundering Spanish galleons. After a brief skirmish, Vane managed to escape with ninety men to resume activity off the Carolina coast.

Legend has it that one of those surrendering to Rogers was Anne Bonney, supposedly the first woman pirate, and daughter of a Charles Towne lawyer. She had eloped with a waterfront character named James Bonney. The couple turned up in Nassau, where they joined the pirates. After Rogers pardoned Anne, she married a rogue named Calico Jack Rackam and resumed pirating, only to be caught. She escaped the gallows in Jamaica because of pregnancy, but evidently had learned her lesson; she returned to Charles Towne and settled down.

Blackbeard's Blockade of Charles Towne

While succeeding in the Bahamas, Rogers only exacerbated the situation off Charles Towne and the North Carolina coast by driving the pirates there. Even before Rogers had actually reached New Providence, many pirates had fled northward, or to the Bay of Honduras. In fact, Charles Towne soon found itself totally humiliated by Edward Teach, "Blackbeard."

Teach [or Thatch; he was known by many names] was supposedly one Thomas Barrow [or perhaps Edward Drummond] born in 1675 in Bristol, England, a port already closely connected by trade with Charles Towne. He had served on a privateer in the West Indies during Queen Anne's War. After the peace, he served under the pirate Benjamin Hornigold, who was based in New Providence. Late in 1716, he was given command of his own ship. She was a French Guineaman captured off St. Vincent and renamed *Queen Anne's Revenge*. Forty guns were mounted on her. One of the first incidents of his command was an encounter with HMS *Scarborough*,[2] which was repulsed after a battle of several hours.

After leaving the Bahamas, he established a base at Ocracoke Inlet. In January 1718, he obtained a pardon from Governor Eden of North Carolina, who was in cahoots with the pirates. The pardon was a cover to be used only if caught. By spring, *Queen Anne's Revenge* was refitted and was harrying vessels off the coast. On one such cruise in the Caribbean, Blackbeard met Stede Bonnet in the Bay of Honduras, and the two returned to Carolina together. Many of the crewmen of the captured ships joined the pirates, and by the time they reached South Carolina, Blackbeard had about 150 men and a fleet consisting of his own 40-gun *Queen Anne's Revenge*, Bonnet's 10-gun *Revenge*, the Jamaican ship *Adventure*, and another sloop.

On May 22, 1718, this fleet appeared off the Charles Towne bar shortly after the rene-

gade pirate Charles Vane had paid a visit and seized several ships. With his fleet Blackbeard captured every vessel that passed by. These included the pilot boat and eight outward-bound vessels. One of the latter was Robert Clark's ship bound for London with Samuel Wragg, a member of the Council of the Province. Blackbeard held Wragg for ransom. He then sent one of the prisoners, a Mr. Marks, into the city in an armed boat with a list of medicines for Governor Johnson to provide the ship. If Johnson failed to comply, he would receive the heads of the prisoners.

Governor Johnson took the matter before Council. Because there was no warship within hundreds of miles and the city lacked money to arm a ship or defend itself, there was no choice but to acquiesce to Blackbeard's demands. They could only hope to seek revenge later.

In the meantime, the pirates who had brought Marks ashore aroused the indignation of the populace by their arrogance, and the city authorities became alarmed that a mob might attack them. The authorities lost no time in collecting the medical supplies the pirates demanded. They were delivered to Mr. Marks to carry to the ships off the bar.

The prisoners on Blackbeard's ship spent several anxious days awaiting the return of Mr. Marks. The small boat was delayed when it capsized in a squall. The pirate chief's impatience led him to threaten his captives with death several times. To bargain for their lives, the prisoners volunteered to guide him into the harbor to sack the city if his men did not return.

Upon the return of his crew and Marks, Blackbeard released the prisoners true to his word, albeit in a half-naked condition. They made their way back to the city, suffering numerous hardships but glad to escape with their lives. For Blackbeard it was a rich haul. The booty from the captured ships included £1500 sterling in specie on Wragg's ship alone. This quenched Blackbeard's thirst for the time being, and he sailed away, leaving the city to lick the wounds of its humiliation.

One who was lucky to escape with the prisoners was Wragg's four-year-old son, William. Educated in England, he grew up to become a stalwart citizen of the colony. Prior to the Revolution, he held many high positions in local government. He remained loyal to King George III and, in 1777, sold his holdings in South Carolina and sailed to England. His ship was lost on the coast of Holland, and he and the entire crew were drowned. King George had a memorial erected to honor his memory in Westminster Abbey.

Blackbeard returned to North Carolina. There, in collusion with Governor Eden and the local authorities, he continued his illegal

This illustration of Blackbeard conjures up a nightmarish vision of the devil reincarnated. Adding to his intimidating looks were the smoking tapers that he placed in his beard.

[2] *Scarborough*, the station ship at Barbados, was a 32-gun, fifth-rate warship 108′ long on deck, measuring 416 tons. Launched at Sheerness Dock Yard in May 1711 (see pages 28–31) she should have easily trounced any pirate ship. Blackbeard's was no ordinary crew, as they were well armed and highly motivated; the gallows awaited them if they lost.

activities at sea while enjoying the benefits of civilization ashore. The law-abiding citizens of North Carolina realized that they could not look to their own government for protection. They sought help from Governor Spotswood of Virginia, who realized the potential threat to his own commerce that the pirates represented. He dispatched two warships of the Royal Navy then stationed in Hampton Roads. They were accompanied by two other ships hired at his own expense. This flotilla caught Blackbeard unaware at Ocracoke Inlet on November 22, 1718. During a fierce battle Blackbeard and several of his men were killed. Those of the crew who did not escape ashore were tried, and many were hanged.

In the meantime, Governor Johnson had lost no time in acquainting the authorities in London of Charles Towne's trials at the hands of the pirate gangs. As usual, his pleas fell on deaf ears, and the colony was left to its own resources. Johnson was no sluggard, though, and would soon show himself fit for the task.

Things were relatively quiet through the summer of 1718, as few cargoes of value passed in or out of the port, but when the ships began to assemble to load the fall crops, the sea rovers returned like bees to honey. Charles Towne was in for an ordeal such as no other English colony in North America had experienced.

Model of a Bermuda Sloop, favorite vessel of pirates because of its speed, nimbleness, and shallow draft.

Stede Bonnet

A key role in the fall battles of 1718 around Charles Towne would be played by Stede Bonnet, a pirate who had been with Blackbeard in June. He was a middle-aged man of means, supposedly from a good background but bored with his life in retirement, and there were rumors that he wanted to flee a nagging wife. Bonnet established himself at Bridgetown in the Barbados after retiring from the British Army with the rank of major. He had little knowledge of the sea, and his first experiences the previous year had resulted in disaster.

Bonnet bought a 10-gun sloop that he named *Revenge*, a name common to many pirate vessels at that time. With seventy hired desperadoes, he left Bridgetown early in 1717. In his first attacks off the Virginia Capes, a number of ships were sacked and burned, and the crews set ashore. From there, he made a call at New York to dispose of his cargoes. Next, he may have put in at Gardiner's Island off the tip of Long Island for provisions, moved south, and appeared off the bar of Charles Towne in August 1717—just as the spring crops were about to leave port. At this time Charles Towne had two channels, one running south by Morris Island, the other east by Sullivan's Island. It was relatively easy in clear weather for one ship to watch both channels and choose the best prey. Bonnet sacked a brigantine, then released it and allowed it to return to the harbor; there the alarm was raised. Another passing sloop he retained for his own use after letting the crew go.

The local authorities were powerless. They could do nothing to protect themselves from Bonnet. Fortunately, he set sail for North Carolina without attacking any more ships. There he refitted *Revenge*, and burned the captured sloop. By that time, his crew had discovered how little Bonnet knew of the sea. It was only his courage, his constant punishments, and his experience as a disciplined army officer that prevented a mutiny.

Bonnet put out to sea, apparently without any destination in mind, and eventually arrived in the Bay of Honduras. It had become the great southern rendezvous point for pirates after Captain Rogers had driven them out of the Bahamas. It had also become a popular refitting base in the winter months when storms ravaged the North Carolina coast. It was there that Bonnet had met Blackbeard, and the two sailed north together. Blackbeard quickly perceived that his companion was no seaman, so he took over *Revenge* by placing Richards, one of his own men, in charge. Bonnet became a virtual prisoner on Blackbeard's vessel in a subaltern position.

The first vessel that was captured when Blackbeard joined ranks with Bonnet was David Heriot's Jamaican ship (probably a

Stede Bonnet, gentleman pirate.

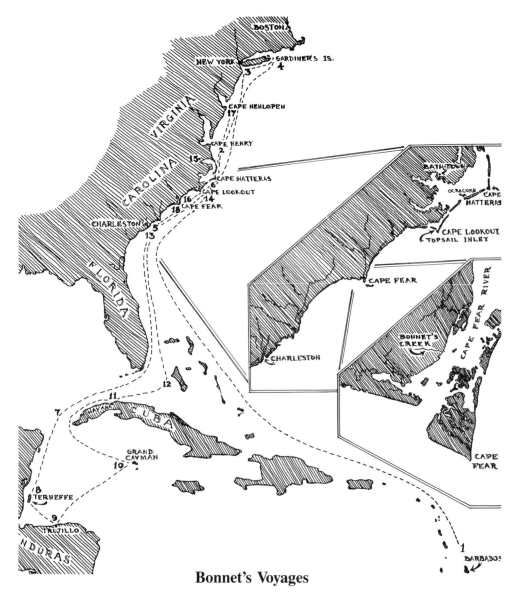

Bonnet's Voyages

1 Early 1717, left Barbados
2 Off Virginia Capes
3 New York and Long Island
4 Gardiner Island
5 August 1717, off Charles Towne
6 North Carolina inlets
7 Meeting with Blackbeard en route to Bay of Honduras
8 At Turneffe
9 At Turkill (Trujillo)
10 Grand Cayman
11 Havana
12 Bahamas
13 May 1718, off Charles Towne
14 Topsail Inlet, North Carolina
15 Pardoned at Bathtown, N. C.
16 July 29, 1718, off Cape Fear, takes *Fortune*
17 July 31, 1718, Cape Henlopen, takes *Frances*
18 August 1718, Cape Fear, careens *Revenge* (*Royal James*)
19 September 27, 1718, battle in the Cape Fear River
20 October 3, 1718, prisoner in Charles Towne

sloop) *Adventure* off the island of Turneffe in the Caribbean. After the pirates captured his ship, Heriot joined their ranks; he played a part in Bonnet's future career. From there they took part in the blockade of Charles Towne in May 1718. Upon leaving Charles Towne, the fleet put in to Topsail Inlet, North Carolina, where it disbanded. Bonnet took this opportunity to avail himself of George I's pardon. To Governor Eden he declared his intent to go to St. Thomas for a privateer commission to sail against Spain. Armed with the proper papers and a pardon, he set out to continue his career as a pirate with the best legal authority available to him.

Returning to Topsail Inlet again, Bonnet found his ship *Revenge* still intact. He recruited a small crew of sailors recently marooned by Blackbeard, including Heriot. From there Bonnet sailed up the coast for four days, seeking Blackbeard to avenge his embarrassment at having been deposed from his own ship in the Bay of Honduras and cheated out of a share of the booty. Renaming his sloop *Royal James* after James II, who was seeking to usurp the throne from George I, Bonnet terrorized the Virginia coast, taking several merchantmen. Five of his men boarded the becalmed *Francis* two miles off Cape Henlopen, Delaware, and overcame the crew. In August 1718, he brought that ship and another captured merchantman, *Fortune*, back to Cape Fear to refit *Royal James*, which was leaking badly. The work proceeded slowly; Bonnet had to capture a shallop in order to use its planking for additional repairs. He released the crew of the shallop, who then spread the word that the pirate fleet was being refitted on the Cape Fear River.

Rhett's Expedition to Attack Bonnet

When word of the pirates reached Charles Towne, which was still recovering from the June humiliation, the city became determined to stamp out the scourge. Governor Johnson feared another blockade by the pirates, but was at a loss as to how to prevent it without any warships in the harbor. Colonel William Rhett, a proud and imperious man of means and Receiver-General of the Province, asked to outfit two vessels for an expedition. When granted permission, he pressed into service the sloop *Henry* under Captain John Masters and *Sea Nymph* under Captain Fayrer Hall. Being the larger, *Henry* became Rhett's flagship, carrying eight guns and seventy men. *Sea Nymph* was armed with the same number of guns and sixty men.

The two vessels were ready on September 10. They were moved across the harbor to Sullivan's Island, where final preparations were made. Just as they were about to leave, a small sloop came in, reporting a more immediate threat—the infamous Charles Vane was once more off the bar with a 12-gun brigantine and ninety men. Having battled his way out of Nassau two months earlier when Captain Rogers arrived to restore authority to the island, Vane had already captured two vessels, one of which was loaded with slaves from Guinea. The slaves had been removed to a sloop commanded by another pirate, named Yeates. Yeates had double-crossed Vane and made off with the booty. Vane subsequently captured the 16-gun *Neptune* and the 10-gun *Emperor* with valuable cargoes.

To Rhett, this news could not have come at a more propitious time; his ships were ready to sail. On September 15, they crossed the bar. Vane had disappeared. Meanwhile, Yeates had put in at the South Edisto River and sent an emissary to the city to request a pardon. Governor Johnson granted it. Vane subsequently was accused of cowardice by his

crew, set adrift, and then rescued by an old friend who turned him in to the authorities at Jamaica, where he was hanged.

When Rhett found nothing of Vane[3] he set out for North Carolina. On the evening of September 26, he sighted the headland to the Cape Fear River. Having no pilot familiar with the channel, Rhett's ships grounded on one of the many sandbars at the mouth of the river. Some distance upstream they could see over a point of land the topmasts of *Royal James* and her two prizes. Since it was late at night before his vessels were afloat, Rhett waited until first light before attacking.

In the meantime, the pirates' lookout reported the appearance of Rhett's ships. Because they could not tell in the darkness if the ships were men-of-war or merchantmen, they sent three armed boats down to reconnoiter. They did not have to get very close to identify them. Realizing the task at hand, Bonnet used threats and fear to exhort his crew to clear the decks and make ready for action.

Rhett's men had seen the scouting boats and prepared for a night action, knowing that certain death would be the cost of defeat. With their superior forces, they were confident of victory. They stood by their arms through the night. All night long the sounds of preparation could be heard on the other side.

Battle in the Cape Fear River

Neither side slept, and by first light everyone was active. The sun was hardly above the headlands before the sails were up on *Royal James*. She came running downstream before an offshore breeze to where the two sloops lay at anchor. With the ebb tide carrying him, Bonnet intended to make a running fight for the ocean. Rhett's ships weighed anchor as Bonnet came around the point of land and closed for action. *Sea Nymph* and *Henry* forced *Royal James* in close to the shore, causing her to run aground. Because the attacking sloops were unable to come about fast enough, they also grounded on the sandy bottom. *Henry* grounded within pistol-shot of *James'* bow, while *Sea Nymph*, trying to cut off her escape, had grounded far ahead, out of range.

At that time, naval battles between small ships were still fought largely by boarding and man-to-man combat; the small 4- and 6-pounder guns that most small ships carried were not able to do appreciable damage. With his ship aground, Rhett ordered that a heavy fire be poured into the enemy with the guns that could be brought to bear. The steady barrage of small-arms fire was more effective, because the cannon could not be operated from the sloping decks in the ebb tide. As the tide went out, both ships heeled over in the same direction; the South Carolinians were at the greater disadvantage with their decks exposed to the enemy, while the pirate had his heeled away, exposing only his sides. The heavy shot from Rhett's ship could take effect on only the hull of the enemy, while his own deck could be swept from end to end. The battle raged for five hours as the tide went out and then came back in. Rhett's men stood to their guns while the enemy availed themselves of the advantage.

---

[3] Rhett encountered one of the vessels that Vane had set free. The master had been deceived by Vane into thinking that Vane was headed south, when in fact he proceeded in the opposite direction. Rhett fell for the ruse and Vane escaped.

The small-arms fire slowly took its toll, and both sides taunted and jeered each other during lulls. As the tide came in, everyone realized that victory would belong to the first afloat. *Henry* slowly lifted first off the bottom. Once free, many of Bonnet's crew opted for surrender; he refused, saying he would fire the magazine and blow them all up. Drawing his pistols, he tried to force his men to fight on, but they had had enough and overpowered him.

While this was going on, Rhett's men repaired *Henry's* rigging and then bore down on *Royal James* to board and subdue her crew. As *Henry* closed, a flag of truce went up. After a few minutes of negotiation, Bonnet's men surrendered unconditionally. It was not until he came aboard that Rhett learned the identity of his opponent. Ten men from *Henry* were killed

and fourteen wounded, several of whom later died; on *Sea Nymph*, two were killed and four wounded. Seven pirates were killed and five wounded, two of whom later died.

Rhett's fleet remained on the Cape Fear River for three days, repairing the ships and making ready for the return voyage. They arrived in Charles Towne on October 3 with the pirate sloop and Bonnet's prizes, *Fortune* and *Francis*, as trophies of war. Two days later the prisoners were landed and kept under heavy guard in the public watch house, a more economical version of a jail. Bonnet, considered a gentleman, was treated to somewhat better accommodations than his crew, much to the later regret of the authorities. He was confined at the house of Marshal Partridge with two sentinels on guard. He was joined a few days later by David Heriot, the sailing master, and Ignatius Pell, the boatswain of *Royal James*, who had agreed to give evidence for the Crown.

Bonnet's Escape

For some reason the trial was delayed for four weeks. During this time, Bonnet's friends, of which there were many in the city, worked to secure his release by any means. Three days before the trial, the guards were bribed with gold, and Bonnet and Heriot escaped during the night of October 24 disguised as women. Pell refused to flee. Governor Johnson offered a reward of £700 sterling for the duo's capture.

They sailed northward along the coast in a boat provided by friends. However, the winds were adverse and after a few days they were forced to return to Sullivan's Island to procure supplies from the city. They had hardly landed before the governor received word of it and promptly dispatched Rhett and a crew to bring them back alive if possible. Rhett crossed the harbor during the night of November 5. After searching for several hours he found the escapees on the north end of Sullivan's Island. Rhett's party promptly opened fire; Heriot was killed and two others were wounded. Bonnet surrendered, and the next day all returned to Charles Towne.

Trial of Bonnet and His Men

In the meantime, Bonnet's crew came on trial before the Court of Vice-Admiralty[4] on October 28. Chief Justice Trott presided, assisted by leading citizens of the province. All but a few were found guilty and sentenced to death by hanging. There never was any doubt that they were all guilty of piracy; the issue before the court was the question of intent. Four of them managed to prove that they did not intend to become pirates, and thus escaped the gallows.

On November 8, two days after Bonnet's return, the condemned men who had been tried and convicted by the court were taken to White Point, then separated from the city by a small creek running along present-day Water Street from whence the street acquired its name. There

[4] See Appendix I on the Vice-Admiralty Courts.

Colonel William Rhett, pillar of the early Charles Towne establishment, warrior, and planter, without whose leadership the early city may have failed.

Battle in the Cape Fear River between Stede Bonnet's grounded *Royal James* in the foreground and Colonel Rhett's *Henry* (also grounded) in the right background.

on a spot below the city, the men were hanged. Their bodies were buried in the marsh below the low-water mark. As this area has long since been filled in with buildings erected, the exact location of the interment is unknown. Local legend has it that it was near the corner of present-day Meeting and Water streets. Some of Charleston's finest current residences may be resting on the bones of Bonnet's men.

Two days later Bonnet's trial commenced before the same court with the same result. Throughout the trial he maintained composure and dignity. He refused to be intimidated by the prosecutor and judge, and he rendered little in the way of a defense. Governor Johnson set December 10 as the day of execution. Bonnet tried every maneuver that he could think of to avoid his fate; he even appealed to Colonel Rhett himself. Two days before his scheduled execution, Bonnet even addressed a suppliant letter to Johnson, begging for mercy. Such efforts aroused some sympathy, but Johnson, well aware of the suffering Bonnet had caused, did not sway. Bonnet soon followed in his companions' steps and was buried in the mud of the Cooper River.

Bonnet's friends had kept the city in a constant uproar while he was awaiting trial. These threats combined to make October 1718 the most difficult month to date for the young city. Almost every night Bonnet's allies caused commotions, accompanied by threats to burn the city down. At that time many of the buildings were made of wood with shingled roofs; a major fire would have been disaster. To make matters worse, the town-watch had been established only a few years earlier and was not sufficiently manned to provide for public safety. The militia guarding Bonnet's crew were able to prevent their release, but bribery could tempt anyone at any time. There were also constant rumors of pirate fleets being prepared to

The hanging of Stede Bonnet at White Point below the Charles Towne city wall, December 10, 1718.

sack the city and release Bonnet and his men. The citizens had as their precedent similar attacks on cities of the Spanish Main in the preceding two centuries.

With Bonnet's demise the courts found themselves deluged with resulting litigation. Many Charlestonians had served in the fight against Bonnet out of patriotic devotion and had not expected to be rewarded, but others went seeking reward. In addition, the owners of *Sea Nymph* and *Henry* had to be compensated. Their captains filed for condemnation of *Royal James*, urging that her prize money be turned over to her captors. Colonel Rhett was the only one on the Cape Fear expedition who did not demand a reward for his part. After a lengthy trial, Judge Trott ruled in favor of the applicants. He decreed that the prizes should be sold, with one-half of the proceeds given to the captors and the remaining half awarded to the original owners of the captured cargoes.

Moody, Vane, and Worley

Bonnet had hardly escaped the previous month when a new threat manifested itself in a reappearance by the notorious pirate, Christopher Moody. He returned to the bar with a 50-gun[5] vessel carrying 200 brigands, and he promptly seized two vessels inbound from New England. Governor Johnson immediately convened his Council and called for quick and decisive action. No help could be expected from the Royal Navy, so the colony was dependent on its own resources. Fortunately the ships used in apprehending Bonnet were still in the harbor, and the Council concurred with the governor in employing them against the new threat. Two merchant ships waiting in the harbor to load the crops then being harvested were also pressed into service. After making an examination of the available ships, the Council selected *Mediterranean*, *King William*, and *Sea Nymph*. To these were added Bonnet's *Royal James*, then being held as a prize. The latter, fitted with eight guns, was commanded by John Masters, formerly captain of Rhett's flagship. *Mediterranean* was fitted with twenty-four guns, *King William* with thirty, and *Sea Nymph* with six. Governor Johnson promised volunteers a part of any booty that might be taken.

Johnson had had a falling out with Rhett over Bonnet's pending fate. (Rhett had felt that he had given his word that Bonnet would not be hanged.) Therefore, Johnson took personal command of this expedition. His example met with a hearty response from the citizens; three hundred men quickly volunteered. Before the ships could sail, the ship captains demanded security on behalf of their owners in the event that their vessels should be damaged or lost. The Assembly voted a bill to secure the shipowners against all losses and expenses that they might incur. These proceedings delayed the expedition for about a week. In the meantime, scout boats were stationed along the shore of the islands at the harbor entrance to watch the enemy's movements and repel any attempts to land. At the same time no ships were allowed to leave port. The scout boats off Sullivan's Island sighted a ship and a sloop

---

[5] It is highly unlikely that any pirate sailed on such a large vessel. A 50-gun warship of the early eighteenth century was a major warship, a ship-of-the line of battle. As such they were usually slow, easily seen, and confined by shallow coastal waters—hardly the type vessel that a pirate would choose. The 50-gun ship that local accounts mention was probably a former merchant ship about 100' long, armed with about half that number of guns.

that came up to the bar, dropped anchor, and attempted to land. The guards prevented a landing by a show of force, and for three days the two craft lay quietly at their moorings, making no movement to arouse further suspicions.

Late on the evening of November 4, the fleet under Governor Johnson's command sailed down the harbor and anchored several hundred yards off Fort Johnson, moving as quietly and inconspicuously as possible so as not to arouse enemy suspicions. They lay at anchor through the night. As the first light of the hazy morning broke, Governor Johnson gave the order to weigh anchor and follow his flagship, *Mediterranean*. The captains, ordered to make no war-like displays, directed the ships out of the harbor with guns covered and crews below decks. The deception was apparently complete, as the unsuspecting pirates thought the four vessels were merchantmen.

The pirate ships quickly weighed anchor and stood in toward the mouth of the harbor so as to cut off any retreat. They ran up the "Jolly Roger" once they were between Johnson's ships and the harbor entrance and demanded the surrender of *King William*. In reply, the King's colors were run up, the gunports thrown open, and a broadside delivered at the closest vessel with telling effect. Before the pirates could recover, the Charlestonians bore down on them and began the battle at close quarters. The hatches were opened and the men poured from below decks while the other vessels joined in the cannonade. Although they were hemmed in between the ships and shore, the pirates skillfully maneuvered and bent on all sails to escape. Johnson signaled *Sea Nymph* and *Revenge* to chase the sloop, while *Mediterranean* and *King William* went after the ship.

The pirate sloop, which carried six guns and forty men, was unable to reach the open sea. She was vigorously attacked, and the battle raged broadside to broadside for most of the morning. Finally, the overwhelmed pirate crew abandoned their guns, seeking shelter below decks. The Carolinians poured over the side and took possession of the vessel. The pirate captain was killed during the fracas, as were some of the few men left above deck. The men who had fled below were clapped in irons. The ship was then triumphantly carried into Charles Towne harbor to the tremendous joy of the inhabitants; the battle had taken place within sight of the city. The celebration rose to a pitch of exultation as the throng along the wharves saw *Sea Nymph* and *Revenge* coming up the channel, the royal ensign at the mast-head signaling victory.

Meanwhile Governor Johnson was having an easier time of it, despite the larger size of his opponent. He had a long and hard chase after the fleeing ship and did not come up with her until the middle of the afternoon. During the pursuit the enemy abandoned the defense and bent every resource on escape. Even guns and boats were thrown over the side to lighten the ship. This effort was fruitless, as the colonists had the faster ships. As soon as *King William* came within range, its crew raked the enemy deck. Two pirates were killed and the "Jolly Roger" came fluttering down.

When the South Carolinians came aboard to take possession they found thirty-six women below decks. The ship turned out to be *Eagle*, bound from London to Virginia and Maryland with one hundred and six convicts and covenant servants for settlers. She had been captured off Cape Henry by the pirate sloop, which was known as *New York Revenge*. *Eagle* was converted to a tender for the sloop and renamed *New York Revenge's Revenge*! A good many of the convicts had joined with the pirates; those who didn't were held prisoner with the women.

Upon his return to the city Governor Johnson was surprised to learn that Moody had not been involved in the battle. The commander of the pirates killed on the sloop proved to be Richard Worley, notorious for having already terrorized the northern coast.

Worley's career as a pirate had spanned only six weeks. He had set out from New York at the end of September 1718 in an open boat with eight consorts. They ran down to Delaware Bay, where they plundered a small vessel. Upon its release, it sailed to Philadelphia and reported the attack. An unsuccessful expedition went out after Worley. In the meantime, he captured a Philadelpha sloop and converted it to his own use. His attacks were so continual during the next few weeks that the governor of Pennsylvania orderd HMS *Phoenix*,[6] then at Sandy Hook, New York, to seek him out. But Worley stood out to sea and escaped.

Worley captured *Eagle* off Cape Henry after a pursuit of over twenty-four hours. At first *Eagle's* crew fought, but on the second day, the "Jolly Roger" so unnerved them that they deserted their posts and fled below. Under threats of death from the pirates, *Eagle* surrendered. Worley subsequently made his way south to Charles Towne. He arrived just as Moody departed, and thus he fell victim to the preparations already made against Moody.

The question remained as to Moody's whereabouts; certainly, he was still free and would seek revenge if these were indeed his men. Governor Johnson maintained the ships in a state of readiness. When the vessel *Minerva* arrived from the Madeira Islands, Captain Smyter reported that he had been taken off the bar by Moody, who had at about the same time learned of the preparations underway in the harbor against him. Therefore, Moody took *Minerva* several hundred miles to sea and plundered and released her. He then set sail for New Providence in order to avail himself of the king's pardon.

The authorities set about dealing with the surviving pirates. Rather than let the badly wounded die uncondemned, they chose swift justice to settle matters. The trial lasted five days; all were found guilty, and Judge Trott sentenced the entire company to death. This series of executions meant that forty-nine outlaws were dispatched within a month. Only nine out of the entire lot had been acquitted.

Governor Johnson's expedition had aroused a great deal of interest because of the nature of the cargo. The ship captains in the expedition expected payment too. *Eagle's* captain and crewmembers who had not joined the pirates fought valiantly to preserve their possession of the ship and its cargo. Her captain, Robert Staples, had been beaten severely by the pirates and died of these wounds before the trial began; but Edmond Robinson, the chief mate, assumed command, engaged legal counsel, and made a hard fight. Governor Johnson had promised all prizes to the volunteers; the plaintiffs fought with determination. The cargo of white indentured servants was even contested, an unusual occurrence in that day. After hearing the testimony, Judge Trott decreed that the servants should be publicly sold and one-half of the proceeds delivered to Robinson as agent for the owners. As for the ship, one-half went to the captors. It was indeed an unusual sale in the annals of slavery in America.

Ramifications in London

These two exploits earned Charles Towne a place in the records of piracy battles, but the danger was by no means past. Each month brought new tales of attacks against vessels off the coast. Governor Johnson was determined to prevent a pirate horde from descending

[6] Later station ship at Charles Town from 1738 to 1742.

upon the town and sacking it in revenge. In February of 1719, the Assembly passed an act appropriating sufficient funds to pay the debts for the two expeditions of the preceding year. Another letter went to the Lords of the Board of Trade, saying in effect that if they did not want to see the colony exterminated and the trade from it extinguished, they had better have a warship stationed at Charles Towne. Johnson further pointed out that during the previous year the colony had provided for the Royal Navy 32,000 barrels of tar, 20,643 barrels of pitch, and 473 barrels of turpentine.

The British Board of Trade, not one to be hurried, moved with unusual slowness in Charles Towne's case. Governor Johnson's letter was sent on December 12, 1718, and it was received the following February 24. The remoteness of the colony must not have made the matter seem urgent, for it was another two months before Johnson's letter was read at one of the Board's meetings. The secretary agreed to recommend to the Lords of the Admiralty that the request for a warship be granted. Finally, on April 29, a letter was sent to Governor Johnson acknowledging that the Lords of the Admiralty had agreed to send a frigate "as soon as possible."

Warships had been stationed in the harbors of the northern colonies since the early years of the eighteenth century. While they were not always present, their existence was a deterrent to pirates. Now at last, the southern colonies received theirs and Charles Towne became the first base. The first Royal Navy Station Ship was *Flamborough*,[7] which arrived on October 5, 1719, under Captain John Hildesley. The pirate threat rapidly subsided. There were other isolated attacks, but they had no lasting effect on the commercial life of the colony. In these random attacks, pirates moved in quickly, captured an unsuspecting ship, and then made off in haste before the alarm could be raised.

Last Pirate Attacks

In one of the pirate episodes of the summer of 1722, the English freebooter George Lowther appeared off the coast, probably when the station ship *Blandford*[8] was away at Halifax, Nova Scotia, for its usual summer refitting. Lowther lay off the bar for several days and then attacked the unsuspecting merchant ship *Amy*, commanded by Captain Gwatkins, as it left the harbor bound for England.

Gwatkins returned the pirates' fire and attempted to close for a fight at close quarters. The tables thus turned, the pirate vessel ran onto the beach and the crew abandoned ship and swam ashore. Unwilling to end the matter there, Gwatkins tried to set fire to the stranded vessel. While engaged in this, he was fired upon from the beach and killed. *Amy's* men retreated to their vessel and resumed their trip. Lowther got his sloop afloat and sailed for a North Carolina inlet, where he spent the winter while his ship was being repaired.

The next attack occurred in May 1723, when Edward Low, a pirate from New England, appeared accompanied by another desperado, Harris. They captured and plundered several

[7] *Flamborough* was a 24-gun, sixth-rate warship, 94′ long on deck. She was launched at Woodwich Dock Yard on January 29, 1707, and rebuilt in 1727 as a 20-gun ship.

[8] The 20-gun *Blandford* was a 375-ton sixth-rate, 106′ long on deck. She was built at the Deptford Dock Yard in 1719 and remained in service until 1742.

vessels coming out of Charles Towne. The captain of one vessel had his ears cut off and his nose slit before being dismissed by the pirates. Three more vessels were seized before the pirates moved on. However, Low's attacks did not cause much consternation in the port, as no news was received of them until some time after he left the area. A month later Low and Harris were attacked and captured by the warship HMS *Greyhound*. They were carried to Newport, Rhode Island, and hanged with their crews.

Blandford brought a number of pirate prisoners into Charles Towne in 1724. Then in 1727, Arthur Middleton commissioned a sloop to cruise against pirates who had recently taken ships off the coast. Another pirate, Nicholas Burnwall, was executed in 1728. Although pirates continued to plague the northern colonies and the Caribbean, South Carolina's relentless defense gave her comparative immunity.

Charles Towne Ramifications of the Pirate Battles

The major repercussion in Charles Towne of the pirate attacks was the rebellion against Proprietary rule in December 1719. The first recommendation for the Crown to assume the management of the colony came at the end of the seventeenth century in Edward Randolph's damning account of the laxness of colonial administration. These critical reports, combined with the cries of the English merchants and shipowners for losses at the hands of pirates and corrupt colonial administrators, forced the Crown to realize that Proprietary rule had to end. Private enterprise had saved the Crown the initial investment in the colony, but it also prevented the allotment of necessary funds for the administration and defense of the colony. It was the refusal of the Proprietors to send or even request aid from the Crown during the Yemassee War and their failure to support the fight against the pirates that irrevocably turned the colonists against them.

In December 1719, the colonists declared James Moore to be governor in the name of the king. Johnson was first offered the governor's seat with the condition that he renounce the Proprietors; this he refused to do, so he was removed from office. A few months later Moore was followed by Francis Nicholson, former governor of New York. He found the colony free of pirates. By this time the colonists had recovered financially and taken strong measures for the common defense.

Conclusion

The nearly simultaneous fight against the pirates and the Indians give testament to the courage of the early settlers of Charles Towne. At the time the colony was not fifty years old. A rigorous discipline had tempered their character. While the land would be relatively peaceful for another fifty-five years, the period of trial and self-reliance just past influenced the colonists to question the ability to govern of any authority three thousand miles distant. These battles were the first of many honorable passages in South Carolina's history, and placed her in the front line of the fight for independence.

Part II

A ROYAL COLONY

The Royal Navy as Guardian

With the end of proprietary government in South Carolina heralding a new era, the colony had survived for almost a half-century by dint of its own self-reliance and resources. It had met and repulsed several threats with very little external aid. The reliance on domestic armed forces for its own protection would form a background that would carry South Carolina to statehood in a new nation.

As the period of Royal government unfolded, the people of Charles Town exchanged a physical threat for a political and economic one. The colony had been dependent on external trade for its economic life before 1720; this dependency would only become greater as English merchants and officials began to dominate the affairs of the colony more and more.

During the 1720s, the Royal Navy station ships began to make regular patrols off the

The Cooper River waterfront of Charles Town in the late 1730s. This stylized view of the prospering city clearly shows the wide variety of vessels using the port, including the sixth-rate warships in the right and left foregrounds (probably *Seaford* and *Phoenix*); several single-masted sloops (the ones with guns were probably the smaller station ships *Spence* or *Shark*); two-masted brigs (right center and extreme right—the brig slightly to the right of center bristling with guns was probably another warship); and the assortment of small craft that used the Lowcountry's rivers as highways. The lack of schooners in the scene is unusual; probably the London engraver was unfamiliar with the colonial type.

Admiralty builder's model of a sixth-rate warship of the 1719 establishment. Since the masts and rigging were a standard formula based on a ship's measurements, builders models omitted them for clarity. Note the short forecastle. The entry port on the gun deck is clearly visible with the oar ports fore and aft of it. Compare this model with the one on page 60.

Carolina coast to ward off pirates and marauding Spanish privateers, and guardacostas. For many years, London had realized the need for station ships; but the combination of European wars, the East Indies Trade, the lack of naval bases, and the distances involved made it very difficult for the king's government to render support for the colonies in general, and South Carolina in particular.

Maintenance had been the biggest obstacle to providing a station ship for the South Carolina coast, for without a naval base nearby, the warships had to return to England for upkeep. The lack of naval facilities meant that each ship on station required an additional one as a backup for maintenance. Later a Royal Navy base was established at Halifax, Nova Scotia, but this was a long way to go for the required annual maintenance on the ships' bottoms. Bottom cleaning was the most time-consuming part of maintenance. While careening was used in remote stations, ship captains did not readily take to it because of the work involved and the stress that it placed on the ship's hull structure and masts.

Due to the distance from the seat of government in London to Charles Town, upon departure from British waters the ship commanders were given general instructions in regard to their duties while on the Carolina station. Much was left up to their own initiative and the local circumstances. At times, naval officers in America took crucial steps without specific directives from the Admiralty. The officers who were sent to South Carolina carried instructions to protect trade foremost, to convoy merchant ships to and from the Bahamas, and to prevent all illicit commerce with the colony. In addition, they were expected to support the

Model of one of George Anson's commands at Charles Town, *Scarborough*. She was a 20-gun sixth-rate of the 1719 Establishment, meaning that the particulars of her design were maintained until

the next Establishment was instituted in 1733. This beautiful model was built by Robert Lightley of Cape Town, South Africa.

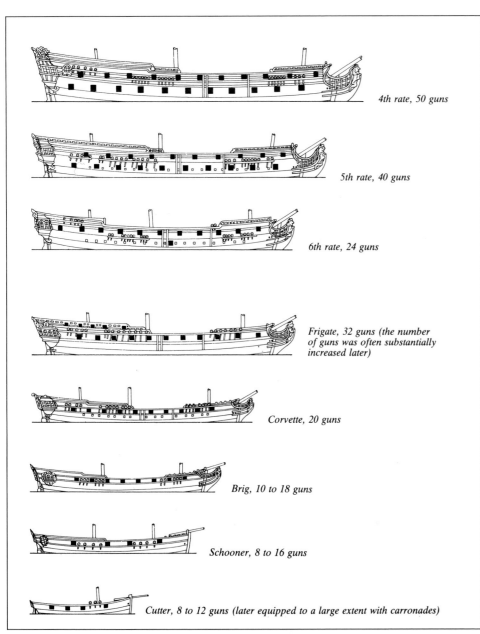

4th rate, 50 guns

5th rate, 40 guns

6th rate, 24 guns

Frigate, 32 guns (the number of guns was often substantially increased later)

Corvette, 20 guns

Brig, 10 to 18 guns

Schooner, 8 to 16 guns

Cutter, 8 to 12 guns (later equipped to a large extent with carronades)

Royal Navy Ship Rating System

In the Royal Navy's warship-rating system, a sixth-rate carried twenty or more guns, a fifth-rate forty or more, a fourth-rate fifty or more, and so forth up to a first-rate, which carried over ninety-eight. In this treatise, however, we are concerned with only the smaller three rates and minor vessels. Anything larger than a fourth-rate warship could not cross the bar into Charles Town harbor. Fourth-rates could do so only when their guns and stores had been offloaded to lighten the ship, thereby reducing draft sufficiently to cross the bar.

governor in the execution of governmental authority and protect the city of Charles Town against attack by the Spanish.

Ships were not expected to remain on station indefinitely, but only until they could no longer stay without a general overhaul in a Royal Navy dockyard. Until the base at Halifax was established, this meant that the ships had to return to England. Bottom cleaning and other relatively simple maintenance could be performed on station, but anything requiring major repairs to sections of the hull had to be performed in one of the Royal Navy dockyards.

Most of the warships assigned to duty in Charles Town were sixth-rate warships, sometimes called *frigates*. The term *frigate* was still loosely applied to any fast, armed ship with a waist and transom stern. The frigates that became famous in the Revolution and War of 1812 were generally not developed until the 1740s, when the French adapted them from the design of their large-armed merchant ships, the French East Indiamen.

George Anson

Little note has been made of these station ships, since their work was largely a matter of routine; however, in June 1724, one man arrived who would permanently leave his mark on Charles Town. His position in the galaxy of flag officers of the Royal Navy would be eclipsed only by Admiral Nelson a half century later.

At the age of twenty-seven, George Anson found himself posted to the Carolina Station in command of the 20-gun, sixth-rate *Scarborough*.[1] Anson was born in 1697, the son of a well-to-do English family. He began his naval service in 1712 on HMS *Monmouth*. By 1716 he had been promoted to the rank of lieutenant. In 1719 Anson received his first command, *Weazle*, on fishery protection in the North Sea. The battles with the pirates had subsided before Anson's arrival; therefore, his official duty in Charles Town was fairly undemanding, and he was noted more for his social than naval prowess. As Mrs. Hutchinson of Charles Town wrote to her sister in London:

> Anson is not one of those handsome men...but I think his person is what you would call very agreeable.... [He] has good sense, good nature, is polite and well-bred...is generous without profusion, elegant without ostentation, and above all, of a most tender, humane disposition.... [H]e never dances, nor swears, nor talks nonsense. As he greatly admires a fine woman, so he is passionately fond of music. He loves his bottle and his friend so well, that they will not be very soon tired of their company,.... [I]f fame says true, he is very far from being a woman-hater, and that now and then his mistress may come in for a share of him.

The governor called upon Anson to help suppress an open rebellion instigated by a man named Smith among the settlers. The local marshal was unable and afraid to arrest Smith, so Anson sent armed boats to arrest him at the Ashley River Ferry; they returned him to Charles Town, where he was tried for high treason.

Anson spent some six years in the city off and on until 1730. In 1725 when Spain made

---

[1] *Scarborough* was originally built as a 32-gun, fifth-rate warship. In 1720 she was rebuilt as a 20-gun sixth-rate. She was not sold out of service until 1739.

an attempt to retake Gibraltar, Anson's ship patrolled against the Spanish and escorted merchantmen clear of the Carolina coast until peace was reestablished. He also commanded *Guarland*, another sixth-rate, after her captain died in Charles Town in July 1728. By that time, *Scarborough* was in such bad repair that she had to return to England. On June 5, 1730, Anson sailed from Charles Town for England in *Guarland*, escorting five merchant ships. This departure signaled the end of his first tour of duty on the South Carolina station.

Between tours of duty in Charles Town, Anson served aboard the 40-gun ship *Diamond*. In the spring of 1732 when intelligence had been received that the Spanish were planning an attack on Georgia, he was ordered to the 24-gun *Squirrel*,[2] another sixth-rate, and instructed to proceed to Charles Town. In the event of a Spanish attack, Anson was directed to call on the other station ships in the American colonies for assistance if necessary.

On his return to Charles Town, starting in June 1732, Anson patrolled the coast and called at various settlements; he found, however, that the inhabitants did not consider that the Spanish posed a threat to them. Other than occasional patrols against the Spaniards who sailed out of St. Augustine, and stray French privateers, Anson remained at anchor in *Squirrel* in Charles Town harbor for long periods of time. But life in port was not without incident. One day, a boat crew from *Squirrel* got entangled in a Vice-Admiralty case of homicide.

A warrant had been filed in the Court of Vice-Admiralty against a Captain Gordon of a merchant ship for a debt of £56. The marshal went out to the ship at anchor in Rebellion Road[3] to serve the warrant. Upon his approach, Captain Gordon threatened the marshal. He retreated, but a shot was fired. It landed perilously near the marshal's boat.

The judge of the Vice-Admiralty Court issued a warrant against Captain Gordon for assault and formally requested *Squirrel's* assistance. When *Squirrel's* boat approached the ship, it too was fired upon by a musket. The boat moved around to the stern where the carriage guns would not bear. As the boat closed, musket fire resumed. *Squirrel's* boat returned fire, killing Captain Gordon. The men in *Squirrel's* boat were subsequently arrested and brought to trial for murder. They were acquitted because they had fired in self-defense.

Anson's prowess at cards was well known, as was his penchant for gambling. Once, a story goes, he had invited a General Lee to dine. After dinner, they sat down at cards. The stakes were high, and the general lost. Shortly after the game, Anson's ship left Charles Town on a patrol. After his departure, a letter was delivered to General Lee. In it, the entire amount that he had lost to Anson was returned. Anson, it seems, invested his profits from playing cards in real estate. If land had been wagered by his opponent, it probably would have remained Anson's.

Anson was a shrewd real estate investor. In 1726 he purchased sixty-four acres of plantation lands. In 1730 it was recorded that 12,000 acres had been transferred to him. When he departed for England in 1730, he appointed an agent to manage his property in the colony. Paying for his property may have caused the tough financial straits he encountered on his return to England. As he mentions in a letter to Sir John Norris:

> The *Happy* sloop has to be relieved, as she has seven years pay due. If I could be continued a year longer here, it would much contribute to the establishment of my affairs, which are yet pretty much distressed.

This distress probably prompted the sale of the valuable forty acres of property known as the "Quarter House Tract" to John Laurens on March 4, 1731, while Anson was in England. It was the location of this property that enhanced its value: it was at the fork of roads leading out of the city.

His last recorded deed is dated May 1735, when his title to an area of Charles Town later known as Ansonborough was certified. Anson supposedly won this property in a card game with Thomas Gadsden, a lieutenant in the Royal Navy and the King's Collector of Customs.

Legend has it that there was a house on the Ansonborough property that Anson occupied. It was situated at the head of a creek that led away from the Cooper River. When his

---

[2] *Squirrel* was a 24-gun sixth-rate that had originally been built as a 262-ton ship. In 1727 she was rebuilt and enlarged to 377 tons at Woolwich. *Squirrel* was sold out of service in 1749.

Left: **Model of an English 20-gun sixth-rate warship of the 1719 establishment. These warships were 110′ long, about the average size of a transatlantic merchant ship. George Anson's commands at Charles Town were vessels of this class. Up to the Revolution, the vast majority of station ships at Charles Town were sixth-rates. At times they were supplemented by smaller warships; only occasionally were larger ones assigned.**

The sixth-rate warship in the first half of the eighteenth century was the "maid of all work" in the Royal Navy. It had a small forecastle deck and a short quarterdeck with accommodations below that for the captain and officers. Most guns on sixth-rate warships were mounted on the upper deck, with only a few (if any) mounted on the lower or gun deck; these sixth-rates were really little more than a scaled-down version of the larger rates and were rigged similarly. As the size of the larger ships decreased, the gun deck became closer to the waterline. Note the top three warships in the sketch on page 29. By the time the basic warship design had been scaled down to a sixth-rate, the gun deck was so close to the water that open gunports on that deck could be a danger to the safety of the ship in a seaway. Therefore, the guns were mounted one deck higher, leaving only an entry port and oarports on the gun deck. The oarports (small row of openings just above the waterline) opened sideways like doors, and the oars were a great asset for getting the ships in and out Charles Town's narrow winding channel under adverse weather or tide conditions in patrolling the inlets along the coast.

Mounting the main battery (mostly 6-pounder guns until 1743, when 9-pounders were substituted) on the upper deck contributed to topheaviness, which had to be countered by heavy ballasting. Consequently the extra weight caused the English sixth-rate warships to be outclassed by the French frigates that were introduced in the 1740s.

Compare this 1719 sixth-rate with the 1745 sixth-rate shown on page 60. Note the longer forecastle and quarterdecks on the latter as the main guns were gradually covered to reduce the exposure of gun crews in battle to enemy fire and falling debris, and to improve the seaworthiness of the vessels.

[3] There is a popular misconception that the main ship anchorage in Charles Town harbor between Shute's Folly and Sullivan's Island, known as "Rebellion Road," received its name from the colonial rebellion in 1775 or the more recent rebellion in 1860. This is incorrect. The anchorage received its name by an act of the Colonial Assembly in 1696, which declared that any vessel that anchored in that location was considered in "rebellion" against the Crown. At the time the roadstead was out of the range of the city's guns. Consequently any vessel anchoring there was outside of the enforcement of the law and thus considered "in rebellion."

Overleaf: **The station ship *Squirrel's* main battery booms out a salute in Charles Town harbor as South Carolina Indian chiefs come aboard much like visiting heads of state. The ship's commander, Captain George Anson, ordered the rare reception, showing his flare for showmanship and the dramatic.**

Mark Myers: 1987

ship was at anchor in the harbor, Anson could be rowed ashore, right up to his own doorstep.[4]

Rose[5] relieved *Squirrel* as the station ship and Anson returned home. He escorted a convoy of seven merchant ships over the bar on May 17, 1735, never to return to Charles Town.

In 1744, the Ansonborough property was divided into lots and sold. It became the first suburb of Charles Town, but of the houses built before the Revolution only the one at 79 Anson Street still remains. The streets were named for Anson and his ships, but only the names of George and Anson streets survive. Peter Warren (later Admiral), captain of the station ship *Solebay* at Charles Town in 1732, was another officer of the Royal Navy to acquire real estate and have a street named in his honor, which also remains.

After he left South Carolina, Anson progressed to greater glory. In 1737, he was appointed to command the third-rate *Centurion*, a 60-gun ship-of-the-line. In 1740–1744, he circumnavigated the globe. Anson's fleet started out with six warships and two supply vessels, but only *Centurion* completed the voyage. In a fierce battle off the Philippines, Anson captured Spain's fabulously rich Manila Galleon. One of the most significant contributions of that voyage was the discovery that citrus fruits would prevent scurvy, a very serious and disabling threat to the crews on long voyages. At least five of the survivors of Anson's crew on his monumental voyage later rose to flag rank in the Royal Navy. This is a notable record; most naval vessels were lucky to produce one flag officer during their lifetimes. They had obviously been schooled by a master!

Anson's accomplishments were rewarded with a fleet command, and in 1747 when his force annihilated that of French Admiral Jonquierre off Cape Finisterre, he was made a peer and First Lord of the Admiralty.

Throughout his illustrious career there can be little doubt that his service on the Carolina station had contributed to his style, his self-reliance, his courage and flare. He left behind him notes, logs, and plans that cartographers later found invaluable in charting the coast. South Carolina may have also invested his leadership ability with some of the frontier spirit and self-reliance that he used on his circumnavigation. He demonstrated John Paul Jones' later remark: "It is well and good that a naval officer must be a capable mariner. He must be that and more"—*much* more, as Anson showed; the South Carolina station undoubtedly was an excellent training ground for him even at a time when the colony was relatively peaceful.

Other Events

In 1728, the second major hurricane struck Charles Town. It flooded the lower floors of the houses and sent the citizens into the upper floors for safety. Twenty-two ships in the harbor were driven ashore. Among them was *Olive* of Glasgow, which was filled with a cargo of rice. She wrecked on White Point at the southern point of the city.

---

[4] Captain Anson's house was supposedly torn down in 1805 to make way for far grander houses (many of which are also now gone), including that of Charles Town's colonial and Revolutionary statesman, Henry Laurens.

[5] *Rose*, a 20-gunner, was another of the sixth-rates that had been rebuilt and enlarged from 273 tons to 377 tons.

Charles Town Station Ships

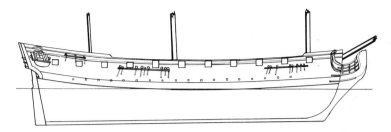

Scarborough, 20-gun, sixth-rate 1724–1728

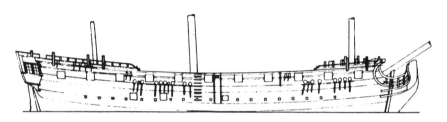

Rye, 20-gun, sixth-rate 1742–1744

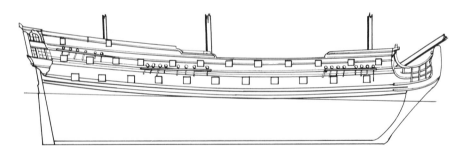

Falkland, 50-gun, fourth-rate 1757, largest station ship at Charles Town

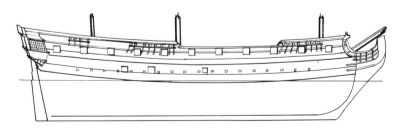

Dolphin, 24-gun, sixth-rate 1760–1761

Trade

Charles Town existed as a trading port and the ships hauled the products of trade in and out of the harbor. The Royal Navy's vessels protected the shipping lanes as well as the city itself. The economic heyday of Charles Town, 1720 to 1820, coincided with the peak of colonial sailing ships. It was necessary for ships of the period to follow the clockwise motion of the prevailing winds in the North Atlantic. This corresponds roughly to the flow of the ocean currents (see front endpapers). Sitting as it does on the west side of this vortex, Charles Town was in a favorable position for ships traversing this route. Ships coming from Europe en route to northern ports could easily stop at Charles Town to load or unload small amounts of cargo. In addition, the city is situated just north of the point where the Antilles and Florida Currents converge to form the Gulf Stream. Taking advantage of these currents and winds, ships heading to Europe from the West Indies, the Gulf of Mexico, and the western Caribbean passed within a few miles of the coast, making Charles Town an easy stopping point for additional cargo.

A sailing vessel bound from Europe to America most often ran down the eastern side of the Atlantic toward the Cape Verde Islands; there it caught the northeast trade winds to push it across the Atlantic—the same route taken by Columbus. As a ship approached the West Indies, it would veer off toward the northwest until it reached the latitude of its destination. Then it would "run down the latitude" until it made a landfall, and from there make for port.

Speed was not a primary consideration of sailing vessels in this period except when pirates menaced the routes. Once the pirates had been suppressed, seaworthiness and carrying capacity returned to paramount importance. Due to the bluff or apple-cheeked bows of these vessels and the poor ability of square-rigged vessels to head upwind, they were dependent upon the wind's direction. The prevailing wind system of the Atlantic Ocean had been realized early in the sixteenth century, and sailing mariners have taken advantage of it ever since.

In winter, ships traveling from Europe to the northern ports of America were driven off the American coast by snow storms and westerly gales. Instead of running off into the Gulf Stream, as sailing vessels did in the nineteenth century, many ships would stand back to Charles Town or the West Indies for the winter and wait until spring to attempt to reach their destinations. Therefore, Charles Town became the "halfway house" between England and the northern ports on this side of the Atlantic.

Progress was slow for these small square-rigged sailing vessels, and navigation was still rudimentary. Therefore, it was difficult for a vessel to manage more than one round trip per year around the rim of the North Atlantic Ocean. A one-way voyage across the ocean would take from sixty to ninety days. Loading and unloading could take several more weeks. The balance of the year was taken for maintenance of the vessel, which in those days was particularly time-consuming because the materials disintegrated rapidly in the salt water, harsh wind, and sun.

Navigation

Voyages were dragged out by anachronistic methods of navigation. Latitude could be determined fairly accurately with a quadrant. Longitude remained largely guesswork until the invention of the chronometer in the mid eighteenth century. Mariners consequently did their sailing by dead reckoning; as they approached land, ship captains became very cautious and slow in their forward movements. Landfalls could be made as much as several hundred miles off, causing additional delays while mariners fumbled around to determine their actual position.

Adding to these troubles were the poor charts, which did little to assist in making a landfall. Seventeenth- and eighteenth-century charts were extremely distorted, especially in their depiction of land masses. It is not difficult to imagine the danger of using one to sail across the ocean. It is amazing that so many more ships were not lost, but sea captains learned to anticipate danger by reading such signs from nature as wave and current action, prevailing wind direction and force, sea and bird life, and cloud cover.

Since latitude could be fairly well determined by navigational instruments that determined the angles of known stars above the horizon, most ships would sail by dead reckoning to a position on the same latitude as their destination. When the desired latitude was reached, they would sail east or west until they made landfall. From the landfall they would sail north or south along the coast to the final destination. Instead of sailing the direct route along the hypotenuse of a triangle, they would sail first along one leg and then along the other—obviously a far greater distance. Ships approaching Charles Town would make landfall anywhere between the North Edisto and Bull's Bay if their navigators were proficient. If not, they could spend several days merely trying to determine where they were.

Pilots

Pilotage is the work of guiding large vessels in and out of harbors. In the eighteenth century in Charles Town this was a risky, competitive business because of the narrow, winding channel leading to the port; the swift currents; and the necessity to wait off the bar in bad weather for an incoming ship to beat the competition to the job of bringing it in. In 1672 the colonial Assembly passed an act requiring that the local pilots use Sullivan's Island as a base of operations.

Pilots had been bringing ships in and out of the harbor since the first days of the colony, when Indian guides performed the duty. In later years, many pilots purchased slaves to do the piloting work. Local laws required that if a black man[1] were piloting a vessel, a white man had to be aboard in charge. Regardless of status, blacks and whites worked side by side on the pilot boats, as they did on the larger vessels.

The pilot's duty was an essential part of bringing a ship in or out of port; few ship captains could keep abreast of changes in the harbor. Sand bars and shoals shifted regularly,

---

[1] Primus Swain was a well-respected freedman, who was a Charleston harbor and coast pilot. He lost his pilot boat *Hornet* in 1820. In 1823 he lost another boat and apparently his life, as accounts refer to the second loss as belonging to the "late black pilot."

and sunken vessels formed new hazards. The financial loss of a grounded or lost vessel was far greater than any piloting fees.

Pilots were cursed and praised. One day they would be blamed for the loss of a ship, and the next praised for saving one. Charles Town pilot John Hogg was drowned in 1730 when the ship that he was piloting was beaten to pieces in the breakers off Folly Island.[2] The next year a ship attempting to follow HMS *Alborough* over the bar was lost for the lack of a pilot. The stranding of the ship *Minerva* in 1737 was attributed to the "unskillfulness of the pilot." In 1755 the station ship *Jamaica* was run ashore by the carelessness of the pilot. *Jamaica* was

[2] In 1700 the ship *Rising Sun* and four other vessels were lost off Folly Island. The ships were en route from Panama to Scotland and had stopped off the bar. Aboard was the Reverend Stobo, who came into Charles Town to preach. Then a hurricane struck. So many bodies washed ashore from the five ships that the island was labeled "the Coffin Land" on maps for a century. One benefit did derive from the loss; the Reverend Stobo went on to become in "a great measure the founder of the Presbyterian Church in South Carolina."

refloated safely, but the next year the same pilot lost the snow *Brothers Adventure*.

Piloting in Charles Town developed in a haphazard manner. At first, anyone with a boat was able to become a pilot. As the colony grew, an apprentice system sprang up based upon practices in England. The pilots would compete with each other for business by waiting off the bar for an incoming ship. The first one to the vessel usually brought it in and collected the fee, some of which went to the government. In this competition, business went to the quick and the maneuverable. Since pilot boats had to remain off the bar in heavy weather, they had to be seaworthy. In order to hold down costs, once the pilot was put aboard a ship, another person on the pilot boat had to be able to manage until either the pilot returned or the pilot boat entered port and anchored. In the early days, when smaller craft were used, the pilot boat was towed in or out of port behind the vessel being piloted.

Being fast and maneuverable, schooners became the favorite pilot boat. The fore-and-aft Bermuda, or gaff-rigged sails of schooners could be easily handled by as few as two or three men. The vessel was steered from a small cockpit behind the main mast. With this rig, one man could handle the boat for short periods of time by reducing the sails. If heavy weather threatened, the boat could be run into a sheltered area in the harbor, the sails lowered, and the vessel anchored. The first recorded powered pilot boat was the 111' screw steamer *Pilot* that was placed in service in 1849, but wrecked three years later.

Sullivan's Island became the base of operations for local pilots, since they could easily put out from there in small craft. As the profession became more competitive, the pilots went further offshore to meet incoming ships, a venture that required larger, more seaworthy pilot boats. Pilot boats did not have to be designed to carry cargo, although some did during the summer off-season, when carrying passengers to outlying islands was also profitable.

Due to the laborious task of getting a sailing vessel in or out of Charles Town's narrow channel, a pilot often found himself aboard a ship for days, awaiting the proper sailing conditions. The extra time consumed did not produce greater fees. These fees were based on the ship's draft. The act of October 18, 1776 called for ships drawing less than six feet to pay a charge of £3, 15s.; those drawing twenty feet paid £65, 15s. These fees increased regularly through the Revolution as costs went up. All vessels paid it, even those owned by South Carolinians.

Warships of the period, even those engaged in attacking the city, also employed pilots. The British campaigns of 1776 and 1780 used

A pre-Revolutionary Charles Town pilot boat meeting an incoming ship off Sullivan's Island.

either Tories who had abandoned the city or naval officers who were familiar with the port.

The pilots depended heavily on the lighthouses and channel markers. The earliest known lighthouse at the entrance to Charles Town harbor was constructed in 1767 at the south end of Morris Island. Little is known about it, other than that it was octagonal in shape and one of the first of eight such structures built in America. Before that, haphazard and fairly unreliable beacon fires were used. Being a prominant landmark, Cape Romain on Bull's Island had one of the early lighthouses that were painted with alternating bands of black and white.

In 1857 a new lighthouse was built to replace the earlier Morris Island structure, which had been destroyed in a storm. This one was 133 feet high and had a new Fresnel lenticular apparatus as its beacon. It was demolished at the beginning of the Civil War, and by April 1861 all lights in Charleston harbor were extinguished.

Ferries were also used in the harbor before bridges were built. They operated out of the creeks as shelter from storms. The first known ferry was in operation across the Ashley River in 1711. In 1828 a steam ferry was in service to Sullivan's Island. In 1830, James Hibben was granted a twenty-one year monopoly to operate a steam ferry from the city to the head of the Wando River. Prior to this, Hibben operated a ferry from Shem Creek to Prioleau's Wharf, the same ferry that had been started in the 1740s by Henry Grey, an officer on the station ship *Rose*.

Ships Used in Trading

From the very first decade of colonization, ships brought in manufactured goods from England and sugar and rum from the West Indies. In turn, they carried away agricultural products. Most of these vessels were quite small, in the ten- to fifty-ton range. Because of the limitation of their size, they came in large numbers in the fall when the crops were harvested. The vessels increased in size over the years, but so did the amount of material to be hauled away. All types of ships called at Charles Town. The largest were ship-rigged vessels (three masts, all of which carried square sails). The larger vessels usually carried goods across the ocean, whereas the smaller ones traded with ports in the other American and West Indian colonies.

At the beginning of the eighteenth century the largest of the ships that called at Charles Town were under 100 feet and displaced about 90 tons on average. They increased to the 125-foot, 150-ton range by the time of the Revolution. These were relatively small for ocean-going vessels of the time, but a few ranged as large as 200 tons. The largest recorded ship that called at Charles Town before 1740 was *Eagle* of Bristol, at 305 tons.

By the 1730s, some accounts report that up to one hundred vessels were in the harbor at one time in the fall. One account says that between 1717 and 1737 the total annual tonnage of ships clearing Charles Town rose by 80 percent from seven thousand tons to a little over

Pilot preparing to board a schooner before clearing the harbor.

Loading cargo onto a trading vessel from a boat.

thirteen thousand tons. Of these figures, 55 percent of the first and 70 percent of the latter tonnage were British owned. At the same time, local ownership of vessels was diminishing.

In addition to cargo, many merchant vessels of the time carried passengers, for as business increased, so did the necessity for travel to Europe. Passengers would usually board the ship from the ship's cutter, which picked them and their baggage up at one of the city's many wharves. The cutter was a utility craft, often painted brown, and also used to haul bulky cargo to and from shore in order to avoid paying the wharfage fees.

The passengers would have to mount the side of the ship themselves while their baggage was hauled up with block and tackle suspended from the main yard. Once on deck they would find themselves in the waist of the ship between the main and foremast, where the main cargo hatch was located. In the hold would be loaded barrels of Jamaica rum, hogsheads of indigo and rice, and other commodities from the colonies.

The quarterdeck was a level higher, extending from the mainmast aft. Through a door the passengers would gain access to their cabins under the quarterdeck. In the very aft portion was the captain's cabin. Each room usually had one window, except for the captain's cabin, which had three facing aft. On each side of the captain's cabin were located the toilets

for the passengers and ship's officers. The crew used the toilets[3] in the bow next to their quarters. In the central portion of the aft quarters was the wardroom, or officers' messroom, with a skylight breaking the ceiling.

Accommodations were far from luxurious. The passage of several weeks in a small vessel brought constant seasickness, poor food, and monotony broken only by the hassle of rough weather.

The European Connection—Bristol and London

In England, the trading ports of Bristol, London, and Cowes dominated Charles Town's trade. Bristol had links with Carolina from the beginning, as many of the original settlers came from that port. Bristol was also Britain's primary slave-trading port. This provided another link to the southern colonies, but throughout the colonial period, London remained the predominant destination for all Charles Town exports.

By the time South Carolina became a Royal Colony, London merchants had realized the advantages of trade with Charles Town. These London merchants had the available finances, access to the source of manufactured goods, shipbuilding, and contacts on the continent where goods not marketable in England could be sold. These were the same advantages that New York would have a century later. In addition, both London and Bristol maintained agents in Charles Town to promote their interests. In the political arena they could easily take their complaints or promotions to the Board of Trade.

British Trade Policy

The English Navigation Acts, the primary regulator of colonial trade, restricted English imports and exports to British ships manned by British subjects. These acts created a monopoly of both shipping and trade for the mother country. The Navigation Acts were begun in the fourteenth century and were augmented, amended, and altered over the years. They matured under the Long Parliament, but the colonists ignored them until the Restoration of Charles II. The new king had the Navigation Acts reenacted and firmly enforced. The colonists chafed under the acts because they restricted colonial trade to the English market at prices established in England without regard to world market forces. By 1672, intercolonial trade was also being discouraged by tariffs. There was a great demand for colonial produce in other lands where people were willing to pay generously. The profits from this potential source of trade fostered a lawlessness that served to encourage piracy and smuggling.

All of the major export commodities of South Carolina were economically interlinked in the colonial period. The years immediately before 1725 marked the culmination of the first stage of development of the agriculture of the colony. In the early 1720s, rice and naval stores competed for top place in monetary value. When the bounty on the latter was removed, it plummeted in value as an export. More planters turned to rice cultivation, glutting the market and bringing down prices. The market strengthened somewhat when direct shipments were allowed to the Iberian Peninsula. Once the bounty was partially restored on naval stores

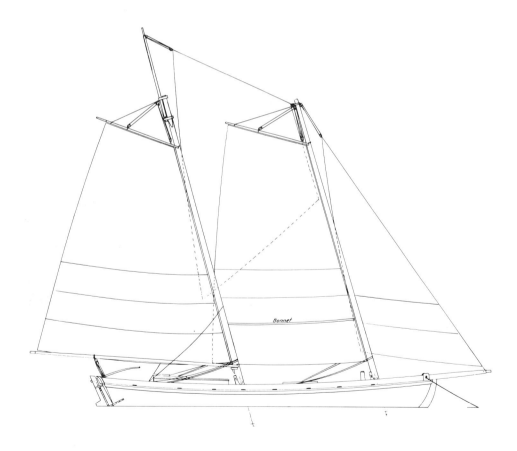

Plan of an eighteenth-century pilot boat.

[3] From this arrangement comes the term *head* meaning "men's latrine," because it was in the "head" of the ship.

and turpentine, that industry revived to some extent. When indigo production began in the 1740s, naval stores dropped; indigo was more profitable and required essentially the same workers and land for cultivation. The colonial legislature's attempts to control or encourage the local economy also led to the development of indigo as a cash crop. Government policy had an overriding effect on economic life in the form of either subsidies or policies that served to restrict or promote competition and profitability.

British trade policy aimed at both regulating and controlling the economy of the empire. While encouraging some pursuits, it also denied British markets to foreign merchants. To the mills of England, the colonies were a source of raw materials and a market for her manufactured goods. Under these regulations, most crops had to be sent to England rather than to more lucrative markets in other countries or colonies. This policy kept prices low for the British market. At the same time, it allowed the colonists to realize the benefits of protection from the British armed forces and the superior quality of British manufactured goods.

British trade policy was not rigid. The colonists lobbied for, and sometimes received, exceptions to the restrictions. For example, in 1730 when the Carolina planters lost European rice markets to the Italians carrying Middle Eastern rice, the Board of Trade granted a special exemption to the product being shipped to ports south of Cape Finisterre on the Iberian Peninsula. Rice was left on the enumerated list, meaning that it first had to be shipped to the mother country before being transshipped elsewhere; this added to its final cost. Shipments going directly to Spain and Portugal were excepted after 1730. By the mid 1730s, 25 percent of the colony's rice was being shipped there. The regulations for this exception were stringent, and penalties for violations were severe.

The Customs Process

By the time Charles Town was founded, world trade was generally well organized. It was not the haphazard affair many would imagine today. When a vessel arrived in port, its captain had to notify the governor or port official, then called a "naval officer." After the ship's captain had given proof that his vessel had been loaded legally in a British port, permission was given to unload. When it was time for a vessel to clear port, a bond was issued. The naval officer or port official made certain that a bond was posted with the customs officials and that all duties had been paid. A bill of lading was prepared in duplicate, one under seal to go with the ship and another for the Collector of Customs in London, sent on another ship for security. A ship that came in without the proper papers for its cargo was subject to drastic measures, which could involve forfeiture of the vessel. As an incentive to ensure compliance, any person who reported an improperly documented ship shared with the governor a portion of the returns from any vessel and cargo condemned for confiscation. Early records show that few vessels' masters and owners were prosecuted for violations.

The books on these transactions were closed quarterly and forwarded to the Commissioners of His Majesty's Customs and Excise and to the Commissioners of the Treasury. To guard against loss of the original, duplicates were sent by another vessel. In the period of 1717 to 1737, an average of 250 entrances and clearings per year were shown; most of them came in the last quarter of the year, when the crops of the colony were ready for export.

While the naval officer often acted as the customs house officer, he was actually the governor's official. On the other hand, the customs officer was the king's official. This system of checks and balances was supposed to assure honesty. Because of the rising value of the goods from the colonies and the lax checking system in London, there was much temptation for fraud and bribery. Although most goods shipped from Charles Town were bulky and heavy and thus not subject to the temptation of smuggling, the goods imported from England were another matter. But only a few cases of smuggling are shown in local court records before 1740, and the records also indicate that no naval officer was ever removed from office for illegal activity.

In the early years the Proprietors' frugal policies did not give their appointed officials the means with which to enforce their own laws, much less those of the Crown. The officials became corrupt and teamed up with the smugglers and pirates. Governor John Archdale was alleged to have allowed Dutch merchandise to be brought into Charles Town from Curacao illegally. The cargo was then reexported to the northern colonies in violation of the Navigation Acts. In the last years of the century, Governor Blake was another who is reported to have headed an effective customs racketeering ring that allowed enumerated goods to be shipped directly to non-English ports instead of first going through British ports. That ring fell apart when he died in 1700. But the problem didn't end; it continued off and on until the Revolution. Evidently either insufficient evidence was available for prosecution, or officials turned a blind eye to the problem.

Colonial Wharves or Bridges

Wharves or docks for ships to load and unload were privately owned in colonial Charles Town, except for the public landing at the Exchange building. Ships paid fees to the owners for their use. To avoid these charges, many ship masters preferred to have their vessels loaded and unloaded from lighters or smaller vessels while at anchor in the harbor. Wharves in colonial America were little more than places for a ship to moor close to the land. While European harbors were beginning to develop such devices as shears (the forerunner of modern cranes) for unloading ships, the colonial wharves continued to rely largely on block and tackles and the spars of the ships as loading and unloading equipment.

Wharves were not constructed on pilings; instead they resembled stone breakwaters. They were called "bridges" after the method of construction. Cribs of palmetto logs resembling log cabins were built on shore and floated to the desired location. Several were placed

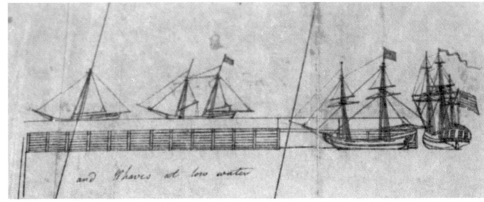

Sketch of a Charles Town wharf on Concord Street near the foot of Pinckney Street at the end of the eighteenth century.

Wharf at the foot of Tradd Street in 1793. Note the three types of vessels at the dock: a schooner, brig, and ship; also note how buildings were constructed on the land end of the wharf.

Stowing barrels in the hold of a trading schooner.

Warping a merchant vessel alongside a wharf. Before the advent of tugboats, merchant vessels had to be maneuvered close to the wharf under sail and then manually pulled the last few yards. Much of this work was made easier by capstans, but adverse winds and tides often made it a difficult process.

An English hoy, somewhat similar to a colonial sloop and rigged as such, but with a rounded bow and stern. The crew and docker are making ready to tie up the hoy to the wharf. This is part of the Deptford Diorama by Robert A. Lightley; scenes similar to this occurred in eighteenth-century Charles Town. Note the device for lifting the barrel off and onto the wagon. Similar devices were used for lifting heavy loads on and off ships alongside a wharf, but they were rare in colonial America.

in a line running toward land. These were filled with stones, usually ships' ballast, until they sank. The line of sunken cribs was connected with a wooden walkway. Some, such as Adger's Wharf (known as Motte's Bridge in 1739 when it was built), were further protected by granite stones placed in a curtain or wall around the cribs. Many of the stones from these colonial wharves or bridges are today in the Battery seawall and under the streets of Charleston.

The largest wharf in Charles Town before the Revolution was Gadsden's Wharf at the foot of Calhoun Street. Completed in 1774 after seven years of work, it was one of the largest in North America. Using his political connections, Gadsden had the city government build a roadway to his wharf along present-day Calhoun Street where a creek stood—little wonder that it still fills with water during heavy rains! Gadsden claimed that at low tide some thirty fully loaded ships could be accommodated at his wharf. However, this claim seems an exaggeration due to the shallow water along the Cooper River waterfront. Other docks of smaller size were constructed along the river. As the Cooper River area filled up, wharves were constructed on the south side of the peninsula into the Ashley River. The wharves of William Gibbes, Thomas Savage, and Miles Brewton were most prominent. The houses that these traders built near their docks still stand.

Early Charles Town Trade

In November 1670, a few cedar planks were sent to England as Charles Towne's first items of export. Shortly afterward furs, skins, and Indian goods were being shipped to England. Meat, lumber, and naval stores were shipped to the West Indies. The vessels returned laden with supplies of rum, slaves, and sugar. Charles Towne's proximity to the Caribbean placed it in the best position to develop trade with that area. This became the early backbone of the colony's overseas commerce. The financial balance of trade with the Caribbean was favorable, bringing much needed specie into the colony; the unfavorable balance of trade with England left that medium of exchange in chronic short supply throughout the American colonies.

In the seventeenth century the Caribbean trade was second only to the export of deerskins to England. Meat was heavily salted and packed into barrels for shipment. In the year 1712–13, over 3,000 barrels of this commodity were exported. This amount fluctuated throughout the eighteenth century, falling to under 500 barrels in the 1730s. Such other foods as corn, peas, and flour were also traded to the islands. While the amount of food exports steadily declined through the colonial period, the islands took over 80 percent of this trade, the bulk going to Barbados and Jamaica.

Early Shipping Firms

Very little is known of the people and firms engaged in colonial Charles Town trade, but several hundred names are known of either whole or part owners of locally owned ships. The choice of investors then, as now, was to become a part owner in several vessels rather than a major or total owner of one or a few. In the first third of the eighteenth century, the Wragg brothers, the Rhett family, and the Holmes family were the largest local shipowners. Samuel Wragg had a large circle of commercial contacts and joined in shipowning consortiums with others outside of the colony. He and his brother Joseph owned small vessels outright and invested with others in larger ships that traded in Europe. They were the only

important mercantile house to survive the turbulent economic times of the late 1720s.

The partnership of Benjamin Godin, Benjamin Dela Conseillere, and Richard Shubrick prospered in the years just prior to 1720 when the pirates were at their peak. Evidently the pirates did not affect the firm adversely or they were in league together. Stephen Godin held down the London end of the firm, which traded regularly with England, and became the

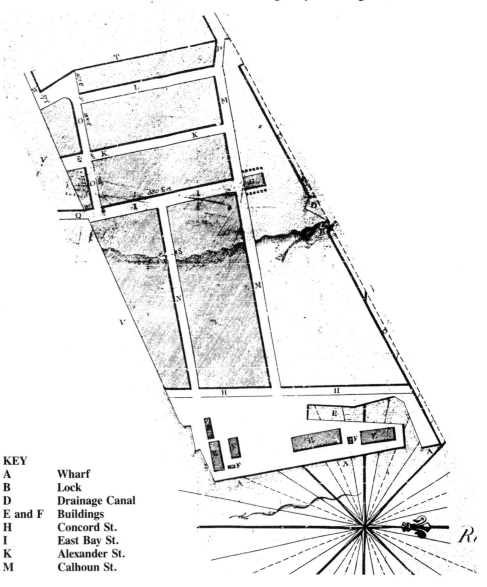

KEY
A   Wharf
B   Lock
D   Drainage Canal
E and F   Buildings
H   Concord St.
I   East Bay St.
K   Alexander St.
M   Calhoun St.

Plat of Gadsden's Wharf at the foot of Calhoun Street prior to the Revolution. This wharf was unusual for Charles Town in that part of it was constructed parallel to the river and it contained a lock that allowed ships to be loaded and unloaded without having to compensate for the rise and fall of the tide. Vessels would move into and exit the lock at high tide. The gate would be closed, leaving the water level inside constant as the tide ebbed and flowed outside.

Council's London agent. The firm of Allen and Gibbon, which owned more but smaller vessels, was also very successful. They transacted business only on this side of the Atlantic. Holmes is also mentioned. His contacts were largely with his home city, Boston. After his death, trade with that city declined. This was probably due to the desire to eliminate the northern ports as middlemen.

The Indian Trade

The Indian trade became lucrative during the young colony's first three decades. Deerskins and other hides were in great demand in Europe. As this trade increased, it constituted a significant portion of England's exports, which were used as a medium of exchange with the Indians. The superiority of English manufactures drew the Indians away from other Europeans. As a result of the Indian trade, Carolina settlers not only came into conflict with the Spanish in St. Augustine, but also had soon penetrated so far inland that they were competing with the French, who had established a colony at Mobile in 1702. The antagonisms arising out of the Indian trade are one of the reasons for the Franco-Spanish attack in 1706.

By the early eighteenth century, South Carolina and New York were the leading English colonies active in the Indian trade. Some 90 percent of the deerskins that left Charles Town went to the ports of Bristol and London. Trade peaked in 1707, when 121,355 deerskins were carried from Charles Town. That yearly volume was never surpassed and the trade subsequently fluctuated. As was to be expected, shipments plummeted during the Yemassee War. With the founding of Georgia in 1733, South Carolina began to lose out to her neighbor, whose geographic location was better situated to take advantage of the trade. Furthermore, Georgia's taxes were lower. As late as 1771, some 70,000 deer and stag hides were still being exported from Charles Town to Europe, but by then it was a small portion of the total exports.

Naval Stores

Due to high labor and shipping costs and the poor quality of colonial pitch and tar, naval stores got off to a slow start as an export. The production of naval stores was more a breakeven situation to keep the farmworkers productive during the winter months between harvest and spring planting. The English authorities recognized this fact in their attempts to promote production.

In the 1690s, the Board of Trade was created to oversee specifically the colonial production of naval stores; soon it expanded into all trade areas. In a report to the Board of Trade in March 1697, Edward Randolph, Surveyor General of Customs for the colonies, called South Carolina the best source for naval stores on the continent; he reported that great advances had been made in South Carolina as a result of the industry and labor of the inhabitants. He went on to say that if London would encourage the production of naval stores with bounties,[4] the colony could send over greater quantities of pitch, tar, and turpentine, as well as rice.

[4] The system of paying bounties was common during the colonial period. Although South Carolina provided financial grants to any person who could produce flax, hemp, linens, thread, and wheat flour, most of these items could not be successfully produced in the colony, even with the bounty. The bounties ceased during the Revolution and were not revived afterward because of the preference for promoting local production by imposing duties on competing imports.

Another stimulus to the local production of naval stores was the Royal Navy's increased requirements during Queen Anne's War. When Sweden, which had been England's primary supplier, became antagonistic, Parliament acted in 1705 by placing a bounty on its colonial production. Exports of the stores, which had been hitherto insignificant due to the cost of shipping the bulky material long distances, were stimulated. Under the law all naval stores shipped to England had to be offered first to the Crown. Bounties were also included for hemp, masts, and yards, but these were not exported to England from Charles Town before 1740.

At first, pitch and tar were the important naval stores; turpentine was added in the 1730s. In 1712–13, some 6,600 barrels of naval stores were exported; the rate increased sharply, and by 1718 the export totaled over 52,000 barrels, or 50 percent of all the naval stores shipped to Britain from the American colonies. These figures do not include those stores that first went north for transshipment. The South Carolina industry peaked at almost 60,000 barrels during the 1724 production year.

Some 70 to 80 percent of the colony's exports of naval stores went to England—so far in excess of her needs that much of it was reexported to the continent. After 1725, the curtailment of the bounty for naval stores caused production to plummet. With the stroke of a pen the Crown removed almost one fourth of the colony's income. By 1727 just under 15,000 barrels were exported. At the same time the Swedes and Russians were lowering their prices, making the colonial product less attractive, especially considering its inferior quality. In order to prevent a complete stoppage of colonial naval stores, a smaller bounty was offered in 1729, with new measures to try to bring the quality of the colonial product up to that of the Scandinavian. The amount exported rose through the 1730s, but never attained more than 50 percent of the peak level of 1724.

Timber Trade

Cedar was the first timber to be exported to England. The West Indian trade had slowly developed this industry, and by 1700 most of the best forests within thirty miles of Charles Town had been cut for export timber and naval stores, and for building construction. The timberlands along the Santee River were the next to be exploited. Starting in the 1740s, the cutting of timber for masts, yards, and bowsprits was begun, although it required considerable capital investment and skilled labor. Processing lumber became an important economic activity in the colony after 1740, when water-powered mills were built along the colony's rivers and streams to process timber. By the 1750s, several million board feet of lumber, as well as thousands of masts and barrels of naval stores, left Charles Town each year.

Rice Trade

Every planter in the colony aimed at self-sufficiency first, and then a cash crop that would produce income to purchase additional comforts and luxuries. Rice provided this first cash crop. A barrel of rice used as seed by the first colonists had failed to yield a successful crop. A second introduction in the late 1680s or early 1690s had met with success; by 1695, rice was firmly established as a major export commodity. However, overproduction led to declines in price.

The Board of Trade placed rice on the enumerated list in 1705, to confine its export to those markets within the British Empire. However, these commodities, including rice, could be sent to England and then reshipped to other countries, thereby increasing the cost but allowing British officials to tax it. At the same time, reshipment provided additional business for British shippers and agents.

In 1700, some 330 tons were shipped. By 1720, the amount exported had increased tenfold; by 1730, that figure had trebled. Rice was the predominant commodity of the colony until the Revolution. Over 70 percent went to England, most of which was then reexported. The remainder went to the West Indies, Spain, and Portugal, which had become a particularly profitable market. There rice was considered a luxury and brought a better price.

Indigo

Indigo failed as a profitable crop in the second year of the colony because the early frosts killed the plants and prevented the fermentation necessary for making the dye. For the next half century the crop remained largely experimental.

In 1739, Eliza Lucas began a series of experiments at her father's plantation on the Wappoo Creek west of Charles Town. She found the Bahama variety of indigo and West Indian methods of cultivation adaptable to the climate. Her father hired a man from Montserrat to teach her how to process the plant. Being French, he was reluctant to reveal the process to the English and deliberately fouled up the process. However, Miss Lucas, then barely 20, eventually managed to gain sufficient knowledge to turn out good dye. In 1744, she harvested the first successful commercial crop. Afterwards indigo problems were more commercial than botanical.

At that time, England imported most of its indigo from French and Spanish colonies. London was concerned with this dependence on the empire's natural enemies for raw materials. Then in 1739, the War of Jenkins' Ear closed British ports to French and Spanish goods. This left indigo a scarce commodity in England, but also depressed rice prices due to oversupply in England as the rice trade with Spain was severed. Needing a new crop and having a virtual monopoly on the indigo market, Carolina planters rapidly increased production. In 1745 the legislature further stimulated production by offering a bounty to farmers who would produce indigo rather than rice. The bounty had to be withdrawn after two years in order to keep the colonial treasury from being depleted! Exports of the dyestuff had risen from almost nothing to 138,000 pounds in less than three years.

The treaty of Aix-la-Chapelle in October 1748 ended King George's War and restored indigo to free-market status. This put Carolina producers on the same footing as their French and Spanish competitors. Consequently, in 1748 exports from Charles Town dropped to less than half the previous year's total. Without market protection Carolina planters failed to compete.

The wartime profits on indigo had been great; with post-war depression, the planters petitioned Parliament for a bounty on colonial indigo. London considered it an advantage to produce the product within the empire, and instituted a bounty of six pence per pound. The bounty did not directly aid the Carolina planters. Instead it allowed purchasers in England to pay a higher price to American suppliers than to foreign suppliers. The net effect was to keep specie in England. The 1749 crop returned to the wartime level of two years earlier, but declined almost steadily thereafter.

In 1754 the renewal of war along the Ohio River valley, and two years later in Europe, once more closed British markets to French products. The Carolina planters now benefited from a wartime market as well as a bounty. In 1757, indigo exports peaked at 876,400 pounds, clearly demonstrating the effect of market protection. With the end of war in 1763, Parliament cut the bounty by a third as an economy measure, but included a six pence per pound duty on foreign indigo. The duty created a trade barrier that foreign producers were unable to overcome. As a result, Carolina dye shipments maintained a high and steady level, averaging nearly 500,000 pounds annually. In 1770, when the bounty returned to its original level, exports rose even higher. By 1775, over a million pounds were shipped to England. This constituted over one third of the colony's exports.

The American Revolution shattered the indigo industry, as southern plantations were thrust into open-market conditions. The first blow came with the Continental Congress' non-exportation resolution, which allowed only rice to be exported from South Carolina. The indigo planters were subsidized to some extent by the rice producers, but devastation was close at hand. Some indigo was sold to France between 1777 and 1780, mostly by government agents to purchase arms. The military actions in the South further destroyed fields, crops, and production facilities.

Under British occupation, indigo had one brief revival with wartime price rises in Britain, limited production in South Carolina, and loss of other foreign sources. The British departure in 1782 brought the final collapse of indigo production. So necessary was the subsidy to its production that indigo all but disappeared by 1800. Britain had new sources in India and the East Indies where they could get a dye of better quality.

Conclusion

South Carolina was destined to be agricultural in its formative years, a factor recognized in London, which added direction and encouragement to the natural tendancy. Toward the final years of colonial status, despite the political outcry for increased freedom, the planters looked for more aid. Even in the eighteenth century when farmers sought government aid and protection, few of them could conceive of an economy free of government control in spite of the clamor of others for political freedom.

Controls meant tariffs and duties, which were intended to regulate trade and raise money for the colonial government. An act passed in April 1740 provided for the collection of duty on spirits and other luxury items. In 1767 an act was passed standardizing port charges throughout the colony. The law listed rates for wharfage on all types of ships, charges for the goods that were landed or passed from ship to ship in the harbor, storage rates, and weighing charges.

The rise and fall of the South Carolina indigo industry is an excellent case of government influencing production, in this case with bounties. Bounties were used to stimulate other products such as hemp, silk, and even wine, but without success. As long as there were a few profitable crops, the incentive to develop others was limited. After 1783, the British used the same bounty to shut out American producers; however, even if the market had been totally free, the American producers could not have competed.

The colonists gained more than profits from the sale of lumber, naval stores, rice, and indigo. Through trade, especially with foreign markets, the colonists broadened their perspective. Additionally, individuals traveling on business acquired entrepreneurial skills and became astute observers of the market climate in other lands. They brought back to the colony the culture and attainments of foreign countries. Those who visited the West Indies and

England brought back to Charles Town the knowledge of things previously unknown or unfamiliar. Although motivated by profit rather than patriotism, the contacts with both neighbors and foreigners would prove of great benefit in the battle for independence.

In spite of the colony's success in developing cash crops, she still imported more than she sold for export. This imbalance created a constant shortage of specie. As early as Governor Robert Johnson's administration, paper credit had to be used to pay taxes and bills due in England. The Commons House of Assembly nimbly managed the paper money in circulation and produced a ratio of seven to one for South Carolina paper to sterling. The planters battled the merchants over the amount in circulation. The legislature usually sided with the former for a higher amount; here was the classic battle between hard-currency merchants and soft-currency farmers.

As cotton would in the next century, a good portion of Charles Town's shipments went to northern ports: primarily to Boston, later Philadelphia, and then New York. From these ports it was shipped abroad. The goods shipped via this indirect route were not as significant as the amount that went directly to London. This route was probably due to the large number of small northern-owned ships carrying the southern intra-colonial trade. As the profit margins on the goods going by the indirect route fell, the route was slowly discontinued in favor of the direct route. As a consequence, Charles Town's trade with her northern neighbors slowly declined over the colonial period.

By the mid-eighteenth century South Carolina's economy was flourishing. In 1770, Charles Town stood third in American seaports in terms of the total tonnage arriving and departing. (Philadelphia was first with 47,000 tons, followed by Boston with 38,000, and Charles Town with 27,000. New York was right behind with 25,000 tons.) Charles Town's total tonnage of direct sailings to London exceeded any of the others; she recorded 109 ships departing, whereas Philadelphia recorded 26. Much of this can be attributed to vessels from the Caribbean putting into Charles Town for additional cargo before setting out across the ocean. These ships probably would not have made the port call if the city had not been so convenient to their normal route.

The early development of trade ensured the survival of the colony and gave it a *raison d'être*. Early self-sufficiency in the production of food guaranteed this survival. In contrast, once gold ran out in the Spanish colonies to the south, the economy became shaky due to the failure to develop a strong local agricultural or industrial alternative. Even today as our nation debates its trade policy, we should remember that these earlier periods of South Carolina prosperity were built on a viable trading system; attempts to erect barriers work to the detriment of all. Fortunately, cotton would rescue the South in the next century as a bulwark of the trading system, but the Civil War would destroy that. With little else to replace cotton, the South would face almost a century of economic depression.

Schooner loading cargo at a pier similar to those that were found on plantations of coastal South Carolina.

Early Shipbuilding in Charles Town

Charles Town developed in the period that Great Britain asserted her predominance as a world power. Sea power enabled Britain to obtain and protect her dominions around the world. Naval stores and other shipbuilding materials became of paramount importance for the maintenance of the Royal Navy. Raw materials for shipbuilding were abundant and accessible in the Lowcountry of South Carolina. The only things lacking for the promotion of local shipbuilding were the manufactured items such as sails, rope, and hardware.

The Carolina climate was best suited to agriculture—an extension of the West Indies plantation economy. Initially the lure of agriculture's profits drew potential investors away from shipbuilding. As a result shipbuilding in the Lowcountry enjoyed periods of prosperity interspersed with years of decline. In spite of these fluctuations, shipbuilding was the largest industry in South Carolina before the American Revolution.

In addition to the competition from agriculture, the sultry summer heat discouraged the heavy manual labor that shipbuilding required. Therefore many shipbuilders employed slaves. These slaves were trained in the trades of the day in order to increase their monetary value for resale or to lease for the income they could produce. The use of slave labor tended to discourage the settlement of free labor in the colony, because the local slave-owning shipbuilders were unwilling to pay the higher wages necessary to attract free labor.

Although Charles Town was tied to the sea, at first none of the vessels using the port was locally owned, much less locally built. The first record of local ownership shows one John Boon purchasing in 1675 a one-fourth interest in *Dove of London* for 5,000 pounds of sugar. Seven years later, Henry Simonds bought a 30-ton sloop in Newport, Rhode Island, and sold a share in it to another Charles Town merchant.

By the end of the 1670s, shipbuilding was underway at Charles Town, albeit on a relatively small scale. By 1680, three or four small vessels were under construction. The industry started first as ship repairing, but by the 1690s shipbuilding was fairly well established. Records indicate that between 1696 and 1698, four ships totaling 140 tons were built, with the largest one measuring 50 tons. This was quite a respectable achievement for a colony that was only thirty years old. For the next ten years the industry languished with an average of only one vessel built each year. During this early period several shipbuilders emigrated to Charles Towne from Bermuda in order to take advantage of the abundance of timber; all timber in Bermuda had to be imported.

Ship Registration

The passage of the Navigation Acts of 1696 required that vessels be registered. Most, if not all, of these first vessels registered in the Charles Town fleet were used to carry bulk commodities from the plantations to docks and ships in the harbor. As the coastal trade developed with other colonies, the locally built ships gradually increased in size.

From these registrations we learn that the largest vessel registered in Charles Town was 50 tons, and the smallest 25 tons. There were ten vessels registered by the summer of 1698, the total amounting to 330 tons, an average of 33 tons each. Seven were sloops, of which four had been built in the colony, two in Bermuda, and the rest in the northern colonies.

Virginia at this time had some 27 vessels after ninety years as a colony, so South Carolina was not doing badly in ship ownership, although she had the smallest locally owned fleet of any American colony. Edward Randolph, in his report of March 1699, said that much of the colony's shipping had been destroyed by French privateers in King William's War (1689–1697) and that this circumstance handicapped the development of the colony. Governor Johnson's report nine years later showed that the fleet had remained static; he reported "not above ten or twelve sail of ships belonging to the province." This was in spite of concessions allowed in the revenue law of May 1703. It specified that dutiable commodities would be assessed at one-half the normal rate if carried in locally owned, locally built vessels.

Ships were built on speculation in the colonies, then sent to Great Britain with both ship and cargo for sale. Colonial-built ships had the advantage of their low cost compared with

Gang of workers replacing the planking on an English vessel. Repair scenes such as this were common in pre-Revolutionary Charlestown.

their European-built competitors. As a result, by the 1730s three-fourths of the British-flag vessels engaged in colonial trade were American-built. Even the percentage of American-built vessels owned in England rose steadily to 40 percent in 1720 and to nearly 70 percent by 1735. This was due in large part to the abundance of low-cost timber in the colonies. America also built ships for other countries. As a rule, English-built ships were larger, averaging in the 90- to 100-ton range in the first half of the century, as they carried most of the transoceanic commerce.

At the beginning of the eighteenth century, shipbuilding in Charles Town was sluggish. Only about half of the fleet that Colonel Rhett used in 1706 to repulse the French were locally built. Shipbuilding was stimulated by subsidy in 1711. The growing naval stores and rice trade also gave a boost to the local fleet. From then to 1720 marked the peak in local building before the 1760s. In the nine years following 1708, the local fleet trebled in size to total 1,143 tons.

In 1715, Benjamin Austin built the 150-ton vessel *Princess Carolina*. He employed eleven other shipwrights plus various mechanics. Probably the first ship built in the colony for transoceanic commerce, she was as large as most ships that then called at Charles Town. This proved that Charles Town shipbuilders were capable of building ships of European standards. She was built of Virginia and Rhode Island oak planking for Samuel Wragg, and Austin captained her on her maiden voyage to England.

In an added inducement to shipbuilding, the Proprietors exempted the local shipwrights from military service in the Yemassee War. Once the war was over, shipbuilders enjoyed a three-year boom. At least 27 vessels totaling 542 tons, more than half of which were schooners and sloops, hit the water. Most were in the 6- to 30-ton range.

The First Decline of Shipbuilding

The boom ended in the economic slump of the 1720s. Even then the health of the shipbuilding industry was closely tied to European economic conditions. Local ownership of vessels declined in the 1720s, and a decline in ownership of the larger oceanic merchant ships followed in the 1730s. In 1718, some twenty-five vessels totaling 942 tons had called Charles Town home. This number declined to ten vessels aggregating 647 tons by 1724. It rose again to seventeen vessels averaging 33 tons apiece in 1737. Large ships were evidently unprofitable for local owners, who were competing with northern- and English-owned bottoms. The small trading vessels remained largely in local hands, as it was difficult for outside owners to compete in the intra-colony trade. By the 1730s, the decline of local shipbuilding was running counter to the expanding export market; thus, an increasingly large percentage of the vessels that called at Charles Town were owned elsewhere; there were no vessels in the local fleet capable of transoceanic voyages, although some managed coastal and West Indian trade. During the three years 1734–36, only four vessels totaling 120 tons were built. This indicates that the rate of construction was a fifth of what it had been twenty years earlier.

Much of the decline in local shipbuilding and ownership can be traced to the fact that

An eighteenth-century shipyard scene, showing an English smack drawn up on a timber cradle that slips freely on wooden balks or rails. These rest on ways sloping down to the water. Note the painter at work under the transom. The smack was a small vessel, similar to a cutter and rigged as such. While this scene depicts the Deptford waterfront near London, the waterfront at Charles Town was for all practical purposes identical. This diorama was constructed by Robert Lightley of Cape Town, South Africa.

there was more profit to be gained from agriculture in the South. A surplus of labor in New England promoted the industry in that area. As an example of the contrasting risks of capital ventures, a merchant could have a 200-ton ship built and ready to sail for £1,200. He would take on greater risks from such sources as storms, pirates, and the other hazards of the sea. The same investment would purchase a 500-acre plantation with upwards of a dozen or so slaves. With rice and then indigo so profitable and ships readily available for charter, the choice of ventures was obvious.

During these early years, the mercantile interests of the colony relied heavily on vessels built and owned in England and New England, where the agricultural attractions for capital and labor were not so strong. The demand for vessels at Charles Town peaked in the fall and winter when the harvested crops were ready for shipment. By 1720, approximately half of the ships calling at Charles Town were registered in England; within the next few years, the number had risen to 70 percent. As late as 1749, Governor James Glen remarked that the colony had a local fleet that did not exceed 1,600 tons. He also reported to the Board of Trade in London that almost 200 vessels had left port in 1749: 68 sailed to Europe, 87 to the West Indies, and 38 to the northern colonies.

King George's War (1739–1748) depressed several previously profitable industries, causing new immigrants to go into ship construction and repair and the production of such naval stores as rope. By 1750, agriculture's lure had lessened, as most of Charles Town's prime cropland had been developed. The naval activities off the coast during the war forced a revival in the colony's ship repair and shipbuilding industries. The large number of enemy privateers that prowled the waters off Charles Town resulted in an increased Royal Navy presence. This in turn increased the need for local ship repair facilities.

Revival

Once the war was over in 1748, a large number of well-trained shipbuilders and artisans arrived in Charles Town and set up shop. Most of them were fleeing from the repeated upheavals and wars in Europe and were attracted by the rising prosperity in South Carolina. They infused the industry with innovations and new skills, while most native builders continued to concentrate on building schooners and repairs. This immigration only partially solved the labor shortage that had plagued the local industry. It was the delays in construction caused by these labor shortages that hindered the industry until the late 1760s.

In 1744, Andrew Ruck petitioned the Carolina Commons House of Assembly for relief from the great number of blacks "employed in mending, repairing, and caulking ships. . .and working at the Shipwright's Trade," adding that as a result, the white artisans "could meet with little or no work to do." Freemen found that slave labor depressed their wages, and this discouraged shipwrights from settling in South Carolina. The local slaveowners tried to squelch the petition by stating that the artisans wanted "extravagant wages," and defended their right to use slaves that they had purchased and trained. As a result of this petition, a committee of the Commons House recommended that a limitation be placed on the number of blacks hired out as shipwrights. In 1751 the Assembly placed a tax on imported slaves. One-fifth of the revenue collected was used as a bounty to encourage shipwrights and caulkers to settle in South Carolina. Three years later the bounty was dropped, as trade and business grew by leaps and bounds and shipwrights began to move into the colony.

Although Charles Town remained the colony's center for shipbuilding, both Georgetown and Beaufort became important secondary sites by the 1730s. By 1745 shipbuilding had started at Winyah Bay near Georgetown and, in July 1748, Benjamin Darling launched the 200-ton *Mary Anne*, one of the largest ships built in the colony before 1750. By the 1760s, shipbuilding on Winyah Bay fell dormant due to the financial instability of some builders and the removal of others to Charles Town.

During the same period Beaufort produced sixteen vessels averaging eighteen tons. The largest ships listed in the colony's registry records were built in the Port Royal area, where facilities were also available for careening vessels. By 1765 ten shipbuilders were active on Port Royal Sound. There in 1772, Robert Watts built the 260-ton *Friendship*, one of the largest ships built in the colony before the Revolution. During the same period John Emrie moved from Charles Town to Beaufort, where he built the 200-ton *Rose Island* in 1766.

Between 1740 and 1779, four shipyards in Charles Town and one in Beaufort produced 24 square-rigged vessels in addition to sloops and schooners. During the same period over 200 schooners (83 schooners and 4 sloops in the 1740s alone) averaging twenty tons each were built. The schooner was the most popular of the locally built craft, handy in the narrow channels of the shoal-ridden coastal waters; with their fore and aft rig, they could steer to windward better than any other vessel. With two masts, the rigging and sails were divided into smaller, more easily handled parts. A small crew could set the sails on one mast and then the other, whereas the single-masted sloop had one large mast, requiring a larger crew to work all the sails simultaneously. Small crews made the schooners economical to operate, and their speed and nimbleness enabled them to escape wartime capture by running upwind or into the shallow coastal waters where larger adversaries could not easily follow.

By analysis of the records of ships owned and registered in Charles Town prior to 1760 one can draw some interesting conclusions. During that period, the vast majority of the locally owned vessels were obviously for use in coastal trading. Most of them were under 50 tons in displacement, in the 10- to 20-ton range—hardly the type to engage in oceanic commerce. Local construction clearly centered around the easily built schooners, which averaged 20 tons. Some 140 of these vessels were built between 1735 and 1760. At the same time only 7 ship-rigged vessels and 25 other ocean-going ships were built. A few built at Hobcaw were in the 175- to 200-ton range.

The majority of new vessels, particularly the large ones, were built at Hobcaw, just across the Cooper River from Charles Town. A few were brought into Charles Town after being taken from the French or Spanish by warships or privateers. Once captured in such a way, the vessel in question had to be condemned by the Vice-Admiralty Court and then sold at auction. This allowed local entrepreneurs the best opportunity to purchase these vessels at good prices; it was difficult for outside buyers to travel to Charles Town for a Vice-Admiralty Court auction.

The list of ships registered to Charles Town owners during the forty years preceding the Revolution shows that most of the larger ones built in the colony, particularly those over 175 tons, were built in the Beaufort/Port Royal area, which had the deepest harbor in the colony. Also a plentiful supply of live and white oak, cypress, and pine was at hand. Because of its remote location away from the primary center of economic activity at Charles Town, and the fact that it was on an island with poor road connections to the hinterland, Beaufort and Port Royal never developed their full potential as a shipbuilding site.

Another shipbuilding location was Bloody Point on Daufuskie Island near Savannah. Here for £1,300 sterling Robert Watts built the 260-ton *Friendship* and *Cowles* for Henry

Laurens and William Cowles of Bristol; Laurens considered this "as cheap or cheaper than building the ship in England." These large ships reflected the pre-Revolutionary joint ownership between Charlestonians and English businessmen.

Before Great Britain won complete control of eastern North America in 1763, large ships were deemed too much of a risk to capture or natural disaster for the Carolina builders and investors. With peace and stability and no enemies within several hundred miles of Charles Town, the investment in large ships became more attractive and brought about a significant construction increase prior to the Revolution. The economies of scale that these large vessels offered served to offset risk of loss, and helped meet the fierce competition in the shipping business.

Simultaneously there was a brisk business in ship repair, which brought large profits to the local shipyards. A damaged vessel arriving in Charles Town had little choice but to pay the exhorbitant local rate for repairs rather than risk a voyage to another repair facility. This area of economic activity required many mechanics—including shipwrights, carpenters, painters, glaziers, ironwrights, sail and rope makers, and cabinetmakers. When the crops were loaded on board as many as 200 vessels in Charles Town harbor each fall, many of these ocean-going ships required repairs before returning to sea.

Of great hindrance to local shipbuilding was the fact that few local leaders either promoted the industry or owned any vessels at this time. Most preferred to charter vessels as they needed them. In 1763, Henry Laurens had a ship constructed in England because he doubted the skill of local builders. But with British shipwrights, Laurens ran into the same trouble that British merchants met when they ordered American vessels—confusion, delays, and cost overruns.

After 1760, the picture changed as the colony's efforts to promote shipbuilding began to bear fruit. Henry Laurens became involved in local shipbuilding. In 1771, he had a ship built for an English business associate and recruited a Philadelphia shipwright to come to Charles Town to construct the vessel. On a visit to England, he promoted the Carolina industry and won another order. In the decade prior to the Revolution, seventeen ocean-going vessels were built and registered in the colony, along with 6,141 tons of other craft. With this construction, South Carolina's shipbuilding ranked about ninth in the colonies. British merchants also began to purchase ocean-going vessels built in South Carolina. Shipbuilding had become the most valuable and prosperous of the mechanic industries during a period of political turmoil for Charles Town artisans.

Between 1770 and 1774 more and larger ships were built and registered in South Carolina than in the preceding decade. The increased activity made Charles Town an important commerce and shipbuilding center at the beginning of the Revolution. The *South Carolina Gazette* of October 25, 1773, commenting on the launch of the 200-ton *Briton* at Hobcaw for the London trade, reported that the colony had "no less than twelve Carolina built ships, constantly employed in the trade between this port and Europe."

Live Oak

One asset that promoted Lowcountry South Carolina shipbuilding in the decade prior to the Revolution was the gradual realization that live oak timbers, when properly cured, were one of the best and most durable shipbuilding materials in the world. This realization came almost at the same time that English and European shipowners began to realize that American vessels built of northern oak were subject to early rot, especially in the frames.

Live oak trees grow in the coastal areas of the southeastern United States, in a rough geographic arc from coastal North Carolina to Texas. The durability of live oak as ship's timber is undoubtedly due to the fact that these trees thrive along the banks of saltwater creeks and inlets.

The wood is light brown with a very hard texture, high tensile strength, and great resistance to rot. Its specific gravity of .80 (water is 1.00) is the highest of any native North American timber. As the wood ages, it increases in toughness; some pieces have been known to become almost as hard as cast iron. As a consequence, it is nearly impossible to cut aged live oak with hand tools. Because the wood does not grow in straight lengths, it is best suited for making the frames of a ship. Today it has little commercial value and thus it is seldom found in a lumber mill.

It is not known when Carolina shipbuilders began to use live oak, but they must have experimented with it early since it was so plentiful in the Lowcountry. In 1737, a Joseph Avery of Port Royal advertised that he had a great quantity of live oak on hand for shipbuilding. In 1747, Thomas Middleton advertised for sale in Charles Town a 40- to 45-ton schooner built of live oak and yellow pine. Shipbuilders who attempted to use imported English oak often found the price of the completed product too high. In order to remain

A sawyer sawing timber into planks from the Colonial Shipyard Scene by Harold Hahn. A sawyer was a skilled craftsman before the advent of water- and steam-powered sawmills. The timber to be cut was either placed across a pit or elevated on two large trestles as shown here. The sawyer stood on top, facing opposite to the direction of the cut. The pit man stood below at the other end of the two-man saw. By alternately pulling and pushing on the saw, they cut the timber lengthwise into planks.

competitive, they were forced to employ native materials. While the twisted, gnarled shape of live oak branches ruled out its use for keels and spars, it readily lent itself to framing materials; the shape of any needed frame or portion thereof and the knees for reinforcing corners were relatively easy to find in standing trees.

The first European record of the superiority of live oak occurred in 1771 when the Carolina-built *Fair American* was lengthened in an English yard. The ship was ten years old and had seen much hard service hauling rice to Liverpool. Roger Fisher, shipwright in charge of the work, was so impressed with her live oak frames and pitch pine timbers that he praised them to the Admiralty as superior to English oak. The text of his letter was added to the third edition of his book, *Heart of Oak, the British Bulwark*, in 1772. Undoubtedly Fisher had much trouble cutting *Fair American's* frames of aged live oak during her lengthening. He found very little rot in her timbers, unusual for a ship ten years old. Carolina shipbuilders could not have asked for a better advertisement. Probably as a consequence of Fisher's report, the Admiralty sent a frigate to the St. Marys River in Georgia to survey the live oaks for ships-of-the-line. One such ship would require the oak from sixty acres of trees. A follow-up survey in 1772 found few planters interested in being lured away from indigo

Colonial American Shipyard by Harold M. Hahn. Note the derrick for lifting heavy objects onto the vessel under construction, and the scaffolding around the hulls to enable workers to get at the sides more easily. The vessel in the background is *Chaleur*, station ship at Charles Town from 1766 to 1768.

The Brown's River Ferryboat, an early eighteenth-century example of South Carolina shipbuilding. While this was not an ocean-going craft, it is the only definite example of pre-Revolutionary South Carolina shipbuilding in existence and is the oldest vessel of colonial manufacture ever discovered in the Western Hemisphere. It was raised from the Black River in Georgetown County in 1976. The boat is the earliest known example of the use of live oak timbers and is believed to have been built as early as 1700. When she burned and sank in 1730, she was carrying a cargo of bricks.

The Colonial American Shipyard diorama by Harold M. Hahn of Lyndhurst, Ohio. The vessels shown on the three building ways are schooners in various stages of construction; most colonial vessels were built in similar fashion. The hull in the foreground is in its first stage, with keel, stern, stempost, and a few frames in position. These frames consist of the floor timbers (bottom just above the keel), two futtocks to each side (scarphed to the floor timbers), and top timbers (scarphed to the futtocks); a total of five different pieces were all scarphed together. The middle vessel shows the completed framework of the hull and the beginnings of the side planking. Note the beams supporting the deck in the top of the hull, with openings for hatches, and the partners around the holes for the masts. The vessel in the background is ready for launch. The hull and hull planking are complete. The Stewart and Rose Shipyard at Hobcaw would have looked very much like this scene.

production to cut the timber. This and the Royal dockyards' bias against American oak saw to it that nothing was done to promote live oak's use in shipbuilding in England.

Charles Town Shipyards

As early as 1702, there had been ship activity at Hobcaw across the Cooper River from Charles Town on the Wando River. Ships were no doubt lured by the deep water and fresh-water spring close to the shore, from which they could refill their casks without having to carry them overland. Another advantage to the location was its separation from the distractions of the city. Workers and crews of the vessels could concentrate on the job at hand.

The French burned the area in 1706, and legend has it that they were attracted by ships under construction. George Dearsley owned the shipyard at this time. After his death his widow married Thomas Bolton, who continued the operation. The ship construction and repairing industry prospered; in 1727, Captain John Gascoigne, surveying the coast in *Alborough*, brought the ship to Hobcaw to be careened and the bottom cleaned.

Thomas Bolton seems to have been primarily responsible for getting shipbuilding going at Hobcaw. Then in 1753, he sold his shipyard to James Stewart and John Rose, two immigrant shipbuilders who had established themselves in Charles Town in the 1750s. Stewart had arrived in 1749, after apprenticing under his uncle, Mungo Murray, at the Royal Naval Yard at Woolwich near London. By 1754 he and Rose were prospering at Hobcaw, and in 1763 they were able to build *Heart-of-Oak* on speculation. Rose went along on her first voyage to London to recruit other mechanics and to sell the ship. Soon after, they built the sloop *Liberty* with a likeness of Colonel William Rhett on the bow. The Stewart and Rose shipyard spread out over a hundred acres with good wharves and other facilities for heaving down as many as three vessels at the same time.

In 1769 Rose retired with a fortune of some £30,000 sterling. He sold the shipyard to William Begbie and Daniel Manson, who had arrived in Charles Town only six years earlier. On November 30, 1769, Begbie and Manson advertised for shipbuilding, heaving-down, and repairing at Hobcaw and for heaving-down, graving, repairing, and mast-making at John Rose's Wharf at Charles Town. This announcement included notice of a good inventory of live oak, cypress, and spars for topmasts, yards, and booms. By 1773 they had built twelve ships at Hobcaw.

Begbie and Manson launched *Magna Carta* of 300 tons measurement in November 1770; the next year, the 200-ton *New Carolina Packet* was launched for the London trade. Evidently the rising friction between the colonies and the Crown extended even to ships' names; *Friendship* and *Carolina* were being replaced by *Liberty*, *Fair American*, and *Oliver Cromwell*. Begbie and Manson, however, remained loyal to the Crown. In 1778, along with other loyalists, they were forced to sell out to Abraham Livingston and the radical boatwright Paul Pritchard, who had arrived in the colony from Belfast only ten years earlier. The property became known as Pritchard's Shipyard. By the time of the Revolution, the shipyard was so significant that a powder magazine and works with barracks had been constructed to protect it. Pritchard leased the site to the State Navy in 1778 and 1779 before the British occupation of the city.

By 1773 there were five shipyards in the Charles Town area, including Clement Lempriere's across the Cooper River on Shem Creek, where *Betsy and Elfy* was built in 1769 for the London trade. Lempriere was a former officer in the Royal Navy who had settled in Charles Town after King George's War. To the north of Charles Town on Dewees' Island there was the small shipyard of Cornelius Dewees. He specialized in building brigantines for the West Indian Trade. Another small shipyard existed on the Stono River.

In 1763 on Charles Town Neck to the north of the city, Robert Cochran established a shipyard on the south side of Shipyard Creek, then known as Long Point Creek, on property inherited by his wife and her sister. Shipyard Creek, though not very wide, provided deep water close to shore, perfect for ships to use while fitting out after launch. The Shipyard Creek location was too small to accommodate growth and too close to the diversions of the city. This led to problems with ships' crews in the yard. It is difficult to imagine the hardships endured in the colonial period, particularly at sea. An ocean voyage was so grueling that crews were often desperate for a few hours of noisy respite in a local tavern. Such "respite" often led to problems for the ships' officers as well as the townspeople. Hobcaw, remote from the temptations of the city across the Cooper River, was the perfect place for shipbuilding and repair. Those shipyards in and closer to the city languished by comparison.

Despite its drawbacks, Cochran was successful on Shipyard Creek and during the Revolution the State Navy leased his yard for two years as a repair facility, but the state abandoned it in favor of Hobcaw in 1779. Cochran operated the yard after the war and in 1788 divided the property between his wife and her sister, with his wife retaining the shipyard location. One of Pritchard's sons leased the yard from Cochran and built several ships at this location before the War of 1812 including the frigate *John Adams*.

Before the War of 1812, the U. S. Navy rented the site as the Charleston naval station. In 1813, Cochran's son C. B. tried to have the navy purchase the land, but Secretary Jones refused, alleging that the asking price was four times the actual value. After the War of 1812, the navy abandoned the site and Charleston as a base.

Another indication of the success of shipbuilding in Charles Town is the advertisements placed by mechanics associated with the industry. Examples include those of the well-known mechanic Joseph Hancock, who had served an apprenticeship in one of the Royal Navy's dockyards; Philip Witherstone, a ship carver from Bristol, England; and Nathaniel Lebby, who in 1763 came to Charles Town from Portsmouth, New Hampshire, where he had become a mast and spar hewer. Three years later, Lebby and many other Charles Town mechanics assembled under the Liberty Tree to protest the Stamp Act under the leadership of Christopher Gadsden, and the death-knell of colonial South Carolina was heard.

Summary

While South Carolina's colonial shipbuilding industry was not as impressive as that of the northern colonies, some of her ships were noted abroad for their quality and durability, and shipbuilding became the colony's largest non-agricultural industry before the Revolution. Shipbuilding in Charles Town had the great advantage of an abundance of superior timber, a growing dynamic trade-oriented local economy, and a great natural harbor. However, the minus factors that shipbuilding had to surmount were a social bias in favor of planting, brisk competition from northern builders, and the discouragement that slave labor placed on the skills and ability of the free artisans, black or white.

King George's War 1739–1748

There was little peace in the world during the eighteenth century. The struggle for supremacy by the major European powers dominated the century. Queen Anne's War ended in 1713, but the decades to 1739 were little more than an erratic armed truce interspersed with periods of conflict. By the late 1730s, British merchants, unable to cut into Spain's monopolies in the New World by peaceful means, were ready to try war. The public, alarmed by the constant tension between England on one side and France and Spain on the other, grew more acclimated to the inevitability of war.

The British Parliament had been increasing its power and authority during the years since the end of Queen Anne's War; in fact, Queen Anne was the last monarch to veto an act of Parliament. It would be Parliament that would vote the final declaration of war in response to the wishes of the Empire, as well as the money to pay for it.

In the years between 1713 and 1737, the Royal Navy had been allowed to decline. As a new conflict loomed larger, it became apparent that it would be a naval war. By 1738, the shipyards of Britain were busy turning out a fleet of new warships, several of which would serve on the Carolina station.

Spanish attacks on British merchant shipping in the West Indies continued unabated through the 1730s, with one outrage leading to another. In 1739, Captain Robert Jenkins, master of the merchant brig *Rebecca* of Glasgow, was detained by a Spanish privateer captain, who cut off Jenkins' ear after mistreating Jenkins' crew. Legend says that Captain Jenkins brought his severed ear to Parliament, which was so outraged that war was declared against Spain in October. France became an ally of Spain in 1744. First known as the War of Jenkins' Ear, it became the War of the Austrian Succession; Austria allied herself with England in the fighting in Europe. In the American colonies, it was known as King George's War.

Attack on St. Augustine

Charles Town's profitable rice trade with Spain was lost as a result of the war, a major blow to the local economy. Worse still, the city feared an attack by the Spanish from their stronghold at St. Augustine. Through the years the trade of Charles Town had suffered heavily from the depredations of privateers operating from there; further problems arose when they raided outlying plantations to loot and steal slaves. War brought the additional threat of invasion by the Spanish army and navy. South Carolina had mobilized in 1737 against a rumored Spanish invasion fleet gathering at Havana, which failed to materialize.

On the other hand, the Spanish had been upset by the founding of Savannah in 1733. They encouraged Indian raids across the St. Marys River against the new English settlements. The English in turn encouraged retaliatory raids against the Spanish towns by tribes friendly to the Crown. The situation was exacerbated by the Spanish promise of freedom to all English slaves escaping across the border—the underlying cause of the slave rebellion of 1739.

These depredations caused a united military effort by Georgia and South Carolina to remove the Spanish threat similar to the northern colonies' combined attack on the French fortress at Louisbourg in Nova Scotia. The English forces were placed under the command of Governor Oglethorpe of Georgia, who had been made military leader of the region in 1737.

Lieutenant Governor Bull pledged £120,000 sterling and 400 men for the expedition. In addition a squadron of English ships and a body of friendly Indians were recruited to help.

Unfortunately Oglethorpe failed to live up to his reputation. Setting out in May 1740, he consulted with neither Captain Pearce of the supporting naval force nor Colonel Alexander Vander Dussen of the South Carolina regiment. Oglethorpe's poor organizational abilities nullified his great energy. He forfeited surprise, antagonized the Indians, and failed to cooperate with the navy. The troops were landed forty miles above St. Augustine, forcing them to march twice as far as necessary. A better plan would have been to sail the ships down the St. John's River to Fort Picolata, from where they could easily march the twenty miles overland to St. Augustine. As it was, the troops arrived for the siege exhausted from a late spring heat wave.

In any event, taking St. Augustine would have been difficult; Oglethorpe rendered it hopeless. He was indecisive, spending several weeks in fruitless bombardment and minor skirmishes around the city. When the siege began in earnest at the end of May, the land forces were supported by a squadron of English warships, that included the sixth-rates *Flamborough*

Castillo de San Marcos, focus of the English colonial attacks in June 1740.

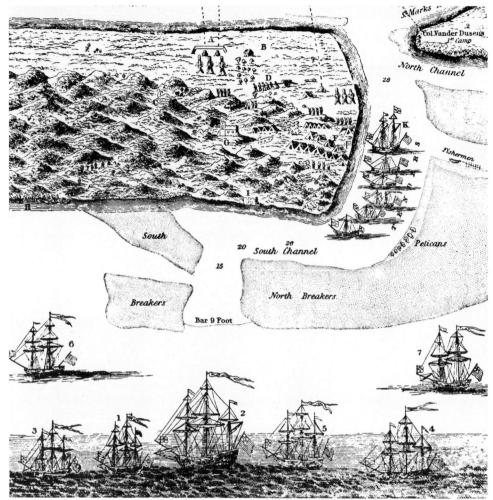

The English fleet and army before St. Augustine, Florida on June 20, 1740 by Thomas Silver, who described the letters and numbers on the sketch as follows:

A The English south trench with three 18-pounders and two small mortars
B Marshy area where English small mortars were located
C Eustatia Island
D Sailors hauling cannon to fire on Castillo de San Marcos
E A north trench with three 18-pounders and a mortar
F General Oglethorpe's camp
G A watchtower taken on June 12
H Soldiers and sailors landing on June 11
I A Spanish sand battery abandoned at the approach of the English
K Captain Warren, commander of the naval force ashore, hoisting the Union Flag on board a schooner
L Wells that supplied water to the ships

Bottom: the English fleet—1-*Flamborough*, 2-*Hector*, 3-*Squirrel*, 4-*Tartar*, 5-*Phoenix*, 6-*Wolf* (sloop), 7-*Spence* (sloop).

and *Squirrel*.[1] At the end of June bad weather forced the warships to sea for safety; this allowed Spanish relief ships to get through the blockade.

Apprehensive of the hurricane season, the English fleet refused to remain beyond July 5, thus sealing the fate of the expedition. Colonel Vander Dussen and the South Carolina troops were the last to break the siege, bringing off the artillery with them. The unsuccessful attack had done little more than antagonize the Spanish; it would only be a matter of time before retaliation came.

The First South Carolina Navy

Building large warships was beyond the capacity of the colony, but they were capable of smaller ones to patrol the coastal waterways. In 1741, the colonial Assembly passed an act to construct galley-type naval craft for the defense of the colony. Other than the earlier scout boats, these were the first local naval craft designed and built from the keel up. This fleet can therefore be considered the origin of the South Carolina Navy.

The Spanish had brought the galley concept to the New World, successfully deploying the craft in support of troop movements near shoal water. The coastal waters of the South Carolina Lowcountry are shallow, laced with narrow, winding, strong tidal creeks. These conditions limited the usefulness of ocean-going craft, as they were vulnerable to ambush; furthermore, their draft limited their movements, and tall trees close to shore blocked the wind, their only means of propulsion.

The few coastal roads were primitive and the rivers and bays of the colony were the primary avenues of transportation. Control of inshore waters in wartime was essential. Row-

---

[1] *Squirrel* and *Flamborough* had been assigned to the Carolina station in the preceding decades. Originally built in 1707 and rebuilt in 1727, they were nearing the end of their service life.

Artist's conception of *Charles-Town* galley.

galleys were perfect for escorting troop movements and, lacking dependence on the wind, could move relatively freely along the coast, their heavy bow guns giving powerful support to forces ashore.

Charles Town shipwright John Yerworth was given a contract to build two "half galleys" (essentially a smaller version of a galley without a quarterdeck) for £3,000 in the colony's currency. Oars provided the main propulsion, with schooner-type or lateen sails supplementing them as wind conditions allowed. In March 1742 *Charles-Town* and *Beaufort* were launched, heavily armed for their size with twelve swivel guns and six light carriage guns, and carrying a crew of fifty men. The hulls were barge-shaped, with shallow, flat bottoms to facilitate operations where vessels of deeper draft could not maneuver.

On April 8, 1744, *Charles-Town* was lost when she was hit by a sudden gale while escorting a sloop over the bar. Ten men were lost, but Commander David Cutler Braddock, and the rest saved themselves in the galley's lifeboat. *Beaufort* served through two wars and was not retired until 1764.

The Royal Navy Station Ships

Other naval activities in King George's War centered around the employment of the Royal Navy station ships used to fend off Spanish invasions, neutralize St. Augustine as an enemy base, and patrol against enemy privateers. The two most notable of these ships were the sixth-rates HMS *Rose* and her sister HMS *Rye*, which were constructed in England during the rearmament period at the beginning of the war. They were 24-gun ships of over 440 tons on a 106-foot long hull, with crews of 160 men. They were small forerunners of the Revolutionary frigates and similar to the earlier station ships of George Anson. Other, but older sixth-rate station ships active at Charles Town during the war were *Seaford*, *Shoreham*, *Phoenix*, *Tartar*, *Flamborough*, and *Alborough*.

Smaller vessels on station during the war included the 10- to 16-gunners HMS *Hawke*, *Spence*, *Swift*, *Spy*, and *Swallow*. Occasionally larger fourth- and fifth-rate warships would make an appearance, including *Loo*[2] and *Adventure*. The impact of these latter ships on the Carolina station was of lesser importance, even though they were effective against the Spanish privateers.

Maintenance was a considerable problem for ships on colonial stations, far from British naval dockyards. Rarely was Charles Town assigned a new warship that had recently received a period of training and "shakedown" in home waters. *Rose*[3] and *Rye* followed this pattern, but most of the others were nearing the end of their service life, being stretched for one last assignment before going to the shipbreakers.

[2] Spelled *Looe* in some accounts.

[3] *Rose* of 1741 should not be confused with the earlier station ship (1734–1738) of the same name. A common practice of the Royal Navy was, and still is, to keep ships with identical names in service. The earlier *Rose*, although taken out of service in 1739, was not disposed of until 1744, meaning that the Royal Navy had two similar ships with the same name at the same time.

Between the departure of George Anson and the advent of the Revolution, the most notable station ship commander was the captain of HMS *Rose*, Thomas Frankland. Like Anson, he was quite popular with the local citizens. He was a son of Henry Frankland, the Governor of Bengal, and a nephew of Sir Thomas Frankland, then a Lord of the Admiralty. At the time, the rich trading grounds of the West Indies attracted naval officers in search of prize money. Therefore, many politically influential officers maneuvered assignments there. Charles Town shared in this hunting ground, and Frankland was not to be disappointed.

Frankland's naval career began in 1731 when he was assigned to the 64-gun *York* and later Anson's *Scarborough*. By 1738 he was promoted to lieutenant. In July 1740, he received his posting to captain, skipping two ranks, thanks to his uncle's influence. He was then appointed to command the new *Rose*. Shortly after her completion in September, Frankland sailed to help escort King George back to England after a visit to his Hanoverian dominions, a signal honor for any naval officer. Frankland then received orders to proceed to the Bahamas to relieve HMS *Spence* as station ship. His orders stated:

> Captains of his Majesty's Ships station'd in America have of late... taken unwarrantable liberty of lying in port with their ships for the greatest part of the time they have remained abroad, to the dishonour of his Majesty's Service, and the disservice of the Colonies for whose protection they were appointed. And... we do hereby strictly charge and direct you to employ the ship... under your Command diligently in the execution of the instructions you have.

Frankland was not to disappoint the Admiralty, though he would spend more time in Charles Town than in Nassau. A corrupt governor of the Bahamas demanded too large a share of the prize funds from the ship captains who brought prizes there.

Bad weather plagued Frankland's arduous passage across the Atlantic. After clearing Madeira, *Rose* lost her foretopmast, then the entire mast, followed by the maintopmast and the mizzenmast. With only the lower mainmast in place, the ship was rolling so badly that the crew could barely secure the wreckage and await better weather before rigging jury masts. Once the jury rig was in place, Frankland set course for Charles Town where he arrived on March 3, 1741. The extensive damage could not be repaired in the Bahamas.

By June *Rose* was repaired and convoyed four vessels to Jamaica. She then put into Nassau. Captain Frankland spent the hurricane season of 1741 at New Providence, lying there from July to October. Subsequently, several weeks were spent cruising about the Bahamas and down to Cuba chasing sails, exchanging news with captains of friendly privateers, and successfully capturing several Spanish merchantmen. In one operation, *Rose* sent her boats in to take a Spanish vessel, but grounded slightly in the process, damaging her keel.

In August of that year, Charles Hardy, commander of HMS *Rye*, was ordered from England to South Carolina to relieve HMS *Phoenix* and *Tartar*. Hardy had been in the Royal Navy almost ten years when he received his appointment to the Carolina station to protect the colony's commerce and harass the enemy at St. Augustine.

Rye anchored off Charles Town on January 13, 1742. Two days later she came into the Cooper River, where she found *Phoenix* and *Rose*. Like *Rose*, *Rye* had also been damaged in crossing the Atlantic and spent three months at Hobcaw having her rigging refitted and bottom cleaned. By March 26, *Rye* was ready for sea, but was shorthanded. Captain Hardy tried to press replacements from the merchantmen lying at anchor, but was foiled by threats of legal action under an act of Queen Anne that forbade the impressment of seamen on the coast of America. Help from the South Carolina Council could not improve the manpower situation until a £5 bounty was offered to entice enlistments.

While *Rye* was en route to Charles Town from England, *Rose* returned to Charles Town from her Bahama patrol. She anchored off the bar on December 30, 1741. A barge was hoisted out and sent in to pick up a pilot. The pilot did not get aboard until the morning of January 2; for unexplainable reasons he then put *Rose* ashore on the north breakers. Fortunately the surf was not too high and she was pulled off the sandbar using her own anchors and capstan. Two days later *Rose* was safe in the harbor at the cost of one anchor that had fouled on the ocean bottom.

Rose was deferred in her maintenance while *Phoenix* was prepared to voyage home for a much-needed extensive refit. Commanded by Charles Fanshawe, the 20-gun *Phoenix* had been one of the Charles Town station ships for almost five years, an unusually long time. In addition to *Rye*, the 24-gun *Flamborough* under Joseph Hamar had been ordered to Charles Town and arrived on February 8, two weeks before *Phoenix* departed.

While *Rose* was being hove down at Hobcaw, her shrouds parted, springing the mainmast and necessitating its replacement. When a new spar was needed the ship had to wait while a tree was cut and the spar shaped. Anticipating future needs, Frankland ordered several extras to be cut.

Rose's First Lieutenant John Bray was injured and disabled in the accident; he was replaced by Midshipman James Allen. Accidents such as this were one of the reasons why ship captains preferred to have their vessels drydocked or beached for bottom cleaning. Unfortunately these were options only for small vessels in Charles Town. Not only were the facilities for heaving down primitive by European standards, but also the new sixth-rates were so stiff that extra effort was needed to heel them over. Allen's inexperience and the time lost on the new spar delayed the refitting process, and Frankland complained bitterly to the Admiralty about the problems of repairing a warship in South Carolina. To complicate matters *Rose's* hull became infested with worms, necessitating extensive repairs two years later.[4]

---

[4] *Rose's* delay in waiting for her turn at Hobcaw caused her to remain at anchor in the harbor. Generally a wooden ship's movement through the water prevents worms from attaching themselves; thus, captains and owners wanted to keep their vessels on the move.

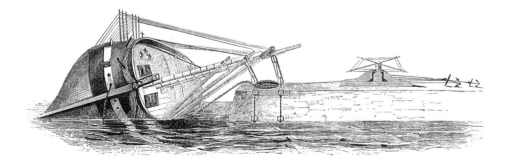

A ship hoved down for bottom cleaning.

On April 24, *Rose* and *Rye* finally departed Charles Town convoying two merchant ships clear of the coast, and then cruising to the south. However, the pilot ran *Rye* aground off Sullivan's Island. The damage that she sustained required a further six weeks of repairs. *Flamborough* took *Rye's* place, but she and *Rose* cruised independently.

On June 4 in the Bahamas between Little and Great Exuma, *Rose* sighted four sail and set out in chase. When the strangers hoisted English colors, Frankland ran a French flag to his mast head. By 11 o'clock she had them within gunshot. *Rose* displayed her true colors, and the strangers hoisted a Spanish flag. The three larger ships bore down to attack. Frankland held his fire until close alongside the leader; he then unleashed a broadside, which the enemy returned.

Frankland continued the unequal battle for three hours. Two of the enemy ships then hauled away, but the third continued the battle; after another hour her crew struck against the captain's wishes. He was Captain Juan de Leon Fandino, one of the most notorious of the Spanish privateer captains, and the man who was reputed to have cropped Jenkins' ear, starting the war!

Frankland quickly manned the prize and took the original crew on board *Rose*. The two ships set off in chase of the fleeing enemy ships, which were really Fandino's prizes. It was not until the next morning that *Rose* overhauled and captured her chase and its consort, a small schooner that had remained out of the battle. The prize also captured her chase and, after rendezvousing at Nassau, the squadron made for Charles Town, arriving on June 18.

Spanish Counter Attack

A Spanish counterstroke to the attack on St. Augustine was delayed for two years by disease, although their privateers occasionally seized merchantmen off Charles Town. On June 4, 1742, Governor Oglethorpe warned the South Carolina Council of the long-awaited attack and requested reinforcements.

Oglethorpe's fears were confirmed when *Flamborough* reported her encounter with Spanish warships off St. Augustine and nearby Matanzas. She had left Charles Town on April 29 with *Rose* replacing the damaged *Rye*. After parting company with *Rose*, *Flamborough* cruised between St. Simon and St. Augustine. At the end of May, while becalmed, she sighted ten small Spanish ships and set out to attack them. Using oars and longboats she got within range and kept up a gunnery duel for several hours, but the ships eventually made it into St. Augustine. *Flamborough* returned to Charles Town on June 8, followed by *Rose* ten days later.

As *Rye* was still being repaired, *Flamborough*, the galley *Beaufort*, and the sloops *Hawke* and *Swift* departed on July 1 to support Oglethorpe. Meanwhile, Frankland took *Rose* to the Bahamas to guard that area from attack.

The Spanish invasion fleet of fifty-six vessels had left Havana early in May. One was wrecked and a storm dispersed the rest, delaying their arrival at St. Augustine. On June 21 nine of the Spanish ships attacked Amelia Sound, but were driven off by the guns of Fort William. Three days later fourteen Spanish vessels entered Cumberland Sound on the southern coast of Georgia and landed troops. Oglethorpe descended upon the relatively small vessels in only two gunboats, fighting his way through and causing them to panic and put to sea.

On June 28 the main Spanish force of thirty-six vessels, joined shortly by ten more, anchored off St. Simon. Sailing past the land batteries and two warships at anchor, a Spanish force of from 3,000 to 4,500 troops—mostly untrained blacks whom the Spaniards hoped would attract the slaves of the British colonies to join them—landed and scattered the opposing British. Oglethorpe ordered his two warships, the 24-gun sixth-rate *Success* and a schooner, to retreat to Charles Town while he retired to Fort Frederica.

There he managed to gather 700 English troops and 70 Indian allies to confront the enemy who had followed him. In the subsequent battle of Bloody Marsh, 3,000 troops of the Spanish main body were repulsed and driven back to their camp at St. Simon.

Led by *Flamborough*, the English squadron arrived off St. Simon on July 13, but they panicked when they saw the large Spanish invasion fleet, and returned to Charles Town. They had not received word that there was no vessel larger than a 20-gun warship in the enemy force. The Spanish were equally alarmed at the sight of the English warships and, having had their troops repulsed at Bloody Marsh, hastily reembarked and departed. Thus ended the last major Spanish threat to Charles Town.

In the meantime, Charles Town authorities were raising a supporting naval force for Oglethorpe by pressing all available ships in the harbor into service. The galley *Charles-Town* was brought down from Dorchester and fitted for sea, and volunteers were offered bounties. The fleet of warships that sailed on July 18, 1742, was the largest that the city had seen. It consisted of *Rye* with six colonial vessels: the 22-gun *Success*, which Oglethorpe had earlier sent north; the 12-gun schooner *Ranger*; the 10-gun brig *Carolina*; a 10-gun sloop; a 6-gun schooner; and the recent prize of *Rose*, the 10-gun snow *San Juan Baptista* taken from Fandino and rechristened *St. John the Baptist*.

On July 26 this squadron arrived off St. Simon and found that the invading Spanish force had departed. Thinking that the Spanish might be headed for Port Royal, the fleet returned to Charles Town at the end of the month. In the meantime, Frankland had received word of the Spanish invasion force when he reached Nassau, and also returned with *Rose* on August 4.

Charles Town Safe

During that first and second week of August 1742, Charles Town harbor hosted the most powerful squadron of warships it had ever seen. While meager by European standards, it must have been an impressive sight to the citizens of the city—four sixth-rate warships, four sloops, and four other smaller warships. As none of them had engaged the enemy, an acrimonious argument between their officers and the colony's Council occurred. It was not smoothed over until Lieutenant Governor Bull returned in mid-August. Captain Hardy, stung into action by criticism from the Council, departed Charles Town for St. Augustine early in August with *Rye* and *Hawke*.

On August 18, Frankland departed to patrol the coast in *Rose* as flagship of a powerful squadron consisting of *Flamborough*; *Swift*; and four provincial vessels, *South Kingston*, *Norfolk*, *Carolina*, and *St. John the Baptist*.

For the next several months the English and colonial warships occupied their time patrolling the coast and keeping an eye on the Spanish forces at St. Augustine. The Carolina galleys were even sent to St. Augustine, operating on the open ocean being a real feat of seamanship for them. At one point, they were used in vain as bait in an attempt to lure the Spanish out to battle.

English reinforcements for Charles Town returned to Virginia and Jamaica, in spite of constant rumors about new Spanish invasions. As a result of the rumors, the English warships kept on a constant patrol between Charles Town, St. Augustine, and Nassau. London also dispatched the larger fifth-rate *Loo* to the Carolina station as a result of the Spanish incursion. She spent much of her time patrolling until she was wrecked on the Florida Keys in February 1744.

The constant cruising did not prevent Captain Frankland from taking the opportunity to marry Sarah Rhett, daughter of Colonel William Rhett, and stepdaughter of the Chief Justice of South Carolina. She was described as a "beautiful and accomplished lady with a large fortune." In due course she bore her husband fourteen children, of whom three sons and six daughters reached maturity.

Charles Town's merchants presented Frankland with a handsome silver bowl as a token of their esteem and appreciation; it was a back-handed slap at Captain Hardy of *Rye*, with whom they were not too pleased. Meanwhile, Hardy's problems mounted, both personal and physical. His ship was blown ashore and grounded in a storm while at Hobcaw. Another grounding off White Point before the eyes of the city caused much embarrassment when all guns and stores had to be offloaded to get her free. Continual desertions and bickering with the city's leaders also burdened his stay on the Carolina station with problems.

Following his wedding, Frankland took *Rose* to Boston for repairs. Here the greater rise and fall of the tide would allow the ship to be hauled ashore and repaired at low tide, precluding the laborious process of careening.

On August 31, 1743, Charles Town was struck by a hurricane. *Rye* was moored with a cable each way, and her lower yards were lowered to reduce wind resistance. *Flamborough*, *Spy*, and *Swift* were unrigged. Most of the merchant vessels and two privateers in the harbor all went around into the Ashley River; three or four remained with the warships in the Cooper River. The gale reached its height shortly after midnight. All but two of the merchant vessels in the Ashley River were driven ashore, while *Rye* sustained only the loss of her pendant.

When the sixth-rate *Tartar* arrived on December 18, 1743 with Governor James Glen, she brought orders for *Rye* to return to England. During December and January a new mainmast was installed; and the ship was heeled and scrubbed for the last time on this side of the Atlantic. On February 7, *Rye* departed Charles Town with a convoy. At the end of April she reached Sheerness and, being in bad need of a refit, was put out of commission.

Captain Hardy became governor of Newfoundland and later New York in 1755. When the French and Indian War broke out in 1756, he became a rear admiral. Hoisting his flag on the 50-gun *Sutherland*, he participated in the final attack on the French fortress at Louisbourg, Nova Scotia. After that he served under Admiral Hawke and participated in the British naval triumph at Quiberon Bay in 1759. He died in 1780, while in command of the Channel Fleet.

Frankland brought *Rose* back from Boston in December and set out on January 13, 1744, for Nassau. After crossing the bar she and *Tartar* went to the aid of the snow *George*, which had grounded off Cape Romain. Then *Rose* set out for New Providence. After cruising through the islands and off the north coast of Cuba where she took several prizes, she returned to Charles Town with one of them on March 12, 1744.

Ten days later, Frankland set out on another cruise through the islands. In Nassau he heard rumors of Spanish plans for a new invasion of Georgia and South Carolina now that France was in the war. Arriving off St. Augustine to check on the Spanish before heading north, *Rose* found *Tartar* and *Flamborough*. Nothing seemed unusual there, so the three warships headed for St. Simons. Here news of the Spanish seemed more ominous, so *Tartar* was left behind while the others returned to Charles Town.

Instant Wealth

Once more *Rose* refitted at Hobcaw as was usual during the hurricane season, when the enemy was less likely to be at sea. By mid-September *Rose* and *Flamborough* reconnoitered St. Augustine and then parted; *Rose* made for Jamaica and arrived on October 28, eight days after a hurricane had struck. All ships in the harbor, including three ships-of-the-line, had been driven ashore or severely damaged.

Six days later, Frankland patrolled through the waters south and west of Cuba in *Rose*. Before daylight on December 1, when they were about eighty miles north of Cabo San Antonio off Cuba's west coast, Frankland found himself almost upon a large ship. In spite of the rough sea, he closed and ran up his colors. Seeing *Rose* closing, the stranger cleared for battle. Instead of surrendering as expected, the strange ship surprisingly ran up the French flag. Both ships opened fire when within pistol shot. Several times Frankland came so close that the hulls scraped together. The battle ran in this fashion until just after noon. When *Rose* came up to deliver another blow, the enemy surrendered.

The fierceness of the enemy's defense is indicated by the French casualties: 116 were killed and 45 wounded, opposed to 5 killed and 7 wounded on *Rose*. Both ships' hulls and rigging were damaged, and the enemy lost a mast over the side.

The prize turned out to be the 20-gun, 400-ton *Conception* out of St. Malo under the command of Adrian Merçan. She was bound from Cartagena to Cadiz via Havana. In her holds lay the reason for the fierce defense she had put up. It was one of the biggest hauls of the war: sixty-eight chests containing 310,000 pieces of eight, items of gold and silver plate, and a large quantity of diamonds and pearls. While it was not the Manila Galleon, it was the stuff that every crewman on a warship or privateer dreamed of taking; it was also more than Charles Town had seen in one haul before or since.

With both ships damaged and in enemy waters and with too many prisoners on his hands—two men for every one of his—Frankland abandoned the prisoners on Cay Sal with provisions. His crew divided up and brought the two ships to Charles Town, arriving two and a half weeks later.

When the booty was hauled up onto the wharf in Charles Town, there was so much that it could not be counted! Instead it was divided up by weight; this resulted in much wrangling among crewmembers, who felt shortchanged. Additional treasures were found stashed away in the ship and in the possessions of the crew. Naturally the governor of the Bahamas was chagrined that the prize was not brought there so that he could get a share. In Charles Town the rarely seen specie was showered upon the merchants, tavern owners, and brothels. This led to a round of temporary prosperity and its attendant inflation.

On June 1, 1745, *Rose* and *Flamborough* crossed over the bar for the last time and set course for England, escorting seven vessels. One of them was *Conception*, which Charles Town merchant John Watson had purchased in the Vice-Admiralty Court proceedings. *Rose* carried much of her treasure, which was estimated at £80,000. Once clear of the coast the

Rose drying her sails and taking on stores while at anchor in the Cooper River with her prize, Conception, at left.

convoy broke up, and each proceeded independently so that the slower vessels would not hold up the faster ones.

Frankland, now a wealthy man in his own right, went on to subsequent commands, but of little note. He became a member of Parliament in 1749 and eventually an admiral, despite an earlier dispute with another admiral that resulted in his court martial. He died on November 21, 1784.

As the war continued, it ruined the rice trade. This led to trading with the enemy at St. Augustine under flags of truce, a crime considered more serious than smuggling. That port had become dependent upon the English colonies for much of its supplies. While Charles Town ships were not the main offender, two local firms were found to have been flagrant in trading with the enemy.

Indigo planters profited immensely from the war, but the mercantile interests found themselves in a depression caused mostly by losses incurred by enemy ship seizures. Losses of cargoes reached alarming proportions. During the war the provincial government was unable to get Parliament to allow the export of rice to northern Europe. This would have relieved that industry. The Indian fur trade and traffic in naval stores remained steady, but were unable to absorb the deficit brought by the decline in rice. High insurance and freight rates made these industries only marginal at best.

Other valuable prizes were brought into Charles Town, but Spanish and French privateers captured their share of English ships off the Carolina coast. The enemy crews also came ashore on the outer islands to forage for food and supplies. The year 1747 was especially bad; one Spanish privateer took a schooner inside the bar, and another drove a Winyah periagua aground and looted her. To help counter these assaults, two large Bermuda sloops, *Non-Pareil* and *Pearl*, were purchased in Bermuda in November 1747, as armed escorts to supplement the Royal Navy station ships.

In his report to the Commons at the end of the war, Governor Glen commented that locally owned shipping stood at only 1,600 tons, as shipbuilding had slackened during the war, probably due to the builders turning to repair work.

The increased governmental war expenditures did benefit a few Charles Town merchants, but not to the extent that it benefited the northern colonies. Through influence with the government at Westminster, one large firm, Nickleson and Shubrick, secured the profitable appointment as "agents victuallers," suppliers of such expendable items as food and supplies for the Royal Navy station ships at Charles Town. It was such a lucrative business that John Nickleson and Richard Shubrick retired to London. Unfortunately, for each successful Charles Town firm there were several that went bankrupt.

The experiences of the station ships at Charles Town point up a few interesting facts. First, manpower for all naval vessels associated with the city continued to be a problem and would remain so until after the War of 1812. Since only bounties could entice volunteers, the Royal Navy impressed seamen against their will, a practice that did not endear the Royal Navy to the local citizenry.

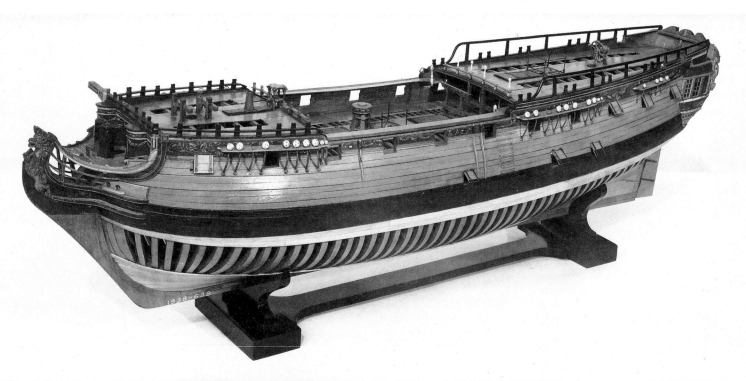

Model of an English sixth-rate warship of the 1745 Establishment. Sixth-rate warships of this establishment were slightly larger than sixth-rates of the earlier establishments. Note the longer forecastle and quarterdeck, which resulted in a shorter waist (open section amidships).

A second factor was the constant maintenance required by the ships, especially bottom cleaning. As a rule, careening, scraping, and cleaning the bottoms was done once a year; however, the tropical environment of Charles Town, especially in the warmer months, required that the sides to about six feet underwater be scrubbed more frequently. Scrubbing did not entail the tremendous expenditure of energy that careening did. Generally, all the crew had to do was shift ballast to one side to raise the other sufficiently clear so that in the ship's boats they could scrub the exposed portions of the bottom. The few feet of a ship's bottom closest to the waterline was the section where most marine growth accumulated.

Occasionally to avoid the labor of scrubbing, merchant vessels would go up the Cooper River to Childsbury, where the fresh water would kill the barnacles and they would eventually drop off. Other vessels would careen on "the hards," places where the river bottom in shallow water was hard enough so that the ship's hull would not sink into the mud. The best "hards" were at the east end of Laurens Street in the city and on Shute's Folly opposite the city where Castle Pinckney was later built. Here the vessels would run aground at high tide. As the tide went out, the bottom would be exposed, allowing maintenance to be performed. As Charles Town's rise and fall of tide seldom exceeds six feet, a vessel of greater draft had to be careened.

A third factor was the general maintenance, which was extensive for a wooden vessel operating in the eighteenth century. Masts, spars, and rigging were in constant need of attention. Sprung or cracked masts required immediate attention and much work; all the rigging and spars on the particular mast had to be unshipped, the sprung mast removed and often replaced, and then the rigging and spars reshipped. It is estimated that before the use of copper plates to protect the bottoms of warships, they were lucky if they spent more than 50 percent of their life "on station," doing the work for which they were designed. Most of the rest of their time was spent in training and maintenance. Little wonder that navies were (and are) so expensive to maintain.

A final and most important point for Charles Town was that the sixth-rates, while rather small warships, were having much trouble getting in and out of the harbor without grounding or hitting the bar while crossing. A ship crossing a shallow area in rough water could have sufficient clearance on paper, but the troughs of the waves might cause her to touch bottom, often with such force as to do serious structural damage. This was a risk no ship captain wished to take. As ships increased in size during the next century, the problems with the bar would only increase.

While King George's War may have seemed a rather minor affair for Charles Town, the increase in naval activity and the potential threat of the Spanish at St. Augustine served as a dress rehearsal for the more important task to come—the American Revolution.

Colonial Privateers

A true privateer was a vessel commissioned by a state or government agency to cruise against its enemies and intercept them. Many carried "letters of marque and reprisal,"[5] which

[5] A letter-of-marque ship, as distinguished from a privateer, was an armed merchant vessel designed primarily for cargo carrying; however, it also had authority to take prizes whenever necessary or possible.

were issued by the governor and council. Privateering was a business proposition supposedly constituted according to legal authority. Once an enemy's vessel (usually a merchantman) had been seized, it had to be brought to the nearest court of the state that had licensed the privateer. Only after due process in court could the seized vessel become the property of the privateer, after which the new owner could sell it or convert it to his own use.

Commissioning a fleet of privateers was the quickest and cheapest way to lay the foundation of a sea-going force. This was particularly true for a colony such as South Carolina, which had no standing navy responsible to the colonial authorities. Furthermore, a privateer provided a way to quick riches for investors and seamen if the cruise was fortunate. These ships sortied to engage the enemy only in order to reap profits for the owners and crews. Speed was their most important characteristic, both for running down prey and fleeing from more powerful enemy ships. Unfortunately, when an ally's ship was seized, the crew was often dispatched by fair means or foul in order to make the seizure defensible in court.

In order to counter the court proceedings, many merchant ships carried several sets of papers so that they could produce the one that would ensure her freedom if captured. There was much double dealing and duplicity in the courts, as well as among the privateers. The arm of the law was often very short in colonial America.

The earliest accounts of privateers at Charles Towne appeared in 1682 when Thomas Newe wrote home to England that there were among the mercantile ships a number of privateers that were "tolerated, if not encouraged." Despite their authoritative "letters of marque," the privateers were little more than pirates. Once they were out of the reach of the arm of the law there was small incentive to adhere to the restrictions of their commissions, especially if a rich ship fell into their hands, be it friend or foe.

With the start of the War of Jenkins' Ear in 1739, Charles Town entrepreneurs lost no time in fitting out privateers to prey on the Spanish and French ships that plied the waters off the coast.

One of the first privateers to set out was commanded by Captain Price. His was really a merchant vessel with a letter of marque, and carried a crew of eleven. While cruising along the coast of Hispaniola, he captured a Spanish sloop valued at less than £1,000 and brought it to Charles Town at the end of December 1739.

A privateer commission was granted in Charles Town on November 22, 1739, to George Austin, merchant, and James Whitefield, shipmaster. They gave a bond of £2,000 and swore to:

> obey all orders from the governor who empowered them to take and destroy
> the ships, vessels, and goods of the King of Spain and his subjects, and
> bring any captured prizes into English ports for adjudication in the Vice
> Admiralty Courts.

They were directed not to convert captured vessels and goods to their own use until they had been adjudged lawful prizes. Furthermore, at least a fourth of their men had to be British subjects, and all laws and customs relating to privateers "must be obeyed."

Following Captain Price was the 70-ton sloop *Sea Nymph*, owned by William Lassere. She returned a Spanish sloop to Charles Town the second week of January 1740. The prize and cargo brought a return of £61,382 in South Carolina currency, a good haul.

The 20-ton Spanish schooner *Cruizer* was rebuilt at Charles Town after its capture. Late in February 1744, *Cruizer* was sent out as a privateer in consort with Captain Richard I'on, who commanded the 14-gun privateer *Assistance*, a Charles Town-built vessel.

A group of local merchants invested in the privateer *Recovery*, but her captain absconded and left American waters. Although *Recovery* eventually turned up in Europe, the merchants lost their investment in her as well as that in her sistership, *Assistance*.

One of the largest Charles Town privateers was the brigantine *Loyal William* commanded by Mark Anderson; she mounted fourteen carriage and sixteen swivel guns with a crew of 100. She sailed from Charles Town on October 17, 1743, under Captain Mark Anderson. In March of the following year *Loyal William* was attacked by several Spanish vessels and compelled to strike when she exhausted her supply of powder.

Late in 1743 Captain I'on relinquished command of *Assistance* before she was absconded, and sailed in command of the privateer *Eagle* in company with the privateer *Hawk*. Together they captured a prize with 25,000 pieces of eight and took her into New Providence.

Late in 1745, Captain Ramsey volunteered to liberate the bar of a Spanish privateer that had been prowling nearby. The authorities gave him a schooner and 60 men. The Spaniard fought him broadside to broadside, but Ramsey boarded and captured the enemy and brought her into the harbor in triumph.

Captain Joshua Wilkinson, who sailed from Charles Town in 1745, met a different fate. He was captured in November by a French warship and had to be ransomed for £510. Also sailing in 1745 was Captain Clement Lempriere in the privateer *Fame's Revenge*.

One of the most exciting careers was that of the galley *Isabella*, which operated out of Charles Town during the war. In 1747 while on a cruise she came upon the schooner *Walker*, which was having a bad time of it at the hands of an 18-gun French privateer. *Isabella* came to the rescue, firing her bow guns, and boarded the French vessel, which struck. The enemy's consort surrendered to *Walker*. The privateer prize turned out to be the Rhode Island ship *Patience*, which had been seized by the Frenchman and turned into a privateer. *Isabella* brought *Patience* into Charles Town on August 21, 1747, while *Walker* carried the other prize, the ship *Mary*, into Frederica. That fall *Isabella* and *Walker* teamed up again to take the Spanish privateer *Conquestador*. *Isabella* chalked up another success in March 1748, when she captured the 300-ton 14-gun French ship *St. Jacques*. After a three-hour battle, *Isabella* brought her into Charles Town.

Other Charlestonians continued to invest in privateers throughout the war, but the initial enthusiasm did not last. It was too risky. By 1745 the issuance of letters of marque had slumped; too few investors had reaped the spectacular bounty they had hoped for. As a matter of fact, most of the prizes were quite small and the value of the cargoes negligible. The Admiralty Court at Charles Town handled only twenty-one enemy ships captured by local privateers over the nine years of privateering.

During the French and Indian War (1754–1763) privateers again fitted out and sailed from Charles Town. The schooner *Major Rogers* under James Rogers captured several ships, among them the sloop *Le St. Ferdinand*, which was later wrecked on the Abaco Island Keys in the Bahamas in July 1762. Her crew barely survived the disaster. Another local privateer was the brig *Charlestown*, which was armed with fourteen 6-pounders and twenty swivels.

As Spain did not officially enter the war until January 1762, enemy privateering against the southern colonies got off to a late start. In fact, Spanish privateers were active for less than a year before peace was signed in 1763. The British expedition against Havana in 1762 further restricted enemy activities off Charles Town. Only St. Augustine was available to the enemy as a nearby privateer base. The population of St. Augustine suffered when the wartime embargo severed their delivery of foodstuffs from the English colonies, their normal source.

As a consequence, few privateers were able to use the port against Charles Town's trade.

In the past French privateers had also used the Spanish bases in St. Augustine and Havana to attack shipping on the Carolina coast. With Spain at peace with England until 1762, French privateers were not the nuisance they had been in past wars. Once Canada was lost in 1760, British expeditions focused on the French possessions in the Caribbean. Once Spain entered the war, St. Augustine quickly commissioned both French and Spanish privateers to attack British shipping in order to supply the city with food. The French 22-gun privateer *La Marianne* ranged as far north as Delaware Bay in July 1762, then appeared off Charles Town and nearly captured two of the port's pilot boats.

In September the small Spanish galley *San Christoval*, which mounted only five guns, ran three small vessels ashore on Folly Island and the South Edisto Breakers. She also captured the polacre *James* off the Charles Town bar. Shortly afterward, the sixth-rate *Success* returned and restored order off the coast.

By October the food situation in St. Augustine was desperate, and two privateer sloops of ten and twelve guns set out in search of provisions. One, the schooner *St. Joseph*, took *Charming Sally* near Havana. Unable to navigate back to St. Augustine, the crew asked directions of a vessel bound for Charles Town; the vessel instead led them into port, where they were promptly seized.

In November 1762, the 20-gun, sixth-rate *Mercury* joined the 10-gun sloop *Bonetta* and the sixth-rate *Success* on the Carolina station. They were unable to prevent *St. Joseph* from chasing a sloop ashore at the mouth of the Santee River. A French privateer took the Charles Town brigantine *Friendship* just off Edisto Beach. She was carried to Bull's Bay and burned. From there, the marauders chased another Charles Town ship, but failed to make a capture. As revenge for the failure, they put in at North Island near Georgetown and took the pilot station's crew and all the station's provisions.

In December the Spanish privateer *Sancta Maria*, commanded by the resourceful Don Martin d'Hamassa, raided the coast off Charles Town. He took the brigantine *Neptune* of Charles Town and the schooner *General Wolfe*, which was worth £3,000—a large sum for her size. *General Wolfe* was employed as a tender for *Sancta Maria*, and together they drove a schooner ashore on North Island and took the 18-gun sloop *Adventure* from Jamaica, which they then converted into another privateer. The prisoners were set ashore on North Island on December 20, and the next day the Spanish took the brigantine *Portsmouth* off Shubrick's (Bull's) Island. On the day before Christmas the squadron of Spanish privateers easily captured the schooner *Mary* of Charles Town off the South Edisto. She was stripped and scuttled. On January 13, 1763, the Spanish privateers set sail for St. Augustine. However, only *Adventure* and *Sancta Maria* made it; *General Wolfe* was lost with her cargo and three of the prize crew.

The Spanish privateer *St. Joseph* was even less successful; not one of her prizes reached home. The station ship *Bonetta* had recaptured one of them off St. Augustine; another lost its way and was taken back to Charles Town; and a third just disappeared. From then until the reestablishment of peace in February 1763, several more vessels were taken off the coast. The station ships were too busy escorting convoys clear of the Charles Town coast to be of much help in fending off enemy privateers, which preyed mostly on the smaller coastal ships.

In 1763, Charles Town merchants breathed a sigh of relief when Florida was ceded to Britain in the Treaty of Paris. Unfortunately, the reprieve would be shortlived; St. Augustine would once again become a base for privateers operating against Charles Town. This time, however, they would be English!

CHARLESTOWN SHIPS 1750–1783

Scale 1″ = 50′

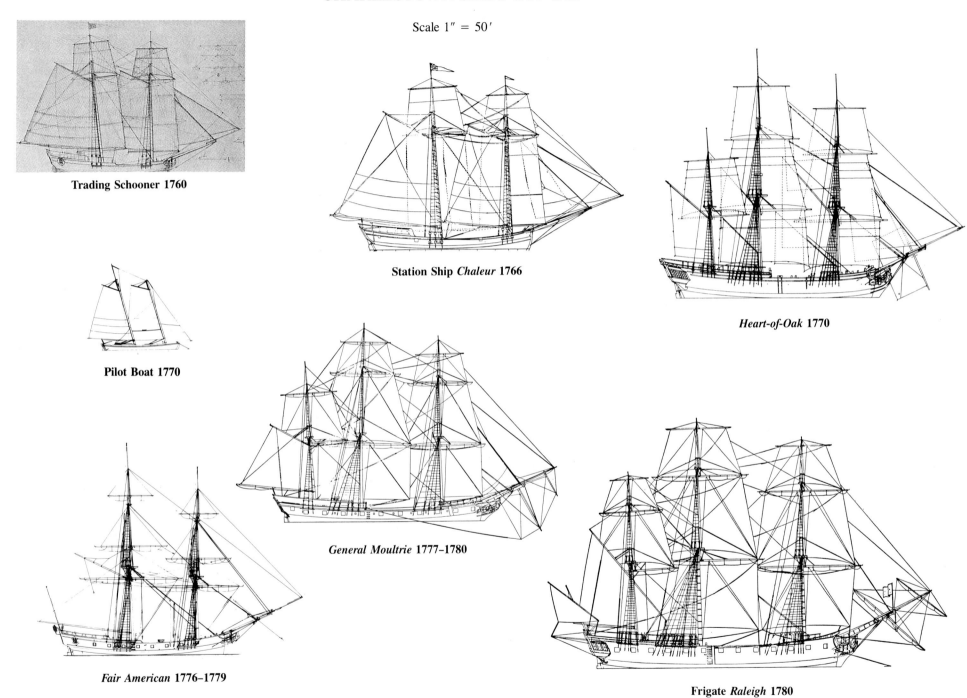

Trading Schooner 1760

Pilot Boat 1770

Station Ship *Chaleur* 1766

Heart-of-Oak **1770**

General Moultrie **1777–1780**

Fair American **1776–1779**

Frigate *Raleigh* 1780

Crown Jewel of British America 1749–1775

Following King George's War the colony of South Carolina was in the throes of vigorous economic growth and political turmoil. As is all too often the case in politics, once the external threat was removed, the internal bickering intensified. The external threat had been Spanish Florida; this threat was removed when Spain ceded Florida to England under the Treaty of Paris in 1763. England, now the dominant world power, tightened control over the colonies with increasingly strict political and economic measures. The rising prosperity in South Carolina and the advantages that it brought made these new measures intolerable to the colonists. Tensions and antagonisms with London were inevitable. However, South Carolina's leaders were of a more conservative temperament than those in Massachusetts; as a consequence, the colony moved cautiously in its resistance to British control.

An unusual degree of economic and political freedom characterized the white man's life in the colony; in fact, they prized freedom as their birthright. This treasured liberty eventually became the catalyst that prompted the citizens to join in the movement to throw off the bond to England; at the same time they continued to enjoy the economic benefits of their ties to the Crown. Colonial liberty rested on British tradition. As the center of the colony's political, economic, and social life, Charlestown was (and still is to a large extent) the most Anglophile city in America. Because of the legacy of slavery, the democratic tradition in South Carolina is given short shrift in many national accounts; but just as the successful English monarchs had done since the time of Henry VIII, those in South Carolina did not make bold political moves without strong popular support and backing from their state assembly. Democratic concepts were recognized and endorsed from the early days of the colony.

In the half century before 1775, the colony of South Carolina grew by leaps and bounds. By mid-century it is estimated that South Carolina had the world's highest economic growth rate; her white citizens were the most prosperous in North America. During this time a free man with determination could make a fortune more quickly in South Carolina than at any other time in her history. The young frontier spirit allowed no preconceptions of a person's rank or background. Men were judged by their character; thus unhindered by class or rank, they were able to attain their fullest station in life by hard work. Because of this prosperity, the people took pride in their English ties. As a consequence, they moved slowly to break them.

Even though the colony was less than a century old, Charlestonians had already established a sophisticated culture. They took pride in displaying their wealth in their houses and public buildings, in the education of their children abroad, and in their support of the arts. By the 1760s, Broad Street had one of the most elegant streetscapes in the British Empire. The aristocracy worked hard, played hard, and enjoyed life with some of the most sophisticated cultural events in the colonies.

The South Carolina plantocracy was the first to use Newport, Rhode Island, as a wealthy social capital for the summer months. From May to October the moneyed elite of Charlestown would flock to the cooler air of Narragansett Bay. The passenger lists of the packet ships plying the waters between Charlestown and Newport read like a "Who's Who" of South Carolina; in fact, Newport came to be dubbed "the Carolina Hospital." Some vacationers would even charter their own vessels rather than use the packet ships for transportation.

Prosperity did not free the city from natural disaster however. The year 1752 saw two major hurricanes strike the harbor. During the first it is estimated that 80 vessels of all sorts were driven ashore; and in the second, 20. On September 15, hurricane winds raged from 4 a.m. until 9 a.m., flooding the harbor. By 11 a.m., all ships were on shore except *Hornet*, and all wharves and bridges on East Bay Street were destroyed; the water had risen ten feet above the high water mark. The Palatine (immigrant) ship *Upton* full of German settlers was driven ashore in a relatively protected area of James Island. It took dozens of slaves several months to dig a channel some three hundred feet long, thirty-five feet wide, and six feet deep to refloat her. Only the station ship *Hornet*[1] escaped grounding by cutting away her mainmast to reduce exposure to the wind and to lower her center of gravity, thus reducing pitching in the swells. Four anchors had to be employed to help her maintain position.

Tornadoes were also of great concern to mariners. In 1761 five vessels were lost in the harbor when two tornadoes struck almost simultaneously. One came down the Wando River and the other down the Ashley. They joined in the middle of the harbor heading seaward, tearing up every vessel in their path. A fleet of 40 ships that were waiting to sail barely missed disaster.

The Slave Trade

After 1748 the Board of Trade located in London began to regulate colonial trade more closely. The various colonies used lobbyists to speak for them, but unfortunately London did not always choose to listen, especially after financial problems began to mount in the 1760s. The bounty on indigo helped the colonial planters to prosper; so, too, did Parliament's removal of the duty on rice imports into England in 1767, which doubled the price that the planters received within five years. Indicative of that prosperity was the fact that in this period the importation of slaves reached a peak.

In 1672, slaves came to Carolina with settlers from Barbados, where slaves had been used extensively in the sugar plantations. In the first decade of the colony, many settlers had had slaves, both Indian and black. Thus established in the very beginning of the colony, the institution of slavery grew to enormous proportions in the Royal period; thus, the black population almost always outnumbered the white. Charlestown's slave trade was the largest and most widely developed in the colonies. Her factors sold slaves throughout the Western Hemisphere.

Slave labor discouraged the immigration of free labor to South Carolina; this forced the users of labor to import still more slaves. In the early years of the colony, rice production was primarily responsible for the vast growth in the number of slaves. At every step of the growing and harvesting process, rice demanded backbreaking hand labor, some of it dangerous. Working in the swamps brought diseases that decimated the slave population, requiring

---

[1] *Hornet* was a 14-gun sloop and at 272 tons the hurricane's winds gave her a buffeting.

The 240-ton ship *St. Helena* built at Beaufort in 1766. This is the only known portrait of a South Carolina vessel built prior to the Revolution. It was meant to please the owner, not present an accurate picture; the number of sails shown is excessive. An unusual feature is the lack of armament of any sort, which would have made her vulnerable to anything that chanced by.

The new governor of South Carolina, the Right Honorable Lord Charles Greville Montagu, second son of the Duke of Manchester, disembarking from *Fonthill* in Charlestown harbor on June 12, 1766. By this time, Charlestown was one of the bright jewels in the crown of the British Empire and at the peak of its economic prosperity compared to the rest of the New World. She was the most important city in Britain's Western Hemisphere possessions south of Philadelphia.

a continuous resupply of workers. And as the rice trade flourished, the demand for more slaves was directly proportional. Therefore, in the first half of the eighteenth century slaves were the single greatest import into the colony. During King George's War, the depressed wartime economy and a prohibitive duty[2] on slaves temporarily reduced the colony's demand for them. But when the war ended, the demand resumed and once the duty on slaves was removed in 1751, demand increased dramatically. The French and Indian War (1755–1763) did not hinder the slave trade; each year from 1752 to 1762, the number of imported laborers surpassed the previous year's number. In 1765, some 8,000 slaves were imported into South Carolina. New arrivals were quartered on Sullivan's Island for ten days to ensure that they were free of infection.

Many of the wealthier artisans of Charlestown invested in skilled slave labor. They would purchase an unskilled slave, train him, and then offer him for sale at a handsome profit or rent his service. This "for-hire" slave labor became the primary competition for immigrant artisans. Shipbuilders used numerous skilled slaves. The keen competition between the artisan owners of "for-hire slave labor" and the free labor market was a deterrent to immigrant free labor. This unfortunately stifled the expansion of the shipbuilding industry, which needed the immigrants' skills.

The Ships That Used Charlestown

As the economy expanded during the last twenty years of Royal government, so did the ships in both numbers and size. Most of the overseas ships calling at Charles Town were English owned, although often some South Carolinians held minor interests in many of them. Business syndicates were popular, allowing entrepreneurs to spread their risks and merchants to make safe, minor investments in vessels rather than take on the burden of total ownership. They could maintain some semblance of control, but retain enough capital to invest in other ventures. By 1775 some 400 vessels were trading with the colony, and at least 10 percent were locally owned. The volume of shipping was as follows:

Ships Entering and Clearing Charlestown

Year	Entering	Clearing
1755	301	281
1760	245	241
1765	450	444
1770	447	427

The rising numbers of ships clearly indicate the colony's prosperity, as the ships were also increasing in size. Only the war year of 1760 showed a decline. A list published in 1757 showed 89 ocean-going vessels of all types at anchor or docked in Charlestown harbor at one time. A similar list in 1766 showed 46 ships, 18 snows, 30 brigs, 1 billander, 47 sloops, and 11 schooners—a total of 153 ocean-going vessels in the harbor on one day. Neither list includes the large number of river and harbor craft that were certainly present.

[2] The first duty on slave imports was levied in 1703 to raise revenue. Later it was used to discourage importation.

Another indicator of the colony's prosperity was the rising level of exports. In 1763 South Carolina exports to England stood at £341,727, and rose to £579,549 by 1775. In that year the ship *Maria Wilhemina* arrived from New York. At 800 tons, she was probably the largest built in America to that time; she was certainly the largest pre-Revolutionary sailing ship to call at Charlestown.

Aiding the growing economy was the rising use of packet vessels, or ships that sailed on a schedule rather than waiting for a full cargo. The first mail packet service began on June 14, 1765, when the snow *Suffolk* departed for Falmouth, England. In 1769 a mail packet service was inaugurated to the West Indies and Bermuda.

Nicholas Pocock and the Charlestown Connection

On December 11, 1766, the ship *Lloyd* arrived from Bristol. While this was little noted at the time, on board as master was Nicholas Pocock, who was already perfecting his skills as a master painter of marine scenes. *Lloyd's* owner, Richard Champion,[3] had christened the

[3] Josiah Wedgwood praised Champion as being a better potter than he, but drove him out of England for crooked dealings. Examples of his work as a potter, made after he settled in Camden, are in the Charleston Museum.

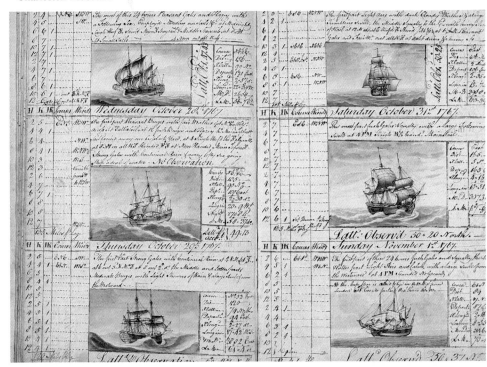

Page from Pocock's log on *Lloyd* en route from Charlestown to Bristol in 1767. In it are noted the condition of the sea and sky and of the ship and its sailing; it also contains sketches of the ship and the set of her sails according to the condition of the wind and sea, an unusual factor.

vessel with his wife's maiden name. Champion's brothers-in-law had already emigrated and lived in the port city; after the Revolution he would follow them, and settle in Camden, S. C.

When *Lloyd* came into the Cooper River, the wharves of the city were full; therefore she had to wait six days for space to load and unload. This operation ultimately took three weeks, during which two members of the ship's crew deserted. On the second voyage in March 1768, five men jumped ship. Thus was the population of the colony growing.

Between 1766 and 1769, Pocock made a total of six trading voyages to Charlestown, maintaining an average of two round trips in a year; at that time one yearly round trip was considered full employment of a vessel. This attested to his skills as a mariner. His logs of these voyages, which still survive in the National Maritime Museum in Greenwich, England, give us a rare insight into the problems and nature of eighteenth-century commerce between Charlestown and Bristol.

A quick passage was the first aim of a voyage, followed by a quick turnaround in port in order to keep port fees at a minimum. The actual time spent was dependent upon whims of the weather, problems in loading and unloading the cargo, and the delay or advance in harvesting the crops for the return cargo. *Lloyd* would arrive in Charlestown carrying dry goods and other manufactured commodities, passengers, and ballast, which would be exchanged for agricultural commodities.

While Pocock is known to few Americans today, students of the Royal Navy in the eighteenth and early nineteenth centuries study his illustrations for their accuracy and aesthetics. The most famous of his paintings was his allegory depicting "Admiral Nelson's Five Flagships." Pocock retired from the sea in 1780, and began exhibiting his work. His first exhibition at the Royal Academy attracted the attention of Sir Joshua Reynolds, and his work was hung there on a regular basis until 1815. Two years later he was afflicted with paralysis and died in 1821, but he had made an invaluable contribution to British marine art.

Here Represented

Pocock's ship portrait of *Lloyd*, a vessel of about 150 to 200 tons with a crew of sixteen men.

Rising Political Conflict

Parliament passed the Stamp Act in 1765. South Carolinians rallied behind the other colonies in opposing the law and instructed their London agent to do likewise. Because of the Navigation Acts, the colonies were already being drained of specie; therefore, they felt they were unable to bear any further taxes.

Before the Stamp Act went into effect in November 1765, the colonies firmly resolved to oppose it; South Carolinians were more passive, leaving strong opposition to their northern neighbors. South Carolinians were too busy making money to get stirred up by political turmoil.

National historians have made much of John Hancock and the other pillars of the Massachusetts colony who led the fight for independence. But they have sadly neglected South Carolina's counterpart, Henry Laurens. If there was any man with the political and economic clout to support his position, Laurens was that man. He had made a fortune in planting and mercantile pursuits and was widely respected both in America and in England as a result of his enormous business contacts. By the time of the Stamp Act, Laurens saw only two alternatives: obedience until the law was repealed, or war. He was too conservative to decide on the latter course; but just as Hancock did in Boston, he would eventually opt for and lead in the fight for independence.

Nicholas Pocock's "Prospect of Charlestown" in 1767, shortly after the end of the Stamp Act Crisis. In the center is *Lloyd*, and at right the Royal Navy station ship, probably the brig *Hornet* or *Sardoine*. To the left is a typical Charles Town schooner of the period; this one is the pilot boat that met *Lloyd* off the bar (see page 36).

Charlestown in 1774 by Thomas Leech. This painting is probably one of the most accurate pre-Revolutionary views of the harbor and city. In the center is the newly constructed Exchange building with the spire of St. Michael's Church to its left and St. Philip's Church to its right. The large building on the right is the Pinckney Mansion, completed in the 1740s and destroyed in the great

fire of 1861. Note the variety of craft in the harbor: ships, schooners, and small craft. The artist apparently came to Charles Town to complete the painting, which was then sent to London for engraving just as the Revolution began.

South Carolina sent three delegates to the Stamp Act Congress in New York that October. One of these was Christopher Gadsden, who, as the rising leader of the artisans of Charlestown, had a solid political base. He can be considered South Carolina's John Adams; like Adams, he had a radical approach to the break with England and was gifted with brilliant oratorical skills. He is remembered as the designer of the Gadsden flag with its "Don't tread on me" motto, which was very popular during the Revolution. Joining Gadsden as delegates were John Rutledge and Thomas Lynch. The Stamp Act Congress sent an appeal to the King and Parliament. South Carolina was not so much opposed to the tax as to the colony's inability to control those who imposed it. Her leaders felt that more taxes would follow if this one were left in place.

In Charlestown, events were moving along with the election of a new Assembly. Then, on October 18, the ship *Planters Adventure* arrived with the stamps and anchored under the guns of Fort Johnson. The following evening a crowd marched down Broad Street to the Cooper River. They carried an effigy of a stamp distributor, which was burned along with a coffin labeled "American Liberty." They also rifled the home of the alleged stamp collector. The royal authorities were powerless to stop them, and Lieutenant Governor Bull ordered the stamps removed to the station ship in the harbor, the 8-gun sloop *Speedwell*.

The newly formed Sons of Liberty forced the stamp collectors to resign. On November 1, when the act was supposed to take effect, the port closed down; this caused havoc with the ships arriving daily to haul away the recently harvested crops. By Christmas, ships packed the harbor, barrels of rice crammed the wharves, and idle sailors roamed the streets. Although ships began to depart empty, neither side backed down until February 3, 1766, when Bull capitulated and issued clearance certificates for the ships by stating that no stamps were available. Parliament repealed the Stamp Act in March, but Charlestown did not receive notification until May 3. When an official copy of the repeal arrived on June 4, the King's birthday, the city celebrated with a holiday; colors streamed from the ships in the harbor, church bells rang, and militia companies stood in review.

South Carolina now had two victories over royal authority; therefore, further defiance would be much easier. A wedge had been driven between the colonies and the mother country, and a bond had cemented amongst the colonies. March 18, the official day of repeal of the Stamp Act, became a national holiday ten years before independence.

However, at the same time Parliament repealed the Stamp Act, it passed the Declaratory Act, which pronounced the American colonies subordinate to the Crown and Parliament. Gadsden and his artisans, who had no intention of relaxing their opposition or vigilance, swore to defend the colony against tyranny. They would need unity to accomplish this; the political fallout of the next few years would affect the artisans most seriously. Their very livelihood would be threatened, but they were bound and determined to oppose the imperious dictates of Parliament.

Parliament had passed another act, effective September 1764, that prevented the issuance of paper money as legal tender in the colonies. The ramifications of this act fell on the debtors of the colony—the mechanics and planters. At first the effect was not noticed; however, after 1765 debts and bills became harder to pay because of the scarcity of specie, which was being steadily drained from the colonies by the trade laws. Payment of wages and business expansion became nearly impossible, and bartering became the order of the day. Many artisans and others were forced out of business. The planters became politically sympathetic to the artisans, but both were opposed by the merchants, who generally remained in the loyalist ranks; their business had suffered less.

The next political upheaval in Charlestown came with the arrival of a new customs collector from England in the spring of 1767. Smuggling had never been much of a problem in South Carolina, but the new collector, Daniel Moore, came determined to tighten up the service and make some money, most likely at the expense of South Carolinians. He enforced the laws so rigidly that he brought a deluge of suits by local merchants. In May, after a mob threatened marines who were inspecting her cargo, Moore ordered the 15-ton Carolina schooner *Active* to be seized. In June, two sloops belonging to Henry Laurens were confiscated by the authorities for engaging in questionable activities. Within six months Moore had to flee. When Laurens brought the matter to court, he won a decision against the customs officials who had seized two of his vessels on minor infractions—similar to cases against John Hancock in Boston. Two more victories were chalked up against British authority, and Laurens became an ardent and noted champion of American rights throughout the colonies.

In the Townshend Revenue Act, effective November 1767, Parliament created a new tax on all glass, lead, paint, paper, and tea imported into America. The merchants were not as agitated by the act as were the artisans who used most of the taxed products in their work. The merchants merely sold the products and could pass along the costs. The Townshend Act was passed largely to make royal officials in the colonies financially independent of the local assemblies. Opposition began in the North and quickly spread South with the nonimportation movement, essentially a boycott of British goods. Through 1768 things worsened in Boston, violence flared, and British troops landed to maintain order and authority.

Governer Montagu dissolved the South Carolina Commons when it unanimously endorsed Massachusetts' acts of defiance and urged joint action to oppose the new duty. Nondorsed Massachusetts' acts of defiance and urged joint action to oppose the new duty. Non-

Station ship *Chaleur* 1766.

importation, the only recourse, led to conflict between the planters and artisans on one side and the merchants on the other; merchants opposed nonimportation, as they would be seriously affected if commerce were halted. A compromise was reached, but enforcement was a problem. Imports from Britain dropped by more than 50 percent, making South Carolina's embargo one of the most effective in the colonies. South Carolina was well on the road to a split with England.

The artisans were delighted by the embargo and welcomed the relief from the deluge of British manufactures. Encouragement of American products became popular. While British merchants were not too badly affected by the embargo, they did persuade Lord North to repeal the act in April 1770. Repeal was another victory for the colonists, although the tax on tea remained. Repeal did bring revival for Charlestown commerce, and the more radical artisan factions went down to defeat in the next election, tempering the colony's politics for awhile.

In South Carolina subsequent bungling by the customs officials and the miscalculations of Governor Montagu further strengthened the hand of the Assembly and disrupted the regular functioning of government during the last six years of the colonial period. The Commons of the South Carolina Assembly broke the governmental deadlock by issuing certificates that could be accepted as legal tender until a tax bill could be passed. The citizens backed the Commons, saying in effect that the Crown could not take away basic rights.

To rescue the East India Company from economic plight, Parliament changed the Navigation Acts, allowing the company to ship tea directly to America instead of first landing it in England. Although this move meant that the colonists could buy tea cheaper, even with the tax, they saw it merely as a move to gain their de facto acceptance of Parliament's taxing authority. The tea tax aroused bitter controversy, as it was considered a fundamental threat to the propertied men of South Carolina who controlled the colony's legislature. They looked upon paying the tax as an admission that Parliament had the right to tax them, even without their representation in the decision-making process.

The colonies took measures to prevent the tea from landing and had it returned to England. Boston and Charlestown were exceptions to these measures. On December 2, 1773, the ship *London* arrived in Charlestown harbor with 257 chests of tea aboard. Two days later a mass meeting revived the nonimportation agreement, convincing the consignees of the East India Company by "threats and flattery" not to receive the tea. The tea, thus liable for seizure for nonpayment of duties, was landed and stored in the Exchange. While the artisan and planter factions debated how to prevent its sale, the tea remained in the Exchange until the Revolution, when it was sold to finance the war effort.

Charlestown, the only port in which the tea was allowed to land, came under much criticism from the other American colonies. It was the conservative nature of the colony's political leadership that allowed the tea to land; Christopher Gadsden and his artisan followers, now called the Sons of Liberty, were at the time little more than a controlled mob with only an indirect influence on politics. They would eventually become a popular rallying point against British rule and an effective counter to the conservative merchant leaders. But at this point, they were fairly powerless against the merchants, who had a monetary interest in the landing and sale of the taxed tea. The merchants reponded to the crisis by organizing the Charlestown Chamber of Commerce, the second such organization in America. Through it, the merchants amassed enough political clout to counter the planters and artisans, and picked two out of five of the S. C. delegates to the Continental Congress.

The violent tea party in Boston brought swift British retaliation. Although it was intended to intimidate the colonies, it had the opposite effect; they unified to support Massachusetts. When news of the British blockade of Boston reached Charlestown on June 3, 1774, a call went out for a convention in protest. Meeting in July, the convention laid the foundation for the quasi-governmental bodies that ruled the colony until an independent government was established by the Provincial Congress on March 26, 1776. Donated goods and supplies were collected in Charlestown and sent north. Then, in September, a colonial congress was called to meet in Philadelphia. Representatives to a general meeting in Charlestown adopted resolutions supporting a Continental Congress. Delegates were given powers to agree to joint measures, but agreement on nonimportation could not be reached.

Henry Middleton, John and Edward Rutledge, Christopher Gadsden, and Thomas Lynch represented South Carolina at the First Continental Congress, which met from September 5 to October 26, 1774. Gadsden and Lynch played important roles in the meeting. Most of the delegates from the other colonies opted for an embargo on exports to England. South Carolina was against this embargo because of the colony's large export crops, and her delegates almost broke up the Congress over this issue. In the end, rice was exempted; the colonies felt that including it would place an unfair burden on South Carolina's export-dominated economy.

Upon the return of the delegates to South Carolina, the general committee promptly called elections for a Provincial Congress to meet on January 11, 1775. When it met, the backcountry representatives made their unhappiness felt over the terms of the association, which included nonexportation of indigo, grown largely in their districts. To placate them, a third of the rice crop was used to compensate those who produced products subject to nonexportation; committees to enforce the nonexportation were also established. The Provincial Congress reelected the same delegation to the Second Continental Congress.

On February 27, 1775, the British House of Commons approved the ministry's plan for reconciliation, saying in effect that as long as the colonies contributed toward the support of the common defense and civil government, they would forgo any tax. The Americans realized that no provisions recognized their right to tax themselves. As long as Royal officials remained judges of the matter, it was open to controversy. Rumors of British plots to foment slave and Indian insurrections swept the colony, and shortly afterward, news of fighting at Concord and Lexington arrived in Charlestown.

Final Break with the Mother Country

The South Carolina Provincial Congress met on June 1. It quickly raised troops, authorized paper currency, and called for elections for a new provincial congress to meet on December 1. A Council of Safety was established to act as an interim executive; loyalists were spurned; and an association was signed pledging to unite to defend America and, if necessary, to sacrifice "our lives and fortunes to secure her freedom and safety." When this council met on June 16, it elected Henry Laurens president. From then until the following March, he was the de facto chief executive of South Carolina.

The new and final Royal governor, Lord William Campbell, arrived on June 18 on the sloop *Scorpion* to an alarmed city. Members of the Commons told Campbell during its last session that all peaceful means had been tried to settle things and that now it was up to the Almighty.

Uniformed men of the South Carolina State Navy with the brig *Notre Dame* in the background. The enlisted ranks wore a motley set of uniforms, according to the policies of the various ship commanders and not the Navy Board of Commissioners. Officers' uniforms were also somewhat haphazard, based as they were upon what the various officers could afford. Only the marines seemed to have a consistent set of uniforms.

The flags left to right are Gadsden naval flag, Fort Sullivan flag, and rice sheaf flag of the South Carolina Navy 1778.

DON'T TREAD ON ME

DARBY ERD

Captain   Seaman   Seaman   Boatswain   5th S.C. Regt., Continental Line

Part III

THE AMERICAN REVOLUTION

The South Carolina State Navy

As the colonies drifted toward war with England, they found themselves totally helpless on the ocean. While all possessed a militia to defend themselves on land, none had a navy; furthermore, only the northern colonies possessed any appreciable number of ships of the type that could be easily fitted for naval service. The various governments found themselves in the alarming position of having to fight the very body they had relied upon for protection at sea—the Royal Navy.

The southern colonies were in an especially perilous position regarding maritime matters. For the preceding hundred years, they had relied on ships from the northern colonies and Europe to carry their trade. They had done little to promote local ownership of ships or to encourage shipbuilding. Yet, they were completely dependent on trade at home and abroad; if it were severed, they would be in great difficulty. Therefore, South Carolina began to expend large amounts of money and energy to build and equip a state navy; few colonies would match her efforts.

There were only a few shipyards at Charlestown, Georgetown, and Beaufort, and they were mostly small enterprises geared to building and repairing small vessels. As a result, the few available shipwrights commanded high wages for their work. The acquisition of ships from local yards was a costly and painful process.

First Warship

Three months after the Massachusetts battles of Lexington and Concord in April 1775, South Carolina commissioned its first ship. As with the other colonial state navies, South Carolina's was largely defensive in nature, designed to protect local trade along the coast.

The first endeavors of the state were to obtain gunpowder for the Continental Army. In July 1775, General Washington was desperately in need of powder, and sent out pleas for supplies; South Carolina responded. The Council of Safety, as of June the colony's executive body, dispatched to Savannah aboard a barge an armed party to join a force there in capturing a British supply ship reported to be carrying the necessary material. Using a Georgia schooner, the forces captured the ship with its 16,000 pounds of powder. South Carolina received over 5,000 pounds of it, and sent 4,000 pounds to Washington's army.

To procure more of the needed gunpowder, on July 25 the Council ordered Captain Clement Lempriere to take the sloop *Commerce* to the Bahamas and seize all available gunpowder there. A former British naval officer and privateersman, Lempriere had become a shipbuilder. On the way to the Bahamas, he seized the British brig *Betsey* off St. Augustine. Lempriere bribed the crew, obtained 12,000 pounds of powder on board, and took it to Port Royal. Upon her return to Charlestown, *Commerce* ended her service in the state navy.

Through the summer of 1775 matters simmered in Charlestown and came to a boil when the Council of Safety learned that Governor William Campbell was plotting with loyalists in the Upcountry. Campbell supposedly was expecting British troops to come to his aid any day. When the Council learned of this plot, it decided to occupy Fort Johnson near the harbor entrance. During the night of September 14, 1775, about 150 men of the Second South Carolina Regiment of Foot under Colonel William Moultrie shoved off from Gadsden's Wharf and drifted down the Cooper River on the ebb tide to James Island. There they landed to the west of Fort Johnson. Moving quickly upon the fort, they found it abandoned; a small garrison of British troops had left after partially carrying out their orders to destroy it. The South Carolina troops hauled up the first South Carolina flag, a navy blue emblem with a silver crescent in the upper right corner. The origin of the crescent is unknown, but it was at the time the insignia of the South Carolina troops. A Charlestown merchant, Theodore Trezevant, had supplied the uniforms and selected silver crescents for the front of the helmets.

The next day Governor Campbell dissolved the Commons House of Assembly. With the great seal of His Majesty's province of South Carolina, he fled aboard the station ship *Tamar*, a 16-gun sloop then anchored far out in Charlestown harbor. *Tamar* met up with another British ship, the 8-gun *Cherokee*, and the two began to harass and occasionally seize ships entering and leaving the harbor. The dissolution of the Assembly and the flight of the royal governor symbolized the collapse of royal authority and the real beginning of the Revolution in South Carolina.

The local authorities were still reluctant to precipitate a break with the Crown. At the same time they were unsure as to how to end the threat posed by the British men-of-war in the harbor; forbidding harbor pilots to serve the ships only increased tensions. Matters swayed back and forth until October, when the state authorities purchased a schooner named *Defence*.

Due to the decline in commerce caused by the British blockade of the harbor entrance, sufficient seamen were readily available for *Defence*. Simon Tufts, a transplanted New Englander, became commander of this first permanent naval vessel; it was anchored between the city and Fort Johnson to intercept surveillance boats from the enemy ships.

In November *Eagle* and *Hibernia*, two pilot boats, were taken into the public service. They were based in the Stono River to avoid British warships off the harbor entrance, and patrolled the coast to warn all vessels to steer for other ports. The Provincial Congress also created a navy department with Edward Blake, a wealthy factor experienced in maritime affairs, as its superintendent.

The Battle of Hog Island

On November 11, the inevitable clash came when *Defence* was ordered to oversee the sinking of four schooners in Hog Island Creek; the sunken ships were to obstruct passage by British ships into the Cooper River. William Henry Drayton, president of the Provincial Congress and a member of the Council of Safety, was on board *Defence*. He was determined to commence hostilities in order to force a stronger public stand on the war. As the schooners were being prepared for sinking, *Tamar* fired six short shots at *Defence*, who returned fire from her longer and heavier guns. *Cherokee* joined the battle, which lasted intermittently until *Defence* withdrew at seven o'clock the next morning. Damage was minor and there were no serious casualties in what came to be known as the Battle of Hog Island. Three of the schooners were sunk in the channel. An armed boat from *Tamar* towed the fourth to shallow water after setting it on fire.

ROYAL NAVY OPPONENTS AT HOG ISLAND

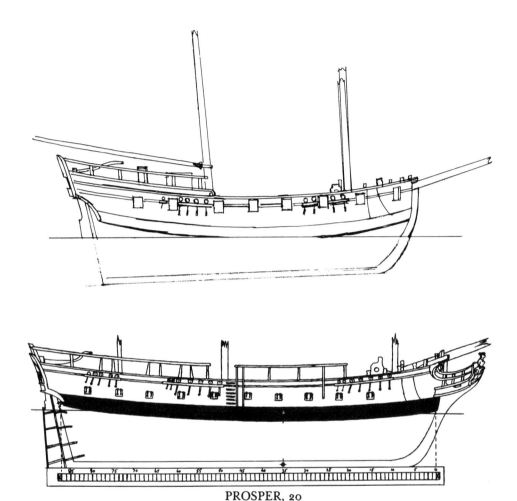

PROSPER, 20

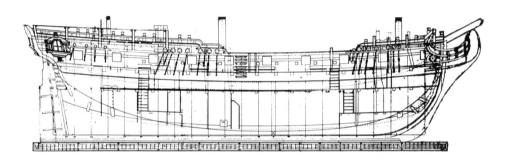

Draughts of HMS *Tamar*, a 343-ton, 16-gun, ship-rigged, sloop-of-war (corvette). Adding to the disparity in size between *Tamar* and *Defence* is the fact that *Tamar* was built as a warship with a trained crew. In addition she was supported by several other warships and armed merchantmen. *Tamar* was launched in 1758 so that by the beginning of the Revolution her life expectancy was nearing an end. She was renamed *Pluto* in 1777.

Conjectural draughts of the former merchant ship *Prosper* and the schooner *Defence* taken in hand as warships for the South Carolina Navy. *Defence* was a sixty-foot-long (keel length) schooner that was converted into a warship by the addition of two 9-pounder guns, six 6-pounder guns, and four 4-pounder guns. She had a quarterdeck (no forecastle), a narrow stern, and a round bow. Her sides were painted black with a good sheer, and her bottom white. The insides of her sixteen gunports were painted bright red. The mainmast was stepped far aft, making her appear shorter than she was.

   Defence had been hastily converted from a merchant schooner and her crew was largely untrained for combat. Therefore, at the Battle of Hog Island, the proper course for *Defence* was to avoid action.

   These were the first vessels of the South Carolina Navy that were capable of ocean cruising for any appreciable time.

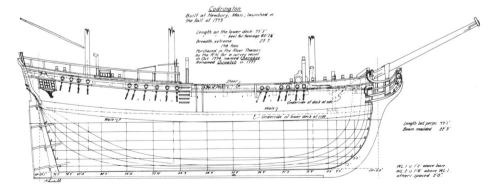

Draughts of HMS *Cherokee*, the former American-built merchant vessel *Codrington*. *Cherokee* had a trained crew and therefore was a functioning warship, which gave her an advantage over *Defence*.

Drayton had achieved his goal of commencing hostilities. The Provincial Congress gave its support by immediately appointing a committee to consider adding ships to the navy. It also recommended that *Prosper*, a British merchant ship then in the harbor, be impressed into service as a warship. The British captain naturally objected, but she was seized and armed with eight 12-pounder, eight 6-pounder, and four other guns, becoming the fourth vessel of the state navy. Obtaining a captain and crew was more difficult. Colonel Moultrie was ordered to detach from his command forty men who were "best acquainted with maritime affairs" and to assign them to *Prosper* for one month. After two other officers declined command, Drayton, who knew nothing at all about ships or sailing, accepted. The Council hoped that his energy and enthusiasm would prove a shot in the arm for the new state navy.

British Harassment

The shots exchanged in the Battle of Hog Island were the only signs of all-out warfare. The British ships offshore were still obtaining supplies from their local agents, and merchant ships were able to enter and leave port at will despite some harassment. The Provincial Congress had even agreed to notify Governor Campbell on *Tamar* before an attack occurred upon the British ships. Both sides seemed reluctant to engage in active hostilities against those who had previously been friends and fellow countrymen.

At the end of November the 10-gun sloop *Scorpion* joined the British blockading squadron, and a few days later one of her longboats captured two schooners as they left the harbor. Now a veritable fleet of the Royal Navy stood offshore; it consisted of three warships, two schooners, two sloops, and a supply ship. To oppose them, the South Carolina State Navy could offer only four ex-merchant ships and the newly acquired shallow-draft coasting schooner *Comet*. She had been refitted as a brigantine by adding square sails to her foremast to make her more maneuverable. *Comet* was armed with a mixed battery of twelve to fourteen 4-pounder and 12-pounder guns.

The local authorities feared bombardment of the city far more than a British invasion. Consequently, new guns were placed around the harbor, and the militia was kept on alert. The authorities also had to counter British forays against outlying houses and plantations, in which slaves and other property had been stolen. The British supply agent in Charlestown, William Price, was ordered to cut off supplies to the blockading ships if the thefts did not cease and the stolen slaves returned. The warning was ignored, and the ban was put into effect, but it was made clear that it would be rescinded if the slaves were returned. Instead of giving in, the British chose to obtain their needs elsewhere. The fleet departed during the first week of January 1776.

In the meantime, on December 22, King George III declared that after the first of the year, all vessels captured by British ships leaving American ports would be deemed lawful prizes. Before that ruling took effect and Charlestown remained quiet, the Council of Safety enlarged and improved harbor defenses while ships of the state navy patrolled against smuggling and other unlawful activities.

The brief period of peace came to an end in the middle of January 1776, when the British squadron returned, augmented by the 28-gun sixth-rate *Syren* and the 16-gun *Raven*. The city went into panic, fearing that the long-awaited bombardment and invasion was about to begin. *Prosper* and *Defence* took up station in the harbor, ferrying troops and supplies to the fort under construction on Sullivan's Island. To everyone's relief, the enemy ships merely remained at anchor for several days and then put back out to sea.

Coastal Operations

With the enemy gone from off the bar, *Defence* and *Comet* made several short cruises along the coast in search of smugglers and other marauders. In late March *Comet* captured the British 10-gun merchant sloop *General Clinton*. Meanwhile, another British warship appeared off the bar, presumably the frigate *Syren*; she had appeared off the North Edisto River while *Defence* lay there in February. *Defence* was taking powder and supplies to the battery stationed at the river entrance. *Syren* armed her boats and sent them in to board *Defence*, which drove them off with grape-shot.

Due to the shortage of seamen, the crews of laid-up ships were constantly transferred to the operating vessels. The switching of men from vessel to vessel diminished the overall efficiency of the crews. In December, Captain Cochran received permission from the Continental Congress to venture north to recruit up to 500 additional men. Massachusetts agreed to allow Cochran to recruit there, as long as he did not take any men from the Continental Army or other forces defending Massachusetts. Two days after the British evacuated Boston on March 17, 1776, Cochran's recruits sailed for Charlestown in the sloop *Providence*; however, they were far less than the 500 men he sought. They included Thomas Pickering from Piscataway, who would later distinguish himself in the service of the South Carolina Navy. Although additional recruits were signed up in Savannah, the state navy's manpower problem continued, and deepened, throughout the war.

The State Navy Takes Shape

In the spring of 1776, the General Assembly passed measures to set up a naval bureaucracy, including a court of admiralty to have jurisdiction over prizes brought into port. The Council of Safety directed the day-to-day affairs of the navy until March 26, 1776, when the new constitution went into effect and the colony officially became a sovereign state ruled by a president and a privy council. In September, President John Rutledge recommended to the legislature an act modeled after one passed in Virginia, setting up a board of commissioners to direct and administer the navy; the legislature passed the act.

Life in the South Carolina State Navy was trying at best. The meager pay was no incentive for naval service; the only inducement was the lure of prize money. The state navy followed the prize money allotment formulas of the Continental Navy: the crew received one third of the prize money for merchantmen captured, and one half of the prize money for warships captured. The remainder went to the state. In 1777, the allotment changed so that crewmembers received one half for captured merchantmen and all prize money for captured warships.

On May 22, an altercation took place off the bar. Returning to port with prizes, *Comet* and *Defence* were met by the 28-gun British sixth-rate *Sphinx* and the schooner *Pensacola Packet*. The enemy took after *Comet* and her prize, the large ship *St. James*, which ran for the bar. The ebb tide caused *St. James*, which drew some seventeen feet of water, to run aground. Coming to assist, *Defence* ran aground also. The enemy made for *St. James*, which was loaded with rum and sugar, and set it on fire. *Defence* fired on the British as best she could until the tide came in and freed her. She was able to seek safety in the harbor, but *St. James* was a total loss.

The first major blow by British forces was about to fall on Charlestown.

The naval Battle of Hog Island commences as *Tamar* opens fire on *Defence* covering the scuttling of four schooners.

Charlestown—First American Victory

"Now bold as a Turk,
I proceed to New York,
Where with Clinton and Howe
you may find me.
I've the wind in my tail, and
am hoisting sail,
To leave Sullivan's Island
behind me."

—Old ballad giving the American version of
Parker's dispatches to the Lords of the Admiralty

During the middle and latter part of 1775, the British army at Boston had been under siege by the Continental Army. As a diversionary maneuver designed to relieve the situation at Boston, the British high command decided to launch an attack against the South. The British were encouraged by the former southern colonial governors, who maintained that the South was a bulwark of loyalty to the Crown that needed only a royal show of strength to be brought back into the fold.

When John Rutledge returned from a long session of the Continental Congress in February, he brought with him warnings of a British move against the South. Meanwhile the British commander in America, Sir William Howe, had selected Major General Henry Clinton to lead an expedition; Sir Peter Parker would be in command of the naval portion, which was then being collected at Cork, Ireland. Upon reaching Cape Fear in March 1776, Clinton learned that the loyalists in North Carolina had been soundly defeated and scattered at Moore's Creek Bridge on February 27.

Clinton reviewed his plans while he waited for Parker, whose force took until mid-May to arrive. It consisted of ten warships and some thirty transports carrying the troops of Major General Charles Cornwallis, who was destined to become a familiar figure in South Carolina before the war was over. The fleet had left Cork in mid-February and encountered heavy weather on the way to Cape Fear. Parker's flagship was the 50-gun *Bristol*, which had been commissioned the previous October at Sheerness. Clinton was inclined to cancel the southern expedition and return north, as his orders read; however, Parker was a weathered old sea dog eager to leave his mark. He sent two ships to scout the Charlestown area. Their report of weak defenses only whetted his ambition. Clinton had no intention of trying to seize the city with the small force under his command, but he reasoned that Fort Sullivan could be captured and held by a relatively small force, effectively bottling up the port. This move would allow him and the main body of his troops to return north; Charlestown would be left to strangle to death.

Charlestown Prepares for Battle

Christopher Gadsden was attending the Continental Congress assembled in Philadelphia, so the state's military preparedness was left to Colonel William Moultrie, an old Indian

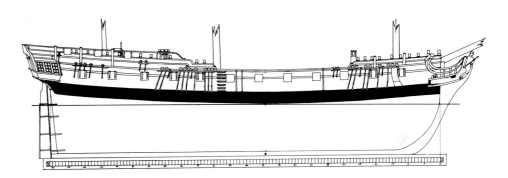

Draught of the frigate *Actaeon*, which grounded on the Middle Ground shoal opposite Fort Sullivan. *Actaeon* was one of a new class of frigates that were being built when the Revolution commenced.

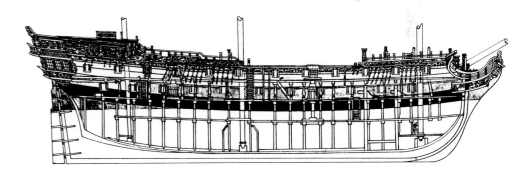

Inboard profile of the 50-gun, 1,049-ton *Bristol*, flagship of Sir Peter Parker in the attack on Fort Sullivan. *Experiment* was similar. With two full decks of guns, they were quite intimidating, even though the fourth-rate, 50-gunners were no longer considered of sufficient power to participate in the line of battle in a major fleet engagement. They were designed as flagships for foreign service. The 50-gunners were smaller and less expensive to build and maintain than ships-of-the-line, yet they were large enough to carry an admiral and his staff and powerful enough to be able to defend themselves against anything that they might reasonably expect to encounter.

fighter who had helped to engineer the seizure of Fort Johnson. Early in March, he and the Second South Carolina Regiment arrived on Sullivan's Island to complete construction of a large fort. They found a number of slaves and artisans who had been working there since January 10. Thousands of palmetto logs were brought to the fort for its construction. The gun platforms were cut from two-inch planks and pegged together. The fort's merlons, or solid intervals between embrasures, stood ten feet higher than the gun platforms. By June only the walls facing the channel on the southeast and southwest sides and the two channel bastions were finished. In the unfinished parts of the fort, heavy planks, seven feet high, stood upright with loopholes provided for riflemen to beat off infantry attacks.

The only entrance to Charlestown's bar for deep-draft vessels was off Lighthouse Inlet between Morris and Folly Islands. Inside the bar off Morris Island was "Five Fathom Hole." From there, the main ship channel led to within a few hundred yards of Sullivan's Island. It then turned west into the inner harbor. The new fort was placed at this key point to allow it to rake an approaching enemy ship's bow with cannon fire. In order to head into the harbor, the enemy would have to make a sharp turn in front of the fort, thus exposing the stern to more raking fire.

Late in May 1776, *Sphinx* and *Pensacola Packet* reconnoitered Charlestown and returned north to Cape Fear after their skirmish with *Comet* and her prize. Charlestonians knew that the main force would not be long in coming.

The British Fleet Arrives

On May 30 Parker's squadron weighed anchor and headed south with Clinton's troops. On June 1 the fleet of fifty sail appeared off the bar to the alarm of the city. However, the arrival of General Charles Lee boosted the morale of the South Carolina troops, for he was considered the best flag officer in the colonial army; he had been considered for the position of commander in chief, which Washington had won. Although his brusque demeanor at first offended the officers, he became highly respected and was thought by many to be equal to reinforcements of 1,000 men.

Lee was appalled at what he found. He termed Fort Sullivan a slaughter pen, but Rutledge refused to abandon it. Though nominally in command of only the Continental soldiers on the scene, Lee was also given command of the South Carolina forces, with orders to

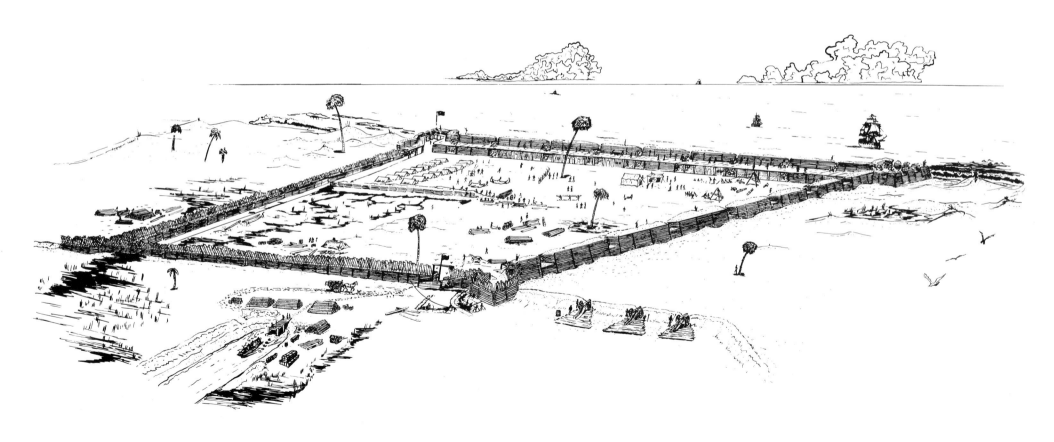

Perspective of Fort Sullivan. Note the uncompleted rear and east sides.

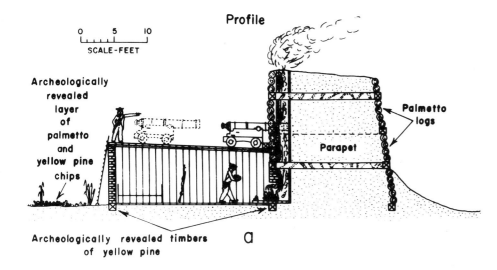

Profile

SCALE-FEET
0   5   10

Archeologically revealed layer of palmetto and yellow pine chips

Palmetto logs

Parapet

Archeologically revealed timbers of yellow pine

a

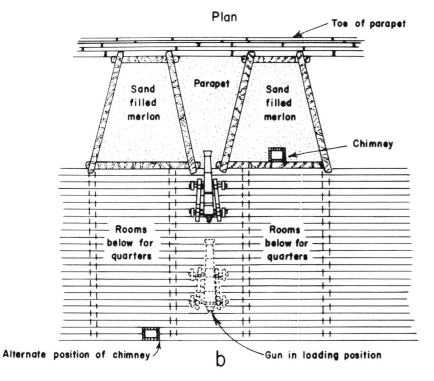

Plan

Toe of parapet

Sand filled merlon

Parapet

Sand filled merlon

Chimney

Rooms below for quarters

Rooms below for quarters

Alternate position of chimney

Gun in loading position

b

Cross section of a gun emplacement in Fort Sullivan.

consult with Rutledge in their handling. Moultrie was so slow in responding to his orders that Lee resolved to replace him; but the British attacked before he could do so.

Lee insisted that the fort be provided with an avenue of possible retreat to the mainland. Moultrie tried to execute the order by constructing a pontoon bridge of planks placed on hogshead barrels. This did not work. The barrels sank if a group of men tried to cross on them. General Christopher Gadsden eventually completed a usable bridge.

During the first week the British took soundings of the bar and placed buoys to guide their ships through the channel. The flagship *Bristol* had to offload her guns onto a transport in order to make it over the bar on June 10 with the deep-draft transports. They anchored with the smaller ships in "Five Fathom Hole" off Morris Island. There *Bristol* reshipped her guns. On June 16 an American sloop arriving from the West Indies with a cargo of gunpowder, arms, and rum was surprised by the British presence. Through the ignorance of her pilot, the sloop grounded while trying to escape. Armed boats from the British fleet burned the vessel, which eventually blew up. Her crew escaped ashore.

In a small sloop, General Clinton took two days to survey the islands to the north. He then decided that a landing on Sullivan's Island in heavy surf in the face of American fire would be hazardous. Long Island, now called the Isle of Palms, was unoccupied. Clinton was told that the inlet between it and Sullivan's Island was only 18 inches deep at low tide; this would enable his troops to wade across. On June 18 after most of the British ships had crossed

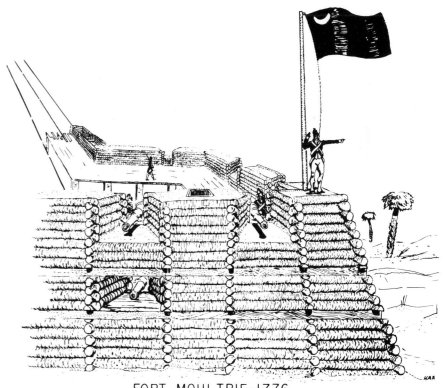

FORT MOULTRIE-1776
A Reconstructive View of the Southeast Bastion

Nicholas Pocock's rendering of Parker's fleet early in the attack on Fort Sullivan. While the artist was not on the scene, he was quite familiar with Charlestown and the ships involved. In the right foreground is *Actaeon* leading the British frigates to attack the west flank of Fort Sullivan; the bomb vessel *Thunder* is to her right. The large warship at center left is probably *Bristol* or *Experiment*, with two frigates to her starboard.

Parker's fleet bombarding Fort Sullivan toward the end of the action after the flood tide had turned the ships' starboard sides toward the fort. This is one of the few good paintings by a participant in the battle, Lt. William Elliott, Royal Navy (fl. 1784–1792). *Bristol* is the large ship to right of center to the immediate left of Fort Sullivan. The three grounded frigates are in the left background. The ship at extreme right is probably the frigate *Active*.

the bar and anchored in Five Fathom Hole, Clinton appealed to the patriots to return to the fold as His Majesty's loyal subjects. When Rutledge rejected the plea, Clinton and 500 soldiers landed on Long Island to face Colonel Thomson's regiment of 300 rangers across Breach Inlet on Sullivan's Island. Much to his consternation, Clinton now found that the inlet was seven feet deep at low tide because of the easterly winds. He described the situation to Parker, who replied that the Royal Navy could take the fort alone.

The square-shaped fort, complete only on the seaward front, did not present an invincible image to the British. The walls were 16 feet wide, constructed of palmetto logs and filled with sand. They rose ten feet above wooden platforms on which artillerymen and their guns were stationed. A motley collection of guns guarded the uncompleted rear of the fort.

Although few of the Americans had much faith in Moultrie's palmetto fort, the commander remained unshaken and Rutledge adamantly refused to order it abandoned. The troops grew uneasy as they anticipated battle, and discipline was strictly enforced. Even the officers were held in line. By late June Moultrie commanded a garrison of less than 400 men with 31 guns mounted in the fort. The guns were mostly British 18-pounders and French 24-pounders.[1] The nineteen 26-pounder French cannon had been given by King George II for the defense of Charlestown. They had come from the French ship-of-the-line *Foudroyant*, which had been captured by the Royal Navy off Barcelona in 1758.

The local citizens cooperated with the military leaders in their preparations for the defense of the city. Lead was gathered and melted into musket balls. Reinforcements of Continental Army regulars arrived from North Carolina and Virginia to aid the threatened city.

On June 16 Major General Charles Cornwallis and his brigade of 2,500 men went ashore on Long Island to supplement the troops landed a few days earlier. Boats from the fleet were to ferry them across Breach Inlet once the warships began the assault on the fort. Across the inlet, Thomson's Rangers were augmented by two cannon and 100 additional men. There Captain De Brahm had erected defensive breastworks of palmetto logs on which were mounted an 18- and a 6-pounder gun. The battle seemed set.

On June 27 the 50-gun *Experiment*, which had arrived two days earlier, came across the bar. The British battle fleet now consisted of the following ships:

Bristol	50 guns	Commodore Sir Peter Parker
		Captain John Morris (killed)
Experiment	50 guns	Captain Scott (killed)
Solebay	28 guns	Captain Thomas Symonds
Actaeon	28 guns	Captain Christopher Atkins
Active	28 guns	Captain William Williams
Syren	28 guns	Captain Christopher Furneaux
Sphinx	20 guns	Captain Anthony Hunt
Ranger	armed ship	Captain Roger Willis
Friendship	armed ship	Captain Charles Hope
Thunder	bomb ship	Captain James Reid
Carcass	bomb ship	Captain Thomas Dring

The British force totaled some 270 guns; in the fort there were only 31.

At 9:30 a.m. on June 28, Parker signaled Clinton that the attack would begin in one hour. An hour later *Bristol* fired a signal gun and the fleet weighed anchor and got underway. Across the cove in Mount Pleasant, General Lee watched the British ships advance toward the fort under topsails with battle flags flying. Off the fort, they maneuvered into firing position, drawing their sails in and letting go their anchors with springs on the cables; this would allow them to turn their hulls to fire in different directions while at anchor. The bomb ketch *Thunder* anchored 3,000 yards from the fort with a supply ship as an escort. In a line west to east opposite the main portion of the fort and 400 yards out, *Active*, *Bristol*, *Experiment*, and *Solebay* took positions slowly. All of this took place in plain sight of the Charlestonians, who feared that the enemy would quickly pull down the world about them—so powerful and invincible did the fleet appear.

At 11:20 Moultrie's men commenced firing with four or five shots at *Active*, the first ship in range. Moultrie then directed his gunners' attention to the flagship *Bristol* and her largest consort, *Experiment*. Ten minutes later *Thunder's* gunners began to lob 13-inch mortar bombs toward the fort. As the British ships maneuvered into position, their broadsides lashed

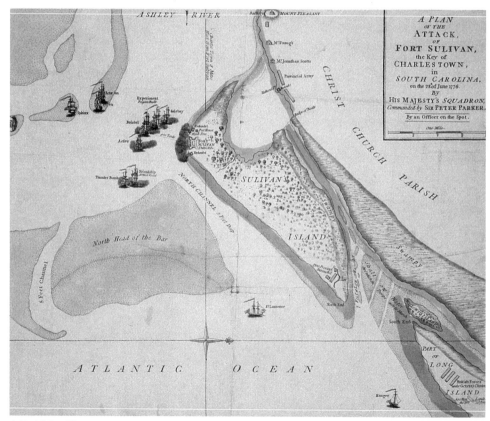

A British officer produced this map of the disposition of British forces. In order to justify Clinton's inability to cross Breach Inlet, it has been shown here as much wider than it was and riddled with deep channels. See the rear endpapers for a correct layout, which has changed little in 200 years.

---

[1] Due to the different methods of measuring pounds in France and England at the time, a French 24-pounder gun was a 26-pounder by British measure.

out with a deep booming retort. The concussion of the discharge filled the American ranks with apprehension; then the walls of the fort shook as the guns hit home. The cannonballs buried themselves in the sand and pulpy palmetto logs with no telling effect on the structure of the fort. When the English gunners across the water heard the cheers of the defenders, they replied with another barrage. The ships shook from the impact as shot after shot from the fort fell upon them. Moultrie's gunners took cool and deliberate aim to make sure that their limited supply of ammunition counted.

Parker's frigates *Syren* and *Actaeon* and the sixth-rate *Sphinx* had been placed westward of the British line to prevent fireships and other vessels from attacking the warships firing on the fort, and to enfilade the fort and cut off any retreat. In taking up their positions, they ran afoul of each other; all three ended up on a shoal called Middle Ground where Fort Sumter was eventually built. At 1:30, *Syren* and *Sphinx* rejoined the battle; *Sphinx* had lost her bowsprit in a collision with her consort. *Actaeon* was hard aground. At about this time, *Thunder* had to withdraw from battle, incapacitated because overcharging of her mortars had broken the supporting beds.

Inside the fort, the gunners stood to their guns. Unfortunately only some 28 rounds of ammunition per gun remained at hand, but the palmetto logs withstood the cannonading and protected the men. Casualties came only from direct hits through the embrasures.

Meanwhile, Colonel Thomson was holding off General Clinton's schooners and boats advancing across Breach Inlet. The British vessels ran aground on sandbars. When the heavily burdened soldiers jumped overboard to wade ashore, they sank over their heads in the treacherous hollows. Artillery and musket fire raked them in the water and few of Clinton's men made it. Those that did withdrew at nightfall.

Early in the afternoon, the fort's flagstaff was shot down and fell outside its walls. Sergeant Jasper leapt over the ramparts, walked the length of the beach in front of the fort, and recovered the colors. He attached them to a sponge staff that was handed to him and firmly planted it in the sand at the top of the wall. He had been exposed to enemy fire the entire time, but miraculously returned to his position unhurt.

The British casualty lists reflected the American fire directed at the largest two ships. Commodore Parker was wounded in the head, and at one point his britches were supposedly rent by the American fire! *Bristol* suffered heavily, especially on her upper deck. Every man upon it was injured or killed. With the frigates aground and Thomson's Rangers holding off the troops of Clinton and Cornwallis, Moultrie's men in the fort were able to concentrate their efforts against the ships in front of them.

At midafternoon, the fire of the fort slackened due to the shortage of powder, but later that day, Lee arrived from the mainland with 700 pounds of powder from the sloop *Defence*. To allow Lee's entrance, some men under Francis Marion had to leave their guns and remove the timber that barricaded the entrance to the fort. When the British saw this, they concluded that the fort was being abandoned; quickly they felt their error. Lee later reported that he found the men "determined and cool to the last degree, their behaviour would have done honor to the most seasoned veteran."

Withdrawal

Around four in the afternoon the tide began to ebb and the British ships put out additional anchors astern. When the fort's fire resumed, one shot carried away the stern anchors on *Bristol*, causing her to drift with the tide,[2] her stern exposed to a murderous raking fire as it swung past the fort. The British stuck to their guns, but by 9 p.m. Parker had had enough;[3] with darkness closing in, he signaled his ships to cut their cables and move out of range before the ebb tide was out. Francis Marion fired the last shot from the fort at the retreating enemy. In the withdrawal, *Active* tailed on shore, but boats of the squadron were immediately sent to her assistance and got her afloat.

Bristol had been hit 70 times and had 40 dead and 71 wounded. Her main[4] and mizzen topmasts were shot away, and the mizzenmast fell over the side the next day before it could be secured. Two lower deck guns were dismounted. *Experiment* suffered 23 dead, 56 wounded; *Active* and *Solebay*, 15 casualties. The captains of both *Bristol* and *Experiment* later died of their wounds. Against these casualties the fort suffered only 12 killed and 25 wounded.

The next morning, Captain Jacob Milligan of *Prosper* led a flotilla of small boats against the stranded *Actaeon*, whereupon her crew set her on fire and took to their own boats. Milligan boarded the burning ship and fired a few of her guns at the damaged *Bristol*. He removed some trophies, including the ship's bell and flag. Later, *Actaeon's* magazine exploded, sending up a pillar of smoke that expanded at the top and seemed to take the shape of a palmetto tree! Sixteen of her guns were later recovered and used to arm shore batteries.

It took Parker's fleet until August 3 to get back over the bar; the flagship became stranded for a while and several ships needed extensive repairs. *Prosper* managed to slip past the British ships and got to sea, seizing a stray brigantine aground off Dewee's Inlet.

After leaving Charlestown the British ships returned north to participate in Lord Howe's descent upon Long Island and the subsequent battles for New York. The fort still stood, but not much else around it did. Moultrie became a general, and the fort was renamed in his honor. As a symbol of the victory, a palmetto tree was added to the center of the state flag. Jasper received Rutledge's sword. The victory was strong tonic for American morale in the North, which was reeling under the British victories.

After the British departure, the southern colonies won a reprieve that enabled them to purchase and transport war materiel from the neutral islands in the West Indies to the beleaguered patriots in the North.

---

[2] Midshipman James Saumarez (later Admiral) made several attempts to reset *Bristol's* cable. Parker promoted him to lieutenant for his actions.

[3] Some seamen of American birth who had been serving in *Bristol* deserted to the American side after the battle. Her crew reportedly said, "We were told the Yankees would not stand two fires [broadsides], but we never saw better fellows." When the fire of the fort slackened and some cried, "They have done fighting," others replied, "By God, we are glad of it, for we never had such a drubbing in our lives. All the common men of the fleet spoke loudly in praise of the garrison"—a note of admiration so frequent in generous enemies that we may be assured that it was echoed on the quarterdeck also. They could allow it, for beyond the mortification of defeat, there was no stain on their own record, no flinching under the severity of the losses. Although a number of their own men were comparatively raw, volunteers came forward from the transports almost as one man when they knew that the complements of the ships were short through sickness. From Clowes, William Laird. *A History of the Royal Navy*, vol. III:379.

[4] Nine shots were found in the mainmast.

The State Navy, Part II

During Commodore Parker's attack in June, the ships of the South Carolina State Navy watched helplessly from the sidelines. *Prosper* was decommissioned, her guns landed to augment the firepower of the forts, and her crew was dispersed among the other active state warships in the harbor. She was never recommissioned, and that fall she was sold out of the service. Only *Defence* was near the battle, at anchor in the cove behind Fort Moultrie. Her part in the battle had been to supply powder to the fort when its supply ran out.

Several days after the battle at Fort Moultrie, one of Parker's transports, *Glasgow Packet*, grounded on the bar. Thomas Pickering, captain of a merchant ship in the harbor, seized an opportunity. Grabbing a flat boat, probably one of those used to haul building supplies to Fort Moultrie, he hastily armed it with an 18-pounder gun and some swivels; then, with twenty-four men, he set out to attempt to capture the grounded ship.

Glasgow Packet was helpless, and there were no other British warships to come to her aid. The stranded ship was refloated on the flood tide and brought ignominiously into the harbor, captured by a barge. The victorious flatboat was then christened *Revenge* and stationed near Fort Moultrie as a floating battery. Pickering was rewarded with command of *Defence*.

On August 5, 1776, the Declaration of Independence was proclaimed in Charlestown with great celebration. At noon, the militia was drawn up on Broad Street, and President Rutledge and other high officials inspected the troops. The document was read to the assembled dignitaries and citizens; it was read a second time at the Exchange, where it was greeted with cheers and cannon salutes.

Later that summer, the 100-ton brig *Islington* was purchased and taken into the state

View of Charlestown from James Island from F. W. Des Barres, 1777. Note the walled defenses of the city along the Cooper River.

navy as *Notre Dame*, with Robert Cochran as captain. *Notre Dame* carried a battery of eighteen 4-pounders and numerous swivels. She was manned by a crew of ninety-four officers and men, including the soldiers from the Fifth regiment. She was low-built, with a pro-

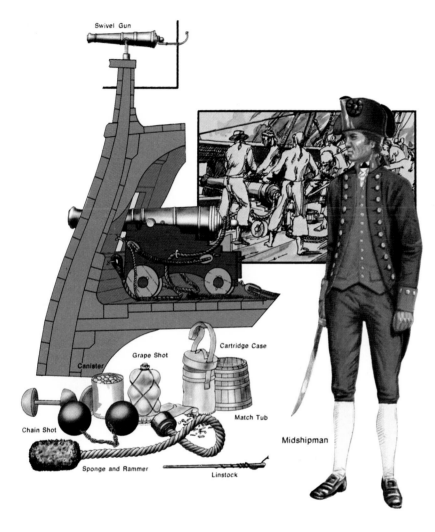

Swivel Gun

Canister

Grape Shot

Cartridge Case

Chain Shot

Match Tub

Sponge and Rammer

Linstock

Midshipman

Guns, Projectiles, and Accessories

Most naval guns were similar in construction and function, differing only in size. Swivel guns, mounted on the bulwarks or in the mast tops, fired a ball weighing from a half to three-quarters of a pound, while frigates carried 18-pounder cannon. Solid shot was generally used in naval engagements. Often the opening broadside was fired with double-shotted guns, two balls fired at once from each cannon. But there were other projectiles used for special purposes. Bar shot and chain shot were fired into the rigging, where they could shred sails and cordage, disabling a ship. Grape shot, canister, and langrage were effective antipersonnel weapons, especially when raked the full length of an enemy ship. Some of the equipment used in working the guns is shown above.

jecting figurehead and a plain stern with yellow moldings. A fast sailer, *Notre Dame* turned out to be one of the most successful vessels in the state navy.

Notre Dame was immediately dispatched to France to take on supplies at the port of Nantes. She was the first American vessel to enter a French port, but she did so disguised as a Dutch vessel. Captain Cochran and his ship remained in France until October in order to confer with the American representatives in Paris, Silas Deane and Benjamin Franklin. On the way back to Charlestown, *Notre Dame* captured the merchantman *Mackerel*, but she was recaptured by the 20-gun sixth-rate *Camilla* off Antigua and the prize crew aboard her was hanged for piracy.

The next year *Notre Dame* put to sea again, under Captain Seymour. She fell in with a British brig of sixteen guns and after a twenty-five-minute battle, the enemy surrendered. Lieutenant Hall from *Notre Dame* was put aboard as prize master. After evading a long pursuit by the 20-gun sixth-rate *Daphne*, he arrived safely in Georgetown, where the brig brought a good return to *Notre Dame's* crew. Subsequently Seymour resigned her command, and Hall took over. He was only twenty-two years old.

That same summer of 1776, *Defence* was converted into a brigantine; yards were added to the fore and aft sails on her foremast. She and the other larger ships supplemented their regular duty by earning money transporting state-owned rice, indigo, and other goods to the West Indies to exchange for weapons. Trade to that section thrived as the colonies brought in war materiels from the neutral Dutch, Spanish, and French islands.

The South Carolina State Navy began to expand its activities by venturing as far north as Virginia and south to Florida and the West Indies. St. Augustine, now a thriving British port, was a popular haunt for state ships who were after prize money. *Defence* left Charlestown on November 6 carrying cargo to the West Indies with orders to scour the coast for enemy ships while en route. While in the West Indies, the ship incurred tremendous expenses that the state government did not completely repay for over eighteen months. However, by February Captain Pickering and *Defence* were back in Charlestown with two prizes.

Shortages of funds, manpower, and equipment plagued the vessels. Men were shifted from incoming ships to join those departing; other ships short of gear had to be augmented. At the end of March 1777, *Defence* sailed on her last voyage, which was to raid enemy commerce. On April 2, a few days out of Charlestown off the Delaware Capes, she fell in with the 44-gun *Roebuck* and the 20-gun *Perseus*. Her poor sailing qualities made her vulnerable. Being unable to outrun such superior adversaries, Captain Pickering struck her colors. He was captured but later exchanged, and returned to New Hampshire; he was killed at sea shortly before the end of the war. *Defence* was taken into the Royal Navy as *Hinchinbrook*.

Later that spring, the brigantine *Comet* also fell in with enemy warships, but she eluded them. Her luck ran out a year later when, under the command of James Pyne, she was captured by the frigate *Daphne*. The British took *Comet* to New York and cut her down to a galley, armed with an 18-pounder forward and six 6-pounders amidships. The forays by state vessels continued until the end of the war. Some of them ranged considerable distances on voyages that lasted two to three months.

Warship Construction

Late in 1776, the state ordered the construction of two galleys, its first locally built warships. Galleys were ideally suited to the narrow, tidal rivers of the coast where winds were unpredictable at best and slaves could be used for rowers. This lessened the manpower requirements. The new galleys were apparently lateen-rigged craft somewhat similar to those built in the 1790s in Charleston. They were manned with twenty oars and carried both carriage and swivel guns. The sterns were transomed with a quarterdeck, probably to offset the weight of the heavy guns in the bow. The balanced weight would have made them stable rowing craft on the inland waterways, but they would have been difficult to sail in anything except calm water and a following wind. The strategy was for these galleys to cover the water flanks of troop movements on land and to keep enemy ships, particularly privateers, from being sheltered in the coastal estuaries.

Only the galley constructed at Beaufort was completed as a galley; she was christened *Beaufort* in 1777. While most of the state's galleys were lateen-rigged, *Beaufort* was probably schooner-rigged with topsails. She was slightly over sixty feet in length, displacing about 100 tons; her armament probably included two 18-pounder guns in the bow, supplemented by swivels mounted aft.

As there was a lull in naval activity off the coast, the other, larger galley ordered built at the state yard at Hobcaw was altered during construction and completed as the 14-gun brigantine *Hornet*. She was scaled down to slightly over sixty feet and launched in November 1778.

Hornet put out on her first cruise in February 1779, just as the war returned to the South. Off the coast of Georgia on April 1 with the pilot boat *Eagle*, she caught the brig *Royal Charlotte* and the sloop *Prince of Wales*, which were ferrying supplies to the British troops in Savannah. After leaving the prizes in Charlestown, *Hornet* herself was captured on April 11 by the same HMS *Daphne* that had captured *Comet* a year earlier.

The State Navy Yards

In the first years of the war the state navy used private shipyards to refit and maintain its vessels. This proved an unsatisfactory arrangement, and in April 1777 the navy commissioners leased the shipyard owned by Robert Cochran on Shipyard Creek for five years at £1,200 per year. The lease included the service of five laborers. This site soon proved to be too small. Therefore, a year later the state purchased a 75 percent interest in the Pritchard Shipyard at Hobcaw. This purchase included the fifteen slaves who were employed there. By 1779, the state navy removed most of its equipment to the Hobcaw site; by that September, only one state vessel remained on Shipyard Creek.

Charlestown's Revolutionary Privateers

While the South Carolina State Navy suffered from an acute manpower shortage throughout the Revolution, the many privateers that sailed from Charlestown did not. Most of these vessels could pick and choose the crew they wanted while other ships languished at dock for want of a crew. Everything depended, it seems, upon the vessel itself and especially its captain. A daring and resourceful commander with a record of prizes and rich rewards could virtually pick the best men on the waterfront for his crew.

Most privateers were financed by local merchants who were interested in potential prize money. Privateers supplemented the navy; in addition to harassing the enemy, they sometimes contributed to coastal defense. Because they did not go out to seek battle with enemy warships, work on them was less dangerous and discipline was more lax. This, plus the prize money profits, made service aboard the privateers more desirable than naval service.

The records of Charlestown's privateers are very sketchy. They come from scanty newspaper accounts, memoirs, and the surviving logs of various ships. While the state issued many so-called "letters of marque," records of only thirty-eight of them survive in the South Carolina State Archives. These cover the period from August 17, 1776, to April 19, 1777. Although information about the vessels is brief, it can be reliably surmised that they were small craft. Only one was a ship, at least half were sloops, and the rest were brigs and schooners.

In addition to the state of South Carolina, the Continental Congress also commissioned several privateers that used Charlestown as a base of operations. The city thus fitted out and sent forth its share of vessels to harass British commerce.

In the days of sailing vessels, it was relatively easy to convert a merchant ship into a warship. The addition of a few guns was all it took. While such a conversion would not enable the vessel to stand up in combat to a warship of equivalent size, it would give it an advantage over an even larger unarmed merchant ship.

In August 1776 the sloop *Swift* under Captain Francis Morgan became the first vessel officially commissioned by the state as a privateer. Morgan did not remain with her long. She was taken over by Captain Andrew Groundwater later that month. Together with the 12-gun sloop *Vixen* under Captain Downham Newton, *Swift* came across the 10-gun schooner *Comet* at Nassau. *Comet* retired under the protection of the harbor's fort and the Carolina sea rovers retreated. Shortly afterward, *Swift* was grounded in a gale on a reef and went to pieces. The captain and crew were taken aboard *Vixen*.

With the shipwrecked Captain Groundwater aboard, *Vixen* continued her cruise. On June 13, she captured the British sloop *Polly*, which was bound for Dublin from Mississippi. The prize was sent into a South Carolina port with her cargo of barrel staves. *Vixen* then joined forces with another Charlestown privateer, the sloop *General Washington* under Captain Hezekiah Anthony. At the end of the month, the duo took the rum-laden sloop *Salley* and delivered it to a safe port. The very next day, July 1, the two encountered a Jamaica fleet of over a hundred ships convoyed by four British men-of-war. After tailing the convoy for four days, the two Charlestown ships managed to cut out and take *Nancy*, a ship bound for London with 250 hogsheads of sugar, 50 of rum, and 80 pipes of wine. Captain Groundwater was put on board *Nancy* as prizemaster, but bad luck continued to follow him; he was captured by the 20-gun sixth-rate *Perseus*.

Several weeks later, Groundwater and nine others either managed to escape or were released from *Perseus* while in Chesapeake Bay. They returned to Charlestown on September 28. He would have been more fortunate to have perished at sea; in March 1779, he and two others were tried on charges of having had treasonable dealings with the British, and he was hanged.

On July 15 *Vixen* took another prize, the British schooner *Betsey*, bound from Antigua to New York with a cargo of sugar; however, the British retook her off Charlestown. After that, *Vixen* seems to have disappeared from the news.

Hezekiah Anthony, captain of *General Washington*, was one of the most successful of the city's Revolutionary privateersmen. Probably a New Englander, he was first mentioned in the minutes of the meeting of the navy commissioners held on December 10, 1776. He had submitted a claim for back pay from a promotion while on a cruise in the brig-of-war *Comet*.

When the commissioners refused the increase and in effect demoted him, Anthony left the service.

In February 1777, Anthony received a privateering commission for the sloop *General Washington*. On her first cruise, she took several prizes carrying general cargo. Some of these prizes were taken with *Vixen*, the rest alone.

On September 7 off Cape Antonio, *General Washington* fell in with the British 12-gun merchant brig *Pensacola* bound for London with a valuable cargo. After a three-hour battle, Anthony was forced to break off; his rigging was badly damaged, but none of the crew was hurt. On September 25 in the Bay of Honduras, *General Washington* took the 300-ton ship *Spiers* bound for Glasgow with mahogany and rum. She also took two brigs. Subsequently she fell in with the armed snow *Peggy* out of London. *Peggy's* main topmast was shot off, but she managed to escape.

General Washington took one more prize, and on October 12 she fell in with *General Howe* bound for New York from Jamaica. In thirty minutes of battle, *General Washington* suffered hull and mast damage; one man was killed and two were wounded. The prize escaped

when its armed escort *Fame* arrived, forcing Anthony to retreat. He dogged the two ships for several days, but they parted when a gale struck.

One of *General Washington's* prizes, *Spiers*, was recaptured by another *General Howe* and taken to St. Augustine. However, while the English prizemaster was ashore, *General Washington's* men onboard seized the opportunity to retake her and brought her to Charlestown. As a reward for his success, Anthony received command of a larger vessel, the 14-gun brig *Polly*.

Another successful Charlestown privateersman was Captain Jacob Milligan. He had led the party that boarded the grounded frigate *Actaeon* after the battle of Fort Sullivan. He subsequently served as a lieutenant on *Prosper* until she was sold out of the service.

In December 1776, Milligan received his commission from South Carolina's President Rutledge to command a sloop named *Rutledge*. The first cruise was quite successful. She took the British brigantine *Endeavor* under the guns of a fort at Barbados, even though a warship in the harbor weighed anchor and gave chase. She then took three more prizes, but one went ashore on Cape Romain. On the approach to Charlestown's bar, Milligan survived

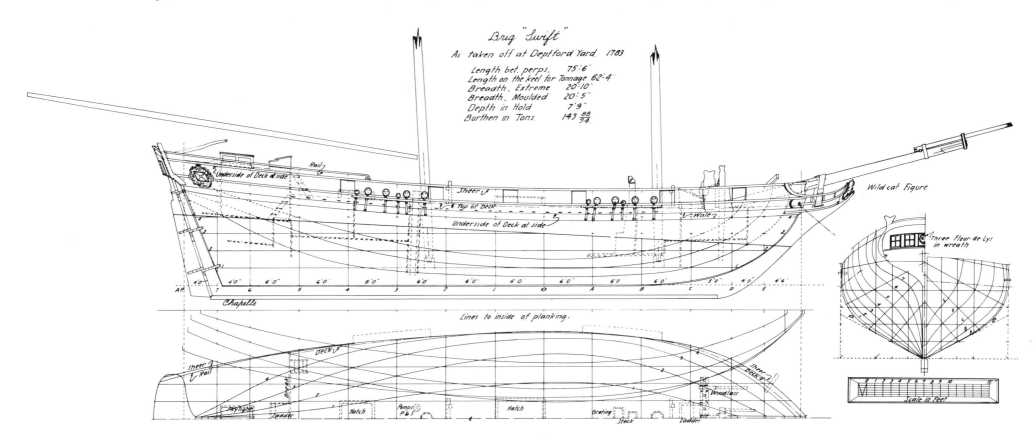

The light-displacement brig *Middleton* built in 1778 and taken into the Royal Navy as H. M. Brig *Swift*. Her fine lines show the high degree of refinement in hull form reached in America during the Revolution. She is typical of the privateer vessels that operated out of Charlestown. As her name suggests, she was probably Charlestown-owned, if not Charlestown-built. *Middleton* was 75 feet long with a 20-foot beam on an 88-ton displacement. She carried ten 3-pounder carriage guns.

In a dramatic victory, the Charlestown privateer *General Moultrie* (right) moves in to rake the British privateer *Wasp* across her bow. This was the hardest fought battle of the Revolution for a Charlestown warship.

a chance encounter with the enemy frigate *Greyhound*, which was disguised as a merchantman. The unsuspecting Milligan came close enough to read the name on her stern before he realized his mistake. Fortunately, she did not give chase.

After another successful cruise in the summer of 1777, Milligan seems to have given up privateering. Captain John Porter assumed command of *Rutledge*. Milligan later commanded the schooner *Margery*, which was captured on May 21, 1778, by the 28-gun sixth-rate *Levant* off the coast of Georgia. *Levant's* captain put Milligan and his men into a boat off the bar, and they made it safely into the harbor. In the summer of 1782, Milligan commanded the galley *Revenge* at Georgetown.

On a cruise in the fall of 1777 under Captain Porter and a large crew, *Rutledge* took several prizes and returned to Charlestown; the following spring she was either captured or sold, for her name disappears from local accounts.

Another privateer schooner, *Priscilla*, had a brief career before being wrecked in the West Indies near Turks Island. Only two of her crew survived. A more daring if not successful vessel was the little *Cotesworth Pinckney*, manned by thirteen men including officers and armed with only two swivel guns and four patteraroes. She sailed late in April 1777 from Charlestown under William Rankin, but was chased into the Cape Fear River by a warship. She then proceeded south and east off St. Augustine. Here she made several attempts to take far larger vessels; she just missed being captured by a 14-gun sloop when a calm allowed her to row off. Chased again by a sloop, *Cotesworth Pinckney* got clear and resumed cruising off St. Augustine. This time persistence paid off; she took the sloop *Mary*.

Two weeks later three sail were sighted at anchor to the north between the St. Marys and St. John's rivers. Rankin stood toward them. One turned out to be the frigate *Daphne*, which gave chase and retook *Mary*. Rankin decided that this was enough and returned home with only six surviving crew members. After one more unsuccessful cruise *Cotesworth Pinckney* became the pilot boat at Sunbury, Georgia, where she was captured and taken to St. Augustine.

Captain Rankin took command of another privateer, the sloop *Elbert*, which was wrecked on Abaco. The crew switched sides, was taken into New Providence, and served on the Jamaican ship *Mary*. She was subsequently captured by the Continental sloop *Providence*. Now in poor health, Rankin went to a plantation on New Providence to recover and disappeared from the news.

The privateer *Volunteer* took two prizes in the summer of 1777, one of which was recaptured. Several weeks later while some 25 leagues off Sullivan's Island, she was hailed by the British 32-gun sixth-rate *Brune*. When *Volunteer* refused to stop, *Brune* opened fire, killing *Volunteer's* captain and sinking the vessel.

In December 1777 about twenty miles north of St. Eustatius, *Experiment* under Captain Francis Morgan met a British 10-gun privateer sloop out of Antigua, commanded by Captain Phillips. When hailed, Morgan replied that he was from Charlestown; the enemy responded with a broadside, and Morgan returned fire. The engagement went on for over an hour. *Experiment* badly damaged her adversary and killed four men, wounded seven. The sloop ceased fire for almost ten minutes; suddenly and without explanation, *Experiment* blew up and sank. Captain Phillips did not pick up the eighteen survivors. Five of them either swam to the enemy sloop or made it to shore. All of the others perished.

Naval schooner of the type most commonly used during the Revolution by both sides as warships and privateers, especially the latter. Easily converted from merchant vessels, these small fast craft were popular for their low cost, speed, and shallow draft. The Charlestown privateers *Margery* and *Priscilla* were probably similar.

After the *Randolph* expedition (see following chapter), *Polly* returned to Charlestown under Captain Anthony. From November 1778 to the following January she made a successful cruise, capturing several vessels. One was the 18-gun ship *Resolution*. During the battle, *Polly* was so badly damaged that Captain Anthony had to abandon her and take over *Resolution* as prizemaster.

Sometime after his return to port in *Resolution*, Anthony took command of the brig *Bellona*. She may have been the same *Bellona* that arrived under the command of Captain George Warren Cross in January 1778, seven weeks out of Nantes. She brought with her the ship *Glorious Memory*, which she had taken off Bermuda. They were pursued off Charlestown by the blockading warships *Carysfort* (28-gun sixth-rate), *Perseus*, and *Hinchinbrook*, each of which fired several shots. Anthony was captured and paroled when Charlestown fell to the British in May 1780. He made his way to Philadelphia, where in October he became captain of the 1-gun privateer cutter *Hazard*. One of the owners of *Hazard* was David Lockwood, who had commanded the frigate *Bricole* of the South Carolina State Navy. After leaving *Hazard*, Anthony commanded two galleys off the coast. The Tory papers of Charlestown complained bitterly about his "crew of free booters and plundering banditti."

When *General Moultrie* was restored to her owners in the spring of 1778, Captain Sullivan was succeeded in command by Captain Downham Newton, formerly of *Vixen*. A storm on August 10, 1778, drove *General Moultrie* ashore on Haddrell's Point, but she was pulled off with little damage. On September 2 she resumed cruising. In less than a month *General Moultrie* was back with a hard-won prize, *Wasp*, a fine privateer brig fitted out in Jamaica with fourteen 4-pounder guns and twelve swivels.

Wasp, which had been fitted specifically to cruise off Charlestown, was a potent war vessel because of her size and power. In the two-hour battle with *General Moultrie*, ten men on *Wasp* were killed and twenty-five were wounded. *General Moultrie* had five men wounded, but none killed. *Wasp's* masts and spars were so shattered that the next morning her foremast and bowsprit fell overboard with the head of her mainmast. Her hull was so battered that the captors were "obliged to bale and pump at both hatchways."

Wasp and *General Moultrie* next sailed together and captured two valuable prizes out of a convoy of thirty-seven from Jamaica, which were escorted by the 20-gun *Ruby* and two armed Indiamen. One of the prizes was the 16-gun *Earl of Chester*, which became a prison ship in Charlestown harbor.

By spring of 1779, privateering out of Charlestown diminished, probably because the war was moving southward and the coast was crawling with enemy warships and British privateers. At some point in 1779 *General Moultrie* went back into state naval service under Captain Simon Tufts [Tuffts], who had been in command of the state's first vessel, *Defence*, at the battle of Hog Island. *General Moultrie* did not fire a single shot at the enemy during the 1780 siege and ended up at the bottom of the Cooper River with most of the state navy.

Wasp lasted a little longer. On July 28, 1780, the British privateer schooner *Highland Lass* put into Savannah and reported that she had been taken on June 12 by the brigantine *Wasp*, "formerly of Charlestown, but then in possession of a Spaniard." On the following day HMS *Richmond* (32-gun fifth-rate) and *Camilla* met and captured *Wasp* and her prize *Highland Lass*.

The South Carolina State Navy took into service as many of the privateers as it could obtain and outfit with crews. These were sent out to attack the now numerous enemy privateers sailing out of St. Augustine and cruising off the Carolina coast. The privateers returned to port with what seemed to be exaggerated tales of large numbers of enemy ships near the coast. But the tales were not exaggerated; a large blow was about to fall. The sloop *Sally* under Captain Stone did escape just as Arbuthnot's squadron (see pages 103–114) appeared off the bar, but she was later captured off Nassau.

There were other Charlestown privateers in the American cause, but they either captured no prizes or made uneventful cruises. A vessel can only battle the enemy if she encounters them, and a combination of factors ensures success: a good and resourceful captain; a trained crew; and good luck.

Although Governor Matthews held privateers in very low esteem, not all privateersmen were greedy men interested only in prize money. Some came close to piracy, but the majority of the city's privateersmen, like their consorts from other ports, were decent men with admirable patriotic motives, in spite of their quest for a fair measure of profit.

Model of a Revolutionary privateer similar to *General Moultrie*.

The *Fair American* and the *Randolph* Expedition

In the naval history of the Revolution many American ships stand out, but few won fame and glory and then disappeared into oblivion quite like the Charlestown-connected brig *Fair American* and her consort the Continental frigate *Randolph*. As with most of the American navies during the war, including South Carolina's, the war at sea was mostly a losing endeavor against overwhelming odds. These two vessels, however, offer one of the few thrilling episodes that occurred in American waters.

The *Fair American*

In the years prior to the Revolution, as the drift to separation accelerated, the name *Fair American* was very popular with colonial shipbuilders—a not-so-subtle rejoinder to the Crown's vexing policies. A 200-ton vessel by the name *Fair American* appears on colonial ship registers as having been built in South Carolina in 1762. Her career until the start of the Revolution is obscure. She was probably the ship that was lengthened in a British shipyard in 1772, when observations on the durability of southern live oak were brought to the attention of the Admiralty. In 1777, a privateer brig by the same name was taken into the South Carolina State Navy and fitted with sixteen guns. The exceptionally fine lines of this *Fair American* proved the skills of colonial designers; they were far from unlearned backwoodsmen capable of building only rough scows.

The *Fair American* that had been lengthened in 1772 was not the Revolutionary War *Fair American*. The earlier one was ship-rigged and the *Fair American* in question here was a short and broad brig with tall masts. She measured between 120 and 160 tons. These qualities made her a good sailer. She carried a battery of eight 4-pounder and six 6-pounder guns. Her crew numbered about 80, with provisions for an additional 26 soldiers of the First South Carolina Regiment to serve as marines. While in the state service, records indicate that she carried 99 men.

Charles Morgan commanded *Fair American* and, along with the 12-gun privateer brig *Experiment* under Captain Francis Morgan, raided Bermuda in the spring of 1777. There they captured several British vessels and seized the fort in the western harbor. They held it for six days, spiked the guns, and destroyed the carriages.

On the way back to Charlestown, they took another vessel and then separated. Off the bar, *Experiment* fell in with a British brig that ran out sixteen guns and commenced firing, backed up by a sloop. Seeing himself about to be overwhelmed, Captain Morgan exchanged a few shots and successfully ran into the harbor.

After parting, *Fair American* stumbled upon a British fleet of almost eighty sail bound for England from Jamaica. As the convoy was only lightly escorted by the 28-gun sixth-rate *Boreas* and the 14-gun sloop *Hornet*, Morgan managed to cut out the schooners *Margery* and *Betsey*. *Boreas* pursued *Fair American*, but Morgan managed to give her the slip and returned to Charlestown with *Margery*. *Betsey* grounded off Stono Inlet and went to pieces, although some of her cargo was saved.

The new Continental frigate *Randolph* under the command of Captain Nicholas Biddle was waiting for *Fair American* in Charlestown. Biddle had reason to believe that *Fair American* had on board four of *Randolph's* crew who had deserted. Morgan refused to stop his ship for a search, so Biddle fired a shot across the bow and forcibly removed the men.

Nicholas Biddle

Biddle, a former galley captain of the Pennsylvania State Navy, was daring, resourceful, and aggressive. He was one of the few bright stars in the Continental Navy along with John Paul Jones, Joshua Barney, and John Barry. He had better qualifications than any other captain in the navy, even though he was only twenty-five years old when the war began. His efforts were no doubt helped by the political connections of his brother, who represented Pennsylvania at the First and Second Continental Congresses and secured for him command of the brig *Andrea Doria* in the first squadron of the Continental Navy. Before the war he had served as a midshipman on HMS *Portland* for fourteen months. On an expedition to the Arctic in 1773 aboard *Carcass*, he served with the future Admiral Horatio Nelson. His nephew, James Biddle, achieved fame as the victor over HMS *Penguin* in the sloop-of-war *Hornet* in 1814. After the War of 1812 James Biddle became a commodore, serving off Africa, in the Mediterranean, in the Pacific in the Mexican War, and on the first U. S. Navy mission to Japan. James' brother, the second Nicholas Biddle (1786–1844), founded the Philadelphia banking empire associated with the Biddle name.

The *Randolph*

Randolph was one of the original thirteen frigates authorized by the Continental Congress for the new Continental Navy in 1776. She was named for Virginia's Peyton Randolph, the late president of the Continental Congress. Of these first thirteen frigates, *Randolph's* original draughts are the only ones that survive. She and her sister, *Washington*, were built at Philadelphia and designed with twenty-six 12-pounders on the main deck and six 6-pounders on the quarterdeck. On Biddle's recommendation *Randolph's* 6-pounders were increased to ten in number.

By the time of the Revolution, the frigate type of warship had reached the point of development that is well known today in ships such as *Constitution* of War of 1812 fame. It was a ship-rigged warship with the main battery of guns on one main, nearly continuously covered gun deck. Most frigates had quarterdecks where smaller guns were mounted and forecastle decks for bow chaser guns. Stern chasers were mounted in the stern on the gun deck. Some small frigates had short quarter or forecastle decks and were more accurately termed *sloops-of-war* or *corvettes*, as their main gun deck was open to the weather. Regardless of name, as a type they were the work horses of most navies, used for patrolling, scouting, raiding, carrying dispatches, and substituting for larger warships when necessary.

Randolph's first attempt to put to sea in December 1776 was thwarted by enemy blockaders, most notably HMS *Roebuck*. On February 6, in consort with *Hornet* and a swarm of merchantmen, the breakout was successful. Thus, *Randolph* became the first American frigate to get to sea. Unfortunately, her sister and two other new frigates were burned when the

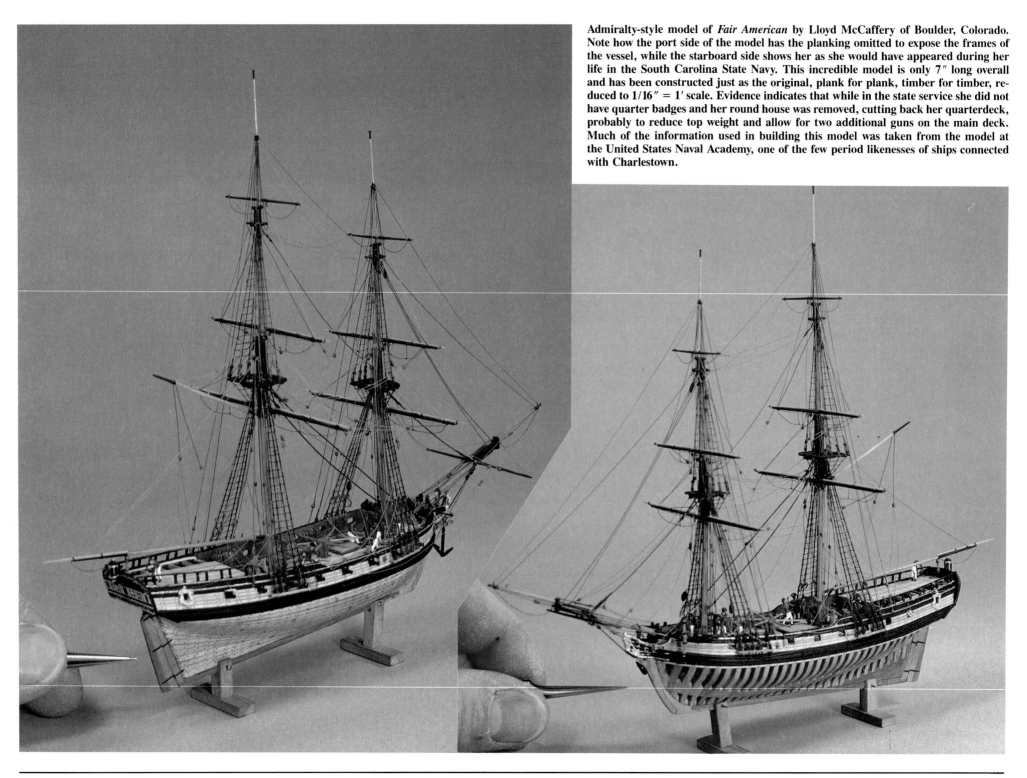

Admiralty-style model of *Fair American* by Lloyd McCaffery of Boulder, Colorado. Note how the port side of the model has the planking omitted to expose the frames of the vessel, while the starboard side shows her as she would have appeared during her life in the South Carolina State Navy. This incredible model is only 7″ long overall and has been constructed just as the original, plank for plank, timber for timber, reduced to 1/16″ = 1′ scale. Evidence indicates that while in the state service she did not have quarter badges and her round house was removed, cutting back her quarterdeck, probably to reduce top weight and allow for two additional guns on the main deck. Much of the information used in building this model was taken from the model at the United States Naval Academy, one of the few period likenesses of ships connected with Charlestown.

Cross Section of frigate *Randolph*

1. Quarterdeck
2. Steering wheel
3. Capstans
4. Ship's boats
5. Belfry
6. Cathead
7. Captain's cabin
8. Captain's bed place
9. Gun deck
10. Riding bitts
11. Galley stove
12. Tiller
13. Wardroom
14. Staterooms
15. Berth deck
16. Hammock
17. Mess table
18. Rudder
19. Cockpit
20. Cable tier
21. Light room
22. Filling room
23. Magazine
24. Stores
25. Shot lockers

British captured Philadelphia a few months later.

For four days Biddle tested the ship's sailing qualities off the Delaware Capes. Once satisfied that she was the best sailer he knew, he ordered the waiting merchantmen to follow him out to sea so that he could escort them clear of the coast. For three days he shepherded them away from land and then sent them on their voyages to Europe and the West Indies. He then turned *Randolph* north to search for the marauding 28-gun sixth-rate HMS *Milford*, which had been plaguing New England. While on this course, *Randolph* sprung and then broke her main- and foremasts due to rotten wood. In her damaged condition, she was prey to any enemy vessel that might happen along. Realizing that the Delaware Capes might be reblockaded and that the enemy had warships off the Chesapeake, Biddle decided to take advantage of the northeast wind and put into Charlestown as a safe haven for repairs. En route, a mutiny by the former English seamen on board was nipped in the bud. On the morning of March 11, 1777, *Randolph* hove to off the bar for a pilot. That afternoon, she passed the guns of Fort Moultrie and anchored in the harbor.

Sojourn at Charlestown

The next day, John Dorsius, one of the joint Continental agents for South Carolina, came on board to greet Biddle and determine his needs. Before *Randolph* proceeded to the Hobcaw navy yard, the sick crewmembers were sent ashore and several visitors were received, including General Moultrie. Although damaged, the brand new ship riding at anchor in the harbor caused quite a stir among the citizens of the city, who had never seen a frigate flying the American flag. Biddle called upon President Rutledge, who ordered the navy commissioners to assist him in every way. Being much respected locally, Dorsius soon had things in order.

New masts had to come from North Carolina, as none was available locally. In the meantime, the ship had to be unloaded, sails mended, the hull cleaned and fumigated. Desertions rapidly depleted the crew due to fever on board, desire for greener pastures, and other reasons. Biddle was undeterred by the task before him, and steady work paid off. Even without masts after a month of restoration, *Randolph* was described in glowing terms by a local citizen: "as noble and complete a ship as one as ever sailed from Britain in every respect." By May, the new masts were in place and the ship was almost ready, except for a crew.

Part of the overhaul included the ship's guns, whose carriages were rotten in places. While the overhaul was being performed, local legend has it that *Randolph's* gunner told one of the blacksmiths of his great attachment for the ship. He said that he would never allow her to be taken by an enemy. If necessary, he would blow her up with his own hands, since his battle station was in the ship's magazine.

Biddle, meanwhile, enjoyed the social scene in Charlestown. He made friends with Rutledge, Drayton, Pinckney, and Moultrie. Another friend was Lieutenant Richard Bohun Baker of the Second South Carolina Regiment, whose ancestral home was Archdale Hall on the right bank of the Ashley River above Middleton Plantation. At Archdale Hall, Biddle met and courted Elizabeth Baker, the oldest sister of Lieutenant Baker. It must have been the right match; the two became engaged before the summer was out.

On June 8, 1777 *Randolph*, fully rigged and overhauled, came down from Hobcaw into the harbor. Here, a lightning bolt struck the new mainmast and splintered it to the deck. While it was being replaced, Biddle set his mind to replenishing his crew, which had diminished to scarcely 100 officers and men while at the navy yard. Even the enlistment bounty customarily paid to new seamen failed to draw recruits away from the privateers.

Randolph was trim in appearance by the first anniversary of the Declaration of Independence and added to the celebration, which included lavish displays of flags and a seventy-six gun salute from the forts. The festivities concluded with a banquet and fireworks such as had never been seen before in the city.

Lightning supposedly never strikes twice; nevertheless, it did. Before *Randolph* could get underway, once again the ship's mast was hit. Biddle enlisted Rutledge's support in obtaining a crew by getting the state treasury to underwrite part of the enlistment bounty. Rutledge was persuaded by his memory of the presence of the 20-gun HMS *Perseus* off the bar that spring. She had taken many of the city's merchant ships as well as their crews, and had to return to the West Indies in order to replenish her own crew. The increased bounty from the state partially succeeded; *Randolph* even gained some recruits from returning privateers. One man came aboard with several of his slaves to be used as crewmen.

Biddle aimed to make sure that lightning did not strike a third time. The new mast was stepped, and a slender iron rod jutted above the main topgallant masthead. A wire led down one of the backstays to the water. Ben Franklin had advocated this device in *Poor Richard's Almanac*, but it had not yet been seen in Charlestown.

On August 18, the frigate dropped down to Rebellion Road to await a fair wind to take her over the bar. It was here that *Randolph* encountered Morgan and *Fair American*. While the southerly breezes held the ship in port, Biddle took the time to exercise the men at the guns and train them in boarding. A square-rigged sailing ship was impossible to maneuver in a narrow channel against the wind. Sometimes they would use kedge anchors, pulled out ahead of the ship with boats, in order to pull the vessel up a channel; however, this was back-breaking work for the crew. Smaller vessels could put out sweeps and row short distances, but *Randolph* was too large and the distance too far for this task.

Finally, a fair wind and an ebb tide allowed the frigate to get over the bar to sea. Once clear she set a course for St. Augustine to search for the richly laden ships that used that port and cruised along the coast of Florida. Biddle's reasoning paid off with the capture of three prizes barely 200 miles south of Charlestown. Because it took sixty of his crew to man the ships and because the frigate's bottom was in atrocious shape from sitting in Charlestown harbor, Biddle was forced to return there, escorting his spoils of war. Barely a week after leaving, the frigate had returned to port with two ships and two brigs. The local citizens flocked to the waterfront to greet *Randolph* and her prizes as they came into the Cooper River.

After the celebration, *Randolph* returned to Hobcaw to be hoved down for a bottom cleaning. In order to heave her down, first the guns and then movable equipment and stores were landed. Heavy tackles had to be rigged to the top of the lower masts, connected to capstans on shore, which were used to pull her over onto her side, exposing her bottom, one side at a time (see page 56). But somehow the restraining tackles on her keel failed and the ship capsized, filled with water, and sank. It took two weeks to raise her.

If embarrassment was high, it was also short-lived; the prizes brought £90,000 sterling, enough to give every member of the crew some real spending money. Most of the money was spent in the city, and some of the officers invested in the state's securities. Naturally, this move endeared them to the local populace, especially those upon whom the crew lavished their gains. Best of all, it gave *Randolph* a good name; finding a crew in the future would be no problem.

Charlestown Blockaded

News of the disasters in the northern campaigns reached Charlestown in October, just as the Royal Navy began to reassert itself in southern waters. In November 1777, a blockade was set up off the bar by the 28-gun sixth-rates *Carysfort* and *Lizard*, the 20-gun *Perseus*, and the 6-gun brig *Hinchinbrook* (the former *Defence* of the state navy, recently captured). Lord Howe had ordered them down from the Chesapeake. To make matters worse, merchant ships were ready to depart from Charlestown with the summer's crops, and ships were expected from Europe with war materiel. The British ships played havoc with the commerce of the city; furthermore, they were reportedly in close and regular communication with Charlestown's large Tory element. General Moultrie alleged in his *Memoirs* that the crews of British boats were in town every night.

During the days of sail, blockading was not a simple matter, even with four warships. Charlestown had four ship channels; guarding all of them would tax the resources of a dozen sailing warships. The guarding warships had to be mounted twenty-four hours a day, and if a ship was spotted, it had to be checked. While one vessel was being checked, another had to take the checker's place. If the wind was poor or disadvantageous, this process could take hours. At night or during storms, poor visibility made the problems greater. Therefore, many vessels got through the blockade while others were captured passing in or out of the harbor.

By the end of November, Charlestown harbor was clogged with ships waiting to sail, their holds filled with spoiling cargoes. Biddle and Rutledge pressed for *Randolph's* overhaul to be completed so that she could be used to drive the enemy away from the bar. The blockade of the port was ruining the local economy and its overseas trade.

The Expedition to Break the Blockade

By December *Randolph* was ready, with a crew on board. With her as a nucleus, the state authorities planned a powerful naval expedition to destroy or drive away the British blockaders. Rutledge proposed that Biddle be in command of a force of four state warships, including two privateers that had been pressed into service.

The brigantine *Notre Dame* was the only vessel of any consequence in the South Carolina State Navy at the time; thus, the privateers *Polly*, *Fair American*, *Volunteer*, and *General Moultrie* had to be purchased to make up the rest of the proposed squadron. In spite of the bounty offered, enough men could not be found. Therefore, *Volunteer* was returned to her owners. Biddle's command included:

Randolph, 36-gun frigate	Captain Biddle
General Moultrie, 20-gun ship	Captain Sullivan
Notre Dame, 16-gun brig	Captain Hall
Fair American, 16-gun brig	Captain Morgan
Polly, 14-gun brig	Captain Anthony

At about 200 tons, *General Moultrie* was the largest ship thus far in the state navy. She was deep-waisted, with a small head and an upright plain stern. She had been built in Charlestown for the navy and steered well. Her guns included twelve short 12-pounders and six 4-pounders, all on the main deck; being unusually high-rigged, she had a number of cohorns in her broad tops. *Polly* was similar to *Fair American* and *Notre Dame*, but she carried only fourteen 4-pounders. She was low-built and a good sailer with a crew of seventy-four.

The local merchants, who had been taking heavy losses, put up a bonus to add to the enlistment bounties so that the ships could be manned quickly. Pressure was put upon General Moultrie, who came up with 150 Continental regulars to serve as marines.

On December 20, *Randolph* anchored in Rebellion Road to bring the crew up to battle-readiness and get them away from the diversions of the city. Three days later, seven British prisoners from *Randolph's* prizes escaped from the city jail, stole a boat, and rowed out to the British ships offshore. They carried with them news of the mounting naval expedition.

One delay after another thwarted departure; throughout January, *Randolph* rode impatiently at anchor. Biddle took time to write his will, leaving a large part of his considerable estate to his betrothed, Elizabeth Elliott Baker. It was as though he had a premonition of impending death, but it was also customary for an officer in wartime to make a will.

In the early morning hours of January 15, 1778, a disastrous fire swept the city, fanned by the northerly winter winds of a passing cold front. It could be seen clearly from the blockading ships offshore. The flames swept down present-day State Street from Queen, and from there down Church Street to the water. It left a large swath of destruction in its path. Many felt that it had been set by British seamen who, disguised as civilians, had rowed in from the ships at sea.

Biddle raced in from Archdale Plantation, but did not arrive until after the flames had almost burned themselves out. A landing party from *Randolph* came ashore to help fight the conflagration. The destruction of some of the ships' supplies plus the need to aid fire victims further delayed the sailing of the squadron.

By the first week of February, the four ships of the state navy joined *Randolph* at anchor in Rebellion Road. As Biddle was rowed to his ship for what would be his last time, he was pleased with the state of his fleet. His crew was trained to perfection. His orders to the other captains contained an omen: he warned them that if "coming to action in the night, be very careful of your magazine."

Sortie

Just after first light on February 12, 1778, the squadron picked up a favorable wind and tide and passed over the bar with some thirteen merchantmen. The enemy ships were nowhere to be seen. The Americans figured that Captain Fanshawe had departed the area after seeing the American warships assembled in Rebellion Road. Actually the British warships were once more loaded with prisoners and short-handed from manning prizes, and had been forced to return to their base.

The squadron sailed east toward Bermuda, then south for Antigua, and from there to the north of Barbados. One prize of no value was taken and burned; another small schooner was made a tender to the fleet.

East of Barbados shortly before dark on Saturday, March 7, 1778, the squadron sighted a large sail to the northeast making for them in the fading light. *Randolph* steered to close with it, the South Carolina ships trailing astern. Both sides were spoiling for a fight. Biddle evidently mistook the suspicious sail for a smaller vessel; it turned out to be the 64-gun third-rate *Yarmouth* under Captain Nicholas Vincent, out of Antigua.

The opening broadsides between *Randolph* and *Yarmouth*. The great disparity in the sizes of the two ships is readily apparent. This is not a period watercolor. It was rendered by the English artist Bevan in the late nineteenth century from written accounts and descriptions of the ships involved. He incorrectly shows the South Carolina ships fleeing at the onset of the contest; accounts indicate that they were closing in in unison against their large antagonist. If they had been successful and carried *Yarmouth* as a prize of war back to Charlestown, they would have eclipsed John Paul Jones' victory over HMS *Serapis* eighteen months later as the greatest American naval victory of the war. Note *General Moultrie* at extreme left.

Bevan's rendering of the destruction of *Randolph*. It is amazing that anyone survived the explosion. Actually the ships were probably closer together, but the much larger size of *Yarmouth* is quite apparent in this scene. These are two of several illustrations by Irwin John Bevan from the Mariners' Museum's collection. Bevan was a Welsh artist with a keen interest in maritime subjects.

Several of his renderings have been reproduced in this book. However, they are portrayed from the British side and in most cases depict American defeats. Nevertheless the watercolors have been used in this volume because they offer a rare link to Charleston.

Disaster

Yarmouth steered for the American ships, thinking they were privateers. At 7 p.m., Biddle backed his mizzen topsail and hove to in order to await the enemy. *General Moultrie* and the other ships astern followed suit, but *Moultrie* was unable to slow quickly enough; she passed ahead of the squadron, only to find herself in the van to confront the onrushing enemy. *Yarmouth* fired a warning gun as she passed and hailed *Moultrie*. Captain Sullivan replied that he was from New York and gasped at the sight of the two-decker in the dim moonlight, as she passed close by, heading for *Randolph*.

Captain Hall in *Notre Dame* also realized the predicament, but he continued to try to maneuver for a raking position under *Yarmouth's* stern. Hearing the discourse, Biddle also noted her size, but his men were ready at their guns. When hailed, *Randolph* ran up the Grand Union flag and Lieutenant Barnes answered clearly enough to be heard astern, "This is the Continental frigate *Randolph*." Then a broadside lashed from *Randolph* into the darkness. *Yarmouth* promptly answered, joining in a continuous roar, but *Randolph's* crew served her guns quickly, getting off more shots per gun than her antagonist.

The ships stood yardarm to yardarm, trading broadsides in the tropical night. *Yarmouth* lost her bowsprit and mizzen topmast. On the lee quarter, *General Moultrie* fired three quick salvos in the direction of the battle. When her crew realized that some of her shots were hitting *Randolph*, they tried to get ahead and engage on the bow. While *Notre Dame* unloaded a broadside into the enemy's stern, *Fair American* and *Polly* struggled to get into range.

Randolph fought ferociously for fifteen minutes, while the South Carolina marines in the mast tops poured a withering fire onto the enemy decks and mast tops. Although wounded in the leg, Biddle continued to direct the battle. A chair was brought to prop him up. Suddenly, *Randolph's* magazine ignited, and in one tremendous flash the ship blew out of the water.

Being to windward, *Yarmouth* escaped the destruction of the explosion; but the concussion stunned her crew and a rain of debris poured upon them. It tore the rigging and sails to shreds. A Grand Union flag, rolled up and unsinged, fell onto her forecastle. *General Moultrie's* young captain broke down at the sight of *Randolph's* destruction. He was almost captured. Since *Fair American* had just come into range when the explosion occurred, Captain Morgan at first thought it was the enemy ship. He realized the truth as he came up to hail Biddle, and quickly made sail to the south behind *Moultrie*. The others sought safety to the west, clapping on a full press of canvas.

Yarmouth attempted to pursue the fleeing South Carolina ships, but the darkness and her shredded sails made the effort fruitless. She hove to and for twenty-four hours her crew repaired her sails and rigging, fearful that a wind would spring up and force her masts over the side.

Although *Randolph* and her crew were destroyed in the explosion, four men from a quarterdeck gun were hurled into the ocean. Somehow they made a makeshift raft out of a spar and other debris and clung to it for four days and nights. On the morning of March 12, they spotted a sail growing larger and larger. A boat was lowered and picked them up. Their savior, however, was *Yarmouth*—still hunting for the South Carolina ships. These four seamen were *Randolph's* only survivors out of a crew of 315, including Captain Biddle, Captain Joseph Ioor, and his fifty South Carolina troops who were serving as marines. *Yarmouth* had only five killed and twelve wounded.

The South Carolina ships cleared out of the area after the destruction of *Randolph*. Simeon Fanning, aboard a schooner that the American squadron had captured, brought word of *Randolph's* loss to Charlestown on March 29. *General Moultrie* and *Fair American* arrived shortly afterward with a valuable merchantman that they had captured en route. *Notre Dame* and *Polly* continued cruising through the West Indies, and off the Isle of Pines they fell in with a British convoy out of Jamaica. They managed to capture three of the vessels and eight others subsequently; however, less than half reached port safely, and one was wrecked on the bar at Georgetown. One of those taken was a ship of twenty guns that was captured only after *Notre Dame's* crew had boarded her.

Epilogue

After the battle, *Fair American* returned to Charlestown for repairs and reprovisioning in April. Subsequently, she continued to transport cargoes to the West Indies to trade for war supplies. En route, she managed to take every enemy ship that she could. In August she returned from St. Eustatius in a convoy with several other Charlestown vessels that were hauling munitions, escorted by the Spanish frigate *Diligente*.

Once again, Charlestown's trade was being harassed by enemy ships off the bar. *Fair American* returned to learn that the Jamaican privateer *Gayton* had taken several vessels. After being quickly unloaded, weapons prepared, and manned with volunteers, she fell down to Rebellion Road to proceed seaward. Early the next morning *Fair American* sailed against the tide, a heavy sea, and a strong easterly wind. The attempt to clear the port under these conditions caused her foremast to spring in the partners, and she was forced to return to port.

On December 22 *Fair American* returned from another trading trip to St. Eustatius. She reported having had a brush the day before off St. Helena's Island with "a long low Virginia-built vessel, mounting only two-pounder guns." When this vessel made aggressive moves against his becalmed brig, Captain Morgan had fired nearly fifty shots before the supposed enemy was able to row out of range.

Captain Morgan went from *Fair American* to command the schooner *Fly*, which arrived in Charlestown with a large supply of military stores on April 14, 1779. She had sailed from the West Indies in company with the privateer brig *Hercules* under Captain Josiah Young, formerly commander of the privateer sloop *Lively*. When *Hercules* came into port from St. Eustatius that September, she brought with her the British armed schooner *Eagle*, which had been sent out from Tybee Island, just south of Savannah a few days before "for intelligence and to look into this harbor."

Fair American ended her connection with Charlestown sometime in 1779. The precise date and conditions are unknown, as the journals of the Commissioners of the South Carolina State Navy covering this period were burned in a fire at the New York Public Library in 1911.

Fair American was captured by the British, probably after her Charlestown owners sold her to northern interests. She ended up as a British privateer operating out of New York. Because of her capture by the enemy, her lines were recorded and a model was built of her in the 1780s in England, probably by her British owner. In 1782, she was at the engagement off the Delaware Capes in which the American privateer *Hyder Ally* under Joshua Barney captured HMS *General Monk* under the nose of the larger British frigate *Quebec*. *Fair American* ran aground early in the action while chasing some American merchant ships, and was unable to aid her consort. Sometime later she was retaken by the Americans, but then disappeared into oblivion, no doubt a victim of the anonymity that faces many warships in times of peace.

The War Returns to the South

By the fall of 1778, the war was at a stalemate in the North, and the British reverted to their original 1776 plan of subduing the southern colonies by tapping the large loyalist population. General Henry Clinton, the British commander-in-chief, ordered Archibald Campbell to take Savannah with 3,500 men supported by a naval force under Commodore Hyde Parker, and then use it as a base for the real objective—an invasion of South Carolina. The American patriots were partially repaying the French for their aid with trade out of Savannah and especially Charlestown. The indigo, cotton, and rice coming from these ports were products that the foreign merchants preferred over cash. More than actual combat, Charlestonians were intent on pursuing the mercantile aspects of the war and the ready profits of privateering. Also working against the patriot cause in South Carolina were the large number of loyalists and those with allegiance to neither side.

Late in 1778, Major General Benjamin Lincoln succeeded Major General Robert Howe as American military commander in the South. Lincoln had achieved recognition as an able commander in the northern campaigns, but he arrived too late to save Savannah. In December, the British forces easily seized it. The South Carolina authorities had tried to raise forces to aid their fellow colonists, but the enlistment drive did not draw sufficient recruits to man ships for the expedition. By the end of February 1779, the entire state of Georgia was in British hands.

With the enemy based next door, naval activity along the South Carolina coast increased dramatically. British privateers out of St. Augustine, who had been active since the beginning of the war, became even more menacing when a secure local base in Savannah was theirs. They used the bays and inlets to harass coastal trade and waited off Charlestown, Port Royal, and Georgetown to attack oceanic commerce.

With the military situation altered and the state facing a possible invasion by land, the state navy shifted its emphasis from ocean vessels back to galleys that could be used to control the coastal waterways and support troop movements.

Ten galleys were authorized to supplement the one in commission. The flatboat *Revenge* that had been stationed as a floating battery behind Fort Moultrie was converted to a galley. Three large barges used to ferry goods to and from plantations were converted to the galleys *Marquis de Bretagne*, *Lee*, and *Rutledge*. They had been large raft-like boats propelled by oars. During the conversion process they were decked over, armed with guns, and fitted with masts and sails. The larger galleys like *Rutledge* had quarterdecks with accommodations below for officers. *Carolina* and *South Edisto* were converted from deeper draft schooners with keels. Their appearance differed from the others, and they were easier to sail than to row.

Each galley was to have a French 24-pounder (26-pounder by English measure) in the bow, but only *Revenge* and *South Edisto* actually did. The others carried two 18-pounders and carriage-type 4- or 6-pounder broadside guns supplemented by swivels. *South Edisto*, however, carried four 18-pounders in her waist.

One of the naval officers who oversaw the work on these galleys was George Farragut, father of the future admiral. He had come to Charlestown in 1776 and served as an officer on the privateer *Vixen*, and was then commissioned a lieutenant in the state navy. He eventually commanded the galley *Revenge*. Before the British moved up the coast to take Charles-

town, Farragut took *Revenge* up the Sampit River at Georgetown, where he concealed her so well that the enemy never discovered her. Once Georgetown returned to American hands, *Revenge* was recommissioned in state service under Jacob Milligan in 1782. In the meantime, Farragut joined Francis Marion's brigade and fought at Cowpens.

The Georgia galleys *Congress* and *Lee* had retreated to the inlets of South Carolina when their state fell to the enemy. On March 21, 1779, while off Yemassee Bluff in support of a ground action, they came upon and attempted to capture the British galleys *Comet* and *Hornet*. But they in turn were surprised when the 74-gun third-rate *Thunderer* came up and turned the tables on the Georgians; the galleys were captured and four men were lost, six were wounded, and ten taken prisoner. The British took *Congress* and *Lee* into service and renamed them *Scourge* and *Vindictive*, apt names for what they were about to inflict on Charlestown.

While the South Carolina State Navy was being enlarged to meet the looming British threat, available ships were sent out to search for enemy vessels. In March, *Hornet* under Captain Pyne fell to the same 20-gun enemy privateer *Daphne* that had captured *Comet*.

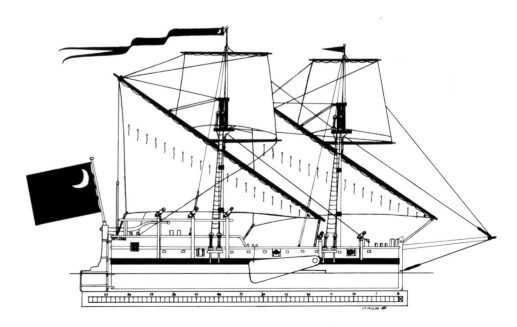

The South Carolina galley *Rutledge* as she may have appeared in 1779. *Lee* and *Marquis de Bretagne* would have been similar but smaller, with one single gun directly in the bow.

Hornet was carried into Savannah; from there she was sent to New York.[1]

In May 1779, General Prevost made his overland thrust from Savannah to the outskirts of Charlestown. General Lincoln's army rushed back from its diversionary attack against Augusta just in time to save the city. A state squadron consisting of the galleys *Rutledge* and *Marquis de Bretagne* and the schooner *Rattlesnake* moved down the Stono River on June 23 to support Lincoln's attack on Prevost's troops at Stono Landing to the south of Charlestown. As the squadron passed the high land on John's Island, they were taken under fire from small arms and field guns of the British troops on land. Once past Stono Ferry (the present-day site of Limehouse Bridge) the South Carolina vessels discovered that Prevost's rear guard under Lt. Col. John Maitland had already withdrawn from the mainland to John's Island after repulsing General Lincoln's attack. The squadron anchored and fired occasional shots into the British camp. Meanwhile, Maitland's forces prepared for the galleys' return to Charlestown by mounting heavier guns on the island along the South Carolinians' line of withdrawal.

The state vessels made the mistake of waiting too long (or not long enough) to begin the journey back to Charlestown. The two galleys and a prize schooner that they had seized got safely past Maitland's guns, even though *Marquis de Bretagne* was damaged and six men were killed. *Rattlesnake* ran aground on the east bank of the ferry and was attacked by Hessian grenadiers supported by two field guns. While *Rattlesnake's* crew beat off the attack, Captain Frisbie considered his situation hopeless and ordered the schooner set on fire and abandoned. The crew made their way back to the American lines on foot.

At the same time, the South Carolina brigs *Notre Dame*, *Beaufort*, *Eagle*, and *Bellona* put to sea to intercept several of Prevost's supply vessels near Stono Inlet. Two of the British vessels were captured and one destroyed; the remaining four escaped.

The Allied Siege of Savannah

Governor Rutledge and the citizens of Charlestown were thoroughly alarmed by Prevost's attack. General Lincoln and Rutledge pleaded with French Admiral Comte D'Estaing, then in the West Indies, to come to their aid. Needing to offset his earlier setbacks, D'Estaing seized the opportunity for what appeared to be a quick victory over the British. Early in September he arrived with 4,000 troops on 51 ships, including 22 ships-of-the line and ten frigates, probably the most powerful naval force ever to assemble off Charlestown. Within a week they were off Tybee, where they caught and captured the fourth- and sixth-rates *Experiment* and *Ariel* and two supply ships.

The state navy placed all available vessels at D'Estaing's disposal. By September 12, sufficient small craft and the pilot boat *Eagle* with pilots familiar with the waters around Savannah arrived from Charlestown to enable most of the French troops to land. Because the large French men-of-war were unable to get upstream to participate in the attack on Savannah, much of the fighting was done by the crews of the smaller South Carolina vessels.

The first state warship on the scene was the galley *Revenge* under William Sisk, fol-

lowed shortly by *Rutledge* under James Pyne. They joined an inshore squadron that included the French transports *Truite* and *Bricole*, which had been selected because of their shallow draft. *Bricole* proved too large to get up to the city. *Truite's* armament was increased considerably for shore bombardment.

Facing the allied warships in the river were the small frigates HMS *Rose* and *Fowey* and several other small vessels, including the former South Carolina *Comet*, now an enemy galley. As the allied war vessels moved upstream on September 19, the British ships dogged their advance. The next day, the British sank *Rose* in the river just below the city to hinder the allied thrust. For the next several days the river fighting between the galleys centered around the wreck of *Rose*.

Truite managed to bypass *Rose* via another channel, and by September 28 was directing long-range fire into the city from beyond Hutchinson Island on the South Carolina side of the river. Distance thwarted *Truite's* firepower, but the South Carolina galleys' fire damaged several buildings.

It was not until October that the South Carolina warships *Notre Dame*, *Beaufort*, and *Wasp*; privateer *General Moultrie*; and galley *Marquis de Bretagne* arrived. They rendered

A modern reconstruction of the British 24-gun sixth-rate *Rose*, which at first dogged the South Carolina galleys attacking Savannah. Due to her age (launched 1749), *Rose* was scuttled in an attempt to block the channel leading to Savannah.

---

[1] *Hornet* and *Comet* of the South Carolina State Navy should not be confused with the Georgia galleys of the same names mentioned in the preceding paragraph. *Comet* mentioned here was the former South Carolina Navy brig that had been captured and taken to New York. There she was converted to a galley and brought south for the assault on Charlestown in 1780.

helpful service to the French by providing ship-to-shore communications and ferrying supplies and troops.

Although ill-prepared and outnumbered by the Franco-American forces, the British land forces put up an excellent defense. The allies now paid for the failure to capture Maitland's force at Stono Ferry; they had successfully reached Savannah through the coastal creeks on September 17. The British were also helped by the able engineer Moncrief, who completed the defensive works; because of them, the allies spent a month investing the city and preparing an attack.

D'Estaing was unable to mount a prolonged siege because his ships were needed in the West Indies and he feared the hurricane season. Therefore, he decided to force the issue with a frontal assault on the British lines on October 9. The attack was easily repulsed and brought 800 casualties, including Polish Count Caismir Pulaski, who died of his wounds on board *Wasp* en route to Charlestown and was buried at sea.

The French ships offshore suffered through several gales, and Pritchard's Shipyard in Charlestown supplied repair timber for spars and rudders. After the French had withdrawn, the remaining South Carolina warships were hit by another storm on November 4. *Rutledge* lost a mast; with another vessel, she was blown into the Savannah estuary and captured. *Rutledge* became HMS *Viper*, and Captain Pyne began his third term of captivity.

The Americans regrouped at Charlestown to prepare for the certain British attack. From now until the end of the war, South Carolina would be the scene of most of the fighting in America, and her battles would turn the tide of the war to the American side. Yorktown would merely be the final blow to the disintegrating British resistance. This fact is lost upon many historians of the American Revolution.

Assault on Charlestown

When General Clinton learned of the British victory at Savannah, he immediately set in motion his plans for an all-out attack on Charlestown. He left New York at the end of December with Lord Cornwallis and 7,000 troops in a fleet of 96 ships under Admiral Marriot Arbuthnot. After riding out a storm off Hatteras, the fleet of transports, supply ships, five ships-of-the line, and five frigates put into Savannah on February 2, 1780. But Clinton had stopped only to reassemble his forces after the storm, and quickly moved northward. On February 10 the fleet sounded the North Edisto River and marked the channel.

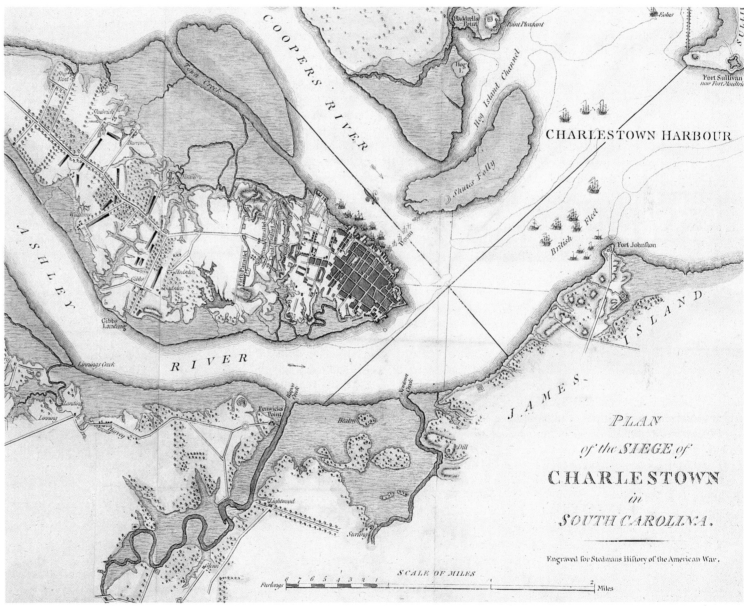

A plan of the siege of Charlestown by the British Army and Navy in 1780. The British fleet is anchored off Fort Johnson and in Rebellion Road (labeled Charlestown Harbour). At lower left Wappoo Creek leads from the Stono River to the Ashley River. Note the American defenses and British siege works across Charlestown neck (see also page 107).

The troops, which included Hessian mercenaries, landed unopposed the next day on Seabrook's (then known as Simond's) Island near Kiawah Island, only twenty-five miles south of Charlestown. Flat-bottomed boats supported by galleys brought more troops and supplies up the Wadmalaw and Stono Rivers as far as New Cut and Stono Ferry. They were mostly unopposed, except at the latter, where an American schooner was burned on February 14. A British row galley accidentally caught fire and blew up near New Cut on February 19.

Two weeks of skirmishing ensued with American forces under General Lincoln across John's Island to Fenwick Hall, Stono Ferry, and the lower Stono River (near the present airport). On February 24, Lord Cornwallis and General Leslie crossed onto James Island at Grimball's Cross Roads (near the new county park). During its advance across John's Island and the Stono River, the British Army was supported on the river flanks by the galleys *Comet*, *Scourge*, *Viper*, and *Vindictive*. *Viper* (the former South Carolina galley *Rutledge*) had been rearmed with two 12-pounder guns, and the other galleys had one 18- or 24-pounder gun; all had crews of fifteen to twenty men, including marines. On February 28 the British van advanced to the harbor side of James Island and the abandoned Fort Johnson. The Continental frigate *Providence* came down from her anchorage off Sullivan's Island and briefly drove them into the interior of the island with cannon fire before returning to her station in Rebellion Road.

During the night of March 6 and 7, Cornwallis and the light infantry, followed by Clinton and a battalion of British grenadiers, crossed Wappoo Creek to the mainland on a bridge that they had built during the preceding week. From here they skirmished with American forces as they advanced up the west side of the Ashley River. A week later at the mouth of Wappoo Creek at Albemarle Point, they erected a battery of six 32-pounder guns taken from ships-of-the line *Europe* and *Raisonable*, then off the coast. These guns were used to fire on the west side of the city, but were primarily used to keep American naval forces out of the Ashley River; thus, the British maintained control of its upper reaches in order to enable the main body of its army to cross onto Charlestown's neck. They erected another three-gun battery a quarter of a mile upstream (site of the present-day Ashley River bridge approaches). These gun emplacements forced the frigate *Queen of France* and other ships stationed at the mouth of the Ashley to weigh anchor and pass around the city into the Cooper River. The American forces had lost all control over the Ashley River, and British galleys were now free to move upriver to support the army's advance onto Charlestown's neck.

It was during Clinton's march up the west side of the Ashley River that General Lincoln lost his best chance to challenge the British while he still had some freedom of movement to do so; later he would become locked within the walls of the city. The British brought small boats (flats or rafts) and the galleys up the Stono River through Wappoo Creek and up the west side of the Ashley under cover of darkness to a point twelve miles upstream. From here, during the night of March 28–29, Clinton's forces were able to cross the Ashley River totally unopposed to commence the direct siege of the city.

Unfortunately, politics forced Lincoln to get boxed in on the city's peninsula. Both he and General Washington preferred to abandon Charlestown to the British and preserve the army to fight when the situation was more advantageous. The South Carolina authorities refused to allow Charlestown to be abandoned to the enemy. Lincoln's only recourse was to concentrate his limited resources on saving the city. Had he forced the issue and abandoned Charlestown, he may well have lost support of the patriot cause in South Carolina and with it, the war. Lincoln was successful in persuading Rutledge and three members of his council

Two French Warships for the South Carolina State Navy

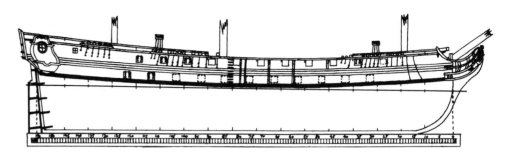

French draught for a 750-ton flute or transport, similar to *Bricole*, which was given to the South Carolina State Navy by France in 1779. *Bricole* was listed in state records as being a 44-gun frigate; however, French records show that she was designed by Giroux, a naval architect who specialized in the flute type of vessel. Flutes were designed to serve as supply vessels for the main body of the French fleet, much as the fleet train serves the U. S. Navy today on far-flung stations.

Bricole was built in Le Havre and launched in 1761. She was 146 feet long, 32.5 feet wide, and drew 16 feet of water. Her original battery consisted of four 12-pounders on the lower gundeck and twenty 8-pounders on the upper gundeck. These were later increased to fourteen 12-pounders and twenty-two 8-pounders. At Savannah, D'Estaing tried to get her upstream in order to bombard the city, but her draft was too deep. Once the siege was abandoned, the extra gunports that had been cut into her hull made her less desirable as a transport; therefore, she was given to the state navy. Her age was probably also a factor in the decision; she was almost twenty years old and in poor repair.

Her narrow beam made her suitable only for harbor defense when heavily armed; the additional weight of so many guns would have made her too limber in a seaway, and thus an unstable gun platform. She could have carried the full 44-gun armament. If so, she would have been slightly inferior to HMS *Roebuck*. Since she was designed as a transport, she would not have had the heavy sides and reinforced spars and rigging to withstand the rigors of combat. Therefore, she would have been at a disadvantage against enemy ships of equal firepower.

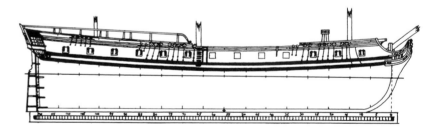

Draught of the 26-gun frigate *Truite* that was given to the state navy by Admiral D'Estaing after the siege of Savannah. *Truite* was built at Le Havre in 1776. She displaced about 580 tons. Like *Bricole*, *Truite* was a transport. At Savannah, gunports were cut only on the port side, and she was used to bombard the city. With the additional gunports, she was no longer desirable as a transport; therefore, she was given to the South Carolina State Navy. The state navy cut additional ports on her starboard side and placed her under the command of James Pyne. Initially they also considered cutting off her forecastle deck and quarterdeck to make her a sloop-of-war or corvette similar to *Ranger*. However, there was not sufficient time or money to accomplish this work.

to leave the city early in the siege, thus maintaining a semblance of civil authority in the rest of the state after the fall of Charlestown. Since the authorities in Georgia had not similarly left Savannah, that state was entirely lost to the British for the duration of the war.

To some, Lincoln was too political, weathercocking to sudden shifts in political opinion; but such a characterization was more the result of the bad fortune that plagued him. He was quite capable, but he lacked the necessary strength to enforce unpopular decisions. He was never held up for public degradation for the disaster at Charlestown, thus showing that he must have possessed qualities of the highest order.

The siege of the city actually began on the night of March 31. The British and Hessian troops erected their trenches and a system of redoubts across the Charlestown neck so quickly and quietly that the American forces were not aware of it until the next day. Ironically, it was April Fool's Day.

Charlestown Prepares for Battle

But the Americans had not been standing idly by. In the fall of 1779, Henry Laurens

Commodore Abraham Whipple's Continental Navy Squadron

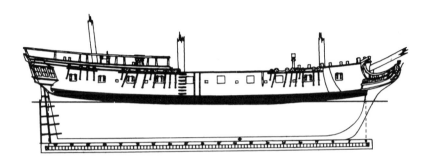

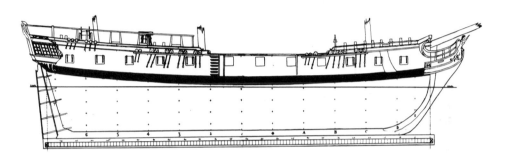

The 18-gun light frigate (or corvette) Ranger. She was typical of the three-masted sloops-of-war first introduced in 1760 for auxiliary purposes. When she arrived in Charlestown at the end of 1779, she was probably the most well-known ship in the Continental Navy. She was built at Portsmouth, New Hampshire, and completed in 1777. John Paul Jones, her first captain, took her to France in November. In February of 1778 at Quiberon Bay, a French warship returned Jones' salute while he was flying the new Stars and Stripes; this is thought to be the first time that the new flag was officially recognized by a foreign government. Two months later, Ranger bested the 20-gun HMS Drake in the Irish Sea. After John Paul Jones left Ranger, she returned to America and came to Charlestown with Whipple's squadron. Upon the fall of the city she was taken into the Royal Navy as HMS Halifax; in poor repair, she was sold out in 1781.

Draught of the Continental frigate *Providence*, built at Providence, Rhode Island, in 1776. Abraham Whipple, her first commander, got her to sea through the British blockade at Newport in April 1777. He took her to France, where she joined *Boston* and *Ranger* in their return to Boston at the end of 1778. In the summer of 1779, *Providence*, *Ranger*, and the frigate *Queen of France* caught a British convoy off Newfoundland and cut out eleven ships, bringing over $1 million in prize money, the largest haul of the war for the Continental Navy. The next year she was ordered to Charlestown, where she became the most active warship in the defense of the city. Upon the surrender of Charlestown she was taken into the Royal Navy as HMS *Providence* and sold out of service in 1784.

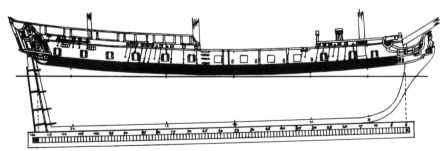

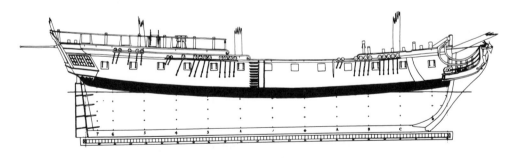

Conjectural draught for the Continental frigate Queen of France. She had been built in France as the privateer *La Brune* and was purchased by Marie Antoinette and given to the American Navy, which renamed the frigate in her honor. The vessel was old and mounted only 6-pounder guns, which were hardly effective against frigates of the day. By the time *Queen of France* reached Charlestown, she was in such bad shape that she was one of the vessels sunk to block the Cooper River.

Draught of the Continental frigate *Boston*, one of the original thirteen frigates ordered by Congress in 1776. She was built at Newburyport, Massachusetts, and first went to sea in 1777. With the frigate *Hancock* she took HMS *Fox*, but fled when all were set upon by two British warships; this allowed *Hancock* and *Fox* to be captured. After a cruise to France, *Boston* was ordered to Charlestown; here she was captured and taken into the Royal Navy as HMS *Charlestown*. She was sold out of the navy in 1783.

had succeeded in persuading the Continental Congress to dispatch a naval force to help in the defense of the South. On December 23, 1779, Commodore Abraham Whipple had arrived in Charlestown with the 28-gun frigates *Providence*, *Queen of France*, and *Boston* and the 18-gun sloop-of-war (corvette) *Ranger*, a squadron that represented a full third of the Continental Navy's warships. This response spoke well of Laurens' efforts and the importance attached to Charlestown, despite the poor faith he and Congress had in the South Carolina State Navy.

The state navy had also been beefing up its forces. In December 1779, four warships were obtained from the French squadron that stopped in Charlestown after the abortive Savannah campaign. One ship obtained was the transport *Bricole*, which was placed under the command of David Lockwood, with intent to convert her into a 44-gun frigate. However, time and money were insufficient for the conversion; therefore, in January the State Navy Board had additional heavy guns mounted on her main deck so that she could be used for harbor defense.

Also obtained was the 26-gun *Truite* (spelled *Trinite* in some accounts). Her command was given to James Pyne, who had been exchanged after losing the galley *Rutledge*. The 26-gun *L'Aventure* and a 16-gun polacre-rigged[2] vessel named *Beaumont* rounded out the French donation.

All of these warships were placed under Whipple's command on February 8, after the departure of the remainder of the French squadron in January. Additional private vessels were purchased, leased, or borrowed. Thus, the South Carolina State Navy boasted a fleet of some fifteen ships and five galleys. However, even with liberal bonuses and lavish supplies of rum, insufficient recruits were attracted to man the galleys *Lee* and *South Edisto*.

Clinton's objective was to besiege the city from the neck while Arbuthnot's fleet controlled the harbor and river approaches. This would sever the land and sea approaches to the city, effectively cutting it off from outside assistance. Lincoln's objective was to keep Clinton confined to James Island while Whipple kept the Royal Navy from crossing the bar or at least coming beyond Fort Moultrie. Lincoln realized that if the British fleet could be kept out of the inner harbor, Clinton could not succeed on land without great difficulty. As Parker had discovered during his attack four years earlier, any ships drawing more than seventeen feet of water could not cross the bar except on the full moon tide. This meant that warships mounting over thirty guns would have to lighten ship to enter the harbor. The task could be accomplished by removing the heavier guns on the lower gundeck and decreasing the ship's stores and supplies. But in such condition, the ships would be very vulnerable to attack. High winds would also pose a threat, as the lightened ships would be unstable, riding high in the water.

Lincoln's plans did not see fruition, as Whipple, typical of the conservative, overly cautious military officer, was not eager to engage the enemy regardless of the circumstances. In fairness, he undoubtedly realized the shortcomings of his ships and the overwhelming superiority of the British fleet. But any excuse sufficed to provide him reason not to attack: his frigates drew too much water to maneuver in the confined water near the enemy working to cross the bar, and his smaller ships were no match for the enemy. Because of the strong current, Whipple also vetoed Lincoln's suggestion that he place his ships off Fort Moultrie

Commodore Abraham Whipple (1733–1819) by Edward Savage (1761–1817), circa 1786. The frigate *Providence* is supposedly the ship in the background.

[2] A polacre was a Mediterranean vessel with tall, slender masts of single poles with no doublings. They were not expected to withstand the heavy weather of the open ocean.

A Plan of the Siege of Charlestown 1780

American Fortifications

Forts

A. Wilkins	10 guns
B. Gibbs	9 guns
C. Fergusons	5 guns
D. Sugar House	6 guns
E. Old Magazine	5 guns
F. Cumming's Point	5 guns
G. West Point	4 guns

H. Hornwork of masonry closed during the siege to form a citadel with stong lines and redoubts. A canal ran from the Ashley to the Cooper River in front. The Hornwork mounted 66 guns.

Other American Defenses

K. Gadsden's Wharf	7 guns
L. Old Indian	5 guns
M. Governors Bridge	3 guns
N. Exchange	7 guns
O. End of the Bay	4 guns
P. Darrell's	7 guns

Q. Boom from the Exchange to Shute's Folly composed of 8 vessels sunk across the channel.

Redoubts and Batteries of the British Army

Redoubts numbered 1 through 6 begun on April 1 for the First Parallel.
o The Second Parallel completed April 19.
p The Third Parallel completed May 6.
q Gun batteries
r Mortar batteries
Upon the surrender of the American forces, the garrison marched out of the city and laid down their arms at I in front of the Hornwork.

A Masterpiece of the Ship Modeler's Art

HMS *Roebuck*, flagship of Arbuthnot's squadron in the Charlestown Campaign. This stunning Admiralty-style model by Harold Hahn of Lyndhurst, Ohio, shows exquisite detail. Along with HMS *Perseus* and *Russell*, she was copper-bottomed, a rarity during the Revolution. In the spring of 1777 she and *Perseus* captured *Defence* of the South Carolina State Navy. Her sister ship was the famous *Serapis*, which John Paul Jones captured in 1779. They were part of a class of 44-gun fifth-rate ships that rendered yeoman service. Typical of the small two-deckers of the period, the guns on the lower deck were so close to the water that they were difficult (if not dangerous) to handle in a seaway with waves washing through the open gunports. *Roebuck* and the later American frigate *Constitution*, also rated at 44 guns, exemplify the transition from two to one gun decks as ship lengths increased in the last two decades of the eighteenth century. *Constitution* carried her 24-pounder weapons on a 1,500-ton displacement; *Roebuck* displaced little over half that, even though her guns were mostly 18 pounders. *Roebuck* arrived off the Charlestown bar on February 25, 1780, and remained until June 8, when she departed to escort 100 ships to New York with the bulk of Clinton's troops.

to aid the fort in opposing the British squadron as it tried to enter the inner harbor. However, he was really more concerned with being cut off from the city with no means of escape. Almost a century of Royal Navy victories over the naval powers of Europe served to cower any potential adversary. In Whipple's case the mere reputation of that prowess succeeded.

Thus, Lincoln allowed the Continental Navy squadron to withdraw to the city and await the enemy. In March after the British squadron crossed the bar, the Americans decided to scuttle *Notre Dame, General Moultrie, Bricole, Truite,* and *Queen of France* in the Cooper River between the city and Shute's Folly, after placing spiked obstructions on their decks ("chevaux de frize") and binding them together by a boom tied to their masts. This barrier of sunken ships would keep Arbuthnot's ships out of the upper Cooper River and allow the river to serve as a route for both incoming reinforcements and possible escape. British land batteries on the west side of the Ashley River made that river untenable for the American ships. In addition, the city side of the Ashley was mostly marsh, therefore less vulnerable to bombardment. Consequently, the American forces were concentrated on the dense and fortified Cooper River waterfront and the land defenses on Charlestown neck.

The scuttling operation all but ended the South Carolina State Navy, leaving only a few smaller vessels and galleys. The remaining Continental warships *Providence, Ranger,* and *Boston,* along with *Beaumont* and *L'Aventure* and several galleys, were stationed behind the boom to defend the city and keep enemy ships from coming through Hog Island Creek. The other vessels were tied up at dock with their guns and crews sent either to join the land fortifications or put to fighting the enemy land batteries around the city. By mid-April all of the warships except *Providence* and *Ranger* were laid up and stripped of their guns and crews. With these additions from the navy, Charlestown's battery on land consisted of some 200 guns, ranging from 2-pounders to 32-pounders. The British and Hessian troops complained more of the heat and insects than they did of American firepower; there seemed to be very little organized resistance except in retreating.

In preparation for the sortie into the harbor, Admiral Arbuthnot shifted his flag to the 44-gun fifth-rate *Roebuck.* For the two weeks preceding the spring tide on March 20, crews worked feverishly to remove the guns and supplies from *Roebuck,* the 50-gun *Renown,* and the 44-gun *Romulus.* Thus lightened, these three fourth- and fifth-rates were moved over the bar; for two more weeks, their equipment and arms were then reinstalled. Six additional 12-pounder guns were installed on *Roebuck* to bring her armament up to fifty guns. At the same time several hundred British seamen accompanied by officers were sent ashore in ships' boats to cooperate with the army. Throughout the entire time the British squadron was vulnerable to an American attack that never came.

Roebuck, Renown, and *Romulus* alone possessed as much firepower as all of the artillery defending Charlestown on land. Their maneuverability allowed them to be concentrated at any point where the water was deep enough, but their wooden hulls were more vulnerable than the masonry and sand fortifications that they would oppose, particularly if hot shot or heated cannonballs were thrown their way. A slugfest between these powerful ships and the fortifications of the city never materialized, but had it come, it would have been a battle royal.

These warships, along with the 32-gun frigates *Blonde* and *Raleigh,*[3] the 28-gun *Virginia,*

and the 24-gun *Sandwich,* gave Arbuthnot a powerful force with which to challenge the defenses of Charlestown. Only the guns of Fort Moultrie stood between Arbuthnot's squadron and the inner harbor, and he would have to pass within a quarter of a mile of it as he came up the channel. Now stronger, the fort was built of brick and palmetto logs 20 feet high, and mounted some forty guns, most of which were 24-pounders manned by 150 men under Colonel Scott.

On April 8 Arbuthnot's ships set sail under a cloud of canvas from Five Fathom Hole off Morris Island. With a favorable wind and tide and occasional rain squalls, they approached the fort at 3 p.m. with guns blazing. Because the transports were following, Arbuthnot decided against anchoring and engaging in a cannonade with Moultrie as Parker had done four years earlier. Instead he chose to run by the fort. Parker's defeat had proved the futility of his course of action; Arbuthnot knew that once his fleet got past safely and into the harbor, Fort Moultrie would be powerless to defend the city.

Vice Admiral Marriot Arbuthnot, commander of Royal Navy forces during the siege of Charlestown. Except for his contribution to the British victory at Charlestown, he had a rather lackluster career.

---

[3] *Raleigh* and *Virginia* were former frigates of the Continental Navy that were captured by the British in 1778.

Panorama of the 1780 siege of Charlestown, as seen from the British lines on Charlestown neck. Visible are the remains of the ships sunk in the Cooper River to obstruct the entry of British warships, seen in the distance off James Island (left). At right are the British gunboats and galleys operating in the Wappoo and Ashley rivers.

Renown brings up the rear of the formation as Arbuthnot's line battles past Fort Moultrie. The British transports are at left. These two paintings by the marine artist Mark Myers, RSMA of Cornwall, England, are among several especially commissioned for this book. The artist went to great lengths to ensure accuracy by obtaining plans of the original ships from the National Maritime Museum in Greenwich, England.

Vice Admiral Arbuthnot's van sails into Charlestown harbor after battling past Fort Moultrie. In the left foreground is the frigate *Richmond* with her crew struggling to clear away the wreckage of her foretopmast after it was shot away by Moultrie's deadly fire. Behind *Richmond* is the damaged transport *Aeolus*. Between *Richmond* and the flagship *Roebuck* (right foreground) are *Romulus* followed by *Virginia*. At extreme right is *Renown* bringing up the rear.

The flagship *Roebuck* and the frigate *Richmond* served as the van, withstanding the heaviest fire of Moultrie's guns. They were followed by *Romulus, Blonde, Virginia, Raleigh*, and *Sandwich*; then the six transports; then *Renown* covering the rear. When the latter passed the fort, she lay to, took in her sails, and poured in several broadsides in such quick succession that the whole ship seemed to flare up. After two hours, the fleet succeeded in passing the fort, and anchored off Fort Johnson. The defenders had caused damage, but not nearly enough. *Renown* suffered most, with seven men killed and twenty wounded. *Richmond* lost her foretopmast, but of the 14 sail in the fleet, only the armed transport *Aeolus* was lost when she was disabled by Moultrie's fire and ran aground off Haddrell's Point. While lying helpless, she was taken under fire by Captain Thomas Gadsden with two field cannon. She was so shot to pieces that her crew set her on fire after her equipment was removed.

Once the squadron anchored, they were taken under long-range fire by batteries in the city. The flagship *Roebuck* was the primary object, but most of the shot fell short and those that did hit were ineffective. Each time the ships dared to approach the city, they were taken under fire; as a result they maintained their station off Fort Johnson for most of the remainder of the siege.

From the steeple of St. Michael's Church, Peter Timothy watched the passage of Arbuthnot's ships and remarked:

> They really make a most noble appearance and I could not help admiring the regularity and intrepidity with which they approached, engaged, and passed Fort Moultrie. It will reflect great honor upon the admiral and all his captains, but 'tis pity they are not friends.

With the serviceable American warships now behind the boom in the Cooper River, the British galleys *Comet* and *Scourge* began to come out of the Wappoo Cut regularly at night to join the British land batteries in bombarding the Ashley River side of the city. Their attacks were so frequent and little opposed that they soon ran low on ammunition.

On April 18 an additional 3,000 British reinforcements arrived from New York. They made the forces besieging Charlestown one of the largest armies deployed during the war. These new troops were used against the American forces across the harbor in Mt. Pleasant. On April 26 the battery at Haddrell's Point fell, and the next day 500 British marines and sailors took the battery at Lempriere's Point at the fork of the Cooper and Wando rivers. They effectively severed the last American link with the outside. This completed the investment of the city.

On April 30, *Renown* and the galley *Comet* ran aground while moving in to attack the bridge battery on Mount Pleasant that guarded the mainland approach to Fort Moultrie. *Comet* was lost and burned, but *Renown* was refloated. On May 7, marines from *Richmond* landed and took the bridge battery without firing a shot. From here they sent a summons to Fort Moultrie to surrender, threatening that refusal would lead to annihilation. Most of the fort's troops had already been removed to the city; those that remained surrendered without firing another shot.

Disaster at Charlestown

Lincoln held on for a few more days, but the end was in sight. The city was hemmed in by a powerful army on all sides and a fleet in the harbor. After much negotiating, Lincoln accepted the British terms and surrendered the city on May 12, rather than have it fall to an enemy assault that could have resulted in its being destroyed, with many civilian casualties.

Charlestown's siege had not been particularly severe. There was no shortage of food or ammunition. What contributed most to the British success was the lack of zeal for the American cause and the number of loyalists in the city. The enemy bombardment, while destructive, did not begin to compare with that experienced by European cities of the period. Most of the fighting in Charlestown took place along present-day Calhoun Street almost a mile from the main part of the city. Warships and galleys of the Royal Navy and gun emplacements on the west side of the Ashley River threw shells into the city, but the damage was more psychological than physical; the main portion of the city lay on the Cooper River side of the peninsula, almost two miles from the enemy guns on the Ashley. Since the main portion of the city that faced the Cooper River was well protected by gun bastions, the city managed to keep enemy warships at a distance. Most of the American losses were from British and Hessian sharpshooters on the main siege line. Their fire was so amazingly accurate that at times American gunners refused to appear before the gun embrasures for fear of being shot down.

With the fall of Charlestown, the American cause received a crushing blow. Not only had 5,500 troops been lost, but also the most powerful squadron yet assembled by the Continental Navy. The state of South Carolina lost not only Charlestown, the most important city in the colonies south of Philadelphia, but also almost the entire state navy, 1,000 seamen, and large quantities of munitions. Not until General Julius White surrendered almost 14,000 Union troops to Stonewall Jackson at Harper's Ferry in September 1862 would more American men at arms surrender in one fell swoop to enemy forces. Since then it has been exceeded only by General Jonathan Wainwright's surrender of American forces on Bataan in April 1942. Thus, Charlestown became synonymous with disaster in the annals of American military history.

Forty-nine ships and some 120 boats of various kinds were taken with the fall of the city. The Royal Navy lost only one ship, with 23 seamen killed and 28 wounded. The South Carolina State Navy did not disappear completely. The brig *Polly* continued to cruise against the enemy as late as October 1781. In addition, the galleys *Revenge* and *Beaufort* were hidden in the state's waterways. Privateers cruising off Charlestown were able to cause the British army serious losses of war materiel.

The British forces settled in for a long occupation in Charlestown under Lord Cornwallis, who from there attempted to subdue the rest of South and North Carolina. General Clinton and the Hessian troops returned to New York a month after the fall of the city. The captured frigate *Boston* became HMS *Charlestown*, and *Ranger* became HMS *Halifax*. Most of the other captured vessels were deemed unserviceable and scuttled.

General Lincoln was sent to New York, where he was exchanged for Major General Phillips in November 1780. Upon rejoining the Continental Army, Lincoln was made a division commander. As second in command to Washington at Yorktown, he won a measure of retribution for his surrender to Cornwallis at Charlestown. How he must have relished seeing Cornwallis take his turn at surrender! After the war, Lincoln served as Secretary of War for two years, and in 1787 was in charge of putting down Shay's Rebellion. He died in May 1810 in his native city, Hingham, Massachusetts.

Alexander Gillon and the Frigate *South Carolina*

No maritime history of Charleston would be complete without reference to the flagship of the South Carolina State Navy, the frigate *South Carolina*. She was the largest ship ever to fly the flag of the Palmetto State, and possibly mounted the largest cannons of any frigate in history. *South Carolina* only once had a glimpse of her namesake state, and that was from a great distance offshore. The state of South Carolina was occupied by the British at the time. Even if it had not been, however, *South Carolina* had too great a draft to have crossed over the bar into Charlestown.

Nevertheless, her influence on South Carolina's naval history during the American Revolution cannot be exaggerated; it was probably greater than that of any other ship associated with the state. Furthermore, she had a direct influence on the subsequent design of the American frigates that won fame during the War of 1812. (Compare the plan of *South Carolina* on page 118 to that of *Constitution* on page 126).

Alexander Gillon Arrives in Charlestown

The history of *South Carolina* begins with the story of Alexander Gillon, the man responsible for bringing her to America and into the South Carolina State Navy. Born on August 13, 1741, in Rotterdam, Holland, Gillon was the son of a Scottish sea captain of French ancestry and his second wife. Although his father died a poor man, young Gillon managed to serve an apprenticeship first with a Dutch shipping company and then with a British concern. He made his first trip to America in 1764 as master of the small merchant brig *Surprize*. The following year he called at Charlestown for the first time. On a subsequent voyage to the city in 1766 on the brigantine *Free-Mason*, one of his passengers was Mary Splatt Cripps, widow of William Cripps of County Kent, England, and daughter of Richard Splatt, a Charlestown merchant. Love must have blossomed during *Free-Mason's* passage; Alexander and Mary were married in July 1766 shortly after they arrived in Charlestown.

Charlestown in the 1760s was rapidly approaching the cultural heights it would achieve before the end of the century and maintain thereafter. Its people were already noted for their politeness and affability; the Carolina colony had managed to avoid the puritannical austerity of its northern neighbors. Attracted by the quality of life in Charlestown, Gillon was certainly influenced by his wife and her father to settle there. He retired from the sea and successfully entered trade, undoubtedly encouraged and assisted by his many European connections and a benevolent father-in-law. By the time of the American Revolution, he had amassed a small fortune and acquired real estate in the proximity of East Bay Street near the Exchange Building and present-day Gillon Street. His real estate holdings were estimated at £30,000 sterling. During 1773 he was among the seventy prominent Charlestonians who founded the city's chamber of commerce. Gillon's charm and affability quickly ingratiated him with the city. He became a leading citizen in every sense of the word.

As tension between the colonies and Great Britain grew during the latter part of 1775, Gillon secured a contract from the Continental Congress at Philadelphia to procure military materiel in Europe for the colonial armed forces. The three ships he dispatched for this pur-

Commodore Alexander Gillon by Gilbert Stuart.

pose returned to America in 1776 laden with cannon, powder, and other military supplies. Upon the formal declaration of war, Gillon organized a volunteer militia company and was later appointed a commissioner of the South Carolina State Navy. With a group of his peers, he supervised the conversion of the impressed merchant ship *Prosper* into a 20-gun ship-of-war for the state navy, despite the protests of its skipper. As his involvement in state politics grew, Gillon served a term in the original General Assembly during 1776, having held a seat in the Provincial Congress, its predecessor. During the following year, he left the mercantile trade entirely in order to devote his full time and energies to the Revolutionary movement. Although he had another opportunity to procure supplies for the Continental Congress, he was concurrently offered the post of Commodore of the South Carolina State Navy. Gillon accepted the position, influenced no doubt by the commodore's share of any prize money obtained.

European Intrigue

Gillon received his commission in May 1778 and was ordered to Europe to purchase and equip three frigates for the state navy, for which the legislature had appropriated a budget of $500,000. As the state's currency was worthless in Europe and there was little specie, the budgeted funds were used to purchase indigo and rice to be sold in Europe for cash. To augment the proceeds of this sale, Gillon was authorized to negotiate loans abroad against the credit of the state of South Carolina. After participating in an attack on three enemy privateers off Charlestown, two of which were captured and brought into port, Gillon got underway for Europe in August. Escorted by *Oliver Cromwell* of the Connecticut State Navy and two sloops, Gillon sailed on *Notre Dame* for Havana; there he established a relationship with the local hierarchy that would prove beneficial later in the war. On the way to France, Gillon encountered D'Estaing's fleet, which detached the 40-gun frigate *La Fortunee* to escort them to Brest. They arrived in January 1779.

Gillon's arrival came at an inopportune time. Since France had recently been placed on a war footing, any vessels he wanted to purchase had already been conscripted by the French government. To make matters worse, the French commercial houses proved unwilling to extend credit beyond 100,000 French livres; the British invasion of Georgia and its potential threat to South Carolina appeared too high a risk. The French government also turned a deaf ear to Gillon's pleas for additional financial aid, probably due to the British threat to the state, the many calls made on her treasury by various American groups pleading for assistance, and her own war status with Great Britain.

Gillon appealed to Benjamin Franklin for assistance with the French, but Franklin felt that his position was to represent the interests of the Continental Congress, not those of the individual states, and he refused to intercede. Gillon took a tactless approach to Franklin, America's elder statesman, by referring to himself as "Ye Superior American Naval Officer in Europe." This led to a lasting personal feud between Gillon and Franklin. John Paul Jones, a naval officer of proven merit and a personal friend of Franklin's, called Gillon the "red-ribboned commodore," because of Gillon's habit of dressing up in elaborate, colorful regalia. After encountering nearly total failure in his efforts to obtain funding in France, Gillon turned to his native land, Holland. He established himself at Amsterdam, where he was soon attempting to pass himself off as an admiral.

In Amsterdam, Gillon found the large frigate *L'Indien*, which had originally been ordered under subterfuge by France for the American Congress with the tacit approval of the Dutch government. John Paul Jones, who was designated by Franklin to command the frigate, described her as "the finest ship that ever was built." What terror Jones and *L'Indien* would have spread through the British Isles if *L'Indien* had become *Bon Homme Richard* instead of the leaky old French Indiaman, *Duc de Duras*. However, when the British learned of her intended ownership, they forced the neutral Dutch to deliver her to the French and to pressure the Americans into relinquishing their claims to the vessel. The French then ceded the warship's title to the Grand Duchy of Luxembourg in a dizzying sequence of events.

The ship had been designed by the innovative French naval architect Louis Boux along the lines of the French Indiamen built prior to the American Revolution for the French Company of the Indies. She was designed to escort merchantmen far from home, specifically to the Indian Ocean. While called a frigate, she was really a ship-of-the line with one main

A sketch of the frigate *South Carolina* dated some ten years after her capture, supposedly done by one of her former crewmen. According to Jean Beaudroit, the French expert on eighteenth-century warships, this drawing indicates some archaic rigging practices for the time. However, experience indicates that sailors' sketches of their ships were most faithful in the rigging, which they knew best. Undoubtedly Gillon and/or Joyner exercised customary ship captain's discretion and made changes to suit their taste. Of note is the extra row of reefing points on the topsails, the spiritsails on the bowsprit, and the lateen rig on the mizzenmast.

gundeck instead of two or three. She was an exceptionally large ship for a frigate, especially at a time when 64-gun ships were still "of-the-line-of-battle" in European navies. *L'Indien* was larger than the typical 50-gunner in all respects and equal to many 64-gun ships-of-the-line in tonnage and size of broadside. As a result, no contemporary frigate could stand up to her alone and she was the most powerful warship in American service during the Revolution.

The most reliable dimensions available for *L'Indien* are those taken by the British Admiralty. Her dimensions were measured as 198′0″ overall, with an extreme beam of 43′3″. Her main deck battery consisted of twenty-eight Swedish 36-pounders (42-pounders by English measure) with a secondary battery of twelve 12-pounders on the quarterdeck and four others on the forecastle. She was capable of delivering a broadside of 600 pounds. The typical British 40-gun frigate of the period could deliver between 250 to 300 pounds. To give some specific comparisons, the 50-gun *Bristol*, flagship during the British attack on Charlestown in 1776, was fifty feet shorter, with a design broadside of slightly more than 400 pounds. So, while *Bristol* carried more guns, her firepower was less than that of *L'Indien* because of the heavier caliber of the latter's guns. The British 64-gun ship *Africa*, built in 1781, measured 160′10″ on deck, with an extreme beam of 44′9″. She originally mounted a broadside of 600 pounds, which made her relatively equal in firepower to *L'Indien*, although she carried twenty more guns, albeit of smaller caliber.

L'Indien was laid down in the spring of 1777 in a private Dutch building yard, supposedly for Louis XVI of France. By May the Marine Committee of the Continental Congress had learned of the ship and the possibility of purchasing her—probably through the efforts of their newly acquired French Agent, Pierre-Augustin Caron Beaumarchais. The American Commissioners in France, Franklin, Silas Deane, and Arthur Lee, then worked to acquire the ship. However, their plans were foiled by British political pressure.

From Beaumarchais or some other ally, Commodore Gillon had obviously received prior information of Louis XVI's intention to cede *L'Indien* to Luxembourg. Otherwise it would have been impossible for him to complete her lease with the Chevalier de Luxembourg on the day of the cession. As Gillon did not possess

the funds to buy the vessel and the Chevalier was not really free to sell her, the two developed a different stratagem. Under their agreement, signed jointly on May 30, 1780 (only eighteen days after Charlestown fell to the British), the state of South Carolina leased *L'Indien* for three years. Gillon was to command her, the state was to maintain her, and she was to be removed from Holland within six weeks.

The frigate's intended objective was to cruise against the common enemies of France and America. All her prizes were to be sent to France under consignment to a specific Parisian banker. Proceeds from successful condemnation hearings on the prizes were to be divided in fourths: one to the Chevalier, one to the state of South Carolina, and two to the

Admiralty-style model of the frigate *South Carolina*. This magnificent model on ¼″ = 1′ scale is some 43″ long overall and represents an investment of 1,000 hours of labor by four individuals over a fifteen-year period. Compare *South Carolina's* (and *Constitution's* on page 126) arrangement of one long main gun deck instead of two gun decks to that shown in the model of *Roebuck* on pages 108 and 109. Both warships were rated at 44 guns, but *South Carolina's* were of heavier caliber. In this ship we can see the transition to longer warships with fewer gun decks. *Inset: South Carolina's* gilded lion figurehead.

Draughts of the *South Carolina/L'Indien*

These French draughts show an elegant ship typical of eighteenth-century warships with their tumblehome on the sides and graceful sweep of sheer, from the beautifully carved headrails and trailboards at her bow to the magnificently sculptured quarter galleries astern. *South Carolina* is a fine example of why the eighteenth century is considered by many to be the epitome of Western man's civilized acomplishment. Note the similarity of *South Carolina's* hull profile to that of *Constitution's* on page 126.

ship's officers and crew. Upon termination of the three-year agreement (or sooner in case of peace with Great Britain), the frigate was to be returned intact to L'Orient, France. Upon signing, Gillon paid 100,000 livres to the Chevalier to bind the agreement; this amount was curiously equal to his French line of credit. The contractual terms stated that if the frigate were lost by capture or Act of God, an additional indemnity of 300,000 livres was guaranteed to Luxembourg. As collateral, Gillon pledged his personal property, as well as that of the state of South Carolina. On the date the agreement was executed, the vessel's name was officially changed from *L'Indien* to *South Carolina*.

Gillon and his colleague, Captain John Joyner, then set out to various French seaports to enlist a crew. At L'Orient, Gillon enticed some sailors away from Jones' new command, the frigate *Alliance*. This did nothing to improve his relationship with the Franklin/Jones faction. Unfortunately, he also became embroiled in the bitter affair between Jones and Pierre Landais over the Frenchman's treachery during the engagement between *Bon Homme Richard* and *Serapis*.

South Carolina was finally manned and provisioned for sea, but a series of mishaps delayed her departure from Amsterdam. Unseasonably low water blocked her passage through the Zuider Zee to Texel, the gateway to the North Sea. This problem was resolved by off-loading most of *South Carolina's* guns and heavier cargo into lighters and then inducing a sharp list in the ship's trim for the duration of the seventy miles of shallow waters.

The year 1780 was now lost for operations, and Gillon went into winter quarters by running the frigate up a well-protected creek until the end of January 1781. These delays caused additional expenditures, and the Dutch would not clear *South Carolina* for departure until Gillon paid them.

South Carolina's great statesman, Henry Laurens, in Paris on a special mission for the Continental Congress, offered to rescue Gillon financially if the ship would take a consignment of goods to Philadelphia. Based on Laurens' offer, Gillon moved the frigate to Texel Roads on March 12 and began final preparations for his departure. However, an old feud resurfaced; Franklin blocked Laurens' advance, stating a fear that "I shall hear of the arrival of that ship in England before she sees America." In the meantime, the private army of 300 men hired for the ship by the Chevalier de Luxembourg arrived at Texel Roads in the middle of June. This increased the pressure for an early departure.

To thwart his Dutch creditors and to avoid possible confiscation of the ship, Gillon got *South Carolina* underway from Texel Roads on August 4 and came to anchor a league off-shore, safely beyond Dutch territorial jurisdiction. There, several American passengers bound for home joined the ship. Among them were Lieutenant Colonel John Trumbull, a noted artist; Charles Adams, the youngest son of John and Abigail Adams of Massachusetts; and, most important of all for the safety of the ship, Lieutenant Joshua Barney of the Continental Navy, who had recently escaped from Mill Prison in England.

Underway for America

On the morning of August 14, Gillon was preparing to depart from the anchorage when a vicious gale struck the ship. The direction of the wind made the treacherously shallow coastal waters of Holland a lee shore and placed *South Carolina* in an exceptionally dangerous position. Gillon was forced to weigh anchor. But he could not reenter the Texel for fear of being seized by the Dutch authorities; nor could he get underway on a safe course down the

English Channel for fear of encountering British warships of superior strength. Therefore, he chose his only remaining option and tacked upwind to keep away from the dangerous Dutch seaboard.

When darkness fell, the ship was perilously close to shore, but continued to stand off Texel Island for nine days awaiting a convoy of two Dutch ships as well as several American merchantmen with Continental stores.

Finally on August 23, to the cheers of the crew, Commodore Gillon ordered Captain John Joyner to set sail and steer northwestward through the North Sea for America.

Several hours later as *South Carolina* closed in on the island of Heligoland in a fog, the weather worsened. Regrettably, Gillon's seamanship and command ability were both lacking at this time of crisis; the big frigate was battered by the rough seas. Her crew abandoned their stations aloft with all hope for survival apparently lost.

Fortunately, Lieutenant Barney came on deck to offer his assistance to the ship's officers. By his authoritative manner, he was able to gain the confidence of the crew, and they responded promptly to his disciplined orders. Barney soon had *South Carolina* under control again, and they safely weathered the Heligoland Bight.[1] Then with the Danish coast looming a few miles ahead and the aid of a friendly windshift, Barney ordered the crew to tack to the northwest and stand out to sea. After gaining a safe offing from the coast of Jutland, Barney worked the ship northward around the Faero Islands, where on August 25 she suffered through yet another severe storm before turning to the south once again.

After storm dangers had abated and *South Carolina* was safely on its way down the west coast of Ireland, Gillon apparently resumed command. It became evident that the large armament of the ship and the extra hands required to work it meant that insufficient space remained for provisions for the transatlantic voyage. Gillon decided to put into La Corunna, Spain, to replenish stores and disembark many of the passengers; although not able to bear a hand in working the ship, they were still depleting her limited supplies. Enroute to Spain he took several prizes, including the privateer *Alexander* (later retaken) and a cutter that he burned. After their arrival in La Corunna on September 23, the condemnations brought £25,000 sterling to *South Carolina's* crew.

South Carolina departed from La Corunna in mid-October, leaving behind more than fifty sick crewmen, the majority of the passengers, several French deserters, and a number of unpaid bills. En route to Santa Cruz harbor, Teneriffe, in the Canary Islands, the frigate captured a brig loaded with salt fish, which was sold upon arrival. Gillon weighed anchor from Santa Cruz on November 24, leaving thirty more ailing crewmen and another string of unpaid bills.

During the last week of December 1781, *South Carolina* at last approached Charlestown, only to encounter an English fleet of thirty-two sail. For five days she successfully dodged them and cruised briefly within sight of Charlestown; those on board could make

---

[1] On the Dutch coast, the morning after the storm of August 14, the wreckage of a convoy of twelve Swedish merchantmen escorted by a 74-gun ship-of-the line was discovered in the vicinity of Texel Island. The Swedish 74 had a yellow lion figurehead similar to that on *South Carolina*. At first it was thought that Gillon's frigate had been lost. Due to the extensive offshore shoals in that area, the Swedish ships broke up in the surf many miles from land and all on board perished.

out Fort Moultrie and the church spires of the town. Finally determining that the city was still in enemy hands, Gillon reshaped his course for Cuba rather than winter in the north.

Cuban Interlude

In order to avoid a chance encounter with British men-of-war, Gillon chose to sail through the Gulf of Providence in the Bahamas, then still relatively uncharted. During the passage, he remained near the foremast while the leadsmen constantly sounded the bottom. While passing through the Florida straits against the Gulf Stream, *South Carolina* came across five Jamaicamen (three ships and two brigs) loaded with sugar and rum. Gillon captured them by a *ruse-de-guerre*, steering into the fleet under the pretext that *South Carolina* was a British man-of-war. A few days later on January 13, 1782, the flagship of the South Carolina State Navy saluted the Moro Castle and entered Havana harbor with her prizes.

During the next four months, Gillon sold the prizes for $91,500; he then careened, refitted, and replenished *South Carolina* at the Spanish dockyard in Havana. In April Juan Manuel de Cagigal, the Spanish Captain-General of Cuba, approached Commodore Gillon concerning an invasion he was planning of the British-held Bahamas. He offered Gillon command of the considerable maritime force of sixty-two vessels, including troop transports and privateers, that was to be employed.

Gillon accepted in exchange for the cost of his refit of 60,000 Spanish milled dollars, part of which he and Joyner had already paid from personal funds. Gillon felt that his assistance would help to rid Charlestown of the British privateers out of Nassau. It also enabled him to return a favor to the Spanish for their friendly assistance to American ships that had put into Havana during the war. Cagigal apparently gave Gillon verbal acceptance of his offer, but failed to put it in writing.

Thus, on April 22, 1782, *South Carolina* became the flagship of the Spanish invasion fleet of some sixty-two vessels, fifteen of which were American privateers transporting 3,000 Spanish troops. Gillon guided the vessels safely through the Northwest Providence Channel and arrived off New Providence Island on May 5. He was aided by the former Charlestown privateer captains Downham Newton, his brother William Newton, and William Woodsides, who had become familiar with the area when aboard *Vixen* and *Swift*. They were now in command of three privateers out of Philadelphia.

Gillon stationed the warships of the fleet around the island and General Cagigal drew up his forces for the attack on Nassau. Cagigal called upon the British Governor General, John Maxwell, to surrender in order to avoid bloodshed. Governor Maxwell, after submitting one unacceptable counterproposal, complied; on May 8 the Spanish forces landed and took possession of the fort and harbor. Gillon cruised off New Providence until all the Spanish ships had safely entered the port of Nassau and then set sail for Philadelphia. Despite the apparent success of the expedition, it ended in acrimony, as did most of the events involving Gillon and *South Carolina*. The state of South Carolina did not receive any reimbursement from the Spanish because Cagigal defaulted on his promised payment, claiming that Gillon had failed to escort his fleet safely back to Havana.

Sojourn at Philadelphia

Off the coast of North Carolina Gillon encountered an American merchant fleet and escorted it into Philadelphia, arriving on the last day of May. Most of the crew left *South Carolina* immediately because their enlistments had expired. Many were foreigners anxious to seek their fortunes in a new land; others merely deserted, having received very little pay or prize money. Gillon then set out to recruit a replacement crew. In the town of Lancaster he enrolled fifty Hessian prisoners who had been captured five years earlier at the battle of Saratoga. Although they were promised repatriation after the battle, the Hessians were still prisoners of war. They represented a volatile asset to *South Carolina*; in a battle with a British ship, it would be to their interest to surrender. All in all, Gillon managed to enlist a motley group of two to three hundred recruits. While few had ever seen the sea, others were deserters from the British Army. The latter had great potential as fierce fighters against the British; if ever captured by the British, they would be hanged.

Enlisting a crew was not Gillon's only problem. The Chevalier de Luxembourg decided to prosecute for his share of the prize money; secured the aid of the French minister to the Continental Congress, the Chevalier de la Luzerne; and brought legal proceedings against Gillon for breach of contract. Robert Morris, the key civilian executive of the Continental Navy, supported the French. He evidently hoped to wrest the ship from Gillon and turn it over to John Paul Jones for an expedition to Bermuda in company with the few remaining vessels of the Continental Navy. After a hearing, Gillon was ordered held until he could post bond. But he thwarted the court proceedings by resigning his command, turning *South Carolina* over to Captain Joyner, and fleeing the city. Prior to his departure, he ordered Joyner to continue cruising until June 1783, when the ship was due to be returned to the Grand Duchy of Luxembourg.

During *South Carolina's* stay at Philadelphia, the young naval architect and shipbuilder Joshua Humphreys had ample opportunity to study her. Humpreys was already responsible for the design and construction of the fine frigate *Randolph*, and may have contributed to other vessels of the Continental Navy. Twelve years later he was employed by President George Washington and Secretary of War Henry Knox to design two classes of frigates for the new United States Navy. The consensus was that the fledgling navy needed ships that would outclass contemporary European frigates. The five vessels that were subsequently built to his plans all bore an ancestral relationship to *South Carolina*, whose size and power had obviously impressed him vis-à-vis other frigates. All proved their worth in the War of 1812; so, too, perhaps did *South Carolina*, in an indirect way.

After being moored at Philadelphia for six months, *South Carolina* was still 120 men short of her full complement. Joyner was determined to put to sea before the coming winter ice could trap her in the river. By then, South Carolina was largely once again in patriot hands, and the British were evacuating Charlestown on December 14; therefore, wintering at Port Royal and receiving proper instructions from the state's political hierarchy was not out of the question. In addition Luzerne's ongoing legal action and its possible outcome of seizure worried him. Therefore, Joyner decided to weigh anchor and head downstream on December 19. *South Carolina* had traveled no more than a few miles when a portion of his hastily assembled crew mutinied. With the aid of his officers and the Hessians, Captain Joyner restored order, but matters worsened as the ship neared the open waters of the ocean. The majority of the crew became seasick, and Joyner discovered that most of the men who had accepted the ship's bounty as able-bodied seamen proved to be no better than raw landsmen.

Meanwhile, once British intelligence agents in Philadelphia had reported *South Carolina's* departure to their superiors at New York, a squadron of three frigates was immediately dispatched to intercept her. They were the 44-gun *Diomede*, the 32-gun *Quebec*, and the

British frigates *Quebec*, *Astrea*, and *Diomede* closing in to capture the frigate *South Carolina*. This painting by the English artist Irwin Bevan gives a good representation of the relative sizes of the ships involved.

32-gun *Astrea*. Fortune favored the British; on their first night at sea, they discovered *South Carolina* convoying a ship, a brig, and a schooner offshore from the Delaware Capes. Joyner was caught with an untrained and unqualified crew. His one hope lay in outdistancing the pursuing frigates. This he was unable to do and, after an eighteen-hour chase, he was forced to clear for action.

As *South Carolina* came to the wind and hoisted her courses in preparation for battle, *Diomede* and *Quebec* closed immediately and opened fire. The results were almost comical. *South Carolina's* sailing master was wounded and went into shell shock, and one of the marine officers fainted at the sight of the blood of a badly wounded man. In the course of the two-hour battle, *South Carolina's* incompetent gunners failed to discharge a single broadside. They had at least managed to fire her stern chasers with regularity during the time the British were closing with her. *Diomede* got off several broadsides, and *Quebec* at least one. Recognizing the futility of continuing the action, Joyner struck his colors. The six crewmen who were killed or wounded were among the last Americans to fall during the Revolution. The British squadron also captured two of the three vessels under convoy. How different *South Carolina's* account might have been had her original captain and crew been aboard. The outcome would probably have been the same, but at least she would have given them a good fight and maintained her honor.

The British took *South Carolina* to New York, where she was condemned and declared a good prize, and a valuation survey was ordered. The survey results suggested that the Dutch may have built her too lightly for her weight of armament; as a result, she had become hogged (bent) along her keel, making the bow and stern ride deeper in the water. The former South Carolina State Navy frigate was purchased for the Royal Navy as a transport, served a short career there, and was then sold to the East India Company. She was broken up by 1786, probably in India. Her ship's bell was found during World War II by American Naval Lieutenant W. L. Carbine. It was being used in India to call workers to their jobs. Upon close inspection he found the words *South Carolina* clearly engraved on its side. Realizing that he may have discovered an artifact of some significance, he purchased the bell and brought it home with him to the United States. A friend later persuaded him to present it to the University of South Carolina during the 1950s.

When *South Carolina* was brought into New York by her captors, some of the ship's crew were impressed into the British services; however, most of them ended up on board the notorious prisoner-of-war ships moored at Walabought Bay, Brooklyn, until the end of the war. Captain Joyner and some of his officers were paroled in New York City. Upon his return to South Carolina in May 1783, Joyner was court-martialed and honorably acquitted. He became a member of the state legislature in 1786.

Gillon's Post-War Political Activities

Joyner's superior, Commodore Alexander Gillon, also returned to Charlestown early in 1783 and spent the remaining years of his life very active in politics there. He became the favorite of the artisans' political faction after Christopher Gadsden fell from their favor in 1778. His career was apparently never jeopardized by the many investigations into his European escapades. Gillon was elected to the Privy Council in March 1783. He plunged headlong into the violent political quarrels of post-war Charleston, which raged throughout the next two years over the confiscation of Tory property. During that time he purchased thou-

sands of acres of confiscated royalist property at dirt-cheap prices, never hesitating to use his political position to protect his gains.

The Chevalier de Luxembourg, by 1784 a prince, continued to press his claims against Gillon and the state. However, in 1783 a committee of the state legislature found his claims invalid. Their reasoning was that Gillon, who had signed the contracts on behalf of himself and the state, had been removed from command of *South Carolina* before the expiration of the three-year lease period. This action, the legislature claimed, invalidated the other provisions of the agreement. Not surprisingly, the prince disagreed and sent Dr. Edward Bancroft to Charleston the next year with full power to prosecute his claim. Gillon spent the spring of 1784 replying to Dr. Bancroft's charges. Later that year a committee of the legislature acknowledged the 300,000-livre obligation for the loss of the ship, but retained the stance that the other claims were invalid. A commission was appointed to arbitrate the matter, but the claims were not finally settled until 1855. During the French Revolution the prince's property had been confiscated; therefore, there was great uncertainty as to whether the proceeds of any claims were due to his estate or to the French government. In the end, the state of South Carolina paid $65,000 to settle the issue, a mere fraction of the true cost of the vessel.

In February 1784 the South Carolina General Assembly selected Alexander Gillon as one of five delegates from South Carolina to the post-war Continental Congress. Earlier that month he had been elected president of the revived Charleston Chamber of Commerce, the organization he had helped to found in 1773. It survived into the early nineteeth century, when it fell victim to the general disruption of trade caused by Napoleon's Berlin and Milan decrees.

In 1786 Gillon was appointed one of four commissioners charged with purchasing the land and laying out the site for the new state capitol at Columbia. The spring of 1787 found him as conservative supporter of the proposed United States Constitution at the Constitutional Convention in Charleston. In the fall he suffered the loss of his wife. Within two years he married Ann Purcell, the second daughter of the Reverend Doctor Henry Purcell, the Rector of St. Michael's Church in Charleston.

The city held Gillon in such high esteem that he was appointed to oversee the arrangements for entertaining President George Washington when he visited the city in May 1791. Two years later, however, Gillon's questionable post-war land transactions were investigated by a legislative committee, which issued a condemnation of his speculation using land indents. Nevertheless, his loyal supporters rallied to his side; in the spring of 1794, he was elected as a delegate to the Third Congress of the United States of America. After his death in 1794 a suit brought by the Commissioners of Public Accounts succeeded in obtaining a judgment of $42,571 against his estate. Many of Gillon's claims against the state of South Carolina were disallowed.

The quixotic career of Alexander Gillon and the frigate *South Carolina* constitute a very vivid chapter in the social and maritime history of Charleston.

The Last Years of the Revolution

After the fall of Charlestown, the British exiled or paroled most of the city and state officials with their families. Those who violated their parole had their property confiscated, were imprisoned, or in the case of Isaac Hayne, were executed.

When the last body of the Continental Army in South Carolina was defeated at Camden three months after the fall of Charlestown, British dominion over the southern colonies seemed assured. However, much as the German Army would do in the Soviet Union in 1941–1944, Britain's repressive policies goaded the political fence-sitters of South Carolina into the Patriot camp. Even before the military showdown at Camden, these policies had South Carolina aflame in the bloodiest statewide civil war of the American experience.

In October 1780, the Continental Congress appointed Washington's "strong right hand," General Nathaniel Greene, as commander in the South. He adroitly avoided pitched battle with Cornwallis' superior forces. This strategy left the brunt of the fighting to be borne by the partisan bands of Francis Marion, Thomas Sumter, and others. In battles at King's Mountain, Cowpens, and hundreds of other skirmishes, these guerrilla bands broke the back of Tory resistance in South Carolina and with it went the British stomach for the American war.

As 1781 dawned, the British had literally been driven from the Upcountry and were being pressed on all fronts in the Lowcountry of South Carolina. Cornwallis pursued Greene's army and the main body of partisans across North Carolina. They offered battle at Guilford Court House on March 15, 1781. While the British won the field, Cornwallis' forces were so weakened that he was forced to begin his long trek to Yorktown and disaster. By summer the remaining British forces in South Carolina had been hemmed into a small area around Charlestown.

In spite of the fall of the capital and the British occupation of much of the rest of the state, a small semblance of a state navy was maintained. The brig *Polly* was still cruising under Captain Anthony as late as October 1781. In May 1782, the galley *Revenge* was fitted out and manned at Georgetown in company with an armed schooner under Captain Jacob Milligan.

Small privateers continued to operate out of the inlets along the coast. They harassed the British supply vessels going in and out of Charlestown. Apparently they were effective; Cornwallis complained bitterly about the loss of supplies and provisions for his army.

On September 3, 1780 off the Grand Banks, South Carolina's distinguished statesman Henry Laurens was on board *Mercury* when it was captured by HMS *Vestal* and *Fairy*. Laurens was en route to the Netherlands to seek aid, and was carrying confidential dispatches

Frigate *Raleigh*, which helped bring the Philadelphia ship *Morning Star* into Charlestown.

His Majesty's 14-gun sloop *Cormorant*, circa 1776. *Cormorant* was built at Ipswich, Suffolk, England, and launched on May 21, 1776. Rated as a 14-gun sloop, she was pierced for 18 guns and is typical of a number of similar corvettes built between 1761 and 1778. On August 24, 1781, along with the armed ship *Sandwich*, *Cormorant* was captured off the Charlestown bar by French ships of Admiral de Grasse, then on their way north to begin the blockade leading to victory at Yorktown.

that fell into British hands. This resulted in a serious rupture of relations between Britain and the Netherlands. Laurens was imprisoned in the Tower of London and was later exchanged for Lord Cornwallis. Laurens' son, Colonel John Laurens, returned to Boston in August 1781 after a successful mission to France. He was aboard a French frigate that convoyed two large transports bringing military stores and specie. He participated in the siege of Yorktown and then returned to South Carolina for the last fighting of the war. He was killed in a skirmish on the Combahee River in the summer of 1782.

As the British were driven out of the hinterland and hemmed up in Charlestown, food was short in the city. An arrangement was made whereby the Americans would sell food to the British in return for clothing and other needed supplies. A British schooner was sent to Georgetown to load rice under a flag of truce, but was seized in the harbor by a North Carolina privateer. It took the intervention of Francis Marion and the governor to clear up the matter.

Tory Privateers

During the British occupation, the large Tory element in Charlestown sent out their own privateers seeking profitable prizes. The Philadelphia ship *Morning Star* had been taken by HMS *Medea*, *Raleigh*, and *Roebuck* and brought into Charlestown. She was purchased by a Tory syndicate and her name changed to *Earl Cornwallis*. After a short voyage of a few weeks, she returned to Charlestown for repairs; while being careened, her topweight proved too much, and she heeled over and sank. The Tory privateer sloop *Lord North* was also lost when it was struck by lightning while at anchor in Rebellion Road on June 30, 1781. The following August, the 32-gun fifth-rate *Thetis* sank at Gadsden's Wharf during a storm.

A very successful Tory naval venture launched from Charlestown during the war centered around the Tory privateer *Peacock* under Captain MacLean and the armed schooners *Retaliation* and *Rose*. In March 1781 this squadron carried a contingent of land forces to capture the town of Beaufort, North Carolina. There they took munitions, goods, and several vessels in the harbor. They then evacuated the town and returned to Charlestown with their prizes on April 24.

The Tories of Charlestown outfitted and dispatched other privateers, but none made a significant impact on the naval side of the war. By the summer of 1782 the British tide was running out and few of their supporters deemed it expedient to invest in such risky ventures.

The End of the War and the British Evacuation

After the victory at Yorktown, General Greene hoped that the French fleet would reclaim Charlestown in an action similar to the role they had played in Savannah, but such was not to pass. Comte de Grasse returned to the West Indies and his disaster at the Battle of the Saintes.[1]

---

[1] After the British surrender at Yorktown, the major fighting in the Revolution turned into a naval war in the West Indies. There on April 12, 1782, in a major fleet engagement at the Saintes Passage between Dominica and Guadeloupe, Britain's Admiral Sir George Rodney smashed through Comte de Grasse's line of battle in the most dramatic naval victory of the war.

By the middle of 1782 the war in America was winding down and the British began evacuating the towns that they could not easily defend. Savannah was given up on July 11, and Charlestown should have followed shortly thereafter; the lack of available ships, occupied on several other fronts, caused a delay. On the morning of September 6, 1782, a heavy firing off the Charlestown bar announced the arrival of Sir Samuel Hood with a fleet to evacuate the city. After three months of negotiation and preparation, the British finally evacuated Charlestown on December 14. As they departed from their defensive perimeter on Charlestown neck, the American troops followed at a respectable distance. The British filed off to Gadsden's Wharf at the foot of Calhoun Street. Their warships and galleys were positioned in the Cooper River to cover the withdrawal in case the Americans attacked the rear guard. Some houses and fences in the area had been pulled down to provide clear fields of fire. The Americans took over the British positions in an orderly manner; in return, the British ships never fired on the city. The entire operation took about four hours.

The British fleet of some 300 sail lay at anchor in a long crescent that stretched from Fort Johnson out to Five Fathom Hole. They were carrying away not only British troops and supplies, but also almost 4,000 Tories and over 5,000 of their slaves and possessions to exile. It took three days for all of the ships to cross the bar.

There was great celebration in the city as it was returned to American hands and the Continental soldiers marched down King Street. The aged, the women, and the children greeted the returning army with open arms. Many had been cooped up in their houses for two years while unwelcome British soldiers occupied most of the premises.

End of the South Carolina State Navy

On March 17, 1783, the General Assembly of South Carolina dissolved the state navy, following terms of the Articles of Confederation that precluded all states from maintaining separate fleets. The state navy had been a tremendous drain on the state treasury, and the return had been relatively paltry; it had done little more than to drive off an occasional privateer and stray British warship.

Building a military establishment from scratch is difficult under the best of circumstances. As South Carolina would find eighty-five years later, building a navy was particularly difficult due to a lack of shipbuilding facilities, locally owned vessels, and a naval infrastructure. Ships take time to build, and warship personnel take time to train. Navies are not built overnight, but slowly over many years if not decades. In the history of the South Carolina State Navy, the lack of good ships and the competition from privateers deterred the recruitment of good personnel. Those that did sign on were more interested in financial rewards than in establishing and sustaining an effective fighting force. The Navy Board had spent most of its time taking stop-gap measures to find seamen and good ships, as well as equipment and provisions for them.

Nevertheless, the shortcomings of the South Carolina State Navy should not deter an objective appraisal of its contributions. It had provided some protection for the state and its trade, harassed British merchant ships, cooperated with land forces, and aided with obtaining needed supplies. The South Carolina State Navy should not be judged by its meager successes, but by the obstacles that it had overcome in its eight years of existence. In the light of these, its successes acquire greater proportion and significance.

CHARLESTON SHIPS 1783–1815

Scale 1″ = 50′

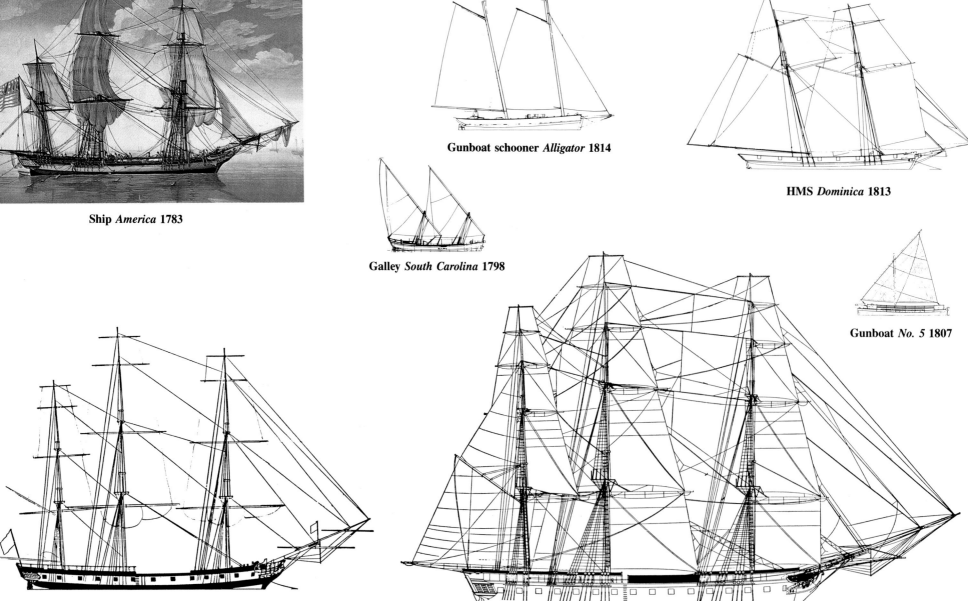

Ship *America* **1783**

Gunboat schooner *Alligator* **1814**

HMS *Dominica* **1813**

Galley *South Carolina* **1798**

Gunboat *No. 5* **1807**

Frigate *John Adams* **1799**

Frigate *Constitution* **1814**

Part IV

A NEW NATION 1783–1815

Like the rest of the country, Charleston emerged from the Revolution in a flourish of patriotism. The city received the first charter of incorporation from the state government; and to go along with the new nation, the spelling of its name was changed from *Charlestown* to the present version—*Charleston*. The euphoria of independence was short-lived as the harsh realities of making a living under new conditions became apparent. Few nations were there to wish America well as she shed the shackles of colonialism. Many powers expected to add her to their empires at some future point. Many citizens at home preferred to withdraw into isolation, but this was neither the temper nor character of the merchants and businessmen who bore the responsibility of economic survival.

America was a sea-minded nation, and its destiny rested as much there as on land. Even before peace was established, shipowners and captains were reestablishing old trading routes and forging new ones. Previously they could depend on the protection of the Royal Navy, but now they were on their own. The disappointing performance of the Continental Navy provided no incentive to the new Congress to establish a federal navy, nor did the dismal record of the South Carolina State Navy make the state legislature feel the necessity to fund a more local fleet. While a few bright stars shone through the clouds of disaster during the years of war at sea, it was hard to see how the outcome would have differed if there had been no American navy, state or national.

Almost from the outset the new nation's commerce was attacked on the high seas or otherwise subjected to insult, forcing ship captains to rely on speed or wits to escape. In 1785 Congress sold off the last warship of the Continental Navy. The southern delegates felt that construction and maintenance of a fleet would benefit only northern interests. Southern states felt they had gained little from naval activities in the past and stood to gain no more in the future.

Shipbuilding in South Carolina had been on an upsurge in the early 1770s, but the war's end brought disaster to local builders. Most of the large locally owned and built vessels had been captured or seized by the enemy, and London capital to build new ones was gone. Furthermore, loyalist promoters left the state. Beaufort, which had been enjoying a pre-Revolutionary boom in shipbuilding, was now having difficulty launching one vessel every two to three years. The war dealt shipbuilding in South Carolina a mortal blow, but it would struggle on for another fifty years before rigor mortis set in.

By the time the new Constitution went into effect the situation had changed little; Indian threats in the West preoccupied the administration of President Washington. From 1783 to 1789 Customs and Navigation Laws were overseen by state and local authorities. Isaac Holmes was the customs collector at Charleston and Captain Robert Cochran was the harbor master. In 1790 Washington appointed Isaac Holmes as customs collector, Isaac Motte as naval officer, and Edward Weyman as surveyor.

The threat at sea grew worse because other nations saw that America could not defend its commerce, thereby making it more vulnerable to attack. Matters worsened in 1793 with the start of war in Europe. Both France and England began to take advantage of American neutrality. To make matters worse, Algeria agreed to a temporary truce with Portugal and turned her corsairs loose on American merchant ships.

Trade

During the first years after British evacuation economic conditions were good, but by 1785 a depression settled over the state. Many old markets were now closed; business suffered until new ones were found. Charleston was not alone in this trouble. Northern states went through the same process, and some endured outright rebellion, most of which was brought on by economic hardship. To exacerbate matters, the legislature, dominated by planters and merchants, resisted reforms and thus continued their conflict with the artisans. Now led by former Commodore Gillon, the artisans allied with the small, non-slave-owning planters of the Upcountry and became fertile ground for the radical propaganda of the French Revolution, much to the consternation of the established business class.

Much has been made of the business turmoil that prevailed under the Articles of Confederation, with many historians showing the Articles' weakness in the retaliatory tariffs of the various states. In South Carolina, however, the legislature was very receptive to promoting fledgling American industry, even in other states. The South Carolina tariff legislation of 1783 began the general policy of allowing American goods to enter the state's ports duty-free, while other nations had to pay to enter their products. Amendments to the act in 1784 renewed this policy. In fact, they even called for refunds on tariffs collected on American goods before the law went into effect and allowed drawbacks on goods that entered the state and were later reexported. In 1787 the last tariff act passed by the legislature before the U. S. Constitution went into effect raised the duty on many non-American goods and imposed new ones on certain luxury items, including coaches, clocks, and jewelry.

Although tariff policy was taken up by most of the other states, South Carolina's port fees aroused anger from her neighbors because instate ships were exempted from some fees. South Carolina used these fees to collect revenue, regulate trade, and pay for port improvements. Most were based upon the vessel's tonnage and/or draft, the latter applying to pilotage costs. The act of March 1785 levied an additional tonnage fee on all vessels entering Charleston to pay for a new lighthouse. Even South Carolina ships paid this.

English bounties on certain products had not only disappeared but had been replaced in many cases by tariffs on American products sent to British markets. The state and national government did not take over the English bounty system after the war, as they found that the same end could be achieved with protective tariffs. They also imposed discriminatory and retaliatory tariffs on countries that did not have a commercial treaty with the United States. Countries that did have treaties received trade concessions under the "most favored nation status." For South Carolina these new trading alignments ended the lucrative Portuguese rice market. While northern states slowly revived from the depression, signs of it lingered in Charleston until 1792, when the European unrest prompted a surge in the demand for American foodstuffs.

The only bright spot was trade with the West Indies, which lacked sufficient foodstuffs and timber resources. However, in July 1783, Britain adopted an Order in Council that closed the West Indian ports to American ships. This order was not meant to discriminate against Americans per se, but was a continuation of the pre-Revolutionary policy of favoring vessels and merchants within the empire as opposed to those outside it. The various American states retaliated with anti-British measures of their own; in South Carolina this took the form of duties on imported sugar, slaves, and rum. West Indian trade began to revive by the time the new Constitution took effect, mostly because the islands exerted pressure when they found they couldn't obtain their goods elsewhere except at great expense.

South Carolina's effective system of inspection of outbound cargoes helped her European trade, because importers knew they could depend on consistency. By 1787 the state was also beginning to delegate tariff and trade matters to the central government, a move that other states were also beginning to realize as important to strengthen the national government financially, increase the nation's prestige in foreign affairs, and present a united front in dealing with Britain's discriminatory policies.

With the end of indigo production in South Carolina at hand in 1796, planters sought a replacement crop. Because rice could be grown only in the wetlands along the coast, another crop had to supplement the interior growers. Eli Whitney's cotton gin, invented in 1793, began cotton's surge as a cash crop. It grew well on the former indigo lands and did not require any production other than removal of seeds. By the end of the century cotton exports reached 6.5 million pounds. The wars in Europe restricted its further development, but after 1815 it would explode.

South Carolina prohibited the slave trade in 1787 and continued the prohibition in 1793 as a result of the slave rebellions in St. Domingue (Haiti). Trade continued to flourish in neighboring Georgia until it was discontinued in 1798. Charleston allowed refugees from the St. Dominguan civil war to bring servants with them, but remained fearful of the propaganda effects that they might have on local slaves. When accounts of Laveaux's July 1794 triumph with black troops on St. Domingue reached the state, there was much consternation that a similar revolt would occur, and efforts were made to suppress the news.

In April 1794 a Spanish prize belonging to the French privateer *la Montagne* arrived in port with a cargo of 75 Santo Dominguan slaves. Blacks from this island were held to be of bad character, no doubt due to the repressive Spanish colonial system. Local authorities accounted for each slave and promptly dispatched them out of the state. In September the brig

The ship *America* of Charleston fishing on the Grand Banks, May, 1789, from the painting by Michele Felice Cornè.

The Port of Charleston, 1789, with the Charleston merchantman *America* in the foreground. The Cooper River waterfront with its wharves, shipyards, and the Exchange Building are in the background. *America* was the ex-British *Pompey* captured during the revolution. This striking scene was recently completed by the eminent English artist Roy Cross, RSMA.

General Pinckney arrived with twenty-two blacks who were similarly dispatched out of the state.

Economics had ended the slave trade in South Carolina, but the rapid growth of the cotton industry brought a demand for additional laborers, and trade was reopened late in 1803. During the next four years more than 39,000 Africans were brought into the state on 202 ship arrivals, 61 of which had originated in Charleston. In 1808 the overseas slave trade ended except for those smuggled in, but trading in native-born slaves continued.

Various Charleston vessels sailed to the west coast of Africa, mostly Gambia. They carried rum, textiles, and various other goods to exchange with the slave traders. Once the slaves arrived back in Charleston, they were quickly auctioned off. Most raw slaves would bring $300 to $400, returning a tidy profit to the investors.

President Washington's Visit to Charleston

The biggest event in Charleston just after the Revolution was the visit of President Washington in May 1791. He arrived with his retinue at Andrew Hibben's Ferry at the mouth of Shem Creek in Mount Pleasant. There a barge awaited him, rowed by twelve sea captains and commanded by Captain Cochran as senior officer and coxswain. The South Carolina coat of arms was emblazoned on the barge's side, beneath which was the inscription "Long Live the President." The oarsmen, among whom was George Warren Cross, wore light blue silk jackets, black Florentine breeches, white silk stockings, and black hats with a wide light blue silk sash. A delegation of local dignitaries was on hand as well as many boats, some of which contained members of the Amateur Musicians Society, who serenaded the President with the popular song "He Comes—the Hero Comes." Despite its historic significance, the barge evidently fell into disuse after this event, as its owner, A. Seixas, put it up for sale in July 1793.

From Shem Creek the President was rowed to Prioleau's Wharf at the foot of Queen Street, where more distinguished citizens met him to escort him to the Exchange for his speech. The city celebrated for several days with many social functions and events.

The previous year, Congress had established the United States Revenue Marine, forerunner of the Coast Guard. Prior to his southern trip, Washington had intended to appoint William Hall master of the Charleston-based revenue cutter[1] in order to please William Loughton Smith, a Federalist member of the House of Representatives. On May 7, 1791, the president was honored at a gala celebration in Charleston. The next day he appointed Captain Robert Cochran to command the first revenue cutter at Charleston. The social gathering changed the president's mind. Cochran had been a political opponent of Commodore Gillon and had even sat on the latter's court martial in 1783 upon his return from the *South Carolina* fiasco. With Gillon's death, Cochran became the foremost naval person in Charleston and received a pension from the legislature.

At this time Charleston was going through the turmoil of converting from state- to federal-administered customs' laws. Naturally each system had its detractors and adherents; the new revenue cutter commander became embroiled in the resultant controversy. With the

state's trade beginning to revive after the postwar depression, many traders were content to transact business under the table rather than risk losing it because of new federal regulations.

Furthermore, American shipowners and masters were being frozen out of the overseas shipping business by foreign shipowners who had connections in Europe. A few months before Washington's visit some forty-one American ship masters had met in Charleston and sent a petition to Congress for relief. Charleston shipbuilders also petitioned Congress for legislation to raise the shipbuilding industry out of the doldrums. Facing these problems, Cochran, then enjoying a prosperous life in middle age, took on the task of completing and commanding the first revenue cutter to be put into service in Charleston. He was fortunate that Hugh George Campbell was chosen as his first mate. Unfortunately, the first revenue cutter, a schooner christened *South Carolina*, was delayed in completion until the end of 1793. In the interim, other vessels were used to patrol the harbor and coast.

South Carolina was less than forty tons and probably around fifty feet in length. She was flush decked, and much like a pilot boat with four swivel guns. Although locally designed and built, she was paid for by the federal treasury. Her diminished size did not befit the status of the nation's fourth port. Other seaports supplemented their federal appropriation in order to build more imposing cutters, but Charleston's depressed economy made that impossible. Even Savannah, a smaller port, had a more impressive revenue cutter. These revenue cutters patrolled the bays and sounds of the coast with instructions to keep on the move as much as possible to control smugglers and enforce the customs laws.

Revenue cutter of the size and type of the first *South Carolina*.

---

[1] These vessels were called "cutters" not because of their rig, but because the revenue vessels employed by the English authorities had been cutter types and the term *cutter* became generic to the duty they performed.

The French Privateers at Charleston

Accounts of two different privateering episodes have now been related, but the one involving the city of Charleston and the French privateers in the 1790s is, to say the least, unusual. When a seaport in one nation harbors the privateers of another nation so that they may cruise against the ships of a third nation that is ostensibly at peace with the first, an unusual situation exists. This situation was not new to international relations or even to Charleston. Almost every nation at war relies on aid, whether direct, indirect, or paid for in gold. Charleston had seen it several times before and would see it again from another side.

War in Europe

The French Revolution was almost four years old when it crossed her borders and inflamed into open warfare with Great Britain. President Washington wisely proclaimed America's neutrality, but he was under great pressure to aid France, his old ally. Huguenot ancestry abounded in Charleston, and citizens were openly sympathetic to the professed aims of Republican France; furthermore, anti-English sentiments hung in the air from the Revolution. With the local economy still suffering from the post-Revolutionary depression, the city was fertile ground for any endeavor that would both satisfy Francophile feelings and boost the sagging economy.

France found herself sadly unprepared at sea. Her navy had been in the forefront of the American Revolution, but had been allowed to go to pieces in the intervening years. Ships were neglected and few new ones built. Furthermore, the French Revolution had decimated the officer corps, which generally held strong allegiances to the Bourbon Crown. With these problems, the French government turned to the traditional way to build a navy quickly—privateers. The geographical position of the few French possessions remaining in the Western Hemisphere precluded their being resupplied or defended by the main force of the navy now blockaded at home. France's American dominions were largely left to their own resources. The merchant vessels caught in these possessions were at great risk from the many English warships in the area. Therefore, many turned to privateering.

Ramifications in Charleston

From the outset of the European war Charleston, with its important position on the flank of the Gulf Stream and the main trade route to Europe from the Caribbean, was high on the priority list as a base for French privateers. On April 8, 1793, Edmond Charles (Citizen) Gênet arrived in Charleston on the French warship *L'Ambuscade* en route to Philadelphia where he had been appointed Minister Plenipotentiary to the American capital. Supposedly under authority from his government, he issued some 250 privateer commissions to various syndicates in Charleston. Within ten days of his arrival five of the privateers had cleared port and *L'Ambuscade* had brought the British brig *Little Sarah* into port. *Little Sarah* was renamed *La Petite Democrate* and sent out privateering.

Gênet's overland trip to Philadelphia was met with celebration and toasts to French liberty; undoubtedly this swelled his vanity. His instructions by the French National Convention were to promote closer trade relations with America, resupply the West Indies colonies, collect French debts, employ American ports for the use of French warships and privateers, and deny British access to them.

After Gênet departed Charleston, the flurry of privateering followed him northward. Gênet left behind the French consul, Michel Ange Bernard Mangourit, to continue the intrigue backed by the consular prize courts he had set up. Mangourit had been at the storming of the Bastille in 1789. In the summer of 1792 he took up a French public relations position in Charleston and began participating in various fêtes to promote the French cause. He solicited gifts of money and goods and organized other activities in support of the new republic. Once war broke out with England he worked just as assiduously against "perfidious Albion." In August 1793 the Jamaican merchant sloop *Advice* was disarmed by local authorities acting upon the insistence of Mangourit's agents.

By June, Washington and his cabinet were so alarmed by Gênet's activities and British reaction that they commenced curtailment measures. First, they agreed to return to the legal owners all French prizes brought into U. S. ports. This proved easier to promise than to enforce. In the meantime the courts gave tacit approval of the French privateers by refusing to grant injunctive relief to the British. Added to this was the case of Gideon Henfield, an officer on the Charleston-commissioned *le Citoyen Gênet* who put into Philadelphia as prize-master of a French prize and was arrested. The jury refused to indict him and set him free amidst great outpourings of public approval for the French cause.

The Supreme Court refused to settle the matter. When Treasury Secretary Alexander Hamilton tried to clarify the neutrality question to local customs officials, he made it only worse by leaving it up to them in regard to privateers. However, Hamilton had a running feud with Charleston's customs' collector, Isaac Holmes, whom he called an anarchist for allowing a few local citizens to flaunt the laws of the nation in order to support the French. Through the summer of 1793 the matter was sorted out by the courts and high officials. By September, French privateers commissioned in American ports had moved on because no authority would allow them to keep their prizes, which previously they had won after sending them into American courts for condemnation. The privateers commissioned in France and her possessions continued to have their prizes favorably disposed of. The unfriendly reception in northern harbors turned the French steadily toward Charleston. Even the reception at Wilmington, North Carolina, was less than cordial.

First Privateers out of Charleston

Through the last half of 1793 French privateers continued to operate out of Charleston and bring their prizes in for disposal. Jean Bouteille, who would become the most successful of the French privateersmen operating out of Charleston, arrived on July 18, 1793. Four days later his *La Sans Pareille* followed the neutral Hamburg (German) brig *Anna Magdalena* out of port and seized her as a prize off the bar. Even this violation of American neutrality failed to dampen Charleston's pro-French sentiment, but the consular prize court released *Anna Magdalena*.

While the northern courts were forcing the French away from their harbors, the British were doing the same in the Caribbean. The Royal Navy, hard pressed to maintain the blockade of France's European ports, set privateers loose upon French shipping in the West Indies. British amphibious assaults had captured all of the French dominions in the Lesser Antilles by the summer of 1794. Only part of St. Domingue and Cayenne remained French, but the latter was hemmed in by Britain's Dutch, Spanish, and Portuguese allies. These events served only to force the French privateers in the Caribbean northward to Charleston.

Popular enthusiasm was kept at fever pitch in Charleston by the news of France's victories in Europe. The triumph at Dumouriez in the Low Countries prompted a two-day celebration in January 1794. Celebration of another victory the next month, at which Charlestonians sang *La Marseillaise*, was reported in the press as far away as Philadelphia.

As Charleston's support for the privateers grew, the city became filled with the soldiers of fortune that flock after such profitable mercenary activities. The sailors' raucous behavior and drunken brawls brought to the surface the first vestiges of anti-French sentiment.

The British did not take matters lying down. In February 1794 the 28-gun frigate *Hussar* appeared off the bar. She hovered for a few days in an attempt to catch any French ships that came by. A few American ships in the harbor that had been violating the British blockade of France were thrown into a panic at the prospects of also being seized. On February 10 *Hussar* signaled the British ships in port to join her and then stood north with the convoy.

British depredations by now had all but severed the flourishing American trade with the British West Indies. War fever was at its peak; many Americans felt a new conflict with England was inevitable. In March Congress passed bills to fortify the harbors of the coast, build a navy for the new republic, and impose a thirty-day embargo on all shipping in American harbors. The embargo was extended to sixty days before its expiration at the end of May. As a result of this legislation, Fort Mechanic was constructed by the city's artisans on Oyster Point below the city.[1] Also built on Shute's Folly was the first structure known as Castle Pinckney, and the second Fort Moultrie on Sullivan's Island. All three forts were earthen and brick fortifications that were destroyed by a hurricane on September 8, 1804. Construction of the forts was accelerated after British warships appeared off the bar and, in full view of the workers on Sullivan's Island, boarded the American ship *Norfolk* and impressed four of her sailors into the Royal Navy.

The embargo was sometimes violated. One instance involved the schooner *Hawke* of Charleston, which cleared port on May 16, supposedly for St. Marys, Georgia. Instead, she sailed to Port-de-Paix, where she was sold to one of the French passengers, Captain Alexander Bolchez.

Holding a legal French commission, Bolchez sailed *Hawke* back to Charleston, where Collector of Customs Isaac Holmes seized the ship. After a lengthy trial in the Admiralty Court, *Hawke* was condemned. The owners appealed to the U. S. District Court, which overturned the Admiralty Court. Renamed *La Parisienne*, *Hawke* then had a long and successful career as a privateer.

Another more serious Charleston matter involved a direct challenge to the authority of the federal government. In 1783 a treaty had been signed with Sweden to exempt her from the embargo. However, certain Charleston citizens were opposed to the exemption and took

steps to interfere with trade. Treasury Secretary Hamilton viewed the situation with alarm and instructed Collector of Customs Holmes to turn over all materials to the federal attorney for legal action.

The embargo brought desired relief for West Indian merchants hungry for trade. One after another the West Indian governors suspended the Navigation Acts for periods of six months to a year. In the week that the embargo ended an estimated 300 ships departed American ports for the West Indies.

Meanwhile, accounts of the excesses of the French Reign of Terror in the summer of 1793 began to reach America. These accounts fanned the flames of rising anti-French sentiments. As a crowning blow, the flagrant violations of American neutrality by Citizen Gênet and his agents, who were hatching a scheme to topple the solidly neutral Washington administration, dampened the anti-British fervor. Through the spring of 1794 matters deteriorated for the French. Alarmed, the Committee of Public Safety in Paris changed its stance and decided to honor American neutrality. It dispatched Jean Antoine Joseph Fauchet to patch up relations and secure the commercial treaty that Gênet had failed to obtain. When he landed at Norfolk in February from the frigate *La Charente*, Fauchet lost no time in proceeding directly to Philadelphia. Gênet, meanwhile, sought and received political asylum; he could not return to France.

An American-built French privateer of the type that used Charleston as a base.

[1] Fort Mechanic was located approximately where East Bay and Atlantic streets intersect today.

not return to France because he had been associated with the regime's predecessors and had failed in his mission.

The East Florida Expedition

In Charleston, Vice Consul Mangourit had been hatching a most ambitious plan—to lead an expedition against Spanish Florida and Louisiana. Governor Moultrie gave tacit approval to the project. Charleston merchants, never at a loss to turn a dollar, raised the prices of supplies that were being purchased for the army and used to entice Creek and Cherokee allies. Before leaving office, Gênet raised a covering naval force of privateers for the campaign.

By the end of 1793 it was obvious that Mangourit's campaign would have to be scaled down to an attack against eastern Florida focused on Amelia Island, where the French hoped to establish a base for French privateers if they were driven out of Charleston. Mangourit pressed into service for the expedition several French privateers that were then in Charleston.

While plans for the expedition were proceeding, Fauchet landed at Norfolk. Before he could dispatch new instructions to Mangourit at Charleston, the expedition to Florida was rushed ahead. It sailed, escorted by two privateers, despite Fauchet's proclamation honoring American neutrality. Mangourit proceeded because he thought that the deteriorating situation in America necessitated a French base free of foreign control.

On March 26, 1794, Citizen Fonspertuis arrived in Charleston to relieve Mangourit. Mangourit delayed the transfer of power; therefore, the vessel sent to recall the invasion arrived too late. But the invasion was a fiasco anyway.

Once at sea, most of the escorting privateers set off on their own to seize prizes; these began arriving in Charleston in May. The so-called troops that were put ashore remained encamped awaiting reinforcements that never came.

These men languished until June 1795, taking refuge on the American side of the St. Marys River. A French consular agent arrived, but only fanned discontent in Spanish East Florida. Late in June an uprising broke out in the area between the St. Marys and St. John's rivers. Much of this area was seized along with Amelia Island, which was taken without a fight. Within three weeks Spanish reinforcements arrived and drove the insurgents across the border into Georgia, thus ending the abortive East Florida Expedition.

Privateering Peaks at Charleston

With the departure of the grain convoy from Hampton Roads on April 17, 1794, and its escort of privateers now pressed into the French Navy, privateering decreased rapidly except in the Carolinas and Georgia. The remaining ones fell victim to Fauchet's campaign to honor American neutrality. New privateers appeared in Charleston, many of them converted from the prizes that the escorts from the Florida campaign sent in. By June the numbers had increased appreciably and Charleston again became their primary base in American waters. Another factor that influenced the South Carolina port was a decision handed down in March by Judge Thomas Bee of the U. S. District Court.

Judge Bee was a wealthy gentleman of the Charleston establishment. He had as much distaste for the aims of the French Revolution as any American Federalist could have. His rulings,[2] the most important of which was *Costello v. Bouteille et al*, threw one barrier after another into the efforts of federal officials to enforce the neutral position of the Washington administration. Bee held that the president's wishes did not have the force of law and were not binding. Accordingly, he denied federal jurisdiction over the activities of the French privateers. Bee also held that the Franco-American treaties were more sweeping than those with other nations. These decisions resulted in a proliferation of privateers, many backed by syndicates of Charleston businessmen and manned by Americans who steered the narrow line between legality and outright piracy.

At the same time the British Vice Consul at Charleston, Benjamin Moodie, who had arrived on February 9, 1794, on *Caroline*, complained of the lack of cooperation from the authorities. To these incidents can be traced part of the difficulties that American shipowners were having at the hands of British warships and privateers. Charlestonians who aided the French apparently were not cognizant of the repercussions of their actions.

One of the more colorful Charleston groups was the syndicate of William Talbot, Edward Ballard, and John Sinclair. As master of an American brig, Talbot had been captured by a British privateer early in the fighting between France and England and was taken into Nassau, where he lost his vessel and cargo to the corrupt prize court. This act turned him against the British and made him anxious to help the French. Returning to Virginia, he met Sinclair and three others who owned the schooner *Fair Play*, which they fitted out as a privateer under French colors to attack the British. Although the furor over Gênet's activities was rising, they were able to arm the vessel and clear her for Guadeloupe. There she received French registry and Talbot became a French citizen. Early in January 1794, *Fair Play*, now renamed *l'Ami de la Pointe-a-Pitre*, sailed on her first cruise. She put into Charleston with nine prizes in time to partake in the Florida expedition, in which she took another rich prize.

In the meantime, Sinclair had obtained a pilot boat in Virginia and a French commission from Admiral Jean Van Stabel, the commander of the grain convoy escort then gathering at Hampton Roads. Admiral Van Stabel employed the vessel, now named *l'Ami de la Liberté*, as a tender.

Once the fleet sailed, however, Sinclair made for Charleston with Ballard aboard. Ballard was put in command when she arrived on April 20. Vice Consul Fonspertuis endorsed Sinclair's commission over to Ballard so that Sinclair could then outfit the vessel that Talbot had recently brought into port as a privateer. Ballard took *la Liberté* to Savannah, where it was armed; then in company with *la Pointe-a-Pitre*, she set out on a cruise. Before returning to Charleston they took several Dutch, Spanish, and English prizes.

Back in Charleston they faced a deluge of suits and libels questioning the legality of their actions. Most were lost by default due to the worthless commissions and citizenships that Ballard held. To make matters worse, one of the syndicate's privateers, the 3-gun *San Joseph*, cleared Charleston for a cruise and fell in with the New Providence privateer *Flying Fish*. After a fifteen-minute battle, *San Joseph* struck her colors and was taken to Nassau.

The British backed up their court cases against *la Liberté* and *la Pointe-a-Pitre* with papers confiscated from *San Joseph* which confirmed the illegality of the capture of several

[2] Judge Thomas Bee's rulings are given credit for laying the foundation for U. S. maritime law. See Melvin H. Jackson's *Privateers in Charleston 1793–1796* (Smithsonian Institution Press, 1969). Much of the information in this section was condensed from this publication with the kind permission of the Smithsonian Institution Press.

of the prizes. *La Pointe-a-Pitre* continued to cruise through the remainder of 1794 under Talbot, but the prizes sent into Charleston and Savannah were returned to their owners. Probably out of frustration, she took the American brig *Neptune* and hauled her into Port-de-Paix in St. Domingue (now Haiti) where the ship and her cargo were subjected to the same type of forced sale that had become commonplace in Charleston and Nassau.

L'Ami de la Pointe-a-Pitre was renamed *l'Egalité* and operated out of Charleston until the end of 1795 under several different commanders. Ballard narrowly escaped being tried for piracy and ended up in debtor's prison. Sinclair went to Norfolk, where he became embroiled in more privateering activities.

The activities of this syndicate may seem unusual in a neutral port at peace. However, they were quite ordinary; the French and their agents used every means to circumvent the law and get both legal and illegal privateers to sea. British agents were sent into the port to watch the activity, and whenever possible, units of the Royal Navy appeared off the bar.

By June 1794, the French were back on the offensive in the Lesser Antilles. Guadeloupe fell to a fierce French attack, saving St. Domingue from complete envelopment after the fall of Port-de-Paix to the British. Supplies for the French garrisons on these islands had originated in Charleston, but munitions were subsequently embargoed by President Washington in May when it was found after the war scare that the nation itself was sadly lacking in these items.

In June Congress passed an act prohibiting the fitting out of a vessel for privateering, procuring one for such purposes, or augmenting the armament of a vessel. This merely redoubled the ingenuity of Charleston privateering entrepreneurs and arms exporters. It also made merchant vessels already armed for self-defense that much more valuable as potential privateers. Warships that had been constructed in northern shipyards during the spring war scare were brought to Charleston and profitably sold to the privateer syndicates. One, *le General Laveaux*, the former American brig *Cygnet*, laid down as a privateer, was brought to Charleston and fitted out at Gaillard's Wharf. British agents reported the ship's supposed conversion to a warship, and the collector of customs seized her. Once her guns were landed she was allowed to proceed to sea, whereupon her guns were brought out to her by lighters and remounted off the bar.

Upon *le General Laveaux's* return to Charleston with the prize *Mermaid*, a libel was filed by the British consul. In the subsequent trial, Judge Bee found that the French ship had been built as a warship and, therefore, there was no reason for her not to proceed to sea as such; he held that her armament was defensive in nature, which it was not. He considered her being rearmed at sea hearsay and awarded the prize to the French.

This was only one of many such episodes following the same pattern. Another vessel, the prize *San Jose*, was fitted out by removing her quarterdeck. Her guns were installed at Rebellion Road and she proceeded to sea. Another case involved a brigantine from Port-de-Paix that was fitted out at Gaillard's Wharf. Once clear of the harbor, her quarterdeck was cut away and thrown overboard, instantly converting her into a flush-deck corsair. Her guns were then hoisted aboard from barges and she was off.

On October 25, 1794, HMS *Hussar* and the corvette *Scorpion* appeared off the bar after capturing the privateer *le Republican* with 33,000 dollars in specie on board. In spite of the best efforts of British agents and occasional visits by their warships, the fitting out and servicing of French privateers continued until the summer of 1795. In January 1795 British units began making more frequent appearances, including HMS *Quebec* and the frigates

Blonde, *Thetis*, and *Terpsichore*. These warships cruised singly or in groups of various size off Charleston and Savannah, but other than infuriating Charlestonians by impressing American seamen from vessels entering and leaving the harbor, their impact was negligible. They did bring the privateer *la Montagne* to bay off Edisto Island and chased two of her prizes ashore.

When the British ships captured *le Republican*, they failed to take *l'Intrepide*, which slipped by them into the harbor with Jean Baptiste Carvin aboard, one of the more daring French captains. He arrived as a passenger from Port-de-Paix to complete the fitting out of two prizes as privateers. One, *le Pichegru* (ex-*Pulaski*), was of particular concern to the British agents; they foiled her departure until January 1795.

Between the fall of 1794 and July 1795 the outfitting of French privateers in Charleston reached its peak. It was a taxing time for British Vice Consul Moodie, who not only had to shepherd cases through the court, but also gather information to prosecute the cases and keep tabs on the British seamen from the French prizes, who had to be maintained for court appearances. On top of this he had to see about getting British ships in and out of port, past the French privateers. Usually British merchant vessels would wait for a British warship to appear off the bar and then sortie or run into the harbor.

The tremendous number of French prizes coming into Charleston also drew British privateers to the bar to intercept them. On April 6, 1795, the Bermudian privateer *Sir Charles*

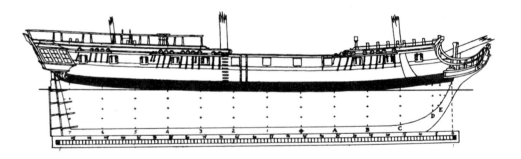

Draught of the Continental frigate *Delaware*, a sister of *Boston* that was captured by the Royal Navy at Charlestown in 1780.

Delaware* was built at Philadelphia in 1777 and came down to attack British forces on the Delaware River in September, only to run aground, surrender, and be taken into the Royal Navy. At the end of the war she was purchased by a Boston widow who renamed her *United States* and employed her in whaling and trading. The ship was then sold to French owners, who renamed her *Le Dauphin* and used her as a whaler. She wound up in Charleston during the 1793 embargo and was sold at auction to Jean Bouteille, who converted her to a privateer. Bouteille removed her quarter galleries and quarterdeck, opened her gunports, and outfitted her once more as a warship. She was painted a somber black to resemble a British-built merchantman. In this guise she could slip unnoticed into a convoy before striking. As such she was the most powerful of the French privateers operating out of Charleston. Her armament as a warship had been twenty-two 12-pounders and six 6-pounder guns, making her a powerful adversary. British agents doggedly kept after her, but after some nine months of sparring through the bureaucracy and the courts she was ready for sea. She did not leave Charleston until 1795 and probably foundered in a gale in the West Indies.

Grey encountered the incoming *Le Brutus*. After a quick encounter the Bermudian was damaged enough to force her withdrawal.

The year 1795 started with Charlestonians still receptive to French aims in the port. Rioting in 1794 had caused sharp public outcry, but matters became very severe in April 1795, when several citizens were stabbed (one fatally) by French seamen. Rewards failed to apprehend the culprits. Another serious outburst took place late that month when two other French seamen were forcibly freed from custody by armed seamen. City Council passed an ordinance prohibiting seamen from appearing on the streets of the city with swords, pistols, or any other offensive weapons.

In the summer of 1795 the privateering out of Charleston fell off as the French offensive in the West Indies made more bases available there. Britain was caught off balance and, being hard pressed in Europe, could not send reinforcements until well into 1796.

The French began the offensive in the spring of 1795—called the "Brigand's War" by the British. The French fomented rebellion among the slaves on the British possessions, creating confusion and fear. One of the first islands to fall was Grenada, which lies near Barbados. In these actions the French privateers carried supplies and arms to both the rebels and the French soldiers aiding them. By April, St. Eustatius and St. Martins had fallen, and in June the British evacuated St. Lucia.

The Jay Treaty with Britain

Throughout 1794 Savannah grew tired of the presence of the French privateers and slowly forced them out. Charleston was gradually moving in that direction, but progress was eclipsed in mid-1795 by the nationwide furor over the Jay Treaty with Great Britain. The treaty had been signed the preceding November, but its provisions were only gradually revealed. The French benefited temporarily from the clamor, although they would ultimately be the loser by its provisions. The American public saw the treaty as a sellout to British arrogance. The full text was published in Charleston on July 12. Article 24 would spell the end of French privateering in American ports, as it prevented their arming, selling of prizes, or provisioning beyond that necessary to reach the nearest French port.

American ships in the harbor lowered their colors the next day in reaction to the treaty. A public meeting on July 16 presided over by the Chief Justice of the Supreme Court, John Rutledge, was held to decide how best to react against the reprehensible treaty. A select committee issued a report on July 24 that urged several changes, including a plea that the president recommend against ratification. Charles Pinckney accused Jay of bartering away the nation's honor for a mess of pottage, urged his impeachment, and led a mob down Broad Street to burn an effigy of Jay at the corner of Meeting Street.

In Philadelphia the French lobbied in vain for the treaty's rejection. The new French ambassador, Pierre Adet, arrived in the middle of the debate—too late to influence a change. He was immediately caught up in the charges leveled at his consul in Charleston, Fonspertuis, who was accused of malfeasance in office and a scandalous public and private life. The ambassador went beyond his authority and sent his first secretary, Victor Dupont, to Charleston as consul. Other than a last vain effort to resuscitate the East Florida debacle, Dupont had a quiet time; the privateers were already transferring to the newly seized bases in the Caribbean. By the end of the year Spain had switched sides and her possessions became available as French bases. A few ships and prizes came into port during the last half of 1795, but by April of the next year the last of them were gone. On June 30, 1796, the collectors of customs were ordered to refuse admission of the privateers of all countries to United States ports.

Charleston Turns Against the French

It took the burning of the the British merchant ship *Arcabessa* off the bar to seal Charlestonians' anti-French feelings. This ship had been bound for London from Jamaica when she ran into a storm off the coast and lost her main and mizzenmasts. She managed to reach Charleston and got across the bar to anchor in Five Fathom Hole on October 13, 1797, unable to proceed further. On October 16, provisions were brought out for her crew. Anchored nearby was a strange schooner with a crew identified as a mixed assortment of outlaws.

British Vice Consul Benjamin Moodie was notified of the situation and called on Governor Pinckney for help. The revenue cutter *South Carolina* was in the harbor. The governor had no authority over her, so he appealed to Collector Holmes to send her out. Captain Cochran prepared to proceed to *South Carolina*, anchored off Fort Johnson. It was not until the next day that she made it to *Arcabessa's* anchorage at Five Fathom Hole, only to find her in flames and the mystery schooner gone.

Fortunately her crew was set adrift at Stono Inlet and made their way to the city, where they reported being sacked by *Vertitute* under Captain Jourdain. The very next day Jourdain took the American vessels *Pallas* and *Mary*. This incident so alarmed Charleston's merchants that two more vessels were readied for revenue service and the ground was laid for the construction of *John Adams*.

The Jay Treaty soured Franco-American relations through 1796. French seizures of American ships in the Caribbean began to accelerate, continuing through 1797. The French prize courts turned out to be more corrupt and arbitrary than the British. American seamen received the brunt of French resentment, which led to the Quasi War of 1798–1800. A new Franco-American treaty was signed and ratified in 1800. Its article 24 called for the admission to each other's ports of armed vessels and their prizes free of duty and examination for lawfulness; upon departure, only warships were required to show their commissions. The terms were an obvious outgrowth of the privateers at Charleston, and were to be of enormous benefit to Americans in the War of 1812, when France's European ports would enable American commerce raiders to rove around the British Isles.

Charleston and the New Navy

When the Third Congress met for its second session in December 1793, the issue of whether or not to have a navy was at the top of the agenda. The Jeffersonian Republicans were more attuned to southern agrarian interests and therefore opposed to supporting a navy, which they considered to be primarily for the benefit of northern mercantile interests. Nevertheless, Washington's message to Congress stated bluntly that if they wanted to secure peace, they had best be prepared for war. In January 1794, a naval bill was passed by a close vote. It called for frigates of forty-four and thirty-six guns. Secretary of War Henry Knox was given the final responsibility for constructing the vessels. He took the advice of naval authorities and approved warships superior to foreign frigates.

Joshua Humphreys of Philadelphia, who had designed and built warships for the Continental Navy, was appointed naval constructor. The able and well-trained Josiah Fox, an English Quaker, became his assistant.

The persons appointed to command the first naval ships recommended southern live oak as a building material. They were not to be disappointed; two of these first frigates, *Constitution* and *Constellation*, are still afloat. The longevity of these ships was quite remarkable for their time. *Congress*, the shortest lived of those that remained in the United States Navy, was not broken up until 1837.[1] In contrast, the average life span of a wooden warship built of oak was ten years.

The drawback for using live oak was the distance of its habitat from the shipbuilding sites. In June 1794, John T. Morgan, a Boston shipwright who had been provisionally appointed constructor at the Gosport (Norfolk) Navy Yard, was sent to Charleston and Savannah. There he sought out property owners and surveyed the live oak and cedar timber that was available. To aid him with making contracts and obtaining provisions and transportation at Charleston were Isaac Holmes, collector of customs, and Daniel Stevens, supervisor of revenue. Unfortunately the landowners in South Carolina held out for more money; therefore, Georgia forests provided most of the timber for the first ships of the United States Navy. To reduce costs, crews of skilled shipwrights were sent to roughcut the wood on the spot and then ship it north.

Work on the ships proceeded slowly because of the delays in cutting and hauling the wood out of the Georgia swamps. Each frigate needed almost 1,000 pieces of live oak, and delivering this much material for six frigates was a slow process. During the summer heat the cutting practically ceased.

It took upwards of two years to get the first frigates into the water. By then French privateers from West Indian bases were seizing American merchant ships. Congress authorized more ships for the navy and created a separate Navy Department with cabinet rank. The Revenue Service (Coast Guard) was placed under operating control of the Navy. Benjamin Stoddert, a capable merchant on the verge of retirement, was persuaded to become the first secretary of the navy. On the day he accepted the position, Congress authorized the president to direct American warships to seize, take, and bring into U. S. ports any armed vessels found hovering along the coast; this action began the Quasi War with France.

Charleston's Revenue Service

That June the small revenue cutter *South Carolina* was sold to make way for the larger brig by that name then under construction. Captain Cochran was given command of the new 14-gun revenue cutter brig, *Unanimity*, the first of the new warships then being built in Charleston shipyards. She had been built of live oak and cedar at Hobcaw by Paul Pritchard. Though Cochran favored the new *South Carolina* then under construction at Hobcaw, he was obliged to prepare the former for service. He was now 63 years old and ready for less strenuous activity than taking a new ship and crew to sea; nevertheless, by late June he had her ready.

The Battle of Dewee's Inlet

Cochran's first assignment was to escort to sea two unwelcome slavers that had arrived from Haiti. The governor refused to allow the slaves on board to land because of the state's anti-slavery laws and sent *Unanimity* to see them clear of the coast. As she beat out of the harbor, the steady breeze carried away her main top gallant mast and fore topsail, forcing her immediate return. Poor workmanship was blamed for the trouble. During July she made several more cruises along the coast without mishap.

That summer HMS *Thetis* had been cruising off Charleston, stopping and interrogating all vessels. At the same time the French privateer *Coffee Mill* had been prowling nearby. These marauders prompted the secretary of the navy to instruct warship captains to call at Charleston regularly. On July 17, 1798, Captain Truxtun anchored the brand new 38-gun frigate *Constellation* off the bar, the stars and stripes snapping proudly in the breeze from her spanker gaff. Truxtun reported that he had seen no French ships.

Unfortunately, *Constellation* and the other new frigates drew over twenty feet of water fully loaded and were unable to cross the bar into the harbor. Instead, they anchored off Lighthouse Inlet and sent their ship's boats into the city. Several citizens who saw the mast tops from the Cooper River docks went over the bar in Swain's pilot boat to visit *Constellation*. They were politely received and handsomely entertained by Captain Truxtun. The citizens were impressed with the twenty-eight 24-pounder guns in her main battery. An account in the *South Carolina Gazette & Timothy's Daily Advertiser* remarked that *Constellation*

> sails remarkably fast, is well manned and is in every respect equipped for the defense and protection of the commerce of the United States. The crew are active, well disciplined men, and appear highly animated in the glorious service in which they are engaged. Captain Truxtun has been five weeks on a cruise, in which time he crossed the Gulf Stream, traversed to

---

[1] *Chesapeake* and *President* were captured by the British during the War of 1812 and broken up in 1820 and 1817 respectively.

The new frigate *Constellation* battling the French only a few months after her visit off Charleston.

Bermuda, then along the coast to St. Marys and up to our bar where he remains to vindicate the honor and dignity of his country on its own waters, where it has so often of late been violated with impunity. We sincerely wish him the success which his patriotism and gallantry merit. . . .

On July 27 the inward-bound *Unanimity* exchanged signals with the departing *Constellation*. Whereas the frigate would go on to fame and glory, another fate lay in store for Cochran and his brig. After stopping briefly in the harbor, she pulled out on July 29 and headed north. A few miles up the coast Cochran spotted two sails, one of which was a sloop-of-war or corvette flying British colors. Suspecting that she was a French privateer, he bore down on her. Off Dewee's Inlet the two came together, crews at action stations, each suspecting that the other was French. As the warships maneuvered in the shallow waters trying to determine the other's identity without revealing their own, the stranger fired a warning shot. When it went unanswered, more shots followed. This time *Unanimity* returned fire.

Captain Cochran apparently panicked and ran for cover in the inlet. He struck the bar as he crossed it and lost about thirty feet of the false keel. Uncertain of the shoals, the opposing captain refused to follow, but continued to fire into *Unanimity* from outside the bar. He ceased fire only when a pilot boat came up and identified his victim. The opposing ship turned out to be HMS *Mosquito*.

Both warships put into Charleston. There the public condemned Cochran for cowardice, and he accused his crew of mutinous behavior. Charges, countercharges, and recriminations flew. When it all settled down, Cochran was cashiered, and became the first officer dismissed from service for cowardice. No protest was sent to the British for attacking an American warship in American waters. Secretary of the Navy Stoddert received word of the incident from the British ambassador, who was the first in the capital to obtain a report of the incident. Stoddert then had to make inquiry to Naval Agent Henry W. DeSaussure at Charleston, who spoke highly of Cochran and recommended that his wish for a court of inquiry be granted. The secretary, however, had made up his mind based on news accounts and the written reports tendered to him, and gave command of the new brig under construction to Captain George Warren Cross.

Cochran continued to run his shipyard. His son C. B. became federal marshal in 1801, mayor of the city in 1806, state treasurer the following year, and president of the Union Bank in 1813; the battle of Dewee's Inlet had clearly left no stain on the family integrity. The captain died at the age of 88 on January 22, 1824, at 24 Society Street in Charleston. His wife died five years later at the age of 91 and was buried beside her husband in the family burying ground on Shipyard Creek.

Charleston's Warships for the New Navy

Of the additional ships authorized by Congress, two were galleys built at Charleston: *Charleston* (ex-*Mars*) and *South Carolina* (ex-*Protector*). They were units of the *Savannah*-class, some 51.75 feet long, 15 feet wide, with a 5-foot draft. Both were lateen-rigged with two masts and carried a bow-mounted 24-pounder gun, five or six small howitzers, and a crew of twenty-nine. These vessels were designed along the lines of the galleys used in the Revolution, with flat bottoms and high, broad bows to carry the weight of the gun, which was mounted so that it could train to either side. The gun's carriage had no wheels, being

mounted on skids whose friction helped to check the recoil. Long rowing hatches where the rowers sat ran the length of the vessel on either side of the masts. The lateen rig had the advantage of simplicity and good sail area with reduced weight. The galleys were poor in sailing upwind, but could be fast in sailing before the wind. *South Carolina* and *Charleston* spent most of their time in the harbor or cruising the inland waterways looking for smugglers. These galleys were all but useless for the navy's needs in ocean patrolling. They were laid up in August 1801 and sold the following February, bringing to an end over a century of use of galleys in South Carolina.

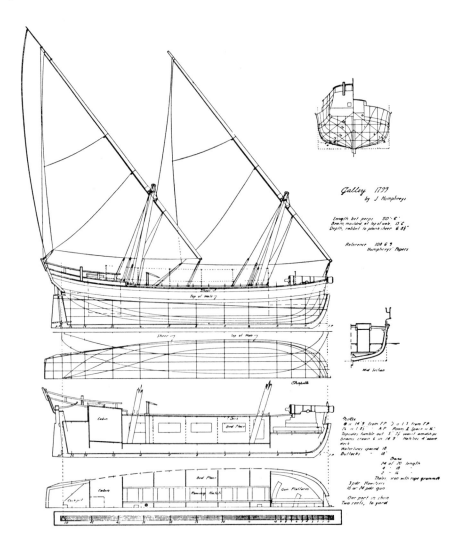

Joshua Humphreys' design for the class of galleys of which *South Carolina* and *Charleston* were units. These warships were designed for river and harbor service and thus useless for the Navy's needs in patrolling on the open ocean.

On September 22, 1798, the new revenue cutter brig *General Pinckney*[2] was launched by William Pritchard at his yard at the foot of Pinckney Street in Charleston. She was an 18-gun brig of 190 tons. In the eighteenth century there was a tendancy to overload warships with guns, but Secretary Stoddert thought that twelve guns, if properly employed, would be sufficient for *General Pinckney*. Her figurehead was a bust of Major General Charles Cotesworth Pinckney carved by George Statler of the firm of Cotton & Statler at 20 Mott Street in Charleston. She was manned by a crew of 140, which included about 20 marines.

With Cochran out of the running, the command of *General Pinckney* went to George Warren Cross, a Charleston privateersman in the Revolution who had been soliciting a naval commission. Cross did not remain commander long enough to see the vessel commissioned; at the end of October he was appointed to superintend the construction of *John Adams*.

Command of *General Pinckney* went to Samuel Hayward, captain of one of the Charleston galleys.[3] *General Pinckney* remained under control of both the Revenue Service and the Navy; the former used her to patrol the coast, and the latter used her to escort convoys. On October 15, 1798, William Crafts was appointed agent of the Naval and War Departments for South Carolina after the death of Henry DeSaussure. On November 19 the new U. S. revenue cutter *South Carolina* was launched at Cochran's Shipyard. As she hit the water, one of the new Charleston-built galleys under Captain Hayward fired a salute. *South Carolina* was a 14-gun brig, 96 feet long on deck. She was one of the first Charleston-built vessels to have a copper-sheathed bottom. *South Carolina* turned out to be a dull sailer and consequently useless; just about anything afloat could outrun her.

Galley Captain James Payne was appointed to command *South Carolina*. In February 1799, she departed on her first cruise. *General Pinckney* joined her the following month in patrolling the coastal waters of South Carolina. Dressed out with flags, both ships attended the launch of the frigate *John Adams* on June 6, 1799, and fired a salute in honor of the occasion.

General Pinckney and *South Carolina* cruised to Havana to escort merchant ships and seize any French privateers that they encountered. For the next three months they patrolled the waters off Cuba. On August 21, they took the French schooner *Adelaide*, which was sent to Charleston. A week later, they captured another French schooner and sent it into Havana. On September 6, they anchored off Fort Johnson. There they discovered that the French schooner had been captured while under a flag of truce. They freed her to return on her mission after Captain Payne of *General Pinckney* was reprimanded for plundering the crew and passengers. Orders were given to restore all articles taken, and "to furnish her with such supplies and provisions as will be fully sufficient to take her back to Santo Domingo and you will give all necessary aid to her captain to expedite her departure."

The next month *General Pinckney* escorted another convoy of merchant ships to Havana with the brig-of-war *Norfolk* under Captain William Bainbridge. In December the two were challenged at Havana by a French schooner whose captain declared that he could "take either of the American brigs singly." Once the Frenchman departed, *General Pinckney* followed, whereupon the former came around and sneaked back into port. As the two passed within musketshot, the crew of *General Pinckney* showed their contempt by manning the yards and giving three cheers.

General Pinckney departed Havana with another convoy of merchant ships. She grounded briefly on the Carrisfort Reef Keys at the end of the month, and lost her rudder, part of the keel, and an anchor. A gale scattered the convoy, and foundered the ship *Mary*. *General Pinckney* was able to rescue one of her survivors. By January 6, 1800, she had anchored in Charleston. With enlistments of *General Pinckney's* crew up, more ships joining the navy, and operations moving further from home, Secretary Stoddert decided that some of the navy's smaller vessels were superfluous, including *General Pinckney*, which was sold by April 1800. *South Carolina* was returned to the Revenue Service, where she remained until 1803, when she too was sold.

The Frigate *John Adams*

The first ships of the U. S. Navy were primarily used to clear the coast of roving French privateers. Once the coast was cleared, naval squadrons were dispatched to clear the French bases in the West Indies. On February 9, 1799, near the island of Nevis, Truxtun's *Constellation* came upon the French 40-gun frigate *L'Insurgente*; after a battle of an hour and a half, the French surrendered. Lieutenant John Rodgers and a prize crew were put aboard the crippled frigate in a heavy sea. After working through the night and two more days, he brought her to St. Christopher with 173 French prisoners locked below decks. Rodgers would later command Charleston's *John Adams* in the Mediterranean.

The battle with *L'Insurgente* was the first between nearly equal combatants for the new navy. In the public's eye, it confirmed the correctness of Congressional support for the fleet, which also indirectly paid its way by saving merchant ship owners additional insurance premiums. Stoddert adroitly made political hay with Congress.

As the new navy's frigates captured the public's fancy, there soon developed a contest between the major seaports to build and donate to the naval service warships that reflected the civic pride of these cities. Charleston was not to be left out. At the end of July 1798, when news of the congressional act authorizing subscription warships reached the city, leading citizens met at William's Long Room and resolved "to appoint a committee to receive subscriptions...for the construction of a ship of war at Charleston." William Crafts, later Naval Agent at Charleston, headed the frigate committee. By August 4, all of the estimated $100,000 cost had been pledged. Donations eventually reached $114,000. The additional funds enabled the construction plans to be scaled up from a 20- to a 24-gun ship. Charleston became the seventh of nine East Coast ports to start construction of a subscription warship for the U. S. Navy.

A meeting on August 8 "resolved to build and equip a vessel of war of not less burthen than 550 tons, to carry 24 guns on the main deck, and of not less calibre than 9 pounders." Henry Laurens, Thomas Morris, William Crafts, Nathaniel Russell, and Adam Tunno were appointed to oversee the work for the committee. Josiah Fox had drawn plans for many differ-

[2] Both *General Pinckney* and the subsequent revenue cutter *South Carolina* were also referred to as double-topsail schooners or "jackass brigs."

[3] The remaining officers on *General Pinckney* were:

Cornelius O'Driscoll	First Lieutenant
James Smith	Second Lieutenant
Lewis F. Raynal	Acting Purser
Joseph Anthony	Surgeon
Benjamin Pearson	Acting Master
Richard Hrabvinski	Midshipman

ent ship types to be built for the navy. Many of these plans were conjectural and never used. The Charleston Frigate Committee looked over several of these and chose the one for a "24-gun ship," as this was the largest warship type that could get over the Charleston bar fully loaded. The plans defined it as a "24-gun ship" because of the number of guns on the main deck, even though additional weapons were carried on the quarter and forecastle decks.

In a letter to William Crafts, Navy Secretary Benjamin Stoddert said that President Adams would accept the frigate offered if she were named *John Adams*, as a frigate then under construction at New York was to be named *Adams*. Constant confusion resulted between the two ships, similar in both name and rate, until the New York frigate was burned in the Penobscot River fiasco in 1814 (see page 152).

Stoddert further suggested that the armament of the Charleston frigate be twenty-four 12-pounders on the main deck, and four or six of smaller size on the quarterdeck. The quarterdeck guns were changed to six 32-pounder carronades, a new type of lightweight gun with short range for action at close quarters. Two long 12-pounders were placed on the forecastle. *John Adams* became one of the first ships of the new navy to be designed with carronades in her armament and the first to get to sea with them.

At the end of August 1798, Stoddert approved the appointment of George Cross as a naval captain, and in October he was ordered to superintend the construction of *John Adams*.[4] Cochran's Shipyard was selected as the building site. Paul Pritchard, Jr., son of William Pritchard, the Hobcaw shipbuilder, was contracted to oversee the work. James Marsh was brought in from Philadelphia as foreman. A shortage of shipwrights in the Charleston area caused other local yards to be subcontracted to handle some of the work. As a result, one yard probably cut the frames for one side of the ship and another for the other side; when the parts were assembled, *John Adams* was slightly wider on the port than on the starboard side. As a consequence she was stiffer (heeled less) on the starboard than on the port tack and tended to list to starboard. One local historian contended erroneously that the ship was built in halves at separate building sites, with one half being taken to Shipyard Creek to be attached to the other half. This is an interesting conjecture; however, with the methods available at the time it would have been nearly impossible to move such heavy parts and join them together with structural integrity. Another theory held that she had one more gunport on one side than on the other, also not true.

The navy became aware of the discrepancy in width during the 1807 refit of *John Adams*. Jeffersonian economy and a subsequent war prevented further investigation. In 1820, after many years of redoubtable service by *John Adams*, the navy began an investigation. By then Pritchard was dead and no construction plans for the ship could be found. In a letter to Charleston's Navy Agent, John Robertson, in 1820,

U. S. brig-of-war *Norfolk*—a conjectural model of the warship that accompanied the Charleston-built brig-of-war *General Pinckney* in patrolling the southeastern coast of the United States and the West Indies in 1799. *General Pinckney* was probably quite similar.

[4] Appointed to serve under Cross were:

Isaac B. Hicbourne	First Lieutenant
William Smith	Second Lieutenant
William Flagg	Third Lieutenant
John Hall	Lieutenant, Marine Detachment
Christopher Gadsden, Jr.	Midshipman
John J. Ellsworth	Midshipman*
Henry Morrison	Midshipman
Joseph Maxwell	Midshipman*
Peter Bonetheau	Midshipman
Maurice Simons	Midshipman
Thomas Devaux	Midshipman
Humphrey Magrath	Midshipman
Peter Trezevant	Purser

* no record of service found

November 1, 1799, the new frigate *John Adams* sails down the Cooper River and returns a salute from Fort Mechanic while merchant ships in the harbor lower their colors in her honor.

James Marsh said that he had laid the ship out in a mold loft but he did not admit that she was the famous "two-sided frigate!" His report goes on to read:

[H]er keel and keelson was of pine, her frame of live oak [which came from St. Simons, Georgia, and was cut in the winter of 1797], with the exception of some of the top timbers which was of cedar, her beams was all of Edisto yellow pine, her plank was all of pine, for bottom ceiling, decks, etc. her harpins round the bows was of live oak, and I think her bends and wales was of this country white oak and was of but short lengths, not being able at that time to obtain long lengths, and the reference at that time was given to the oak in reference to long lengths of pine. . . : [H]er lower or birth [berth] deck beams, was dovetailed into [I] think clamps and not kneed. Her gun decks, as well as her quarter decks and forecastle decks was all kneed. As best I can recollect, I think the draught was 86

feet keel straight-rabbit, but owing to the length and goodness of the stuff that was scarphed together for the keel, the Committee thought proper to have her built 5 feet longer than the draught which was accordingly done and thereby added one more (gun) port than was laid down in the draught. I think she was 32 feet beam, 12 feet lower hold, 6 feet to the gun deck and 5 feet 10 inches waist. She was a ship calculated for the Charleston bar and consequently of a light draft of water. She was very fleet on the river for a ship of war of her size.

The additional five feet and one gunport that Marsh mentions as being added to the ship's length were undoubtedly used to increase and improve the accommodations rather than increase the number of guns. The additional space for living quarters made her a popular flag vessel throughout her life span.

In November 1798 the thirty or so ship carpenters from northern shipyards that were hired to supplement the local workers, both freemen and slaves, arrived on the ship *Romulus* from Boston. On November 10, 1798, the keel for the new frigate was laid. It was set on the building ways and the floor timbers and frames of live oak attached on top.

Much of the pine timber for the ship was cut in the fall and winter of 1798–99, along the Edisto River. Shipbuilding timber was normally cut in the winter when the sap was down, as there would be less moisture in the wood to dry. Much of the wood was freshly cut and unseasoned; as a consequence, no effort was made to cover the hull. It was built in the open so that the wood could season. When it was discovered that insufficient knees and beams were on hand, additional ones were cut in the spring of 1799.

The construction proceeded quickly in the cool Lowcountry winter. The ship was supposed to be copper-bolted, but such bolts were not available locally, so iron bolts were used to attach the stem, stern, and keel pieces. The planks were fastened to the sides with composition spikes and trunnels. These must not have adversely affected the structure of the ship, as she remained in service until 1867.

To show the pride of the city in the new ship, the foremost ship carver in America, William Rush of Philadelphia, was commissioned to carve the bust of President John Adams for the figurehead. The Charleston firm of Cotton & Statler carved the trailboards, transom, quarter gallery, and other decorations.

Through the spring of 1799, the hull took shape, the raw lumber being shaped into carefully flowing lines with gunports checkering the sides. Finally, when the big day of the launch arrived, the crowd assembled, but as the shores and hull blocks were knocked away, the great bulk moved down the ways about ninety feet and shuddered to a halt. The soft ground gave way beneath the weight and stopped her advance toward the water. Her ways were taken apart and reassembled with proper support so that on June 5, 1799, two days after the first attempt, *John Adams* was introduced into her element. One observer wrote that she hurried from the ways before all of the shores and blocks could be knocked away, and nine workmen still under her barely escaped unharmed.

Coming by land and water, a large crowd of spectators gathered for the event, despite the distance of three miles from the city proper. Governor Rutledge, Major General Charles Cotesworth Pinckney, Brigadier General William Washington, and other leading citizens attended. A band played patriotic tunes, and refreshments were served to the spectators by the subscription committee; toast after toast was downed to celebrate the event. As *John Adams* hit the water, the brigs *General Pinckney* and *South Carolina*, dressed in bunting

The second launch of *John Adams*, at Norfolk in 1830, this time as a second-class corvette. Her original launch at Charleston in 1799 was probably identical, with similar crowds in attendance.

and flags, fired a federal salute. Dressing ship in the tradition of the time included flying the national flags of all maritime powers, including France, the war with which was the catalyst for the event!

Once the ceremonies were over the completed hull was taken to a fitting-out pier for coppering, masting, and rigging. Then, on July 16, she dropped down the Cooper River with the ebb tide and tied up at Gadsden's Wharf where the lower masts and rigging were stepped in place with heavy lifting shears much like modern cranes. As she came down, the vessels in the harbor lowered their colors in her honor and citizens on the shore cheered.

Riding proudly on her native waters, the new ship must have stirred the pride of every Charlestonian, as she was the most powerful warship built in Charleston to that date. A steady throng came to see and remark on the ship for which they had paid. Once the lower masts were in place she was taken back to Cochran's Shipyard, probably to be heaved over and have sheets of copper nailed to the underwater portion of the hull to protect it from teredos, barnacles, and other marine growth. Then she came down the Cooper River for the final time and anchored off Prioleau's Wharf at the foot of Queen Street. There the job of completing the ship continued. The top masts and yards of Lowcountry heart pine were swung into position and miles of cordage from the rope walk in Columbia completed her rigging.

While the original plans of *John Adams* have not been found, from a list of her spars we can determine that the ship followed contemporary improvements in rigging, including a flying jib-boom, dolphin-striker, and spanker sail on the mizzenmast. In addition the waist, previously open in frigates, was probably fitted with fixed beams and wide gangways on either side, linking the forecastle and quarterdeck.

At Mr. Crawford's Tavern on the southeast corner of Governor's Bridge (Market Street) and East Bay Street, Captain Cross and his officers opened a "rendezvous" to enlist the 220-man crew for *John Adams*. A shortage of labor in Charleston caused delays in recruiting a full crew. On July 17, the forty marines assigned to the ship arrived on the packet *Ann* from Norfolk, but had to be quartered at Fort Moultrie until the ship was ready. They consisted of a sergeant, corporal, drummer, fifer, officer, and thirty-five privates.

Through the summer of 1799 the final touches were put on the ship. Her long guns arrived from the foundry at Cecil Furnace, Maryland, on the merchant ship *South Carolina*; her carronades came from England, as they were a new type of gun unavailable in America. When the guns were lifted into place on their carriages, their broadside (firepower) of almost a quarter of a ton of metal made her one of the most powerful ships in the U. S. Navy.

By October 1, 1799, *John Adams'* captain received final orders from Secretary Stoddert to join the U. S. squadron patrolling off Puerto Rico. On October 18, a final notice was published for financial claims against the committee paying for the ship, and by October 25 she was ready for sea. *John Adams* weighed anchor on November 1, to drop down to Rebellion Road to await a favorable wind in order to sail out of the harbor. On passing the city she fired a grand salute that was returned by Fort Mechanic on White Point, to the hearty applause of proud Charlestonians on the shore. The harbor was busy that day with nearly a hundred ocean-going vessels and numerous coastal craft joining in the salute to the new warship. The strong easterly wind forced her to anchor off Fort Johnson rather than risk grounding in tacking through the narrow channel out to the bar.

On November 14, 1799, the ship weighed anchor again and passed Fort Johnson, which fired a salute as she passed; it was returned gun for gun. She gave a good account of her sailing qualities; under topsails, spanker, and jibs she made seven knots on the trip to Five

Fathom Hole, where she anchored overnight. The next day the anchor was once more upped and she put out over the bar. The pilot, Mr. Delano, remarked that she would "equal any ship in the Navy, and he never saw a ship answer her helm so quickly or slip through the water against the tide so rapidly." While her speed would prove her one of the fastest ships on the Guadeloupe Station, *John Adams'* topside weight would make her roll in a good (top-gallant) breeze—in some cases to the point of putting her maindeck gunports under the waves. A sailing warship depended on a certain degree of stiffness to make it a stable gun platform in battle. Much of this lack of stiffness in *John Adams* can be traced to James Marsh's decreasing the deadrise, thereby reducing her draft[5] and raising her center of gravity. Exacerbating her rolling was the added topside weight of the guns on her quarterdeck and forecastle. Until they were removed permanently after her 1829–1830 rebuilding, *John Adams* rolled excessively. Without them she proved to be a remarkably stable warship requiring little or no ballast.

[5] Marsh had to reduce her draft somehow in order for *John Adams* to cross the Charleston bar fully loaded. Decreasing the deadrise was the easiest way; otherwise, he would have had to build a smaller ship. The frigate committee did not wish to do so.

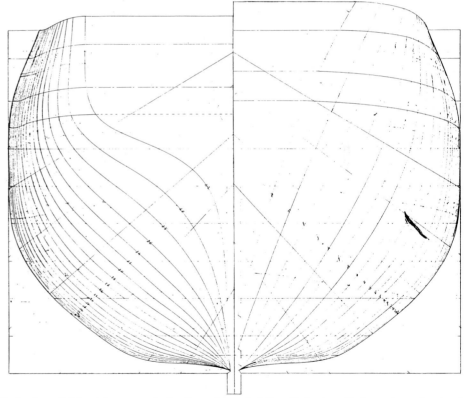

Body plan of *John Adams*—probably the only part of the ship's plans that survive—showing her configuration as built in Charleston. Note the lack of deadrise on the bottom of the hull and the tumblehome on the side.

The new frigate outsailed all vessels she saw as she proceeded from Charleston to Puerto Rico on the first leg of her voyage to the Guadeloupe Station. On December 16, 1799, she recaptured the brig *Dolphin*, which had been previously taken by a French privateer, and sent it to Charleston. *Dolphin* eventually brought $1,017.31 in prize money to the ship's company. Six days later *John Adams* put into Basseterre, St. Kitts, after a minor altercation with Spanish authorities in Puerto Rico over the detention of a landing party searching for supplies. At St. Kitts, three proud new American frigates rode at anchor, showing the nation's resolve to rid her merchant fleet of the French menace.

In January 1800, *John Adams* captured a Spanish three-masted lugger bound for Puerto Rico as the prize of a French privateer. Captain Cross put Midshipman Humphrey Magrath on board; with a prize crew he took her to Charleston. From there he obtained passage on a merchant vessel back to St. Kitts to rejoin *John Adams*.

For the next several weeks *John Adams* patrolled the waters around St. Kitts. By the end of January a fleet of American warships had gathered there to form the Guadeloupe Station under Commodore Truxtun in the frigate *Constellation*. One of *John Adams*' officers wrote to a friend in Charleston:

> I have the pleasure to inform you that *John Adams* has been more generally approved of here, than any ship of her force belonging to the United States, that has been at the island, and the English captains in particular are much pleased with her. When we sailed from Charleston the ship was too light, we have since taken in twenty tons more ballast and completed our water for another cruise, and now she sails much faster, as we had experienced in bearing up from the Old roads to Basseterre, when we had an opportunity of trying her with the United States schooner *Enterprize*, reputed to be the fastest sailer on the station, yet she could not gain upon us. *John Adams* does credit to Charleston.

In March *John Adams* recaptured the American merchant brigs *Hannibal* and *Atlantic* from the French. Then on April 4, she ran down and captured the 8-gun French privateer schooner *Le Jason* between Martinique and St. Lucia after a chase of four hours. In an attempt to escape, *Le Jason* hove six of her guns over the side. *Le Jason* was a new Virginia-built pilot schooner, coppered to the waterline and completely fitted, typical of the American-built vessels the French had purchased in the 1790s to prey on British merchant shipping. She was sent to Charleston and eventually brought $3,389.88 in prize money for *John Adams*' crew.

On April 15, 1800 *John Adams* put into St. Thomas with a convoy of sixty-one American merchant vessels. After turning them over to the U. S. brig *Pickering* she returned to the Guadeloupe Station. While at St. Thomas an officer wrote to Charleston that "we have been in company with several British warships and have outdone them all in sailing."

On June 13 *John Adams* captured the French privateer schooner *Le Decade*. However, as she was not worth the time and trouble of a journey to an American prize court, she was sold at St. Kitts.

Through the summer of 1800, *John Adams* engaged in routine patrols; by that time, the numbers of American warships on the scene had reduced the French menace to almost zero. On November 22, she sailed with a convoy from St. Pierre, Martinique, for the United States, arriving in Charleston on December 15, with forty sail in convoy after a cruise away from home of 397 days. During that time *John Adams* had spent only thirty-five days in harbor, a unique statistic in our early navy.

In January 1801, Captain Cross took leave and eventually was discharged from the navy. He and his family are buried in the graveyard of St. Michael's Church. Lieutenant William Smith was placed in charge of the ship while she underwent repairs from the long cruise. In June the fleet was cut back to peacetime strength, so Smith took *John Adams* to the Washington Navy Yard to be placed in ordinary for possible future use. Other less desirable ships were sold or returned to their owners.

By 1800, both France and America had tired of the conflict and commenced diplomatic negotiations, although French privateers would continue to harass American ships off and on until 1815. An agreement was reached in October, and while it took another year to work out the details, the war was over by year's end. The war had been a success; it had proven the usefulness of the American Navy. Stoddert had worked wonders in setting up the new Navy Department, overseeing the purchase, construction, and dispatch of over thirty warships. Thousands of men had been trained and brought into the service. He guided legislation through Congress that would shape the future of the U. S. Navy. None of this would have been possible without the successes at sea, in particular those of Truxtun, who had bested the French in two battles that captured the public's fancy and generated naval support in Congress.

Other Naval Activities

Part of this public support of the new U. S. Navy was reflected in the 1799 act to expand the fleet through construction of six 74-gun ships-of-the-line. One of the timber contracts for these ships was awarded to Colonel Thomas Shubrick of Bull's Island to procure sufficient live oak timbers to construct the frames for two battleships.

Unable to obtain sufficient skilled labor in Charleston, Shubrick hired sixty-five ship carpenters from Newburyport, Massachusetts. Unfortunately five of them died on the job. To help them, forty local slaves were leased as carpenters. The 74-gun ship type was one of the largest sailing warships and one of the most complex of all sailing ships of the time, and American builders had built only one at Portsmouth, New Hampshire, in the Revolution. As a consequence the immense amount of timber required (34,000 cubic feet of wood per ship or 680 mature trees) was underestimated; Shubrick could provide sufficient timber for only two-thirds of one of the ships. Compounding the problems was the fact that much of the live oak on Bull's Island was found to be rotten. This was discovered only after the trees had been cut down, for the rot works from the core outward. In the end Shubrick paid out $22,000 in expenses and received from the government only $17,000. Adding to the unfortunate circumstances, Congress never appropriated the money to actually build the ships until 1813. However, by then the wood was well seasoned, so despite Shubrick's troubles, the first three American 74's lasted well over their fifty-year life expectancy.

The young nation was now moving beyond infancy. A functioning central government was in place with a navy to aid the nation's resolve to protect its rights. Charleston's citizens and shipwrights had done their part in launching the fleet by capping a long and successful period of shipbuilding. Unfortunately they would not carry forth very far into the new century; Charleston shipbuilding had reached its zenith with the construction of *John Adams*.

The Charleston-built frigate *John Adams* in the Mediterranean in 1837. By this time the ship had been rebuilt as a second-class corvette (sloop-of-war), with her quarter and forecastle decks removed. She retained much of her original appearance, as her masts, rigging, and the number of gunports on the main deck remained unchanged. With her Charleston-built top decks re-moved, she sailed far better and reportedly more than held her own against the larger frigate *Brandywine*. This illustration by the Neapolitan ship portrait painter Cammilleri can be con-sidered highly accurate.

1800–1812, Years of Turmoil

With the French menace gone from the coast, America settled into a period of peace that was to be quickly interrupted. Charleston was enjoying a decade of prosperity that would end as she joined the rest of the nation in the turmoil that led to war with England. Charlestonians would help lead in this period of difficulty, and Charleston would play its part in building ships and serving as a base of operations for the approaching conflict.

With Jefferson's election in 1800, the supporters of the new U. S. Navy became most uneasy. Jefferson and his southern agrarian allies had fought naval construction over the course of the preceding six years; to them, it was nothing more than a federal subsidy of northern shipping interests. In the last days of Adams' administration the departing president bowed to the inevitable and signed a bill that reduced the size of the fleet to thirteen frigates. Seven of these were laid up in ordinary, including his namesake, *John Adams*, and the remaining six were on active service, but with two-thirds complements.

War With Tripoli

Charleston's interest in the Tripolitan War was much like that of the other American seaports—in the ships and men who served. A war thousands of miles across the Atlantic was a large feat for a new nation. However, its navy, while hardly a decade old, possessed a fine fleet of ships and the men and officers to serve on them.

The war started over the Barbary Pirates' age-old custom of seizing foreign ships and crews and holding them for ransom—a concept alien to America. When several of her merchantmen were affected, war was declared. War operations started poorly. As most U. S. Navy operations in the Mediterranean since, the officers looked upon duty there as a chance to see the sights and hobnob with Europe's elite. Retaliation against the pirates was lackadaisical at best in the first months. It fell upon Charleston's *John Adams* and her new captain, John Rodgers, to reverse the falling American fortunes. In August 1802, *John Adams* was recommissioned at the Washington Navy Yard, where she had lain in ordinary for over a year. After taking on provisions at Norfolk, the ship left Hampton Roads for the Mediterranean on October 22, 1802.

John Adams arrived at Gibraltar on November 17, and joined her sister subscription frigate, the New York-built *Adams*. That ship was now under the command of Charlestonian Hugh G. Campbell, who had been first mate on the first revenue cutter *South Carolina* at Charleston only five years earlier. Campbell's successful tour as captain of *Eagle* in the West Indies had won him a frigate command.

John Adams spent the subsequent months refitting and resupplying after the Atlantic crossing. The winter weather in the Mediterranean was so bad that a blockade of Tripoli was impossible. Except for a brief four-day stint in February, it was not until May that *John Adams* took station off Tripoli.

On May 9 while alone off Tripoli, *John Adams* engaged in a cannonade with forts and gunboats in the harbor for most of the afternoon. The firing on both sides was ineffectual. The next day a few more shots were exchanged, and three days later a strange sail was seen to the east; *John Adams* set out in pursuit. After two hours the sail hove to and was identified as the 28-gun Tripolitan warship *Meshouda*, which had recently been blockaded by the American squadron at Gibraltar. She was the former American ship *Betsey* of Boston, captured by the enemy in 1796 and converted to a warship. The prize was taken to Malta, and on May 21, 1803, *John Adams* sailed with the frigate *New York* and schooner *Enterprize* for Tripoli. For the next several weeks they sparred with the Tripolitan batteries and gunboats while maintaining the blockade. Early in June Commodore Morris and Captain Rodgers even went into Tripoli under a flag of truce in an attempt to negotiate a peace.

On June 21, 1803, the enemy gunboats in Tripoli harbor got underway and a large polacre-rigged ship fired on *Enterprize*. *John Adams* came up in support. The enemy ship ran ashore, the crew abandoned her, and she subsequently blew up. This ended another enemy nuisance. With this action *John Adams* had eliminated the two largest warships in the bashaw's navy. A few days later *John Adams* sailed for Malta and up the Italian coast, around to Gibraltar, and home. In October at Tangier Bay, Campbell relieved Rodgers as captain.

In the meantime, Jefferson had dispatched a new commodore, Edward Preble, to take charge in the Mediterranean. Before he arrived, the fine new frigate *Philadelphia* grounded on a reef off Tripoli. Helpless, she was set upon by the corsairs and Captain Bainbridge was forced to surrender. When the tide came in, the prize was refloated and taken into Tripoli harbor. At a single stroke the enemy possessed one of the most powerful ships in the American fleet.

Preble lost no time in getting to Tripoli, where he saw the enemy's new prize. The northerly winter winds made it impossible to maintain a proper blockade, so Preble withdrew to Syracuse after capturing the small ketch-rigged vessel *Mastico*.

Here it was decided to use *Mastico* to slip into Tripoli harbor and burn *Philadelphia*. Renamed *Intrepid* and commanded by Stephen Decatur, *Mastico* was loaded with combustibles and, accompanied by *Siren*, sailed to Tripoli in February. Charlestonian Ralph Izard, son of the statesman of the Revolution and a midshipman on *Constitution*, went with Decatur on *Intrepid*. Using a pilot from Palermo who knew the waters around Tripoli and spoke Arabic, they entered the harbor on the evening of February 7, 1804, and pulled alongside the anchored ship. Within fifteen minutes they routed the crew, set the ship afire, and were off—using sails and oars as the enemy forts opened up on them. *Philadelphia* lit up the southern sky as they rejoined *Siren* and returned to the cheers of the squadron at Syracuse. Britain's Admiral Nelson called it "the most bold and daring act of the age," a fitting tribute from an able naval commander.

With *Philadelphia* out of the way, Preble got down to work. Realizing that only force would bring the bashaw to terms, he obtained six gunboats and two bomb ketches from the Kingdom of the Two Sicilies. By the end of July the force off Tripoli consisted of 1,600 men aboard *Constitution*, three brigs, three schooners, two bomb ketches, and six gunboats. Opposing them were walled forts with 115 large guns and 25,000 men, as well as a naval force of nineteen gunboats, two galleys, two schooners, and a brig.

The battle on August 3 was dramatic but accomplished little, although the American gunboats took several prizes. Mindful of *Philadelphia's* fate, *Constitution* stood off shore. The other ships supported the gunboats as they battled the enemy. A second attack four days later and two subsequent attacks were equally unsuccessful in subduing the Tripolitans. There-fore, one September night *Intrepid*, loaded with explosives, sailed into the harbor in an effort to destroy the fort. She mysteriously exploded short of her goal, killing the crew.

In the meantime *John Adams* had spent the winter and spring of 1804 refitting at the Washington Navy Yard. In June of 1804, she left Hampton Roads under the command of Isaac Chauncey, carrying supplies for the fleet in the Mediterranean. In order to provide more room for these supplies, her guns were struck below and their carriages shifted to the frigates *Congress* and *Constellation*, which were to return them to *John Adams* in the Mediter-ranean. On August 8, 1804, four days after the bombardment of the forts, *John Adams* arrived off Tripoli and anchored alongside the frigate *Constitution*. Without her gun carriages *John Adams* had to stay on the sidelines, but some of her crew went to supplement those in the active ships.

Shortly after this, Commodore Samuel Barron relieved Preble, who returned home in December on *John Adams*. Realizing that Tripoli could not be taken by naval assault William Eaton and a handful of marines went to Egypt to assist in trying to overthrow the bashaw. After spending several months crossing the Sahara the force attacked the fort at Derne and, with naval support from *Argus* and *Hornet*, took it on April 28, 1805.

Commodore Barron realized that only a large land force could move against Tripoli from Derne, and that was beyond his resources. Bowing to the inevitable Barron proposed $60,000 in cash for peace and the release of Bainbridge and his men. Tired of war, the bashaw eventually struck a deal. Commodore Rodgers then moved onto Tunis and forced the bey to agree to a peace. The American presence in the Mediterranean was then reduced; by spring of 1805, it was down to three ships, a result of Jeffersonian economy. In 1807, when the *Chesapeake-Leopard* crisis struck (see pages 151–154), the few American warships[1] in the Mediterranean were recalled. They did not return until 1815.

In spite of cost-conscious Congress, the war remained popular with the public even after the loss of *Philadelphia*. If anything, it boosted European respect for America and made other nations think twice before waging war against the new nation. It was also a proving ground for the American Navy, who would engage in a conflict soon to follow against Britain.

In June 1805, *John Adams* returned to the Mediterranean under Master Commandant John Shaw, spent three months on patrol with other American warships, and then returned to Washington in November. For the next four years she was laid up there, having her forecastle and quarterdeck removed to be converted into a corvette. It was there in 1807 that Josiah Fox noted that she was wider on one side than the other. In the conversion process her entire top-side was replaced, one of several rebuildings that the ship would receive in her sixty-eight-year lifespan. Fox also shortened the overhang of the stern and noted that her frames and planks in the lower part of the hull were all in sound condition—the Carolina live oak and heart pine had held up well.

Once the Tripolitan adventure was over, most of the naval fleet was mothballed or laid up in ordinary. Jefferson was no sluggard in naval matters, despite his early opposition to the expenditure of funds necessary to maintain the young navy. He sent a proposal to Congress

for an elaborate covered drydock at Washington. It was to be some 800 feet long and would accommodate up to a dozen frigates. Keeping them dry could greatly increase their "in ordi-nary" lifespan. Naturally, when Congress balked at the half-million-dollar price tag, the measure died.

Jefferson's Gunboats

Jefferson's naval ideas were numerous. His most controversial naval policy was the re-placement of larger ocean-going warships with swarms of gunboats. Gunboats were nothing new in navies at the time, but Jefferson's plan was to make them "the fleet" rather than an adjunct to the larger warships. Their inability to cruise on the open ocean made them fit into a purely defensive role with its political considerations. Many gunboats were built through four different congressional appropriations. All of them together would not have equalled the cost of a single frigate, but at the time they were all that Congress would authorize. In retro-spect, naval historians have criticized the gunboat policy, but at the time the nation did not have the resources to build a large fleet, and America enjoyed natural naval protection geo-graphically; all potential aggressors had to cross 3,000 miles of ocean. Furthermore, a large

Model of a double-ended, lateen-rigged Jeffersonian gunboat based on a design by Commodore Barron. Gunboat *No. 2* was similar. She survived two Atlantic crossings only to succumb in a gale when en route from Charleston to St. Marys, Georgia, in 1811. She rolled over in a heavy sea. The crew below panicked and opened the hatches; she filled with water and sank.

[1] One ship was *Constitution*, commanded by Hugh G. Campbell, who had had a meteoric rise through the navy's ranks. Charlestonian Ralph Izard would become her first lieutenant (executive officer) in 1810.

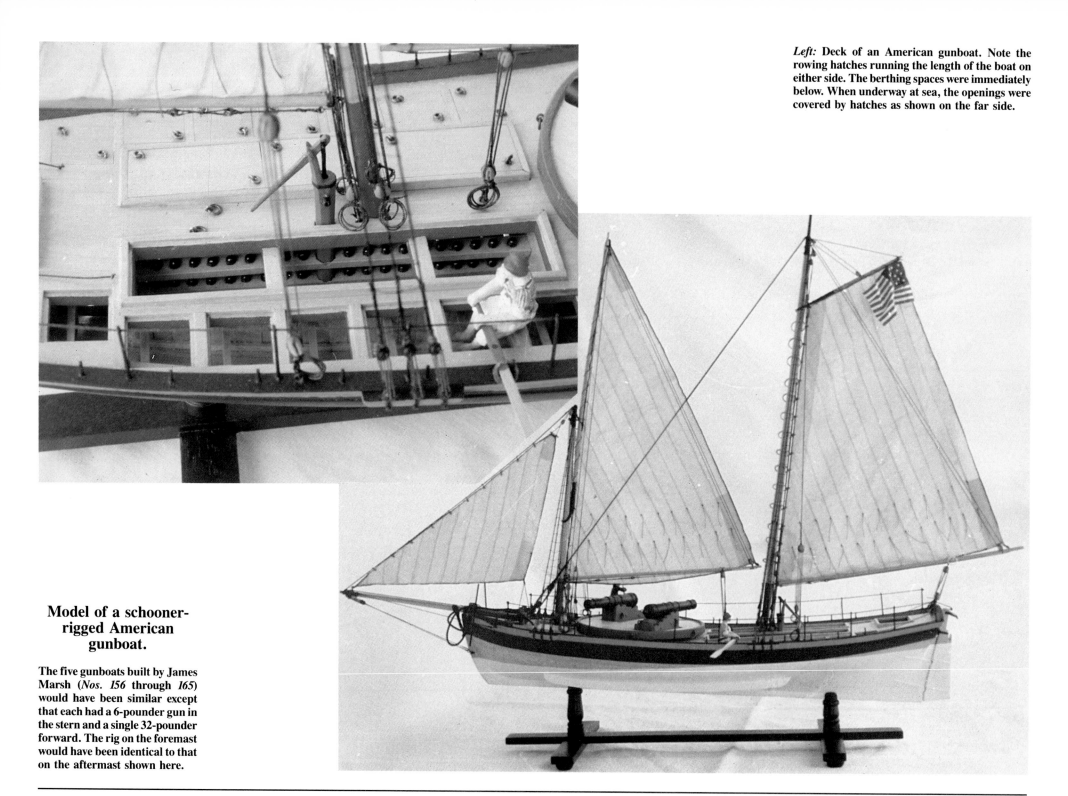

Left: Deck of an American gunboat. Note the rowing hatches running the length of the boat on either side. The berthing spaces were immediately below. When underway at sea, the openings were covered by hatches as shown on the far side.

Model of a schooner-rigged American gunboat.

The five gunboats built by James Marsh (*Nos. 156* through *165*) would have been similar except that each had a 6-pounder gun in the stern and a single 32-pounder forward. The rig on the foremast would have been identical to that on the aftermast shown here.

The ship *Three Sisters*, built in Charleston in 1800 of live oak, displacing 201 tons. She was originally built as a brig, but on a voyage to the Mediterranean in 1801 she sought refuge from pirates at Barcelona for over a month; during that time she was rerigged as a ship. Thomas Ogier, a Charleston merchant, was her owner and John Bonnell was master on her first voyage. She continued trading out of Charleston with ports in France, and by 1804 had made seven complete runs. It was on one of these voyages that this watercolor was painted by John Elne Toulso in April 1802.

fleet build-up would have served only to alarm, if not antagonize, Britain. After the Battle of Trafalgar in 1805, Jefferson realized that no one could or would challenge Britain's dominion of the seas in the foreseeable future.

Once Jefferson sold his gunboat idea to Congress, two experimental ones were built at Washington and Norfolk and put into service in the summer of 1804. These boats mounted one large cannon in the bow, carried crews of up to thirty-five men, and used both sails and oars for propulsion. With oars they could set upon enemy warships becalmed or in confined coastal waters and batter them at their weak points.

Five different designs were used and over a hundred gunboats built in various places along the coast, including Charleston. In this way each seaport was protected by its own gunboat squadron.

With Jefferson's inauguration, William Smith became Naval Agent at Charleston, and to him fell the task of constructing the local gunboat squadron. During the summer of 1804 the first gunboat arrived for the Charleston station. She was gunboat *No. 1* under Sailing Master John P. Lovell—one of the experimental ones that had been built at Washington. She then proceeded to Savannah, where she was driven ashore in a storm but was refloated. Humphrey Magrath assumed command in November and brought her to Charleston for repairs, ostensibly in preparation for a voyage to the Mediterranean, but *No. 1* was not considered seaworthy for the trip. She was then joined by gunboat *No. 2* commanded by Ralph Izard and ordered to remain on the Charleston station to enforce quarantine laws. After several changes of commanders, Lt. James Biddle arrived in Charleston in October 1805 to take over. His uncle, Nicholas, had nurtured a fond following in the port city during the Revolution. James would go on to fame in the naval service during the War of 1812 and afterwards.

In January 1805 Lieutenant Nathaniel Fanning arrived in Charleston to superintend the construction, equipping, and outfitting of a gunboat then being built by Paul Pritchard at his shipyard at Fair Bank Plantation on Daniel's Island. Fanning was much pleased at what he found, saying:

> [The gunboat has the] stoutest and best materials in her frame of any vessel I ever knew of her size.... [H]er timbers are throughout as well as her plank large enough for a sloop of war and has been thus far faithfully built. She is the...very best boat on every account for carrying guns, and for safety at sea, of any one which has hitherto been built in the U. S. She is in fact so large, buoyant, and burthensome that she might with a skillful navigator on board double Cape Horn and proceed around the world with perfect safety.

The vessel was built slightly larger than the plans and fitted with a transom rather than a pointed stern. She was some 71 feet long and 18 feet wide, with a six-foot, two-and-a-half-inch depth of hold. She was launched on March 3, 1805, when she became gunboat *No. 9*. Due to her large size and seaworthiness she was armed with two 32-pounder guns (one at each end) and rigged as a fore-and-aft ketch. In other words, her rig was much like a schooner, but the forward mast was taller than the aftermast. On May 8, 1805, gunboat *No. 9* under Lieutenant Samuel Elbert and *No. 2* under Midshipman Ralph Izard departed Charleston for the Mediterranean. They arrived at Gibraltar after a passage of twenty-seven days—no minor accomplishment for such small vessels on the open ocean.

The gunboats rendered good support of the larger ships on the Mediterranean station.

Then in May 1806 in Gibraltar, pursuant to instructions from the secretary of the navy, Commodore Rodgers ordered the brigs-of-war *Vixen* and *Argus*; bomb ketches *Spitfire* and *Vengeance*; the cutter *Hornet*,[2] and gunboats *No. 2, 3, 4, 5, 6, 8, 9,* and *10* to return to Charleston for reassignment. This reduction of the Mediterranean fleet was part of Jeffersonian economy. Rodgers warned the commanders of the various vessels:

> The climate of South Carolina is at best unhealthy in the summer...and more particularly so in the vicinity of Charleston, [so] I am induced to surmise to you the propriety of the vessels lying at Sullivan's Island, where you will find the air much more wholesome than higher up the river, however as this place abounds with shellfish, you will find it absolutely

[2] This vessel was a new cutter purchased in the Mediterranean, not *Hornet* mentioned on page 153.

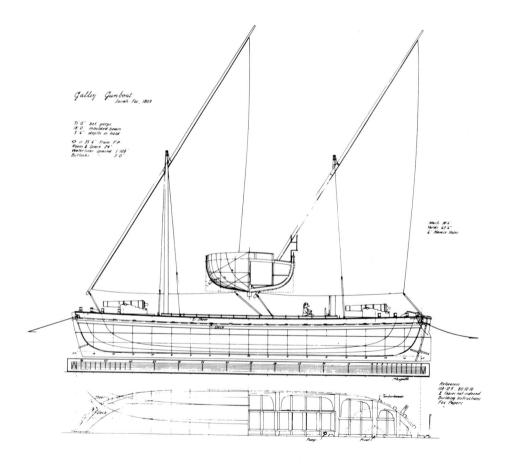

Josiah Fox's plan for a 71′ galley gunboat. Gunboat *No. 9* was similar, except that she was rigged as a fore-and-aft ketch with a transom stern and one rowing hatch on the centerline.

necessary to abstain from eating them, during the hot weather, particularly the oysters and crabs.

During the last week of May and the first of June 1806, the various vessels got underway; after taking on water in Madeira, they arrived in Charleston in mid-July. Gunboats *No. 2, 3,* and *9* were then permanently reassigned to Charleston and laid up in ordinary under Lt. Christopher Gadsden. Gunboat *No. 2* was brought across the Atlantic by Midshipman Ralph Izard, Jr., and *No. 3* by Sailing Master Humphrey Magrath. *No. 2* parted company with the others en route and towed gunboat *No. 9* part of the way. The other vessels proceeded to Norfolk and New York on July 27, after resupplying. Two officers in this squadron, Isaac Hull, captain of *Argus*, and Lieutenant James Lawerence, commander of gunboat *No. 6*, would leave their mark on the U. S. Navy.

Nathaniel Ingraham had arrived in Charleston several years earlier and became Navy Agent in 1807. He had served on *Bon Homme Richard* in 1779 under John Paul Jones in the battle with HMS *Serapis*. He established a permanent home in Charleston, and his son later commanded the Confederate ironclad squadron. Shortly after his arrival, he oversaw construction of five new gunboats by James Marsh that had been approved by Congress in 1807. Ingraham had been ordered the previous summer to assemble the materials for their construction. The draughts of the boats were sent to Charleston, but plans for the deck layout were left up to Ingraham, the only requirement being that they accommodate two 32-pounder guns, one at each end.

This group of gunboats was based on a plan drawn up by Commodore James Barron. They measured sixty feet on deck with a sixteen-and-a-half-foot beam. They probably had a square or transom stern and were schooner-rigged. Once construction started Ingraham evidently felt that the three-ton gun mounted aft was too heavy; it was reduced to a 6-pounder, with the forward 32-pounder on a pivot that could be trained through 360 degrees. Its carriage rested on a wrought iron circular track inlaid in the deck. The bottoms of these gunboats were copper sheathed. They were completed early in 1809.

Under the command of Lieutenant John Kerr, *No. 157* was lost on the South Breakers of the Charleston bar on May 17, 1811. After the boat rolled over, the crew clung to the bottom for several hours. Fishing boats standing by were unable to rescue them because of the surf. Some sailors managed to swim to safety, but only eight of the crew of twenty-two were saved.[3] Two fishing boats were lost on the bar in the same storm. The other gunboats served through the War of 1812, and were then sold out of the service in 1815. Several became merchant vessels carrying cargo in the coastal trade.

Other Operations

One intersting aside that occurred in Charleston during Jefferson's administration concerned the merchant ship *Resolution*. On October 26, 1803, she arrived from New London

---

[3] One sailor remarked after being rescued from *No. 157*,

> I would to God that those who planned and who still persist in this species of naval defence, were compelled to man these boats themselves. . . . They [are] wretched machines and consign our unfortunate seamen to certain death and disgrace.

and anchored in the Cooper River with a cargo of live lobsters. On October 28 all hands were employed in taking them into the city market. A fish stand was set up for three days and the crew made a profit of $76. Charlestonians liked lobsters as much then as now! On November 1 they went hunting up the Wappoo Creek. For the next few days the ship's boats put out to fish offshore and returned to the city market every few days with a load to sell.

Other nautical activities at Charleston in the first decade of the nineteenth century centered around the usual ship disasters. Several of these were caused when vessels attempted to leave or enter port without pilots—a risky situation for even a skilled mariner in Charleston's winding channel. On October 14, 1805, the 12-gun, 423-ton British ship *Northumberland* bound from Jamaica to London under the command of Captain Gibbs went aground on the North Breakers of the South Channel of the Charleston bar. She was a total loss, including her cargo of sugar, rum, cotton, and logwood. The sloop *Republican* under Captain Myers put out of Charleston for Savannah on June 7, 1812. She went ashore on the Stono breakers. Except for her sails, rigging, and a small part of her cargo of rice which were salvaged, she was a total loss.

The *Chesapeake-Leopard* Affair

While Jefferson and the Congress argued the pros and cons of the gunboat navy, a new crisis was brewing. The U. S. Navy had relied on volunteers and monetary inducements to raise crews. In the Royal Navy, the press gang had forcibly handled recruitments. Naval life at that time was hard, with long periods at sea, low pay, and brutal discipline. Desertion was high, and seamen stayed away from His Majesty's Service in droves. The demands for manpower that the European war generated meant that British ships were almost always cruising shorthanded. Thus, they often resorted to impressment of crewmen from merchant ships. English merchant ships were not the only ones to suffer this humiliation. Ships of other nations, including America, were often stopped and the crews searched for British subjects. Any that were found were added to the warship's crew, and all too often it did not take much more than an accent to determine arbitrarily that a man was British. Naturalization was not recognized—once an Englishman, always an Englishman.

In the first ten years of the Napoleonic Wars more than 2,000 men were taken off American ships. In the ten years prior to the War of 1812 that number tripled, even though a third of those impressed were later released. Large numbers of British seamen, surely many of whom were deserters, made their way into the U. S. Navy. In fact, it is estimated that a third of *Philadelphia's* ill-fated crew off Tripoli were English.

The Royal Navy did not hesitate to meet its manpower shortage by ruthless impressment of any able-bodied seaman who came their way by fair means or foul. The first incident involving impressment from an American warship was the removal of fifty-five men from *Baltimore* in 1798, which resulted in her captain's dismissal from the U. S. Navy. The secretary of the navy sent instructions to ship commanders that such actions were to be resisted with all due force. Another incident off Cadiz in 1805 involving gunboat *No. 6* under James Lawrence en route to the Mediterranean resulted in reiteration of this instruction.

Matters rested for about two years until the frigate *Chesapeake* under Master Commandant Charles Gordon and bearing the flag of Commodore James Barron was readying for a cruise to the Mediterranean. Her newly recruited crew included three deserters from HMS *Melampus*. England made diplomatic protests to no avail, as Barron asserted that the men in

During the summer of 1805 the frigate *Adams* (above) and the sloop-of-war *Hornet* cruised off the coast with instructions to protect all vessels against armed aggression. *Adams* had just departed the Charleston bar on October 5, when a 12-gun French privateer appeared and boarded every vessel coming or going. On October 12 the French attempted to board *Two Friends*, which was in company with the British ship-sloop (corvette) *Peterall*; after a battle of twenty minutes the privateer hauled off after the loss of some men and damage to her hull. *Adams* returned to the bar on November 12 and remained there for several weeks, supported by Lt. Biddle in gunboat *No. 1*. No incidents were reported. *Adams* even towed gunboat *No. 1* down the coast to check out the privateer base then in operation at St. Marys, Georgia. No sooner had *Adams* departed than

Hornet arrived under Master Commandant Isaac Chauncey. In view of the recent visit of the French privateer, the South Carolina Insurance Company persuaded Chauncey to escort a convoy of American merchant ships from Charleston northward.

Hornet departed Charleston with the merchantmen on the day after Christmas 1805, but ran into a gale off the Frying Pan Shoals on the North Carolina coast. She sprung her mainmast and returned to Charleston for repairs. In January *Hornet* was once more at anchor in the harbor with her mainmast now stripped. A new spar was obtained from Simons Landing and stepped in place; by early February 1806, *Hornet* departed Charleston for New York.

After service in the Mediterranean, *Hornet* returned to Charleston after a forty-day crossing from Malaga under the command of Master Commandant John H. Dent, who would command the Charleston station during the War of 1812. As she came into the harbor on November 29, 1807, she exchanged a seventeen-gun salute with Fort Johnson. She then proceeded to the Navy Yard for repairs to her sprung mainmast, bowsprit, and rigging, which had been damaged in a storm. The next month *Hornet* was placed in ordinary at Charleston, where she remained for one year; she was then recommissioned and returned to service. *Hornet* enforced the embargo act off the coast, and during the War of 1812 she was the victor over HMS *Peacock* in 1812 off Brazil and HMS *Penguin* in 1815 in the South Atlantic.

Shown above is Lloyd McCaffery's masterpiece of *Hornet's* sistership, *Wasp*, rigged as a three-masted ship. This exquisite miniature ship model gives an excellent idea of *Hornet's* general appearance. Shortly after leaving Charleston, *Hornet's* rig was altered from a brig to that of a ship as shown here.

question were Americans who had been impressed into *Melampus*. As a result the British commander of the North American Station issued orders to his captains that should they meet *Chesapeake* at sea, they were to search her for deserters—an unprecedented measure in maritime history.

At the end of June, *Chesapeake* got underway from Norfolk with gear and supplies piled haphazardly on her decks and her cannons not even properly mounted. Her captain figured that this material could be stowed during the voyage, as she was already late to take station as a relief for *Constitution*, which had been in the Mediterranean since 1803.

As the ship passed Cape Henry she was pursued by the British 50-gun *Leopard*.[4] After several hours, *Leopard* closed on *Chesapeake's* starboard quarter and asked her to stop, which *Chesapeake* did. Well aware of the controversy over his three alleged deserters, Barron had done nothing to have *Chesapeake* prepared for action during the pursuit. He also noticed that the British ship had her guns run out with the tompions (plugs in the muzzles) removed, a sign of hostile intent.

A British officer came on board *Chesapeake* and demanded to search the crew for the deserters. Barron refused. Only then did he begin to prepare for action, but it was too late. Once her officer returned aboard, *Leopard* poured three broadsides into the helpless ship, which finally struck her colors. Only one shot was returned. The three men in question were then removed, and a fourth taken for good measure. *Chesapeake*, with three men killed and eight wounded, limped into Hampton Roads the next day.

The news rocked the Jefferson administration. On July 2, Jefferson issued an unenforceable proclamation prohibiting British warships from entering American waters and demanding that those present leave. What was left of the Mediterranean squadron was summoned home. This incident left no doubt in Jefferson's mind that war with England was coming, and spurred him to rearm the nation on land and at sea. However, Jefferson's idea of building more gunboats was not an effective solution; a far better strategy would have been to construct larger warships for commerce raiding. The *Chesapeake-Leopard* affair also spurred the construction of forts along the coast. Castle Pinckney in the form it still stands today was constructed in Charleston harbor. In addition Charleston's Washington Light Infantry was founded. The helmets of their present uniforms contain a patch of leopard skin to commemorate the rally to arms.

The Embargo

The impressment of seamen was bad enough, but the seizure of ships and cargo added to the conflict between America and Britain. With Britain and France at war, American shipowners found lucrative business in carrying cargo to both countries. This trade led to the risk of seizure by the other. America stood by the "freedom of the seas" doctrine, which was not recognized in Europe. After the battle of Trafalgar in 1805, Britain enforced a close blockade of European ports. The defeated French Navy was powerless to intercept merchant ships putting into English ports, but did continue to harass American ships. Hoping to strike at British pocketbooks, Jefferson signed the Embargo Act in December 1807; it virtually

prohibited American foreign trade. Neither this act nor the new gunboats had the desired effect; Britain and France continued to seize American ships according to their own rules. However, the Embargo Act hit Charleston hard. The city's trade declined sharply along with that of the other American ports. One who took note of the embargo's effect was the future governor and senator, Robert Y. Hayne. He saw unemployed sailors and other tradesmen in Charleston pressed almost to the point of starvation. The embargo and the year 1808 are considered the beginning of Charleston's decline vis-à-vis the other ports of the nation (see pages 171–174). Rather than cope with the troubles, many of the city's leading merchants simply retired, leaving a vacuum of leadership that was eventually seized by outsiders who did not have the same broad support of the business community. Thus, the city lost her direct links to Europe. When trade shifted to New York, much of Charleston's European trade also shifted, siphoning off part of the profits.

In 1809, newly elected President James Madison replaced the embargo with a nonintercourse act that excluded trade with only Britain and France. Then, the next year trade was reestablished, but only on the condition that American rights be respected. Any infringements would be just cause to sever any commercial relationships. France accepted the conditions later that year, but American relations with England worsened to the point that the American minister in London was ordered home.

Sliding Towards War

With Madison's inauguration, Secretary of the Navy Paul Hamilton of South Carolina sought to reactivate the frigates that had been laid up in ordinary. He also sent a bellicose message to his ship captains, directing them to be vigilant and to expect action at any time:

> If within one marine league of the coast of the United States any British or French armed vessel should molest any of our merchant vessels you will use all the means in your power to defend and protect such merchant vessels. . . .

In the summer of 1810, Hamilton divided the operating fleet into a northern and southern division. The northern one, under Commodore John Rodgers, included the frigates *President* and *Constitution* and the smaller warships *John Adams* and *Siren*. The southern squadron consisted of the frigates *United States* and *Essex* and the smaller warships *Hornet* and *Argus*.

Also attached to the southern squadron were *Wasp* under Jacob Jones and the sloop *Ferret* under Christopher Gadsden at Charleston. In June of 1810 these last two vessels were joined by the U. S. schooner *Revenge* under Lieutenant Commander Oliver Hazard Perry. Perry was ordered to take *Revenge* from Charleston to Spain's Amelia Island in Florida, to take possession of the American ship *Diana*, held there by her captain who had run her away from her American owners under British colors. Perry boarded *Diana* with the tacit approval of the Spanish, despite the presence of the British brig *Plumper* and the schooner *Jupiter*. He manned *Diana* with a prize crew and sailed her to Cumberland Island, Georgia. Perry was supported by three American gunboats from St. Marys, Georgia, which Perry had enlisted in order to prevent any interference from the British warships.

While off Cumberland Island on July 20, *Revenge* fell in with the British 16-gun brig *Goree*, whose commanding officer, Captain Byng, tried to compel Perry to come aboard his vessel in order to identify himself. Instead, Perry sent Lt. Hite, who told Byng that a commander of an American warship in Spanish or American waters was "not obliged to answer

---

[4] While rated as a 50-gunner, *Leopard* was actually smaller (1,025 tons to 1,127 tons) and weaker in broadside (495 pounds to 543 pounds) than *Chesapeake*.

any questions put to him by the Royal Navy." Meanwhile, Perry sent his crew to action stations. Although Byng seemed satisfied by Lt. Hite's answers and sailed off, the feeling on *Revenge* was that if it had come to blows, "our gallant commander would have succeeded. . . . [H]is cool self-possession and admirable command of gesture inspired every soul with enthusiastic confidence. . . ," a premonition of the events that would unfold on Lake Erie four years later, when Perry's tacit victory message to his superior, General Harrison was, "We have met the enemy and they are ours!"

In August 1810 *Revenge* was refitted at Charleston and sailed to rejoin Commodore Rodgers' squadron, which was patrolling from Cape Henry to the Canadian border. At the same time Hugh G. Campbell, now a commodore, returned to Charleston to command the coast from Wilmington, North Carolina, to St. Marys, Georgia. In December 1811 the schooner *Enterprize* and brig *Vixen* were assigned to the Charleston station. The former remained only a few months before she was transferred to New Orleans, but returned in 1814 after her victory over HMS *Boxer* to act as a Coast Guard vessel until the end of the War of 1812. Christopher Gadsden won command of *Vixen*.

The navy's warships were now patrolling the coast. In February 1810 the frigate *President* under William Bainbridge called off the bar to pick up Secretary Hamilton's family and transport them to Annapolis. Subsequently Commodore Rodgers moved his flag to *President*. In May 1811 off the Chesapeake Capes he pursued a British warship in the dark. Thinking it was *Guerrière*, which had recently impressed a seaman from an American ship, Rodgers realized that he would have to fight to retrieve the seaman. Both ships refused to answer when hailed. A shot was fired and cannonading ensued for forty-five minutes. The next morning the stranger was identified as the British corvette *Little Belt*, cut to shreds with thirteen men killed and nineteen wounded; *President* had one man wounded. Refusing aid, *Little Belt* returned to Halifax. Except for New England, which was still smarting under the effect of the embargo, Rodgers was toasted by the nation for avenging the *Chesapeake*. Madison refused to apologize to Britain. Undoubtedly America had had enough and was ready for war.

The drift to war accelerated on the frontier. Settlers living in Spanish Florida were encouraged to revolt, and *Vixen*, with Hugh Campbell aboard as commodore, patrolled off St. Augustine with two gunboats out of Charleston. The elections of 1810 had confirmed the nation's sentiment, and the War Hawks, led by South Carolina's young congressman, John C. Calhoun, urged the nation to battle.

Secretary Hamilton tried to persuade Congress to build more ships, but his efforts were narrowly defeated. Hamilton had the full support of Langdon Cheves of South Carolina, now chairman of the Committee on Naval Affairs. Early in 1812 Cheves' committee again recommended increasing the fleet by ten 38-gun frigates, building a dry dock, and stockpiling timber. Cheves argued that England would have to build three ships with which to oppose each American in view of the distance from home: one on station, one for refit, and one en route to and from action. Despite the War Hawks' support, the bill was defeated in the House on January 17 by the narrow margin of 62 to 59. The current naval appropriation was then cut; thus died the last chance to build up the navy for the looming war.

Madison sent a message to Congress in April 1812 recommending an embargo. In reality, it was a measure designed to call ships home prior to hostilities so that they would not be caught in foreign waters when war was officially declared. The next month Congress authorized the president to call up 100,000 militiamen for six months' service. On June 18 Congress declared war.

President James Madison's first Secretary of the Navy, Paul Hamilton of South Carolina.

The War of 1812

The American Navy was ill-prepared for war. The years of gunboat building had left many of the larger ships laid up or in limited service. The "Jeffs," as the gunboats were known, proved to be useless, spending most of their time at dock. No new vessels had been built since 1806, and only ten frigates, two sloops, six brigs, and assorted smaller vessels were in service. Many of these were in poor condition. However, two battle squadrons were available, one at New York under John Rodgers and another at Norfolk under Stephen Decatur, Jr. Both were in a high state of readiness with crews eager for action.

Three days after the declaration of war on June 18, 1812, Decatur's squadron joined Rodgers' ships at New York and the next day Rodgers led them to sea in *President* to try to catch the British Jamaica convoy. Two days out they came upon the frigate *Belvidera*. Although unaware of the declaration of war, *Belvidera's* crew made every effort to escape. She threw anchors and gear overboard to lighten ship. As *President* closed, her bow chasers opened up. Rodgers came forward to supervise the action, whereupon a gun blew up, killing one man and injuring thirteen, including Rodgers. In the confusion *Belvidera* escaped along with the Jamaica convoy.

At the same time *Constitution* under Isaac Hull was involved in her famous escape from a British squadron off Barnegat, New Jersey. After returning to Boston for supplies she went on to defeat HMS *Guerrière* in August, bringing the nation its first of a string of victories that would firmly establish the U. S. Navy's prestige. The euphoria of victory helped Congressman Langdon Cheves steer through Congress two new ship construction measures, which finally led to the building of ships-of-the line and six 44-gun frigates, one of which was named *Santee* for South Carolina's principal river.

U. S. Naval Operations at Charleston

Compared with the two British attacks and other naval activity around Charleston during the Revolution, the War of 1812 was relatively quiet. The Royal Navy had its hands full fighting Napoleon in Europe; consequently, British strategy was merely to contain the Americans while subduing the French.

No battles were fought on South Carolina soil, but the state furnished 15,000 soldiers for the nation's defense. The third regiment of state troops was stationed at Mount Pleasant in support of Fort Moultrie, where stands today the only monument in the southeastern United States to the War of 1812.

In March 1812, Captain John H. Dent was appointed to command the naval station at Charleston. He had served on many naval ships since 1798 and had commanded both *John Adams* and *Hornet*. At Charleston he found a few gunboats and the 12-gun brig *Vixen*. His first assignment was to break up a smuggling route through Port Royal to Augusta that had developed due to the embargo; however, the outbreak of war quickly ended this nuisance.

British warships had been patrolling off Charleston and the other American ports since the end of the Revolution. In the spring of 1812, Charlestonians did not take the war rumors seriously; they preferred to engage in commercial pursuits. Thus, Captain Dent hoped that some hostile act would precipitate some local war fever.

Dent's hopes were partly answered by Lieutenant Christopher Gadsden of *Vixen*. Gadsden, a native of Charleston, had been appointed a midshipman in 1799, served on the frigate *Boston* in the Mediterranean, was promoted to lieutenant in 1807, and then given command of gunboat *No. 9* on the Charleston station. In 1809 he commissioned the 12-gun cutter *Ferret* at Norfolk and cruised the coast of the Carolinas and Georgia, enforcing the embargo.[1] While approaching the Charleston bar in *Vixen* in May 1812, Gadsden encountered HM Sloop *Colibri*. Both ships beat to quarters and they remained within pistol shot for half an hour but, as war had not been declared, they eventually pulled away without incident. If they had come to blows the 185-ton, 14-gun *Vixen* would have been hard-pressed to stand up to the 365-ton, 18-gun *Colibri*. Gadsden was promoted to master commandant in July but fell ill and died of yellow fever on August 28. It was a sad loss of a promising officer. His midshipman and sailing master on *Vixen*, William B. Hunter, later served under Charles Stewart on *Constitution* when she captured the British warships *Cyane* and *Levant* in 1814.

At the start of the war Britain lacked sufficient ships to watch the entire coast. She also hoped to encourage a New England secession movement and refrained from imposing a tight blockade north of Cape May, New Jersey. New England ships were carrying cargoes of food to Wellington's troops in Spain. But Britain's policy toward Southern ports was another matter; where war sentiment was high, the blockade was tight. In July 1812, shortly after the war started, a relatively weak blockade was instituted off Charleston by *Colibri* and three British brigs. Twelve merchantmen were captured that summer. The enemy ships were able to stand in close to shore; evidently they had on board pilots who knew the local coast.

Captain Dent had to rely mainly on his own resources; the navy was in no position to raise the blockade at Charleston or any other port. He took into service the revenue cutter *Gallatin*,[2] a schooner that had been purchased at Norfolk in 1807 for the Charleston Revenue Station. On August 6, 1812, while on a cruise out of Charleston, *Gallatin* captured a British privateer-brig after an 8-hour battle. Unfortunately, on April 1, 1813, *Gallatin* was destroyed by a magazine explosion in Charleston harbor while she was anchored off Blake's Wharf. She sank in minutes, her stern and quarterdeck having been blown away by the explosion.

Dent also purchased two schooners. One was a prize of *Nonpareil*, which was purchased, renamed *Ferret*, and armed with eight 6-pounder guns and a long 12 that rotated in all directions. She was ready for service in November and was stationed at Beaufort under John Smith. *Ferret* gave excellent service until February 2, 1814, when she wrecked in a gale on the north breakers of the Stono Inlet while returning to Charleston for supplies.

Dent's second vessel was the 230-ton *Carolina*, built by James Marsh and purchased while under construction. She was approximately ninety feet long with a twenty-four-foot beam, mounting twelve 12-pound carronades, and three long 9-pounder guns. *Carolina's* only commander was John D. Henley,[3] an in-law of Commodore John Rodgers. In 1813 *Carolina*

---

[1] *Ferret* was subsequently altered to a brig and renamed *Viper*.

[2] She was named for Jefferson's Secretary of the Treasury, Albert Gallatin.

[3] In December 1817 on *John Adams*, Henley was commodore of the squadron that captured Amelia Island.

captured the British schooner *Shark*; then in August of that year she was transferred to Louisiana to patrol against pirates. There she led the naval attack on Jean Lafitte's base at Barataria Bay in 1814.

The British army landed south of New Orleans, and *Carolina* joined other naval units in harassing their advance. In one attack she poured cannon fire into a British encampment lacking artillery support. Reinforced with heavy guns, the British got their revenge on December 27, 1814, as *Carolina*, becalmed in the Mississippi River, drifted within range. Five enemy guns opened fire, setting her on fire with hot shot. Unable to counter effectively with only one gun, the crew abandoned ship. Shortly afterward, *Carolina* blew up. Her crew joined General Jackson's forces in repelling the final attack on New Orleans on January 15, 1815.

In December 1812, Dent also purchased the privateer *Nonsuch* after her voyages had earned owner George Stiles some $119,500. Built at Baltimore earlier in the year, she had sent in seven prizes plus the cargo from another. At first Dent used *Nonsuch* to ferry supplies to Fort Johnson. Then, on a cruise in April, she sent in the British privateer schooners *Sancho Panza* and the 8-gun *Caledonia*. The latter resisted only seven minutes, during which nine men were killed. While approaching the Charleston bar on June 13, 1814, *Nonsuch* was pursued by a larger British warship and had to jettison her guns in order to escape after she grounded on a shoal near Stono Inlet.[4]

Late in 1812, Secretary Hamilton made two attempts to raise the blockade of Charleston. He ordered a squadron of American warships to swoop down off the bar to try to catch the British blockaders napping. The first attempt was to involve Commodore Bainbridge with the frigate *Constitution* and sloop-of-war *Hornet*; unfortunately Bainbridge sailed before receiving the orders. A similar order to Captain Porter in the frigate *Essex* was also missed. At Charleston, Dent was much frustrated by their failure to arrive; he had pilots awaiting them off Cape Romain.

In March 1813 Commodore Decatur, fresh from his victory over HMS *Macedonian*, proposed a similar move to raise Lord Townsend's blockade of Charleston, using the frigate *United States* and the brig *Argus*. Nothing ever came of it, as Decatur was unable to escape the blockades of New York and

New London, and *Argus* succumbed to HMS *Pelican* while stretching her luck on an otherwise very successful cruise around the British Isles.

While 1812 had ended on an upbeat note, 1813 became a more sobering year. Hamilton was replaced by Secretary of the Navy William Jones, a Philadelphia sea captain[5] and merchant who pushed through the naval expansion bill and improved the expanding department's administration. He had a good grasp of the overall situation; wisely, he sent the few large

---

[5] Jones spent the decade from 1785 to 1795 in the Charleston-to-Philadelphia coastal trade, so he was familiar with the Carolina Lowcountry.

His Britannic Majesty's ship-sloop *Colibri* taking a passing merchant ship off the Charleston bar shortly after the beginning of the War of 1812. *Colibri* had been captured from the French in 1809 in the West Indies and remained a nuisance off Charleston until she was destroyed on the Port Royal bar in 1814. This illustration incorrectly depicts her rigged as a brig.

---

[4] After the war *Nonsuch* accompanied *John Adams* under Commodore O. H. Perry on an 1819 diplomatic mission to Venezuela. *Nonsuch* carried Perry up the Orinoco River to meet with Simón Bolívar; on the return, Perry came down with yellow fever and died on board *Nonsuch* within minutes of reaching *John Adams*. In 1826 *Nonsuch* was broken up at Boston.

Model of the brig-of-war *Vixen* by Robert Lightley of Cape Town, South Africa. This model was constructed piece by piece, just as the original. She was a small, trim vessel designed for speed. *Vixen* had been built as a schooner-of-war at Baltimore in 1803. She was altered to a brig in 1807 at the Washington Navy Yard; the conversion spoiled her fast sailing qualities. Note the tall masts and short yards. Charleston's Christopher Gadsden commanded the ship until his untimely death in August 1812.

Stern of *Vixen* model.

After Gadsden's death, George Reed was ordered to command *Vixen*. She left port in the middle of October. On November 22, while on the way back to Charleston after taking no prizes, she sighted a strange sail approaching. Reed made sail to escape, thinking it was a British warship. By 10 a.m., *Vixen* was slowing due to light and variable winds, and Captain Reed ordered the sweeps (oars) out. The situation improved, and a fresh wind came up at two in the afternoon. By three, *Vixen's* crew set to lightening ship, heaving the anchors over, followed by the water, spare spars, main armament, and some of the ammunition. When this did not help, the wedges were knocked out of the mast and the rigging loosened to increase flexibility, all to no avail. At three-thirty the enemy tried a ranging shot, and an hour later they were close enough to present their broadside. Finding it impossible to escape or resist so superior a force, Reed fired a gun on the lee side of his ship as a signal of surrender and hauled down the colors (above). His captor was Sir James Yeo in the 32-gun frigate *Southampton*,[6] which had left the blockade of Charleston only a few days previously.

Five days later a storm hit the two ships as they headed through the Crooked Island Passage in the Bahamas. *Southampton* hit a reef off the Conception Islands and went down in heavy seas. *Vixen* wrecked shortly afterward. A few of her men survived, including Captain Reed, who later died in a British prison at Spanish Town, Jamaica.

[6] *Southampton*, built in 1757, was the first true frigate in the Royal Navy. Her fifty-five-year service was unusually long for a wooden warship. Sir James Yeo subsequently led British naval forces in the fighting on Lake Ontario.

ships on commerce-raiding missions rather than having them remain at home to fend off what was truly a superior enemy. At the same time he sent officers to build fleets on the Great Lakes and slowed construction of the ships-of-the-line; they were, after all, ambitious projects that would take too long to build to affect the course of the war. Instead, he focused on the construction of smaller warships designed for commerce raiding.

Charleston's Privateers

Word of the declaration of war reached Charleston within six days. Eight days later Congress passed legislation enabling the commissioning of privateers to attack the enemy. Local syndicates quickly took three schooners into hand to outfit as letters of marque. The first two were 40- to 50-ton pilot-boat schooners.

Crews for these and subsequent privateers were largely French nationals who had served in privateers off the American coast and in the West Indies for the past twenty years. Their French bases were under constant attack by the British; by operating out of American ports, they could have some degree of security while refitting their vessels to accomplish the same end—attacks on British shipping.

With its harbor, shipping, and shipbuilding, Charleston should have been a hot bed of American privateering activity during the War of 1812. The thirty or so vessels sent out were far short of potential. Like any other business, privateering required investment capital and entrepreneurial ability, both of which were lacking in the South for most nonagricultural commercial ventures.

Nonpareil was the first privateer to sail. On July 10 she put out to sea. She must not have presented a very intimidating sight, since her sole weapon was a mere six-pounder—undoubtedly a long gun on a four-wheel carriage or on a slide, either of which enabled it to be fired from any available gunport. The slide-mounted guns were on a sliding carriage that turned on a circular metal track in the deck. This was a forerunner of the pivoting slides used on heavy guns of the Civil War. These guns were common in the low-bulwarked pilot-boat privateers; the pivot mounting allowed the gun to fire over the very low rails or sides of the vessel.

Four days after leaving Charleston, *Nonpareil* sent in as a prize the 66-ton schooner *Lelia Ann*, which was purchased at auction in Charleston by the U. S. Navy and commissioned into service as another vessel named *Ferret*.

Nonpareil next sailed for Bermuda, where she fell in with the 12-gun British brig-of-

Charleston's second privateer was *Mary Ann*, which left port on July 18, 1812, under the French captain, John P. Chazal, who would become Charleston's most successful privateersman of the war. *Mary Ann* was a 50-ton schooner, mounting one 4-pound gun with a crew of fifty. She returned a month later with two brigs, having burned one and released another with her prisoners. The prizes, *Honduras Packet* and *Amelia*, were displayed at Prioleau's Wharf to the delight of the city.

At the end of August *Mary Ann* put out again, this time to the waters off Jamaica. Here she fell in with and captured the 12-gun ship *Phoenix* after a running fight of seven hours, three of which were spent in close engagement. Prizemaster McIver and his crew sailed *Phoenix* to Charleston, arriving on October 15, 1812, after a close engagement with a 28-gun British frigate, which they fought off broadside for broadside. Evidently the British warship was escorting a convoy, for after three hours of sparring she stood off. With her mizzenmast almost shot away, *Phoenix* was chased over the Charleston bar by an enemy brig, only to be fired upon by Fort Moultrie.

***Mary Ann* returned to the waters off Jamaica on May 5, 1813, where she is shown being pursued by the British ship-sloop *Sapphire* and the 18-gun brig-sloop *Forester*. After a running battle of an hour and a half *Mary Ann* was compelled to strike to the superior force. Three men were killed and five wounded.**

war *Decouverte*, which she mistook for a merchantman. Captain Martin and the crew of *Nonpareil* closed and attempted to board, whereupon they learned their mistake and were captured. Providence smiled upon them, for they were exchanged in November and eighteen of them arrived in Charleston in the cartel (flag of truce) schooner *Nassau*.

The privateer schooner *Rapid* left Charleston under Charles Francis Broquet on August 18, 1812, the same day that the frigate *Constitution* was engaged in what was to be the first major American naval victory of the war over HMS *Guerrière* off Nova Scotia. *Rapid* fought, boarded, and burned a British privateer in the Bahamas. After that she sent the 2-gun schooner *Comet* into Savannah. Then off the coast of Louisiana, she was chased by the British corvette *Herald*. Too much sail was crowded on in an effort to escape, and *Rapid* capsized. Her crew was saved by the enemy.

In the fall several other privateer schooners cruised out of Charleston with varying success. Off Savannah on her second cruise, the 3-gun *Hazard* battled the 8-gun privateer *Caledonian* out of New Providence in order to take her charge, *Albion*. The failing light allowed the escort to escape, even though both were larger than *Hazard*. *Albion* was taken into Savannah and *Hazard* returned to Charleston. She made another cruise under Peter Lamason, but in 1814 was captured near Barbados by the British, who referred to her as a "Cartagenian privateer."[7]

On September 7, the schooners *Eagle* under Captain Connolly and *Lady Madison* left Charleston together. *Lady Madison* parted company with *Eagle* and returned to Charleston on January 22, 1813. She reported that *Eagle* had taken several prizes, including the 14-gun British privateer *Perthshire* that was retaken by HM sloop *Fawn* and sent to Kingston. Two members of the American prize crew were hung for piracy.

John Chazal took the larger schooner *Defiance* out in December 1812. After putting into Wilmington for repairs, Chazal sailed in company with two other privateers. They captured one prize, but it was retaken. Then *Defiance* engaged in a useless battle with a large Spanish ship, which Chazal thought was English! Several of Chazal's men were killed in the battle, and then the ship pulled off. On March 15, *Defiance* fought another bitter battle with the larger brig *Nimrod*. Chazal was unable to escape, due to a damaged main boom that reduced his speed. Five of his men were killed and ten wounded, including himself. *Defiance* was taken into Port Royal, Jamaica, and ended up in the British service because of her speed. Chazal and two of his officers were exchanged, and they reached New York at the end of April.

Also leaving Charleston in December 1812 was the ship-rigged *General Armstrong*, under Captain Sinclair of New York. She was one of the largest (over 200 tons) and unluckiest of the local privateers. She had come to Charleston several years before the war. *General Armstrong* was French-built and her sharp lines and strong, fine frames made her an excellent privateer. When taken in for fitting-out as such, she had been altered from a brig to a ship-rig by stepping a third mast.

There were several ships named *General Armstrong* during the war, the most famous of which fought off a squadron of armed British boats at Fayal in the Azores. The Charleston *General Armstrong* mounted 16 six-pounder guns and was manned by 120 seamen.

General Armstrong set out to do her hunting in European waters and touched at a

Charleston's third privateer out was *Poor Sailor*, with one six-pound gun and sixty men. She damaged her rudder on the way out and again off Wilmington, where she put in for repairs. Then, off Wilmington, she sent in the brig *William* with a cargo of rum. Late at night on September 21, a British officer and boat crew put into Sullivan's Island and passed themselves off as *Poor Sailor's* crew. They replenished their water supply at the Towers Hotel, and the next day the deception was discovered; all that was seen off the bar was a 14-gun British brig-of-war!

In the meantime, the real *Poor Sailor* was being set upon by the sixth-rate *Garland*. After a four-hour chase followed by a flat calm, *Garland's* boats were lowered and, under the command of the senior lieutenant, William Lenthall Brake, they boarded and captured *Poor Sailor* (above).

---

[7] The term *Cartagenian privateer* was a euphemism for pirate. The Spanish colonies of Latin America were beginning their struggle for independence. As did the American colonies of the eighteenth century, many commissioned privateers to sail against their enemies. Many of these privateers were little more than pirates carrying state commissions. Cartagena, later Colombia, was the most notorious for commissioning quasi-pirates as privateers. More would be heard from them after the War of 1812.

French port after being chased by an English frigate. Her only prize was the brig *Tartar*, which was loaded with rum. As *Tartar* and her prize crew approached the South Carolina coast homeward bound, they were chased by a British warship. The prize master chose to run her into Georgetown without a pilot and ran aground on the shoals of North Island. To console her crew, some of her cargo was offloaded before she went to pieces. Their subsequent hangovers are not recorded.

Meanwhile, *General Armstrong* had endured a de facto mutiny off the Cape Verde Islands. Captain Sinclair had been steering the ship for African waters and allegedly ran low on food. The crew petitioned him to return to France or home for additional supplies, but he refused. He was locked in his cabin until she reached Wilmington, North Carolina, where he had the crew arrested. The subsequent legal proceedings were dismissed by the secretary of the navy and most of the men ultimately reached Charleston, but *General Armstrong* never sailed again as a privateer. She ended up as a merchantman and was lost in 1818 carrying cargo from Charleston to Havana.

Peter Sicard took command of the smaller 67-ton schooner *Lovely Cordelia*, armed with one six-pound gun. She sailed from Charleston on June 27, 1813, and did not return until October. Most of that time was spent off Jamaica, where she took some fifteen small vessels, which were either burned or ransomed by their owners. One, the armed brig *Arab*, was taken after a brief action and sent to the United States with a prize crew. Several times *Lovely Cordelia* engaged in action with enemy ships and once with a coastal battery. Upon her return to Charleston, she was sold at Fitzsimmons' Wharf, and her privateering days came to an end.

While the exploits of these privateers may not seem very significant, they do show that Charleston was a busy port during the War of 1812, a period that scarcely warrants a paragraph in most histories of the city. The most dashing accounts of Charleston's wartime privateers belong to two superb vessels that give sound testimony to the capability of local shipbuilders, since they were both Charleston-built.

The Privateer *Decatur*

The larger of the two Charleston-built privateers was the 223-ton[8] schooner *Decatur*, built by Pritchard and Shrewsbury. She was 113 feet long (90′ keel) with a 28-foot beam, copper-fastened and coppered below the waterline. *Decatur* was launched on March 12, 1813. She got to sea at the end of May with a largely French crew of 140 men, commanded by Dominique Diron.

Diron was a tough and able ship handler. As commander of the French privateer *Superbe* in the West Indies, he had fought off two British warships for two days in September 1806. Eventually he had to run *Superbe* ashore. He and the crew escaped, and he subsequently came to the United States, where he was given a command.

Diron took *Decatur* southward to the rich hunting grounds of the Caribbean. Off Surinam some seven weeks out of Charleston, *Decatur* took her first prize, the 210-ton British

The privateer schooner *Stephen Decatur* when she put into Salem, Massachusetts. There is some question as to whether this is the Charleston *Decatur*, as the original caption refers to her as *Stephen Decatur*. The Charleston *Decatur* was in Charleston on May 15, 1813, the date indicated on the painting. There could have been only one privateer commanded by a Captain Diron at the time and that was the Charleston ship. Therefore it is reasonable to assume that this painting depicts the Charleston privateer *Decatur*.

[8] The tonnage figure quoted here is taken from newspaper accounts. Based upon her length and beam her tonnage measured:

396 Charleston Customs House tons
371 Carpenter's tons
375 British tons

schooner *General Horsford*, which made it back to Savannah and was then purchased by the U. S. government.

Late in the morning of August 5, 1813, *Decatur* spotted a schooner-of-war escorting a merchant ship. As *Decatur* came abreast of the warship, she hoisted enemy colors. The two sparred for another thirty minutes, firing an occasional shot from their long guns. Diron sized up the situation and decided to attack the warship in order to gain her charge as a prize. He ordered the decks cleared, guns loaded, ammunition and small arms brought up, and hatches closed to prevent the faint-hearted from seeking shelter below. By 2 p.m. all was ready. As the opponents closed, they lashed out with their long guns—*Decatur's* crew used their larger gun with telling effect. Initially Diron kept his distance because of the heavier firepower of the enemy's short-ranged carronades, but he then made several attempts to get close enough to board over the stern, avoiding the broadside guns. At the same time, the British schooner was aiming its fire to disable Diron's spars and rigging, to prevent his escape. Each time Diron got close enough, only small arms could be used as the two vessels came at each other end on. Occasionally a shot rang out from the "long Tom." Finally, *Decatur* came up on the port tack to present her bow to the enemy. As she did this, *Decatur* received an ineffective broadside into the rigging and ran up on the enemy's stern, piercing the mainsail with her jibboom. Both vessels were inextricably entangled.

The two crews poured in a steady barrage. Then the enemy dropped alongside *Decatur*, and the latter's drummers beat the charge, sending her crew over the side. Fortunately the smoke obscured the Americans from the British small-arms fire. Once the firearms were expended, the crews went at it with cutlasses, swords, and anything else at hand. Only when the schooner's captain and senior officers were killed were her colors hauled down by the Americans. The warship's charge, *Princess Charlotte*, escaped to England with news of the battle.

The prize turned out to be the British schooner-of-war *Dominica* with eighty-three men under Lieutenant George Wilmot Barrette. She was armed with twelve 12-pounder carronades, two long sixes, a brass four-pounder, and a 32-pound carronade on a pivot. *Decatur* had only six 12-pound carronades and one 18-pounder on a pivot.

Dominica was formerly the French *Duc de Wagram*, captured in 1809 off Guadeloupe. The Royal Navy was so impressed with her design that the Admiralty ordered her to England to have her lines recorded. She was then commissioned the next year as HMS *Dominica* to replace a vessel of that name that had been lost in a hurricane off Tortola in 1809.

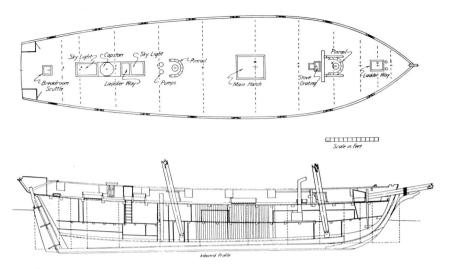

Inboard profile and deck layout of His Majesty's schooner *Dominica*. The schooner-rigged privateers operating out of Charleston would have had similar arrangements.

Decatur **running her bowsprit through the mainsail of H.M. schooner *Dominica* on August 5, 1813.**

Charleston's privateer *Decatur* leads her prize HMS *Dominica* and the merchantman *London Trader* up the Cooper River on August 20, 1813. Note the naval tradition of flying the captured vessel's colors under the victor's flag.

Dominica was probably one of the vessels built on the Chesapeake Bay that the French purchased during the Napoleonic Wars to replace their losses. Ships built in this area were noted for their fine lines and speed. This attracted foreign buyers, most notably the French, who purchased them to prey on British shipping in the Caribbean.

The *Decatur–Dominica* engagement was one of the bloodiest naval actions of the War of 1812; the Americans had nine killed and sixteen wounded, and the British had twenty-three killed and forty-two wounded. This comprised two-thirds of the latter's total crew and 42 percent of the total crews involved.

It must have been quite a sight when the schooners came up the Cooper River on August 20 after eighty-five days at sea. *Dominica's* Cross of St. George flew below the Stars and Stripes as she led in another prize, *London Trader*, which had been taken the day after the battle.

Unfortunately *Decatur's* luck ran out. A week later a fierce hurricane struck Charleston with considerable loss of life. Several vessels were torn from their moorings and run ashore, and others were damaged to varying degrees. A large prize brig anchored in the harbor as a prison ship holding many of *Dominica's* crew was driven ashore on James Island. *Decatur* and *Dominica*, which were tied up at Lathrop's Wharf, were torn away and deposited on Prioleau's Wharf. The prize *London Trader* was also torn away and driven into the packet ship *Belle*, stoving in the latter's starboard quarter and her own port quarter and receiving much other damage in the process. *Mary Ann's* prize, *Phoenix*, which had been repaired at Pritchard's Wharf, was sunk.

In February 1814, *Decatur* returned from her second cruise empty handed, and sailed on her last at the end of March with the privateer *Roger*. She was pursued by an enemy brig and escaped only by throwing two of her guns overboard to lighten ship. That summer as she was pursuing two rich prizes off Haiti's north coast, a frigate appeared to windward and bore down quickly. A freshening breeze failed to reach *Decatur* in time, but she bore off and the chase lasted some eleven and a half hours. Finding that she could not outrun the larger ship, *Decatur* cleared for action. Only after being crippled by the superior firepower of his much larger adversary, the powerful 38-gun frigate *Rhin*, did Diron strike his colors.

Meanwhile *Dominica* was repaired after the storm. Renamed *Dominique*, she sailed from Charleston on May 21, 1814, but only twelve hours out *Dominique* was taken by the 18-gun brig *Dotterel*, the 18-gun ship-sloop *Morgiana*, and the 58-gun *Majestic*. Reinstated in the Royal Navy as *Dominica*, she was lost off Bermuda in August 1815.

The Privateer *Saucy Jack*

War rumors in the spring of 1812 had prompted the Pritchard and Shrewsbury Shipyard on the Cooper River, like many of their northern counterparts, to construct on speculation a vessel specifically designed for privateering. By the time war actually commenced, the vessel was nearing completion. On July 4 an announcement was made soliciting investors to subscribe to the fitting out of a privateer. Thomas Hall Jervey was appointed captain. He had been first mate on the schooner *Galliot* when she capsized in a squall in 1798. With other survivors, he was picked up by the brig *Apollo*, but then removed by HMS *Edgar* and impressed into the Royal Navy. These experiences had made him eager to strike back at Britain.

The new schooner was launched on August 6 and christened *Saucy Jack*. Her private flag bore the words "never despair." Displacing 170 tons on a ninety-foot length, she was designed to mount sixteen guns, although only seven were mounted at first. She carried a crew of 150 men.

The first privateers had departed Charleston without fanfare, but *Saucy Jack* demanded a celebration because she was Charleston built, owned, and manned. When she put to sea on August 30 under a press of sail, the city and the news media were there to wish her success. They were not to be disappointed.

Saucy Jack took the 14-gun brig *William Rathbone* near Demerara, British Guiana, with a cargo worth £40,000; however, both the brig and the 28-man prize crew were retaken by HM brig *Charybdis*. *Saucy Jack* took several other small vessels, but only one made it back to Charleston. On October 25 she returned to Charleston. As she sailed up the Cooper River, banners streaming in the fall breeze, she fired a salute. The wadding from one salute almost started a fire when it landed on the shore just north of Broad Street.

Captain Jervey left *Saucy Jack* after her first cruise to become captain of gunboat *No. 10*. Later he was appointed Charleston's surveyor and inspector of revenue.

Saucy Jack put to sea again in December under Peter Sicard, who had sailed under Chazal on *Mary Ann*. She took two small schooners and, with the New Orleans privateer *Two Brothers*, took the brig *Antrim* in the Bahamas after a two-hour battle. A week later, they captured the ship *Mentor*. Both prizes were taken to New Orleans, where they brought $150,000. On the way home *Saucy Jack* encountered the Spanish ship *LaVicente*, which fired on her, mistaking her for a French privateer. After a spirited battle, the Spanish ship struck. Captain Sicard let her proceed, after offering assistance. When *Saucy Jack* reached Charleston in April, Captain Sicard left her for another privateer.

When Captain John P. Chazal took command of *Saucy Jack*, the right man and the right ship had finally come together. After augmenting her armament by one long gun, he took her out on her third cruise on June 12, 1813. Four days later to the north of Haiti she was pursued by the 18-gun brig *Persian*, which ran aground and was lost on the Silver Keys. *Saucy Jack* took a number of small prizes, as well as the ships *Eliza* and *Louisa* and the brig *Three Brothers* in August. On the way to Charleston, these three ran into an enemy convoy escorted by a ship-of-the-line and a brig-of-war, which set out in pursuit. Unable to save the slow *Louisa*, Chazal removed her prize crew and set her on fire; she eventually blew up. The wind died, so the ship's boats were manned in the effort to pull away from the pursuers. The next day, after a chase of thirty-one hours, the British abandoned the pursuit. On the following day *Saucy Jack* put into St. Marys, Georgia. There in September, a storm drove her into the marsh, but she was refloated.

Returning to the West Indies in October, *Saucy Jack* took several more prizes and had a brief battle with a Spanish ship, which mistook her for a Cartagenian privateer. In another encounter she took the 16-gun Nova Scotian brig *Sir John Sherbrooke*; after surrendering, it accidentally discharged a gun into *Saucy Jack*, who retaliated with a broadside in return. By mid-December she was back in Charleston, and at the end of February she put out again. Early in March Chazal had an altercation (most likely a clash of personalities) with Captain Samuel C. Reed of the American privateer *Boxer*, and the two captains parted company on very bad terms. Reed would go on to fame in the New York privateer *General Armstrong*, and is credited with the invention of lightships and the arrangement of the stars in the American flag.

At the end of March, *Saucy Jack* turned upon a brig that was pursuing her; after a battle of several hours, the brig surrendered. She proved to be the Spanish privateer *San Juan*. Chazal installed a prize crew and headed into port. However, when the two were pur-

Saucy Jack returns to Charleston from her first cruise on October 25, 1812 with her prize, the little sloop *Brothers*.

sued by a warship, Chazal removed his men and put her crew back aboard, abandoning her because she was too slow to keep up with *Saucy Jack*.

At the end of April, *Saucy Jack* spotted a large ship and, after twenty-four hours, came upon her. Chazal opened fire and was answered with a broadside. The wind died, and *Saucy Jack* peppered her from astern. Stern chasers replied for over an hour. When the wind sprang up again, Captain Chazal pulled alongside and boarded. After a heated defense, the ship surrendered. It was the 540-ton *Pelham* with a good cargo of dry goods bound for Port-au-Prince from London. On May 20, 1814, the two pulled into Charleston to the awe and admiration of the city. The large prize was almost new and well outfitted.

Saucy Jack was now a celebrated vessel, and men were eager to serve on her. When she opened a rendezvous to solicit crewmen for her next cruise, 130 men signed up in six hours, a record for the city. She left port on July 30 and returned to Savannah with two prizes ten days later. There on September 20, she was struck by lightning. Two men were killed, and her foremast and yards were badly damaged. Additionally, the lightning bolt passed out of the ship through the stem, shattering it and causing a bad leak.

Saucy Jack was quickly repaired and returned to her hunting grounds off Jamaica. She took one prize and on November 2 off Cape Tiberon, Chazal spotted two ships and gave chase. Both shortened sail and maneuvered into position for combat; Chazal determined that one mounted sixteen guns and the other eighteen! Despite being outgunned, *Saucy Jack* closed and prepared for boarding the closer ship, HMS *Volcano*. She was a bomb vessel, full of British troops hiding below decks. They were being carried to Jamaica after their recent attack on Washington and Baltimore. Chazal bore off in the nick of time. The two pursued him for an hour before he was able to get out of gun range.

Saucy Jack was lucky to survive; the skirmish left her rigging and spars cut up, and eight men were killed, fifteen wounded.

Four days later Chazal met and took the ship *Amelia* after a brisk engagement of nearly an hour at close quarters. Her cargo was dry goods, the most valuable of which was off-loaded onto *Saucy Jack*. A few days later *Amelia* had to be given up and burned upon the approach of a British warship, as she lacked the speed to escape.

Saucy Jack hove into Savannah on November 28 with the schooner *Jane* as a prize. *Jane* and the goods of *Amelia* brought approximately $75,000. On the last day of the year *Saucy Jack* put into Charleston, unaware that the Treaty of Ghent had ended the war. Word of peace did not reach the city until February 14, 1815. Captain Chazal settled in Charleston after the war. The home that his widow built on Anson Street after the great fire of 1838 still stands.

***Saucy Jack* shown fighting off the British bomb ship *Volcano* in the Windward Passage on October 31, 1814.**

Other Operations

While the warships and privateers of both sides were busy in the waters off Charleston, the coastal islands also felt the presence of the British blockaders. On August 18, 1813, a group of small boats from these blockading warships put a landing party ashore on Dewee's Island. They burned small craft and buildings, and foraged among nearby farms. A similar incident occurred at Hilton Head four days later by seamen from H.M. Brigs *Moselle* and *Colibri*. No troops were available to defend these outer islands because of a conflict over Governor Alston's authority to handle the state militia. However, once word came in of these depredations, the conflict between the governor and the militia was put aside in favor of defending the coast.

Moselle and *Colibri* put into Port Royal Sound just before sundown on August 22, 1813. They anchored for three days, putting men ashore to forage at Captain Pope's plantation on Hilton Head. By August 25 a storm developed and, not wishing to be caught in an enemy estuary during a storm, the two ships weighed anchor and put out to sea. As they crossed the bar, the smaller ship, *Colibri*, struck bottom and grounded. Her crew jettisoned her guns in a fruitless effort to free her. When that did not succeed, they cut away her masts, again in vain. Ultimately she was torn to pieces by the breakers after her crew was rescued by her consort. After riding out the storm, *Moselle* put into Port Royal for repairs. She departed before American gunboats could arrive to attack.

Gunboat *No. 166* had been decked over, converted into a schooner, and renamed *Alligator*. On January 29, 1814, three British warships chased her into Stono Inlet. That night *Alligator* anchored near Cole's Island. Armed boats carried 140 marines to attack her. In the skirmish she ran aground, but drove the enemy away after thirty minutes of grape and musket fire. *Alligator's* commander, Richard Bassett, was promoted to lieutenant for the successful defense. On June 30, 1814, *Alligator* was hit by a tornado in Port Royal Sound and capsized

On August 11, 1813, His Britannic Majestey's brig-sloop *Moselle*, on blockade duty off Charleston, chased a vessel flying Spanish colors across the bar. Another ship lay anchored off Fort Moultrie waiting to sail. The humiliation of allowing a vessel through the blockade was too much, so Captain John Moberly brought *Moselle* to and anchored in calm seas off the bar. Late that night, the boats were hoisted out, armed, and sent into Charleston harbor under the guns of Fort Moultrie. Here they boarded, took over the ship, and sailed it out of the harbor under American colors as a *ruse de guerre*. The prize, the American ship *Eastline*, bound from Charleston to Gothanburgh with rice and cotton, joined *Moselle* off the bar at 8:30 a.m. *Moselle's* barge was lost in the breakers, but the crew was rescued.

with the loss of twenty-three officers and men. Fourteen were saved. She was raised and refitted in July 1814.

In March 1814, the frigate *Constitution* under the most able ship handler of that famous warship's career, Charles Stewart, anchored off the bar at Charleston. She refitted and replaced her rotten masts while her crew recovered from scurvy. When the weather freshened and there seemed to be no activity off the port, she struck down her topgallant yards, reefed her topsails, and eventually made off for Boston. There she spent the remainder of the year tightly blockaded.

Charleston's redoubtable frigate *John Adams*, now in a jack-ass configuration,[9] played

[9] "Jack-ass" configuration means that she had a quarterdeck but no forecastle.

a part in the signing of the Treaty of Ghent. She carried American peace commissioners Henry Clay, Jonathan Russell, and John Quincy Adams to Texel, Netherlands, under a flag of truce. The ship had spent the entire war bottled up at New York. She had gone there in July 1812 after her jack-ass conversion at Boston. On the way to New York through the Hell-gate, her captain, Master Commandant Charles Ludlow, reported:

> [S]he cannot pass for more than a tolerable sailing merchant ship and so crank that a ship of 20 guns ought to take her, in what would generally be called a topgallant breeze. . . . I will give up her command with much pleasure. . .as a corvette she will answer as a vessel of war, but at present she is unworthy of the name of an American ship of war.

Evidently the replacing of the ship's quarterdeck had added so much topside weight that it impaired her sailing qualities. She was stripped of her crew and most of her guns and equipment, which were sent to Lake Erie, where they contributed to the American victory in 1814.

In January 1815, before news of peace reached South Carolina, a patrol squadron under Captain Dent came upon the 36-gun frigate *Hebrus* anchored off Edisto. Her boats and crew were ashore foraging and replenishing her water supply. Lieutenant Laurence Kearney captured forty men and two boats from the shore party, including a carronade and six brass swivel guns. A similar incident happened a few days later, in which another shore party from *Hebrus* was taken.

Summary

The end of the war brought a wave of nationalism that precluded talk of laying up the fleet. In fact, the wave of popular support for its victories brought expansion for the U. S. Navy. The victory also brought the end of the new republic's infancy. America was now firmly established with respect abroad, and its navy deserved much of the credit. Charleston's contribution, the frigate *John Adams*, was far more significant than most histories recognize. The ship would continue to render valuable service, though overshadowed by the larger new ships that were joining the fleet.

While Charleston's contributions in the War of 1812 may seem lackluster, her privateers' contribution to the war had been their success in eroding British war resolve. It was this battle fatigue that ultimately led to peace. With the sailing success of *Saucy Jack* and *Decatur*, the city's shipbuilders had shown that they could build a warship equal to the best.

On November 2, 1813, while patrolling off Charleston, H.M. brig *Recruit* saw a strange sail to the north near Cape Romain and set out in chase. It was the American schooner *Inca*. *Recruit* was joined by the brig-sloop *Dotterel*. After exchanging broadsides, they drove *Inca* ashore. Boats were put out to attack, as the water was too shallow for the British warships to follow. Under a continuous supporting fire, the boats moved in for the battle. The American struck her colors, and the crew took to the boats and got ashore. By late afternoon *Inca* had been floated free. She had been bound from France to Charleston, carrying dry goods and wine. Her defeat followed a pattern that the British blockaders had been pursuing for most of the summer, i.e., using armed boats to attack smaller vessels seeking shelter in the shallow coastal waters.

CHARLESTON SHIPS 1815–1860

Scale 1″ = 50′

Steamer *Union* 1852

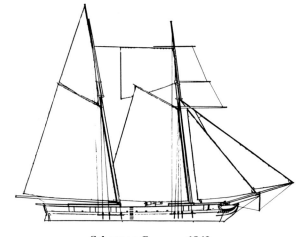

Schooner *Grampus* 1843

Revenue Cutter *Marion* 1826

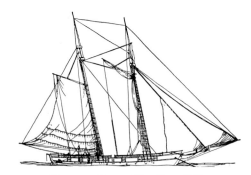

Revenue Cutter *Hamilton* 1853

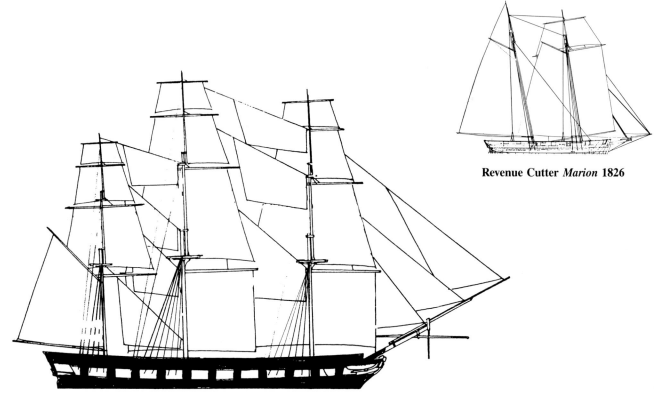

Ship *John Ravenel* 1847

Topsail Schooner *Louisa* 1826

Part V

CHARLESTON'S DECLINE 1815–1860

Peace and Recession

With the conclusion of the War of 1812, Charleston entered a period of peace and relative prosperity. Her history until then had been disrupted by wars of varying intensity and duration. The year 1815 began almost a half century period when, unlike the early history of the city, war would have no direct effect on Charleston's economic activity. It would be the half century dedicated to commerce.

With peace Charleston would face serious challenges brought on by Western economic expansion after the end of the Napoleonic Wars in Europe. Two factors mitigated against her progress: changing sea routes and fierce competition from other rising seaports in the region. Charleston would begin this period as the fourth most important seaport in the nation, but end it as only third most important in the South.

If the primary feature of Charleston in the eighteenth century had been economic expansion, the primary feature of the nineteenth would be economic decline when compared to the growth of the rest of the nation. The century did get off to an excellent start; the period from 1795 to 1819 can be correctly characterized as the golden years of Charleston's commerce.

Several factors go into making a seaport.[1] One is a good natural harbor with anchorages and enough depth to allow ships to get in close to the shore to load and unload. Another is good connections with the hinterland by water or land in order for goods to be brought to and from the harbor. Until 1815 Charleston had only mediocre connections with the Upcountry; the Ashley and Cooper rivers, the city's primary feeder routes, were navigable for about 50 miles inland. Roads were primitive and where good ones existed it would take many wagons to transport enough cargo to load or unload an average ship. The city fathers showed excellent foresight in encouraging the construction of canals to reach further. This goal was realized in the late 1820s, when the first railroad in America was constructed to bring the upland cotton to the port. Plans called for this railroad eventually to reach over the Appala-

chian Mountains. However, as these regions developed, competing ports on the Gulf of Mexico siphoned off the potential commerce.

Despite her expanding horizons several factors served to restrict Charleston's expansion vis-à-vis the nation's rapid growth in commerce during the second quarter of the nineteenth century. One was the opening of the Erie Canal in 1830, linking New York City with the upper Mississippi valley system via the Great Lakes. Another was the natural position of New Orleans at the mouth of the Mississippi River. New Orleans and New York thus drew off any commerce that Charleston would hope to gain by a railroad over the mountains. As a result they grew in importance, while Charleston stagnated. By 1798, New York had already become the foremost port in the nation. After the War of 1812 her shipping entrepreneurs moved quickly to form the first transatlantic packet service, begin construction of the Erie Canal, and then establish packet service to Southern ports.

Another factor working against Charleston was the shallow entrance to the harbor. This prevented ships with a draft of over 16 feet from entering port except at high tide. With the end of the Napoleonic Wars in Europe, engineering and science made rapid strides on all fronts; naval architecture was no exception. Increases in size of ships and innovations such as steam engines came in rapid succession. Twenty-three feet became the average draft for the large antebellum sail and steam ships. Thus, Charleston's twelve- to seventeen-foot bar (low to high tide) precluded entry for all but the smallest ocean-going ships. The seriousness of the problem was highlighted when the Ravenel Company's superb new ship *John Rutledge* had to be sold after two voyages because she could barely slide over the bar at high tide. Because the large ships were denied access to Charleston, Charleston was denied the commerce they offered.

From 1820 to 1830 the commerce of the city declined steadily in comparison to the other American ports. Renewed involvement in shipping by Charleston merchants came after 1845, but it was hardly enough to keep pace with other cities, much less restore Charleston's economy to old levels. By 1820 New Orleans had become the leading port of the South and, by 1850, Mobile was next. Savannah, even with her great river leading to the interior, remained slightly behind Charleston, but her competitive spirit made her a serious and bitter rival—even to this day. She never failed to let shipping companies know of Charleston's defi-

---

[1] These factors are pointed out here rather than earlier because in the period after 1815, transportation developments (railroads and canals) would make any seaport in the southeastern United States a potential rival. Before 1815 Charleston and most other seaports were usually confined to the commerce of a particular area rather than that of a region or nation.

ciencies while boasting of her own river links to the interior. When yellow fever hit both cities in 1854, they competed with publicity declaring themselves to be healthier places to conduct business.

Unfortunately, the Savannah/Charleston rivalry hampered establishment of regional shipping ties to Europe. Because no Southern seaport except New Orleans could hope to develop overseas trade alone, any new shipping firm had to have a regional concept. Despite protestations to the contrary, leaders of the other Southern ports saw Charleston's interests in pan-Southern commerce as nothing more than ploys to push their own efforts aside.

Successful, locally owned shipping companies with direct links to Europe remained a steadfast goal of the city's leadership throughout the first half of the nineteenth century. But there were repeated attempts and only few successes in Charleston. Many factors combined to thwart this goal, among them the shallow bar, the lack of ship owners, and New York's preponderant leadership. The Charleston Chamber of Commerce was reestablished through an act of incorporation from the legislature in 1823. Originally it was intended as little more than a court of arbitration for commercial disputes, but over the next four decades merchants gradually transformed it into a potent lobbying vehicle to help arrest the city's decline.

Influence of the Gulf Stream on the Trade of Charleston

Northern seaports were aided in siphoning off Southern trade after 1795 by ship navigators' newly acquired understanding of the principles of thermal navigation, a method of determining navigational position by measuring water temperature, and the growing use of chronometers for determining longitude. Both freed sailing vessels from dependence on southern trade winds. Mariners no longer needed to travel in a clockwise pattern around the perimeter of the North Atlantic.

The understanding of thermal navigation began after the Revolution when Benjamin Franklin published a chart of the correct outline of the Gulf Stream. In the early nineteenth century longitude was still a rough science, since chronometers were so expensive that many ships were not able to carry them. They did not come into widespread use on American ships until prior to the War of 1812. Even then they were costly and difficult to adjust, and their reliability was questionable. However, by measuring the water temperature and consulting published temperature tables, a ship approaching the east coast of North America could determine its east/west position in relation to the Gulf Stream. As a vessel moved from the colder water of the central Atlantic into the Gulf Stream, a marked rise would occur in the water temperature. The reverse would occur as the ship moved out of the Gulf Stream into the coastal waters. Temperature tables thus fixed the ship's position in conjunction with the known latitude.

Precision in navigation and its revolutionary impact on trade routes began slowly, since the methods used did not become popular until 1816, when Jeremiah Thompson, Isaac Wright, and others established a packet line between New York and Liverpool. Gradually they and other packet lines began to dominate East Coast commerce with Europe. The New York packet lines hastened Charleston's decline from a major way station to a minor position on the outskirts of transatlantic thoroughfares.

The use of northern sea routes was further encouraged by the gradual climatic warming of the North Atlantic waters after 1750. The change allowed sailing vessels heading to America from Europe to traverse higher latitudes. Thus, they could take advantage of the prevailing

Icelandic low-pressure system, whose winds blew toward the west for much of the year. Prior to this warming trend, a ship's rigging and sails became useless when they froze solid in the subfreezing weather of these northern latitudes.

Therefore, after 1800 a sailing ship leaving the English Channel no longer had to travel almost to the tropics to begin its journey across the Atlantic. By precise navigation in conjunction with wind and current charts, a ship's captain could keep his vessel to the north of the Gulf Stream, pushed along by the Icelandic winds and then the Labrador Current, thus reaching the east coast of North America at a higher latitude—New York! The crossing between Europe and New York was shortened by over 50 percent and the Southern ports were bypassed. By the second quarter of the nineteenth century, a sailing ship could make the round trip from England to New York in less time than it could make a one-way passage from England to Charleston.

As they increased in size, sailing ships also tended to increase in speed, seaworthiness, and the ability to head into the wind. This last development allowed square-rigged ships to sail closer than 70 degrees to the eye of the wind. Consequently, if the ship's destination was upwind, tacking would allow her to make some headway until the wind's direction became more favorable.

Other Factors in Charleston's Decline

In the eighteenth century Charleston's business community was led by strong, influential men such as Gadsden, Laurens, and Manigault. After the Revolution their descendants entered the more prestigious professions of planting and the law. Many potential leaders who might have replaced them were Tories and had fled or been discredited. The consequent vacuum was filled by such non-natives as Nathaniel Russell and others, who came from Northern states generally as agents for the commercial houses of New York. Some saw this non-native blood as a stimulus to local entrepreneurial ability. Others resented it and refused to cooperate, especially the planters. This period saw a large influx of New Englanders into the entire South, but Charleston's proud, established society was the most difficult for Yankee traders to penetrate. Thus she retained her Southern character, making her a natural advocate in the fight against Northern commercial aggression. By mid-century native talent was again in the forefront.

Casting its cloud over this period was the slavery issue. Charleston became more withdrawn and less receptive to new ideas, especially those advocated by outsiders, no matter how well intentioned. The attempted slave revolt of Denmark Vesey in 1822 reinforced this siege mentality, and the legislature in 1822 and 1823 passed Seamen's Acts requiring that free blacks on vessels entering the port remain aboard or be quartered in jail until departure. The act contained a stipulation that the ship's master pay the freedman's board. If not paid, the freedman could be sold into slavery to pay the costs! This law was tested by a black on a British vessel, but was eventually upheld on a technicality. The net result was that ships with freedmen in the crew did not call at Charleston, adding to the decline of the city's commerce. In the spring of 1823, Secretary of State John Quincy Adams persuaded the South Carolina authorities to suspend the Seamen's Law. By that summer, free black sailors were again on the streets of the city.

Most of these adverse developments occurred just after the Revolution. The post War of 1812 cotton boom was financed on a mountain of paper credit, which touched off the Panic

Charleston harbor circa 1831 by S. Bernard. Castle Pinckney is at the right with the steeple of St. Michael's Church visible above its left side. The bustle of shipping in the harbor seems in contrast to the city's decline during the preceding decade. While the Northern coastal cities changed, Charleston retained its colonial character and to this day more resembles southern Europe than America.

of 1819. The subsequent decade in Charleston was financially bleak. Fewer than one in three local merchants survived the depression of the 1820s. The state's poorly developed banking system exacerbated the financial problems. In addition the spendthrift habits of the planters drained specie from the state. It is estimated that they spent a half million dollars annually on their vacations in Newport, Rhode Island. Problems deepened in the financial panics of 1837 and 1857, which dealt severe blows to the city's economy. On top of this, the great fire of 1838 left three million dollars in losses and 6,000 homeless.

The city did have a great resource in its strong, able leadership. Consequently, the antebellum period shows a remarkable degree of ingenuity and courage in arresting the city's economic decline in relation to the rest of the nation—an accurate gauge of the ability and ingenuity of the Charleston entrepreneur.

Timber Trade

In the first part of the nineteenth century the activity of the port was centered largely around the growth of the cotton trade. However, timber, which had been profitable in the early years of the colony, also contributed to the total trade volume of the new state and followed its time-honored pattern of sale to the West Indian market. By 1815 Martin Strobel had built the first steam sawmill in Charleston and by 1825 at least four of these modern facilities were in operation, in addition to the older water-powered mills. One of the largest lumber mills was run by Gibbes, Williams and Company, at the corner of Tradd and Council Streets. The sawn timbers produced there were shipped to both domestic and overseas destinations from the company's wharf on the Ashley River.

In a related development, the demand for southern live oak had burgeoned after the War of 1812. This demand was sparked by the fame achieved through the use of this unique material in the victorious American frigates and the practical need for a tougher and more durable timber for the larger class of merchant vessels then under construction.

Sadly, few Southern shipyards benefited from the exploitation of this native product. Instead, Northern shipbuilders sent crews into the coastal forests much as the U. S. Navy had done in the 1790s. As early as 1816 a noted Boston shipbuilder, Ebenezer Coffin, began to send his crews to St. Helena Island, South Carolina. There Coffin's laborers worked for two months, cutting live oak and making ship frames. This practice presented a sound solution to the enforced inactivity in the Northern shipyards during the harsh winter months; many workers saw this off-season work as a chance to maintain a livelihood. At the same time it eliminated a local middleman in the shipyard's source of supply.

One northern firm, the Swift family from Falmouth on Cape Cod, harvested timber from the sea islands in the Charleston area, primarily near Port Royal. From Charleston they shipped live oak north to their shipyard. However, the profitable South Carolina live oaks were almost gone due to colonial shipbuilding; therefore, the Charleston activity was quite small when compared to the massive operations of this family and other "live oakers" that denuded the Georgia, Florida, and Gulf Coasts before the Civil War.

In the last part of the 1850s, lumber production and export steadily declined by about a third from its peak. The loss was due to the city's decline as a port, to overcutting of timber in the state, and to the less than honorable treatment West Indian merchants received at the hands of the Charleston agents.

Cotton Trade

Southern prosperity from 1815 to 1860 was built on the rapid expansion of the cotton trade. Cotton so dominated this period that it was the single most important unit in American commerce. While the first cotton shipment left Charleston for England in 1785, it remained a minor export until Whitney's cotton gin revolutionized the business in 1793. By then the war in Europe severely limited its demand, but peace brought rapid expansion. In 1815, Charleston led all Southern ports with six million dollars in cotton exports, followed by New Orleans with five million dollars, and Savannah with four million dollars. In 1822, New Orleans overtook Charleston and by 1836, Mobile wrested third place from Savannah; four years later, Mobile surpassed Charleston. By 1840 the score was New Orleans, 34 million dollars; Mobile, 12; Charleston, 10; and Savannah, 6. That order was maintained until the outbreak of the Civil War, when it changed to New Orleans, 108; Mobile, 38; Charleston, 21; and Savannah, 18.

Rice and timber continued to account for part of Charleston's trade, but dependence on "upland" cotton from the Piedmont of South Carolina was so great that it made the city quite vulnerable to the economic contraction of the 1820s. This recession/depression was first caused by overproduction and then the opening of new cotton-growing regions to the west, served by New Orleans and Mobile.

Loading Cotton at Charleston

This 1878 scene shows methods relatively unchanged from those used in the antebellum period. Only the ship being loaded would have been different.

The packet ship *Commodore Perry* of the "Ship Line," under Captain F. W. Moores. This illustration is attributed to the great French marine painter, Antoine Roux, Jr., in honor of her 90-hour passage from Charleston to New York in August 1822. *Commodore Perry* was built at New York in 1816. She displaced 262 tons on a 92-foot length with a 25-foot beam—quite small for the period. Her draft of 12 feet, 9 inches easily allowed her to cross the Charleston bar. She was the second packet of the Charleston Ship Line, and served between 1822 and 1827. The "A.1" on her foretopsail indicates (for the attraction of passengers) her Lloyds of London insurance rating.

In the eighteenth century the bulk of Charleston's trade went directly to Europe, but by 1850 some 84 percent of its imports and 64 percent of its exports went through Northern ports, even though there was more than enough business for direct service. Coastal trade on small ships continued from colonial times because of the shallow bars in the harbors of Charleston and other Southern seaports. This profitable trade was centered first in Boston and then New York, because of their ships and shipbuilding. Charleston had shipped the first load of cotton to Liverpool in 1785. But a second shipment arrived the following month via New York, and that was the beginning of the roundabout trade that was to swell to such tremendous proportions in the next century. Savannah sent her first shipment in 1790, but by then New York and Philadelphia were dominating the trade. By 1822 some 55 percent of New York's exports to Liverpool were Southern products, most notably cotton and naval stores.

Normally, ships loaded with cotton would leave Charleston for Liverpool or Le Havre, where they would pick up general freight for the return voyage to New York. Here the freight was offloaded and the ships came to Charleston in ballast or with some freight. Many ships would take cotton from Charleston to New York, where it would be placed in larger ships bound for Europe. In this way New York maintained a stranglehold on Southern commerce on both legs of the transatlantic run. By the time Southerners realized what was going on, the New Yorkers were taking up to 40 percent of every European dollar paid for cotton! Without the cotton, Northern ships would have been hard pressed to earn a profit on the return voyages. However, Southern lack of interest in mercantile pursuits persisted, allowing Northerners to run away with the lion's share of the business.

While New York cornered much of the cotton market to Europe, it also had through its association with many Charleston shipping firms and agents an interest in the cotton that was shipped directly from Charleston to Europe. These Charleston agents would go north during the summer slack season to cement business relationships and cultivate new ones. This was especially strong before the banking system was well developed in the state in the late 1830s.

The first stage in that relationship was between the planter and the "factor" who was resident in such inland towns as Columbia. These factors were in many cases Northerners who had established New York connections before coming to the South. The key to their success was their ability to offer credit in the form of advances against the next year's crop, as the average planter was usually a year in debt. This vicious circle arose from the expansionist desire to acquire more, whether it be land, slaves, or whatever. New York's increasingly important position as a financial center placed it in an advantageous position to benefit from the planters' credit needs.

From the inland factors the cotton passed to other Northerners in Charleston for shipment to New York against their accounts, which were usually large for they, like the planters, borrowed to finance their transactions. Others would ship it to Boston for the New England mills. Therefore if New York did not get the cotton, as a financial center it got the interest on the advances against cotton, the insurance premiums for shipping it, and other business opportunities.

In 1825, one of the first and biggest cotton speculation fevers swept the industry. It started in Liverpool when traders discovered that the inventory of the English mills was one-third below normal. British cotton traders began buying up the staple and dispatched agents to New York and the cotton ports to do the same. Once the news hit the Southern ports, speculators moved inland to buy up cotton. Then the bottom fell out of the Liverpool market. Because the telegraph was still in the future, it took weeks for the news to move across the

Atlantic to New York and then down to the cotton regions. By mid-summer the cotton market was prostrate, and many fortunes had been lost. There were other speculative fevers, but none reached the level of the 1825 boom and bust cycle.

Early Steamboats

Robert Fulton placed America's first successful steamboat in operation on the Hudson River in 1807. Steamboat use spread to many of the country's waterways, including those in Charleston.

The first in the Lowcountry was the 152-ton *Enterprise*, built at Savannah in 1816 for the inland river trade serving both Savannah and Charleston. In June of that year the Charleston Steamboat Company was formed and contracted with John O'Neale to build the 160-ton steamer *Charleston* as a ferry to Sullivan's Island. She entered service in 1817, but her weak engine caused her to be removed from service in 1820. The company also built the more successful *Georgia*, which served until 1831.

The first ocean-going steamship, *Savannah*, paid a visit to Charleston in 1819, just prior to her maiden voyage to Liverpool. She was an ordinary sailing merchant ship of the day, but fitted with steam-driven paddle wheels for auxiliary power. This adaptation was the idea of Captain Moses Rogers of Cheraw, South Carolina. On April 14, *Savannah* anchored off the Charleston light and at 6 a.m. the pilot came on board. At 9 a.m. the ship got up steam and by 11 hauled up to the city wharf. On May 1, she returned to Savannah where President Monroe came on board on May 11. On May 24, she got underway for the historic voyage to Liverpool.

It is not known if the significance of this historic vessel made an impression on Charleston's leadership, because the national depression that started with the financial panic of that year put an end to any local business expansion. Steam tugs, ferries, and river steamers were already operating in the harbor and on the inland waterways. They quickly replaced small craft as the principal carriers of produce until the railroads came along. These steamers brought goods to the East Bay wharves, which competed with King Street retail shops as the main center of business activity in Charleston.

By the early 1830s all of the state's major rivers were being served by inland steamers, which greatly shortened the passage time between plantations and the Charleston docks. Accidental explosion of the boilers seemed a common problem with early steam-powered engines of all types, and ships were no exception. One of the first steamers to end in this manner was the previously mentioned *Enterprise* on September 10, 1816, shortly after entering service. Fortunately no lives were lost.

The Charleston-built *Macon* was not as lucky. She was built by Paul Pritchard in 1826 with a walking-beam engine common to American antebellum sidewheelers. *Macon* was destroyed by an accidental explosion on February 5, 1835, which killed four people. An even greater toll was fourteen dead when the steamer *Marlboro* exploded at Charleston in 1853. The early steam engines were so prone to problems that for the first half century, insurance companies allowed the steamers a better rate if they were also equipped with sails to return to port if their engines failed.

The use of steamships in coastal service progressed more slowly because of the treacherous passage around Cape Hatteras. In 1820 coastal steamship service began with the 702-ton paddlewheeler *Robert Fulton*, out of New York to New Orleans with stops at Charleston

steamer to be constructed specifically for ocean service. She was never profitable, as she did not sail on a schedule and passengers would not wait for her if a sailing ship was ready. Losing money, she passed out of service in 1825. It would be another decade before Charleston saw steam packets on a regular basis. By 1826 steamers began to be used in the irregular coastal trade. There were fourteen of them running along the coast to Charleston and Savannah. Nevertheless, sailing ships would still dominate the trade until the 1850s.

Coastal Packet Service

The 1817 success of the Black Ball Line, New York's first packet service to Liverpool, led to the organization of coastal packet lines to Charleston and other ports. A packet ran on a fixed schedule rather than waiting for a full cargo before sailing. These lines operated much like regional and transcontinental airlines do today; as such, they regularly fed cargo to New York, supplying the main shipping trunk across the Atlantic to Europe.

Robert Fulton, the first steamship to be placed in American coastal service. At times she cut the Charleston to New York run to three days versus twice that for a fast sailing ship. In 1825 *Robert Fulton* ended up as a second-class frigate in the Brazilian Navy.

Two decades would pass before Charleston entrepreneurs successfully stepped into this field; therefore, these first years of the coastal packet business were dominated by Northern interests. But because Charleston was a major stop on most runs from New York to New Orleans, all vessels had to be designed to get over the Charleston bar; this limited their size. Consequently, coastal packet ships were generally smaller than those on the transatlantic run from New York to Europe.

On March 4, 1822, metal magnate Anson G. Phelps joined with Bouker & Hopkins of New York to set up the first real coastal packet service. It was called the Charleston Ship Line or "Ship Line," as it was popularly known in Charleston. The first packets were *President*, *Commodore Perry*, *Amelia*, and *Franklin*, which had been in the coastal trade for several years. These were fairly small, ship-rigged vessels of 200 to 260 tons. For 33 years they provided the first and most regular packet service to the South.

On average two packet ships would leave Charleston each week during the "cotton season." During the summer months when there was little to haul, only about two departures per month were scheduled. Other vessels came and went too, but these were of the "unscheduled" variety.

Packet vessels did not take all of the New York-Charleston trade. Of the eighty-eight vessels arriving in New York from Charleston in 1827, only thirty-five were packet ships. All ran on lines established within that decade, primarily by Northerners. The New or Brig Line (also called Bulkley Line) was founded in 1822; the Union Line of Schooners was established in 1823, but discontinued in 1826.

NEW YORK—CHARLESTON PACKET LINES 1819–1826

Line	Vessel Types			
	Brigs	Schooners	Ships	Sloops
Ship Line 1826	2	2	13	2
New Line or Brig Line	7			
Union Line 1826		7		1
Benjamin Smith's Line				2

This table shows that the packet lines were popular and grew quickly. The Ship Line advertised weekly sailings on Monday from Charleston and Thursday from New York. By 1825 the sailings were every four days. Other lines offered similar service, but were limited to the October-April period when the cotton crops were harvested and exported. During the rest of the year the Charleston service was curtailed, except during the summer when a number of Charlestonians went north for business and to escape the heat.

The packet ships quickly cut a normal New York to Charleston trip from ten days down to an average of six, depending upon the weather and the speed of the vessel. They carried cargoes of cotton, rice, and hides, and most of the ships had deck cabins for passengers. Ships exclusively for the passenger trade did not begin to call at Charleston until mid-century. By 1855 steamships had driven sailing ships out of the coastal packet trade; although the latter departed on schedule, they would often arrive several days late depending on the weather.

Hurricanes struck the city in 1824 and 1830, wrecking several ships. The brig *Romp* went ashore on the mud flats near Haddrell's Point in September 1824, a total loss including her cargo of salt. In the hurricane of August 1830 the brigantine *Atlantic* was sunk at the foot of Vendue Range with her cargo of 300 barrels of sugar.

The Railroad and the Port

The depression of the 1820s had cut South Carolina's import business by half and exports by a third. Cotton exports had doubled from other Southern ports, but Charleston's had grown by only a third. The Chamber of Commerce took note of these statistics with alarm. They saw the newly invented steam engine mounted on rails as a means to transport cotton from the prospering, newly cultivated lands in the upper part of the state to the port. Even though no railroads had yet been built in the United States, knowledge of them was quite extensive from British accounts.

Charleston's merchants and business leaders were never lacking in entrepreneurial ability. Most realized that if they did not develop rail connections to the port, Savannah would. They saw the port as a perfect link between railroads and ships. Without such transportation, growth of the port of Charleston would be hindered. The state-sponsored canals and roads had been unsuccessful in bringing new commerce into the city. Railroads seemed the answer.

Charleston merchant Alexander Black was the moving spirit for a railroad. But a debate ensued for several years. Late in 1827, the ball got rolling with an appeal to the legislature for a feasibility survey for a canal or railway between Charleston and Augusta. This was not passed because the recession had discouraged further state involvement in transportation projects; however, the legislature did pass an act to incorporate The South Carolina Canal and Railroad Company.

In 1828 the project was promoted, and the public viewed a model of the proposed railroad with much excitement. Based on information on British railroads, a Chamber of Commerce committee reported that a railroad was preferable to a canal. It estimated a 19 percent return on an investment of $600,000—a large sum for the time, but a large return too. The local newspapers touted the project as a chance to recall the city's departed prosperity and on March 17, 1828, the subscription books were opened. Construction of the first 140-mile leg of the line to Hamburg, S. C. (near Aiken) was begun on January 9, 1830, starting at Line Street in Charleston. By May 1831, some 65 miles were under construction. A year later work had progressed all the way to Hamburg, and the railroad was in operation for the first fifteen miles out of Charleston. Ezra L. Miller of Walterboro financed construction of the first locomotive engine, called the "Best Friend of Charleston." Built at the West Point Foundry in New York City for $4,000, it arrived in October 1830 on the Charleston Ship Line's *Niagara*. On October 3, 1833, the entire line was completed and opened for passenger service. The governor and his party left Charleston at 5:45 a.m., arriving at Aiken at 5:00 p.m., proving the speed, practicality, and convenience of locomotive power.

The final cost of the first 140 miles of track ran to just under a million dollars; despite the cost overrun the project was a business success. The original company survives today as part of the Norfolk-Southern System.

But success did not preclude problems and opposition. The city fathers refused to allow the steam engines into Charleston, fearing that cinders in the exhaust would start fires. This refusal was enthusiastically supported by the drayage firms, who probably lobbied city council to pass the restrictions so that they could share in the lucrative business of hauling cargo between the docks and the train terminals. Later when this fear was alleviated, the tracks still did not reach the harbor because the matter became embroiled in a conflict between competing mercantile interests—the factors on East Bay Street and the retailers on King Street. By 1860, the tracks still did not reach to the waterfront.

The Nullification Controversy

Southern representatives in Congress had not looked favorably on a protective tariff on imports from the beginning of the union. Most of them did support the 1816 tariff bill, influenced by the national euphoria at the end of the War of 1812, the strong economic conditions that prevailed, and the expectation that the South would become a manufacturing center. However it quickly became apparent that free labor in the South could not compete with slave labor, and that slaves made poor mill workers.

Import tariffs had been deemed a temporary measure, but they became not only permanent but expanded; there were calls for increases in the duties, and each successive tariff bill extended duties to include additional products. The economic recession that began with the Panic of 1819 exacerbated the conflict over the tariff question. South Carolina's politicians blamed their economic woes on the tariff when the problem was at home (see pages 171 to 174).[1] While cotton stood at 30¢ a pound, the South was for the tariff; however, when it fell to 20¢ they were against it and, as it fell to 10¢, secession and nullification permeated the air.

Southerners wanted to export their crops and purchase cheaper manufactured products from Europe. Northern interests wanted a protective tariff to help them as their infant industries developed. Southerners found themselves selling their agricultural products on an open market abroad and having to buy dutied imports or higher priced Northern manufactured goods on a closed market. Because Britain purchased the majority of the cotton crop each year, the South felt obliged to buy British manufactured goods for fear of losing that market.

The planters of South Carolina dominated the state economically and politically. Thus, they called the tune, leaning toward nullification and states' rights. The merchant classes were largely unionists, but they had been weakened severely by the business depression. Political domination by the planters prompted the merchants' politicalization. Record voter turnouts characterized elections in 1830 and 1832; offices were bitterly contested, and party alignments sprang up quickly. Exacerbating the matter was corruption, which became the order of the day and grew worse into the 1830s. Vote buying, wholesale intimidation of voters, and other schemes to alter electoral results were prevalent.

While the planters and merchants opposed the protective tariff, a few Charlestonians realized that the economic consequences of nullification would be worse. The city would be cut off from the rest of the nation, and business would flee to Savannah. The nullifiers swept the state elections of 1832, but business interests continued to have a moderating influence on politics through the remainder of the antebellum period. As in the rest of the nation, they began to dominate city government completely by the 1840s, and exercise some moderation on state government as well.

The passage of the Tariff Act of 1828 was the straw that broke the camel's back and precipitated the Nullification crisis. South Carolina leaders, especially Senator Robert Y. Hayne and Vice President John C. Calhoun, decried the act as unconstitutional; to them, it was nothing more than a federal subsidy of Northern manufacturing interests. Calhoun asserted the individual states' rights to nullify acts of Congress; for this specific act, that meant not paying the duties. The matter was debated back and forth, culminating in President Jackson's heated Jefferson's Birthday exchange with Calhoun. To the president's statement that "the Union, it must be and shall be preserved," Calhoun retorted, "The Union, next to our Liberty, most dear."

The stormy debate prompted the passage of the less stringent Adams Tariff in the spring of 1832, but the duties were not significantly lowered. After the "States' Righters" won the fall elections, Governor James Hamilton, Jr., led the state legislature in declaring on November 19, 1832 that the Tariff Acts of 1828 and 1832 were null and void, effective February 1 of the following year. During the fall and winter of 1832-33, South Carolina took steps to prevent or nullify the collection of allegedly oppressive federal tariff duties within its borders.

U. S. schooner *Experiment*, one of the warships that President Jackson sent to Charleston to enforce the tariff laws.

---

[1] Practically a repeat of what is happening today in regard to foreign imports. South Carolinians in the 1820s found it difficult to cut back on their good life, just as Americans are today, and in the late 1820s the "chickens came home to roost." Unfortunately those who do not understand history are condemned to repeat it.

President Jackson's reaction was to reinforce army units in and around the state. In order not to unduly precipitate a conflict, all U. S. troops were removed from the city and sent to the forts; there the waters of the harbor would separate the opponents. A quarter of all artillerymen on active duty in the U. S. Army eventually arrived at Castle Pinckney and Fort Moultrie. Naval vessels were also dispatched to Charleston harbor to enforce the customs laws. The prospect of civil war was great.

Hamilton turned over the governership to Robert Hayne on January 4. Hamilton tested the president's resolve by dispatching his brig *Catherine* to Havana. There she was loaded with sugar, only to be intercepted late in February and the sugar off-loaded and stored in Fort Moultrie.

Hayne raised a 25,000-man, minuteman-type militia to counter the federal forces then gathering at Charleston. These troops were haphazardly organized and most came from the ranks of the regular militia, but uniforms were the order of the day at social gatherings throughout the state.

In January 1833, the 18-gun sloop-of-war *Natchez*; the schooner *Experiment*; and five revenue cutters: *Gallatin*, *Alert*, *Jackson*, *Dexter*, and *McLane*, began intercepting inbound ships off the bar to collect customs duties. Also included was the USS *Franklin*, the only steam-powered warship in the U.S. Navy. The naval portion of the squadron was under the command of Commodore Jesse Elliott.[2] On January 13, *Natchez* grounded while entering port and was stranded for six days before she could anchor in Rebellion Road.

On the night of February 16, a fire broke out in Charleston. Lieutenant David Farragut, the future admiral, then an officer on *Natchez*, was sent into the city in the ship's launch and cutter with fifty sailors to help extinguish the flames. Unarmed troops from the forts in the harbor also rendered assistance. The military's aid made a favorable impression; they spent the rest of their stay attending parties and dances.[3]

One fete was hosted by Dr. Joseph Johnson, a prominent unionist ally of Joel Poinsett, at Belvidere, his villa on the Cooper River about three miles above the city. Festooned with flags, *Experiment* came up the river for the festivities and

anchored by the villa. On board was General Winfield Scott, who was ostensibly on a national inspection tour, but had remained in Charleston during the crisis. General Scott remained in Charleston until April 4, when he departed on *Natchez*.

Another soiree was hosted by Duncan Nathaniel Ingraham, future Confederate naval commander at Charleston. His wife was Harriott Horry Laurens, granddaughter of Henry Laurens and John Rutledge.

By February, South Carolina's leaders had begun to cool on the nullification matter, as they realized that the other Southern states were not behind them. That same month, Henry Clay introduced a compromise tariff bill in Congress, which was signed by the president in March. With this act, the nullification crisis became merely an ominous prelude of what was to transpire thirty years later.

U. S. ship-sloop (corvette) similar to *Natchez* on which Farragut served at Charleston in 1833.

[2] As commander of the brig-of-war *Niagara*, Elliot almost lost the Battle of Lake Erie in September 1813. Only when Commodore Perry left his battered flagship *Lawrence* at the height of the battle and rowed over to *Niagara* did Elliott's ship enter the thick of the action and turn the tide.

[3] Some credit Farragut's reception by the citizens of Charleston and his father's Revolutionary ties to the city for his later refusal of the Charleston command during the Civil War. If he had taken the command, there is no doubt that the unsuccessful April 1863 naval attack on the harbor would have been repeated, probably successfully.

The Struggle to Revive Commerce

As the local economy recovered from the 1820–1830 depression and the success of the railroad seemed assured, local merchants began to awaken to what New York was doing to them in the direct shipping business to Europe. Around 1834 Charleston shipping interests began to pioneer efforts to start direct packet and steamer connections to Europe, thus eliminating middlemen in New York. One of the first attempts was led by local merchant Jacob C. Chamberlin, who received a charter from the legislature in 1836 and purchased two ships. Unfortunately, the ships were never able to maintain regular service; consequently, the firm succumbed to the nationwide economic panic of 1837. Others, though, were waiting in the wings to take advantage of the temporary setback that New York shipping had also suffered in the 1837 panic.

Another Charleston group founded the Planters & Merchants Steamboat Company in 1837. They purchased the ships *Osceola*, *Anson*, and *Swan*. Poor management and losses, however, contributed to the company's demise by 1841. Henry Shultz, a German immigrant from Augusta, also received a charter and loans to found a shipping company in 1835, but it never got into operation.

A third effort was made by James Hamilton, Jr., one of Charleston's biggest capitalists,

and Gazaway Bugg Lamar, a Georgia financier who would become a successful blockade runner. In 1834 at Savannah, Lamar had financially backed the first commercially successful steam-driven metal-hulled riverboat.[1] In 1836 the two formed the Savannah and Charleston Steam Packet Company and bought the steamer *Pulaski* for $50,000 to run between Liverpool, Savannah, and Charleston. Although this venture also went down in the 1837 panic, Hamilton and Lamar did continue to operate the ship in coastal passenger service to Baltimore, after trying to sell it to the Texas State Navy. In June 1838, *Pulaski* went down in a fiery explosion off the coast. Her loss, combined with that of the steamer *Home* the year before off Hatteras, in which nearly a hundred lives had been lost, destroyed public confidence in passenger steamships. It would be another eight years before *Southerner* of the Adger Line restored that lost confidence.

In October 1839, several local commercial firms announced the formation of a consortium to begin packet service to Liverpool the following February. However, their four

[1] Named *John Randolph*, she was wrecked off Sullivan's Island in 1865.

TWO EARLY STEAMSHIPS THAT DESTROYED PUBLIC CONFIDENCE

Left: The paddlewheel steamship *Home* (see also page 187).

Right: The paddlewheel steamer *Pulaski* of the Savannah & Charleston Steam Packet Company. She was a 687-tonner built of wood by John A. Robb of Baltimore in 1837–1838 and put into service on May 2, 1838. She was 203 feet long with a 225-horsepower vertical or walking-beam engine. On June 13, 1838, she left Savannah with 90 passengers, picking up 65 more in Charles-

ton. About 45 miles south of Cape Lookout that night, her starboard boiler exploded. It tore up the promenade deck, wrecked the starboard side amidships, and demolished the bulkhead between the forward cabin and boiler room. The hull subsequently broke into three parts. Within 45 minutes all except the bow had sunk. It remained afloat for several days, and was sighted by the schooner *Henry Cameron*, which picked up thirteen survivors. Sixteen more saved themselves in *Pulaski's* boats, and thirty others floated to shore on two rafts. Ninety-five lives were lost.

vessels (*Liverpool*, *Medora*, the Charleston-built *Thomas Bennett*, and *Chicora*) made only infrequent trips in 1840. Other attempts with European firms also failed.

Charleston had been once again affected by the malaise of the national and world economy. While the spirit of commercial venture and innovation was bright in the city, the nation-wide panic of 1837 and the subsequent depression of 1839–43 created an environment that made it impossible for such ventures to succeed. Unfortunately, they also pointed up the South's dependence on Northern mercantile houses.

But the 1839–43 depression waned and local interest in shipping ties to Europe picked up again; by 1850, it was stronger than ever. James Gadsden purchased a British ocean steamer to attempt to open direct service between Charleston and Europe. Charles G. Baylor, then U. S. Consul at Amsterdam, even got Dutch merchants to offer cash advances to Gadsden for direct shipments of cotton. But Gadsden was unable to secure enough local business for his firm, which ultimately went the way of the others.

In December 1851, local businessmen Henry W. Conner, George A. Trenholm, and others incorporated the Atlantic Steam Navigation Company, using tax exemptions and an interest-free state loan of $125,000. The Jabez Williams Shipyard of Williamsburg, New York, built the first steamer at a cost of $200,000. She was a propeller-driven, ship-rigged vessel named *South Carolina*, 200 feet in length and displacing 1,301 tons. She was launched on October 11, 1851, completed shortly afterward, and left New York bound for Charleston in January 1852, arriving to much celebration.

In February she hauled her first cargo of cotton and rice to New York, where she turned around at a leisurely pace for the return trip. On April 7, 1852, she left Charleston bound for Liverpool with a full load of cotton. Embarrassment struck, as the fully loaded ship, riding lower in the water, grounded on the treacherous bar and damaged her propeller. She was pushed over the bar and changed course for New York. The repairs to the ship took considerable time and expense; a month later, she was still in drydock. Her owners must have given up on her, as she was sold at auction for $105,000 on June 11, 1852—a considerable loss. The fiasco ended the company, whose total losses were estimated at $400,000. *South Carolina's* engines were removed in 1853, after she was purchased by George A. Trenholm. He subsequently sold her. She spent the remainder of her life as a sailing ship on the Liverpool to Melbourne emigrant run and was broken up in 1887. Her thirty-four-year life proved that Charleston's attempt at an Atlantic liner produced a superb sailing ship, but a poor steamer.

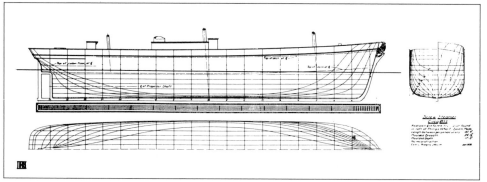

Hull lines of an early screw steamer similar to, but smaller than, *South Carolina* (151′ versus 200′).

The failure of *South Carolina* was probably due to inexperience and poor management. Her long turnaround periods pointed up a lack of organization. If the company had started with smaller vessels or sailing ships and built up from there, the prospects might have been more promising. Thus ended Charleston attempts at direct transatlantic steamship service to Europe, which can be summarized as follows:

Charleston & Liverpool Line 1835
(organized by J. C. Chamberlin; proposed 4 ships, purchased 2)
  American & German Trading & Insurance Company 1835
(organized by Henry Schulz; proposed 2 ships)
  Savannah & Charleston Steam Packet Company 1836
(organized by J. Hamilton, Jr.; purchased 1 ship)
  Liverpool & Charleston Packet Line 1839–40
(organized by three Charleston firms; purchased 4 ships)
  South Carolina Atlantic Steam Navigation Company 1851
(organized by H. W. Conner and G. A. Trenholm; proposed 2 ships, purchased 1)
  Hamburg & Amsterdam Line 1851–52
(organized by C. G. Baylor and J. Gadsden; purchased 1 steamer)

Attempts at a Naval Depot

Since 1720 the port of Charleston had been home to warships assigned to protect trade. Only during the decade of 1783 to 1793 had no warships been assigned to the port. During the following two decades warships arrived, but they were largely a local effort in the national service; that is, they were largely built, manned, and financed locally. The national bureaucracy tightened control after 1800, and local efforts waned. Warships continued to use the port, but the overall presence declined, especially when their need lessened with the end of the War of 1812.

During the War of 1812, Congressman Langdon Cheves tried valiantly to have a navy yard established at Charleston. However, even as chairman of the House Ways and Means Committee, he was unsuccessful. Money was short and resources needed to be channeled elsewhere.

With the end of the war, naval operations out of Charleston were abandoned as an economic move. Then in 1819 Congress authorized the West India Squadron to suppress the piracy of the privateers of the newly independent republics of Latin America. Many of the ships seized were sent into Charleston for adjudication in the Admiralty Court. Additionally, the smaller warships of the squadron frequently came into the harbor to replenish supplies or handle administrative matters.

After 1812, the U. S. Navy began constructing large ships; these were unable to use Charleston's harbor because of the shallow bar. Nevertheless, Charleston's political and business leaders continued to try to designate the city as a naval depot. The logic was apparent: there were no naval bases south of Norfolk until the 1830s. The local leaders' efforts centered around the feeling that if the Navy came, it would bear the cost of making and maintaining harbor facilities and improvements.

Use of protective tariffs, long a bone of contention in the South, became widespread in this period. Southerners complained bitterly about the large sums their ports collected in

Assembly of the U. S. West India Squadron, painted in 1822 by John Christian Schetky. The three-masted ship in the right midground (under the tip of the bowsprit of the schooner in the foreground) is Charleston's redoubtable *John Adams*. She was Commodore David Porter's flagship in 1822 when he commanded the squadron. These warships made good use of Charleston as a port for replenishment and administrative matters.

tariffs with very little federal funds received in return. For Charleston, a naval depot seemed a logical trade-off. However, everyone in public life knew that competition for federal money to advance state and regional causes was a game with high stakes in money and reputations, much as it is today.

The first effort to establish a naval depot came in the legislative session of 1823, with the appointment of a commission to get a depot located in Charleston. The commission received broad support. Freshman Congressman Joel R. Poinsett; Congressman James Hamilton, Jr.; and U. S. Senator Robert Y. Hayne served as the intermediaries.

Hayne had been a big Navy booster since before the War of 1812, when he had come under the influence of then Congressman Langdon Cheves. As U. S. Senator from South Carolina in 1823, he became a friend of Secretary of the Navy Samuel L. Southard. The two became allies because they shared a desire to expand and improve the service. Hayne

In March 1843 the Norfolk-based schooner *Grampus* capsized in a gale and was lost with all hands while on a cruise out of Charleston. Designed by Henry Eckford and built at Washington in 1821, she was considered one of the fastest schooners of her day. She is shown here in action, capturing the Puerto Rican privateer *Palmira* while operating with the West India Squadron in 1822.

consistently boosted the Navy's efforts in the Senate. He had arrived in Washington as the initial postwar naval support was on the wane as a result of several factors: 1) the panic of 1819; 2) the demand for internal improvements; and 3) bad publicity from quarrels and duels among officers, such as the one in which naval hero Commodore Stephen Decatur was killed by Commodore James Barron over the *Chesapeake-Leopard* affair. Hayne set about to reverse this decline. His efforts were mostly administrative improvements and policy changes. In 1827, he was among the first in Congress to propose legislation authorizing the establishment of a naval academy. The bill lost by only two votes.

In 1824 Congress appropriated $5,000 for a survey of Charleston; St. Marys, Georgia; and Pensacola. The harbor was extensively surveyed the next year by Navy Agent John Robinson, James Marsh, and Master Commandant Lawrence Kearny. The report pointed up the harbor's sheltered anchorage, easy defense, good timber, and cheap labor. Nine places were suggested for the proposed navy yard: Shute's Folly (Castle Pinckney); Lempriere's Point at the mouth of the Wando; Strobel's Mill on Cumming's Point; Cochran's old shipyard site on Shipyard Creek; Hampstead at the mouth of Town Creek; Marsh's Island at the mouth of Town Creek; a tract of land on the Cooper River just north of Calhoun Street; Mey's Wharf at the foot of Pinckney Street; and Marsh's Wharf nearby.

Hayne was assured privately that Charleston would be designated a second-class naval station for smaller warships of the West India Squadron. However, although President Monroe held contrary views, in 1825 a bill was introduced to establish a navy yard and depot at Pensacola. This appropriation caused Secretary Southard to reverse his position in 1828, leading to a falling out with Hayne, who then opposed Southard's South Seas exploring expedition of 1829. Hayne did remain supportive of Navy matters by introducing several reform measures as the naval expert in Congress, but he was never successful on the navy depot question. He resigned from the Senate in December 1832 to become governor of South Carolina.

The matter died for several years, due largely to the nullification controversy. However, Joel Poinsett appealed to Vice President Van Buren, saying that a navy yard would bring white shipyard and dock workers into the unionist camp. In the latter part of the 1830s, local leaders made four separate appeals for a naval installation.

Nevertheless, even with Poinsett as secretary of war in President Van Buren's administration, all of the efforts came to naught. Part of the failure can be attributed to the frugal nature of Congress, which chose to consolidate its Southern naval operations at Pensacola.

In February 1837, Congressman Pinckney of South Carolina introduced an amendment to the Naval Appropriation Bill calling for the purchase and construction of a naval base at Charleston. The amendment proposed $50,000 for the purchase of land, construction of a drydock, and authorization for personnel. It was voted down at the end of the month.

Additional obstacles to Charleston's efforts to establish a naval yard arose when other cities in the region began competing. Both Georgia and North Carolina entered the battle, touting their own ports as superior candidates. After twenty years of trying, local leadership took a different tack and set about to dredge the harbor channel in an effort to attract the Navy. Despite these unsuccessful efforts to establish a naval yard, Charleston remained relatively active as a Navy port. The smaller warships called regularly, and local naval agents continued to be appointed. However their work was quite small compared to that of the period prior to 1815. Most of the naval receiving ships (administering ships) in Charleston were schooners and other small vessels.

Ending the Plague of the Shallow Bar

The failure of the city's political leadership to attract a naval depot had a positive side. Business leaders had long regarded port improvements as a major priority, but an engineering report of 1851 cast a pall of doom when it reported:

> All the channels [across the bar] have not only decreased in depth, but have changed unfavorably in position. . . . [T]his information imparts no hope for an improvement by the action of nature, and the demands of commerce call for artificial means to be adopted, even though the effect should result in but temporary benefit.

With this report in hand local merchants now embarked on their own efforts to dredge the harbor entrance, hoping to lure the Navy and improve commerce.

Henry Gourdin, now president of the Charleston Chamber of Commerce, convinced the government and business leaders of the city and state to back the bar-clearing project because of the potential to the state's commerce. A Chamber of Commerce committee on "The Improvement of the Charleston Bar" managed to have the federal government conduct a coastal survey in order to study the matter. The survey, led by Navy Lieutenant John N. Maffitt, reported that the Sullivan's Island Channel was feasible for dredging with a cut through the Drunken Dick Shoal, which separated its deep water portion from that of the northwest approach. The Sullivan's Island Channel was renamed in honor of Maffitt. Maffitt's plan was opposed by Army Captain Albert H. Bowman, who in the previous decade had supervised construction of a series of breakwaters on Sullivan's Island to protect Fort Moultrie. He recommended a straight cut along the line of deepest water in the Sullivan's Island Channel, directly to the harbor.

The differing opinions resulted in the formation of a new commission, which made its own study and ultimately adopted Bowman's plan. Following federal approval of the commission's recommendations and assurances that the Army Corps of Engineers would participate in the project, the Charleston Chamber of Commerce authorized dredging operations. In the Rivers and Harbors Act of 1852, Congress allocated $50,000 for the work.

For the remainder of the decade various private and public agencies fought over who would control the work. In 1853, the Charleston City Council pledged $45,000 to purchase a Patent Steam Dredge Machine from Jason C. Osgood of Troy, New York, who had designed the first hopper dredge in the United States. He was providing similar machinery to Savannah. The state also chipped in, and the dredgeboat *A. H. Bowman*, named for the engineer in charge of the project, arrived in July 1854. She could steam at eight knots and remove up to 100 cubic yards of bottom material per hour, using a continuous chain of buckets. *Bowman* suffered mechanical and jurisdictional problems over the next year, and was never able to remove more than 450 cubic yards of material per day.

By now Gourdin had made deepening the harbor channel a personal cause, and refused to let the matter die. He managed to get legislative support for a new harbor commission that proposed using a new machine invented by Nathaniel H. Lebby of Charleston. Lebby's concept for dredging was based on his patented centrifugal pump that was used to drain rice fields. There he had probably observed considerable silt entrained in the water. Army

Captain George W. Cullum saw a working model of Lebby's dredge and improved it with a powerful propeller, a bin or hopper for dredged material, and a pump six feet in diameter with a 19-inch suction. Theirs was the world's first hydraulic suction dredge, a radical departure from mechanical dredges that relied on cumbersome dippers or ladder buckets.

With a contract from the city to dredge the channel, Charleston machinists James and Thomas Eason had the experimental dredgeboat *General Moultrie* built in New York, incorporating Lebby's ideas. *General Moultrie* began operating in Charleston in February 1857, but due to stormy weather, inexperience in operating the new machine, and frequent breakdowns, little was accomplished until June. From then on, progress was rapid; even heavy seas presented no problems.

General Moultrie cleared 190,000 cubic yards of silt from the channel at a price of 66¢ per cubic yard. Her success made her the forerunner of modern dredges used by the Army Corps of Engineers. Maffitt's Channel was cleared and ships of full draft were using the port on a regular basis by 1860.

Along with these efforts, waterfront businessmen were constantly seeking improvements to the harbor in the form of wharves, docks, and warehouses. Harbor improvements were especially wanted after an economic revival in the last half of the 1840s. To enhance Charleston's reviving commerce, Congress appropriated money for a new customs house; it cost over two million dollars to construct, but was not completed until after the Civil War.

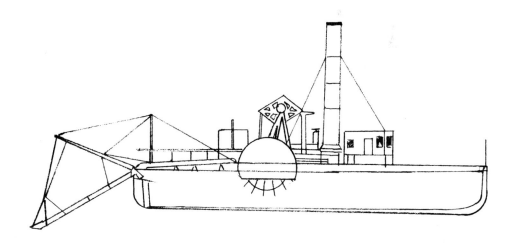

The dredgeboat *General Moultrie*.

The paddle-steamship *Southerner*. She displaced 785 tons and was 191 feet long on deck with a beam of over 30 feet and a 14-foot draft.

Local Efforts at Coastal Service

The coastal shipping trade remained the province of Northern interests until the 1840s. Because of the shoals and rough waters, the lanes around Cape Hatteras were as treacherous as any at sea. In fact, marine insurance underwriters considered sailing from Charleston to New York riskier than sailing from either to Liverpool; their rates reflected this risk from actual losses.

But coastal steamship service was still more profitable for Charleston entrepreneurs than transatlantic service had been, even though they were not the first into the business. Between 1836 and 1838, five steam packets were put into service on the New York to Charleston run by James Allaire and Charles Morgan of New York. Then Wetmore and Cryder put two steamers on the New York to Charleston run in 1838. These first vessels were relatively small and lightly built, and could not withstand the heavy seas that often plagued the coastal waters in winter. Many would be forced to put into ports along the coast to ride out the storms; this disrupted their schedules. Other firms, however, added steamships to their schedules during the busy fall and winter seasons. Steamship service developed somewhat as passenger jet service did in the 1950s: some firms, such as Allaire, made a grand entry, resulting in disaster from an untested machine; others came in more conservatively, creating new machines by adding to existing but tested devices.

The first coastal steamer in service after the 1820 *Robert Fulton* was *Home* of Allaire's Southern Steam Packet Company. *Home* was built by Brown and Bell of New York in 1836–1837. After several runs she encountered a gale to the north of Cape Hatteras in October 1837 and began leaking badly, probably the result of a previous grounding. The rising water extinguished her boiler fires, so she made for shore under sail and touched bottom just as the waves were coming over her decks. Within half an hour the surf tore her into matchwood. Ninety-five people died, including Allaire (see page 181). Although Allaire had been the driving force behind the Southern Steam Packet Company, his partners attempted to keep it going by placing the larger *Neptune* in service in 1838. However, the loss of *Home* was followed by that of *Pulaski* the following year. The two disasters dealt steamship service a blow; it took ten years to recover public confidence. The Southern Steam Packet Company bowed to the inevitable and sold its steamships *Neptune*, *New York*, and *Columbia* in 1839.

By the late 1840s Charleston businessmen began to cut into the coastal trade with some success. James Adger, the Gourdin brothers, and William S. King joined with Spofford, Tileston, and Company of New York to establish the New York and Charleston Steamship Line, or Adger Line, in 1845–46. In later years it became known as the Clyde-Mallory Line, whose ships docked at Adger's Wharf.[2]

---

[2] It was at Adger's Wharf in 1850 that the solid black barge landed with the remains of John C. Calhoun for burial in St. Philip's Churchyard.

Adger's Wharf as it appeared shortly before the Civil War. The steamship is probably *James Adger*.

Steamship *Northerner* of the New York and Charleston Steamship Line (Adger Line), built in 1847.

The 1,151-ton sidewheeler *James Adger*, third steamship to be built for the New York and Charleston Steamship Line (Adger Line) and named for Charleston businessman and merchant James Adger, the company's founder and major stockholder. The ship was built in the summer of 1852 by the noted New York shipbuilder William H. Webb. She joined *Marion* on the New York to Charleston run. For much of her pre-war service she was used by the Spofford, Tileston Line on the New York to New Orleans run with stops in Charleston. When Fort Sumter was fired upon in April 1861, the ship happened to be in New York. She was seized and converted into USS *James Adger*, a blockading warship with a battery of eight 32-pounder guns.

In the fall of 1861, she crossed the Atlantic in search of the CSS *Nashville* after the latter broke out of Charleston. She spent most of 1862 on blockade duty off Charleston, where she helped to capture several blockade runners. After a refit in Baltimore early in 1863, she escorted the new monitor *Montauk* to Port Royal and the Ogeechee River in Georgia. There *Montauk* destroyed the former Confederate cruiser *Nashville*. In April she became flagship for Admiral DuPont as he made the final preparations in the North Edisto River for the ironclad assault on Charleston. After the attack she helped to tow the crippled monitors to Port Royal. *Passaic* was so badly damaged that *James Adger* had to tow her to New York. From there she joined the blockade off Wilmington, where she helped to capture the blockade runners *Robert E. Lee*, *Kate*, *Ella*, and *Cornubia*. After the war *James Adger* was sold to James Campbell, who refitted her and put her back into the New York to Charleston coastal run. In 1878, worn out, the ship was taken to Boston and scrapped.

The first ship to enter service for the New York and Charleston Steamship Line was *Southerner* on September 12, 1846. For the first nine months of her life she was the only American steamship in ocean service anywhere. William H. Brown of New York was the builder, with engines supplied by the Novelty Iron Works. With superior design and experienced shipping agents, she rendered successful service every two weeks in and out of Charleston. *Southerner* was not a particularly large vessel for ocean commerce (191' long, 785 tons), but was of a new and remarkably successful design; she set the pattern for American coastal steamships for the subsequent decade. While her heavily built wooden hull was that of a typical sailing ship, the masts and rigging were sparse. The paddle boxes were not added to the hull, but incorporated into it, with the hull planking curving around the guards to increase their strength.

The crew was traditionally placed in the forecastle and the first-class passengers in the stern. On either side of a grand salon, the thirty-two staterooms ran fore and aft with portholes for each. Forward of the boilers on the lower deck was another cabin with berths for 100 to 150 additional passengers in two classes.

On September 12, 1846, *Southerner* began her maiden run from New York to Charleston, arriving in 60 hours. Thereafter she made the run every two weeks. In November she showed the superiority of a steamship by not having to remain sheltered from a gale in Delaware Bay; 140 sailing ships did. Her best time was 55 hours, and she took up to 70 hours in bad weather. Her speed, comfort, and reliability attracted both passengers and shippers of cargo. *Southerner* spent a profitable decade steaming between New York and Charleston. Her only serious accident occurred on October 4, 1850, when she rammed the bark *Isaac Mead* head on, splitting *Mead's* hull down the middle. *Southerner* quickly launched her Francis-type galvanized metal lifeboats, which were able to pick up only nine of the thirty-three passengers and crew of the sunken vessel. The metal boats in use on *Southerner* were far more durable than the traditional wooden boats, which were easily damaged and often leaked like sieves after sitting on the decks of ships.

In 1857 Spofford, Tileston sold *Southerner* to S. L. Mitchell, who put her on the Savannah run. In September she ran into the same gale off the South Carolina coast that sank the larger *Central America* with such tragic losses. *Southerner* put into Charleston badly beaten up, with her stack, paddle boxes, and boats gone. Part of her cargo had to be tossed overboard. She was patched up for the return to New York, where she was deemed unfit for further service and broken up in 1858.

After only ten voyages by *Southerner*, a second ship, *Northerner*, was laid down and commenced service in October 1847. *Northerner* was the slightly larger of the two, at 203' on a 1,012-ton hull. Both ships carried weekly passenger and freight service, sailing every Saturday. Together they pioneered the rapidly expanding coastal service that during the following decade would bring the end of the coastal sailing packets.

The immediate success of these ships was noted. In 1850 the firm accepted a lucrative offer for *Northerner*, and she departed for gold rush service on the Pacific coast. An even larger steamship, the 1,200-ton *Union*, and the smaller 900-ton *Marion* joined the coastal run the following year. *Marion* was built by Jacob Bell of New York and remained on the New York-Charleston run until the start of the Civil War.

James Adger entered service in 1852 and *Nashville* in 1854. When these were all on line, Charleston sailings increased to twice a week, and connections were available from Charleston to Havana and New Orleans. The new steamships offered both the safety and reliability that their smaller and lighter predecessors had not. They also had greater speed from more powerful engines.

As was customary for the times, the firms owned only a small percentage of the ships themselves. The vessels were often owned by outside investors, who then leased them to the firm. Some 70 percent of the Adger Line remained Charleston-owned; stockholders eventually included John Fraser and Otis Mills, the prosperous builder of the Mills House Hotel, who also purchased *General Taylor* to accommodate his company's extensive flour and corn shipments to the West Indies.

The federal government had stepped into the shipping picture to some extent in 1836, when a mail subsidy was authorized for ocean steamers in retaliation for a similar British move that placed American firms at a disadvantage. Naturally the first choices for implementation were the established New York lines. Consequently, the New York firms got the federal government to underwrite their enterprises to many millions of dollars, thus placing newcomers at a greater disadvantage. Charleston merchants, however, rallied to the flag when the Collins Line of New York was almost driven out of the transatlantic business by Britain's Cunard Line; they joined in the petition to Congress for a subsidy to the Collins Line.

The only Charlestonian to win a similar mail subsidy was Moses Cohen Mordecai in 1847, for his new steamship service to Havana. Even his subsidy was not very favorable. Mordecai and Company was probably the most successful of the Charleston-based and owned coastal shipping lines. Its service to Havana and Key West was profitable, allowing the firm to add new steamers regularly. Often, Mordecai had extra steamers available to take over in the event of delay or accident; these surplus ships were also frequently chartered to other firms.

In 1848 Mordecai joined forces with Spofford, Tileston and Company based in New York. Together they attracted passengers and freight with regular sailings. The first ship ordered for their combined enterprise was the previously mentioned paddlewheeler *Union*, which was built by William H. Webb in 1850. She differed from her two predecessors in that she had two side-lever engines instead of one. *Union* displaced 1,200 tons on a 215-foot hull. She remained on the Charleston run until 1856, when she was sold to Austrian interests for service in the Adriatic Sea.

In 1848 Charleston businessman Frederick Richards tested the waters for congressional support for a subsidy similar to that awarded the Collins Line. However Charleston Congressman William P. Miles found support on the wane, and in 1858 Congress voted out all mail and steamer subsidies.

Other Charlestonians active in shipping included William C. Bee, who entered the factoring business in 1831 with James Ladson. In the 1850s Bee formed his own firm with Theodore D. Jervey. They became agents for the Importing and Exporting Company of South Carolina, which had much success during the Civil War (see pages 278 and 281-289). Another active person was James Macbeth, a cotton broker and commission merchant whose successful business allowed him to purchase the ship *Switzerland* and other vessels in 1852.

The Hugh E. Vincent family of ship chandlers owned several vessels in coastal service in the 1850s. Other smaller firms included one run by John W. Caldwell, which provided direct service to growing Florida ports. His Florida Steam Packet Company, chartered in 1851, had several ships in operation by 1858. Backers of the Florida Steam Packet Company included the pillars of the Charleston business community.

Isabel of the Mordecai Line, named for Mordecai's wife. She was built in Baltimore in 1848 by Levin H. Dunkin, the first ocean-going steamship built in that city. *Isabel* was 210 feet long, 33 feet wide, and drew 21 feet, 6 inches. She was powered by a 500-horsepower engine built by A. & C. Reeder of Baltimore, who overhauled it in 1857. Mordecai employed her on his lucrative Charles- ton to Havana run with *Governor Dudley.* The start of the Civil War found her in Charleston, where she was purchased by John Fraser and Company and converted to the blockade runner *Ella Warley.* She made three successful round trips through the blockade, but was captured by USS *Santiago de Cuba* while bound from Havana to Charleston on April 24, 1862.

Sullivan's Island (left). Her cargo had to be unloaded and her passengers transferred to *James Adger.* On January 29, 1861, three steamers were able to pull her off, but the hull was strained and leaking. *Columbia* was undergoing repairs in New York when the fighting started and was pressed into the Union's service. Spofford, Tileston, and Company abandoned Charleston and shifted their terminus to Havana. Late in May 1861, *Columbia* began her Cuban voyages, and then to New Orleans once that city returned to federal control in April 1862. After the war she returned to the Charleston service as part of the Clyde Line and was not broken up until 1875.

Right: The steamer *Columbia* passing Castle Pinckney. *Columbia* was built by William Collyer in Greenpoint (Brooklyn), Long Island in 1857 for the Spofford, Tileston Company's transatlantic service. She was about 10 percent larger than her more famous consort, *Nashville.* *Columbia* made her maiden run to Charleston in May 1857 under Captain Berry in less than fifty-two hours. She was slightly damaged by the same storm that sank *Central America* off Charleston in September 1857. From then until January 1861 she remained on the New York to Charleston run. While exiting Charleston harbor through Maffitt's Channel in January 1861 she ran aground on

Shipbuilding

The flurry of ship construction in the late 1790s that helped to launch the new U. S. Navy began to languish in the years following the War of 1812. It never died completely, but its health was always in jeopardy.

Ship repair remained the primary occupation of the surviving shipyards in Charleston harbor. To enhance the repairing service, the business establishment financed construction of three floating drydocks and two marine railways between 1834 and 1860. The largest drydock was built in 1850–51 by Mordecai and Prevost to service their own vessels. James Marsh's Shipyard had the other two.

By 1848 there were five shipyards in Charleston, which employed 160 white and black mechanics. Repair was their mainstay, although an occasional river steamer was launched. Four of these shipyards were still operating at the outbreak of the Civil War.

William (Hobcaw Bill) Pritchard inherited the Pritchard Shipyard in Mt. Pleasant upon his father's death in 1791. It passed through several hands, and finally shut down in 1831; the site then became known as "Shipyard Plantation." William's brother Paul leased the Cochran Shipyard after the Revolution and operated there as well as at his Fairbank Plantation on Daniel's Island for many years. At the latter, which was often used for constructing small craft, gunboat *No. 9* was built for the Navy in 1805. At Pritchard's death in 1815, Fairbank contained 378 acres, five shipjoiner slaves, several buildings, and equipment.

After the War of 1812, Charleston shipbuilding enjoyed a brief surge as many river steamers and schooners were built. However, the depressed economy of the 1820s dealt it, along with the city's business at large, a blow from which it never recovered. Some 120 shipwrights were listed among the artisans of the city, but many were out of work and left Charleston permanently.

James Marsh, who had come to Charleston from Philadelphia to be foreman for the construction of *John Adams*, purchased William Pritchard's other shipyard at the foot of Pinckney Street. Nearby streets still retain the names Marsh and Pritchard streets. Before the War of 1812 Marsh had become Charleston's premier shipbuilder, a position he retained for some fifty years. Using machinery supplied by the Eason Brothers, he erected the first floating drydock in the area in 1846 and another in 1851. Marsh was buried in St. Michael's Churchyard in 1852, leaving considerable real estate and securities as well as several slaves employed in the shipbuilding trades.

The Eason Brothers also built several river steamers prior to the Civil War and helped install machinery in the Confederate ironclads during the war.

River Steamer *Darlington* built in Charleston for Jacob Brock in 1849, for service on the Pee Dee River. Here she hauled cotton to port from the Cheraw and Society Hill cotton-growing areas, returning with goods for the plantations. Due to the shallowness of the Pee Dee River, after three years *Darlington* went to the St. John's River in Florida, where she was quite successful and remained in service until 1874. She was 133 feet long, 30 feet wide, and drew over 8 feet of water. *Darlington* could carry up to 40 passengers in cabins above her freight deck and was typical of the antebellum steamers such as *Planter*, *Marion*, and *Etiwan* that were built in Charleston.

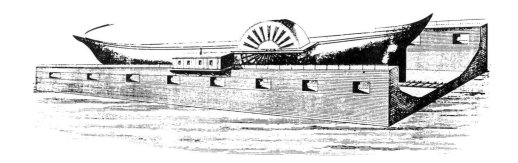

Perspective of a Balance Floating Dry Dock circa 1850 of the type that the Marsh Shipyard used. This type ship repair facility has had few fundamental changes in over a century of use.

School ship *Lodebar* anchored in the Ashley River at the foot of King Street as part of the first floating marine school in America. It was first recommended by the Chaplain Reverend W. B. Yates in March 1856 and, under the sponsorship of the Charleston Port Society, was in operation in May 1859. Her commander was Captain M. L. Aimar, who with a teacher, boatswain, sailor, and sixteen pupils constituted the crew of the schoolship. It was afterward increased to twenty-five students and a mate, who signed on for three years. *Lodebar* would occasionally sail on short voyages to acquaint the cadets with ship handling. The daily routine was quite stringent in the tradition of Southern military schools of the nineteenth century. In 1861 some of the students volunteered for Confederate service and *Lodebar* was put to use in the defense of the harbor. When Charleston came under bombardment in 1863, *Lodebar* was sold and the school moved to Orange-burg, S.C.

Left: Pupils at their studies on *Lodebar*.

PART OF CHARLESTON'S IMMIGRANT CONNECTION

Diorama of the port scene at the Alten Hafen in Bremerhaven, Germany, circa 1840. Here emigrants shook off the dust of Europe before embarking on voyages to America, many of which came to Charleston on ships such as *Copernicus* and *Johann Friedrich*.

Above right: The German ship *Copernicus*, used to ferry immigrants from Bremerhaven to Charleston in the 1840s and 1850s. She was built in 1835 for Reederei N. Gloystein & Sons. One of her captains was Heinrich Weiting, who died in Charleston in 1868 and is buried in Bethany Cemetery. It is estimated that three-fourths of the native Germans living in Charleston came on ships commanded by Weiting.

Right: The German bark *Johann Friedrich*, also employed as an immigrant ship between Bremen and Charleston in the 1840s and 1850s. She was built in 1835 for Reederei N. Gloystein & Sons.

Other Events

Maritime matters in Charleston during the antebellum period were not totally devoted to business affairs. There were the usual number of storms and disasters. One of the most tragic involved the revenue cutter *Hamilton*, a unit of the highly successful *Morris Class*, modeled after the Baltimore Clippers. For twenty years she had been stationed at Boston, but in 1851 she was transferred to Charleston and placed under the command of T. C. Rudolph.

From the beginning of the Coast Guard, movements of the cutters had been under the orders of the various port collectors of customs, who were

Revenue cutter *William Aiken*, the ex-pilot boat *Eclipse* that was purchased for service in 1853 after *Hamilton* was wrecked outside the harbor (see also page 211).

political appointees with little knowledge either of ships or of their employment. For several days in December 1853 the weather at Charleston had been poor, but the collector kept badgering Captain Rudolph to get to his station off the bar. Rudolph was known for his recklessness and temper; angered at the tax collector, he said on December 9, 1853, that he would go to sea that night or "go to Hell." Putting to sea in the face of the storm, *Hamilton* suffered damage to her rigging and became unmanageable. Rudolph attempted to anchor off Kiawah, but the chain parted and the cutter was driven on the shoals—a total loss. The crew took to the two boats, but both capsized. A sole surviving sailor managed to lash himself to one of the boats and was picked up later. For political reasons, the collector's responsibility in the disaster was never made a point of inquiry.

One of the most dramatic disasters of the decade was the loss of the mail steamer *Central America* off the coast of South Carolina during a hurricane on September 12, 1857. Scores of lives and several million dollars in bullion that her passengers were bringing home from the California gold fields were also lost. Her captain unwisely thought that his ship was strong enough to go through the storm rather than altering course to go around it. Fortunately the women and children on board were saved when the male passengers and crew sacrificed themselves for their safety.

Revenue cutter *Hamilton*. Her sister, *Gallatin*, served off Charleston during the Nullification Crisis in 1833.

End of the Antebellum Era

The last half of the 1840s marked the last great antebellum period of economic activity in Charleston. By then merchants began to displace the planters at the top of the economic ladder. Mercantile pursuits became socially acceptable, encouraging more promising entrants. Then, after 1845, maritime prosperity began to return. In 1854, the locally registered shipping tonnage approached and then exceeded the 1815–19 period. While these were improvements, they were not equal to the dramatic national growth during the same period. By 1860, the Charleston-owned merchant fleet numbered between twenty and twenty-five ocean-going ships and numerous coasters. The exact number is difficult to determine because most ships had several owners, some of whom were not Charlestonians; however, it is estimated at 65,000 tons, a pittance compared to New York's 1.4 million.

While direct transatlantic steamship service did not become a reality before the Civil War, Charleston's leadership in other shipping ventures placed the city at the forefront of Southern commerce on the Atlantic coast. Thus, when direct links to Europe became a necessity in 1861, the city's businessmen were experienced and had enough capital to implement it quickly. Without these abilities the blockade-running business may never have reached the levels it did, and Charleston would not have been at the center of it; in the first two years of the war, Charlestonians controlled ten out of every eleven runners.

These efforts prove that business apathy in Charleston was not what most social historians of the time have painted it. Capital may have been a problem and business expertise was lacking, but entrepreneurship and political support from the legislature were not. In turn, large Northern and foreign firms did not seek to compete against Southern business on the local scene, but worked with them. Charleston's businessmen took advantage of the room and opportunities left open to them and forged several business alliances with Northern firms.

Agricultural interests had lent support to earlier efforts to set up transatlantic service, realizing that (as was the case with the railroads) a thriving shipping industry would benefit them directly. The failures and rising power of the urban commercial interests soon appeared to be a potential threat to the planters' political dominance of the state. Planter support therefore waned and local shipping agents were so accustomed to sending their cargoes to Europe via New York that they were reluctant to change. This conflict was exacerbated by the urban-commercial versus rural-agrarian conflict over mutually beneficial goals. Adding fuel to the conflict was the Upcountry's resentment of Charleston, which continues to this day. By the 1850s, the sides were irrevocably divided; but as the inevitability of civil war loomed, many of these planters realized their mistake.

The 576-ton American ship *Claudius*. Under the command of John J. Scobie, she was lost on the Stono Breakers on January 29, 1843, thirteen days from Boston bound to Charleston with 200 bags of coffee. Within two days the ship was driven well up into the breakers, but still had not broken up. She was finally abandoned on February 2 after her crew, cargo, and gear were taken off.

Leading Charleston Shipping Firms

John Fraser & Company; Fraser, Trenholm & Company

In the city's history no firm dominated the Charleston waterfront more than the cotton factors, John Fraser and Company. Originally founded in 1803 as Fraser and Means, the company became over the next half century one of the wealthiest and most respected importing and exporting firms on the East Coast. In Liverpool its office was known as Fraser, Trenholm and Company, and in New York as Trenholm Brothers. When Fraser died in 1854, George Alfred Trenholm, who was described as "a prince among merchants," became senior partner and renamed the firm Fraser, Trenholm and Company. Trenholm enjoyed almost unlimited credit abroad and had extensive holdings there and in America. He had started in the firm as a clerk at an early age. In 1828, he had married Anna Hilen Holmes, and in 1845 they made their home at what is now the Ashley Hall School for Girls on Rutledge Avenue.

The three interlocking firms of John Fraser and Company; Fraser, Trenholm and Company; and Trenholm Brothers purchased several ships and had part interests in others. One of Trenholm's vessels, the 583-ton ship *Delia Maria*,[3] wrecked off Hilton Head on September 7, 1854 while on a voyage from Liverpool to Charleston. Trenholm was aboard during the ordeal. Even though *Delia Maria* was fully insured, Trenholm saw to it that she was salvaged, carried into Charleston, and sold at auction. By 1860, the firms had five vessels in service:

[3] Built at Richmond, Maine, in 1850.

Eugene L. Tessier, a Frenchman, who commanded John Fraser and Company's sailing ship *Emily St. Pierre* in the Charleston trade. Tessier would go on to become a successful blockade-runner captain for Fraser, Trenholm and Company.

George Alfred Trenholm, dominant force of the antebellum Charleston maritime scene.

The Fraser, Trenholm and Company packet ship *Susan G. Owens,* built by Samuel Butler at Baltimore in 1848 for Benjamin Buck. She carried passengers to San Francisco in 1849, but spent most of the next decade on the Liverpool to Baltimore run. She was purchased in 1860 by Fraser, Trenholm and put on the Liverpool to Charleston run. Once the war began, *Susan G. Owens* was sold.

Eliza Bonsall[4]	1,265 tons, 192.5 feet long, built in Bath, Maine in 1855
Emily St. Pierre[5]	884 tons, 178 feet long, built in Bath, Maine in 1854
John Fraser	863 tons, built in Bath, Maine in 1854
Susan G. Owens	730 tons, built in Baltimore in 1848
Gondar	643 tons, built in Newcastle, Maine in 1847 by P. Curtis

Some of these ships operated under the Liverpool-Charleston Line, a packet service inaugurated on July 5, 1860, for which Fraser, Trenholm was the agency. In August 1860 the Liverpool-Charleston Line became the Southern Line of Packets. The ships sailed from Liverpool on the 5th and 20th of each month.

The firm was on the verge of establishing regular steamship service between Charleston and Liverpool when the Civil War started. In the summer of 1860 the *Charleston Daily Courier* boasted that John Fraser and Company was having constructed an iron propeller ship capable of stowing up to 4,000 bales of cotton. The ship was being built exclusively for trade between Liverpool and Charleston. With their experience and capital, this firm had the best prospects of succeeding in direct steamship service between Europe and Charleston. If the South had won the war, this company could well have become the premier steamship company for the Confederate States of America, with headquarters in Charleston.

Trenholm was active in state politics and served on several boards, including that of the Bank of Charleston and the South Carolina Railroad. In 1864–65 he served as Secretary of the Confederate States of America; as a result, he was subjected to brutal conditions when he was imprisoned after the war.

Ravenel & Company

In eighteenth-century South Carolina, planting and the professions were the exclusive occupations of the gentry. When John Ravenel, then a very young man, proposed to sell his patrimonial acres and become a merchant, he met with strong family opposition. He was persistent, however, and in conjunction with Samuel N. Stevens established the firm of Ravenel & Stevens. The name was changed to Ravenel, Stevens & Company when Ravenel's brother William entered the firm. Upon Stevens' death, it became Ravenel Brothers & Company; John Ravenel's sons F. and Frank G. also became partners.

They dealt largely in cotton and were very active in importing as well. Large quantities of woolen cloth were brought in from Rhode Island and England. "The business was enlarged and extended yearly; it was very profitable," said William Ravenel, by whom this branch of the business was begun and managed. Until the 1830s the Rhode Island business was handled by Howland, Ward, and Springs, which imported heavy cloth for slave garments and fine woolen goods from the Hazard Brothers firm in Rhode Island.

The Ravenel business increased still more when they acquired ships, an interest in which the younger members of the firm were especially active. At one time they owned

major interests in seven vessels,[6] all square-rigged ships, named *John Ravenel*, *John Rutledge*, *Yemassee*, *Wateree*, *Lydia*, *Mackinaw*, and *Muscongus*.

The first four were built for the firm. *John Rutledge*, a very handsome vessel fitted to take cabin passengers, was over 1100 tons; she was 175 feet long and 37 feet wide, drawing 23 feet at full draft. *John Rutledge* was launched in Baltimore on August 29, 1851. Since her draft proved too deep for the Charleston bar except on spring tides, she was sold after two voyages.

John Ravenel, a 700-ton ship built along the lines of a packet ship, was constructed in Baltimore and launched on October 31, 1846. On September 17 of the next year, she arrived in Charleston on her first voyage from Europe, carrying the family of John Siegling, a prominent King Street merchant and musician.

These vessels regularly sailed from Charleston to different European ports with cotton, rice, and naval stores. They would return with varied cargoes, including woolen goods (especially the heavy grey cloth worn by the slaves, known as "Welsh plaids"), blankets, linen, tin, hardware, slates, and salt. "For many years," said William Ravenel, "a ship was sent every year with cotton to St. Petersburg, which then went to Sweden and returned to Charleston with a cargo of Swedish iron to be sold in South Carolina and Georgia."

When the city government sold off lots on lower East Battery in the 1830s, William Ravenel constructed at number 13 a fine Greek Revival house overlooking the harbor. From there he could note the comings and goings of his ships. Later from Ravenel's roof, guests watched the opening shots of the Civil War. The impressive front columns fell during the earthquake of 1886, and were never replaced.

When John Ravenel retired from the firm in 1850, William Ravenel continued the shipping business with his two nephews under the name of "Ravenel & Company." William Ravenel also joined Cleland K. Huger to form Ravenel & Huger, a firm that took over the cloth business. During the Civil War William Ravenel was a major stockholder in the blockade-running company called The Importing and Exporting Company of South Carolina.[7]

Street Brothers

The recession of 1820 was in full swing when young Timothy Street arrived from Connecticut and opened a ship agency business, Timothy Street and Company. His brother Thaddeus and another partner eventually joined him. The firm was one of the backers of the first railroad, and *Niagara*, one of its agency ships, brought the "Best Friend" locomotive to Charleston from New York. When Timothy Street died on a business trip to New York in 1833, many of the ships in the harbor flew their flags at half mast in tribute, for by then he and his firm were well known up and down the coast.

The firm carried on as Street and Boinest, then H. T. Street & Brothers, and finally Street Brothers, which survived until recent years. Since part of their operations included piloting, one of their boats, *Pride*, engaged in blockade running during the first year of the Civil War, when a sailing vessel could run the blockade with little risk of failure.

[4] Named for Edward Leonard Trenholm's wife, Eliza Bonsall Holmes.

[5] Named for George Alfred Trenholm's daughter, the ship had a figurehead of her namesake that was carved by Charles S. Sampson of Bath, with stern carvings of the coats of arms of Georgia and South Carolina.

[6] A small share of the investment in these ships was owned by the captains.

[7] At the outbreak of the war the Ravenel ships were sold, with the exception of *John Ravenel*, which was burned at the Northeastern Railroad wharf when Charleston was evacuated in February 1865. The Ravenel business was thus destroyed. It was dissolved when the junior partner, Frank G. Ravenel, was killed at Malvern Hill in 1862.

The sailing ship *Mackinaw* of **Ravenel & Company**. She displaced some 1,094 tons. In 1855 *Mackinaw* was part of the Baltimore Line of Packets.

John Ravenel in the Bay of Naples in the 1850s.

CHARLESTON SHIPS 1861–1865

Scale 1″ = 50′

Steamer *Star of the West* **1861**

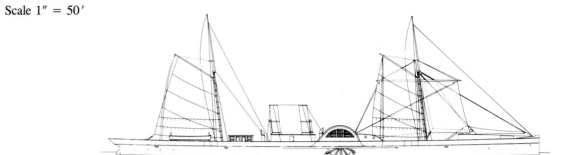

Blockade Runner *Mary Bowers* **1864**

Monitor *Passaic* **1863**

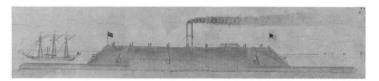

Ironclad Steam Ram *Palmetto State* **1862**

Blockader *Memphis* **1864**

River Steamer *Planter* **1862**

Ironclad Frigate *New Ironsides* **1863**

Torpedoboat *David* **1863**

Submarine *Hunley* **1864**

Part VI

THE CIVIL WAR 1861–1865

Opening Guns at Fort Sumter

During the years of the "Pax Britannica" from the defeat of Napoleon in 1815 at Waterloo to the invasion of Belgium in 1914 with which World War I began, the wars of Western man were relatively short and lacked the bitterness that characterized most conflicts. The exceptions were the War of the Triple Alliance (1865–1870) in South America between Paraguay on one side and Brazil, Argentina, and Uruguay on the other; and the American Civil War or, more correctly named, the War for Southern Independence. The Confederate States of America was fighting strictly for its independence, *not* to overthrow the government of the United States, as the term *civil war* implies. However erroneous, the term has become ingrained in the language to such a point that now it cannot be avoided.

The American Civil War attracts more world interest today than any other conflict of

Confederate Charleston as seen from Fort Johnson with Castle Pinckney at right. This serene view belies the threatening war, while depicting a city heavily engaged in commerce with river steamers (the steamer at left is probably *Charleston* or *Edisto*) moving about while ocean-going and other vessels ply the harbor waters. The square-rigged sailing ship tied up on the city's water-front to the right of center (above the revenue cutter's bowsprit) is *John Ravenel*, and at right (to the left of the steamer to the left of Castle Pinckney) is John Fraser's *Gondar*, all that remained of Charleston's antebellum ocean-going sailing ships.

the American experience, and any other war of the century following 1815. It was the first of the new and the last of the old wars. It saw the introduction of many innovative weapons, such as ironclads, machine guns, and rifled weapons. Yet, there were no fronts established across the entire breadth of the borders that separated the two warring nations. Instead, armies operating in general theaters took to the field and fought for victory. In addition, the style, leadership ability, and chivalry of the Southern leaders have piqued the curiosity of historians ever since.

Advances in Ordnance

The rapid engineering strides Western man was making after the Napoleonic Wars were by no means limited to industrial and mercantile pursuits. The tools of war and destruction were also advancing, especially in the field of rifled artillery. Before the American Revolution, frontiersmen had brought the Kentucky rifle into the military field. Adapting the rifled concept to artillery was not difficult; the problem was to perfect a projectile that could be loaded easily, yet fit the bore tightly enough so that the rifling would engage the projectile to impart spin to it.

Experiments in the 1840s led to the development of a projectile that had bands of soft copper or lead. Upon firing, these bands would expand and engage the rifling. By 1860 Robert Parrott had developed the Parrott rifled gun of cast iron with a reinforced breech; this weapon would become the mainstay of Union long-range artillery. The Confederate equivalent was the Brooke rifle, an accurate, modern weapon that fired explosive shells and solid shot. The American Civil War would be the proving ground of these weapons, which would in turn sound the death knell for the hitherto impregnable forts and fortifications of masonry construction.

Union ordnance continued to make advances throughout the war as new and larger weapons were designed, including the Gatling and Rodman guns, and as machinery was adapted to warfare in the form of steam-powered ironclads and railroads. The Confederacy was by no means lax, but the South's agrarian economy lacked the industrial base to develop and manufacture these weapons easily or in any quantity.

These new weapons offered a prelude to the coming firestorm in sea warfare when a Russian squadron annihilated a Turkish fleet at the battle of Sinope in November 1853. The Russian ships used high-explosive shells to shoot the wooden Turkish ships to pieces with virtual impunity. This battle signalled the end of wooden warships.

Charleston at the Center of the Rising Storm

As the "Cradle of Secession," Charleston became a psychological symbol to both the North and the South. As a blockade-running port in the first two years, Charleston drew the main force of the Union Navy to her bar; then during the last two years of the struggle, more innovations in naval warfare would occur in Charleston harbor than in any other seaport in the Western Hemisphere and possibly the world—a testimony to the symbolic value that both sides attached to the city and the resolve of her sons in her defense. Charleston harbor would introduce and prove in battle torpedoboats, submarines, mines (called torpedoes at the time), steam-powered ironclad fleets, and the first modern naval blockade.

Charleston's role in the Confederate War has been given offhanded treatment in deference to the great strategic battles before Richmond and the campaigns in the West. Both sides

fought valiantly for this city, symbolic of secession. She endured a siege of 587 days, exceeded in modern times only by the Soviet defense of Leningrad in World War II. Actually, from the time of the Federal landings at Port Royal on November 7, 1861, until the evacuation of Charleston on February 18, 1865, there were few periods when the noise of gunfire could not be heard on her streets.

As an ominous prelude to the coming storm, the National Democratic Party had held its convention in Charleston in April 1860. The Southern states split from the national party and fielded their own candidate for president. This act all but guaranteed a Republican victory. Once Lincoln was elected in November, the South Carolina General Assembly unanimously called for a convention on secession. It met at Charleston and passed the Ordinance to that effect on December 20, 1861. By February, other Southern states had joined South Carolina in forming the Confederate States of America, with its capital at Montgomery, Alabama. When Virginia joined the Confederacy in April, the capital was moved to Richmond.

Charleston's Federal Garrison Consolidates

Once South Carolina departed from the Union, Major Robert Anderson, commander of the small U. S. military garrison at Fort Moultrie, found himself in a tenuous position. Rather than try to remain there, on December 26, 1860, Anderson withdrew to Fort Sumter, then nearly completed at the south side of the harbor entrance. The next day South Carolina units occupied the abandoned fort, as well as other Federal installations in Charleston, including the Federal Arsenal on Ashley Avenue and Castle Pinckney in the harbor. The latter

The steamship *S. R. Spaulding* in Charleston harbor. She was a new iron steamer, 218′ long, built at Wilmington, Delaware in 1859. For $10,000 the New England delegates to the 1860 Democratic Convention chartered *S. R. Spaulding* and lived on her for eighteen days while attending the convention. Note the walking beam for the paddle wheels behind the smoke stack.

had the distinction of being the first Federal installation taken by the South and also of never having fired a shot in anger in almost 200 years of existence.

Once the 150 or so Federal troops in the Charleston area were consolidated in Fort Sumter, South Carolina authorities began to surround it with batteries. Early in January 1861, a group of Citadel cadets were sent to a point on Morris Island out of range of the guns of Fort Sumter to build and man a battery of four 24-pounder field howitzers to guard the main ship channel. At the same time in Washington, General Winfield Scott, the senior army commander, prepared the steamer *Star of the West* to sail from New York to Charleston with reinforcements for Sumter's garrison. *Star of the West* was a sidewheeled passenger steamer on the New York to New Orleans run; she was chosen to transport recruits because, as a merchant vessel, she would not arouse suspicions. However, the colony of Southern sympathizers in New York quickly passed word of her preparation to Charleston.

Left: Steamship *Marion* departing in February 1861 from Fort Sumter for New York. *Marion* was one of the Spofford, Tileston and Company's New York to Charleston coastal packet sidewheel steamers. She was a 900-ton vessel with a 198-foot hull, built by Jacob Bell of New York in 1851. *Marion* went into service on the New York to Charleston run that summer and remained there until the start of the war. In February 1861, before the opening bombardment of the war but after South Carolina seceded, *Marion* removed the dependents of Fort Sumter to New York. Once the war began, she was taken into the Federal service, participating in the seizure of Port Royal in October 1861, and the Farragut expedition against New Orleans in April 1862. When that port was reopened to commerce, *Marion* became the first steamer to serve the New York to New Orleans run. In April 1863 she hit a submerged rock in the Bahama Channel and sank, a total loss. No lives were lost and her cargo was eventually salvaged.

Below: Fort Moultrie (at right) booms out a challenge to *Star of the West*.

Once he saw the walking beam, Major Anderson realized that *Star of the West* was not a warship coming to his aid, and consequently not of much help in replying to the fire of the South Carolina guns along the channel leading to his fort.

Star of the West (see page 203) was a fairly typical pre-war coastal steamer.

First Shots

Once word of *Star of the West's* sailing reached Charleston, the South Carolina authorities took up the channel buoys, extinguished the light in the Morris Island lighthouse, and removed the lightship from Rattlesnake Shoal. In addition, a pilot boat and the steamer *General Clinch* with twenty militiamen were sent to guard the waters off the bar during darkness.

Captain McGowan brought *Star of the West* to the Charleston bar before dawn on January 9, 1861, but it was daylight before her leadsman found the channel across the bar. The pilot boat saw *Star of the West* as she pressed on toward the fort. The guardship *General Clinch* fled up the channel toward the harbor, firing rockets and flares to sound the alarm.

Ashore on the dunes of Morris Island, the Citadel cadets watched *Star of the West* advance and readied their guns. As she drew abreast of their position, they shot a cannonball across her bow. The hoisting of a larger American flag to the masthead was answered by more shots, some of which hit her side. Several more shots followed, but the old 24-pounder guns, designed for an earlier day and an earlier conflict, could not do enough damage to stop the ship.

Ahead lay Fort Moultrie and a new challenge to *Star of the West*. McGowan had to swing his ship within a half mile of Moultrie's powerful guns. A puff of smoke belched from Moultrie's ramparts and then another. A huge splash near *Star of the West* unnerved McGowan. No reply of assistance came from Fort Sumter's Union garrison. More shots followed, but

they were wide of the mark. This fire plus the continuing barrage by the cadet battery proved to be enough for McGowan. He decided not to take another chance. He put her wheel hard a starboard and, with the ebb tide behind him, quickly recrossed the bar, followed by a few parting shots.

South Carolina soon afterwards took the steamers *Aid* and *Marion* into service as guardships to assist *General Clinch* and *Nina* in protecting the harbor. Additionally, four old hulks were brought from Savannah, loaded with granite, and sunk in the main ship channel to keep out warships of large draft. Unfortunately, the swift currents quickly swept away their superstructures, nullifying their effect.

As the lame-duck Buchanan administration retained control of the U. S. government, the firing on *Star of the West* did not precipitate war. However, it did demonstrate South Carolina's determination to secede. Buchanan preferred to let Lincoln handle matters when he assumed the reins of government in March.

The Noose Tightens

Guns from Forts Moultrie and Johnson were aimed at two sides of Fort Sumter. Large undefended gaps remained in the sides of Fort Sumter that faced the harbor and the ocean. To safeguard the unprotected harbor side, Captain John Hamilton, CSN, suggested building a floating battery based on ironclads, similar to those used by the British and French in re-

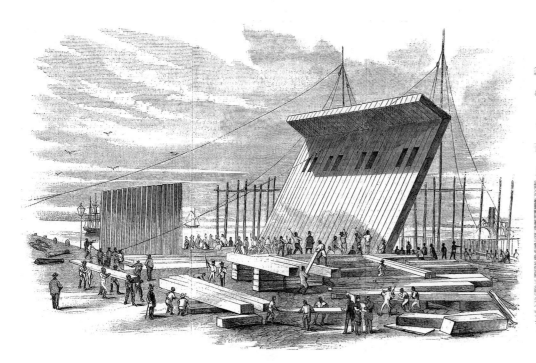

Construction of the floating battery in Charleston harbor.

The floating battery with Dr. DeVega's hospital attached at the rear.

ducing Russian batteries at Kinburn in 1854 at the beginning of the Crimean War.

The state of South Carolina appropriated $12,000 for the ironclad floating battery project, and Hamilton supervised the construction on the city's waterfront. The floating battery was not much more than a large barge about forty feet wide and eighty feet long, with an eight-foot draft. The bow was covered with one-inch railroad strap iron, slanted and greased to deflect incoming shot, and it had four embrasures for two 42-pounder and two 32-pounder cannons. At the stern a hospital and sandbags counterbalanced the weight of the guns. By March 15 the battery was completed, but it was greeted with much skepticism. Southerners christened it "the slaughter pen" because they feared that it would be a sitting duck, unable to deflect enemy shot. Others feared it might tip over. To allay those fears, the floating battery was grounded at the west end of Sullivan's Island early on the morning of April 10 just before the Fort Sumter bombardment. She remained there until destroyed by a storm late in 1863. A similar iron-shielded battery was mounted on land at Cumming's Point to fire on Fort Sumter.

Upon the establishment of the Confederate States of America in February, President Jefferson Davis had dispatched Brigadier General P. G. T. Beauregard, an 1838 graduate of West Point, to assume command of military operations at Charleston. Beauregard inspected the batteries aimed at Sumter and was shocked at the unpreparedness that he found. The artillerymen were untrained and the structures of the guns were vulnerable to counterfire. Furthermore, ranging shots had been taken infrequently. If the order to attack Sumter had come earlier, the South Carolinians would have probably been not only repulsed but humiliated.

Almost at once Union troops at Sumter noticed renewed energy on the shores opposite them. Through spyglasses they could see that someone with a knowledge of engineering was directing the construction of batteries facing them. That, of course, was General Beauregard.

To guard against a night relief force coming to the aid of Sumter, four huge Drummond lights were obtained to illuminate the harbor. At the end of March, Fort Sumter's supplies and communications with Washington via the mails and telegraph were severed. The ring of steel tightened.

Meanwhile, the newly inaugurated Lincoln administration was planning a relief expedition to depart by early April from New York. Captain Gustavus Fox, head of the expedition, was instructed to bring relief supplies and troops to Fort Sumter, even if he had to "use his entire force to open a passage. . . ." An officer from Washington personally conveyed this message to Governor Pickens and General Beauregard in Charleston on April 8. As tensions mounted through the first two weeks of April, ranging shots began to be taken on Fort Sumter from the various Southern batteries. From the preliminary shots, Major Anderson and his men got an idea of what they were to face. Knowing that the relief force was on the way, both sides made last-minute preparations.

On April 10, President Davis directed Beauregard to demand the evacuation of Sumter; if refused, he was to proceed with its reduction by force. General Beauregard spent the morn-

Citadel cadets firing on *Star of the West* from the Morris Island battery.

ing of April 11 ensuring that all was ready. That afternoon, he sent word to Anderson to evacuate, or hostilities would commence. Anderson refused.

With the fort all but ringed by enemy batteries, Anderson decided to try to reduce casualties by not manning the heavy guns on the fort's barbette. A crossfire would make this the most dangerous position in battle, because shells that passed over the fort would explode among artillerymen on the far side of the fort's walls. This limited Sumter's armament to the lighter guns on the first tier, which were primarily intended to repel infantry attacks. The second tier was incomplete, and the embrasures sealed. The small garrison of the fort, only one-tenth of its intended complement, could man only a few guns anyway.

The Union Is Dissolved

At 3:30 a. m. on Friday, April 12, 1861, a final demand was made on Anderson to evacuate. Again he refused, and the Confederates announced that the bombardment would begin in one hour. The two sides shook hands and the boat bearing the Southern officers pulled for Fort Johnson. As it was rowed the last mile they must have reflected on the momentous events the harbor had seen and wondered about those that were unfolding.

Precisely at 4:30 a. m., a ten-inch mortar from Fort Johnson sent a shell in a perfect curve that arched up and over Fort Sumter, exploding above the fort's parade ground. The War for Southern Independence was on!

The other forts and batteries around the harbor quickly replied, but the fire was slow until first light, a half hour later. The Confederate mortars made brilliant displays, as shells burst within the fort where Anderson's men crouched in the casemates. Because there were no candles left to illuminate the loading operations, no fire came from Fort Sumter until 7:00 a. m., when the sun was high enough to pass natural light over the fifty-foot walls of the fort. The 32- and 42-pounder guns in the lower tier of Sumter did very little damage to the Confederate batteries, and the latter could do very little harm to the men behind the thick walls of Sumter.

The citizens of Charleston had thronged to the waterfront the day before in anticipation of the opening guns. When rain began to fall that night, they dispersed; then, the opening concussions rattled windows and shook houses, alerting them that the long-anticipated conflict had finally begun. The crowds on the battery were awestruck at the display of ordnance, but there was little cheering. Perhaps they were too sobered by the cataclysmic events unfolding before them.

With practice the Confederate fire improved as the day went on. Most of the initial shots had passed over Fort Sumter. By afternoon they were ripping into the parapet with telling effect. The supposedly fireproof barracks were ignited by hot shot from Moultrie's furnaces, which had been going since the previous night. Several times the fires in Sumter were extinguished.

The Union relief expedition had arrived off the bar just before the first gun. They anchored to await warships that would blast their way in. However, a mix-up in orders had sent the warship *Powhatan* to Pensacola, and it was not until after Fort Sumter surrendered that the mistake was realized.

By afternoon, the fort's ammunition began to run low. Anderson ordered the return fire slowed, and then had it stopped at nightfall. The Confederates also stopped, but mortars continued to fire at fifteen-minute intervals throughout the night. When fire resumed the next morning, the barracks were ignited, sending flames leaping over the parapet. Anderson's men quickly removed what powder they could from Sumter's magazine and then barred the entrance with earth. As the buildings were consumed, the heat within the casemates became intense. The ready ammunition was thrown out of the gunports into the water to keep it from detonating, leaving only a few rounds with which to reply to the Confederate fire.

The Confederate gunners assumed that Anderson's men were perishing in the flames, but cheered their enemy's courage whenever a gun discharged from the fort. Around noon the magazine caught on fire, sending showers of sparks and flaming timbers over the fort. Onlookers felt that no one inside the fort could survive, but occasionally a gun would discharge. After another hour, the flagstaff was shot away. Again the Confederate fire ceased, but resumed when Peter Hart and several privates raised the flag on a spar.

Model of Fort Sumter as it appeared prior to the opening bombardment of April 12, 1861. The largest guns in the fort had been mounted on the barbette, or top tier, where their elevation would give them a commanding view of any attacking naval force. Unfortunately for the Union defenders, to have manned these guns in the face of the intense Confederate fire would have been foolhardy. Note the barracks lining three of the five interior sides of the fort. Fort Sumter was designed to defend the harbor entrance from naval attack. As a consequence, the weakest side was at the rear of the fort away from the ship channel (left rear). Located here along the "gorge wall" was the longest barracks building, containing officers' quarters. The only heavy ordnance mounted on this side was on the barbette. Unfortunately for the subsequent Confederate defenders of the fort, this weak wall faced Union batteries mounted on Morris Island in 1863. Note the cannon imbedded into the earth of the parade ground, intended to fire as a mortar on Cumming's Point. Smaller 32-pounder cannon were mounted in the lower tier of the fort to repel waterborne infantry attacks. They were also effective in ricocheting fire against ships. The uncompleted embrasures of the middle tier were largely filled in or left open. Major Anderson had sufficient troops to man only a small portion of the fort's total firepower.

The citizens of Charleston gather on the rooftops along the harbor to watch the firing on Fort Sumter.

Beauregard's aide-de-camp, Colonel L. T. Wigfall, rowed across to Sumter from Morris Island and managed to enter the fort for a conference with Anderson, who finally agreed to evacuate. The relief force could be seen merely sitting off the bar. If they were not going to assist him, then Anderson must have figured that it was no use to continue resistance. At 1:30, after thirty-four hours of continuous bombardment, the fort's flag was lowered and replaced with a sheet.

Early on Sunday morning, Charleston harbor was thronged with boatloads of people viewing the smoldering fort. That afternoon, as the Citadel cadets held a dress parade on the battery, people arrived from as far as fifty miles, to view the waters that had once again made history.

At 11 a. m. the steamer *Isabel* pulled up to the wharf at Fort Sumter to convey the garrison out to the relief force off the bar. Anderson was allowed to salute the flag on departure. On the forty-seventh discharge the gun accidentally fired, killing one of the Union gunners. The salute continued nonetheless, but for only 50 guns instead of 100. By 4 p.m. the garrison had marched aboard *Isabel*, but with the tide now low, she was aground. Anderson and his men witnessed the Confederates taking possession of the fort to much fanfare and celebration. The flags of the Confederacy and the state of South Carolina were raised, and the Palmetto Guard occupied the fort.

Early the next morning *Isabel* got underway. As she steamed slowly past Morris Island, the Confederate gunners, with heads uncovered, lined the beach in silent tribute to Anderson and his men. They were put aboard *Baltic* in the relief force and sailed to New York, where they received a heroes' welcome.

The North perceived the Confederate bombardment of Fort Sumter as aggression, and the population quickly galvanized for war. Lincoln issued the call for volunteers, and citizens flocked to restore the nation's honor. In contrast, the South perceived the attack on Fort Sumter as a cleansing of Southern territory of an enemy garrison. The Southern populace was equally galvanized by the call to arms. Thus commenced the bitterest war of the American experience.

Charleston and the Confederate Cruisers

Commerce raiders such as *Alabama*, *Florida*, and *Shenandoah* captured much of the Southern public's fancy when the Civil War was extended to the high seas. However, other cruisers were also busy and occasionally used Charleston as a base. The first of these Charleston cruisers were the pilot boats commissioned by the Confederate government as privateers. Although the Paris Convention had outlawed privateering, the United States was not a signatory. Therefore, Confederate President Jefferson Davis felt safe in issuing letters of marque to business syndicates to outfit warships as privateers.

On May 18, 1861, Charleston pilot boat *Number 7* received her privateer commission. She had been built in Charleston as *Savannah* for pilots Green Fleetwood and Elijah Broughton. She sailed over the bar on June 1, armed with an old 18-pounder gun, circa 1812. She captured the brig *Joseph* of Rockland, Maine, and sent it into Georgetown as a prize bringing $30,000; thus, *Joseph* was the first vessel taken by a Confederate privateer in the Atlantic. Shortly afterward, *Number 7* was overhauled due to mast damage sustained in a storm; she subsequently was taken as a prize of the U. S. brig *Perry*. *Number 7's* crew was taken to New York. The Lincoln administration treated them as pirates and tried them as such. The

Northern press clamored to hang them, but the Confederate government threatened retaliation should they not be accorded the rights of prisoners of war. They were eventually removed to a military prison.

Even more disastrous than *Number 7's* fate was that of the schooner *Petrel*. She had been built as the Charleston pilot boat *Eclipse* and then taken into the revenue service as a cutter in 1853 after the loss of *Hamilton*. The South Carolina authorities seized her after secession and renamed her *William Aiken*. She was subsequently purchased by a group of investors, who commissioned her as a privateer, armed with two small pivot guns. She set out over the bar in July 1861. At daylight the day following her departure, she was spotted by the U. S. 52-gun frigate *St. Lawrence*. After a brief pursuit, *Petrel* ran up the stars and bars and sent a shot through the massive warship's mainsail. In response *St. Lawrence* lobbed an eight-inch shell on the schooner's bow, sinking her in thirty seconds.

The schooner *Sallie*, which set out in September, fared better, taking three prizes before returning home.

The forerunner of the first real cruisers of the Confederate government was *Nashville*.

The Charleston pilot boat *Savannah*.

The USS *St. Lawrence* sinking *Petrel* on August 1, 1861.

CSS *Nashville* on November 19, 1861, twenty-four days out of Charleston, burning the American merchantship *Harvey Birch* in the English Channel.

Charleston's John Grimball and CSS *Shenandoah*

Above: During the summer of 1864 the Confederate naval agent in England, James D. Bulloch, laid plans to buy a vessel for use against the American Pacific whaling fleet. One of his agents found and purchased the wooden steamer *Sea King*. Another agent, Henry Lafone, purchased a smaller vessel, *Laurel*. In October *Laurel* met *Sea King* off Madeira with *Sea King's* six 68-pounder cannon and 100 seamen. Included among her officers were James Iredell Waddell as captain and Charleston's John Grimball as gunnery officer. *Sea King* became the CSS *Shenandoah*; once her armament was aboard she headed for the Pacific. Once in the Pacific *Shenandoah* single-handedly wiped out what was left of the American whaling fleet. Her crew did not learn of the end of the war until June 1865, whereupon *Shenandoah* made for London—the last ship to fly the Confederate flag on the high seas. This painting of *Shenandoah* by Rear Admiral John W. Schmidt shows her burning a group of Union whaling ships in the harbor of Ponape, Guam, on April 9, 1865, the day General Robert E. Lee surrendered at Appomattox.

Right: Photograph of John Grimball of Charleston, taken while gunnery officer on *Shenandoah*. Grimball graduated from the U. S. Naval Academy in the class of 1852, the same class as George Dewey of Spanish-American War fame. His pre-war service included *Macedonian*. In 1862 he served on the ironclad *Arkansas* in the Mississippi River campaigns before Memphis and Vicksburg. Cornered by Farragut's fleet off Vicksburg, *Arkansas* escaped in a daring charge through the enemy fleet, but was subsequently scuttled. Some of her crew were sent to serve with the Charleston ironclad squadron. After the war Grimball settled in New York and became a successful attorney. Late in life he returned to Charleston with his bride to rear his family.

She was an 1,800-ton sidewheel steamer built for the New York-Southhampton-le Havre run by Spofford, Tileston and Company of New York in 1853. *Nashville* was considered the finest steamer on the Atlantic Coast before the war. In February 1861 she made her last New York to Charleston run and arrived with a complete outfit of arms that had been purchased in Liverpool. The start of hostilities caught *Nashville* at Charleston, where she was seized by the Confederate government. Although she was a large ship, her decks were too weak to support heavy ordnance. Therefore, two brass twelve-pounders were mounted, no match for the enemy's heavy ordnance. Her captain, R. B. Pegram, then set sail for England to have her decks strengthened, a task that could not be done in Charleston.

On the night of October 26, 1861, Pegram slipped *Nashville* past Fort Sumter in the dark. Unfortunately poor weather had blown one of his marker boats away from the channel across the bar. This caused Pegram to lose his way and the ship ran aground. Backing off he tried again, only to ground once more. With the moon now rising to reveal his position to the blockading enemy, he backed off and once more pushed ahead, forcing the ship over the bar with her powerful sidewheels. The enemy slumbered on as *Nashville* fled over the horizon. Pegram stopped briefly in Bermuda before crossing the Atlantic.

On November 21 *Nashville* arrived at Southhampton, becoming the first Confederate warship to show the flag in Britain. She had just missed the former Charleston steamer USS *James Adger*, now outfitted as a warship. It had been dispatched across the Atlantic to capture her!

The following April *Nashville* tried to return to Charleston. She was no longer a cruiser, but a blockade runner renamed *Thomas L. Wragg*, owned by John Fraser and Company. The blockaders thwarted her way, so she put into Wilmington. In June 1862 she made another attempt to enter Charleston, only to be spotted and pursued by *Keystone State*, the fastest blockader on the Charleston station. For eighteen hours the chase went on, with the distance closing and both ships discharging gear and cargo. The crew of *Thomas L. Wragg* threw over most of her million-dollar cargo and tore up the deck cabins for firewood. Drinking water and anchor chain were thrown off of *Keystone State* to lighten ship. Finally, *Thomas L. Wragg* slipped into a rain squall and eluded her pursuer under cover of darkness.

On the next try into a Confederate port, *Thomas L. Wragg* made for Obassaw Sound at the mouth of the Ogeechee River south of Savannah. Here her cargo was removed by lighters and taken upriver to the rail crossing. John Fraser then sold her to a syndicate that fitted her out as a privateer. In February 1863, while sitting off Fort McAlister in preparation to sail in this new role, she was set upon by the monitor USS *Montauk* and blown to pieces.

Another Charleston-connected vessel was *Georgiana*, built at Glasgow in 1862 by Lawrie and Company under the name *Louisiana* to confuse Union agents. She was a moderate-sized iron ship some 207 feet long, with a cargo capacity of 407 tons and a top speed of over 14 knots. *Georgiana* made an unlikely blockade runner because her fifteen-foot draft limited her to deep channels. Because of this limitation and the fact that her decks were capable of bearing the weight of guns[1] the Union agents in England considered *Georgiana* to be destined to become a commerce raider. Recent research indicates that she was designed to carry up to 14 guns and over 140 men, which would have made her a more powerful cruiser than *Alabama*.

In January 1863 *Georgiana* arrived in Liverpool to take on cargo. Here she was seen displaying a Confederate flag, a fairly common occurrence in the pro-Southern port. Union agents thoroughly checked out *Georgiana*, and British authorities, convinced that she was not armed,[2] allowed her to sail under the command of Captain Dickenson, a retired British naval officer.

Once at sea two of the field pieces in *Georgiana's* cargo were mounted on deck for defense. On arrival at Nassau in March she was reinspected. Here a Union agent sent a report to Washington stating that once *Georgiana* arrived in a Confederate port she would be armed as a commerce raider and renamed *South Carolina*.

On March 15 *Georgiana* cleared Nassau for Charleston. Three days later she arrived off Dewee's Inlet and began her approach to Charleston via Maffitt's Channel. Off the Isle of Palms she was spotted and fired upon by the former yacht *America*, now serving as a blockader. *Georgiana* refused to stop and was also taken under fire from USS *Wissahickon*, which practically swung alongside the fleeing ship. Once *Georgiana* was hit, Dickenson ordered the safety valves on the boilers tied down in an effort to increase steam pressure and speed. As *Georgiana* pulled ahead the USS *Housatonic* and several other blockaders barred her path. At the same time a lucky hit from *Wissahickon* crippled the fleeing ship.

Captain Dickenson stopped the ship, ostensibly to surrender. The blockaders moved in and launched boats to take possession of *Georgiana*. They rowed up, only to be met by a hail of small arms fire as Dickenson plunged full speed ahead. Fearful of hitting their own boats, the blockaders withheld fire. With escape impossible, Captain Dickenson turned *Georgiana* toward shore. She grounded a mile off shore and 3.5 miles from Breach Inlet. The crew flooded the ship, lowered the boats, and rowed ashore. A prize crew came aboard and tried to pull *Georgiana* off, but failed because of the amount of water in her hold. They did find the liquor, and made off with it after *Georgiana* was set afire. The ship burned for three days as her cargo of munitions detonated. The Union sailors were thrown into irons by their own captain for being drunk and disorderly.

Georgiana remained there as a hazard to navigation. In May 1863 as the blockade runner *Norseman* departed Charleston at high tide, she plowed into the wreck. On August 31, 1864, as the blockade runner *Mary Bowers* (see page 203) made for Charleston, she literally threw herself on top of the wreck of *Georgiana* and also became a total loss. Barely five weeks later, *Georgiana* claimed her third victim, *Constance Decimer*, at the time inbound from Halifax with a cargo of munitions. Thus *Georgiana's* loss became a quadruple blow to the Confederacy.

---

[1] Confirmed by recent diving excursions on the wreck by Dr. E. Lee Spence.

[2] Under international law, a neutral country could build merchant ships for a belligerent, but not warships. Therefore, warships were constructed supposedly for other neutrals or as merchant vessels. As the latter they had to leave England unarmed.

The Fall of Port Royal

After the capture of Fort Sumter by the Confederacy the war passed to other theaters, and Charleston received a reprieve. The peaceful interlude would be all too short; soon events would unfold in rapid succession to bring calamity to the city of secession.

Almost as soon as the blockade had been proclaimed in April 1861, Lincoln appointed a Blockade Strategy Board to make recommendations as to the best way to enforce it. One of the board's first suggestions was the seizure of Port Royal, South Carolina; its large, deep harbor made it an excellent candidate for a base for blockading warships on the South Atlantic Coast.

The Southern military strategists also realized Port Royal's importance and took steps to fortify it. Unfortunately, through the summer and fall of 1861, all that could be accomplished was the erection of earthen forts at each side of the entrance—on the southern side, Fort Walker on Hilton Head; and on the northern side, Fort Beauregard on Bay Point. These

forts were over two miles apart across the expanse of water, preventing a coordinated defense; furthermore, they were assigned a motley collection of second-rate ordnance. General Beauregard, still in command of the Confederate forces on the South Carolina coast, wanted to place the best rifled ordnance in the forts and station a floating ironclad battery between the two. Unfortunately, neither was available.

By mid-September Union leaders began planning the expedition against Port Royal. Secretary of the Navy Gideon Welles began assembling the most formidable naval armada ever to sail under the American flag. By mid-October the Northern press was reporting its presence and destination, saying that it was to serve as a base for the blockade of Savannah and Charleston.

Under the command of Commodore Samuel Francis DuPont, the fleet consisted of fifteen warships carrying 148 guns, with some as large as the new XI″ Dahlgrens, and thirty-

DuPont's "circle of fire" with Fort Walker at right and Beauregard at left. Note the Union transports standing by in the background.

six transports carrying almost 13,000 troops under Brigadier General Thomas W. Sherman. During the last half of October the ships began to assemble at Hampton Roads, Virginia; on October 29, they put to sea. Three columns of fifty-one ships stretched for six miles. The 44-gun steam frigate *Wabash*, a sister ship of the later famous *Merrimack*, served as flagship.

On the second day out, the ships ran into a full-fledged gale and for two days rode out mountainous seas while continuing southward. On November 1 the storm scattered the entire force, but only a few were lost.

Once off the Port Royal estuary, the Union ships were opposed by Commodore Josiah Tatnall's mosquito fleet of three gunboats from Savannah, along with the newly constructed forts. The opponents sparred for two days to little effect, except to give the Union forces a fairly accurate appraisal of the fort's strength.

DuPont had expected to begin the attack on the forts on November 5, but his flagship grounded and the next day the heavy weather prevented an attack. November 7 dawned clean and calm, an excellent day for accurate shooting from the ships. With *Wabash* leading the way, the Union warships steamed up the channel between the forts. Then they turned to port to attack Fort Walker, which was already hitting the flagship. As the fleet bucked the flood tide and the range dropped to 600 yards, *Wabash* slowed and unleashed her broadsides in such quick succession that the gunners in the fort had to take to their bombproofs. Astern, *Susquehanna* joined in the cannonade; for twenty-five minutes the ships remained almost stationary, smothering the fort with shells.

Inside the fort the gunners were plagued by defective ammunition that quickly rendered their best guns useless. However, they continued to fight back. But once the enemy gunboats joined in an enfilading fire, it was all over; the fort had no traverse barriers. Nevertheless, with a large shell coming in at an average of one per second, the green gunners stood to their stations and fought back more or less as a point of honor. After four hours, ammunition ran low and the fort's garrison retreated.

That afternoon the Union army landed and took possession of Fort Walker; however, for all practical purposes it had been destroyed in the cannonade. Across the estuary, Fort Beauregard had fired its one rifled gun at long range until it burst. Once the garrison realized that Fort Walker had fallen, they abandoned Fort Beauregard and retreated to the mainland.

The capture of Port Royal Sound was one of the first Union victories of the war, and Beaufort became the first Confederate town to be permanently occupied. Panic swept Charleston as rumors spread that the enemy army would march in and level the city; the reality was that General Sherman was consolidating his position on Hilton Head.

On November 5, 1861, shortly before the attack on Port Royal, a little-known Confederate general named Robert E. Lee had been placed in charge of defending the coasts of South Carolina, Georgia, and Florida. He arrived after the loss of Port Royal, which had brought the sobering realization of the ability of enemy warships to attack at will along the coast. Lee became pessimistic about the ability of land defenses to withstand the force of heavy guns aboard mobile warships. As a consequence, he withdrew Confederate troops from the sea islands and held them in reserve to defend the Savannah and Charleston railroad line. Therefore, the sea islands became something of a "no man's land." Lee's strategy was to move Confederate soldiers at will to various points along the rail line; he felt that once enemy troops were away from the support of their warships, the Southern troops could deflect an enemy thrust inland on more equal terms. This tactic became the focal point of coastal strategy throughout the rest of the war.

The Great Fire of December 11 and 12, 1861

While Charleston was not directly affected by the fall of Port Royal, its indirect effect was devastating. Refugees from surrounding plantations poured into the city. By December, hundreds had gathered. On December 11, 1861, a cold front passed through the Lowcountry. Near a sash and blind factory at the east end of Hasell Street, a group of black refugees from the sea islands built a fire to cook and keep warm. The fire soon got out of hand and ignited the nearby building.[1] The northeast wind fanned the blaze into a conflagration that quickly spread to the City Market.

With most of the city's young and able men away at war, the firefighters were short-handed. General Roswell Ripley arrived on the scene and ordered that houses on State Street in the path of the fire be dynamited to stop it. Unfortunately his orders were not carried out, and sparks and burning embers continued to rain upon structures downwind. Soon the Circular Congregational Church and the S. C. Institute Hall on Meeting Street were on fire. The Circular Church's steeple and bell crashed into Meeting Street shortly after midnight. The gas works on Church Street soon added to the blaze. By luck and hard work, the Mills House Hotel at the corner of Meeting and Queen streets was saved when guests, including General Lee, hung wet blankets out the windows. A path of fire raged between it and the Unitarian Church on Archdale Street.

As the fire moved from the commercial to the residential areas, draymen made fortunes transporting household goods from homes in its path. Ripley's orders to dynamite several wooden structures downwind on Queen Street were carried out. Unfortunately, the flames and cinders reached so high into the sky that they jumped these buildings and were soon raining on the Cathedral of St. John and St. Finbar on Broad Street.[2] The fire subsequently crossed Broad Street and burned a path all the way to the Ashley River. By dawn one-third of the city lay in ruins, with a swath of destruction from river to river. To this day a person with a keen eye for architecture can trace the fire's path by noting the mediocre post-war buildings that were built in the burned area; in contrast, many fine antebellum buildings remain in the unaffected sections of Charleston on either side of the fire's path.

People from all over the state and the South responded with aid. The following Sunday, the congregations of the Catholic and Circular Churches doubled up in Hibernian Hall, with the former service being preached on the second floor, while the latter was held on the first. The Northern press termed the fire a vindication sent by God for Charleston's part as the "Cradle of Secession." The most moving reminder of this fire are the Matthew Brady photographs of the city, taken in 1865.[3]

---

[1] Some accounts say that the fire may have been set by Union sailors who rowed ashore from the blockading ships, much as British sailors were supposed to have set the fire that burned much of Charleston in 1778. Other accounts point out that the operator of the sash and blind factory was accused of not having banked his furnaces properly.

[2] Unfortunately, the insurance on the Cathedral had lapsed only a week earlier. Consequently a permanent structure was not rebuilt until almost thirty years later.

[3] The best display of these photos can be seen in the Colony House Restaurant on Prioleau Street in Charleston.

Looking south down Meeting Street in 1865. In the distance is St. Michael's Church painted black to make it less conspicuous to Union gunners on Morris Island. The structure with the scaffolding is the remains of the Circular Church. To the right is the damaged Mills Hotel. It survived the fire, enemy bombardment, and the earthquake of 1886, only to succumb to the wrecking ball in 1969. Amazingly the vast majority of wartime destruction in Charleston was caused by the great fire of December 1861 and not by the Union bombardment of 1863–1865.

The Sinking of the Stone Fleet

Once the cruiser *Nashville* and the blockade runner *Gordon* managed to elude the blockading ships and depart from Charleston, it was readily apparent that the blockade was not as tight as the U. S. Navy had intended. In spite of their lack of steam engines, the coastal schooners also managed to slip in and out of the harbor and inlets along the coast, particularly at Bull's Bay.

In an effort to deny Confederate shipping the use of Charleston and Savannah as ports, Assistant Secretary of the Navy Gustavus V. Fox developed an elaborate scheme to sink old whaling ships in the channels leading into the two harbors. It was hoped that these sunken hulks would make the channels impossible to traverse, at least by ocean-going vessels.

The discovery of oil in Pennsylvania in 1859 led to a collapse of the New England whaling fleet. Kerosene quickly replaced the need for expensive whale oil. By the summer of 1861 large numbers of New England whaling ships were sitting idle in the harbors of New Bedford, New London, and Nantucket, even though quite a few were pressed into service as war transports.

On October 17, 1861, Secretary of the Navy Gideon Welles directed the secret purchase of twenty-five vessels, primarily laid-up whalers. A subsequent purchase brought the total number of vessels up to forty-five. The price for the first group averaged about $10 per ton, showing that they were near the end of their useful life. As the first group sailed prior to the purchase of the second group, the price went up. Speculators had gotten into the market and driven the price up to $20 per ton.

All usable equipment on these ships was removed and sold and the holds were filled with granite blocks. A five-inch hole was bored in each ship's bottom and fitted with a lead pipe and plug valve to allow water to be let into the hold. Once the plug was removed, the vessel was expected to fill and sink within fifteen to twenty minutes. Captains and nine- to ten-man crews were hired for each of the vessels.

The first fleet of twenty-five whalers departing from New Bedford as a unit created a great deal of excitement, much like an armada sailing to war. As the vessels passed down Buzzard's Bay, crowds of spectators thronged the shore and guns were fired in salute. Not about to remain in any sort of formation once clear of the port, the captains made a beeline for Port Royal, turning the cruise into a yachting race.

The first ships began to arrive at Port Royal on December 5, 1861. Due to the rigors of the long voyage, old age, and poor maintenance, they were ready for Davy Jones' locker. Those in the worst condition were sunk as jetties or piers at Port Royal and Tybee near Savannah. Several arrived without sufficient ground tackle to anchor and had to be fitted with such.

Once in harbor at Port Royal, the fleet became wind-bound by the easterly winds that often blow along the coast in winter. By December 17, the weather had cleared with a light westerly breeze, and the fleet raised anchor. Sixteen of the old whalers proceeded out of Port Royal harbor, some under tow because their sails and rigging were in such poor shape. Others appeared as if they were survivors from the Continental Navy. Unwilling to risk cruising at night, the armada anchored.

The scene of wreckage and desolation as some of New England's finest ships go down off Charleston.

At dawn the fleet proceeded up the coast escorted by gunboats, including *Ottawa*. The wind was so light that none was able to make the bar. They anchored for a second night with their escort now brought up to eight gunboats, most of which were little more than token warships—all that was needed to keep local units of the Confederate Navy at bay. By the afternoon of December 18, the first part of the armada reached its destination to find that the Confederates had destroyed the lighthouse on Morris Island. Only by its rubble could they determine its former location.

Charleston's Main Ship Channel, which ran south parallel to the shore of Morris Island, was chosen for the resting place of the hulks. One gunboat crossed the bar to guard against a Confederate attack, and the cutters from *Florida* were launched to mark either side of the channel over the bar.

Off and on during the day the Confederate steamer *Emma Davis* sortied from her station off Fort Sumter to check on the proceedings. Lacking sufficient armament to challenge the escorts, she retreated under the guns of Fort Moultrie.

By afternoon the tide was high and the ships proceeded over the bar. Only two ships were settled in position by dark, but the job continued in the moonlight; one after another, the old whaling hulks were towed across the bar and anchored in checkerboard positions perpendicular to the channel. Then the valves were opened to let the sea into their holds. As each one began to settle, her crew brought their belongings on deck and were taken off in one of the cutters of the escorting ships. By midnight seven hulks were in their final resting places in the channel, some lying askew with the sea flowing over their decks, others in an upright position.

This first group were sunk in two lines, and the second group of nine ships were sunk in three lines; the lines overlapped so that even the most nimble blockade runner could not weave its way through. The next day the last were towed in and sunk, and the masts were cut away. What was left was an unbelievable sight: hulks lying in every position across the channel, some on their port side, others on their starboard. Some were submerged forward, others aft. The sea swept over some, and others were on upright keels; all spouted water from their sides as the water raised and dropped them upon the bottom. Only *Robin Hood* remained relatively intact, to serve as the repository for material from the other ships that was deemed too worthless to carry north, but still of value to the Confederacy. Once this material was on board *Robin Hood* and the other hulks were sunk, she was towed away and set on fire at dusk. She burned until midnight, her fires lighting up the sky.

The commander of Fort Sumter, Major T. M. Wagner, watched the proceedings but did not have the means with which to oppose them. The sunken ships eventually broke up in the swift currents; within a week, very little could be seen of the remains. By mid-February they had entirely disappeared. Evidently, the great weight of their ballast caused them to settle into the soft channel bottom and eventually be swallowed up.

But blockade runners continued to slip in and out of Charleston. Therefore, on January 26, 1862, a second fleet of twenty ships, brigs, and barks were sunk in Maffitt's Channel between the Isle of Palms and Rattlesnake Shoal. For this undertaking, the weather was less than favorable. One ship broke her moorings and was swept out to sea, but was retrieved several days later. One broke loose after her valve had been opened; before she sank, she was swept away to sink offshore in the wrong position.

The operation brought expected criticism from the South and generated much sympathetic sentiment abroad. The Northern press however, extolled the act, saying that a "rat-hole" had been plugged. Such optimism was not to prevail. By May 1862 the Federal Coastal Survey noted that "...twenty-one feet at low water may be carried passing north of the shoal and south of the southern-most wreck." In 1863 the U. S. Engineering Department reported that "...nothing in shape of channel obstruction...could prevent or seriously retard the passage of our fleet up to Charleston...." The coast survey soundings for 1863, which were made in great detail, do not indicate the slightest remains of sunken wrecks in any of the channels. Apparently, the Stone Fleet disappeared long before the end of the war. The stone-filled hulks sank so deep in the mud that they actually deepened the channels that they were intended to block!

Some credit the storm of protest from abroad for influencing the North to cancel plans to sink additional vessels in Southern harbors. Mere practicality shows that as an impediment, the sunken ships were not successful; therefore, further hulks would have only been a waste. However, the operation did provide a stopgap remedy that allowed the Union Navy some time to build additional warships to man the blockade.

Sailors pull away from a sinking whaler.

The Steamer *Planter*

Between the 1861 bombardment of Fort Sumter and the ironclad attack in April 1863, Charleston harbor was much like any port at peace, with blockade runners arriving to discharge cargo, inland steamers carrying goods to and fro, and the ironclads and forts guarding over the process.

One of the inland steamers serving the port was *Planter*, which had been built in 1860 by F. M. Jones and his brother at their yard on Haddrell's Point. *Planter* was a 300-ton, 147-foot sidewheeler. She had one wood-burning boiler driving two engines supplied from Northern machine shops. Her shallow draft and speed made her especially valuable in the shallow waters of the Lowcountry, where she picked up cotton and produce from the outlying plantations and brought it to the docks in Charleston. She could be seen trundling down the Wappoo, her decks piled high with cabbages for the city's markets. She was manned by a black crew under Captain C. J. Relyea.

One of *Planter's* crewmen was Robert Smalls of Beaufort, a slave owned by Henry McKee. The owners of each slave in the crew received a rental payment and each slave also was paid a weekly cash wage. Smalls was not the usual unskilled slave. His initiative and resourcefulness enabled him to work his way up to become a first-class pilot for inland waters. Captain Relyea's hat was the symbol of his authority, and Smalls used that point in his plan to run *Planter* out of the harbor at night to the blockading fleet off the bar in a daring bid for freedom.

Complicating Smalls' plan was the fact that *Planter* also served as dispatch boat for Confederate Brigadier General Roswell S. Ripley, who was in charge of the Confederate forces defending the inner harbor. As such, her berth was at the Southern Wharf (near the present-day Shrine Temple), a well-patrolled area.

By early 1862 Union forces had consolidated their position at Port Royal and began moving up the coast toward Charleston. In January and February they had advanced to the North Edisto River. General Robert E. Lee, the Confederate area commander, decided not to contest the advance and ordered a strategic withdrawal from the coastal areas south of Charleston toward the interior. There Confederate land forces would not have to face the guns of the Union Navy. Working their way up the coastal islands, the Union forces neared Charleston in the spring of 1862. By May they had advanced as far as the Stono River and enemy warships began to test Confederate defenses.

On May 12, 1862, *Planter* was sent to Cole's Island in the lower Stono River to pick up four cannon and transport them to Fort Ripley, the Middle Ground Battery in the harbor between Castle Pinckney and Fort Sumter. Confederate forces were abandoning Cole's Island in anticipation of a major Union assault. *Planter* returned to the city from her mission late in the day, so Relyea tied her up for the night. The officers went ashore, but the crew remained aboard; at 3 a.m. Smalls gave the order to fire up the boiler. Thirty minutes later they cast off and moved out into the harbor in the moonlight. *Planter* moved up the Cooper River and alongside the steamer *Etowah*, on which the wives and children of the crew were waiting. Once all were aboard, the steamer headed for the harbor entrance, and at 4:15 a.m. they passed Fort Sumter. Smalls stood in the pilot house, wearing Relyea's hat. He gave the correct signal with the steamer's whistle to the fort's sentry and proceeded on toward the ocean.

A post-war view of *Planter* bringing cargo to the Charleston docks.

Planter steaming past Fort Sumter as Captain Robert Smalls rings up full speed ahead to make good his escape from Confederate Charleston. This painting by artist Peter Dewitz of Augsburg, Germany, captures the excitement and daring of Smalls' feat. The v-shaped wall in front of the superstructure was to protect the engine spaces from gunfire.

Evidently thinking that *Planter* was carrying supplies to Morris Island or relieving one of the guard ships in the channel, the sentry made no challenge, but noted the passage in the log.

All steam possible was made and a white sheet replaced the Stars and Bars on her flagstaff. Instead of turning right and heading down the Main Ship Channel, Smalls headed straight down the Swash channel so as to be out of range of the guns on Morris and Sullivan's islands. The nearest blockader, USS *Onward*, beat to quarters upon *Planter's* approach and sent over a boarding crew, to which Smalls surrendered his vessel.

Even worse for the Confederates than the loss of *Planter* was the loss of the four large rifled cannon she had on board; they were to be used for the harbor defense.

Smalls was praised by Commodore (later Admiral) DuPont for his deed. He and his crew received their freedom and a share of the prize money; Smalls' share amounted to $1,500. Smalls told DuPont of the evacuation of Cole's Island and DuPont immediately set in motion the forces to land on James Island.

Guarded by a flotilla of gunboats and the powerful steamer *Pawnee*, 10,000 Union troops were landed on James Island near the mouth of the Stono River.[1] The plan was for this army to march across James Island to Fort Johnson following Clinton's 1780 invasion route. Here they could bring up powerful batteries and control Charleston's inner harbor. If

the plan had been successful, incoming supplies from blockade runners would have been cut off, and Charleston rendered useless as a port.

Confederate forces quickly threw up defenses across James Island from the Stono to the summer resort of Secessionville, named for the antisocial habits of its eighteenth-century founders. Fort Lamar stood at the eastern end of the Secessionville defenses, and upon it fell the brunt of the Union assault on June 16. The enemy troops came on the run before dawn and quickly overpowered the outer pickets of the Confederate lines. Once the surprise was over, the Southern troops fought valiantly and threw them back; there were heavy Union losses.

The fighting on James Island quickly became a stalemate, and at the beginning of July, the Northern troops withdrew, leaving only the U. S. Navy to guard the lower Stono River. *Planter* was taken into the service of the Union Army and rendered valuable help in coastal South Carolina's shallow rivers. In 1863 *Planter* was taken to Philadelphia, where her smokestack was moved behind the pilot house for better visibility forward. After the war she was taken to Baltimore, repurchased by her original owner, John Ferguson, and returned to service in South Carolina. On March 25, 1876, during a spring gale, *Planter* went to the assistance of the schooner *Carrie Melvin* in distress off Cape Romain. During the rescue attempt, *Planter* grounded on a bar near Cape Island. Before she could be refloated, the storm's waves tore her to pieces, but her machinery was later salvaged.

After the war Smalls entered politics. He served first in the legislature and then in

[1] To make sure that Smalls' escape was not a trap, the Union warships shelled Ft. Palmetto on Coles Island for two days to make sure that it had been evacuated by Confederate forces.

Almost within sight of Charleston, Union troops brave artillery and rifle fire in frontal assault on Fort Lamar at the battle of Secessionville on June 16, 1862.

Congress, continuing until 1887, some ten years after Reconstruction had ended. He rose to the rank of major general in the state militia and was appointed collector of customs at Beaufort in 1889, serving until 1913. He died in 1915.

Capture of the Gunboat USS *Isaac Smith*

One of the more unusual events that occurred during the Civil War was the capture of a warship by land batteries. This feat was the direct result of the Union evacuation of James Island in July 1862. The U. S. Navy gunboats that were left to guard the lower Stono River became bolder as they sallied upriver, shelling Confederate positions.

One of the most daring of these Union gunboats was the steamer *Isaac Smith*, which often shelled Fort Pemberton with her eight 8-inch guns and one 30-pounder on her bow. Her shallow draft of nine feet made her quite adept in the Stono River.

Naturally the Confederates wished to stop these activities. Their consequent plan was to allow *Isaac Smith* to proceed upriver after guns and sharpshooters had been masked along both sides of the river.

On January 28, 1863, Confederate guns were hauled overland to the banks of the Stono River. Two were placed near abandoned Fort Pickens, and two further upriver at Thomas Grimball's on James Island. Field batteries were brought across John's Island to Paul Grimball's farm and placed on high land just above Abapoola Creek. Here the river swung to the east, and these guns on the outside of the river's bend had a clear upriver and downriver view to the east and south.

Late on the afternoon of January 29, the Confederate artillerymen were routed out with an alarm spread by an officer riding full speed on horseback, Paul Revere style. *Isaac Smith* was almost opposite the John's Island guns, proceeding upriver in broad daylight past the hidden batteries. For some reason *Isaac Smith's* lookouts had failed to see the Confederate guns. Once she anchored she was taken under fire by the battery on Grimball's plantation. She returned a broadside and headed downriver under a hail of gunfire. As she approached the batteries on John's Island, they swung around and opened up at almost point-blank range, as the Confederate sharpshooters in the trees swept her decks with a withering fire. Before she got much further, three shots disabled her engines. Rather than blow up the ship, her captain dropped anchor and ran up a white flag. Twenty-five of her crew of 119 were killed or wounded; only one Confederate was lost.

Once in Charleston, *Isaac Smith* was christened CSS *Stono* and put to use as a guard boat. Her speed made her a suitable blockade runner, but on her first attempt she was stranded on the breakwater at Fort Moultrie. She was safely removed and spent the rest of the war in Charleston harbor, only to be burned upon the city's evacuation.

The USS *Unadilla* anchored in the Stono River below Charleston to support Union army operations on James Island and guard against an attack by Confederate ships. Note the XI″ Dahlgren just forward of the smoke stack. On the bow is a rifled Parrott gun.

Caught in the Confederate crossfire, *Isaac Smith* attempts to reply and flee the scene.

Charleston's Ironclad Squadron

Just as the Mexican War served as a training ground for the officer corps of both sides in the American Civil War, the Crimean War between Russia on one hand and Britain, France, and Turkey on the other from 1854 to 1856 saw the introduction of ironclad naval craft that would revolutionize the war at sea in the American Civil War. These first ironclads were no more sophisticated than the floating battery used in the initial assault on Fort Sumter in 1861, but their impact was not lost upon Confederate naval leaders as they sought a way to neutralize the advantage of the Union Navy.

During the spring and early summer of 1861, the Confederate leadership was concentrating on strengthening the land forces. Not realizing the part that sea power would play in the war, they started the Confederate Navy slowly. Secretary of the Navy Stephen R. Mallory not only had to start a navy from virtually nothing, but also constantly had to justify its importance to the Confederate cabinet. Mallory was convinced from the beginning that his navy could equalize the superior numbers of Union warships only through innovation—the construction and deployment of ironclads.

John Porter, Confederate Naval Constructor at Norfolk, also felt that ironclads were the answer. In 1854 the British and French had successfully used ironclad craft against Russian forts; furthermore, the subsequent launching of the French ironclad *Gloire* in 1859 and Britain's HMS *Warrior* in 1860 had revolutionized naval warfare. These warships were primitive, but powerful prototypes. They resembled wooden sailing frigates with steam engines for auxiliary power and iron on the sides for protection. Porter decided to take their design one step further; he discarded the sails and relied totally on steam engines for propulsion. This was not a new concept; he had suggested a similar casemated harbor defense craft to the Russian Navy fifteen years earlier. Porter's design for the Confederacy included inclined armored sides; thin armor on inclined sides would afford the same protection as thick vertical armor, yet reduce the topweight of the craft, making it more seaworthy.

Construction started on a few large ironclads at Memphis and New Orleans. Experiments on wooden ships began as well; the burned-out hulk of the steam frigate *Merrimack* was moved into drydock at the Gosport Navy Yard in Norfolk to examine its conversion potential. Along with most sailing ships of the United States Navy, *Merrimack* had been burned when Virginia seceded because the Union knew that Gosport was indefensible from land without powerful support, which was unavailable in April 1861. Rather than see the ships fall into Confederate hands, the naval yard commander torched all except the two that he was able to tow away.

Of the major warships burned at Gosport, all except *Merrimack* were obsolete sailing men-of-war. Her primary asset was her steam plant. While somewhat old and in poor condition, it was relatively intact. The South had a dire shortage of steam machinery; therefore, *Merrimack* was a gift horse. Porter saw great potential in rebuilding her as an ironclad.

News of the construction of Southern ironclads spread quickly, and in February 1862 Commodore Duncan N. Ingraham, Confederate naval commander at Charleston, was instructed to negotiate a contract with one of the city's shipyards to build an ironclad. In March 1862 the keel was laid for a small coastal defense ironclad steam ram—the first warship to be constructed at Charleston since the War of 1812. Although it was authorized by the state of South Carolina, the Confederate government eventually paid for it.

Charleston Builds an Ironclad

A few days before the CSS *Virginia's* electrifying triumph at Hampton Roads in March 1862, Miss Susan Lining Gelzer of Charleston wrote a letter to the *Daily Courier* suggesting that the ladies of Charleston emulate the example of the ladies of New Orleans and raise money to construct a gunboat to defend the coast. The ladies of the state subsequently raised some 15 percent of the $200,000 needed to build the first ironclad. She was to have been named *Charleston*, but in deference to the ladies' wishes she was named *Palmetto State*.

Marsh and Sons, who were to become the Confederate Navy's shipwright at Charleston, built *Palmetto State* at their yard at the foot of Market Street (site of the present-day passenger ship terminal). A second ironclad, *Chicora*, was started some six weeks later by the rival Eason Shipyard, located at the foot of Exchange Street. Eason was considered the state of South Carolina's shipwright. *Chicora* was launched on August 23, 1862, and commissioned the following month.

These two warships were built from John Porter's design for the so-called *Richmond* class of Confederate ironclads. They were a smaller version of *Virginia (Merrimack)*, to be used for harbor defense. *Richmond* had been built at Gosport in the spring of 1862 and launched just as McClellan's troops occupied Norfolk at the start of the Peninsula campaign against the Confederate capital at Richmond in May. *Virginia*, famous for being the first ironclad warship used in combat against other warships, had to be blown up to prevent capture, as her draft was too deep to allow her to retreat up the James River. *Richmond*, of shallower draft, was towed up the James River to her namesake city to spend the rest of the war guarding its river approaches. She was one of the first ironclads designed and built by the Confederacy from the keel up solely as an ironclad. *Richmond's* design was a great influence on the subsequent Confederate ironclads.

There was great rivalry between the two Charleston shipyards over which one would turn out better ironclads. Accounts of the period describe the ships as well constructed. Porter himself evidently came to Charleston during their building and commended Eason for following his plans so closely. *Palmetto State's* launching on October 11, 1862, extended into a great social fete in Charleston. Despite threatening rain, every dignitary in the area was present. Miss Gelzer broke the traditional champagne bottle on the ship's prow as *Palmetto State* slid into Charleston harbor. *Chicora*, now completed, came up the harbor with colors flying fore and aft to salute her consort. As *Chicora* approached the newly launched *Palmetto State*, "the assembled multitude broke forth in loud and prolonged cheers for *Chicora* and her energetic builder."

Completion of the ships was delayed while builders awaited delivery of the armor from the rolling mills. In the iron-hungry South, armor came from railroad track that had to be taken up and sent to the Tredegar Foundry in Richmond or the Atlanta Rolling Mill to be rolled into twenty-foot lengths, approximately seven inches wide and two inches thick. The finished armor was then sent to the shipyards, where it was spiked or bolted onto the wooden casemates. The armor rails were laid first horizontally and then vertically, giving the iron-clads four inches of protection. The decks and the area to five feet below the waterline had one layer.

For some reason *Palmetto State* differed from her sisters in that she had an octagonal casemate and her pilot house was placed abaft the stack. This was probably to enable the pilot to relay commands directly to the engine room below.

New engines for the ships were unavailable, so secondhand machinery from small steamers was installed. These weak engines could move the heavy ironclads at a top speed of only about five knots, which was barely enough to make headway against an ebb tide. In one account, *Chicora* was unable to maintain station off Fort Sumter and was compelled to drop anchor to avoid being swept out to sea. Even with the engines helping, anchors still dragged in the ebb tide. The underpowered engines also contributed to the ships' poor steering, as enough headway could not be made to allow the rudders to be very effective.

Within the ships' armored casemates were mounted four guns—rifled 6.4″ Brookes fore and aft and two VIII″ Dahlgren smoothbores, one on each broadside. The fore and aft guns could also be pivoted on slides to fire through gunports on either broadside as necessary. A full salvo of three guns could be delivered against an opponent; however, like a sailing warship, the entire vessel had to be maneuvered to aim such firepower. Once three guns had been brought to bear on one side, it would take several minutes to shift the fore and aft guns to the other side if needed. These guns were sometimes landed to augment shore batteries, so the exact armament of each vessel was changed from time to time.

Like the blockade runners, the ironclads were painted a pale blue-grey or "blockader's blue." This color was found to make the vessels less noticeable in the vast expanse of Charleston harbor. However, paint was in such short supply in the South that they quickly became a rust brown.

The ships were well officered and manned, with a higher-than-normal proportion of professional seamen among the 120 to 150 men on board. Some came from the recently destroyed ironclad *Arkansas*, which had fought Farragut's fleet as it pushed up the Mississippi from New Orleans. In his book *Iron Afloat* (University of South Carolina Press, 1985), William Still terms the Charleston Ironclad Squadron "probably the most efficient in Confederate naval service." The ships were among the cleanest in the Southern navy, something in which their crews took pride. If the naval phrase, "a clean ship is a good ship" has any merit, these must truly have been among the best in the Confederate service.

Command of *Palmetto State* went to Lt. Commander John Rutledge, direct descendant of the state's Revolutionary leader. *Chicora's* command was won by the dashing Virginian Lt. Commander John R. Tucker, a veteran of thirty-five years of service. He became commodore of the squadron in March 1863 when Ingraham stepped down. The sailors called him "handsome Jack" and considered him one of the most capable and energetic officers in the service.

By mid-October 1862 the new ships were completed. Having returned from the Western front to reassume command of Confederate forces in South Carolina, General Beauregard, who had a keen appreciation of sea power, was eager and ready to employ the new ironclads.

Author's model of the Confederate ironclad steam ram *Chicora*. Note the spar torpedo at the bow and yardarm for signal flags on the stack. The *Richmond* class ironclads were among the first warships to depend entirely upon steam for propulsion, to employ blisters on the sides at the waterline to defend against torpedoes, and to mount the conning position high in the forward part of the ship protected by armor. These three features would influence warship design into the nuclear age.

The crews worked up the ships and exercised the guns; by January 1863 their morale was at its peak and they were ready for battle.

Commodore Ingraham

Palmetto State bore the flag of sixty-year-old Commodore Duncan L. Ingraham, son of one of John Paul Jones' officers on *Bon Homme Richard*. A native Charlestonian, he commanded the naval forces at Charleston. Ingraham had entered the U. S. Navy as a midshipman in the War of 1812, and had served on the frigate *Congress* and then on the Great Lakes. Ingraham went on to command the brig *Somers* during the Mexican War.

Ingraham was the hero of the Koszta affair. A Hungarian emigré, Martin Koszta had been a follower of Louis Kossuth in the ill-fated Hungarian revolution of 1848. He then fled to America, and in 1850 began proceedings to become an American citizen. In Smyrna, Turkey, on June 21, 1853, he was seized by a boat's crew from the Austrian brig *Huzzar* because he had made insulting remarks about the emperor while in America. Captain Ingraham, who was present in the 20-gun sloop-of-war *St. Louis*, demanded Koszta's release and prepared to attack *Huzzar*. Koszta was then surrendered and returned to America. Congress awarded Ingraham a gold medal for his prompt and decisive action. The Koszta incident is a

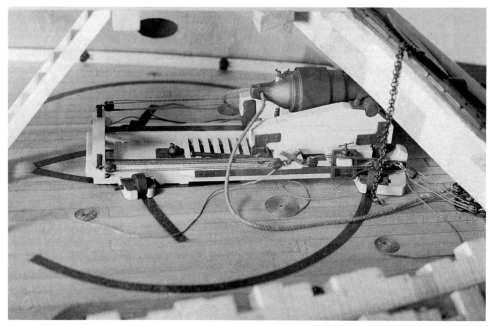

Forward pivot gun on a *Richmond* class Confederate ironclad. Note the iron rails on the wooden deck. The gun's slide rolled on the iron tracks laid on the wooden deck. Upon firing, the gun and its carriage recoiled on the slide. The gun was then reloaded before being rolled forward to the firing position.

Detail of the casemate of *Chicora*. Note the pilot house and steering wheel below it.

CSS *Chicora* at dockside shortly after completion. This is the best and one of the few known photographs of a Confederate ironclad while still flying Confederate colors.

good example of what John Paul Jones meant when he said that a naval officer must be more than a good and capable mariner. A ship commander far from home in the days of sail had to be able to exercise quick and decisive judgment, for he could not expect instructions from superiors when confronted with fast-moving, unusual situations.

At the start of the Civil War Ingraham resigned his commission in the U. S. Navy and returned home to command Confederate naval forces in Charleston. He supervised construction of the ironclads.

Sortie

Ingraham knew the limitations of his ships—slow speed, unseaworthiness resulting from top-heavy weight, and restricted arcs of fire for the guns. Therefore, it took a little prodding from General Beauregard to convince him that action was the best course. Bad weather persisted throughout January, and he postponed action; rough waves outside the harbor could have easily caused his ships to founder. By the end of January the weather improved, and on January 28, an unsigned letter in the Charleston *Courier* questioning Ingraham's lack of action prodded him to move. Time was running out for the Confederate ships. The new federal ironclads were already arriving at Port Royal. For days rumors had swept the Charleston waterfront of an impending attack on the blockading fleet. These rumors were fed by the ships' crews openly slushing down the exterior of the casemates with dark grease, a hopeful attempt to deflect enemy shot.

Commodore Duncan Nathaniel Ingraham at the time of the Koszta incident.

At about 10:00 p.m. on January 30, 1863, Commodore Ingraham came on board his flagship, and an hour and a half later *Chicora* and *Palmetto State* got underway. The commodore, captain, and two pilots manned the pilothouse. It was a calm and bright moonlit night and the ships, burning soft coal, left a huge black trail behind. The ships proceeded slowly so as to arrive off the bar at 4:00 a.m. for the high tide. Several unarmed steamers with about fifty soldiers followed to man any prizes, but they did not cross the bar.

Scattering the Blockading Fleet

The crews of the ironclads went to their action stations after passing Fort Sumter. The gunports were tightly shut so that no light would be emitted. On the inside the battle lanterns cast a pale, weird light on the gun deck. As the ironclads approached the bar they saw the steamer *Mercedita* a short distance outside and steered straight for her. She had been a thorn in the side of the blockade-running business. Nine months earlier *Mercedita* had captured *Bermuda*, the first real blockade runner to enter the Confederacy.

Mercedita had just returned to her anchor after a wild goose chase earlier in the evening and did not see the onrushing *Palmetto State* until too late. Captain Stellwagen hollered, "What ship is that?" His answer was the sound of a falling gunport shutter and a thundering roar from the ram's forward gun. At the same instant *Mercedita* was struck by the ironclad's prow on her starboard quarter, heeling her over to port.

The shell penetrated the starboard side and went through the port boiler's condenser and steam drum. It exploded against the port side and blew a hole four or five feet square. *Mercedita* was unable to get off a shot in return. As the forward part of the ship filled with steam, Stellwagen struck his colors. Captain Rutledge of *Palmetto State* directed him to send a boat alongside. When the boat was lowered, it immediately began to sink because the half-awake crew had failed to put a plug in the bottom. That was quickly rectified and her executive officer was led to Commodore Ingraham, who accepted a verbal parole for the surrender of the ship and crew. Captain Stellwagen honored his word and with due formality he and his crew were routinely exchanged in April.

In the meantime Captain Tucker had taken *Chicora* past her consort to starboard and engaged in a gunnery duel with two other blockaders, *Quaker City* and the paddle steamer *Keystone State*. *Quaker City* took a shell in her engine room. Having heard *Palmetto State's* shot at *Mercedita*, Captain LeRoy of *Keystone State* ordered his crew to action stations. When *Chicora* loomed up out of the mist, LeRoy opened fire. Tucker, meanwhile, was advised by his pilot not to ram *Keystone State*, as *Chicora* might not have sufficient power to pull clear of the sinking ship. Instead, he engaged in a gunnery duel and got off three telling shots from his port broadside. *Keystone State* turned seaward, quickly came up to twelve knots, and left her antagonist behind. As the distance opened and the gathering light improved visibility, *Keystone State* turned back to attack. Turning the tables, she tried to ram *Chicora*. The range rapidly closed as both sides exchanged fire. A shot from *Chicora* passed through both steam drums in *Keystone State's* engine rooms, scalding and killing several men. Additional shells crashed into her hull and exploded on her deck, and steam escaping from below added to her crew's confusion. Water poured into her bilges from two holes below the waterline and caused her to heel to starboard.

As *Keystone State* slowed and turned to escape, *Chicora* took up a raking position several hundred yards astern. Before additional shells could be pumped into her, Captain

CONFEDERATE NAVAL TRIUMPH

Breaking the Blockade at Charleston

CSS *Palmetto State* rams the USS *Mercedita* on January 31, 1863 while her sistership, *Chicora*, engages *Keystone State*.

LeRoy hauled down his flag. However, his chief engineer reported that the engines would work for a few more minutes on their vacuum, and, before Lieutenant Bier from *Chicora* could lower a boat to take possession, the blockader got up steam and slowly moved away. *Chicora* hesitated before resuming fire on a ship that supposedly had surrendered. As the gap widened, Captain Leroy rehoisted his colors, resumed fire with his rifled gun, and escaped. The steamer *Memphis* towed him to Port Royal. Thus the Confederates were cheated

Mercedita **strikes to** *Palmetto State*.

of their second prize. Forty-seven were killed and wounded on *Mercedita* and *Keystone State*, while the Confederates had no casualties.

Daylight dissipated the ironclads' opportunity for surprise, and the blockading ships maneuvered to keep away from them. The blockaders fled southward, and the ironclads turned to the east and north in search of new prey. A few shots were exchanged at long range with *Housatonic*, *Quaker City*, and *Augusta* before they withdrew. Other ships were engaged at long range, but they all made off to the south at high speed and the slow rams were unable to pursue. By mid-morning the horizon was clear and the two ironclads anchored off Maffit's Channel under Confederate land batteries to wait seven hours for the next high tide to carry them over the bar.

During the day, the French and Spanish consuls were brought out to see that the blockade had been broken; the British consul went out aboard HMS *Petrel*, which was then at anchor in the harbor. Under international law a thirty-day grace period had to follow before a broken blockade could be reestablished. If such a grace period had been allowed at Charleston, vast quantities of material would have flooded into the Confederacy overnight. While the consuls saw no blockaders in sight, the Lincoln administration adamantly refused to acknowledge that their blockade had been broken. No foreign government contested their position.

The undamaged blockaders remained hull down on the horizon to watch and await developments at a safe distance. A haze allowed them to creep in slowly and retake their blockading positions later in the day. As the ironclads came into port that afternoon they were saluted by the forts in the harbor, and throngs of people came to the wharves to cheer them as they docked. The following Tuesday the people of Charleston publicly celebrated the victory with a ceremony at St. Philip's Church.

After the sortie of January 31, 1863, "ram fever" swept the officers and crews of the blockading ships off Charleston. They overestimated the Charleston ironclads, and thus were reluctant to challenge them. They also demanded more Federal ironclads as support.

The Counterforce Arrives

A few days after this sortie the new Union ironclad frigate *New Ironsides* joined the blockade off Charleston. She was similar to the French *Gloire* and HMS *Warrior* and was the most powerful warship in the Union Navy. Soon the new monitors joined her. The new Federal ships were marvels of steam machinery. The Confederate ironclads had no hope of successfully challenging them because they were covered with eight-inch armor. Furthermore, shot from the monitors' eleven- and fifteen-inch guns would have easily penetrated the Confederates' defensive shields. The turrets could swing in 360-degree arcs of fire, while the casemates of the Confederate ships were seriously limited in their arcs of fire.

The Charleston ironclads were relegated to the inner defenses of the harbor. They took their stations off Fort Johnson in order to be in position to attack any enemy ships that might make it past the guns and obstructions between Forts Moultrie and Sumter. Each night at least one of them would anchor in the channel between these forts to discourage any nighttime venture toward the city by the Union Navy. Before long a monitor would anchor opposite them to guard against any seaward venture by the Confederates.

In the spring of 1863, after *Palmetto State*'s weak engines had prevented her from successfully ramming and sinking *Mercedita*, the Confederate ironclads were fitted with spar torpedoes. These torpedoes consisted of egg-shaped or cylindrical copper vessels containing

from sixty to seventy pounds of explosives fitted onto twenty-foot spars attached to the bow. A hinge on the bow would lower the spar beneath the water and, when contact was made with an enemy ship's hull, the torpedo would explode with deadly effect.

By summer it became apparent that one of the main defects of the Confederate ironclads was habitability. The enclosed structure with its iron skin had few openings for natural air flow except through open gunports and hatches in the spar deck (the deck on top of the casemate). These openings allowed very little air to circulate below decks, and made the engine rooms a veritable incinerator in summer. Cowl and canvas vents were deployed, but they helped very little. Regular duty on these ships became both uncomfortable and boring, although sea duty was probably far more desirable than service on land in the Confederate army.

On August 30, 1863, *Chicora* and *Palmetto State* rescued more than 600 Confederate soldiers from a sinking transport that had been fired into by mistake and sunk by the guns of Fort Moultrie. That fall *Chicora* alone backed up the repulse of the enemy boat attack on Fort Sumter; although the ironclads were unable to engage the enemy's front-line warships, they remained a threat to anything of lesser fighting ability. By 1864 the boilers and engines of *Chicora* were all but useless. As a consequence she became little more than a floating battery in the harbor, but her crew occasionally provided valuable service on the torpedoboats and the naval units ashore.

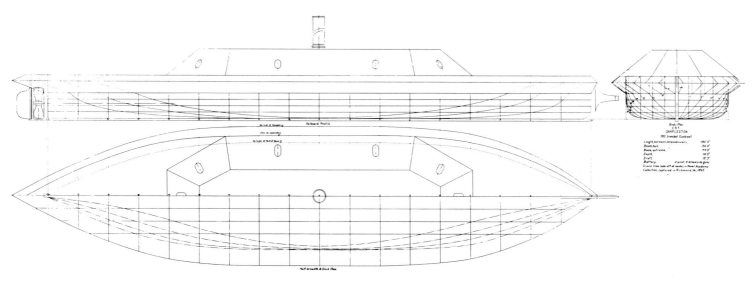

Plan of the ironclad *Charleston*, completed in 1863.

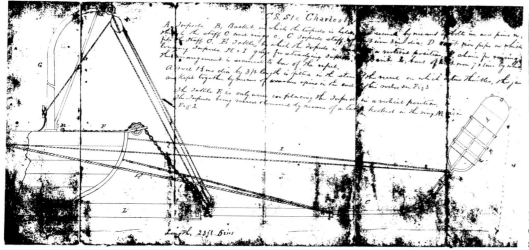

Profile and perspective of the spar torpedo arrangement on CSS *Charleston*. The torpedo cylinder was placed in the basket arrangement at the end of the spar. Note the hinge (K) on the ship's stem, which allowed the spar to be raised and lowered.

Conrad Wise Chapman's Panorama of Charleston harbor as seen from Fort Johnson, probably in the summer of 1864, with the ironclads *Chicora* and *Charleston* at anchor. Note how their haze grey paint has rusted to an unsightly brown. In the left background is Battery Ramsay on White Point in the city; at right is Castle Pinckney. It is amazing how little the city's skyline has changed in the intervening 123 years.

Subsequent Charleston Ironclads

The ironclad *Charleston* joined the squadron early in 1864 as flagship. She was a slightly larger version of *Palmetto State* with an octagonal casemate and an extra gun on each broadside. *Charleston* was built by James M. Eason for the state of South Carolina. Her keel was laid in December 1862 and she was launched a year later, at which time she was turned over to the Confederate States Navy. Some 180' long, *Charleston* carried four Brooke rifles on her broadside and two IX″ smoothbores on pivots fore and aft. In 1864 her captain rigged a type of barrel contact mine that was to be rolled off the stern, but this was never used.

Charleston had a marine detachment and her only real action came in 1864 when she thwarted an enemy boat assault on Fort Johnson from Morris Island. *Charleston* placed herself at the head of Vincent's Creek as the three Union regiments were moving out. She greeted them with double-shotted main battery guns and rifle fire from her marines on the spar deck. In quick order the enemy was soundly repulsed.

A fourth Charleston ironclad, *Columbia*,[1] was built by F. M. Jones, launched on March 10, 1864, and completed late that year. Her machinery was supplied from the machine works at Columbus, Georgia. Engineers from the Georgia facility came to Charleston to supervise the installation. *Columbia* was the largest ironclad built and commissioned in the Confederacy. She was similar but slightly larger than the Confederate ironclad *Tennessee* of Mobile Bay fame, with pivot guns on each quarter and one gun on each broadside. Six-inch armor made her the only ship in the Charleston Squadron that could hope to stand up to the enemy ironclads. Her marine detachment was recruited in Columbia and Raleigh.

Unfortunately *Columbia* struck a sunken wreck off Fort Moultrie shortly after being commissioned. She could not be freed before the city was evacuated, but was stripped of her guns and some armor. The Union Navy refloated *Columbia* in March 1865, and as she was not seriously damaged, she steamed out of the harbor to Norfolk on her own power. Arriving on May 25, *Columbia* was taken into drydock for repairs, but was decommissioned on June 15 and sold for scrapping on October 10, 1867. Some Charleston accounts refer to her as *Ashley*.

Accounts indicate that two other ironclads were under construction in Charleston at the end of the war. These were to be units of the *Milledgeville* class, an enlarged version of the *Richmond* class with four guns (one on each quarter). One was launched in October 1864 at James Marsh's shipyard, but the other never got off the stocks at Kirkwood & Knox's shipyard at North Dry Dock Wharf. Their completion was probably delayed because of a shortage of armor, guns, or machinery. Had they been completed and joined the ironclad squadron, the outcome of the action at Charleston would not have been altered.

At Christmas 1864, U. S. General William T. Sherman ended his march across Georgia from Atlanta to Savannah. The Confederate naval forces at Savannah covered the retreat of their army into South Carolina and set fire to their ships. The personnel then walked to Hardeeville, S. C., caught the train to Charleston, and joined the ironclad squadron. Their respite was brief; on February 1, 1865, Sherman turned his army north into South Carolina.

It was assumed that Sherman would head for Charleston, but instead he turned inland for Columbia. Confederate authorities decided to withdraw military personnel from Charleston and send them inland to reinforce the army in front of Sherman's advance. President Davis urged Commodore Tucker to make one last foray against the enemy, but Tucker wisely refused a last effusion of blood. As Confederate forces withdrew from Charleston on the night of February 17, 1865, naval personnel set fire to the shipyards. The next morning the ironclads were burned one by one. At about 9:00 a.m. *Palmetto State* blew up on the Cooper River waterfront near the foot of Calhoun Street. It sent a concussion over the entire city. A cloud of smoke lingered briefly over her grave and then dispersed. *Chicora* followed shortly afterward. *Charleston* held out until 11:00. Her explosion lifted the casemate out of the hull, and showers of hot metal set the docks afire. The city fire department saved the nearby gas works and the wharves. After the war the wreckage of these ironclads was destroyed or broken up.

While the Charleston ironclad squadron did not attain an outstanding war record, it did achieve the classical status of a "fleet in being." In other words, its potential threat tied down a counterforce of enemy front-line warships that the Union could have employed elsewhere. Union Admiral David G. Farragut had been prepared to move against Mobile in 1863. He was delayed because the ironclads he planned to use were tied down at Charleston. If the Union ships had been removed to Mobile, the Confederate ironclads would have become at once the dominant naval force at Charleston. The Union Navy could not allow this; therefore, Mobile received an additional year of use as a blockade-running port.

The threat posed by Charleston's ironclads also indirectly brought triumph to the Confederate ironclad *Albemarle*, which was built in a cornfield on the Roanoke River near North Carolina's Albemarle Sound. *Albemarle* caught the Union Navy by surprise in April 1864, and they could spare no monitors from the Charleston blockade to counter her. In two sorties against the blockading fleet, *Albemarle* sank one warship, damaged several others, and caused consternation far beyond her meager capabilities. She was finally brought down by a spar torpedo attached to a steam launch, a forerunner of the PT boats of World War II.

The other Confederate seaports possessed ironclad squadrons of varying size. Charleston had built and commissioned the largest number of ironclads in the South. Only the James River Squadron, which defended the capital, came close to equaling it; for daring, initiative, and professionalism, however, the James River Squadron remained second.

While Charleston's ironclad squadron cannot claim to have prevented the capture of the city by the Union Navy, its presence helped to deter a concentrated naval attack such as those that resulted in the captures of Mobile, New Orleans, and Fort Fisher at Wilmington. Because of the multitude of weapons in the Charleston arsenal—primarily the ironclads with their threat of a second sortie—the main body of the Union Navy was forced to remain as a counterforce off the bar for two years after the spring of 1863. At the time, this counterforce was considered the most powerful fleet in the world. Had Charleston fallen to assault, it would have quickly moved on to roll up the other Confederate seaports and bring a speedy end to the war. Therefore, Charleston, with its many and varied defenses, stymied the Union Navy with its almost unbroken string of naval victories during the war.

---

[1] Not one photograph or contemporary illustration of this ironclad has been found. Some of *Columbia's* guns may be seen today at the Washington Navy Yard.

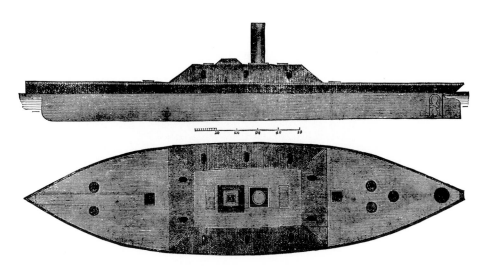

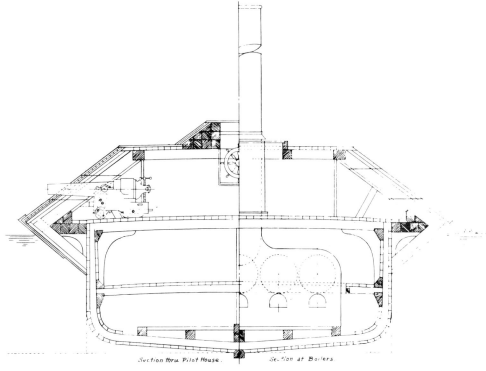

Above: Plan and Elevation of the Confederate ironclad ram *Columbia*.

Right: Transverse section of the CSS *Columbia* at the midship point. Note the incline of the casemate to deflect enemy shot, the thickness of its wood backing, the shallow deadrise (flat bottom) to give her more freedom in shallow water, the blister on the waterline to protect against torpedoes, and the arrangement of the pilot house and boiler.

Section thru. Pilot House.   Section at Boilers

C.S.S. COLUMBIA .Built at Charleston, S.C.

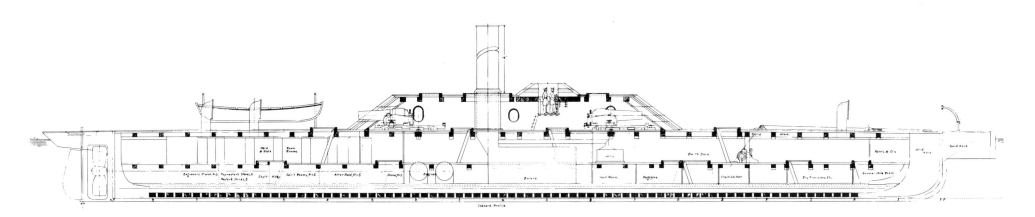

Inboard Profile.

Inboard profile of the ironclad *Columbia*, completed in Charleston in 1864. She was the most powerful ironclad built in the Confederate States of America for the CSN. Of special interest is the holdover from sailing ship days of berthing the crew forward and the officers aft. At first glance the Confederate casemate ironclads would appear to be more seaworthy than their Union counterparts, the monitors. Upon closer inspection, it can be seen that they had the same (if not less) freeboard and their heavy armored casemates rendered them top-heavy and thus vulnerable to capsizing in rough water.

The Confederate ironclad *Columbia* patrolling off Fort Sumter late in 1864 with *Chicora* astern.

By the spring of 1863 the Union and the Confederacy were on a full war footing and flexing their muscles for the summer campaigns that would decide the course of the war. Charleston, the symbol of the Confederacy, was a significant target. Her capture or neutralization would render a psychological blow to the Southern cause, since she was both the "Cradle of Secession" and the most important port available in the Confederacy for blockade runners.

First Offensive Use of the New Union Ironclads

Lincoln and his cabinet were fully aware of the importance of a victory at Charleston. Ironclads became front-line warships after their first naval battle at Hampton Roads in 1862. As a result the Union Navy began immediate construction of an ironclad squadron, and the seizure of Charleston was to be their first mission.

The Union ironclad *Monitor* became the prototypical ironclad for the Union Navy because of her success at Hampton Roads against the Confederate *Virginia*. As with most new vessels, *Monitor* had inherent design problems. These defects were ironed out of subsequent monitor types. Their turret armor was increased to eleven inches; the pilot house was moved to a better position atop the turret; and their armament was increased to the heavier XV″ Dahlgrens (throwing a 440-pound projectile), supplemented by an XI″ Dahlgren. Instead of an XI″ Dahlgren, the monitor *Patapsco* had an VIII″ Parrott rifle (throwing a 155-pound shell).

Opposing them, the largest guns of the Charleston forts were X″ Columbiads (throwing 128-pound projectiles) and VII″ Brooke rifles (throwing 100- to 133-pound shells). The

Southern artillery was too small to pierce the opposing ships' main armor. The North assumed it would be a simple operation to run into the harbor, pound the forts to rubble while the ships' crews remained safe inside their iron boxes, and accept the surrender of Charleston when the Confederates had had enough.

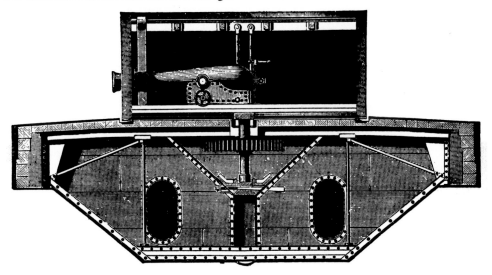

Transverse section of the original *Monitor* based on a plan that her designer, John Ericsson, had offered unsuccessfully to Napoleon III in 1854 to help France defeat Russia in the Crimean War.

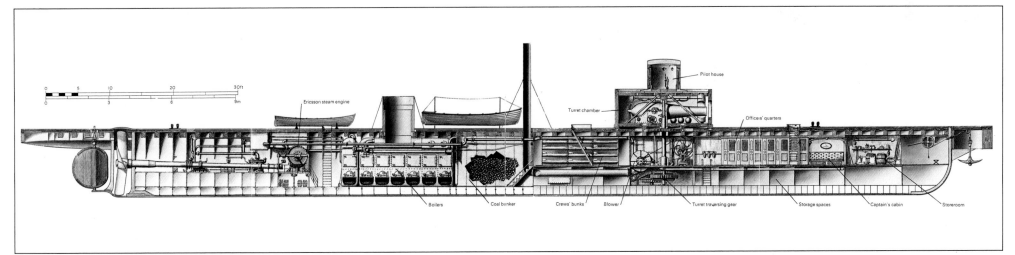

Longitudinal section of a monitor of the *Tippecanoe*, class showing the combination wood and iron construction. *Passaic* class monitors, which bore the brunt of the Charleston blockade, were similar. The main differences were that the crews' quarters on the *Passaics* were forward of the **turret and the turret consequently further aft. The low silhouette gave enemy gunners one target, the well-armored turret. The low freeboard would plague her sisters in heavy weather off Charleston. The simple design allowed for fast construction time.**

For the Charleston campaign the Union ironclad squadron assembled at Port Royal. The original *Monitor* was to lead the force, but en route to Charleston she was lost in a storm off Cape Hatteras. In February the new ironclad frigate *New Ironsides* joined the Charleston blockade. She was designed and completed with masts, spars, and sails, but these were quickly discarded; her sole means of propulsion was her steam engine and single propeller. Her wooden sides were protected by 4.5″ rolled iron plate. Her armament included seven XI″ smoothbores on each broadside, and two VIII″ or 200-pounder rifles on pivots fore and aft. She displaced 3,500 tons, a sizeable ship for the day considering her 16-foot draft, which would barely allow her to cross the bar at low tide. As the spring of 1863 approached, the squadron increased in number. When the new monitors joined the South Atlantic Blockading Squadron, it became the world's most powerful naval force afloat.

To lead this force the Union Navy rewarded Commodore DuPont for his success in seizing Port Royal in 1861 by promoting him to rear admiral. Being an astute judge of leaders, he chose some of the best Union ship commanders for his ships.

By late March, DuPont assembled his force of nine ironclads in the estuary of the North Edisto River, scene of so many earlier maritime threats to Charleston. The fleet included seven monitors, *New Ironsides*, and the double-turreted ironclad *Keokuk*. All of them carried the most powerful naval guns available—a total of twenty-two XI″ Dahlgren smoothbores, seven XV″ Dahlgren smoothbores, and three 8″ Parrott rifled guns.

Charleston Braces Itself

On the other side, the South considered the looming battle a symbol of Southern independence and freedom, a modern David and Goliath confrontation. Throughout 1862 and early 1863 the harbor defenses were being strengthened; by April 1863 no other city in the Confederacy had better defenses. Beauregard was not about to allow himself to be boxed in on the peninsula as General Lincoln had in 1780. Instead, he intended to meet the enemy well away from the city in order to spare it needless destruction, to surrender any land so long as the port was kept open for blockade runners. Within a ten-mile radius of Charleston there were approximately sixty batteries, but troops were sufficient to man only those on the actual front lines. As a result, it was largely up to Charlestonians to defend themselves.

While the forts in the harbor had seventy-six pieces of artillery, they were not of sufficient strength to cause appreciable damage to the monitors' armor. In addition, the turrets on the monitors presented too small a target for anything but point-blank range. But if the Union ironclads were able to steam past the harbor forts, they would be met on the inside by a ring of fire from batteries on the city waterfront, James Island, Castle Pinckney, and Fort Ripley built on a nearby sandbar. If they ran this gauntlet and landed, the city was to be defended street by street.

Both sides seemed pessimistic as the day of reckoning approached: DuPont because of the four unsuccessful trials his monitors had with Fort McAlister on the Ogeechee River in Georgia during the first three months of the year; the Confederates for their relatively weak ordnance.

No battle since the first one of the war had captured the Northern public's imagination as the one pending at Charleston. With baited breath they followed press reports of the gathering battle, much as they would a crusade; if Charleston fell, the end of the war would be in sight—or so they thought. President Lincoln and Secretary of the Navy Gideon Welles had to press DuPont for action. He had no definite plan of attack, nor had he bothered to gather much intelligence to enable him to carry one out. General Beauregard, meanwhile, spurred

Interior of the turret of the monitor *Passaic*.

Interior of the turret of the monitor *Montauk*.

Confederate defenses by building new batteries and sowing the channel with torpedoes.[1] He also developed other elaborate new obstructions, including the placement of buoys in the channel so that the gunners at Fort Sumter, Morris Island, and Fort Moultrie would always know the exact range to the attacking ships. The strong currents in the channel between Forts Sumter and Moultrie, however, carried away torpedoes planted there. The defenders subsequently placed a crude rope barrier supported by empty barrels in the channel. The sight of a rope and barrel barrier caused DuPont much trepidation; flimsy though it actually was, it appeared formidable.

[1] These torpedoes were stationary and thus more like modern mines.

DuPont's squadron underway for Charleston. In the left foreground is *Passaic*, pitching in the moderate sea. In the right background are *Keokuk*, *New Ironsides*, and *Nantucket*.

The Ironclads Assemble

On April 5, 1863, the squadron and its supporting ships began to assemble off Charleston's bar in clear view of the forts. Drawing less water than any of the other ironclads, *Keokuk* was sent ahead to find the channel and replace the buoys. Proceeding up the Main Ship Channel, *Keokuk* found an easy and unobstructed entrance with eighteen feet of water in the shallowest places. She replaced the buoys without opposition. The next day, the rest of the warships crossed; however, hazy weather forced them to rest at anchor off Morris Island before proceeding further. That night a blockade runner slipped past the anchored ships, mistaking them for Confederate ironclads! Even the main battle force of the United States Navy was unable to cork the flow of blockade runners into Charleston.

Tuesday, April 7 broke clear and mild. All was made ready for action on board the ironclads and in the forts. DuPont's plan was to pass the outer batteries and move around Fort Sumter. He would take up positions on the fort's north and west sides within the inner harbor and either force it to surrender or reduce it to rubble. After the surrender, the fleet was to attack Morris Island, supported by five wooden gunboats: *Canandaigua, Housatonic, Unadilla, Wissahickon,* and *Huron* held in reserve outside the bar.

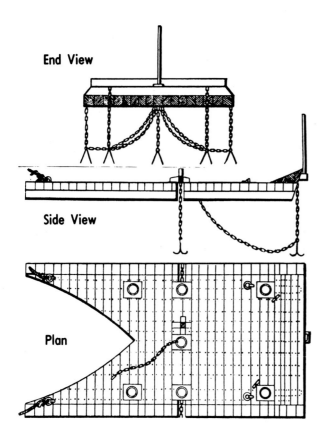

End View

Side View

Plan

Weehawken's minesweeping "devil," also called "the alligator."

The ironclads advanced in line ahead as follows:

First Division

Weehawken	2 guns	Captain John Rodgers
Passaic	2 guns	Captain Percival Drayton
Montauk	2 guns	Captain John L. Worden
Patapsco	2 guns	Captain Daniel Ammen

Flagship

New Ironsides	16 guns	Captain T. Turner

Second Division

Catskill	2 guns	Commander G. W. Rodgers
Nantucket	2 guns	Commander D. McN. Fairfax
Nahant	2 guns	Commander John Downes
Keokuk	2 guns	Commander A. C. Rhind

Captain John Rodgers was selected to lead the column in the new monitor *Weehawken*. He was a perfect choice, daring and resourceful but hindered by Admiral DuPont's lack of resolve. Worden, commanding *Montauk*, had commanded *Monitor* in the battle with *Virginia* at Hampton Roads thirteen months earlier. Percival Drayton in *Passaic* was from one of South Carolina's leading families, but had chosen to remain with the Union. The names of all of these ship captains would go on U. S. Navy destroyers in the twentieth century.

The squadron decided to wait until after high tide at 10:20 so that the ebb tide could aid steering and keep any disabled vessel from drifting into the harbor. At 12:15 the signal to advance was finally given, but was delayed when *Weehawken's* anchor became fouled in the torpedo-protection raft ("alligator") at her bow. Once the problem was resolved, the fleet began the advance against the ebbing tide at 1:45.

The Advance to Battle

By 2:30 the garrison of Fort Sumter had completed the midday meal, and the long drum roll for action stations began. Morale was high and the men, in dress parade uniforms, responded quickly but their cheers were supressed by good discipline. From the ramparts of Sumter flew the Confederate garrison flag at the northern salient, the flag of the state of South Carolina at the southwest salient, and the regimental flag at the southeast salient. The fort's commander, Colonel Alfred Rhett, ordered a salute of thirteen guns—one for each state in the Confederacy. On the ramparts within earshot of the enemy, the regimental band played "Dixie."

The ironclads moved over a glassy sea with a slight swell. As they passed Battery Wagner, a hush seemed to fall as each side withheld fire. On both sides sightseers—correspondents on the blockading ships outside the bar and citizens on Charleston's Battery, the city's rooftops, and windows that commanded a view—hung in suspense. Just inside the rope

Opposite: **The height of the battle, with the Union ironclads pressing their attack on Fort Sumter. In the foreground is the flagship *New Ironsides*, which remained distant from most of the action. The distance in this illustration has been radically compressed in order to show the details of the fort and the ships involved.**

Tom Freeman
© 1986

obstructions in the channel the Confederate ironclads paced their beat to attack any enemy vessels that made it past the forts.

As *Weehawken* came abreast of Sumter at 2:50, a shot from Fort Moultrie broke the calm. It fell short because the ships were still beyond range, but *Passaic* answered and *Weehawken* opened up on Sumter as she passed a buoy in the turn of the channel 1,120 yards distant. Already aimed at this point, the upper guns of the fort opened up by battery. They were followed by those of the other forts, and the gunners cheered between salvos. Because of the extreme range these initial shots caused little damage.

The battle, showing the correct distances involved. Fort Sumter is in the center background, Fort Moultrie at right, and Fort Johnson at left. Note the tugboat in the foreground standing by to assist any disabled warships.

Union Disarray

The First Division of the Union squadron was in disarray. At the middle of the column, *New Ironsides* seemed to hesitate as to which way to proceed. This caused confusion in the entire battle line, and *Catskill* and *Nantucket* had minor collisions with the flagship. Those aboard the flagship thought that she was standing into shoal water. As *New Ironsides* drifted away from the fort, she passed over the boiler torpedo the Confederates had sunk. However, the firing mechanism failed. The flagship finally signaled the others to disregard her movements. DuPont seemed unable to control the forces he had set in motion; he relied upon Rodgers to lead the way, and in the smoke and confusion, the flagship was unable to signal an advance effectively. *Weehawken* also hesitated before proceeding into the harbor, fearing the line of barrels in the channel. The Second Division became similarly confused.

Confederate Order

Within the fort the garrison served their guns with perfect order, using the range markers set in the channel as guides when firing at the ships. *Weehawken's* first shot passed over; a second sprayed the barbette nearby with brick fragments; and a third exploded near the water's edge, sending a cascade of spray over the top of the fort.

Another shell pierced the walls and set bedding on fire, but the flames were quickly controlled. Shortly afterward a mine exploded near *Weehawken*, throwing up a column of water and lifting her slightly. As the lead ship, she received the concentrated fire of the forts for the first part of the action. Captain Worden stated in his report that "the accuracy of the shooting on the part of the rebels was very great." Indeed it was, as of the over 2,000 shots fired by the forts, almost 25 percent found their mark—excellent shooting, considering such small targets.

At first, the firing of the fort's forty guns was fast paced; the simultaneous hit of several

DuPont's Second Division advances to the attack on Fort Sumter at 3:30. The flagship *New Iron-sides* drifts aimlessly, while the monitors *Catskill* and *Nantucket* push ahead. This scene from the London *Illustrated News* of May 9, 1863 clearly reflects a British interpretation of the repulse of the Union Navy. The Royal Navy was quite interested in developments and deployment of new naval technology during the war. Note the small targets that the monitors presented, a clear advantage in combat.

relatively small shots on the monitors made up for the lack of heavy guns. Early hits on each ironclad were relatively harmless, but as the pounding continued, parts began to loosen, armor unbolted, and machinery lost its alignment. Soon smoke from the guns in the lower tier of Sumter lingered in the air, obscuring the vision of the gunners on the barbette. Therefore, they began to fire singly when ready, and the firing became more deliberate, accurate, and effective. The forts also benefitted from a new device invented by Lt. Col. Joseph A. Yates of the First Regiment of S. C. Artillery that allowed the guns to be trained to follow the moving ships and remain on target. This was a forerunner of modern fire control systems.

The crews of the leading monitors had their hands full, running ships and escaping shots that crashed into them at the rate of one a minute. Using the disengaged side of the turrets, they tried to signal each other and sound the bottom. They were hampered by the frailties of their machinery; two of the eight guns in the First Division became disabled. Loading, aiming, and firing heavy guns on moving warships was proving to be more difficult than anyone had previously believed. Collectively, the Union ironclads got off only one shot per minute during the first twenty minutes.

After *New Ironsides* had signaled the squadron to disregard her movements, the Second Division advanced into action. By 3:35 *Catskill* entered the action, followed by *Nantucket* and *Nahant*. *Keokuk* then pushed to the fore, leading her companions to a station six to nine hundred yards from Sumter. With the entire squadron in action, the sky filled with smoke, and shot and shell exploded the waters. Under constant Confederate gunfire, *Passaic* moved away from the forefront to inspect her damage, *Patapsco* ran aground briefly, and *Nantucket* lost the use of one of her XV″ guns after its third discharge.

Commander John Downes took *Nahant* into the heaviest fire from Sumter. He fired only fifteen times, and the fort jammed *Nahant's* turret with three heavy blows and put her steering gear out of commission. This caused her to drift nearer to the forts than any of the others. Shells sheared off bolt and rivet heads on the pilot house; the pilot was knocked senseless and the quartermaster was wounded, and finally only Commander Downes remained in the pilot house. The approaching flood tide threatened to carry the ship into the inner harbor in a disabled condition. At the last minute her steering was repaired, and she retired from action.

Keokuk, with her relatively thin armor and fixed barbettes, made the turn in the channel and came at Sumter bow on, receiving concentrated fire from both sides of the channel. Her guns were silenced after only three shots. After some 25 to 30 minutes of this one-sided pounding, Commander Rhind was glad to escape without going down or being captured. His vessel was riddled by more than ninety hits, nineteen of which were at or near the waterline. As her crew worked feverishly to plug the shot holes, she was barely able to keep afloat through the night. When the wind picked up early in the morning, she sank off Morris Island.

The flagship *New Ironsides* had remained approximately a mile away from the forts. She made one attempt to close the range, but withdrew when the forts concentrated their fire on her. She was not badly damaged, although she received some ninety hits and delivered only seven shots, all at Fort Moultrie.

Retreat

By 4:30 DuPont had had enough and signaled withdrawal to all ships. The squadron ceased fire, but the forts continued until the ships were out of range. Thirty minutes later, the monitors made their way past the flagship, which then followed. Darkness fell as they reached their anchorage and the captains came on board the flagship to report their damage. Some had disabled guns, loose armor, and other injuries—all gave testimony to the effectiveness of the Confederate fire. Nevertheless, only one man was killed and twenty-two wounded on *Nahant* and *Keokuk*. DuPont had planned to resume the attack in the morning, but these grim reports changed his mind. When the fleet weighed anchor and departed for Port Royal, the garrison at Fort Sumter turned out for a dress parade, followed by another salute of thirteen guns, with all flags flying in defiance.

The three damaged monitors proceeded to Port Royal five days after the battle. *New Ironsides* remained off the bar with the blockading force. The four undamaged monitors had to seek shelter in the North Edisto River off Rockville when the weather turned foul. There, the Confederates planned to attack them with torpedoboats. The attack might have succeeded had a deserter not revealed the plans to the enemy the night before.

Fort Sumter had withstood the enemy cannonade. Such powerful hits to a masonry fort were quite new. This had never been experienced before in warfare; the British had employed nothing larger than 68-pounder guns in their bombardment of the Russian forts at Sebastopol in 1854, and the Russian structures had easily withstood them. The massive walls of Fort Sumter with their piers and arches trembled to their very foundations at the impact of the XI″ and XV″ shot. In a few places the damage was severe enough so that if the firing had continued it would have caused serious damage. This was to occur later in the year. As a whole, the fort had lost none of its fighting capacity. Fifteen hits had been severe. Some thirty-four actual hits were found on its face, although some were the cumulative effect of multiple hits and about twenty harmless grazes or nearby bursts. Four Confederates had been killed and ten wounded, most in an accidental explosion in Battery Wagner.

The battle had been dramatic in appearance, but casualties had been light. It remains to this day a record test of armored machinery versus masonry fortifications. The U. S. Navy had not exhibited the vigor and persistence that previously had distinguished it, and that would mark its campaign against Mobile the next year. Next to the battle at Hampton Roads in March 1862, the repulse of the ironclad squadron at Charleston was the most severe defeat for the Union Navy during the war.

The accuracy of the Confederate fire greatly impressed both the enemy and foreign observers on the scene, particularly considering the small targets that the monitors' turrets presented. Collectively, the forts had delivered some 2,206 shots at the fleet, which replied with 139, mostly at Sumter. The Confederate ammunition was replaced with two days' production from the works in Augusta. The victory was a tonic to Southern morale in that spring of 1863; the summer would follow with showdowns at Chancellorsville, Vicksburg, and Gettysburg.

For Charleston, the victory showed the resolve of both the city and the state when under duress. Moreover, the geography of the harbor entrance, which had been such a hindrance to its ocean commerce, had for the third and hopefully the last time worked to the city's advantage by warding off an enemy naval attack.

Furious at the poor showing, President Lincoln and Secretary Welles replaced DuPont in June. For eight months they suppressed official reports of the battle from the public.

The Recovery of the Guns of *Keokuk*

Few histories mention the episode surrounding the recovery of the guns of the Union ironclad *Keokuk*, which was sunk off Charleston in 1863. Yet for ingenuity and skill it remains one of the most daring and successful feats of the Confederate War. Amazingly, no casualties were suffered by either side.

On April 7, 1863, during the Union ironclad attack on Fort Sumter, Commander A. C. Rhind took *Keokuk* to within a half mile of the Confederate guns. His ship was riddled at point-blank range with some ninety hits. With great effort the crew kept the vessel afloat during the night. By 7:30 the next morning, when high tide and the wind created rough seas, she sank in an upright position in eighteen feet of water some 1,300 yards off the southern end of Confederate-held Morris Island. At low tide the tops of her casemates were barely visible; at high tide only the top of her riddled stack could be seen.

Admiral DuPont issued orders for the destruction of the sunken ship and its huge XI" Dahlgren smoothbore guns, but heavy seas prevented their execution. Thus, when the Union squadron departed the Charleston bar five days after the battle, the guns remained intact

within the sunken hulk. Officers from both sides examined the wreck from small boats and all considered it impossible to salvage the guns. Union officers thought that the guns of its blockading fleet would thwart any Confederate attempt to do so. On one occasion, the fleet did challenge Colonel Rhett when he came from Fort Sumter to have a look around. Fortunately, *Chicora* came up in time to rescue Rhett's party, firing on the enemy at long range.

General Beauregard was not as easily discouraged as other Confederate officers often were. The guns on the sunken ship were better than any of his, and so he directed that an attempt be made to salvage them. On April 19, Major D. B. Harris, chief engineer on Beauregard's staff, and Brigadier General R. S. Ripley, commander of the Confederate forces in the harbor, paid a visit to the wreck. They decided that recovering the guns was feasible.

Beauregard placed Adolphus W. LaCoste, a civilian rigger in the Ordnance Department, in charge of salvaging *Keokuk's* guns. LaCoste's skill in moving and mounting heavy ordnance was necessary to the success of the operation, as the guns were fourteen and a half feet long and three feet in diameter, weighing approximately eight tons each. LaCoste and

***Keokuk* sinking off Morris Island.**

his hand-picked crew were escorted out to the wreck in barges from Fort Sumter. Just outside the bar lurked the blockading fleet and *New Ironsides*. Normally, the blockading ship nearest the wreck stayed some two miles distant. This was to ensure its own safety from an attack similar to the sortie by the Charleston ironclads on January 31, 1863. With the powerful USS *New Ironsides* now off the Charleston bar, there was nothing to prevent a blockader from crossing the bar and approaching *Keokuk*.

Small, armed Union boats, capable of moving in at any moment and seizing all of the Confederate workers, plied to and fro among the warships. A Confederate covering force stood by to delay any such move and allow the expedition's work crew to reach Morris Island, slightly over half a mile away, in safety.

Keokuk's turrets were conical, with an upper diameter of fourteen feet. The tops were exposed for only two hours at each low tide. Even then, a heavy sea could make the work impossible.

The first job was to remove the tops of the turrets. Each night at low tide men carrying crowbars, sledge hammers, chisels, and wrenches were put onto the wreck. The armed boats of the covering force then stood off to the channel side of the wreck to keep watch on the enemy blockaders. The work had to be done secretly, with no noise or lights to alert the enemy.

It took over two weeks to cut an opening in the tops of both turrets large enough to remove the huge guns. First, two layers of one-inch iron had to be removed from the top; then the closely set, inch-thick supporting girders had to be cut in two places and removed. Finally, the one-inch iron ceiling had to be taken off. Once all of this was gone, the guns lay exposed.

They were positioned on their carriages and slides in the dark confines of the turret. Before they could be lifted, the two massive square caps of brass holding them onto the carriages had to be removed. To accomplish this the men took turns diving underwater; they each had time to make only one turn of the cap before coming up for air. Once the brass caps were removed, the elevating screw had to be removed from the cascabel at the rear end of each gun.

Finally LaCoste and his men were ready for the real work of lifting the eight-ton monsters clear of the turrets. Final preparations were made and the night of May 2 chosen for the expedition. An old hulk, formerly a lightship used at Rattlesnake Shoal to the north of the harbor, was made ready to hoist and transport the guns. On its bow projected two twenty-foot timbers, fourteen inches square, partially supported by stays rigged to a jury mast and fitted on the outer end with lifting tackles. The bow was weighted down with 1,500 sandbags to aid in the final lift that would clear the guns of the water. The steamer *Etiwan* was selected to tow the hulk to the scene, escorted by the ironclads *Chicora* and *Palmetto State*.

As the Confederates lay about the wreck they could see the blockading ships and their picket boats offshore, but Morris Island must have provided perfect protection, as there were no interruptions from the blockading ships. While the crew may have regarded this as a sign from heaven, a more likely explanation is that the eyes of the enemy ships were turned seaward in search of incoming blockade runners.

The hulk was secured to the first turret. The sling from the bow timbers' tackle was lowered to the gun in the turret and made fast. When LaCoste gave the order to hoist, the men heaved and strained, tightening the ropes; slowly the great gun rose. Soon, the lower block cleared the water, followed by the breech of the gun, muzzle down.

Finally, with the blocks closed up, the breech was clear; but the muzzle was still inside the turret. The sandbags at the bow of the hulk were then shifted to the stern, causing the bow to rise slowly. When all the bags were moved, the men positioned themselves aft. LaCoste checked the gun's position; unfortunately, the muzzle was still banging against the inside of the turret, just inches from the top.

The first streaks of light appeared in the eastern sky. *Etiwan* signaled to ask if all was ready for departure, and the ironclads started moving toward Sumter. LaCoste cursed in frustration, but no one gave the order to cut the prize loose. Suddenly, a large wave lifted the old hulk and carried the gun clear of the turret! Murmurs of congratulations passed around the ship. Quickly, the hulk was cut loose from the wreck, *Etiwan* came alongside, and all were off in haste to safety. As they passed the forts in the gathering light, the garrisons came up to cheer their success.

Three nights later, the second gun was recovered without incident. LaCoste, now ill from exposure, passed the job to his brother. On May 6, only three weeks after the work began, the Charleston papers announced the recovery of the guns. One gun was mounted at the eastern angle of Fort Sumter, where it remained until the ironclad attack of September 1 and 2; it was then moved to Battery Ramsay in White Point Gardens. At the end of the war it was either destroyed or sold for scrap. The other gun was mounted in Battery Bee on Sullivan's Island. Abandoned by the Confederates in 1865, the gun was eventually hidden by shifting sand. In 1898 it was rediscovered and dug up by troops on the island, who loaned it to the city. It was mounted in White Point Gardens in August 1899 and remains there to this day. Except for two inferior Blakeley rifles imported from England, the guns on *Keokuk* were the heaviest ones the Confederates had to defend the harbor. Thus, Admiral DuPont's Charleston record received another blemish!

Author's model of *Keokuk* in battle trim.

Keokuk reflected the early thinking of the U. S. Navy as it attempted to determine the best type ironclad to build. *New Ironsides* and *Keokuk* became one of a kind when the *Monitor*-type clearly demonstrated its superiority with its shallow draft and steam-driven revolving turret. *Keokuk* is more correctly described as a citadel-type ironclad, in that her turrets did not turn. Instead the turrets each had three gunports similar to those on the fore and aft end of the Confederate ironclads, and the gun inside had to be manually positioned to fire through one of the three gunports.

Opposite: Keokuk's **first gun breaks the surface.**

Attack and Stalemate

The Battle for Morris Island

When the Union ironclad squadron was repulsed in April 1863, Federal commanders decided to renew the land assault on Charleston. But they were not anxious to take on the Confederate army on anywhere near equal terms without naval support; Confederate troops had successfully repulsed their first infantry attempt on Charleston in June 1862 at the battle of Secessionville on James Island. By the same token General Beauregard was not anxious to get bogged down in a protracted siege across several miles of front lines on James Island. His strategy was to tie down the enemy with as few troops and as far from Charleston as possible, while keeping the port open for blockade runners.

Morris Island, a small and uninhabited barrier island, lay at the southern entrance to Charleston harbor across a shallow expanse of water from Fort Sumter. Here Citadel cadets had fired the opening shots of the war at the steamer *Star of the West* and additional batteries at its northernmost point had fired on Fort Sumter. Since then, the island had remained rather quiet.

In May 1863 the Union Army chose Morris Island as the next point in the assault on Charleston. Here their infantry would have point-blank naval support and, once the island

was taken, large ordnance could be landed. They hoped to reduce Fort Sumter by long-range artillery fire as they had done to Fort Pulaski outside Savannah two years earlier. Once Sumter was reduced to rubble, they figured that the fort would either surrender or be taken by an infantry assault launched by boats. Once in possession of Fort Sumter, they could use their ordnance to seal the entrance to Charleston harbor to blockade runners. General Beauregard was glad to oblige them on Morris Island, since it would keep the enemy army bogged down on a narrow front far from the city, requiring relatively few Confederate defenders.

Folly Island lay to the south of Morris Island across Lighthouse Inlet and contained no Confederate defenses. Therefore, Union commanders chose it as the staging ground for their assault on Morris Island. The Confederates prepared defenses on Morris Island in anticipation of the attack. They built rifle pits at the southern end to repel a landing from Folly Island. Further up at its narrowest point, about 1,300 yards from Cumming's Point at the northern end, they built the "Neck Battery" (later Battery Wagner, named in honor of Lt. Col. Thomas M. Wagner of the First Regiment of the S. C. Artillery, who had lost his life when a gun accidentally burst at Fort Moultrie). The battery was armed with thirteen guns, the largest a ten-inch Columbiad—good for repelling an infantry assault, but inadequate for use against Union ironclads.

Battery Wagner from the Main Ship Channel.

Union forces were beefed up on Folly Island in preparation for an amphibious assault on Morris Island. Union intelligence always overestimated Confederate strength defending Charleston. Because of withdrawals to other theaters of operation, mostly in Virginia and Tennessee, Confederate forces around Charleston numbered just under 6,000 men by the summer of 1863. Half of these were encamped on James Island to guard against a repeat of the Union attack that had led to the Battle of Secessionville. The remainder manned the harbor forts, including Morris Island, and a handful were held in reserve to guard the rivers north and south of Charleston against enemy naval forays.

By the second week of July Union forces had set up forty-seven guns on Little Folly Island, adjacent to Folly Island, nearest Morris Island. On July 10, they opened up on the Confederate positions on Morris Island, while Admiral Dahlgren led the monitors *Catskill*, *Nahant*, *Montauk*, and *Weehawken* to bombard them from the sea. Though smothered by enemy fire, the Confederate gunners stood valiantly to their posts. After three hours of fire the Federal infantry assault began from boats that were waiting in Lighthouse Inlet. The Southern troops were unable to put up much of a fight after the shelling and fell back to the safety of Battery Wagner. The monitors shelled the island ahead of the advancing Union troops, but Battery Wagner opened up on them once they came within range. The flagship *Catskill* drew most of the fire, receiving over sixty hits.

That night Union reinforcements were brought over to Morris Island for another assault on Battery Wagner the next morning. At the same time, the Confederates reinforced their garrison.

Union heavy artillery was brought over to the south end of Morris Island and placed less than a mile from Wagner. For a week the Union battery and their ironclads pounded Battery Wagner. By July 17, some forty guns of various types and caliber were installed on Morris Island; the next day the tempo of the bombardment picked up. *New Ironsides* moved in close to the beach and blasted Battery Wagner at point-blank range.

During the bombardment, Confederate troops protected themselves in bombproof shelters or were dispersed behind sand dunes and the fort's parapets. Some of the guns were buried in the sand to protect against damage from the enemy fire. By late afternoon the shells were dropping in rapid succession. At dusk the shelling ceased and the assault by some 6,000 Federal troops began.

The Confederate troops took up their positions, unearthed their guns, and poured out a terrific fire. They were assisted by heavy guns from Forts Sumter and Moultrie, which fired at the beach in front of Battery Wagner. As enemy troops poured down the beach, huge holes were blown in their ranks. A few troops made it to the top of the parapet before being killed; the rest broke and fled. The repulse was accomplished despite the fact that the North Carolina troops defending Battery Wagner refused to come out of the bombproofs! The Union casualties were over 1,500; the Confederate, 188.

After this bloody disaster the Union commander, General Quincy A. Gillmore, settled down to reduce Wagner by bombardment. For weeks it was pounded by guns on shore and water. Five hundred Confederates garrisoned the fort and another 500 were held in reserve amongst the sand dunes outside. Union trenches were dug to enable troops to get closer to the fort without being hit. From here sappers were to blow up the outer works. By the first week of September the constant pounding had reduced Wagner to ruins and silenced most of its guns. Rather than lose the men to an assault, General Beauregard withdrew them from Morris Island on the night of September 6. The next morning Federal troops stormed into an empty fort.

Reducing Fort Sumter

With Morris Island completely in Union hands, the next and last obstacle in their path was Fort Sumter. During September 1863, the Union Navy and Army seemed to be holding a contest to decide which would have the honor and glory of taking Sumter. Even before Morris Island had been taken, Union batteries were constructed and intermittently fired on Sumter at ranges of up to two miles. These were large rifled guns similar to those used against Fort Pulaski, designed to fire long distance with accuracy and destroy masonry forts.

Anticipating bombardment, General Beauregard and his chief engineer, Colonel D. B. Harris, decided that Sumter was untenable as an artillery position. Consequently, most of her guns were removed and the casemates made more resistant to gunfire by being filled with a mixture of sand and water-soaked cotton bales.

Union troops storm across Lighthouse Inlet and ashore on Morris Island under cover of artillery fire from Folly Island (foreground).

On August 17, two Union Parrott rifles began firing on Sumter, one with solid shot to destroy the fort's masonry, the other with percussion shells to kill personnel. Other Union batteries followed, and the ordnance eventually totaled eighteen rifled guns. The ironclads *Passaic* and *Patapsco* assisted in the attack on the first day. Only the captured *Keokuk* gun replied in defense of the fort. The shooting lasted continuously for several days. On August 21, when the fort ceased replying, Union General Gillmore threatened to open fire on the city unless Sumter was evacuated.

Gillmore's demand was refused. Therefore, he ordered open fire on Charleston shortly after midnight from the "Swamp Angel" battery in the marsh near Morris Island, four and a half miles from the city. On August 23, after firing 36 rounds, the gun burst. New guns were emplaced on Morris Island to continue the long-range bombardment. Compared to the destruction of the great fire of December 1861, the damage from these guns was negligible. It did force the evacuation of civilians from the area south of Calhoun Street.

Union Ironclads Attack

Not to be outdone by the Union Army, Admiral Dahlgren joined the bombardment by ordering five monitors, with sandbags placed around vulnerable points, to take up position within 800 yards of Sumter. He did not want to repeat DuPont's failure. Consequently, he drove his men hard to capture Sumter. As the ironclads moved into position and began firing, the Confederate batteries on Sullivan's Island joined Sumter in returning fire. This was the last artillery fire from Fort Sumter, which was by now reduced to a mass of rubble. A half million pounds of shells had been expended in the effort.

With *Weehawken* aground (left), Admiral Dahlgren leads his other ironclads in a diversionary attack on Forts Sumter and Moultrie.

On the night of September 1 and 2, Admiral Dahlgren took the ironclads in for an attack on the fort. *Weehawken* moved in first, followed by the others; they anchored across the channel within 500 yards of the target. Finding that Sumter did not reply, the ships came closer and closer, firing at point-blank range. Even *New Ironsides* moved in, and her broadsides lit up the night. In the darkness the Confederates on Sullivan's Island returned fire. The constant roar routed the citizens from their beds, and they came to Charleston's Battery to watch the spectacle.

When the tide began to change Dahlgren ordered the ships to cease fire and return to their anchorage. The firepower of this naval attack surpassed that of the April bombardment. Sumter's east wall was breached in several places.

After Battery Wagner was evacuated on September 6, Admiral Dahlgren decided to try a frontal assault on Sumter, which involved crossing a mile of water from Cumming's Point. By now Sumter was little more than an infantry outpost; all guns had been dismounted, removed, or otherwise incapacitated. But Beauregard ordered that it be held at all costs, as it was the very symbol of the Confederacy.

Weehawken Grounds

On September 7 *Weehawken* was sent to mark the channel around Cumming's Point in preparation for the assault. In the process, she ran hard aground and failed to get off at high tide. The Confederates did not realize her plight, for Dahlgren used the other ironclads to make a day-long diversionary attack on Fort Moultrie.

Tugs attempted all that night to free *Weehawken*, but she remained hard aground. By mid-morning the Confederates realized her predicament and began shooting at long range, trying to hit her underside, which was exposed at low tide. Once more Dahlgren moved on Fort Moultrie to divert the fire. *Weehawken* joined in the cannonade, and one of her shots hit a box of ammunition. It exploded, killing sixteen men and wounding twelve. The concussion within the fort stilled its fire for quite a while, and the broadsides of *New Ironsides* tore through the buildings inside.

Fort Johnson was in the best position to disable the stranded *Weehawken*, but her few guns were short of ammunition; furthermore, the only one really capable of doing damage was mounted on a broken carriage, making accurate shooting impossible. At 1:00 p.m. the fleet withdrew due to low ammunition; shortly afterward, *Weehawken* floated free and fired a parting shot at Moultrie. As she steamed through the fleet to her anchorage she was cheered by the crew of each vessel.[1]

---

[1] *Weehawken* continued to serve on the Charleston station for another three months. On December 6, 1863, she was anchored off the southern end of Morris Island taking on supplies in a moderate gale. At 2:00 p.m. she hoisted a distress signal. Before boats could reach her, she was sharply down by the bow; within five minutes her stern heaved into the air and she sank, taking sixty men with her. With Morris Island in Federal hands, no attempt was made by the Confederates to salvage her guns.

Few of the survivors could provide an explanation for her loss. A board determined that supplies that were being taken in the forward hatch had settled her by the head, and the loss of freeboard allowed waves to break over the bow and down the hatch. *Weehawken's* loss, as well as that of the original *Monitor* off Hatteras in December 1862, showed the basic unseaworthiness of the monitor design. One foot of freeboard allowed very little reserve buoyancy. Once it was compromised, the ship was in extremis.

Repulse of the Boat Attack on Fort Sumter

Once *Weehawken* was free, Admiral Dahlgren sent another demand for the surrender of Fort Sumter. Major Stephen Elliott, the fort's new commander, replied, "Inform Admiral Dahlgren that he may have Fort Sumter when he can take it and hold it!"

Dahlgren figured this as mere bravado and proceeded to launch an amphibious assault. He assigned Commander T. H. Stevens to the task, telling him that since there was no more than a corporal's guard at the fort, all he had to do was walk in and take possession. Now that the Union Army had occupied Morris Island, Gillmore was prodding Dahlgren to push on with the Charleston attack. Both wanted the honor of taking the historic fort, but the Army backed out when it could not command the operation.

The Confederates had by no means abandoned Sumter. The garrison was supplied with grenades, and wire entanglements were placed along the shoreline. One-third of the troops manned the parapets, and the remainder were held in reserve under cover within the rubble to repel any assault.

On the afternoon of September 8, signalmen on the Confederate ironclad *Chicora* intercepted messages[2] from Admiral Dahlgren to the effect that the assault would occur that night. The plan was to send armed boats across from Cumming's Point and land on the southern angle of the fort between the east face and the gorge wall.

That night boats with 500 armed sailors were towed by the tugboat *Daffodil* to within 400 yards of the fort and cast loose. As they pulled for shore in the dark, they were unaware that they were under surveillance. Waiting for them was a "corporal's guard" of the Charleston Battalion, 320 strong and spoiling for a fight! Major Elliott withheld fire until they were only a few yards from the shore. Then grenades, fireballs, and brickbats descended upon them. Anchored nearby, *Chicora* opened up with cannister and grape shot from her broadsides, and Forts Moultrie and Johnson joined in with long-range artillery.

The sailors scrambled for cover in the crags of the rubble, and those who could even-

tually surrendered. The supporting boats pulled off without attempting a landing, leaving behind 6 killed, 2 officers and 17 men wounded, and 25 missing, while 10 officers and 92 men, as well as 5 Union launches, were captured and sent to Charleston; there were no Confederate losses. Once again the U. S. Navy had been humiliated in Charleston. Both Gillmore and Dahlgren had gained more respect for the Southern defenders.

Stalemate

The repulse of the boat attack was followed by a lull in the action, which both sides used to reinforce their defenses. Two brigades were sent from Virginia to reinforce the Confederate positions. However, Union reinforcements stood at over 22,000 men by the end of September. Most of the Union troops remained inactive on Morris and Folly Islands; had

Union sailors storm ashore under a hail of gunfire and brickbats in a valiant attempt to take Fort Sumter.

---

[2] They were using a codebook recovered during the salvaging of *Keokuk's* guns.

they been properly and aggressively employed, they could have broken through the thin defenses south of Charleston and ranged almost freely among the outlying settlements. One of the Confederate brigades was sent to Tennessee before the year was out.

Fort Sumter endured another bombardment and another attempted boat assault, but both had negligible effects. The land operations of the siege of Charleston stalemated, with the higher command echelons of both sides deteriorating into personality conflicts. The Union Army was reluctant to take the offensive against inland points where naval support was impossible, and the Union Navy was reluctant to employ warships in confined waters where Confederate torpedoes might be effectively used. Thus, the battle at the harbor entrance became a cat-and-mouse game, as the Confederates employed new weapons to dislodge the enemy warships, and blockade runners boldly ran in and out of the harbor through a formidable fleet of enemy craft. It was guerrilla warfare on the water. The Union Navy ruled by day and the Confederates employed daring ingenuity by night, but the irony was that the world's most powerful battle fleet was unable to cross the last mile of water necessary to capture Fort Sumter and close Charleston to blockade runners.

Overleaf: The Bombardment of Fort Sumter, **attributed to John Ross Key (1837–1920), 1865. This painting was originally rendered for Admiral John A. Dahlgren. Looking toward the east out to sea, it shows the second great bombardment of Fort Sumter in October and November 1863, and gives an excellent panoramic view of the stalemate at the mouth of Charleston harbor during the last two years of the war. Union troops were totally stymied in their attempt to cross the mile of open water between Cumming's Point and Fort Sumter. The gorge and eastern walls of the fort show the effect of Union artillery fire from Morris Island that commenced in July 1863.**

Below: **Panoramic view of the interior of Fort Moultrie on November 16, 1863, looking southward, showing Union ironclads firing at Fort Sumter (right background). This beautiful painting by Conrad Wise Chapman gives an excellent portrayal of the confrontation between forts and ironclads. By this time the main armament of Fort Sumter had been withdrawn to Fort Moultrie.**

Note on the key guide the focal points of the battles that raged around the mouth of Charleston harbor from 1863 to 1865.

KEY GUIDE (for overleaf)

A Confederate ironclads
B Fort Johnson
C Battery Beauregard
D Fort Moultrie
E Fort Sumter
F Union monitors
G Battery Gregg, Cumming's Point
H *New Ironsides*
I Battery Wagner
J Shell Point
K Marsh
L Martello Tower

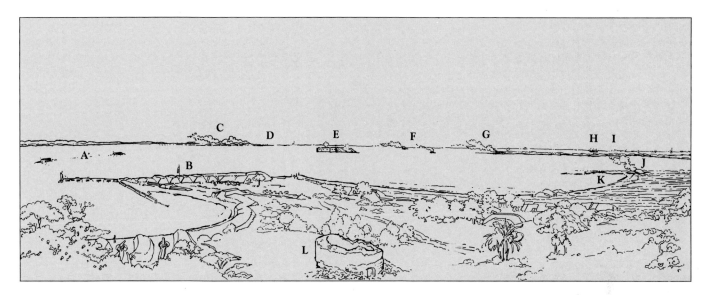

Confederate Torpedoes

The Confederate Navy had no comparable front-line warships to match those of the Union Navy; however, they were not lacking in ingenuity to even the odds. One of the most feared of their new weapons was the torpedo (mine). As early as March 1839, Charles Goodyear[1] experimented with an underwater explosive device in Charleston harbor, although it was little more than a 75-pound keg of powder placed against the underside of a schooner—hardly combat conditions.

As with ironclad warships, the Crimean War saw the introduction of torpedo warfare. The Russians used primitive torpedoes to keep the Franco/British fleet at bay off Kronstadt in the Baltic. The Allies attempted to counter them by employing the earliest known mine-sweeping devices.

The Confederates first used torpedoes in the James River near Jamestown, Virginia, in 1862. Two kegs of powder connected by a rope were set loose to drift with the tide into any ship in its path. Despite this initial failure, the potential was recognized; that year a Torpedo Bureau was established in Richmond with a branch in Charleston. The Charleston

---

[1] Goodyear had invented the vulcanization process for rubber, and the Charleston test was designed to show its suitability for underwater use in diving gear. He had no affiliation with the present rubber company, but it took his name.

Sinking torpedoes in the channel off Fort Sumter.

branch had control over not only the contact and remote control mines, but also booms across the channel and pilings driven into the channel bottoms to obstruct the passage of ships.

General Beauregard considered one torpedo in Charleston's channel worth five heavy Columbiad guns on shore. A properly placed charge of less than a hundred pounds could blow a hole in a ship and sink it in short order, whereas five guns did little damage to a monitor except at point-blank range.

Early Charleston torpedoes were mounted on wooden raftlike frames that were sunk in shallow water with the explosive charge on the top. These frame torpedoes carried a small charge, were clumsy to handle, and shifted at the whim of waves and currents. These deficiencies led to the use of boilers, kegs, and other contraptions filled with powder and anchored in channels.

Confederate torpedoes took many forms—from the cylindrical charges mounted on spars at the bow of the Confederate warships to rafts and kegs of explosives set in the channel. The latter consisted of many forms of explosives in two main types of torpedoes—those exploded by contact and those exploded by electrical charge from cables on shore.

An electrically fired torpedo had failed to destroy *New Ironsides* during the attack in April 1863. Subsequent investigation showed that the cable leading to it was twice as long as necessary; as a result, the electrical current lost most of its power traveling through it and was insufficient to detonate the charge.

The torpedoes fired from shore by remote control were usually the larger, stationary type placed on the channel bottom. These were few in number due to the larger amounts of powder they required and the lack of sufficient cable to fire them. They scored no successes, but did deter the enemy psychologically. Those detonated by contact were usually smaller, and floated on or just below the water's surface. Because they came in actual contact with the target, they required less explosive force than the remote-control variety to do the same amount of damage. Either type could do lethal damage to most ships.

Fear of these weapons was the leading factor that kept the Union Navy out of Charleston harbor. While the monitors would often go within a half mile of the guns of Forts Sumter and Moultrie, fear of the torpedoes deterred them from venturing further. If a torpedo exploded against a monitor, the crew had little chance of escape before she sank, because these ships had so few hatches and so little reserve buoyancy.

During daylight hours Union ironclads would steam boldly near the forts, but once darkness fell they would withdraw to a safer distance because of the fear of attacks by Confederate torpedoboats. As a consequence blockade runners were able to slip in and out of Charleston until the last days.

But the torpedoes presented many problems to the Confederates as well. They could sink both friend and foe, as was the case of the Confederate steamer *Marion*. In addition, they required constant maintenance and replacement. The wooden ones were attacked by wood borers, and the metal ones were corroded by salt water. The currents and waves buffeted them around, occasionally setting them off or casting them adrift to wreak havoc wherever they landed. The Confederate crews who placed them and the Union crews who removed them required more courage than skill.

The Federal Navy used several devices to protect their ships. One of these was the "alligator," a minesweeping raft that was attached to the bow of *Weehawken* during the attack of the ironclad fleet in April 1863. The "alligator" proved to be more trouble than it was worth. Boat crews were eventually dispatched to sweep for mines with long poles or grappling hooks.

The only successful use of Confederate stationary torpedoes in the Charleston campaign occurred on the evening of January 15, 1865. A Union flotilla that included tugs, scout boats, and the monitors *Patapsco* and *Leigh* was making a routine foray near the harbor entrance. *Patapsco* was equipped with a new minesweeping device—little more than an x-shaped pair of logs at the bow with nets suspended to scoop up floating torpedoes. The monitors maneuvered in the waters between Forts Sumter and Moultrie, directing the boats and drifting with the tide. *Patapsco's* minesweeping device failed. As she reached a point 700 yards from Sumter, a mine blew a hole on the port side near the turret; she sank in less than a minute. Forty-four men survived in the lifeboat, but sixty-two men were lost.

At the end of the war, as in most modern naval wars, minesweeping crews were sent to remove leftover mines in the harbor. A few minesweepers had close encounters, but none were lost. Unfortunately, some Confederate torpedoes still remain today in Charleston harbor; therefore, the saga may not be over.

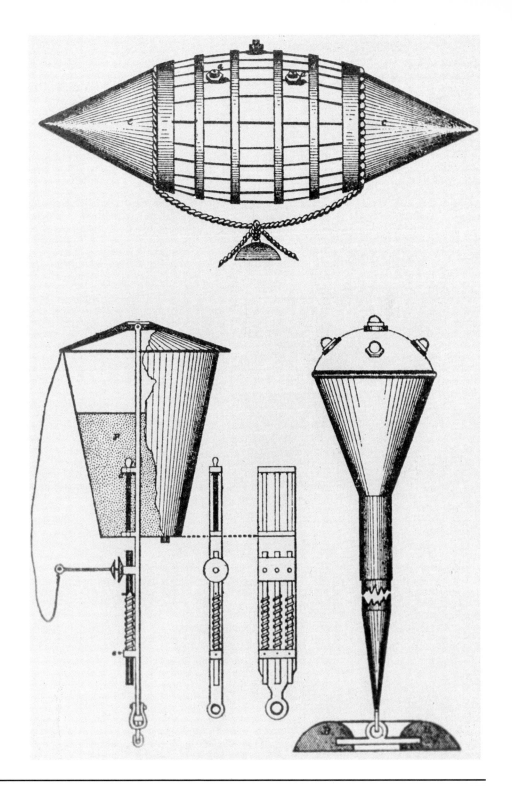

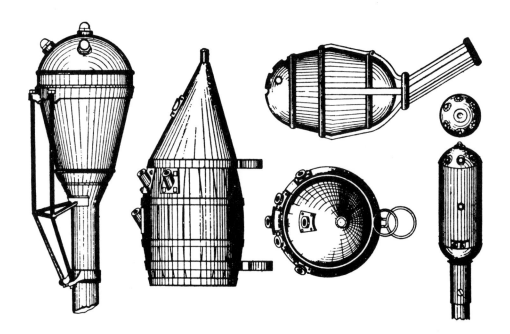

Left: **Variety of ram or spar torpedoes. Type at left was used on the Charleston and James River ironclads. The type at right, containing up to 70 pounds of powder, was carried by torpedoboats.**

Right: **Beer barrels with wooden cones attached (top) made excellent buoyant torpedoes and carried up to 120 pounds of powder. When the iron cap of Singer's torpedo (bottom left) was knocked off, it would pull the lanyard and fire the primer. An antisweeping device was sometimes attached to the buoyant torpedo shown at the bottom right.**

The *David* Torpedoboats

Early in the war the Confederate government promised to pay to the inventor of any device that would destroy Union blockaders a reward of up to 50 percent of the value of the vessels destroyed. As the blockade and siege of Charleston tightened in 1863, Theodore D. Wagner of John Fraser and Company offered a bounty to anyone who would sink a blockading ship. The price placed on *New Ironsides* was $100,000 in gold; a monitor was $50,000; and a wooden warship such as *Housatonic* was $25,000. The bounties were a bargain for the Confederacy; it would cost much more to build new warships capable of sinking the blockaders. The incentive spurred the development of several nautical contraptions. After all, it was similar private enterprise that was working wonders in bringing supplies through the blockade.

One such device spurred by the reward was the series of torpedoboats known as *Davids* from the Southern Torpedo Company of Charleston, a firm funded by Theodore D. Stoney, Cap Chevis, Theodore Wagner, Dr. St. Julien Ravenel, and others. The torpedoboats were based on a design by Ross Winan of Baltimore and refined by Dr. Ravenel of Charleston and David C. Ebaugh[1] of Maryland. Ebaugh, who was head mechanic, claimed that the boats were named for him; legend, however, has it that Dr. Ravenel's wife suggested the name of the biblical David because of the Goliaths that the boats were to face.

Early Confederate Torpedoboats

The South was behind in the contest at sea and therefore forced to turn to such innovative devices as torpedoboats to try to equal the odds. A torpedo was designed by Captain Francis D. Lee, who tested it against a barge in Charleston harbor using an old dugout canoe pulled by oarsmen. The test was a complete success. The charge blew a hole in the barge, which quickly sank. General Beauregard was so impressed that he ordered a squadron of the boats to be built.

In March 1863, Lt. William T. Glassell and a seven-man crew took a large rowboat armed with one of Captain Lee's spar torpedoes out of the harbor to attack the enemy fleet. Offshore they bore down on the sidewheeler *Powhatan* on a calm, moonless night. Once the rowboat was spotted, one of the rowers panicked and in an effort to move away backed on his oar rather than pulling ahead. By the time the boat could be put back on course it was drifting by the target with the tide and all surprise was lost. Once clear of *Powhatan*, the torpedo was cut away and the crew pulled for home.

When Secretary Mallory learned of Union preparations for an ironclad assault on Charleston, he devised a scheme for Confederate marines to board the monitors at their anchorage. Three companies of marines were sent from Drewry's Bluff, Virginia. The plan was to sneak up on the enemy at night with about fifteen rowboats armed with spar torpedoes. Ten to twenty men from each boat would board a monitor and scale the smoke stack to throw bottles of sulphur, gunpowder, and wet blankets down it to suffocate the enemy crew. They would then batter down the stack and clog it with a metal plate over the opening. At the same time army units from the Confederate boats would attack the turret, pilot house, ventilators, and hatches in similar fashion. The turret would be jammed with iron wedges, hatches nailed shut, and the pilot house and vents covered with tarpaulins.

Exercises were conducted in March to refine the tactics. Once the Union ironclads arrived off Charleston, they attacked so quickly that all the armed boats could do was stand by inside the harbor to attack any disabled enemy ships. When the ironclads were repulsed the boats massed behind Cumming's Point under Commodore Tucker to execute their attack. All preparations were readied for the evening of April 12. As the crews awaited low tide,[2] news arrived that the enemy had left. Shortly afterward the Confederate marine battalion returned to Drewry's Bluff.

Torch

The aborted attempt on *Powhatan* convinced the Confederate leaders that only steam-powered torpedoboats could be successful. *Torch* was the first experimental torpedoboat. She was little more than a large boat some twenty feet long with an underpowered old engine from the Savannah tugboat *Barton* that had been refurbished by Cameron & Company of Charleston. With General Beauregard's support, F. M. Jones, the ship carpenter, started work on her late in 1862; he completed the hull the following spring. Her armament was a torpedo with a thirty-pound charge mounted at the end of a twenty-two-foot spar attached to the bow.

Captain Lee had trouble obtaining armor for *Torch* due to Confederate iron shortages; therefore, when she was ready for service on August 1, she lacked armor. As a result *Torch* rode high in the water and had to be heavily ballasted with granite. Her trial run around the harbor was a complete success. With the struggle for Morris Island at its height that month, *Torch* was sent into action immediately. On August 20, 1863, James Carlin, commander of the blockade runner *Ella and Annie*, took her out to attack *New Ironsides*. He stopped at Fort Sumter to pick up a guard force of eleven soldiers under Lieutenant E. S. Fickling and then steamed out of the harbor.

When they were a quarter of a mile from the target, Carlin lowered the torpedo boom into the water and came up to full speed. When the gap lessened to forty yards, the watch on *New Ironsides* hailed Carlin. *New Ironsides* was parallel to his course of attack, and Carlin ordered a right turn, which the helmsman failed to execute until too late. In order to

---

[1] In 1855 Ebaugh had established a lumbering business in the St. John's section of Berkeley County, but the onset of war ruined it. From the end of the war until 1891 he worked in the fertilizer business in Charleston and then became general manager of a plant in Greenville.

[2] Low tide would restrict the enemy ships' movements around the bar. Once the tide began to flood, returning to the harbor would be easier, especially with any enemy ships that could be captured.

avoid the ship's anchor chain, Carlin ordered the small engine to be stopped. It could not be restarted until *Ironsides* was at action stations.

Rather than reattack an alerted enemy, Carlin threw rosin into the boiler fire. This poured out a dense cloud of smoke, enabling *Torch* to escape unscathed through a hail of gunfire. After stopping to return the guards to Fort Sumter, she returned to port and oblivion.

Building *David*

Torch had failed because of her weak engine. So torpedoboats with more power were needed. The Ravenel & Stevens Company had lime works at Stoney Landing, where David Ebaugh was also working as superintendent of the Confederate nitre works. While on furlough from his duties at the Confederate hospital in Columbia, Dr. St. Julien Ravenel approached Ebaugh with his idea of a boat to carry the newly invented torpedo. Ravenel had in mind a manually powered, propeller-driven boat. Ebaugh pointed out that many men would be required. The size of the necessary crew would make the vessel too large. He then suggested a "segar" shaped hull driven by a steam engine. Dr. Ravenel thought this would be too large and noisy, but Ebaugh convinced him that a small engine could be used, and the sound could be mechanically deadened. Riding low in the water, its chances of sneaking up on an unsuspecting blockader would be much better.

Construction of the first *David* was begun with slave labor in May 1863 under a nitre shed at Stoney Landing. Ebaugh obtained a discarded small double engine from John Chalk, who was master of machinery at the Northeastern Railroad Shop in Charleston. The engine had been used to run the machinery at the railroad shop before being replaced by a larger one. Chalk altered the old engine to fit the dimensions of *David's* cigar-shaped hull. Such shape, similar to that of a modern nuclear-powered submarine, showed Ebaugh's remarkable grasp of hydrodynamics. *David's* 18-foot midsection swelled to 5.6 feet in diameter. The pointed ends were large pine logs that had been turned with rabbets or grooves to receive the ends of the hull planking. The round frames were made of 1.5-inch oak planking, doubled and riveted, to which the 1.5-inch hull planking (which ran the entire length of the hull) was riveted.

The hull had an open slot in the top for a cockpit. To keep water out, a coaming was built around the perimeter of the opening a foot or so high. The pilot sat in the middle and steered the vessel with his feet. Ballast tanks allowed the vessel to be lowered in the water so that only the smokestack and the coaming around the cockpit were visible. Air pumps would remove the water, and raise the vessel for the trip to and from the scene of combat. The spar for the torpedo, which carried seventy pounds of explosive, was to be mounted on a hinge at the bow. A line attached to the front enabled it to be raised above the water for normal steaming. For attack, the torpedo would be lowered to six feet underwater so that it would explode below an ironclad's defensive armor.

The completed hull was brought down the Cooper River to Charleston for the installation of the machinery. Here it was hoisted out of the water by a crane onto the Northeastern Railroad Wharf, placed on a flat car, and taken to the railroad shop. At this point much doubt was expressed about its seaworthiness. Ebaugh pointed out that eight to nine tons of

New Ironsides **fitting out at the Cramp Shipyard in Philadelphia in 1862. Before her arrival on the Charleston station, her masts and spars were removed and pole masts for signal flags (seen here) were substituted. The "X" on the stern marks the location of the wardroom. The black vertical lines on her hull indicate the fore and aft ends of the armor belt.**

David refitting at Atlantic Wharf on October 25, 1863, after her attack on *New Ironsides*. This is one of a number of paintings that Conrad Wise Chapman rendered of the Charleston area during the war. The bulk of his wartime scenes can be seen in the Museum of the Confederacy in Richmond, Virginia.

Allegorical scene of Lt. Glassell's attack on *New Ironsides*. Glassell is shown firing his shotgun at the officer of the deck at the same time that the explosion of his torpedo rips the water alongside **the enemy flagship. These incidents actually happened within a few seconds of each other. The moonlight casts an eerie glow over the ruins of Fort Sumter, while a monitor stands nearby.**

The ex-blockade runner *Memphis* in American service as a blockader. *Memphis* was an iron screw steamer that had been built in 1862 at Dumbarton, Scotland. She was employed as a blockade runner and as such was captured by the USS *Magnolia* off Charleston on July 31, 1862. She was taken into the U. S. service as USS *Memphis* and spent most of her service on routine blockade duty in the North Edisto River. She was attacked there by *David* on March 6, 1864, but the weapon failed to detonate despite three attempts.

ballast would be needed to lower *David* to the proper level in the water.

By the summer of 1863 Charleston was under long-range bombardment from Morris Island, and a sense of urgency crept into the project. A boiler from Fort Sumter was installed in the forward part of the cockpit to power the steam engine in the rear, which turned the two-bladed propeller. Once the machinery was installed, *David* was returned to the dock and relaunched. Only about two tons of ballast could be obtained here—not enough to submerge the craft properly; therefore, she was brought down to the Southern Wharf, where the ironclad *Charleston* was being completed. There, about seven more tons of iron were added. When the hull was completely loaded with fuel, it sank to the proper depth in the water.

On a test run to Fort Johnson and back, *David* reportedly made a respectable speed of ten knots. The Confederate Navy then took her over and placed the torpedo on the bow at the end of a 20-foot stationary iron pipe 2.5 inches in diameter. Ebaugh had arranged the torpedo on iron pipes installed on both sides of the hull and attached to trunions so as to enable the crew to raise the torpedo out of the water when moving and lower it for attack. The Confederate Navy covered the top of the hull with strips of plow steel 5 to 6 inches wide and approximately 0.25 inches thick, running below the waterline. They also painted her "blockader blue."

Attack on *New Ironsides*

Lt. W. T. Glassell was chosen to command the vessel. J. H. Tombs, assistant engineer of *Chicora*, and fireman James Sullivan came aboard to man her engine and boiler. J. W. Cannon, the pilot of *Palmetto State*, was in charge of navigation. Just after dark on October 5, 1863, *David* cast off from her wharf; she was then towed by a steamer to a point off Fort Sumter. From there, she proceeded out of the harbor on the ebb tide. The light north wind barely rippled the water's surface and the stars shone through the slight haze. They passed the line of enemy picket boats without being discovered and made for the line of blockaders off Morris Island. Even in the calm sea, the open cockpit shipped water; the crew had to bail constantly.

Around 8:30 p.m. Glassell picked out the hulk of *New Ironsides* and steered for her with

his feet. When barely a hundred yards away, he was spotted and hailed. He cocked his shotgun, and, at forty yards, dropped the questioning officer of the deck. Ordering the engines to be stopped, Glassell drifted the last few yards. Suddenly an explosion ripped the water under *New Ironsides'* starboard quarter. Water cascaded into *David's* cockpit and down her stack, dousing her boiler fires. Rocking helplessly in the water, she came under small-arms fire as the enemy crew recovered from their shock.

Glassell, Sullivan, and Tombs grabbed floats and plunged into the water. Tombs managed to reach *New Ironsides'* anchor chain and hung on for dear life. Cannon, unable to swim, clung to *David's* side away from the fire. Once the torpedoboat drifted out of range

Original *David* lying abandoned on Chisolm's Causeway at the west end of Tradd Street at the end of the war.

he climbed back aboard, relit the boiler, and got underway. Seeing *David* still afloat, Tombs struck out for her through a hail of small-arms fire. Glassell and Sullivan had been captured, but by a stroke of luck *David* made it back to Atlantic Wharf, through fire from the enemy picket boats.

New Ironsides was equally lucky. The torpedo had run too close to the surface and detonated against her armor plate. The 80-pound charge was unable to penetrate the reinforced wooden sides because it hit where a structural bulkhead butted against the hull. This absorbed most of the explosive force. *New Ironsides* eventually had to leave station and return North for repairs to her hull and engines, which had been badly shaken by the concussion. Ebaugh maintained that if *David* had used his moveable rig for the torpedo it would have exploded under the ironclad's armor belt and sunk her.

This attack on the Union flagship caused Admiral Dahlgren to order all ironclads at anchor on close-in blockade to deploy iron nets around them to protect against future attacks by stealth. Dahlgren commented in his report that he had never seen a weapon work so well on its first trial! To reinforce security further, small boats circulated about the Union ironclads from dusk to dawn, aided by calcium-fired searchlights. From now on, there was little rest at night amongst the blockaders' crews. Dahlgren also had to abandon his plan of sending *New Ironsides* up the Stono River to shell Charleston from the rear.

As a prisoner of war, Lt. Glassell was later exchanged for the captain of *Isaac Smith*, which had been captured earlier in the year in the Stono River. Glassell was then assigned to the James River Squadron and was in command of the ironclad *Fredericksburg* when Richmond fell.

General Beauregard was so impressed with the potential of *David* and *Torch* that a torpedoboat school was established at the foot of Hassell Street in Charleston. There new

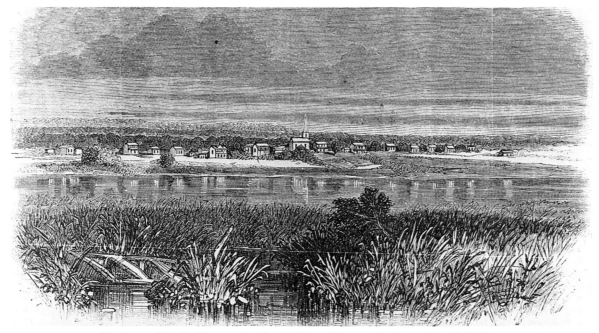
The town of Rockville near the North Edisto River at the time of the Civil War.

crewmen were trained for the additional torpedoboats that were being built. When the city came under bombardment the school was transferred to the Ashley River side of the city.

Attack on *Memphis*

A steel shield was fitted over *David's* upper works and a cap was placed over the smokestack to prevent her boiler fires from being doused. On the night of March 4, 1864, under the command of Tombs, *David* steamed slowly down the North Edisto River to attack the former blockade runner, now the blockader USS *Memphis*, which was anchored near Rockville. Unfortunately, *David's* pumps failed and she could not submerge to the attack level. The mission had to be aborted. She took shelter in the marsh along the river's edge further upstream, and the next night the mission proceeded according to plan.

Tombs approached *Memphis* in the darkness and plunged the torpedo into *Memphis'* port quarter, but it failed to explode. By this time the intended victim was returning heavy small-arms fire, which was deflected by *David's* new shield. *Memphis* slipped her cable and got underway immediately, but *David* made a sharp turn and rammed *Memphis* in the starboard quarter. As *David* passed, her stack scraped the stern counter of *Memphis*, but the torpedo again failed to explode. *Memphis* steamed away, firing her guns. Fortunately, they were not sufficiently depressed to hit the torpedoboat. So determined were Tombs and his crew that they made a third attempt through a hail of gunfire, but it was a glancing blow under the counter and also failed.

David made off, dodging fire from *Memphis'* large guns. The torpedo was examined at Charleston. The leaden covers to the detonators had been flattened by the blows on the hull of *Memphis*, but a defect in the explosive had saved her.

A few weeks later a similar attack was made on the steamer *Wabash* off the bar, but a storm had created heavy swells that forced *David* back into harbor before she was able to get close enough to detonate her weapon. This was the extent of her active career. Later she would be used to tow the Confederate submarine *Hunley* around the harbor. On one occasion *David* almost fouled *Hunley's* torpedo, which would have blown up both craft.

More *David*-type torpedoboats were built; by war's end eight or nine were scattered around Charleston harbor. Among them was an ironclad monster some 150 feet long. One was found at Bennett's sawmill and two on the causeway to Chisolm's mill at the west end of Tradd Street; one of these was the original *David*. Three were raised and repaired. One of these ended up at the Naval Academy in Annapolis and another went to the Brooklyn Navy Yard. The third was lost on *Mingoe* off Hatteras while being carried North.

As a result of the near-success of the Charleston squadron, foreign navies became interested in torpedoboats. Within a decade the major naval powers built an assortment of torpedoboat craft. As the type developed over the remainder of the century, larger ones became known as destroyers, and smaller versions led to the high-speed torpedoboats used so successfully during both World Wars, especially by the Italians. Today almost every nation with a warship in the water has some sort of torpedoboat with missile launchers. All of this arose from the initial ingenuity and daring of a few Charlestonians attempting to defend their city.

The Confederate Submarine *Hunley*

Of all of the vessels associated with Charleston none has won as firm a place in the naval and maritime history of the world as that of the Confederate submarine *Hunley*. Like the Revolutionary War frigate *South Carolina*, *Hunley* was designed and built elsewhere; however, *Hunley* gained her fame in Charleston.

The story of *Hunley* begins in New Orleans in 1862. New Orleans was a great loss to the Confederacy, not only because of her geographic position at the mouth of the Mississippi River, but because of her importance as a manufacturing center. The city had started slowly in preparing for the war, but by early 1862 a number of innovative naval craft were under construction there, including several ironclads. Had they been completed, they might have repulsed Admiral Farragut's assault on the city in April. Another of these craft was the semi-submerged ironclad ram *Manassas*, which did participate in the attempt to repulse Farragut's fleet as it came upstream toward the city. Similar to her was the submarine torpedoboat *Pioneer*, then under construction by John K. Scott, Robin R. Barrow, James McClintock, and Baxter Watson. She was twenty feet long with a fish-like curving hull, with room inside for a crew of three.

On a test run in Lake Ponchartrain in March 1862, *Pioneer* successfully destroyed a barge. However, when Farragut's forces attacked the city the following month, the boat was not sent into action; instead, it was sunk to prevent capture.[1]

Joined by Captain Horace L. Hunley, Watson and McClintock then went to Mobile and constructed a new torpedoboat in the machine shops of Park & Lyons. It was built of iron some twenty-five feet long,[2] five feet wide, six feet deep, and tapered at each end. It was both larger and more streamlined than *Pioneer*. Unfortunately, it was lost en route to Fort Morgan to pick up the crew to attack the blockading fleet.

The third boat built was slightly larger than her predecessor. Eventually named for her designer, she was built of galvanized boiler iron. The boiler was cut in half horizontally and two twelve-inch-wide iron strips were inserted between them. Then the sections were riveted together and the ends tapered. The new boat ended up thirty-five feet long,[3] four wide, and five deep. A bulkhead was placed at each end to form water ballast tanks to raise and lower her in the water. Flat castings were attached to the outside of the bottom and fastened by bolts that passed through stuffing boxes inside. These could be cut loose to lighten the boat in an emergency.

A seacock was connected to each water tank to supply water for sinking the boat; force pumps were installed to release the water to raise it to the surface. A mercury gauge open to the sea was attached near the forward tank to indicate the depth of water. Lateral fins five feet long and eight inches wide were secured to the sides, operated by a lever amidships. By raising or lowering the ends of the fins as the boat moved through the water, the depth could be changed without disturbing the water level in the ballast tanks.

The rudder was operated by a forward wheel that controlled levers for turning it. Eight men worked a crank that manually powered the boat by means of a propeller. It revolved in a wrought iron ring that prevented it from being fouled by ropes. In calm water the crew's best speed was about four knots, not enough to buck the tide in Charleston harbor. The men sat crowded along the port side. Two oval hatches on top provided access and the coamings underneath had glass windows for sighting. Immediately aft of the forward hatch there was an air box into which were inserted two four-foot lengths of 1.5-inch pipe with elbows. These could be raised in order to replenish the air inside when the boat was submerged— a forerunner of the modern schnorkel.

The initial weapon was a copper cylinder that held a ninety-pound charge with percussion and friction primers set off by flaring triggers. This weapon was dragged behind the submarine on a 200-foot line. The boat was to dive under the target, dragging the charge into it. When it exploded against the enemy's side, the submarine would be surfacing on the other side, out of harm's way. In operations at Mobile this maneuver worked well in smooth water; in rough water it failed, so a twenty-two-foot spar torpedo was substituted at the bow. The strategy was to attack an enemy with the spar fixed at a 45-degree downward angle[4] so that the explosion would blow a hole in the victim near the keel, and thus not draw the submarine into the sinking ship. Even with this arrangement the danger of the exploding torpedo sinking the submarine was still too great, so a horizontal spar was substituted. The new strategy was to drive the torpedo into the side of an enemy ship. A spike at the torpedo's front would hold it in the target's hull. The submarine would then back off, unwinding a cable by which the torpedo was detonated after the submarine had reached a safe distance.

An eight-man crew operated the boat; six of them were crankers who manned the propeller. The captain steered and handled the boat forward, and the second officer manned the air supply and air tanks aft and pitched in to help the crankers. Once the crew was on board, the hatches would be closed and secured and a candle lit. Then the ballast tanks were flooded until the top of the hull was about three inches underwater. The seacocks were then closed and the boat put underway. When they had gained sufficient headway, the fins would be used to adjust the depth, using the mercury gauge as a guide. When stationary, the ballast tanks would have to be pumped dry in order to raise the boat to the surface.

What emerged from the Mobile machine shop was a remarkably advanced weapon. In terms of design, subsequent submarines seemed to regress; eighty years would elapse before they would have an underwater breathing apparatus or a hydrodynamic hull form. *Hunley's* hull shape was designed primarily for movement underwater. Until the advent of the comparably shaped World War II German Type XXI U-boat, submarines were considered surface

---

[1] Today the original vessel can be seen on Jackson Square in New Orleans.

[2] Thirty-six feet according to another account.

[3] There is much debate over the exact dimensions of the third submarine. General Beauregard describes her as twenty feet long, a dimension corroborated by witnesses on the USS *Housatonic*. Other accounts list her as anywhere from thirty to forty feet long, a dimension substantiated by projecting the Chapman painting on page 267.

[4] The further underwater that a hole is blown in the side of a ship, the faster it will sink; additionally a smaller charge is required, due to the increase in water pressure.

ships that merely submerged for battle. Therefore their hull shapes were more adept at surface than underwater operations.

Move to Charleston

Off Mobile the chances for this slow-moving "fishboat" to attack the blockading force were slight. It was decided that the Union monitors anchored at their close-in blockading stations off Charleston would be better targets. Therefore, General Beauregard had the submarine sent to Charleston on two flatbed rail cars. It arrived on August 15, 1863, at the height of the battle for Morris Island.

In Charleston Lieutenant John Payne, CSN, and seven former New Orleans longshoremen volunteered as a crew. On August 30, while she was at dock at Fort Johnson, a swell from a passing steamer swamped the boat, and five of the men inside drowned. Payne managed to escape by squeezing out of the hatch.

At this point the "fishboat" became known as the "Coffin Ship." Nevertheless she was raised and brought to the wharf at Fort Johnson.

A regiment of the South Carolina infantry had watched as the decomposing bodies of her crew were removed from the hull and placed in their coffins. Only the eyes of the regiment moved as they stood at attention as their commander related the morbid details. At the end of his discourse, he asked any who wished to volunteer for the next sortie to step three paces forward. The colonel stepped over the pine boxes and looked toward the submarine; it appeared, when he looked back at the regiment, that no one had stepped out of the ranks to volunteer. However, this was because the entire regiment had advanced three paces forward, so determined was their resolve on behalf of the Confederate cause.

The Death of Hunley

General Beauregard decided to turn her over to her designer and a volunteer crew from Mobile known as the "Hunley and Parks crew." The "fishboat" now became known as "the submarine torpedo boat" *H. L. Hunley* in honor of her designer. These men were well acquainted with the vessel and well qualified to operate her. They made several successful practice dives under the Confederate Navy's receiving ship *Indian Chief* in the harbor. On another test dive under the ironclad *Charleston*, *Hunley* tried the original towline method but stuck briefly in the mud on the harbor bottom, so this method was permanently discarded.

On the morning of October 15, 1863, the submarine cast off from her dock at Fort Johnson and proceeded to dive under *Indian Chief*, anchored in the Cooper River between Adger's Wharf and Castle Pinckney. *Indian Chief's* crew followed her bubble trail in the water as she submerged. Suddenly it stopped and air cascaded up from below—disaster had struck.

The submarine failed to surface, and Hunley and eight others were lost. It took a week to raise the boat, and when the hatches were opened a macabre scene greeted the salvagers. The unfortunate crew were contorted and twisted with blackened faces that expressed their final terror. Their bodies were buried with military honors in Magnolia Cemetery.

Evidently the boat had submerged at too steep an angle, and the bow was buried in the mud. Parks had managed to pump the aft tank dry and raise the stern, but Hunley did not close the forward seacock to pump that tank dry. Both he and Parks were found in their respective hatchways, where they had loosened the bolts but had been unable to force the hatch covers off because the water pressure was too great at that depth. The weights on the bottom had been loosened but not released.

In light of these conditions one theory is that Hunley's familiarity with the boat had evidently made him forgetful. Once submerged the tanks were probably given a few strokes to eject some of the water; the fins could then be used to bring the boat up the rest of the way. This would have made it physically easier on the crew. As in most training dives Hunley then partly turned the fins to go down. Needing more ballast, he opened the seacock. As she went down darkness descended, and Hunley fumbled to relight the candle; meanwhile the tank flooded and the boat plummeted down, sticking bow first in the bottom of the harbor.

Determined to Succeed

In spite of her macabre history, there was no shortage of new volunteers; however, General Beauregard considered the boat too dangerous and decided to use her only as a surface torpedo ram, not a submarine. Lieutenant George E. Dixon, a mechanical engineer from Alabama who had helped build the boat, was chosen to command. W. A. Alexander,[5] who had also helped build her, became second officer. She was manned with volunteers from *Indian Chief*. The submarine was moved to Mt. Pleasant, where Dixon and Alexander set up the first submarine school to train the new crew.

By now the Union blockaders were aware of the Confederate torpedoboats and sub-

[5] Alexander's account of *Hunley's* design, construction, and operation give a valuable insight into this unique vessel.

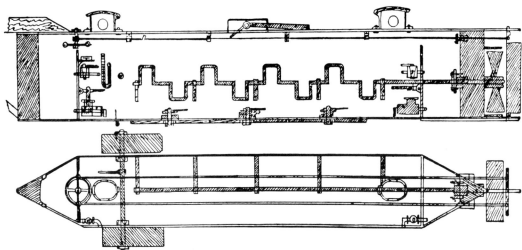

Alexander's sketch of *Hunley*. While not to scale, it gives a good idea of *Hunley's* interior arrangement.

marine inside the harbor and began to anchor further offshore. While this helped the blockade runners, it also made it more difficult for *Hunley* to reach the enemy. In order to get closer to her targets, the boat was moved to the inlet behind Sullivan's Island and moored off Battery Marshall.

By now chain booms, picket boats, calcium lights, and boat howitzers were protecting the Union monitors that anchored close to the harbor entrance at night. The blockading ships further out were unprotected. Admiral Dahlgren also ordered them to anchor in relatively shallow water so that the "diving torpedo" could not pass under them and they could be more easily raised if they were sunk. The frigate *Wabash*, about twelve miles out, became *Hunley's* target. In smooth water the submarine could make about four miles an hour, but rough water cut that considerably. To shorten transit time to the attack point, she would go out on the ebb and return on the flood tide. It was essential to travel on moonless nights, since *Hunley* could not risk being seen on her final attack run.

The crew's routine was to leave quarters in Mount Pleasant after lunch, walk to Battery Marshall at the north end of Sullivan's Island, take the boat out, and practice in the back inlet. At dusk bearings would be taken on the blockading ships as they went to their night stations. The boat would then depart after dark, steering for a previously chosen target until exhaustion of the crew and approaching daylight compelled its return. Once back, the crew would return the torpedo to the magazine under guard at Battery Marshall, and walk the seven miles back to quarters at Mount Pleasant to cook breakfast.

In an experiment one evening, *Hunley* dove and surfaced many times in the inlet; then the hour was noted and the boat sank to the bottom. After twenty-five minutes the candle went out due to insufficient oxygen. During much of the time underwater, the men were working the propeller cranks. Meanwhile, Confederate soldiers who were watching on the beach sent word to Charleston that *Hunley* had again been lost with all hands; but she surfaced after two hours and thirty-five minutes underwater. A new record had been established.

During January 1864, the contrary wind and cold made it difficult for *Hunley* to get far enough out to attack. Usually four nights per week were all the crew could stand. For after rowing six or seven miles, they were forced to return to port by the approach of dawn. In order to conserve the crew's strength the headquarters were moved from Mt. Pleasant to Sullivan's Island.

Destruction of *Housatonic*

On the night of February 17, in spite of the moonlight, *Hunley* put out in a calm sea. Off the Isle of Palms she came across the steam sloop-of-war *Housatonic*, long a nemesis to Charleston. At 8:45 p.m., about two and a half miles off the bar, a lookout on the blockader spotted something that resembled a floating log. It was making for the starboard quarter. Battle rattles sounded action stations, the anchor was slipped, and the engines backed down in an attempt to run down

the suspicious object, which was now making for the sloop's stern. Guns were brought to bear, but they could not be depressed sufficiently to hit the target. An explosion just behind the mizzenmast ripped apart the night and threw water and timber as high as the mast head. *Housatonic* lurched over to port and then settled by the stern into thirty feet of water. She went down quickly in shallow water and took five of her crew with her. The rest of her men took to the rigging and were saved.

Amazingly enough, none of her consorts were aware of the disaster. Captain Charles C. Pickering mustered a crew for one of the boats and rowed over to the USS *Canandaigua* a few hundred yards away for help. Forty of the survivors ended up on the old Charleston-built *John Adams*. She had been a training ship at the wartime Naval Academy at Newport, Rhode Island, but was sent to the Charleston blockade in 1863, supposedly as the Union's rejoinder to Charleston's role in the secession.

The explosion had shattered *Housatonic*. Everything aft of the mainmast was damaged.

Two Confederate veterans of the Charleston Campaign, *Hunley* alongside the CSS *Chicora* on February 14, 1864, just three days before her historic exploit against *Housatonic*. Note the small amount of the submarine visible above the surface of the water and the size of the men in relation to the vessel.

The quarterdeck was gone, and even the rudder post and screw were broken. She was the first warship to be sunk in combat by a submarine, a feat that would not be repeated until fifty years later in the early days of World War I.

But *Hunley* had disappeared. Both sides remained unaware as to what had happened. The next day a court of inquiry absolved *Housatonic's* captain for the loss. The Confederates left the beacon lights on at Battery Marshall for the returning *Hunley*, but days passed with no sign of her.[6] Finally, ten days after the attack, a group of Union prisoners told the story of *Hunley's* last exploit and the sinking of *Housatonic*.

After the war, government divers clearing the wartime wrecks from Charleston harbor never found *Hunley*.[7] Conjecture remains that Dixon was spotted on the surface as he made the final run in to strike *Housatonic* under her stern. Unaware that the enemy had slipped his chain and was backing down, Dixon failed to move aside and the two collided suddenly; either the explosion mortally damaged the submarine or the sinking ship drew her down with her. One theory held that the submarine was drawn into the sinking warship and sank with her, and that post-war salvagers mistook the hull for a loose boiler. Others say that she made off in a damaged condition, only to sink before reaching Breach Inlet and now lies buried in the shifting sand.

The wreck of *Housatonic* was moved and deposited a few hundred yards off the Isle of Palms. Then *Hunley* was forgotten. After World War II, when modern submarines began to receive notoriety, another search was mounted for *Hunley*. Even sophisticated magnetic detecting equipment was unable to locate her. By now she is probably mere fragments of rust beyond possibility of salvage.

Following the Civil War, experiments continued with submersibles, but progress was slow because of their danger and the complexity of submergence technology. By the end of the century, most major navies of the world had submarines of some sort. However, it was not until Germany made major use of them in World War I that their capabilities were appreciated. Today, the modern missile-firing submarine has the ability to end life on the planet; these complex weapons systems can trace their beginnings to the CSS *Hunley* and Charleston harbor.

Author's model of the U. S. steam sloop-of-war *Housatonic*. She was one of the original 90-day gunboats built in 1861–62. Her sister, *Juniata*, was in Farragut's squadron at Mobile Bay in 1864. This model shows her peacetime rig. On blockade duty the sides of *Housatonic's* hull were painted blockader blue and her topmasts were struck below. By 1864 the blockading ships relied almost totally on steam for movement; sails were rarely used except on the open sea, and for blockade work were more of a hindrance than a help.

---

[6] Confederate signalmen at Battery Marshall claim to have seen *Hunley's* signal after the attack, but what they evidently saw were the lights of the Union boats searching for survivors of *Housatonic*.

[7] One post-war government diver claimed to have found *Hunley* and looked inside, where he saw the skeletons of the crew sitting at their positions.

Conrad Wise Chapman's famous painting of *Hunley* at Mount Pleasant on December 6, 1863, after having been salvaged from her fatal dive in Charleston harbor, in which her designer and namesake, Horace L. Hunley, perished. It is because of Chapman's sketches and this painting that we have a relatively clear idea of what this famous craft looked like. The discerning eye of a submarine historian will note the similarity of *Hunley's* hull shape to that of the World War II German Type XXI craft—one the most advanced submarine hull shapes before the advent of the U. S. Navy's modern teardrop design. This pioneer craft was quite advanced in hydrodynamic concept.

Charleston and the Blockade Runners[1]

When the Confederate War commenced, Southern leaders realized that they would have to obtain most of their military supplies from abroad; the South lacked sufficient industry to support a modern war. Thus, ports like Charleston became the Confederacy's lifeline of supply for the tools of warfare.

At the start of the war the Southern states not only lacked a navy, but also did not have much of a merchant marine. Firms such as the Ravenel Company were few and far between, as Southern commerce relied almost totally on Northern- and British-owned ships to haul its cargo.

While cotton was an important political and economic weapon, it had also lulled the Southern states into an agricultural system almost devoid of a manufacturing base. Practically all manufactured goods were imported from the North or Europe. To compound the weakness further, the Southern ports had few direct links with Europe. Most imports were first landed at New York and then distributed from there by rail or on smaller American coastal vessels. Most foreign vessels that arrived at Charleston came in ballast to haul away the cotton crop. When the war started and this trade was interrupted, the South had to start trade with Europe largely from scratch.

Because Charleston firms such as John Fraser and Company had tried during the 1850s to start direct steamship ties to Europe, the city was in a much better position than other Southern ports in regard to European connections. As a result of railroad expansion and the efforts of a wealthy and energetic merchant class, Charleston was on the verge of expanding her overseas shipping and actually placing steamships in service when the war started.

From mid-1858 to mid-1859, the port of Charleston imported one and a half million dollars in goods and exported over twenty-one million dollars worth. These figures were slightly ahead of Savannah's but far behind New Orleans', which totaled twenty million in and one hundred seven million out. While Mobile exported almost twice as much as Charleston, the latter was still considered the Confederacy's number two seaport and certainly number one on the South Atlantic coast. At the same time Charleston's customs collections totaled only $299,339 to New Orleans' $2,120,058 and New York's $35,155,452. Boston, at slightly over five million in customs receipts, collected more than all of the Southern ports combined. Philadelphia was also slightly ahead of New Orleans. In terms of trade the disadvantages between the two sections were enormous, but the South had an enormous balance of trade surplus that contributed immensely to her prosperity and the conviction that cotton was indeed king.

Blockade Proclaimed

After the firing on Fort Sumter, President Lincoln proclaimed a blockade of the Southern coast. Initially, the Confederate government expected the blockade would be so weak that foreign merchant ships would easily break it. If this did not happen, the predominant Confederate view was that the Royal Navy would intercede, sweeping aside the U. S. Navy to open the Southern ports. Southern expectations rested on the delusion that Great Britain could not and would not live without the South's cotton. For in 1859 Great Britain imported some 78 percent of the South's cotton crop and employed almost five million people in manufacturing cotton goods. The English cotton mills returned a profit of £59 million (approximately $300 million), a substantial sum for the period.

After Lincoln proclaimed the blockade in April 1861, a fifteen-day grace period followed for all foreign ships to depart Southern ports and for the word to be promulgated overseas. According to the Declaration of Paris, this grace period was to commence only after the blockade was physically in effect at each port and the local authorities had been notified. While the United States was not a signatory of the treaty, Lincoln and Secretary of State William H. Seward based the blockade on its provisions. Once established, the blockade could force an incoming ship to be searched and, if found to be carrying war materiel, seized. When the proclamation reached Charleston, the foreign ships scattered and Charleston shipowners promptly sold most of their ships. *John Ravenel*, laid up for repairs, was one of the few caught in the harbor for the duration of the war.

Most observers thought that the North would adopt a "cabinet blockade," whereby squadrons of warships would operate on the high seas merely as a deterrent to incoming foreign vessels; however, such a quasi-blockade was not Lincoln's intent. Instead, he meant to strangle Southern trade by posting warships off all major shipping centers.

This first blockade of modern times was enforced by steam-powered warships. Most Southern trade went by sailing ships, easily overtaken by steamers, especially if the wind was not favorable. The Union Navy blockade utilized many of the steamers that had hitherto provided the sea links between the North and the South. As warships they were not very threatening, but they were all that was needed to deter or overtake a sailing vessel or destroy a lightly armed cargo-hauling steamer trying to break the blockade.

The Royal Navy did not follow through on Southern expectations. In fact, both England and France declared their neutrality in May 1861, preferring to wait out the results. By then all of the 1860 cotton crop had been shipped overseas; therefore, it would not be until the fall that the blockade's effect would be felt on England's cotton mills. And so once again, Southerners hoped for British intervention, figuring that once the European countries exhausted their cotton supply on hand, they would break the blockade in order to obtain more.

Blockade Instituted

On the morning of May 11, 1861, the Federal steam sloop-of-war *Niagara* appeared off Charleston to wait out the fifteen-day grace period and enforce the blockade. All passing

[1] Much of this section has been compiled from *Lifeline of the Confederacy: Blockade Running During the American Civil War* by Stephen R. Wise, Ph.D., which will soon be published by the University of South Carolina Press. Other sources also contributed to the material herein.

ships were notified of the pending blockade. One of the few front-line steam warships of the U. S. Navy, *Niagara* was considered fast and powerful for her day, a definite asset for a blockader. However, her draft of over twenty-four feet made her ill-suited for the shallow waters off Charleston.

At first the blockade was weak, but the South lacked the ships to challenge it, and foreign merchant ships lacked the will to do so. Through the summer of 1861, the blockade tightened as more ships joined. On May 31, *Vandalia* joined *Niagara*. On August 21, she captured the Charleston schooner *Arthur Middleton* as it tried to run the blockade.

But blockade duty was terribly monotonous. Although they had to be ready at a moment's notice to chase a suspicious vessel, the blockaders grew complacent at the lack of challenge. By day they anchored and allowed the crews to rest. At night they became vigilant. False alarms were frequent; every shadow seemed

The Charleston schooner *Arthur Middleton*, captured off the bar by *Vandalia* and *Roanoke* on August 21, 1861.

U. S. steam sloop-of-war *Niagara*, the first ship to arrive off Charleston to enforce President Lincoln's blockade. Together with HMS *Agamemnon* she helped to lay the first transatlantic telegraph cable in 1854. In 1861 *Niagara* was one of the U. S. Navy's warships that had been deliberately scattered overseas by Buchanan's Secretary of the Navy Toucey, in anticipation of Southern secession. She was in Japan when the Southern states seceded, but was hurriedly recalled when Lincoln took office.

to be a blockade runner, and on occasion the blockading ships accidentally fired on each other. In foul weather, the ships would move a mile or so further from shore so that, in case the engines or anchors failed to hold, they would have time to react before being driven ashore.

From the blockading ships' position off the Charleston bar, surveillance and capture were not easy. They had to cover a thirteen-mile arc of ocean off the harbor entrance extending from Folly Beach to the Isle of Palms. The wooden steamers and sailing ships on blockade duty could not risk the narrow confines of the four channels leading into the port at night for fear of grounding. In addition if they got too close to shore, they would come under the fire of Confederate batteries, some of which had a five-mile range. At first only a handful of ships were available to cover this distance. As more ships joined the blockade by the end of 1861 it appeared to become more effective, but the Confederates merely escalated with better ships and crews. By late 1862 it had become apparent that the blockade was not as effective as hoped, even though upwards of twenty ships were on blockade duty at various times! Therefore Charleston became the first assignment for the Union ironclad squadron (see pages 235 to 238). With their heavy armor, these ships could anchor close to the Confederate batteries. However, Southern torpedoes and torpedoboats diminished their strategic edge, and the blockade continued as a cat-and-mouse game.

The blockade brought mounting supply and trade shortages in the South, as no ocean-going steamers entered or cleared a Confederate port during the summer of 1861. Some 253 sailing vessels, mostly small coastal schooners, managed to elude the blockading

Blockade runner unloading a cargo of cotton at Bermuda and preparing to take on a cargo of munitions. Note the two stacks for her boilers, an indication of her superior speed to outrun blockading warships; narrow hull, low to the water; and large, powerful sidewheels.

ships and sail in and out of South Carolina ports, but their cargoes were not enough to sustain even the peacetime South, much less the demands of the war effort. As the blockade increased in effectiveness, the numbers of these blockade-running ships declined drastically to 145 in 1862, 55 in 1863, 14 in 1864, and 5 in 1865.

Some of these blockade runners, such as *Palmetto* and *Pride*, were former Charleston pilot boats. The blockade had ended most of the pilots' normal work of bringing ships in and out of port; as entrepreneurs, they therefore turned to other means to sustain themselves, including blockade running.

After the neutral foreign ships departed, the Confederate ports were left with a mixed assortment of vessels. Only six oceanic steamers were available in the entire South; of these, *Nashville* and *Isabel* were at Charleston. There were other steamers, but all were of either the inland or coastal variety, too small for efficient transoceanic work.

The few steamers in Southern ports were seized by the military either to be outfitted as warships or to be used in carrying supplies for the army. *Nashville* became a Confederate warship. The owners of other types of ships were unwilling to risk their vessels running the blockade, for they were convinced that it would be only a matter of time before European intervention came. In an effort to hasten that time, an informal embargo of cotton was introduced with the tacit approval of the Confederate government. Unfortunately, Europe's refusal to bow to king cotton was not apparent to Richmond until later, when much time had been lost.

The First Real Blockade Runner

Despite mounting shortages, the summer of 1861 was by no means an entirely wasted period on the part of the Confederacy in their effort to obtain war supplies. Since foreign countries refused to extend diplomatic recognition to the Confederate States of America, she had to turn to private firms and individuals to obtain war materiel. The most important of these was the Charleston-based John Fraser and Company, which had been established early in the century as a leader in the North Atlantic shipping business. When the Frasers retired from the company in the 1850s, the senior partner was George Alfred Trenholm. In Liverpool, he had established Fraser, Trenholm and

Company. That office was run by Charlestonian Charles K. Prioleau, who became a British subject for the purpose of aiding the South under legal cover.

At the start of the war the Fraser, Trenholm companies operated five sailing ships between Charleston, Liverpool, and New York, and were also working to establish a direct steamship line between Charleston and Liverpool (see pages 198-200). Trenholm was a pillar of the local establishment and "master of the local banking and cotton trade." He commanded equal respect in England, where his efforts and connections would prove invaluable to the Confederacy.

After South Carolina seceded from the Union, but before actual fighting started, Fraser, Trenholm brought in several shipments of munitions. One item, an up-to-date Blakely gun with a supply of ammunition, was donated to the Confederacy in time to be mounted for the opening bombardment of Fort Sumter. The other ordnance was sold at tremendous profit, giving Trenholm an idea of what was to come. Once the blockade was announced, the firm terminated its active shipping business but continued to take orders and prepare shipments to be ready for any contingencies, whether it be wartime demand for munitions or normal peacetime commerce. Trenholm offered the Liverpool branch as a financial agent for the

The perfect type vessel for blockade running, *Presto* (see also page 288) shown here taking on cargo. She was low to the water, shallow-draft, fast, maneuverable with her sidewheels, and her blockader blue paint scheme rendered her almost invisible at night.

Confederacy. For a 1.5 percent commission, bonds and specie deposited with the company in Charleston would allow letters of credit to be issued in Liverpool, which the English banking houses honored. The extended credit allowed Confederate agents and missions in Europe to purchase sorely needed war materiel.

The most pressing needs of the Confederacy were infantry rifles and field cannon with which to arm its 100,000-man army that was massing to repel the Union forces. Confederate military agents arrived in England early in the summer of 1861, and set to work employing British agents as fronts for their efforts. By late July warehouses across England began to fill up with war materiel consigned to the Confederacy, but the agents were at a loss as to how to move it further. Then Prioleau offered the Confederate agents part of the cargo space aboard a Fraser, Trenholm steamer that was readying for a run to the South. The rates were high, but the agents had no other choice.

Prioleau had purchased and outfitted five vessels to run the blockade. Two had been built in the preceding decade and two more were still on the stocks, while the last was yet to be built. The first to be ready was the new iron-hulled *Bermuda*, built at Stockton-on-Tess and registered to one of Fraser, Trenholm's English cotton brokers. English agencies were used to confuse the Union as to her real ownership, a method regularly employed throughout the war with only minor success.

By August 1861 *Bermuda* was loading goods and munitions. Eugene L. Tessier was picked to bring her into the Confederacy (see page 198). Most of the cargo consisted of civilian goods that Fraser, Trenholm planned to sell in the South for large profits. The munitions included eighteen rifled field cannon and 6,500 Enfield rifles. Even Wade Hampton had space consigned on board for weapons for his legion.

Bermuda evaded the blockade and arrived in Savannah on September 18, the first real blockade runner to arrive in the Confederacy. Even before her cargo was offloaded various government agencies began to fight for it. The governor of Georgia even tried to get it. The Confederate general in Savannah seized the Enfields for Georgia regiments, but the rest of the weapons made it to northern Virginia. The civilian goods were snapped up by both merchant and government accounts. Late in October *Bermuda* was loaded down with over 2,000 bales of cotton and headed for England. In mid-November this cargo was sold in Liverpool for a handsome profit.

The *Bermuda* venture proved not only that the blockade could be broken successfully, but that a fortune could be made doing it. It also ended the cotton embargo. Patriots, merchants, and entrepreneurs got the profit message. A stampede ensued in England to get into the blockade-running business; one company raised capital of £2 million almost overnight!

The Realities of Blockade Running

Most histories of this aspect of the war point out that the long Southern coastline was a blockade runner's heaven; however, the economic and logistical facts point in another direction. Bringing war supplies through the blockade involved great risk and getting them to the fronts posed even more problems. Southerners were confident that the Union could not control the entire coast, but the Union was not overwhelmed by geography; they set priorities by blockading the main ports.

Smaller ports, although unguarded, were impractical. The size of the Southern blockade runner limited her ability to sail into a small inlet such as Rockville or McClellanville. With the developments of the steam age, ships had grown considerably in size; they now required deep harbors and docking facilities. If a steamship put into a small coastal town, the drayage of the area would be taxed for months just to haul the cargo away. Then there was the problem of hauling in cargo to load for the outward trip. Therefore, railroads and inland steamers for hauling large amounts of cargo in and out became as necessary a part of blockade running as the ocean-going ships themselves.

There were only some nine Southern ports on the Eastern seaboard that could handle the ships: Norfolk, Richmond, Morehead City, Wilmington, New Bern, Charleston, Savannah, Brunswick, and Fernandina. By the end of 1861 only Charleston and Wilmington were usable. The rest of the seaports were occupied or effectively closed by the enemy's ground and naval forces. Rail crossings of the larger rivers such as the Ogeechee in Georgia and the Santee in South Carolina were available. With some difficulty, shallow-draft blockade runners could pull up to the rail crossings in these rivers and unload their cargoes there.

Bringing an ocean-going vessel into a seaport is no simple matter in daylight, but taking a blockade runner into Charleston in total darkness was nearly impossible. Experienced captains could navigate a ship by the set of the current and the contour of the bottom. Buoys had been removed and lighthouses extinguished shortly after secession. The Confederate Signal Corps had replaced them with new beacons; still, only skippers thoroughly experienced with the coast could be depended on to guide vessels into port at night.

The strategy of these blockade-runner captains was to arrive about 90 miles off the coast at dusk. Then, after the moon had set around midnight, they would make landfall some ten to twenty miles north or south of the harbor entrance, such as off Kiawah or Bull's Island. Then they would work toward the harbor entrance close to shore, just outside of the breakers. Coming from the north, they would be under cover of Confederate land batteries that could hold the blockaders off shore. Coming from the south they could hope to be mistaken for Union vessels, due to the large numbers of blockaders on station. With the advantage of speed and surprise, many runners passed on through the blockade unnoticed. Others could make a mad dash for safety once the alarm was given by a blockading ship's signal rockets. It is amazing how few were caught in relation to the total number of voyages made throughout the war.

A certain type of vessel was required to ensure the maximum chance of blockade-running success. Shallow draft was important; therefore, propeller-driven vessels were undesirable because their propellers required deep water for efficiency. Thus, some blockade runners regressed in terms of marine engineering; outdated by some twenty years and thus less efficient in power output and more vulnerable to gunfire, sidewheelers became the blockade runners' choice. They had the advantage of being able to drift with the tide and, once discovered, attain maximum speed faster than screw-driven ships; consequently, they were able to dash past blockading ships. Sidewheelers could also free themselves more easily from sandbars by working their paddlewheels in opposite directions in a rocking motion. They also had great maneuverability; by reversing one sidewheel, the ship could literally pivot on its axis. Twin-screw vessels could pivot as well, but not as quickly. The first twin-screw blockade runner was *Flora*, which in January 1863 made the first of several successful trips into Charleston. Both types of runners were used, since each had advantages and disadvantages.

The sidewheelers most sought by the blockade-running firms were those built after a style first perfected on the Clyde River in Scotland. They had long, low, iron hulls, narrow beams, powerful engines, and light drafts for fast speed. Fraser, Trenholm and Company, the first to recognize the potential of these vessels, purchased *Herald* early in 1862 from the Dublin and Glasgow Steam Packet Company; she was the first Clyde Steamer to be taken into the blockade-running trade. By the end of the year many similar vessels were being outfitted in Liverpool and Glasgow as runners for various consortiums. The staterooms were removed to increase stowage capacity, stacks were adapted so that they could be lowered while running the blockade, and masts and spars were put on hinges so that they could be lowered when not in use.

Different color schemes were tried. The early vessels were black. But when black was determined to be too discernible at night, shipbuilders turned to light blues and greenish grays ("blockader blue"). These lighter colors worked so well that the ships could pass close to the enemy without being detected. The light color blended in with sand dunes on shore and at times made the runners appear to be clouds of mist moving over the water.

Even fuel could help camouflage. Smokeless anthracite coal was preferred, but it was in short supply. Therefore, soft coal had to be used, especially while on the open sea when the ships were less likely to be seen.

The time of greatest danger for the runners was in daylight hours between ports. Being sighted by an enemy cruiser often led to a test of speed between the two. Although the fastest Union ships patrolled the waters off Nassau and Bermuda, the runners could usually stay out of gun range of most enemy cruisers until dark or they could try to reach the safety of neutral waters. To save weight, the runners themselves carried no guns. In addition, most crews were Southern civilians or neutrals; as such, they were subject to charges of piracy if they engaged in shooting on the high seas. The entire blockade-running business was run according to the rules of international law.

Motives and rewards for running the blockade were many, but money provided the greatest incentive. The business, certainly profitable, also became romantic and even surprisingly safe. Prize money, still in use in the U. S. Navy, lured gun crews to hold their fire until there was absolutely no other way of stopping a runner. The officers and crews of the blockading ships wanted the prize money offered by the government both for the ships and the cargo, especially the cotton carried on outbound vessels.

The lure of quick profits drew blockade-running crews and officers from many nations, and particularly from England, where most of the ships originated. Because Confederate crewmen were subject to the draft, quite a few became British subjects. Thus, if they were captured by the Union Navy, their foreign citizenship enabled them to be detained for a few weeks at most. Once released, they returned to Nassau and often rejoined the trade. In contrast, as Confederate citizens they would become prisoners of war if captured.

John Fraser and Company and Fraser, Trenholm and Company reaped vast profits from blockade running. While government supplies took up more and more space in the ships on inbound voyages, the space on outbound vessels was available for profitable cotton. A successful round trip voyage would not only pay for the ship and its operating costs, but also render a possible profit of $100,000. This was certainly not a bad reward for patriotic duty! As Rhett Butler said in *Gone with the Wind*, there was money to be made when countries were being born and when they were dying. It was difficult to see whether the Confederacy was in its infancy or old age in 1862, but there was money to be made and lots of it.

The most prized ship officers were pilots and captains who were familiar with the waters around Charleston and Wilmington. They could command a king's ransom for taking a runner in and out. The Lockwood brothers, Louis Mitchel Coxetter, and Henry Sterling Lebby of Charleston often caused bidding wars between companies for their services. In the spring of 1862 Thomas Lockwood received $2,000 in gold per trip as commander of *Kate*. By the end of the war some captains were receiving $5,000 in gold for one voyage. Native Southerners were preferred over foreigners as ship captains, as it was felt that patriotism would lead them to take greater risks to deliver their cargoes.

The Nassau and Bermuda Staging Areas

By November 1861 with Port Royal in enemy hands, the port of Savannah was doomed. Overnight, Nassau and Bermuda were transformed into staging areas for the blockade-running business, and enemy cruisers began patrolling nearby waters; some even anchored in the harbor.

In Bermuda and Nassau Confederate blockade-running companies, using British firms

The blockade runner *Aries*, which made a successful round trip into Charleston late in 1862. Of special note are her hinged masts and telescoping stack, both in the lowered position to reduce visibility.

Blockade runner unloading her cargo of cotton at Bermuda. Tied to the dock at right is the former yacht *America*, in Confederate service also as a runner. She was subsequently captured and converted to a blockader. *America* participated in the destruction of *Georgiana* off the Isle of Palms (see page 214).

The blockade runner *Economist* leaving Charleston for Liverpool via Nassau on April 1, 1862, carrying cotton that the blockade runner *Fingal* was unable to get out of Savannah once that port was closed by the fall of Fort Pulaski. To the left is Fort Sumter in Confederate hands after the opening shots of the war. This 1864 painting by William York shows her under the English merchant colors of her alleged owners, a trick often employed to prevent captured ships from being confiscated. *Economist* made two trips to the Confederacy. On one trip she brought in iron plates for the ironclads being constructed in Charleston. She spent the balance of the war ferrying supplies to Nassau and Bermuda from England.

for fronts, maintained bases complete with warehouses for holding goods. British and other neutral ships brought the goods first to these ports, then the runners carried them the last few hundred miles to a Confederate port, usually Charleston or Wilmington.

Before the war Nassau had been a colonial outpost with few vessels calling there. The Royal Navy maintained a coaling station and naval base in its well-protected anchorage. The war ended its sleepy existence much as it did Wilmington's. Nassau was only 500 miles, or three days steaming, from the main Confederate seaports; therefore, by using its harbor as a distribution point under British neutrality, blockade runners had more fuel space available aboard ship for money-making cargo.

Just as boom towns sprang up in the gold rushes of the American West, Nassau was transformed into a raunchy, bawdy town almost overnight. Women came from the brothels of Europe to relieve the sailors of their money, which was said to be as plentiful as dirt. The banks could not hold all of the gold, which was dumped down by the bushel and guarded by soldiers!

Charleston Enters the Business

Charleston's first serious blockade-running attempt was with the ex-steamer *Gordon*, renamed *Theodora*. In October 1861, the Confederate commissioners to Europe, Mason and Slidell, arrived in Charleston to run the blockade on the cruiser *Nashville*. Since she was so closely watched by the Union ships, they turned to the smaller but faster steamer *Theodora*, then owned by a syndicate headed by F. T. Porcher and used as a picket boat in the harbor. The commissioners received permission to charter *Theodora*, but the price was too high; George Alfred Trenholm stepped in and offered to pay half the cost if he could use cargo space on her return voyage to Charleston. The offer was accepted and on the morning of October 12, the ship slipped out of the harbor under Captain Thomas Lockwood and moved down the coast to Nassau and Cuba. From Havana, Mason and Slidell booked passage on the British steamer *Trent* bound for Southhampton. In the Bahama Channel north of Cuba, *Trent* was stopped by the USS *San Jacinto*. The commissioners were removed under threat of force and carried away to prison in New York. Britain protested loudly,

claiming her neutrality had been violated. British troops were sent to Canada in anticipation of war. Because Lincoln could not afford to take on another adversary, the Confederate commissioners were released.

Louis Mitchel Coxetter had also disembarked from *Theodora* in Cuba. He was probably the most knowledgeable steamboat captain on the southeast coast, and would become the top blockade-running captain of the war.

In Havana, *Theodora* took on a return cargo of weapons and civilian goods. She slipped up the east coast along the inland waterways, and arrived in Charleston on November 4.

Captain Thomas Lockwood

His legendary trips in and out of Charleston, Wilmington, and Savannah earned him the title "father of the trade." He made his name in *Kate*, and at the end of the war he returned *Colonel Lamb* to England.

Captain Robert Lockwood was one of Charleston's most successful blockade-runner captains. He commanded *Margaret and Jessie* on several successful runs until her capture off Wilmington. Exchanged, he proceeded to England. There he was supervising the construction of the last class of blockade runners when the war ended. After the war he returned to Charleston and joined the coastal steamer service under the Adger Line, which was later bought out by the Clyde Line. As captain of *City of Columbia*, he and his little terrier "Dandy" drowned off the Delaware coast when the ship sank after a collision.

Her success made Confederate officials and private interests realize the potential of fast, smaller steamers.

On December 10, *Theodora* limped into Nassau from Charleston, having barely survived a violent storm. Already in port was *Gladiator*, a new runner, preparing for a run to Charleston under Robert Lockwood, brother of *Theodora's* captain. *Gladiator* found herself blocked by faster Union warships standing off shore from Nassau. Because of her slow speed, she was deemed unsuitable for blockade running and was put to use on transatlantic supply missions to England.

John Fraser and Company now began to buy up the few remaining steamers left on the southeast coast to use on runs between Nassau and Charleston. At Charleston *Isabel*, *Cecile*, and *Carolina* were purchased. The first, renamed *Ella Warley*, slipped out for Nassau in December 1861 with almost a thousand bales of cotton to exchange for civilian goods. While in Nassau the vessel was registered under the English flag to give it immunity from seizure on the high seas. However, this immunity did not apply when the ship was obviously in a declared blockade area.

Despite the profits, risks were high. Between April and June of 1862, Fraser, Trenholm lost three new steamers with valuable cargoes on their first attempts to enter Charleston. These and other failures during that spring and early summer forced the company to realize that the days of the large deep-draft steamers successfully running the blockade were at an end. While other syndicates would still use the larger, slower steamers for blockade running, Fraser, Trenholm shifted to the newer runners that began to come on line in the summer of 1862.

Before dawn on May 26, 1862, the USS *Huron* spotted a long, low steamer just about to enter Charleston. Firing her forward rifle, *Huron* chased the steamer seaward. After a four-hour chase, *Huron* overhauled and captured the blockade runner *Cambria*. She was a valuable prize, as her holds were filled with rifles, saltpeter, muslin, and medicines.

Charleston's Heyday as a Runner Port

The first months of 1862 saw a marked increase in blockade-running activity through Charleston in spite of the Union occupation of the sea islands southward to Savannah. A newspaper article in the Philadelphia *Daily Evening Bulletin* on February 17 declared that no fewer than 65 vessels had run the blockade in and out of Charleston since the beginning of the war. This report raised such a furor in Washington that there were calls in Congress for an investigation of the Charleston blockade's inefficiency. As an offshoot, a Congressional resolution was passed instructing the Committee on Naval Affairs to inquire into the matter. The resolution was a stinging rebuke to Admiral DuPont, the first of many public outcries that would cast a pall over his command of the South Atlantic Blockading Squadron. Although Secretary of the Navy Gideon Welles defended DuPont, the Charleston station remained the focus of much official criticism.

By the spring of 1862, Savannah, New Orleans, Fernandina, St. Augustine, Brunswick, and Jacksonville had all been captured or evacuated. So had the inner sounds of North Carolina, which cut the port of Beaufort off from the interior. The closing of these ports made more Union ships available for blockade duty off Charleston and Wilmington. The fleet off the Charleston bar became the largest of all the blockading squadrons. It was also the most controversial because of DuPont's failure to stop the blockade-running traffic.

On April 21 the following ships were on duty off the harbor entrance:

Steamer *James Adger*[2]	Commander John B. Marchand
Steamer *Augusta*	Commander Parrot
Steamer *Alabama*	Commander Lanier
Steamer *Huron*	Commander Downes
Bark *Roebuck*	Lieutenant George A. Trundy
Steamer *Pocahontas* (off Stono)	Lieutenant Balch
Bark *Restless* (off Bull's Bay)	Lieutenant Conroy
Ship *Onward* (off Bull's Bay)	Lieutenant Nickels

The first of the new class of blockade runners was the Dublin ferryboat *Herald*, which Prioleau had purchased by coincidence in January 1862 before the spring disasters. She was fast, and she drew only ten and a half feet, allowing her to use the shallower channels into Charleston and Wilmington. She arrived in Charleston under Captain Coxetter in July, beginning a successful season for the company. Fraser, Trenholm was now paying the best wages for the best captains. Having now acquired the best ships, it maintained its position as the premier blockade-running company. In fact, Fraser, Trenholm became so closely linked with the Confederate government that the company may as well have been an arm of the government.

In the spring of 1862 *Kate*, under command of Thomas Lockwood and named after

---

[2] On March 18, 1862, the USS *James Adger* stopped the John Fraser Company ship *Emily St. Pierre* as she neared the Charleston bar. Captain William Wilson claimed that he was not attempting to run the blockade, but was merely off course en route from Calcutta to a United States port. As *Emily St. Pierre* was on a list of suspected Confederate vessels and was carrying contraband, she was ordered to Philadelphia for adjudication. En route Captain Wilson, his steward, and cook overpowered the prize crew. With the aid of four men in the prize crew, the seven sailed the large vessel 3,000 miles to Liverpool.

George Alfred Trenholm's wife, became the stalwart of Fraser, Trenholm's runners. She established so regular a run that she earned the name "packet." It was *Kate* that brought the munitions for the Western Front that supplied General Johnston's army at the battle of Pittsburg Landing (Shiloh). That summer *Herald* and *Leopard* joined Fraser, Trenholm's fleet and rang up a long list of successful runs. Although their runs never equaled those of *Kate*, they had twice her cargo capacity.

On *Kate* Thomas Lockwood's skill in moving through the blockade became legendary. He made almost twenty runs in and out of Charleston and Wilmington and one to the supposedly closed port of Savannah! He reportedly received $2,000 per trip as commander of *Kate*. The government even entrusted him with special cargoes, including gold. Although the Yankees never could catch him, fate dealt him a bad blow. In November *Kate* hit a snag in the Cape Fear River and sank, a total loss.

Other blockade-running companies competed with Fraser, Trenholm in the early months of 1862. One of the first was started by J. A. Enslow, a Charleston commission merchant. He purchased the steamer *Governor Dudley* and renamed it *Nelly*. On her first run, she carried 313 bales of cotton to Nassau. She made five profitable trips before running aground

off Long Island (Isle of Palms) on May 25. Her cargo on that final voyage was saved and sold at huge prices. Her hull and engines were salvaged six days later and sold for $1,700.

Another early entrant was the Importing and Exporting Company of South Carolina, run by William Bee and Charles Mitchell and nicknamed the "Bee Company." John Fraser and Company was the largest shareholder in this friendly rival's operations. Its initial subscription of $100,000 was easily met. The funds were used to purchase the steamer *Cecile* (from John Fraser and Company) and the schooner *Edwin*, complete with their cargoes of cotton, rice, and turpentine.

The two vessels cleared Charleston early in April and arrived safely in Nassau. *Cecile*, under Captain James Carlin, returned at the end of the month, but *Edwin* under Captain N. C. Gambrill ran aground off Morris Island. Although her cargo was saved, she was a total loss. The round trip for *Cecile*, however, returned the original investment plus a profit. Subsequent trips yielded more profits. On June 18 on her way back to Charleston on her sixth trip, *Cecile* was lost on the Abaco Reef. This loss momentarily stopped the company until additional ships could be purchased, but it had repaid its original investment almost two fold and still had capital with which to purchase new steamers!

Large crowds would gather at the Importing and Exporting Company's auction block on Bull Street to bid on the products that slipped in through the blockade. Initially they were sold in package lots. This allowed only the rich with ready cash to buy. The general public was then forced to buy their necessities at inflated prices from middlemen. A cup of brown sugar might cost as much as $10, and quinine, which sold in Nassau for $10, would bring up to $500 in Charleston. In an effort to reduce inflation, William Bee initiated retail sales in the fall of 1863. These "Bee Sales" provided the public with direct access to imported articles. By the summer of 1864 they were discontinued, because the Union blockade tightened, curtailing runs through Charleston.

Domestic firms were not the only ones who were in the blockade-running business. An English firm jumped in with the steamer *Memphis* (see page 260). She and *Thomas L. Wragg* approached Charleston from Nassau on June 22. Union blockaders spotted *Thomas L. Wragg*, forcing her to turn back. She was almost back to Nassau before she could shake off the pursuing *Keystone State*.

In the meantime *Memphis* eluded the blockade and entered Maffitt's Channel, only to run aground off Sullivan's Island under fire from Fort Sumter. The next morning Union

Blockade runner *Anglia*, which was captured in Bull's Bay on her fourth run by USS *Restless* and *Flag* on October 19, 1862.

blockaders tried to destroy *Memphis* with gunfire, but were held at bay by the Confederate forts until the cargo was offloaded and she was towed into the harbor. Her slipping through the blockade was an immense embarrassment to the blockaders; with her large size and high freeboard, she should have been easy to spot. But she eluded them again in the early morning hours of July 31, when she slipped out through Maffitt's Channel unseen. The Union blockade failed to note her absence from the harbor the next day; however, about forty miles southeast of Cape Romain *Memphis* was sighted by the USS *Magnolia*, which gave chase. After two hours of hard steaming, *Magnolia* opened fire. As the shells began to explode close to the starboard quarter, *Memphis* hove to and surrendered.

Failure of *Memphis* and her subsequent English-backed consorts can be traced to the use of deep-draft, high-freeboard steamers, now easy prey for the blockaders. The Navigation Company of Glasgow purchased the light-draft *Minho* from John Fraser and Company, and she proved more successful. *Minho* made several trips before the end of 1862, generating an excellent return and profits to buy additional vessels. However, on an inward trip in October, she ran aground off Sullivan's Island. Her engines and part of the cargo were saved, but the hull was too badly damaged to salvage. Their next two vessels, *Pearl* and *Iona*, were lost before reaching Nassau. A fourth, *Thistle*, made it into Charleston in January, but she too ended up on Sullivan's Island. John Ferguson salvaged her, but she was captured by the USS *Canandaigua* on her outbound voyage. The risks were increasing for light-draft ships too.

Through 1862 the success rate was two out of three trips, allowing a blockade-running company an excellent return on its investment. The risks were high; of the thirty-six vessels running the blockade that year, twenty-eight were lost. However, the lure of good profits kept the business going.

Runs out of Charleston carried the least risk of capture. Since the Confederate military in the forts at the harbor entrances could provide detailed information as to the disposition of the blockading ships to a departing runner, fewer were caught. In 1863, only 11 outbound ships were lost out of 168 attempts to clear Wilmington and Charleston, while 36 out of 204, or three times as many, were lost trying to enter.

By the fall of 1862 the armed forces of the Confederacy were totally dependent on a steady flow of supplies from Europe. The loss of manufacturing bases in New Orleans and Memphis increased their needs. To compound the problem the government was unable to force the blockade-running companies to carry munitions into Southern ports. The problem of transporting munitions got worse as the year wore on because of the danger of transporting explosives, the weight of weapons, and the higher profits possible on civilian goods. Thus, by the end of 1862 government agents in Nassau were able to ship only about half the munitions on hand in warehouses there.

It had finally become apparent that England's need for cotton would not entice her to join forces against the Union. The Confederacy was beginning to feel the crunch of war. Shortages were being felt everywhere in the South, while needed supplies built up in Nassau and Bermuda due to insufficient numbers of runners. To make matters worse Confederate finances in Europe had run out, and creditors were demanding payment. To put finances in order, cotton became the financial medium of exchange in Europe for the Confederacy, much as rice and indigo had been the medium during the Revolution. Mill owners and speculators purchased cotton bonds against future deliveries of the staple, largely to ensure a supply for their mills.

The French steam corvette *Milan* and HMS *Petrel* at anchor in Charleston harbor early in 1863.

Neutral Warships and the Blockade

The Union blockaders had more than blockade runners to worry about. Another nuisance for them was neutral warships. Just as warships of the United States Navy were pulling into Nassau to replenish supplies and to carry dispatches to the American consul, neutral warships were allowed to penetrate the blockade and do the same at Charleston. While not a common occurrence, these visits continued until Charleston harbor became a dangerous shooting gallery. In May 1862 HMS *Racer* mingled with the blockading ships before proceeding into Charleston to meet with the British consul.

In June 1862 after the battle of Secessionville on James Island, the French warship *Renaudin* anchored with the blockaders. This worried the senior Union officer; with operations intensifying around Charleston, the Union suspected that such neutral warships were passing information to the Confederates. A further fear was that they might be caught in a crossfire, causing a diplomatic incident. The British consul at Charleston, Robert Bunch, was an outspoken Southern sympathizer; therefore, Secretary of State Seward asked the British ambassador in Washington for Bunch's recall. When it was refused, HMS *Rinaldo*, the next British warship to approach Charleston, was denied entry to the harbor. She had to anchor off Rattlesnake Shoal from June 8 to 10, but she sent her ship's launch into Charleston to communicate with the consul, who sent return messages out to *Rinaldo* on a tugboat under a flag of truce.

On June 19 the Union blockaders did allow the French warship *Renaudin* to pass through into the city with dispatches for the French consul. Though a warship in name, she was little more than a dispatch boat. The Union feeling was that the French were not aiding the Confederacy as much as the English; no blockade runners had been discovered with French registry. *Renaudin* remained for two days and then sailed to Port Royal.

HMS *Racer* returned to the Charleston bar at the end of June and was forced to anchor outside with the blockading squadron. During the night of June 27 she flashed one of her large, brilliant lights. This alarmed the blockading ships, as they thought that it was a signal to the runner *Memphis*, which was then in the harbor preparing to come out. The next morning a Charleston tug flying a Union Jack and a white flag brought a pilot out and *Racer* was allowed to pass into the harbor. She departed Charleston the next day for Port Royal without incident.

As Union ironclads began to appear off the Charleston bar and a naval attack seemed imminent, the visits of neutral warships to Charleston were curtailed. If any neutral warships had been present in the harbor during the subsequent ironclad attacks and any Union ironclads had penetrated the Confederate defenses, they would have been caught in a deadly crossfire.

Other Blockade-running Firms

In the final months of 1862 and early in 1863 there was a substantial increase in blockade running supported by the private sector and the Confederate government. Even the state of North Carolina got into the business, in order to bring in clothing and equipment for state troops; theirs was ultimately the most successful of the government-run blockade-running operations. As a result, North Carolina troops were among the best equipped in the Confederacy. Throughout the war, the Confederate government itself remained unable to get a significant blockade-running operation underway. Both private and government-sponsored

THE HUNTERS AND THE HUNTED

The Fraser, Trenholm blockade runner *Princess Royal* that was captured on her first attempt into Charleston on January 29, 1863, by USS *Unadilla* (see page 223). She is shown here in the guise of a blockader as she was taken into the Union Navy after capture. Later she was renamed *General Sherman*, and after the war she was wrecked off Cherry Grove, South Carolina.

The steamship *Eagle*. At the beginning of the war she was taken into the Union service as USS *Rhode Island*. In May 1863 she chased and captured the Charleston runner *Margaret and Jessie* in the Bahamas.

ships competed for the same things: cargoes, crews, captains, pilots, supplies, and financing. With ships in short supply, the newer entrants into the business had to content themselves with the cast-offs of older companies, and it was these ships that accounted for most of the losses.

Joining the other companies at Charleston (see pages 278 and 279) were the Steamship Charleston Company, the Palmetto Exporting and Importing Company, the Chicora Importing and Exporting Company, and the Atlantic Steam Packet Company of the Confederate States. Most private firms entered the business solely for profits; however, a few such as Fraser, Trenholm also had patriotic motives, and others did it to obtain cotton for their mills in Europe or to bring goods to their businesses in the South. English and even Canadian firms began to dominate the business because they had better sources of capital, ships, and supplies. These firms took advantage of English shipbuilding advances and purchased British goods at the best prices. While they could not buy cotton as advantageously as their Confederate counterparts, they made up for this by purchasing cotton bonds, which guaranteed them valuable return cargoes. Some made money by hauling cargo to and from the West Indies or selling cargo space to the Confederate government.

In the spring of 1863 one of the most successful blockade-running firms was the Importing and Exporting Company of South Carolina (I. and E. Company). It resumed business after being stopped when its first ships were captured late in 1862. Shortly afterward it was incorporated and sold $200,000 worth of stock (later increased to $700,000). William Bee became president and William Ravenel, W. P. Magrath, Benjamin Mordecai, C. T. Mitchel, E. L. Kerrison, and Theodore Jervey served on its board. These men, knowledgeable of the cotton trade, were closely associated by family ties and decades of mutual business interests in the shipping field.

The I. and E. Company purchased *Ella and Annie*, *Alice*, and *Fannie*. In early April, *Ella and Annie*, one of the first runners to use "blockader blue" camouflage, made her first run into Charleston. Her sister ships joined her two months later, ultimately providing the greatest service, with eleven and ten round trips respectively. *Ella and Annie* made four runs before being captured in November 1864 off Wilmington. She subsequently was taken into the U. S. Navy as the USS *Malvern*, flagship of Admiral David D. Porter for the duration of the war.

These three ships made the I. and E. Company of South Carolina one of the most successful. *Ella and Annie* alone could turn a profit of just under $200,000 for one round trip, and each of the other two could turn over $100,000 per trip. For each share originally purchased at $1,000, the company paid out total dividends of $9,000 and £120 sterling!

The I. and E. Company also had William Denny and Brothers of Dumbarton, Scotland build to their specifications *Ella*, *Caroline*, and *Emily*. *Ella* made only two runs between Wilmington and Nassau before running aground and being destroyed on December 1, 1864,

Captain Frank Bonneau of *Ella and Annie*.

The Importing and Exporting Company of South Carolina's highly successful *Ella and Annie*.

while trying to enter Wilmington. Part of her wreck still remains submerged off Cape Fear, North Carolina. *Caroline* made several runs before returning to England in March 1865.

George Carlin, the firm's foremost skipper, was sent to Scotland to oversee the construction of the new runners. Frank N. Bonneau and other captains had varying degrees of success, but tightened blockade conditions toward the end of the war diminished their chances.

Another successful Charleston firm was the Chicora Importing and Exporting Company of South Carolina. Archibald Johnson, a local merchant, was president. He was backed by George W. Williams, a leading Charleston banker, and Theodore Wagner, one of Trenholm's partners in John Fraser and Company. Chicora began in September 1862 with *Antonica*, formerly *Herald* of John Fraser and Company. Her success enabled the firm to purchase *Havelock* in England. They brought her into Charleston as *General Beauregard*. Louis Coxetter took her on a long and profitable career. In May 1863 Coxetter brought in the underwater cable to be used with the mines in Charleston harbor (see pages 254 and 255).

Another success was the Charleston Importing and Exporting Company, whose stock by early 1864 had increased 800 percent in value!

Early in 1863 John Fraser and Company actively entered the business by assembling several vessels at Nassau. The first one, *Stonewall Jackson*, was sighted as she approached Charleston on her first trip, run aground off the Isle of Palms, and burned. However, the firm had better luck with the second vessel, *Margaret and Jessie*, supposedly one of the finest vessels to be used in the trade. She made four voyages to Charleston under Captain William Wilson. Then in May the Union cruiser *Rhode Island* (see page 280) chased her and ran her aground off Eleuthera, but she was salvaged and repaired in Nassau. She was then sold to the I. and E. Company. There under Captain Robert Lockwood she continued

her highly successful career until October, when she was captured by the Union after an all-night chase while trying to enter Wilmington. She then became the gunboat USS *Gettysburg*.

Another John Fraser success was *Elizabeth* under Thomas Lockwood. By the fall of 1863 she was one of the company's few ships in operation, the others having been lost or sold. On September 26 she ran aground while trying to make the Old Inlet into Wilmington. Lockwood burned her and escaped ashore.

Charleston's Flow Slows

Up until the first half of 1863, Charleston remained the South's main blockade-running port. The private companies were based in Charleston, while Wilmington was the home of operations run by the various agencies of the Confederacy and the state of North Carolina. From January to the end of June 1863, some forty steamers entered Charleston harbor and thirty-two cleared, taking out 29,000 bales of cotton (about 10 percent of the annual prewar rate) and bringing in numerous civilian goods. Auctions took place daily, as the blockade-running firms competed with each other for the remaining funds of the South's merchants. The city's wharves were constantly crowded with ships of all kinds—including warships, blockade runners, inland steamers, and ironclads. The harbor was so congested that on June 9, 1863, the outward-bound runner *Alice* hit the ram of the ironclad *Chicora*, ripping a long gash in her own hull, which flooded the rear compartment. *Alice* was forced to return to dock to be unloaded and repaired.

Charleston so dominated the early blockade-running trade that Union capture of the

John Fraser and Company's blockade runner *Margaret and Jessie*, supposedly one of the finest vessels to be used in the blockade-running business.

Monitor *Catskill* destroying the blockade runner *Raccoon* under the guns of Fort Sumter on July 19, 1863.

William Aiken Walker's view of one of the ironclad attacks on Fort Sumter early in 1864, as seen from Charleston's Battery seawall. The citizens in the foreground do not seem too concerned about the enemy ironclads breaking through into the inner harbor. Note the Confederate iron- clads waiting off Fort Johnson on James Island to the right, and the other ships in the harbor, including the Confederate gunboat *Juno* in the foreground. *Juno* (as *Helen*) successfully ran the blockade in March 1864, only to be lost in a gale before reaching Nassau.

city would have been regarded in England as the deathblow to the Confederacy, and would have done more than any other thing to discourage foreign support. In addition, Northern morale would greatly benefit by the fall of the cradle of secession. With both these factors in mind, Lincoln and his cabinet began planning a major attack on the city in 1862. By June, Federal troops had moved up the coast from Port Royal, but were stopped just short of the city at the battle of Secessionville. Land operations bogged down, and Federal ironclads were called in to end the stalemate. The April 1863 attack was one of the Union Navy's few major defeats of the war. Little prodding was needed in Washington to organize a new attack. The plan resulted in a joint army-navy attack on Morris Island on July 10, 1863. Battery Wagner held them off for two months. Confederate defenses were then shifted to Sullivan's Island, and obstructions and torpedoes were placed in the harbor entrance. By the time Sumter had been pounded to rubble, the other defenses were so strong that the Union Navy never again attempted to enter the harbor in force.

The attacks had failed to capture the city, but they did severely limit blockade-running activity. With the capture of Morris Island at the harbor's southern entrance in September and the emplacement of Federal batteries on Cumming's Point, accurate land-based Union artillery fire was brought to the harbor entrance. Between July 10 and September 18, 1863, only four vessels entered and cleared Charleston. From then until March 4, 1864, no vessels left or entered.

With the temporary closure of Charleston, all major blockade-running activity moved

A blockade runner ramming and sinking a picket boat from the steam frigate *Wabash* off Charleston in the fall of 1863.

north to Wilmington. The fall of 1863 was a bleak period for blockade running. By November and December most of the active runners were captured, leaving only a handful in service. These losses came at a time when the demand for munitions was greatest: the losses at Gettysburg, Vicksburg, and then Chattanooga had to be replaced.

To make matters worse, Confederate finances in Europe were in disarray; discouraging war news caused cotton bonds to sell at a fifth to a third below discount. In August 1863, in an attempt to prop up cotton bond values by inceased cotton deliveries to Europe, the war department in Richmond consigned one-half of all outward cargo space to the government at a favorable rate. With this action the government began to regulate the blockade-running business; later, it prohibited the importation of certain types of luxury and other civilian goods and allotted itself inward cargo space at favorable rates. The Confederate government also involved itself in the blockade-running business by constructing and operating its own fleet of ships. By so doing, the government freed itself of the demands of private shipowners.

By the beginning of 1864, food, leather, and cloth were in short supply for the Confederate Army because production centers for these goods were under enemy control. Imports now had to meet these needs. Meat shortages would plague the Confederacy for the duration of the war, forcing the South to make large purchases abroad. Other needs worsened as private shipowners outbid the government for rail space to haul cargoes of cotton and fuel coal to the ports. The problems extended to just about every aspect of the operation of blockade runners that conflicted with the other needs of the Confederacy. This was nowhere more apparent than in the problems of hauling military supplies to the war fronts over an overtaxed transportation system. Furthermore, the cotton growers became more reluctant to sell their crops for government bonds and demanded cash instead, further pressing the treasury.

Union picket boats from the blockading fleet on duty off Fort Sumter. Their mission was to serve as a first warning of Confederate torpedoboats' attempts to attack the blockading fleet and of blockade runners' attempts to sail from Charleston.

Conrad Wise Chapman's depiction of the sentry and flag of Fort Sumter symbolizing Southern defiance in the face of defeat. This well-known painting gives an idea of the number of vessels engaged in the blockade of Charleston. While in daylight these vessels may have been intimi-dating, at night it was a different story. The low freeboards and camouflage paint of the blockade runners rendered them almost invisible. This, combined with their speed and knowledge of the waters, made them fantastically successful in slipping in and out of Charleston.

Charleston's Final Surge of Glory

Charleston reentered the blockade-running business on March 4, 1864, when the dredge-boat *General Moultrie* cleared for Nassau. She was a small, slow vessel, but her shallow-draft enabled her to maneuver her way out past the blockade. She kept close to the shore of Sullivan's Island, protected by its Confederate guns, and slipped out without being spotted by enemy lookouts on Morris Island. However, once safely in Nassau *General Moultrie* was sold; her slow speed made her vulnerable as a runner. Five days later she was followed by the runner *Helen* (ex-*Juno*). Under the command of Philip Porcher, she ran into a gale when only two days out of Charleston, broke in two, and sank, leaving only two survivors. This disaster demonstrated another risk of these lightly built vessels that were designed and built for steaming in protected waters. They were vulnerable on the open sea; several were lost without a trace.

Charleston's revival as a port centered around the daring of the native ship captains, new runners that were faster and lower to the water, enemy complacency, and Southern desperation. The Importing and Exporting Company of Georgia under Gazaway B. Lamar led the revival. In the summer of 1863, this firm purchased several steamers in Great Britain. The first to reach the South was *Little Ada*, which entered the Santee River in February 1864 and unloaded her cargo at McClellanville. Here she got embroiled in a controversy over whether she would haul out cotton belonging to the state of Georgia or that belonging to the Confederacy. While the administrative battle raged, a real battle ensued; three armed boats from the USS *Winona* moved to seize *Little Ada*. Before the Federal boats could haul her away, a Confederate field battery arrived and drove the enemy off after the Union sailors unsuccessfully tried to burn the ship. Eventually the administrative battle was won by the Confederacy, and *Little Ada* left loaded with government cotton. In mid-June she survived a heavy gale and reached Nassau. Unfortunately, on her next voyage she was captured by the Union while trying to reach Wilmington.

In addition to *Little Ada*, the Importing and Exporting Company of Georgia had three other vessels on line by the summer of 1864. Two were lost in August; one of them, *Mary Bowers*, ran on the wreck of *Georgiana* off the Isle of Palms. Their most successful ship was *Little Hattie*, captained by Charlestonian Henry Sterling Lebby. She would survive the war in Southern service after ten trips.

Another Charleston success during the last half of 1864 was the Charleston Importing and Exporting Company. They had made a mark the preceding year, but had been forced to shut down due to the loss of vessels. In 1864, the company incorporated to raise new capital, and their first steamer in operation was the paddlewheeler *Syren*. Her captains were noted for daring and audacity; during one period they made three round trips through the blockade, while other runners, waiting for better conditions, never left port. *Syren* was so successful that the company never needed to purchase another ship, and by war's end the investors had reaped a 100 percent return on their initial investment! In the fall of 1864, shares that had originally sold for $1,000 commanded $3,000 on the open market.

Throughout 1864, other Charleston blockade-running firms were also succeeding in spite of the enemy pressure on the city from Morris Island. The Chicora Importing and Exporting Company had two new steamers, *Chicora* and *Wando*, in operation. Louis Coxetter, who continued to reign as the master of blockade running, commanded *Chicora*. The Importing and Exporting Company of South Carolina was also turning a profit through the spring and summer of 1864. Their ships *Alice* and *Fannie* made a total of 44 successful trips. Their profits were used to purchase bonds and new steamers.

Although these companies were chalking up successes, John Fraser and Company remained the leading firm. After reaching a low point in the fall and winter of 1863 with only *Bendigo* in service, the company bought five new ships in 1864. From January 1 to September 1, they made 36 trips with only 2 losses.

USS *Pawnee* anchored in the Kiawah River on blockade duty south of Charleston in 1864.

The blockade runner *Chicora* running from the blockade fleet past Morris Island into Charleston. Built by William C. Miller & Company of Liverpool as *Let Her Be*, she was renamed *Chicora* on her arrival in the Confederacy. She was one of the most successful of the Charleston runners during the last months of the war. *Chicora* survived the war to be sold at Halifax and later was taken up the St. Lawrence River to Montreal. There she was cut in half and reassembled at Buffalo, New York. *Chicora* served on the Great Lakes as an excursion boat until 1919. Her hull survived as a barge until 1939.

Thomas Lockwood, now known as "the father of the trade," went to England during the summer of 1864 to supervise the construction of two new large steel runners for the firm, *Hope* and *Colonel Lamb*. Lockwood's being spared to go to England demonstrated the firm's high regard for him and showed that individual Charlestonians were involved in all facets of the business. *Hope* and *Colonel Lamb* were the first of the final generation of iron- and steel-hulled blockade runners being built on the Clyde and Mersey Rivers in England, and were designed to carry upwards of 1,500 bales of cotton. With such capacity they could give half their cargo to the Confederate government and still make, in one round trip, enough profit to recover the investment.

Through the summer of 1864, Union pressure built up around Richmond and Atlanta, and Confederate supply trains ran continuously to both fronts. As the defenses of these two cities continued to hold, so did Confederate finances and loans in Europe; however, once Atlanta fell, the finances came on troubled times. When news of the fall of Mobile and Atlanta reached Liverpool, it produced a financial panic that plunged the price of cotton.

To make matters worse, a yellow fever quarantine in Nassau and Bermuda increased the roundtrip interval from two to eight weeks. The Confederacy, nearing demise, was desperate for supplies. The blockade runners kept the supplies flowing, but delivery was slow and risks were heavy.

After the fall of Fort Fisher at Wilmington in January 1865, only Charleston remained as an East Coast blockade-running port. However, it remained a difficult one to use because Federal forces controlled the southern harbor entrance. Of the thirty-eight runs into Charleston in 1864, twenty-four were made by John Fraser and Company's *Fox*, the Chicora Importing Company's *Chicora*, the Steamship Druid Company's *Druid*, and the Charleston Importing and Exporting Company's *Syren*. Some of the other runners that were thwarted in entering Charleston put into Georgetown and the Santee River.

Sic Transit Gloria

Once Wilmington was closed, more blockading ships shifted to Charleston, making the port more difficult to use. However, for profit or patriotism, a few remaining captains were willing to try. In January 1865, seven made it in and six out. By February Sherman began his move into the state, and the end was in sight; only one runner came in and seven left. *Rattlesnake* ran aground off Sullivan's Island and was lost. Others trying to enter were driven off by the increased number of blockaders. On February 16 *Syren* entered on her thirty-third trip, making her the most successful runner of the war. She failed to get underway before the city was evacuated the following night, and thus was captured. The last ship to

Midship deck area of the blockade runner *Presto* looking aft. Note the binnacle and steering wheel on the open deck between the paddle boxes. From here the captain had a clear view of the water around the ship with which to maneuver through the blockading fleet.

The blockade runner *Presto* being shelled and destroyed by a monitor after she ran aground off Fort Moultrie on February 2, 1864. About a week after this incident the commander of the Union blockading squadron learned why the soldiers of Fort Moultrie had braved the heavy cannon fire of his fleet to save articles from the wreck. *Presto* carried a large quantity of liquor, the first thing that salvage crews looked for. The Union officer claimed that if he had known how drunk the Confederate soldiers had been during the days immediately following *Presto's* loss, he could have captured the entire island!

leave Charleston was *G. T. Watson*, which pulled away from a flaming wharf on February 17 and three days later docked at Nassau with the news of Charleston's fall.

As at Wilmington the new port commander at Charleston kept most of the channel signal lights in operation after the Union took control. The night after the city's fall *Deer* made her way to the harbor mouth from the north. Her captain noticed that the light on the north end of Sullivan's Island was out but he continued on, only to run aground at the harbor's entrance. Officers from the monitors stationed in the channel rowed out and took possession of the ship.

Postscript

With the fall of Charleston, blockade running ceased at Bermuda and Nassau. The Confederate armies had become totally dependent on materiel brought in through the blockade; therefore, they would last only as long as supplies already in the pipeline held out. Once that supply was exhausted, the Confederate army's fate was sealed.

The Union blockade officially ended in June 1865. Out of some 1,300 blockade-running attempts to enter the ports of the Confederacy, over 1,000 had been successful. The average life span of a runner had been two round trips, enough to turn a profit. Of the estimated 300 steamers used, approximately 136 had been captured and about 85 destroyed. Over 400,000 bales of cotton had been hauled out to finance the war effort, compared with the pre-war figure of over three million bales for 1860 alone (although the price of war cotton was considerably higher).

Naturally private blockade-running firms such as Fraser, Trenholm and Company went bankrupt. Once the Confederacy surrendered, their blockade runners and supply steamers that hauled cargo to Nassau and Bermuda fell drastically in value. They were also left with war materiel stored in warehouses, and the new runners that were under construction. If the South had won the war, this Charleston firm may have become the new nation's premier transatlantic shipper. So, Charleston lost in many ways by the Confederate defeat. Fraser, Trenholm tried to continue operations, but the United States government sued it in the English courts to take possession of all Confederate property in that country. When the Federal government was successful in its suit in May 1867, the firm declared bankruptcy. John Fraser and Company managed to hold on until 1872.

Other blockade-running firms closed down when the war ended rather than try to continue in other pursuits. Of the foreign companies, only the Anglo-Confederate Trading

Company came out with an overall profit, even though it was forced to sell its specially built vessels at a substantial loss.

The other Charleston-based firms also closed their offices. The Importing and Exporting Company of South Carolina concluded operations in January 1866 with Theodore Jervey as its last head. A dividend of £20 sterling and $2,000 in Confederate currency was paid to each shareholder, bringing total dividends to £120 sterling and $9,000 per share. After the war the company sold off its property in Europe and paid a final dividend of £70 sterling before closing its books.

The Chicora and Charleston Importing and Exporting Companies also repaid their investors and gave them a profit. The former made one final payment of $100 in gold after the war, when it sold off its property in England and the steamer *Chicora* at Halifax.

While the profits of these firms were considerable during the war, their obligations were greater once the war was over. Many of their assets plummeted in value, leaving little to cover the debts. Specially built high-speed vessels designed for blockade running had limited peacetime use. Once the war ended, large numbers of these vessels were put up for sale, further depressing prices.

Rumors persisted in Europe throughout the war that if the Confederacy lost, the United States government would assume its obligations. This did not come to pass, and Europeans who held Confederate money and cotton bonds found them worthless overnight.

Blockade running was a good example of private enterprise and entrepreneurship in action. Without the blockade runners, the South would not have survived the second year

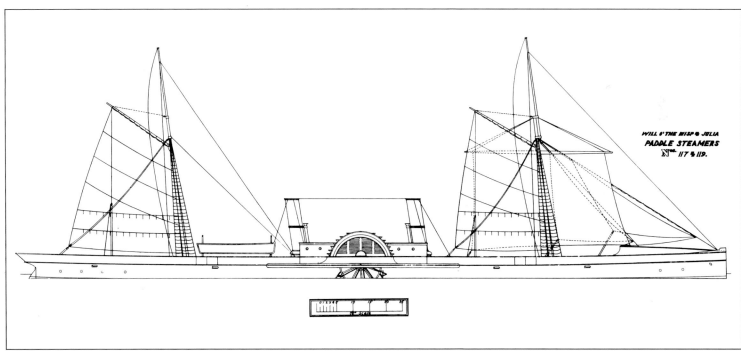

Plan of the blockade runner *Julia* by William E. Geoghegan. She was built by Simons and Company of Renfrew, Scotland, and made two trips into Charleston in November and December 1864. On her second trip out she ran into a gale and sought shelter in Bull's Bay, only to run aground and be captured by small boats from *Acadia*.

Henry Sterling Lebby was another of the redoubtable Charleston blockade-runner captains. A James Island native born in 1829, he commanded the John Fraser and Company ship *Gondar* on the Charleston to Liverpool run before the war. Two of his brothers were surgeons during the war and a third served on runners. His first war command was the privateer *Sallie*, which he took out of the North Edisto River on October 9, 1861, and captured several small prizes. *Sallie* was spotted by a blockader on the way back into Charleston. Lebby made a dash for Lighthouse Inlet between Folly and Morris Islands, bringing her through the surf and bumping the bar as she crossed amid shellfire. Captain Lebby later turned to blockade running, commanding *Mary Wright*, *Little Ada*, *Charleston*, *Scotia*, *Lily*, *Florie*, and *Lillian*, which was named for his daughter. In October 1862 he ignominiously lost *Scotia* in Bull's Bay after the sailing blockader *Restless* cut off her escape. Once in the bay, armed boats from the latter seized the ship, but Lebby and his passengers escaped ashore. No doubt he had no desire to fall into enemy hands again; while crossing the Atlantic in July 1862 on the British brig *Lilla* to Nassau, he had been captured when the ship was seized by an American warship and taken to Boston. Lebby managed to escape by donning an enemy officer's uniform, and was soon back in business.

His reputation for coolness and daring won him command of the Importing and Exporting Company of Georgia's steamer *Little Hattie* in 1864. His escapades on this vessel show why the owners preferred native Southerners to foreign captains, as they would take greater risks to get their cargoes through. On one occasion when being hotly pursued, he ordered that bacon be tossed into the boiler fires to get every ounce of speed. Her last voyage through to Charleston in

January 1865 was typical. By then some eighteen blockaders lay off Sullivan's Island and the Isle of Palms. Lebby chose to drift through the outer line with the wind and tide. With her blockader blue paint, *Little Hattie* looked like a cloud of mist drifting above the water. She was spotted some 200 yards from the second row of enemy ships. The alarm was given and she was taken under fire. Lebby poured on the steam in a mad dash for Charleston harbor. Just below Fort Sumter came the real challenge; in her path were two boats filled with armed men. She passed them in a hail of small-arms fire, which wounded several on board, including the helmsman, who lost several fingers.

Ahead lay the final challenge—an enemy monitor anchored in the channel. *Little Hattie* bore down on her, a bone in her teeth; Lebby figured that the best course was to pass so close that the enemy would have touble swinging his turret to bear as he passed. As *Little Hattie* came up, those on board could hear the commands of the turret officer to the gun crew in the monitor's turret. One after another the huge guns belched out fire and smoke. Both shots missed and in triumph *Little Hattie* steamed up the channel to the docks. A week later she repeated the stunt, delivering a cargo of cotton to Nassau. She was there when Charleston fell. *Little Hattie* was sold to other interests and Lebby continued his career at sea on the steamer *E. B. Souder*. He died in 1898 in Staten Island, New York, and is buried in the Presbyterian Churchyard on James Island.

The scene opposite by noted marine artist Tom Freeman shows *Little Hattie* as she passed the final hurdle on her last run into Charleston.

The blockade runner *Little Hattie* docked in Halifax, Nova Scotia, probably in late August or early September 1864 while on her way to Nassau to begin blockade-running operations in and out of Charleston and Wilmington.

of the war, as home production never was able to supply even half of the nation's military needs. By the summer of 1862, the flow of supplies they brought in enabled the Confederate armies to stand up to the numerically superior Northern armies. This supply was maintained until Charleston, the last East Coast port, fell to the enemy.

In most accounts of Confederate blockade running, Charleston has been given cursory treatment at most. However, it was the initiative of Charleston's entrepreneurs that was predominantly responsible for getting the business going as quickly as it did. Men such as Prioleau, Trenholm, and Bee had sprung immediately into action with remarkable alacrity when it became apparent that the very existence of the Confederacy was dependent upon the services that they could provide. They had been involved in the city's shipping business for decades. Without their experience and contacts in England, blockade running would have had a slower start; as a result the Confederacy may well have fallen at an earlier date. Once New Orleans fell in April 1862, no other Southern seaport had the overseas contacts that Charles-

ton had. If Charleston also had fallen early in the war along with New Orleans, it is questionable as to whether blockade running would have made as large a contribution to the Southern war effort as it did.

Charleston's leadership in the naval and shipping field was firmly established by its role in the Confederate War, no matter the outcome. The initiative, daring, and patriotism of the city's leadership kept the port in Southern hands and made it an asset in the Confederate war effort to an extent that few other Southern cities achieved. As was true over the course of most of the city's maritime history, much of this effort came from men who worked individually, motivated by patriotism and profit, for they believed firmly in their city and its cause. To a large extent it was not a coordinated, united effort, but Charleston's leaders historically have been individuals who generally worked in small groups to improve both the city and themselves.

Colonel Lamb, one of the last generation of blockade runners. In her, Thomas Lockwood approached Charleston during broad daylight on November 4, 1864. When the blockaders took off in pursuit he led them on a merry chase seaward. Once darkness fell he turned on full speed, circled to the north around them, and entered Charleston unnoticed. Docking at 11 p.m., she was unloaded and set out at 3 a.m. in a fog. The fog suddenly lifted but the ship easily outran the blockaders. *Colonel Lamb* made several other successful trips into the Confederacy, was never caught, and was the first of the few Confederate ships that returned to England at the end of the war.

Charleston's Battery, February 1865, with the conquering fleet at anchor in the harbor beyond. The ship in the center background is probably the redoubtable Charleston-built *John Adams*. After four years of valiant struggle, Charleston and the Confederacy succumbed to the inevitable. Much of the city lay in rubble, its commerce swept away, its wealth destroyed. Revival would be a long, slow process that spanned almost a century. The influx of the Navy during World War II would be the city's Marshall Plan. As a consequence while most American cities tore down their architectural heritage and rebuilt, Charleston would be too financially prostrate and would have to make do with its inheritance. Her citizens became more frugal, husbanding their resources for a new era when Americans would awaken to what they had destroyed of their respective cities' heritage; in contrast, Charlestonians would find themselves in possession of the finest collection of antebellum American architecture in the nation. This would be their *physical* inheritance; the *intangible* inheritance—their culture, heritage, and legacy—would make up the richest part of the social fabric of modern Charleston.

Appendix I

VICE-ADMIRALTY COURTS

The Vice-Admiralty Courts were set up under English law to handle violations of the Navigation Acts: piracy, treason, felony, murder on the high seas, and maritime cases in general. Additionally, the prizes of both privateers and warships were disposed of in these courts. Under Admiralty law, once a vessel was abandoned or taken under conditions of war, it was no longer the property of the owner. Instead, it was available to anyone who could salvage or carry it into port. This law served as an incentive for salvagers and other parties to seize or save a vessel, thus opening up another entire line of disputes to be handled by the Vice-Admiralty Courts.

For the first thirty years of the colony's existence the duties of the Vice-Admiralty Court were handled by the common law courts. By 1696, a separate court to handle maritime disputes in the colony was necessary, but its jurisdiction was not clearly defined, because the Proprietors considered it their private domain. The Board of Trade in London settled the question in regard to South Carolina by establishing a Court of Vice-Admiralty in Charles Towne in 1697 with Joseph Morton as judge, Thomas Carey register, J. Amory advocate, and R. Pollinger marshal.

These officials and their successors were appointed by the Admiralty in London on the recommendation of the Proprietors until 1719. The whole system was something of a muddle. The governors of the colonies often received conflicting orders telling them in one dispatch to try pirates locally, and in another instructing them to send the culprits to London for trial.

The Navigation Act of 1696 was the first drastic change in the relationship between the Crown and the proprietary colonies. With the enforcement responsibilities more clearly defined, the governors were subject to fine if they defaulted in their duty. Much of this change was a result of corruption in the collection of duties and frauds perpetrated by various governors and their associates in South Carolina—especially Governor Blake and Joseph Morton of the Vice-Admiralty Court (1696–1700). Their family ties to Cromwell were probably the source of their anti-Crown activities. Blake's death in 1700 brought the collapse of his clique, and complaints of customs' racketeering soon ceased; however, they revived again in the next decade and remained a problem as long as the Crown had jurisdiction over South Carolina.

By 1716, with the resurgence of pirate activity in South Carolina a complete reorganization of the court became necessary. Nicholas Trott, the Chief Justice of the Province, was authorized by Lord Carteret, the President of the Board of Proprietors, to sit as Judge of the Vice-Admiralty Court at Charles Towne. Carteret's authority to appoint Trott to the Vice-Admiralty Court was doubtful, as the courts were under authority of the Crown, not the Proprietors. Britain, however, was giving little attention to her colonies, and Trott was not one to let this impede his power to put the court into operation.

The procedure for trials of murder, piracy, and felony on the high seas went according to the common law. The process was as follows: a grand jury, consisting of thirteen to twenty-three members, was sworn in; the advocate general then presented indictments against the suspects; if a true bill was found and the defendants pleaded not guilty, they were brought before a jury for trial and the jury's decision was final. The other cases were tried according to civil law, without a jury.

Trott ruled the court with an iron hand; very few of the guilty were allowed to escape justice. His first trial in November 1716 resulted in the acquittal of nine men accused of seizing a vessel belonging to two Charles Towne merchants. Another group was tried the next year, found guilty, and executed for taking the vessels *Turtle Dove*, *Penelope*, and *Virgin Queen*. He subsequently presided over the trials of the pirates. With strength and character, he saw that these villains received proper legal justice. Any show of weakness on the part of the Court would have led to continued piracy that victimized Charles Towne merchants. Furthermore, respect of the citizens for the Court would have eroded.

After the supression of the pirates, the Vice-Admiralty Court settled down to such fairly routine matters as prize cases and violations of the Navigation Acts. They also handled many cases of illegal trading involving ships that had not been built in England, that were owned outside the Empire, or that were manned with crews of less than three-fourths Englishmen.

Judge Trott became corrupted by power; his excesses and abuses were one of the factors that precipitated the colony's revolt against the Proprietors in 1719.

Appendix II

ROYAL NAVY STATION SHIPS AT CHARLES TOWN[1]

SHIP	GUNS	CAPTAIN	ARRIVED	DEPARTED
Flamborough	20	John Hildesley	5 Oct. 1719	14 July 1721
Blandford	20	William Martin	8 June 1721	6 Sept. 1724
Scarborough	20	George Anson (William Boutflower)	10 June 1724	27 July 1728
Shark	14	George Sclater	13 Aug. 1725	23 June 1727
Fox	20	Thomas Arnold	9 June 1728	4 May 1732
Guarland	20	Daniel Morris DD 12 July 1728 (William Boutflower) (George Anson)	8 July 1728	5 June 1730
Alborough (surveying)	20	John Gascoigne	29 Nov. 1728	7 May 1734
Happy (surveying)	10/16	Wm. Douglas (James Lloyd)	29 Nov. 1728	12 May 1735
Lowestoft	20	Matthew Norris	20 June 1730	16 Nov. 1731
Cruiser	10	Thomas Billop	21 Oct. 1730	5 Apr. 1731
Fox	20	Thomas Arnold	14 Dec. 1730	25 June 1732
Solebay	20	Peter Warren	26 Dec. 1731	25 June 1732
Squirrel	20	George Anson	18 June 1732	17 May 1735
Shark (Bahamas)	8/2	Richard Symonds	29 Nov. 1733	18 June 1739
Rose	20	Charles Windham	3 Apr. 1734	6 July 1738
Hawk (Georgia)	6/10	James Gascoigne (John Nevinson)	1735	1738
Seaford	20	Hon. Henry Scott (Lord Deloraine)	1 Oct. 1737	10 Oct. 1739
Phoenix	20	Charles Fanshawe	5 May 1738	22 Feb. 1742
Spence (Bahamas)	6/10	William Laws	11 Oct. 1738	16 Jan. 1741
Tartar	20	Hon. Geo. Townsend	12 Sept. 1739	17 Oct. 1741
Rose (Bahamas)	24	Thomas Frankland	3 Mar. 1741	1 June 1745
Rye	24	Charles Hardy	15 Jan. 1742	7 Feb. 1744
Flamborough	24	Joseph Hamar	8 Feb. 1742	1 June 1745
Swift (North Carolina)	12/12	Wm. Bladwell	14 Feb. 1742	23 Nov. 1743
Hawk	10/12	Henry Bruce DD 12 June 1742 (Edward Keller) (Arthur Forrest)	2 Mar. 1742	4 Nov. 1742
Shoreham (Jamaica)	32	Thomas Brodrick	13 Oct. 1742	3 Nov. 1742
Spy	8/12	James Newnan	13 Oct. 1742	20 Sept. 1744
Loo[2]	44	Ashby Utting	18 Oct. 1743	5 Feb. 1744 (wrecked)
Tartar	20	Henry Ward	17 Dec. 1743	8 Nov. 1746
Swallow	10	Andrew Jelfe	1744	24 Dec. 1744 (wrecked)
Alborough	24	Ashby Utting DD 7 Jan. 1746 (Peter Robertson) (Michael Everitt) (Thomas Innes) (George Darby)	26 May 1745	7 May 1749
Adventure	24	Joseph Hamam	18 Sept. 1747	19 Mar. 1748
Rye	24	Charles Wray	8 May 1748	21 Nov. 1750
Arundel	24	John Reynolds	9 Aug. 1748	10 May 1751
Glasgow	24	John Lloyd DD Sept. 1748 (Thomas Hallum)	14 Sept. 1748	11 Oct. 1748

[1] This list was compiled by Commander W. E. May of the Royal Navy, who was Deputy Director of the National Maritime Museum, Greenwich, England, for seventeen years until his retirement at the end of 1968. It is reprinted with the kind permission of the *South Carolina Historical Magazine*.

The ships on this list include those that were sent to cover North Carolina, South Carolina, Georgia, and the Bahamas as a group and those that visited Charles Town while not actually assigned as station ship.

The letters *DD* after an officer's name are the traditional abbreviation for "Discharged-Dead." The names within parentheses are reliefs who joined during the assignment as replacement for the name immediately above.

[2] Also spelled *Looe* in some accounts.

SHIP	GUNS	CAPTAIN	ARRIVED	DEPARTED
Otter	10/14	John Ballett	1 Mar. 1749	10 May 1750
		DD 7 May 1749		
		(Michael Kearney)		
Scorpion	10/14	Elias Bate	22 June 1750	18 Apr. 1753
(North Carolina)		(John Randall)		
		(John Russell)		
		DD 22 Dec. 1752		
		(William Wilkins)		
Hornet	10/14	John Holwall	30 June 1750	19 Dec. 1753
		(James John Purcell)		
Mermaid	24	Edward Keller	12 Aug. 1750	3 June 1753
		DD 10 Sept. 1750		
		(Elias Bate)		
		DD 26 May 1752		
		(John Holwall)		
Shoreham	24	Julian Legge	28 July 1753	21 Feb. 1755
		(William Marsh)		
Jamaica	10/14	Thomas Riggs	14 Sept. 1753	7 Sept. 1757
(Bahamas)		DD 11 Feb. 1754		
		(Samuel Hood)		
		(Samuel Thompson)		
		(Henry Richard Dubois)		
Baltimore	10/14	Coll Macdonald	17 Sept. 1753	6 May 1757
		DD 8 Sept. 1753		
		(Henry Richard Dubois)		
		(William Charles Ellis)		
		(John Ommancey)		
		(Maurice Suckling)		
		(Thomas Owen)		
Port Mahon	24	Robert Hughes	28 Oct. 1754	8 Nov. 1754
Syren	24	Charles Proby	15 Nov. 1755	14 May 1758
Winchilsea	24	John Hale	1 June 1756	Aug. 1758
Falkland	50	Francis S. Drake	28 Aug. 1757	11 Sept. 1757
Port Mahon	24	Samuel Wallis	5 Nov. 1757	25 May 1758
Nightingale	24	James Campbell	12 Feb. 1758	25 May 1758
Penguin	24	Robert Man	13 May 1758	28 Feb. 1759
Surprise	24	Charles Antrobus	15 May 1758	28 Feb. 1759
Zephir	10/12	Wm. Greenwood	20 June 1758	11 Jan. 1762
(North Carolina)				
Scarborough	20	John Stott	3 Nov. 1758	31 May 1761
Hunter	10/14	William Adams	10 Dec. 1758	11 Apr. 1759
(Bahamas)				
Success	24	Paul Henry Ourry	1 Apr. 1759	23 May 1759
Mermaid	24	James Hackman	1 Apr. 1759	23 May 1759
Trent	28	John Lindsay	23 Oct. 1759	6 Apr. 1760
Mermaid	24	James Hackman	11 Nov. 1759	2 Jan. 1760 (wrecked)
Albany	14/14	John Jervis	2 Apr. 1760	6 Apr. 1760

SHIP	GUNS	CAPTAIN	ARRIVED	DEPARTED
Mercury	24	John Faulknor	1 Nov. 1760	23 Feb. 1761
Dolphin	24	Benjamin Marlow	23 Dec. 1760	22 June 1761
Nightingale	24	James Campbell	7 Jan. 1761	7 Feb. 1762
(North Carolina)				
Success	24	George Watson	10 Mar. 1761	30 May 1761
Dolphin	24	Robert Keeler	6 Jan. 1762	9 Mar. 1762
Bonetta	10	Lancelot Holmes	21 Mar. 1762	11 Dec. 1763
		(John Corey)		
Success	20	John Botterell	15 Aug. 1762	10 Dec. 1763
Epreuve	14	Peter Blake	24 Aug. 1762	1763
Mercury	24	Sam. S. Goodall	18 Nov. 1762	2 Feb. 1764
Nightingale	24	Lord Wm. Campbell	9 Feb. 1763	28 Apr. 1763
Tryal	14	James Wallace	7 Aug. 1763	24 July 1766
Hornet	14	Jeremiah Morgan	27 Sept. 1763	20 Dec. 1767
(North Carolina)				
Speedwell	8	Robert Fanshawe	14 Oct. 1763	24 July 1766
Viper	10	Jacob Lobb	23 Oct. 1763	10 July 1766
Escorte	14	Thomas Foley	7 Jan. 1764	17 June 1767
Sardoine	14	James Hawker	25 July 1766	22 Nov. 1767
Chaleur schooner		Lt. T. Laugharne	1 Nov. 1766	1 June 1768
(Florida and Bahamas)				
Cygnet	18	Philip Durell	1 July 1767	14 July 1768
Fowey	24	Mark Robinson	28 Oct. 1767	22 Jan. 1771
Martin	14	Thomas Hayward	25 Nov. 1767	21 Oct. 1771
(North Carolina)				
Bonetta	10	James Wallace	26 Nov. 1767	9 May 1772
Viper	10	Robert Linzee	17 Apr. 1769	6 Sept. 1771
		(Thomas Porter)		
Tryall	14	William Phillips	9 Oct. 1769	6 Nov. 1769
St. Lawrence sch.		Lt. Ralph Dundas	9 Nov. 1769	3 June 1774
(Florida and Bahamas)				
Gibraltar	20	Sir Thomas Rich	12 June 1771	27 Apr. 1773
Mercury	20	Robert Keeler	31 Aug. 1771	8 May 1772
Kingfisher	14	Thomas Jordan	11 Nov. 1771	19 May 1773
(North Carolina)		(Jacob Lobb)		
		DD 20 Feb. 1773		
		(Joseph Peyton)		
		(George Montagu)		
Tamar	16	Charles Hay	5 May 1772	30 Mar. 1776
(North Carolina)		(John Crosse)		
		DD 10 Aug. 1773		
		(Joseph Peyton)		
		(James Montagu)		
		(Edward Thornborough)		
Savage	8	Hugh Bromedge	7 Nov. 1772	4 May 1774
(Florida and Bahamas)				
Glasgow	20	William Maltby	29 Oct. 1773	19 Sept. 1774

Appendix III

CHARLESTON-BUILT SHIPS 1670–1865

This list is far from complete, being a compilation of those vessels known to have been built in the Charleston area. For example, one writer states that between 1735 and 1760 South Carolina builders constructed 140 schooners, 7 ships, and 25 other small ocean-going vessels. Most of these were undoubtedly built in the Charleston area. The two- and three-digit numbers following the name of each vessel refer to the tonnage. No vessels under ten tons are considered on this list prior to the Revolution and none under twenty-five tons after 1776. The pre-Revolutionary displacement figures given here are based on measurements of the ships; actual tonnages could have been as much a one-third higher.

YEAR	NAME	TONNAGE	TYPE	PLACE OF CONSTRUCTION
1696	Joseph	50	sloop	[unknown]
1696	Ruby	30	sloop	"
1697	Sea Flower	30	sloop	"
1698	Dorothy and Ann		sloop	"
1712	Charles Town Galley	120	ship	"
1714	Elizabeth	90	ship	"
1714	Sarah	10	sloop	"
1715	Princess Carolina	150	ship	"
1715	Recovery	30	sloop	"
1715	Alexander	10	sloop	"
1715	Glasgow	30	sloop	"
1716	Ruby	50	ship	"
1716	John	60	sloop	"
1716	Benjamin	15	sloop	"
1717	John's Adventure	50	snow	"
1717	John and Mary	10	sloop	"
1717	Recovery	30	sloop	"
1717	Mary Ann	30	sloop	"
1717	Industry	15	schooner	"
1717	Lucrecia	15	schooner	"
1718	Mermaid	80	snow	"
1718	Betty	30	sloop	"
1718	Elizabeth	15	sloop	"
1718	Providence	10	sloop	"
1718	Rogers	10	sloop	"
1718	St. George	15	sloop	"
1718	Mary	15	schooner	"
1719	Tryall	10	sloop	"
1719	Betty	10	sloop	"
1719	Ann	14	sloop	"
1719	Mulberry Tree	20	schooner	"
1720	Kingston	40	sloop	"
1722	Lucia	10	sloop	"
1723	Johnson's Adventure	20	sloop	"
1724	Gay Ladies	50	sloop	"

YEAR	NAME	TONNAGE	TYPE	PLACE OF CONSTRUCTION
1730	Princess Carolina	90	ship	[unknown]
1730	Queen Carolina	10	sloop	"
1731	William	70	brig	"
1731	Pick Pocket	20	sloop	"
1732	Bold Robert	12	schooner	"
1733	Exchange	20	sloop	"
1733	Oglethorpe	40	schooner	"
1734	Recovery	30	sloop	"
1735	B. William	30	sloop	"
1735	Rebecca & Mary	10	sloop	"
1736	Badger	50	schooner	"
1736	Sea Flower	15	schooner	"
1736	[unknown]	12	?	"
1738	Anne	50	brigantine	"
1739	Carolina	40	brigantine	"
1740	Sally	20	schooner	"
1742	[pilot boat]	10	schooner	"
1743	Charming Peggy	20	schooner	James Island
1743	Good Intent	25	schooner	James Island
1743	Panther	25	schooner	James Island
1743	William	40	sloop	
1744	Charles	25	schooner	
1744	Koulikan	20	schooner	James Island
1744	Lilly	10	schooner	James Island
1744	Molley	30	schooner	
1744	Swallow	20	schooner	Ashley River
1744	Winyaw Merchant	20	schooner	James Island
1745	Friendship	15	schooner	Hobcaw
1745	House Carpenter	6	schooner	Dorchester
1745	Nancy	30	schooner	Dorchester
1746	Charming Nelly	25	schooner	James Island
1746	Charming Peggy	130	ship	
1746	Mary	25	schooner	Hobcaw
1746	Nancy and Betsey	80	brigantine	James Island
1747	46' keel		schooner	Thomas Middleton
1747	Martha	16	schooner	
1747	Mary	80	bilander	
1748	Charming Betty	35	sloop	James Island
1748	Elizabeth	30	brigantine	James Island
1748	Entireprize	35	schooner	
1748	Friendship	20	schooner	
1748	Hector	60	bilander	James Island
1748	Pheasant	10	schooner	

YEAR	NAME	TONNAGE	TYPE	PLACE OF CONSTRUCTION
1749	*African Packet*	19	schooner	
1749	*Live Oak*	125	ship	James Island
1750	*Confidence*	20	schooner	
1750	*Hopewell*	20	schooner	James Island
1751	*Harriot*	20	sloop	Cooper River
1751	*Jenny*	28	sloop	
1751	*Molly*	30	schooner	James Island
1751	*Two Sisters*	10	schooner	
1751	*William*	20	brigantine	James Island
1752	*Chance*	30	schooner	James Island
1752	*Charming Betsey*	90	snow	James Island
1752	*Charming Nancy*	130	ship	James Island
1752	*St. Andrew*	19	schooner	James Island
1753	*Betsey*	45	schooner	
1753	*Indian Land*	20	schooner	
1753	*Molly*	60	brigantine	James Island
1753	*Stono*	16	schooner	James Island
1754	*Charming Sally*	16	sloop	
1754	*Dove*	15	schooner	James Island
1754	*Trial*	20	schooner	
1755	*Sally*	15	schooner	James Island
1755	*Two Brothers*	30	schooner	James Island
1757	*Blakeney*	18	schooner	
1757	*Speedwell*	14	schooner	Wadmalaw
1759	*Dolphin*	20	schooner	James Island
1759	*Henrietta*	20	schooner	James Island
1759	*Margaret*	15	schooner	
1759	*Polly*	15	schooner	James Island
1759	*William and Catharine*	20	schooner	James Island
1760	*Eagle*	10	schooner	
1761	*Live Oak*	20	schooner	Dorchester
1763	*Heart of Oak*	300	ship	Rose-Hobcaw
1763	*King George*	160	ship	Emrie
1765	*Polly*	16	schooner	James Island
1767	*Industry*	12	schooner	
1767	*Liberty*	160	ship	Rose-Hobcaw
1769	*Betsy and Elfy*		ship	Lempriere-Hobcaw
1770	*Diligence*	40	snow	Begbie and Manson
1770	*Exchange*	20	schooner	
1771	*Magna Carta*	300	ship	Begbie and Manson
1771	*New Carolina Packet*	300	ship	Begbie and Manson
1771	*Greyhound*	12	schooner	Hobcaw
1772	*Betsey and Sally*	16	schooner	
1778	*Sally*		schooner	Lempriere
1778	*Hornet*		brig	Cochran
1784	*Palmetto*		schooner	Pritchard
1784	*Governor Middleton*			Pritchard-Hobcaw
1790	[unnamed]		brig	Hobcaw
1793	*Eliza*		ship	Hobcaw
1793	*South Carolina* [revenue cutter]		schooner	
1798	*Victoria*		brig	Pritchard
1798	*Unanimity* [revenue cutter]		brig	Hobcaw

YEAR	NAME	TONNAGE	TYPE	PLACE OF CONSTRUCTION
1798	*Charleston*		galley	Hobcaw
1798	*South Carolina*		galley	Hobcaw
1798	*General Pinckney*		brig	Pritchard-Charleston
1798	*South Carolina*		brig	Cochran's-Pritchard
1799	*John Adams*	540	frigate	Cochran's-Pritchard
1800	*Three Sisters* [later rerigged as ship]		brig	
1800	*Horizon*		ship	Hobcaw
1802	*Middleton*		ship	Wm. Pritchard
1804	*St. Andrew*			Hobcaw
	[unnamed]		ship	Wm. Pritchard, Sr.
1805	*No. 9*		gunboat	Pritchard-Fair Bank
1806	*Paul Hamilton*		brig	Paul Pritchard, Jr.
1808	5 gunboats			James Marsh
1809	*Rice Bird*		ship	James Marsh
1811	*Gadsden*		ship	
1812	*Saucy Jack*		schooner	Pritchard & Shrewsbury
1812	*Governor Middleton*		brig	Pritchard & Shrewsbury
1812	*Carolina*	230	schooner	James Marsh
1813	*Decatur*	240	schooner	Pritchard & Shrewsbury
1815	[unnamed]		brig	Pritchard & Knox
1815	*South Carolina*	306	ship (whaler)	
1815	*Caroline*		ship	Wm. Smith, Jr. (Mazyckb.)
1816	[unnamed]		brig	Robert Eason (Wraggsb.)
1816	*William & Henry*		schooner	Poyas (South Bay)
1816	*Industry*		schooner	
1816	*Experiment*		schooner	Saltus
1817	*Alciope*		pilot boat	Mason's
1817	*Charleston*		steamboat	John O'Neale
1817	*Carolina*		steamboat	Pritchard & Knox
1817	*Georgia*		steamboat	Wm. Pritchard, Sr.
1818	*Altamaha*		steamboat	Pritchard & Knox
1818	*Ockmulgee*		steamboat	Paul Pritchard
1818	*Samuel Howard*			Paul Pritchard
1819	*Columbia*		steamboat	James Marsh
1819	*Pee Dee*		steamboat	Marsh & O'Neale
1820	*Carolina*		brig	Robert Eason
1820	*James Stoney*		schooner	Black & Westrevelt
1820	*Col. Simons*		schooner	Poyas (South Bay)
1821	*Sea Gull*		brig	
1823	*William Lowndes*		steamboat	Paul Pritchard
1824	*Pendleton*		steamboat	O'Neale & Bird
1825	*Macon*		steamboat	Pritchard
1840	*Thomas Bennett*		ship	Thomas Bennett, Bull St. on Ashley River
1840	*Chicora*			
1850	*Marion*		steamer	
1860	*Planter*	300	steamer	F. M. Jones
1862	*Chicora*		ironclad	Eason Shipyard
1862	*Palmetto State*		ironclad	James Marsh
1863	*Charleston*		ironclad	Eason Shipyard
1864	*Columbia*		ironclad	F. M. Jones

Appendix IV

CHARLESTON SHIPYARDS

NAME OF YARD	LOCATION	OWNER	DATES OF OPERATION	NAME OF YARD	LOCATION	OWNER	DATES OF OPERATION
Black & Westrevelt	Saltus Wharf South Bay St., Charleston		1820	O'Neale's Shipyard	Charleston (near Strobel's Sawmill)	John O'Neale	1816–182[?]
Cornelius Dewees	Dewee's Island	C. Dewees	170[?]	also worked with James Marsh later O'Neale & Bird			1819 1824
Eason Shipyard	Wraggsborough, Charleston [later moved to Exchange Street]	James Eason	1815–1865	Poyas Shipyard	South Bay St., Charleston		1816
Hobcaw's Shipyard	Hobcaw	G. Dearsley	1705	Pritchard's Shipyard	Fair Bank, Daniel's Island (Wando River)	Paul Pritchard	180[?]
Bolton Shipyard	"	T. Bolton	173[?]–1753		also at Gadsden Wharf, Charleston		1818–1825
Rose Shipyard	"	J. Stewart J. Rose	1753–1769	Pritchard's Shipyard	Pinckney St., Charleston	Wm. Prichard	177[?]
Begbie and Manson	"	Wm. Begbie D. Manson	1769–1778	Pritchard & Shrewsbury			180[?]
William Pritchard's	"	P. Pritchard Abe. Livingston	1778	Pritchard & Knox			1815
State Navy Yard	"		1778–1780	Shipyard Creek	Shipyard Creek		170[?]
Johnson & Taylor	"		180[?]	Cochran's Shipyard	" "		1763–1778
				State Navy Yard			1778–1779
F. M. Jones and Brothers	Haddrell's Point, Mount Pleasant		185[?]	Cochran's Shipyard leased by Paul Pritchard	" "		1783–1816 1790s
Lempriere's Shipyard	Shem Creek, Mount Pleasant	Clement Lempriere	174[?]	U. S. Naval Station	" "		180[?]–1816
				Shipyard	Stono River		
Marsh's Shipyard	Market Street, Charleston	James Marsh	180[?]–1865	Smith's Shipyard	Mazyckborough, Charleston	Wm. Smith	1815

Chicora and *Palmetto State*.

Appendix V

CHARLESTOWN PRIVATEERS IN THE REVOLUTION[1]

Privateers with S. C. Commissions

NAME	TYPE	CAPTAIN

1776 Commissions

NAME	TYPE	CAPTAIN
Swift	sloop	Charles Morgan
		Francis Morgan
		Andrew Groundwater
Peggy	sloop	Andrew Groundwater (1777)
		Thomas Cheney
Active	brig	Charles Morgan
Chance	brigantine	Jacob Johnston
Hope	snow	John Hatter
Liberty	ship	William Galvar
		Thomas Sherman (1777)
Rutledge	sloop	Jacob Milligan
		John Porter

1777 Commissions

NAME	TYPE	CAPTAIN
Polly	brig	Paul Preston
		Josiah Darrell
		Hezekiah Anthony
Hibernia		[?] Stone
Gen. Washington	schooner	Samuel Stone
Sea Flower	sloop	William Cannon
Betsy	sloop	James McKenzie
		Benjamin Hazell
Allston	sloop	William Thompson
May	schooner	John Roberts
Molly	brig	Gaspard Gourlaver
Priscilla	schooner	Yelverton Fowkes
Recontre	sloop	Jean Derris Martin
Little Charles	sloop	John Middleton
Friendship	sloop	Nathaniel King
Alice	sloop	John Porter
Liberty	sloop	John Thomas
Sally	schooner	Thomas Hook
Amity	brigantine	George Cross

NAME	TYPE	CAPTAIN
Gen. Washington	sloop	Hezekiah Anthony
Vixen	sloop	Downham Newton
America	brigantine	Thomas Smith
Active	sloop	John Osborn
Intrepid	sloop	Jasper Amand Renault
Fair American	brigantine	Charles Morgan
Lively	sloop	Josiah Young

Other American Privateers Commissioned at Charlestown

NAME	TYPE	CAPTAIN
Bachelor	schooner	Nathaniel Bentley
Cotesworth Pinckney		William Ranking
Elbert	sloop	William Ranking
Volunteer	schooner	Eliphalet Smith
Experiment	brig	Francis Morgan
Volunteer	ship	Philip Sullivan
General Moultrie	ship	Jacob Johnston
		Philip Sullivan
		Downham Newton
		Simon Tufts
Bellona	brig	George Cross
		Hezekiah Anthony
Hercules	brig	Josiah Young
Wasp	brig	
Rachel	sloop	Jeremiah Dickinson
Family Trader	sloop	William Allen
Sally	sloop	Benjamin Stone
Medley	brig	Charles Dawson
Sally	brig	Joseph Evans
Witch	schooner	Samuel Spencer

Charlestown's Tory Privateers

NAME	TYPE	CAPTAIN
Earl Cornwallis	ship	
Peggy	schooner	[?] Manson
Sir Samuel Hood	ship	Robert Schaw
Peacock	ship	Duncan MacLean
Retaliation	schooner	
Rose	schooner	
Surprize	whale boat	

[1] The above lists are far from complete and were compiled by Harold Mouzon from local newspaper accounts and the lists of commissions of the state.

CHARLESTON PRIVATEERS DURING THE WAR OF 1812[1]

NAME	COMMISSION DATE	TONNAGE	ARMAMENT	CAPTAIN
Nonpareil	7-8-12	19	1-6	H. B. Martin
Mary Ann	7-13-12	50	1-4	J. P. Chazal
	11-18-12		1-9c	John Jousett
Poor Sailor	7-16-12	45	1-6	Philip McLachlin
Elizabeth	7-27-12	87	1-6	R. W. Cleary
			2-4	(letter of marque)
			2-swivels	
Saucy Jack	7-28-12	170	9-12	Thomas H. Jervey
	10-31-12		1-12l	Peter Sicard
			6-12c	
	6-8-13			John Peter Chazal
Rapid	8-15-12	43	1-6	Charles F. Broguet
Hazard	9-15-12	55	1-6	John Dennis
	6-12-13			Peter Lamson
Lelie Ann	9-9-12	60	1-6l	John Smith
Gen. Armstrong ship	11-23-12	205	16-6	John Sinclair
Hazard	12-5-12	55	3-[?]	Placide Le Chartier
Defiance	12-5-12	75	2-[?]	J. P. Chazal
Charlotte	12-5-12	100	2-4	Jonathan Bowers
Erie ship	1-15-13	508	4-9	Henry Robinson
Amiable ship	1-15-13	278	6-[?]	George Taylor
Matilda	1-15-13	181	11-[?]	Henry H. Rantin
Garrone	1-15-13	295	2-12c	James Forsyth
Tom	3-6-13	286	5-12c	Thomas Wilson
			1-9	
Decatur		240	1-18l	Dominique Diron
			6-12c	
Lovely Cordelia	6-16-13	67	1-6	Peter Sicard
Eagle	6-28-13	54	1-6	Peter Lafete
Minerva	11-6-13	72	1-3	John Peters
G. Washington sloop	11-13-13	74	1-[?]	Joseph Fellows
Black Suche sloop	11-13-13	23	2-swivels	John Graves
Rapid	12-9-13	67	1-6l	Joseph Bruchett
Advocate	1-4-14	53	1-9	Ambrose Dough
Liberty	1-21-14	55	1-6l	Alexander Bolcher
Dominica	[?]-14	203	12-12c	Bonfeu [or Bufean]

[1] Compiled from *Privateers of Charleston in the War of 1812* by Harold A. Mouzon, the Historical Commission of Charleston, S. C., 1954. All are schooners, unless otherwise noted after the vessel's name. The letter *l* or *c* after the size of the gun refers to long gun or carronade; i.e., *12-9c* would designate twelve 9-pounder carronades, and *6-6l* would designate six 6-pounder long guns.

Appendix VII

STEAM BLOCKADE RUNNERS TO ENTER AND CLEAR CHARLESTON[1]

1861

Theodora (ex-*Gordon*)	Oct. 12	for Nassau
Nashville	Oct. 29	for Liverpool
Theodora (ex-*Gordon*)	Nov. 4	from Havana
Ella Warley (ex-*Isabel*)	Dec. 2	for Nassau
Theodora (ex-*Gordon*)	Dec. 4	for Nassau
Theodora (ex-*Gordon*)	Dec. 21	from Nassau

1862

Ella Warley (ex-*Isabel*)	Jan. 2	from Nassau
Kate (ex-*Carolina*)	Jan. 12	for Nassau
Nelly (ex-*Governor Dudley*)	Feb. 8	for Nassau
Cecile	Feb. 20	for Nassau
Ella Warley (ex-*Isabel*)	Feb. 27	for Nassau
Nelly (ex-*Governor Dudley*)	Mar. 6	from Havana
Economist	Mar. 14	from Bermuda
Kate (ex-*Carolina*)	Mar. 24	from Nassau
Nelly (ex-*Governor Dudley*)	Mar. 25	for Havana
Cecile	Mar. 28	from Nassau
Economist	Apr. 1	for Nassau
Cecile	Apr. 5	for Nassau
Thomas L. Wragg (*Nashville*)	mid-Apr.	turned away
William Seabrook	Apr. 15	for Nassau
Kate (ex-*Carolina*)	Apr. 17	for Nassau
Nelly	Apr. 19	from Havana
Ella Warley (inbound)	Apr. 24	captured
Cecile	Apr. 27	from Nassau
Cecile	May 3	for Nassau
Nelly	May 3	for Nassau
Stettin (inbound)	May 24	captured
Cecile	May 24	from Nassau
Kate	May 25	from Nassau
Nelly (inbound)	May 25	wrecked
Minho	May 25	from Nassau
Cambria (inbound)	May 26	captured
Patras (inbound)	May 28	captured
Elizabeth (inbound)	May 29	captured
Cecile	May 30	for Nassau
Kate (ex-*Carolina*)	June 2	for Nassau
Minho	June 4	for Nassau
Memphis	June 23	from Nassau
Herald (I)	July 3	from Nassau
Thomas L. Wragg	early July	turned away
Lloyd	July 7	from Nassau
Emilie (*William Seabrook*)	July 7	captured
Herald (I)	July 21	for Nassau
Memphis (outbound)	July 21	captured
Tubal Cain (inbound)	July 24	captured
Hero	July 25	from Nassau
Scotia (I)	July 26	from Nassau
Leopard	Aug. 3	from Nassau
Columbia (inbound)	Aug. 3	captured
Minho	Aug. 3	from Nassau
Lloyd	Aug. 14	for England
Herald (I)	Aug. 18	from Nassau
Leopard	Aug. 28	for Nassau
Minho	Aug. 28	for Bermuda
Leopard	Sept. 2	from Nassau
Scotia (I)	Sept. 26	for Nassau
Leopard	Sept. 30	for Nassau
Herald (I)	Oct. 13	for Bermuda
Ouachita (inbound)	Oct. 14	captured
Kate	Oct. 15	from Nassau
Minho (inbound)	Oct. 20	destroyed
Anglia (inbound)	Oct. 24	captured
Scotia (inbound)	Oct. 24	captured
Kate (ex-*Carolina*)	Oct. 29	for Nassau
Herald (I)	Nov. 1	from Bermuda
Leopard	Nov. 10	for Nassau
Aries	Nov. 15	from Nassau
Antonica (ex-*Herald*)	Dec. 20	from Nassau
Aries	Dec. 20	for Havana
Nina	Dec. 27	for Nassau
Leopard	Dec. 27	from Nassau
Antonica (*Herald I*)	Dec. 27	for Nassau

[1] Reprinted from Stephen R. Wise, Ph.D., *Lifeline of the Confederacy*, University of South Carolina Press. All dates are given as accurately as possible, but may be in error. *Inbound* and *outbound* in parentheses refer to the fact that the vessel was entering or leaving Charleston at the time of capture or loss. The *for* or *from* before the port name in the righthand column refers to the port that the vessel was bound *for* out of Charleston, or bound *from* into Charleston.

1863

Leopard	Jan. 5	from Nassau
Antonica	Jan. 13	from Nassau
Leopard	Jan. 14	for Nassau
Hero	Jan.	from Nassau
Tropic (ex-*Huntress*)	Jan. 18	burned
Pearl (inbound)	Jan. 20	captured
Calypso	Jan. 22	from Nassau
Flora (I)	Jan. 24	from Nassau
Nina (inbound)	Jan. 25	foundered
Douglas	Jan. 27	from Nassau
Thistle	Jan. 29	from Nassau
Princess Royal (inbound)	Jan. 29	captured
Calypso	Feb. 5	for Nassau
Hero	Feb. 7	for Nassau
Flora (I)	Feb. 11	for Nassau
Annie Childs	Feb. 11	from Nassau
Thistle	Feb. 13	grounded
Margaret and Jessie	Feb. 13	for Nassau
Ruby (I)	Feb. 14	from Nassau
Stonewall Jackson (ex-*Leopard*)	Feb. 14	from Nassau
Ruby (I)	Feb. 15	for Nassau
Stonewall Jackson	Feb. 21	for Nassau
Havelock	Feb. 24	from Nassau
Ruby (I)	Mar. 1	from Nassau
T. D. Wagner (*Annie Childs*)	Mar. 3	for Nassau
Hero	Mar.	from Nassau
Ruby (I)	Mar. 7	for Nassau
Flora (I)	Mar. 15	from Nassau
Gertrude	Mar. 16	from Nassau
Ruby (I)	Mar. 17	from Nassau
Calypso	Mar. 18	from Nassau
Georgiana (inbound)	Mar. 18	destroyed
Ruby (I)	Mar. 19	for Nassau
General Beauregard	Mar. 19	for Nassau
Flora (I)	Mar. 19	for Nassau
Gertrude	Mar. 23	for Nassau
Hero		for Nassau
Antonica	Mar. 23	from Nassau
Eagle	Mar. 24	from Nassau
Margaret and Jessie (*Douglas*)	Mar. 24	from Nassau
Hero	Apr. 1	for Nassau
Margaret and Jessie	Apr. 6	for Nassau
Ella and Annie (*W. G. Hewes*)	Apr. 10	from Nassau
General Beauregard (*Havelock*)	Apr. 12	from Bermuda
Stonewall Jackson	Apr. 12	destroyed
Ella and Annie	Apr. 18	for Nassau
Calypso	Apr. 20	for Nassau
Antonica	Apr. 20	for Nassau
Eagle	Apr. 26	from Nassau
Ella and Annie	Apr. 28	from Nassau
Ella and Annie	May 5	for Nassau
General Beauregard	May 7	for Nassau
Cherokee (*Thistle*) (outbound)	May 8	captured
Eagle	May 8	from Nassau
Norseman	May 13	from Nassau
Antonica	May 13	from Nassau
Calypso	May 15	from Nassau
Ella and Annie	May 20	from Nassau
Margaret and Jessie	May 20	from Nassau
Kate (II)	May 20	from Nassau
General Beauregard	May 20	from Nassau
Calypso	May 21	for Nassau
Antonica	May 21	for Nassau
Fannie	May 23	from Nassau
Alice	May 25	from Nassau
Elizabeth (*Atlantic*)	May 26	from Nassau
Margaret and Jessie	May 31	for Nassau
Stono (*Isaac Smith*)	June 5	destroyed
Raccoon	June 11	from Nassau
Antonica	June 11	from Nassau
Ruby (I) (inbound)	June 11	destroyed
Fannie	June 14	for Nassau
Margaret and Jessie	June 16	from Nassau
Raccoon	June 18	grounded
Alice	June 18	for Nassau
Kate (II)	June 19	for Nassau
Ella and Annie	June 21	for Nassau
Antonica	June 21	for Nassau
Elizabeth (*Atlantic*)	June 21	for Nassau
General Beauregard	June 23	for Nassau
Alice	June 27	from Nassau
Fannie	June 28	from Nassau
Margaret and Jessie	July 7	for Nassau
Alice	July 7	for Nassau
Fannie	July 8	for Nassau
Juno	July 8	from Nassau
Antonica	July 10	from Nassau
Charleston (inbound)	July 11	captured
Margaret and Jessie	July	for Nassau
Raccoon (inbound)	July 19	destroyed
Alice	July 22	from Nassau
Fannie	July 23	from Nassau
Antonica	Aug. 3	for Nassau
Alice	Aug. 15	for Nassau
Spaulding	Aug. 16	from Nassau
Fannie	Aug. 22	for Nassau
Spaulding	Sept. 18	for Nassau

1864

Presto (inbound)	Feb. 4	destroyed
Little Ada (entered Santee R)	Feb.	from Nassau
General Moultrie	March 4	for Nassau
Helen (*Juno*)	March 9	foundered
Rothersay Castle	Apr. 10	from Nassau
Mars	Apr. 10	from Nassau
Rothersay Castle	May	for Nassau

General Whiting	May 14	from Nassau
Mars	May 26	for Nassau
Fox	June 8	from Nassau
Fox	June 10	for Nassau
Little Ada (cleared Santee R)	June 10	for Nassau
Prince Albert	June	from Nassau
Fox	June 26	from Nassau
Druid	July 1	from Nassau
Fox	July	from Nassau
Fox	July 22	for Nassau
Druid	July 26	for Nassau
Prince Albert	July 26	for Nassau
Syren	Aug. 11	from Nassau
Druid	Aug. 11	from Nassau
Fox	Aug. 22	for Nassau
Syren	Aug. 23	for Nassau
Druid	Aug. 24	for Nassau
Fox	Aug. 31	from Nassau
Mary Bowers (inbound)	Aug. 31	destroyed
General Whiting	Sept. 1	for Nassau
Druid	Sept. 6	from Nassau
Fox	Sept. 9	for Nassau
Syren	Sept. 9	for Nassau
Syren	Sept.	from Nassau
Syren	Sept. 27	for Nassau
Kate Gregg	Sept.	from Nassau
General Whiting	Sept. 21	from Nassau
Syren	Sept. 23	from Nassau
Fox	Sept. 28	from Nassau
Fox	Oct. 3	for Nassau
Constance (inbound)	Oct. 6	destroyed
Syren	Oct. 9	from Nassau
Chicora	Oct. 10	from Nassau
Coquette	Oct.	from Nassau
Flora (II) (inbound)	Oct. 22	destroyed
Coquette	Oct. 23	for Nassau
Chicora	Oct. 27	for Nassau
Syren	Oct. 27	for Nassau
Kate Gregg	Nov. 1	for Nassau
General Clinch	Nov. 3	for Nassau
Druid	Nov. 3	for Nassau
Fox	Nov. 4	from Nassau
Colonel Lamb	Nov. 4	from Nassau
Colonel Lamb	Nov. 5	for Nassau
Julia	Nov. 5	from Nassau
Chicora	Nov. 7	from Nassau

Julia	Nov. 18	for Nassau
Syren	Nov. 20	from Nassau
Druid	Nov. 26	from Nassau
Beatrice (inbound)	Nov. 27	destroyed
Syren	Dec. 1	for Nassau
Kate Gregg	Dec. 1	from Nassau
Laurel	Dec. 1	from Nassau
Chicora	Dec. 14	for Nassau
Fox	Dec. 15	for Nassau
Kate Gregg	Dec.	for Nassau
Laurel	Dec.	for Nassau
Julia	Dec.	from Nassau
Syren	Dec. 20	from Nassau
General Whiting	Dec. 23	for Nassau
Julia (outbound)	Dec. 23	captured
Syren	Dec.	for Nassau
Chicora	Dec. 25	from Nassau
Fox	Dec. 27	from Nassau
G. T. Watson	Dec. 27	from Nassau

1865

Carolina (put into Georgetown)	Jan.	from Nassau
Little Hattie	Jan.	from Nassau
G. T. Watson	Jan. 2	for Nassau
Fox	Jan. 2	for Nassau
Chicora	Jan.	for Nassau
Caroline	Jan.	for Nassau
Syren	Jan.	for Nassau
Fox	Jan. 18	from Nassau
Coquette	Jan.	from Nassau
Syren	Jan. 23	from Nassau
Chicora	Jan.	from Nassau
G. T. Watson	Jan. 24	from Nassau
Syren	Jan.	for Nassau
Fox	Feb.	for Nassau
Coquette	Feb.	for Nassau
Little Hattie	Feb. 2	for Nassau
Druid	Feb. 4	for Nassau
Chicora	Feb. 12	for Nassau
Celt (outbound)	Feb.	grounded
Rattlesnake (inbound)	Feb.	destroyed
Syren	Feb. 16	from Nassau
G. T. Watson	Feb. 18	for Nassau
Deer (inbound)	Feb. 18	captured

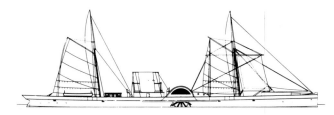

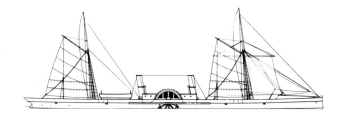

Bibliography

"An Account of the large Rebel Frigate, named the *South Carolina*, from the laying of her Keel until her Capture." *The Political Magazine*: New York 438–440, June 1783.

"Account of the Loss of the *Randolph* as Given in a Letter from Rawlins Lowndes to Henry Laurens." *South Carolina Historical Magazine* 10: 171–173.

Admiralty Survey of the frigate *South Carolina*. 16 January 1783.

Albion, Robert Greenhalgh. *The Rise of the New York Port (1815–1860)*. Devon: David & Charles Publishers, 1970.

Alexander, W. A. "The *Hunley*, The First Confederate Torpedo Boat." *The Mobile Daily Herald* 6 July 1902.

Allen, Joseph. *Memoir of the Life and Services of Admiral Sir William Hargood*. London: Henry S. Richardson, 1841.

Alsop, James. "South Carolina in the Caribbean Correspondence of Secretary of State Sunderland, 1706–1710." *South Carolina Historical Magazine* 83:12–14.

Altman, James D. "The Charleston Marine School." *South Carolina Historical Magazine* 88:76–82.

Anson, George. Captain's Letter Book: 1724–1730.

Anson, Walter Vernon. *Life of Lord Anson*. 1912.

Azoy, A. C. M. "Palmetto Fort, Palmetto Flag." *American Heritage*, October 1955:60–64.

Bargar, Bradley D. *Royal South Carolina 1719–1763*. Columbia: University of South Carolina Press, 1970.

Barnwell, Joseph W. "The Evacuation of Charleston by the British in 1782." *South Carolina Historical Magazine* 11:1–26.

Barrow, Sir John. *The Life of Lord Anson*. London: John Murray, 1830.

Bennett, John. "Charleston in 1774 as Described by an English Traveler." *South Carolina Historical Magazine* 47:179–180.

"Blockade Runner Who Was Never Captured." *The News & Courier* (Charleston) 19 April 1914.

Botting, Douglas, ed. *The Pirates*. Alexandria: Time-Life Books, 1978.

Boudriot, Jean. Letters to the author and John F. Millar.

Bridenbaugh, Carl. "Charlestonians at Newport, 1767–1775." *South Carolina Historical Magazine* 41:43–47.

Bridwell, Ronald E. "Shipbuilding in Colonial South Carolina." Paper presented at the Citadel Conference on the South, May 1985.

Bright, Leslie S.; Rowland, William H.; and Bardon, James C. *C.S.S. Neuse, A Question of Iron and Time*. Raleigh: North Carolina Division of Archives and History, 1981.

Brown, Harold E. Letter to the author.

Brugh, Daniel A. *British Naval Administration in the Age of Walpole*. Princeton: Princeton University Press, 1969.

Bull, Elias B. Correspondence with the author.

"The Burning of Legareville." *South Carolina Historical Magazine* 50:117.

Burton, E. Milby. *The Siege of Charleston 1861–1865*. Columbia: University of South Carolina Press, 1970.

Canfield, Eugene B. *Civil War Naval Ordnance*. Washington: Naval History Division, Navy Department, 1969.

_____. *Notes on Naval Ordnance of the American Civil War 1861–65*. The American Ordnance Association, 1960.

Chapelle, Howard I. *The History of the American Sailing Navy*. New York: W. W. Norton & Company, Inc., 1949.

_____. *The History of American Sailing Ships*. New York: Bonanza Books, undated.

_____. *The Search For Speed Under Sail 1700–1855*. New York: W. W. Norton & Company, Inc., 1967.

"Charleston Manufacturing on the Eve of the Civil War." *Journal of Southern History* 26.

Charnock. *Biographia Navalis*, vol. IV.

Chatard, Dr. Ferdinand E. Correspondence with the author.

Childs, St. Julien R. "The Naval Career of Joseph West." *South Carolina Historical Magazine* 71:109–116.

_____. "The Petit-Guerard Colony." *South Carolina Historical Magazine* 43:1–17.

Clark, William Bell. *Captain Dauntless, the Story of Nicholas Biddle of the Continental Navy*. Baton Rouge: Louisiana State University Press, 1949.

Clowse, Converse Dilworth. "The Charleston Export Trade 1717–1737." Ph.D. dissertation, Northwestern University, 1963.

Coggins, Jack. *Ships and Seamen of the American Revolution*. Harrisburg: Stackpole Books, 1969.

Coker, P. C. "Charleston's *Richmond* Class Ironclad." Unpublished manuscript.

Cordingly, David. *Nicholas Pocock 1740–1821*. Cambridge, England: Conway Maritime Press, 1986.

"The Daring Adventures of a Blockade Runner." *The News & Courier* (Charleston) 5 April 1914.

"David C. Ebaugh on the Building of the *David*." *South Carolina Historical Magazine* 54:32–36.

Denney, William H. "South Carolina's Conception of the Union in 1832." *South Carolina Historical Magazine* 78:171–183.

Dudley, William S. Letters to the author.

_____, ed. *The Naval War of 1812, A Documentary History*. Washington: Naval Historical Center, 1985.

Dunlop, J. G. "Spanish Depredations, 1686." *South Carolina Historical Magazine* 30:81–89.

Dunne, W. M. P. "The South Carolina Frigate: A History of the U. S. Ship *John Adams*." *The American Neptune* XLVII, no. 1:22–32.

Easterby, J. H. "Shipbuilding on St. Helena Island in 1816." *South Carolina Historical Magazine* 47:117.

Edson, Merritt A., Jr. Correspondence with the author.

_____. "*Fair American*, Brig, ca 1776." *The Nautical Research Journal* December 1984:207–208.

Fairburn, William Armstrong. *Merchant Sail*. Lovell: Fairburn Marine Educational Foundation, Inc., 1945–1955.

Farley, M. Foster. "South Carolina War Hawks." *South Carolina History Illustrated* August 1970:33–39.

Feldman, Clayton A. "Building the *Fair American*." *Model Ship Builder Magazine* 32:36–44, 47:13–21.

Fleetwood, Rusty. *Tidecraft, the Boats of Lower South Carolina and Georgia*. Savannah: Coastal Heritage Society, 1982.

Florance, John E., Jr. "Morris Island: Victory or Blunder?" *South Carolina Historical Magazine* 55:143–151.

Floyd, Viola Caston. "The Fall of Charleston." *South Carolina Historical Magazine* 66:1–7.

Forbes, Allan. *The Log of the State Street Trust Company*. Boston: State Street Trust Company, 1926.

Fraser, Charles. *Reminiscences of Charleston*. Charleston: Garnier & Company, 1854.

Gallardo, José Miguel. "The Spaniards and the English Settlement in Charles Town." *South Carolina Historical Magazine* 37:49–64, 91–99, 131–141.

Goldenberg, Joseph A. *Shipbuilding in Colonial America*. Charlottesville: University of Virginia Press, 1976.

Gosse, Philip. *The History of Piracy*. New York: Tudor Publishing Company, 1934.

Greb, Gregory Allen. "Charleston, South Carolina, Merchants, 1815–1860." Ph.D. dissertation, University of California, San Diego, 1978.

Grimball, Berkeley. "Commodore Alexander Gillon of South Carolina." Master's thesis, Duke University, 1951.

Grinde, Donald A., Jr. "Building the South Carolina Railroad." *South Carolina Historical Magazine* 77:84–96.

Hahn, Harold M. *The Colonial Schooner, 1763–1775*. Annapolis: Naval Institute Press, 1981.

Hamrick, Tom. "To Sink a Yankee Ship." *South Carolina History Illustrated*, November 1970:23–30.

Harleston, John. "Battery Wagner on Morris Island 1863." *South Carolina Historical Magazine* 57:1–13.

Harrison, Alfred C., Jr. "Bierstadt's *Bombardment of Fort Sumter* reattributed." *The Magazine Antiques* February 1986:416–422.

Haywood, C. Robert. "Mercantilism and South Carolina Agriculture 1700–1763." *South Carolina Historical Magazine* 60:15–28.

Heaps, Leo. *Log of the* Centurion. London: Hart-Davis, MacGibbon, 1973.

Heyl, Erik. *Early American Steamers*. Buffalo, 1953.

Higgins, W. Robert. "Charles Town Merchants and Factors Dealing in the External Negro Trade 1735–1775." *South Carolina Historical Magazine* 65:205–217.

Hilborn, Nat and Sam. *Battleground of Freedom, South Carolina in the Revolution*. Columbia: Sandlapper Press, Inc., 1970.

_____. "A Show of Strength at Sullivan's Island." *South Carolina History Illustrated*, August 1970: 11–19.

Holcombe, Robert. "Confederate Ironclads." *Warship International* 1980 no. 4:394.

Holmes, Henry Schulz. "The Trenholm Family." *South Carolina Historical Magazine* 16:154–155.

Hough, B. F. *The Siege of Charleston*. Albany: J. Munsell, 1867.

Hover, Otto. *Von Der Galiot Zum Funfmaster, Unsere Segelschiffe in der Weltschiffahrt 1780–1930*. Norderstedt: Verlag Egon Heinemann, 1934.

Hughson, Shirley Carter. "The Carolina Pirates and Colonial Commerce, 1670–1740." *Johns Hopkins University Studies in Historical and Political Science* V–VII (1894):240–370.

Ivers, Larry E. *Colonial Forts of South Carolina 1670–1775*. Columbia: University of South Carolina Press, 1970.

Jackson, Melvin H. *The Privateers in Charleston 1793–1796*. Washington: Smithsonian Institution Press, 1969.

Jeffries, John H. "Maryland Naval Barges in the Revolutionary War." Duplicated, 1978.

Jervey, Theodore D. "Items Relating to Charles Town, S. C., from the Boston *Newsletter*." *South Carolina Historical Magazine* 40:73–78.

Johnson, John. *The Defence of Charleston Harbor 1863–65*. Charleston: Walker, Evans & Cogswell Company, 1890.

Johnson, Joseph, M. D. *Traditions and Reminiscences Chiefly of the American Revolution in the South*. Charleston: Waler & James, 1851.

Jones, Kenneth R. "A Full and Particular Account of the Assault on Charleston in 1706." *South Carolina Historical Magazine* 83:1–11.

Kennett, Lee. "Charleston in 1778: A French Intelligence Report." *South Carolina Historical Magazine* 66:109–111.

Kern, Florence. *The United States Revenue Cutter* South Carolina *1793–1798*. Washington: Alised Enterprises, 1978.

King, Irving H. *George Washington's Coast Guard*. Annapolis: U. S. Naval Institute Press, 1978.

Kyte, George W. "Thaddeus Kosciuszko at the Liberation of Charleston, 1782." *South Carolina Historical Magazine* 84:11–21.

Langley, Harold D. "Robert Y. Hayne and the Navy." *South Carolina Historical Magazine* 82:311–330.

Lapham, Samuel. "Notes on Granville Bastion (1704). *South Carolina Historical Magazine* 26:221–227.

_____. *Our Walled City 1678–1718*. Mt. Pleasant, South Carolina: Society of Colonial Wars, 1970.

Leary, Lewis. "Philip Freneau in Charleston." *South Carolina Historical Magazine* 42:90–91.

Leland, Jack. "Bull's Bay Provides Sanctuary to Variety of Wildlife." *The News & Courier* (Charleston) 10 November 1986: 2–B.

Lewis, Charles Lee. *David Glasgow Farragut, Admiral in the Making*. Annapolis: U. S. Naval Institute Press, 1941.

Macarthur, Antonia. Letters to the author.

Maclay, Edgar Standton. *A History of the United States Navy from 1775–1901*. New York: D. Appleton and Company, 1904.

Madaus, Michael. *Rebel Flags Afloat*. Winchester, Massachusetts: Flag Research Center, 1986.

Mariners' Museum Staff, Newport News, Virginia. Correspondence with the author.

Martin, Sidney Walter. "Ebenezer Kellogg's Visit to Charleston, 1817." *South Carolina Historical Magazine* 49:2–13.

Mathews, Maurice. "A Contemporary View of Carolina in 1680." *South Carolina Historical Magazine* 153–159.

Maury, Lt. M. F. *Wind and Current Charts*. 1853.

May, Commander W. E. "Captain Frankland's *Rose*." *The American Neptune*, January 1966:37–62.

_____. "Captain Charles Hardy on the Carolina Station 1742–1744." *South Carolina Historical Magazine* 70:1–19.

_____. "His Majesty's Ships on the Carolina Station." *South Carolina Historical Magazine* 71:162–169.

McCrady, Edward. *The History of South Carolina in the Revolution 1780–1783*. New York: Paladin Press, 1902.

McIver, Petrona Royall. *History of Mount Pleasant, South Carolina*. Charleston: Ashley Printing and Publishing Company, 1960.

Melvin, Patrick. "Captain Florence O'Sullivan and the Origins of Carolina." *South Carolina Historical Magazine* 235–249.

Middlebrook, Louis F. *The Frigate* South Carolina. Salem, Massachusetts: The Essex Institute, 1929.

Millar, John F. *American Ships of the Colonial and Revolutionary Period*. New York: W. W. Norton & Company, Inc., 1978.

_____. Correspondence with the author.

_____. *Early American Ships*. Williamsburg: Thirteen Colonies Press, 1986.

Minchinton, Walter E. "Richard Champion, Nicholas Pocock, and the Carolina Trade: A Note." *South Carolina Historical Magazine* 65:87–97, 70:97–103.

Moffatt, Lucius Gaston, and Carriere, Joseph Medard. "A Frenchman Visits Charleston, 1817." *South Carolina Historical Magazine* 79:136–154.

Molloy, Robert. *Charleston, A Gracious Heritage*. New York: D. Appleton-Century Company, Inc., 1947.

Moore, Jamie W. *The Lowcountry Engineers*. Charleston: U. S. Army Corps of Engineers, 1981.

Morgan, Thurman T. "John Rivers and the Voyage of the *Three Brothers*." *South Carolina Historical Magazine* 80:267–272.

Mouzon, Harold A. *Privateers of Charleston in the War of 1812*. Charleston: The Historical Commission of Charleston, S. C., 1954.

_____. "Privateers of Charles Town in the Revolution." Unpublished, South Carolina Historical Society.

_____. "The Ship *Prosper*, 1775–1776." *South Carolina Historical Magazine* 59:1–11.

"Necessity is the Mother of Invention." *Port News* (Charleston) January 1987:32–33.

Nepveaux, Ethel S. *George Alfred Trenholm and the Company That Went to War 1861–1865*. Charleston: Comprint, 1973.

Nicholson, Charles W. "The Journal of Frederick William Muller." *South Carolina Historical Magazine* 86:255–281.

Olsberg, Nicholas. "Ship Registers in the South Carolina Archives 1734–1780." *South Carolina Historical Magazine* 74:189–279.

Parker, Captain William Harwar. *Recollections of a Naval Officer*. New York: Charles Scribner's Sons, 1883.

Paullin, Charles Oscar. "Naval Administration Under Secretaries of the Navy Smith, Hamilton, and Jones, 1801–1814." *United States Naval Institute Proceedings* 32:1313.

Perry, Milton F. *Infernal Machines*. Baton Rouge: Louisiana State University Press, 1965.

Peterson, Mendel L. "The Last Cruise of H.M.S. *Loo*." Smithsonian Institution Miscellaneous Collections 131, no. 2, 23 Nov. 1955.

Petit, Percival. *The Hanging of Stede Bonnet, Gentleman Pirate*. Charleston: 1953.

_____, ed. *South Carolina and the Sea*, vol. I–II. Charleston: Maritime and Ports Committee, 1976 and 1986.

Pierce, Jane. "A Brief Study of the Beginning Period of Regular Packet Service Between the Ports of New York and Charleston." Paper Presented to the Faculty of the Munson Institute of American Maritime History, 18 July 1966.

Pine, W. Morton. "History Rides the Winds to Colonial Charleston." *South Carolina Historical Magazine* 87:162–175.

Pritchard, Paul. Will, 1814.

Quattlebaum, Paul. *The Land Called Chicora*. Spartanburg: The Reprint Company, 1956.

Ravenel, Henry E. *Ravenel Records*. Dunwood: Norman S. Berg, 1971.

Redfield, William C. "Civil Engineering." *Journal of the Franklin Institute*, July 1846:1–9.

Log of HMS *Renown*. Kew: Public Record Office, 8 April 1780.

Log of HMS *Rhin*. Kew: Public Record Office, 4–7 June 1814.

Log of HMS *Richmond*. Kew: Public Record Office, 8 April 1780.

Ridgely-Nevitt, Cedric. *American Steamships on the Atlantic*. Newark: University of Delaware Press, 1981.

Riley, Edward M. "Historic Fort Moultrie in Charleston Harbor." *South Carolina Historical Magazine* 51:63–74.

Ripley, Warren. *Battleground, South Carolina in the Revolution*. Charleston: Post-Courier Publishing Company, 1983.

_____. *Charles Towne, Birth of a City*. Charleston: Evening Post Publishing Company, 1970.

Ripley, Warren, and Wilcox, Arthur M. *The Civil War at Charleston*. Charleston: Evening Post Publishing Company, 1966.

Rogers, George C., Jr. *Charleston in the Age of the Pinckeys*. Norman: University of Oklahoma Press, 1969.

_____. "The Charleston Tea Party: The Significance of December 3, 1773." *South Carolina Historical Magazine* 75:153–168.

Rosen, Robert. *A Short History of Charleston*. San Francisco: Lexikos, 1982.

A. S. Salley, Jr., ed. *Journal of the Commissioners of the Navy of South Carolina*. Columbia, 1913.

_____. *Records in the British Public Record Office Relating to South Carolina 1691–1697*. Columbia: Historical Commission of South Carolina, 1931.

_____. "The Spanish Settlement at Port Royal, 1565–1586." *South Carolina Historical Magazine* 26:31–40.

Säyen, John, Jr. "Oared Fighting Ships of the South Carolina Navy, 1776–1780." *South Carolina Historical Magazine* 87:213–237.

Sellers, Leila. *Charleston Business on the Eve of the American Revolution*. Chapel Hill: University of North Carolina Press, 1934.

Sharrer, G. Terry. "Indigo in Carolina, 1671–1796." *South Carolina Historical Magazine* 72:94–103.

Siebert, W. H. "Spanish and French Privateering in Southern Waters, July 1762 to March 1763." *Georgia Historical Quarterly*, September 1932.

Simons, Katharine Drayton. *Stories of Charleston Harbor*. Columbia: The State Company, 1930.

Simons, R. Benthan. "A Charleston Forty-Niner." *South Carolina Historical Magazine* 57:156–178.

Skelton, Lynda Worley. "The Importing and Exporting Company of South Carolina (1862–1876)." *South Carolina Historical Magazine* 75:24–32.

Sloan, Edward. Correspondence with the author.

Smith, D. E. Huger. "Commodore Alexander Gillon and the Frigate *South Carolina*." *South Carolina Historical Magazine* 9:189–219.

_____. "The Luxembourg Claims." *South Carolina Historical Magazine* 10:92–115.

Smith, Henry A. M. "Charleston and Charleston Neck." *South Carolina Historical Magazine* 19:28–29.

_____. "Charleston—The Original Plan and the Earliest Settlers." *South Carolina Historical Magazine* 9:12–17.

_____. "Hog Island and Shute's Folly." *South Carolina Historical Magazine* 19:87–94.

Smythe, Augustine T., Jr. *Torpedo and Submarine Attacks on the Federal Blockading Fleet off Charleston*. Charlottesville: University of Virginia Press, 1907.

Spence, E. Lee, B.I.S., M.H.D. *Shipwrecks of Charleston Harbor*. Charleston: Shipwreck Press, 1980.

_____. *Shipwrecks of South Carolina and Georgia 1520–1865*. Sullivan's Island: Sea Research Society, 1984.

Steedman, Marguerite Couturier. "The Ladies Build a Gunboat." *Sandlapper Magazine*, September 1968, 57–63.

Stern, Van Doran. *The Confederate Navy—A Pictoral History*. 1962.

Stevens, Michael E. "To Get as Many Slaves as You Can: an 1807 Slaving Voyage." *South Carolina Historical Magazine* 87:187–192.

Still, William N. *Iron Afloat, The Story of the Confederate Armorclads*. Columbia: University of South Carolina Press, 1985.

Stuart, Charles B. *The Naval Dry Docks of the United States*. New York: D. Van Nostrand, Publisher, 1870.

Stuckey, Heyward Alexander. "The South Carolina Navy and the American Revolution." Master's thesis, University of South Carolina, 1970.

Stumpf, Stuart O. "Implications of King George's War for the Charleston Mercantile Community." *South Carolina Historical Magazine* 77:161–188.

_____. "Edward Randolph's Attack on Proprietary Government in South Carolina." *South Carolina Historical Magazine* 79:6–18.

_____. "South Carolina Importers of General Merchandise, 1732–1765." *South Carolina Historical Magazine* 84:1–10.

Sullivan, David M. "The Confederate States Marine Corps in South Carolina, 1861–1865." *South Carolina Historical Magazine* 86:113–127.

Symonds, Craig L., ed. *Charleston Blockade, the Journals of John B. Marchand, U. S. Navy 1861–1862*. Newport: Naval War College Press, 1976.

Thomas, John P., Jr. "The Barbadians in Early South Carolina." *South Carolina Historical Magazine* 31:84–85.

Thompson, Edgar K. "George Anson in the Province of South Carolina." *The Mariner's Mirror* 53:3.

Tobias, Thomas J. "Charles Town in 1674." *South Carolina Historical Magazine* 68:63–74.

Topping, Aileen Moore. "Alexander Gillon in Havana, 'This Very Friendly Port.' " *South Carolina Historical Magazine* 83:34–49.

Townsend, Leah. "The Confederate Gunboat *Pedee*." *South Carolina Historical Magazine* 60:66–73.

"George Alfred Trenholm and the *Economist*." Historic Charleston Foundation. Unpublished, undated notes.

Uhlendorf, Bernhard A. *The Siege of Charleston*. Ann Arbor: University of Michigan Press, 1938.

Wallace, David Duncan. *South Carolina, A Short History 1520–1948*. Chapel Hill: The University of North Carolina Press, 1951.

Walsh, Richard. *Charleston's Sons of Liberty, A Study of the Artisans 1763–1789*. Columbia: University of South Carolina Press, 1959.

Waring, Joseph I., M. D. *The First Voyage and Settlement at Charles Towne 1670–1680*. Columbia: University of South Carolina Press, 1970.

Wehman, Howard H. "Noise, Novelties and Nullifiers: A U. S. Navy Officer's Impressions of the Nullification Controversy." *South Carolina Historical Magazine* 76:21–24.

Weir, Robert M. *"A Most Important Epoch," The Coming of the Revolution in South Carolina*. Columbia: University of South Carolina Press, 1970.

Wilcox, L. A. *Anson's Voyage*. London: G. Bell & Sons, 1969.

Wilson, Rhet. "Down to the Sea in Ships, A History of South Carolina Tidecraft." *Coastal Heritage Magazine* 7:1983.

Wise, Stephen R. *Lifeline of the Confederacy: Blockade Running During the American Civil War*. Columbia: University of South Carolina Press, forthcoming.

Withington, Sidney. *Two Dramatic Episodes of New England Whaling*. Mystic, Connecticut: Marine Historical Association, 1958.

Wood, Virginia Steele. *Live Oaking, Southern Timber for Tall Ships*. Boston: Northeastern University Press, 1981.

Young, Rogers W. "Castle Pinckney, Silent Sentinel of Charleston Harbor." *South Carolina Historical Magazine* 39:1–14, 51–67.

Zeigler, John A. "The Pritchards of Hobcaw." *South Carolina Magazine*, October 1958, 14–21.

Zornow, William Frank. "Tariff Policies in South Carolina 1775–1798." *South Carolina Historical Magazine* 56:31–44.

Sources for Illustrations

Dust Jacket (front cover): Roy Cross, RSMA, from the author's collection.

Dust Jacket (rear cover), 1 (center, left), 19, 220: Courtesy of Rob Napier, Newburyport, MA.

Dust Jacket (rear flap), 266: Photo by John O'Hagen, courtesy *Southern Accents*, Birmingham, AL.

i: Collection of Congressman Arthur Ravenel, Jr., Charleston, SC.

ii, iii, 98, 99, 121, 142, 152, 157, 159 (top right), 160, 161, 167, 168, 169, 184, 186, 260: Courtesy of the Mariners' Museum, Newport News, VA.

v: Old engraving courtesy of the South Caroliniana Library, University of South Carolina, Columbia, SC.

vii: Old engraving courtesy of the Jack Patla Company, Charleston, SC.

ix, 63 (lower left): Drawing by Erik A. R. Ronnberg, Jr., courtesy of Model Shipways, Bogota, NJ.

xii (left), 1 (right, top): Franco Gay, Roma, Italy.

xii (right), xiii (left and top), xx, xxi (right): E. W. Petrejus, *Modelling the Irene*, courtesy of Uitgeversmij., De Esch' B. V., Hengelo (O.), Holland.

xiii (lower right), xiv (left), 63 (top and center), 126, 170 (three in upper right corner): Howard I. Chapelle, *The History of American Sailing Ships*, courtesy of W. W. Norton & Company, NY.

xiv (right), 116, 126 (upper left), 128, 149, 157, 162, 175, 177, 188, 197, 212, 273, 280 (left): Courtesy of the Peabody Museum of Salem, MA, photos by Mark Sexton.

xvi (top): Colonial National Historical Park, National Park Service, Yorktown, VA.

xviii (left): Drawing by Walter E. Channing from *Live Oaking, Southern Timber for Tall Ships* © 1981 by Virginia Steele Wood. Reprinted with the permission of Northeastern University Press, Boston, MA.

xix (top), xxi: Reprinted from *Ships and Seamen of the American Revolution* with permission of Stackpole Books, Harrisburg, PA.

xix (lower left), 1 (left top, bottom, and center): William A. Baker from *Colonial Vessels*, courtesy of Conway Maritime Press, London and Mrs. Ruth Baker, Hingham, MA.

3, 13: Musée du Louvre, Paris.

5: Courtesy Erik A. R. Ronnberg, Jr., Rockport, MA.

7, 50 (left), 54 (right): Darby Erd, Columbia, SC.

8: Charleston Postal History Museum, Charleston, SC.

9, 18, 20, 24: Emmett Robinson, Charleston, SC.

11, 84: Library of Congress, Washington, DC.

14, 30, 60, 65, 91: Science Museum, London.

15, 23, 66, 137, 141, 228, 239, 245, 291: Tom Freeman, from the author's collection.

22, 36, 86, 103, 110, 250, 251: Carolina Art Association/Gibbes Art Gallery, Charleston, SC.

27, 187: Charleston Museum, Charleston, SC.

28 (top), 67, 68, 69, 76 (upper right), 107: National Maritime Museum, Greenwich, England.

28 (bottom), 40 (right), 41, 46, 47, 148, 158, 159 (left): Robert A. Lightley/UCA Studios, Capetown, South Africa.

29: From *Historic Ship Models* by Wolfram zu Mondfeld, © 1985 by Argus Books Ltd. Reprinted by permission of Sterling Publishing Co., Inc., Two Park Avenue, NY 10016.

32, 33, 58, 59, 76 (upper left), 78, 90, 112, 113, 164, 166: Mark Myers, RSMA, from the author's collection.

34: Brian Lavery, London.

37, 40 (lower left), 45, 49, 50 (right), 51, 72, 92: Harold Hahn, Lyndhurst, OH.

38, 76 (lower right), 89: From *The Search for Speed Under Sail 1700–1855* by Howard I. Chapelle with the permission of W. W. Norton & Company, NY.

39, 40 (upper left), 42: Courtesy Robert King, Charleston County RMC Office.

53: Castillo de San Marcos National Monument, St. Augustine, FL.

63 (left center, top, and right), 126 (all except upper left). 130, 138, 150: From *The History of the American Sailing Navy* by Howard I. Chapelle by permission of W. W. Norton & Company, NY.

70, 71: Courtesy of the Museum of Early Southern Decorative Arts, Winston-Salem, NC.

74: Darby Erd, courtesy of the Company of Military Historians, Westbrook, CT.

76 (lower left), 79 (top), 104, 105, 134: From *Early American Ships* by John F. Millar, courtesy of Thirteen Colonies Press, Williamsburg, VA.

79 (lower): From *The Wooden Fighting Ship in the Royal Navy* by E. H. H. Archibald, courtesy of Blandford Publishing Ltd., Dorset, England.

80, 81: Drawing by Stanley South from *Palmetto Parapets: Exploratory Archeology at Fort Moultrie, South Carolina, Anthropological Studies No. 1,* South Carolina Institute of Archaeology and Anthropology, Columbia, SC, 1974.

82: Nicholas Pocock from the collection of the South Caroliniana Library, Columbia, SC.

83, 275, 283: Historic Charleston Foundation Collection.

87, 95 (right): National Park Service, U. S. Department of the Interior.

94, 153: Lloyd McCaffery, Boulder, CO.

95 (upper left): Independence National Historical Park Collections, Philadelphia, PA.

101: John F. Millar, courtesy South Carolina Historical Society.

102: John F. Millar, Williamsburg, VA.

106: United States Naval Academy Museum, Annapolis, MD.

111: New York Public Library.

115: Courtesy of Berkeley Grimball, Charleston, SC.

117: Walter Kahn, Westport, CT.

118: From *Souvenirs de Marine*, volume V, Paris.

123, 202 (left): Smithsonian Institution, Washington, D.C.

124: Derek Gardner, RSMA, courtesy of the Polak Gallery, London.

129: Roy Cross, RSMA, from the collection of Eugene B. Sydnor, Jr., Richmond, VA.

132: From *Privateers in Charleston 1793–1796* by Melvin H. Jackson, courtesy of the Smithsonian Institution Press, Washington, D.C.

140, 147: U. S. Navy, courtesy of the Hampton Roads Naval Museum, Norfolk, VA.

143, 217, 261: The National Archives, Washington, D. C.

145, 191, 199: Maryland Historical Society, Baltimore, MD.

163 (top): From *The Baltimore Clipper* by Howard I. Chapelle.

170 (upper left), 182: From *American Steamships on the Atlantic* by Cedric Ridgely-Nevitt, courtesy of Associated University Presses, Cranbury, NJ.

173: Yale University Art Gallery, New Haven, CT.

174, 194, 203, 205, 210, 211, 219, 222, 236 (left), 240, 246, 247, 248, 249, 254, 282 (left), 284, 288 (right): *Harper's Weekly Magazine.*

179, 203 (*Passaic, Memphis, New Ironsides,* and *Palmetto State*), 237, 280 (right), 281, 286: U. S. Navy.

181: From *Early American Steamships* by Eric Heyl.

183: CIGNA Museum and Art Collection, Philadelplhia.

189: Collection of Robert Adger Bowen, Macon, GA.

192 (left), 206 (top), 211, 224: From *Frank Leslie's Illustrated Newspaper.*

192 (right), 198 (left), 223 (right), 238, 255, 262, 264, 269 (top), 276, 293: *Post-Courier* Collection, Charleston, SC.

193 (top), 203 (*Planter*): Edward Sloan, Jr., Greenville, SC.

193 (bottom): From *The Naval Drydocks of the United States* by Charles B. Stuart 1870, courtesy of Chuck Haberlein, Navy Department, Washington, DC.

195 (left): Deutsches Schiffahrtsmuseum, Bremerhaven, West Germany.

195 (right): H. & E. Scheidulin, Bremen, West Germany.

196 (right), 206 (bottom), 236 (right), 278: *The Soldier in Our Civil War.*

198 (right): Mrs. Ethel S. Nepveaux, Charleston, SC.

201, 202, 287: Private Charleston collection.

203 (upper right), 230 (top), 289: by William E. Geoghegan, courtesy of Sail and Steam, Norfolk, VA.

203 (*David*): Courtesy of Robert Holcombe, The Confederate Naval Museum, Columbus, GA.

203 (*Hunley*): Courtesy of David Merriman, Virginia Beach, VA.

204, 241, 269 (left): *The London Illustrated News.*

208, 213 (left): Courtesy of Captain Malachi J. Collet, USNR, the Citadel Museum, Charleston, SC.

209: Courtesy Charleston Post Card Company, Inc., Charleston, SC.

213 (right), 226 (right), 230 (bottom), 243, 257, 259: Collection of Dr. Charles V. Peery, Charleston, SC.

221, 234: Peter Dewitz, from the author's collection.

223 (left), 277: Military History Institute, Carlisle Barracks, PA.

225: Photo by Gregg Vicik, courtesy of the Mariners' Museum, Newport News, VA.

226 (left), 271, 288 (left): New Hanover County Museum, Wilmington, NC.

227: Collection of Nathaniel I. Ball III, Charleston, SC.

229, 265, 299: Courtesy of Daniel Dowdey, Columbia, SC.

231, 258, 267, 285: Courtesy of the Museum of the Confederacy, Richmond, VA.

233 (top left): From *The Defence of Charleston Harbor 1863–65* by John Johnson.

233 (bottom and right): Lines by William E. Geoghegan, courtesy of the Smithsonian Institution, Washington, D.C.

235 (bottom): From Warship Profile 36, *United States Navy Monitors of the Civil War* by Commander William H. Cracknell, USN.

251 (top): Picture key reproduced by permission of the Magazine *Antiques*, New York, NY.

270, 274: Courtesy of Michael Wall, Salem, MA.

290: Nova Scotia Maritime Museum, Nova Scotia, Canada, courtesy of Thomas Morgan, M.D.

Index